Interior Design Reference Manual

Third Edition

David K. Ballast, AIA
NCIDQ Certified #9425

PROFESSIONAL PUBLICATIONS, INC. • BELMONT, CA

How to Locate and Report Errata for This Book

At Professional Publications, we do our best to bring you error-free books. But when errors do occur, we want to make sure you can view corrections and report any potential errors you find, so the errors cause as little confusion as possible.

A current list of known errata and other updates for this book is available on the PPI website at **www.ppi2pass.com/errata**. We update the errata page as often as necessary, so check in regularly. You will also find instructions for submitting suspected errata. We are grateful to every reader who takes the time to help us improve the quality of our books by pointing out an error.

INTERIOR DESIGN REFERENCE MANUAL
Third Edition

Current printing of this edition: 1

Printing History

edition number	printing number	update
2	2	Minor corrections.
2	3	Minor corrections.
3	1	Fully revised and reorganized. Reflects 2003 IBC.

Printed in the United States of America

Professional Publications, Inc.
1250 Fifth Avenue, Belmont, CA 94002
(650) 593-9119
www.ppi2pass.com

Ballast, David Kent
    Interior design reference manual / David K. Ballast. -- 3rd ed.
        p. cm.
    Includes index.
    ISBN-13: 978-1-59126-047-9
    ISBN-10: 1-59126-047-7
    1. Interior decoration--Study and teaching--United States. 2. National Council for Interior Design Qualifications (U.S.)--Examinations--Study guides. I. Title.
NK2116.5.B35 2005
747.076--dc22
                                                        2005044744

TABLE OF CONTENTS

LIST OF FIGURES

PROFESSIONAL PUBLICATIONS, INC.

LIST OF TABLES

PREFACE AND ACKNOWLEDGMENTS FOR THE THIRD EDITION

As the National Council for Interior Design Qualification (NCIDQ) examination continues to evolve, the *Interior De-sign Reference Manual* will also evolve to meet examinees' needs. NCIDQ regularly commissions practice analysis studies of the profession every five years to make sure the exam accurately reflects the knowledge and skills interior designers need to practice responsibly and to protect the health, safety, and welfare of the public. The current specifications of the exam are based on the *Practice Analysis Study for the Profession of Interior Design* completed in 2003 for NCIDQ. For more information about the exam and NCIDQ, visit NCIDQ's website at www.ncidq.org.

The latest practice analysis study indicated that the exam correlated strongly to what professionals do in daily practice. The study also was used to determine the number of questions related to each area of practice.

Because the specifications and format of the exam have changed since the first two editions of this book, I have reorganized and greatly expanded the *Interior Design Reference Manual*. Comparing this

new edition with the previous ones you will notice several changes. First, I have completely reorganized the book by grouping chapters into sections and task areas to reflect the organization of the exam. This will enable you to focus your study on those areas that are of most interest. Second, I have greatly expanded the material in most of the chapters, attempting to cover all the knowledge and skill areas listed in the exam specifications. Third, I have added a new chapter on sustainable design and included information on energy conservation and "green" design in many of the other chapters.

As always, it is impossible to precisely match the organization and content of a review book with the actual exam because of the overlap of subject matter found in the various sections and because of the vast range of knowledge that can be tested. However, the new organization of this edition should help you focus your study on those areas you feel deserve extra study. The expanded material in each chapter will also give you a good idea of the content you should expect to see on the exam. As you review these materials, if you feel you are weak in any one area, use the Recommended Reading list at the back of the book for suggestions on additional study material.

Remember as you take the exam that even though you think you may have good grasp of the information and knowledge in a particular subject area, be prepared to address questions on the material in a variety of forms and from different points of view. For example, you may have studied and know definitions, but can you apply that knowledge when a question includes a definition-type word as part of a more complex situation-type of question? For practice, be sure to try the sample questions at the end of each chapter.

Also, be prepared for what you may consider ambiguous questions with no clear answer. These are the questions that usually have a word like "best" or "most" in the stem of the question. Although they may seem aggravating at best and unfair at worst, they do test your ability to discriminate among fine shades of meaning. For these, be sure to read the question carefully. For practice-related questions, if you have had a lot of professional practice experience it is sometimes best to forget the way you respond to questions in actual practice and answer a question based on the "book" answer instead.

As the time for taking the exam nears, stay up to date by reviewing the NCIDQ website at www.ncidq.org and PPI's website at www.ppi2pass.com. And try to relax as much as possible. Combined with an appropriate educational background and practical professional experience, this book will provide you with the knowledge and confidence you need to pass the exam. Good luck!

I would like to thank several people who helped me in the development and publication of this book. My first thanks go to Loren Swick at NCIDQ for his suggestions and support of the initial effort many years ago. Michele Guest did a thorough reading of the first manuscript and offered many helpful suggestions. Nancy Barsotti's comments also helped steer the direction of portions of the book. My thanks also to Todd Bostick at NCIDQ for his assistance in later revisions to this book.

All of the people at Professional Publications were of immense help in the original publication of this book, especially my editor, Wendy Nelson, and production editor, Lisa Rominger. Thanks are also due to Karie Youngdahl for the always arduous task of copyediting, Jennifer Pasqual Thuillier for the illustrations, Shelley Arenson for typesetting, and Jessica R. Whitney-Holden and Russ Beebe for proofreading.

For assistance for the second edition of this book I would like to thank Jessica R. Whitney-Holden, Kate Hayes, Chuck Oey, Yvonne Sartain, Heather Kinser, and Cathy Schrott.

Now that the book is in its third edition, I would like to again thank Heather Kinser and Cathy Schrott. Also helping to get this latest edition into print were Pamela E. B. Henley, ASID (technical reviewer), Sarah Hubbard (editorial manager), Miriam Hanes (typesetter), and Tom Bergstrom (illustrator).

David K. Ballast, AIA

INTRODUCTION

ABOUT THIS BOOK

The *Interior Design Reference Manual* gives a thorough review of the topics covered on the National Council for Interior Design Qualification (NCIDQ) examination. Chapters are organized according to the exam specifications, to encourage a straightforward and focused study experience. After reviewing the materials, candidates can get a feeling for what to expect on the actual exam and test their current knowledge by answering the sample questions at the ends of the chapters. Detailed answers are also provided. In addition, this book includes a sample practicum with solutions.

The following exam topics are included.

Section I: Principles and Practices of Interior Design

      practice area 1:   Programming
      practice area 2:   Schematic Design
      practice area 3:   Design
                             Development

Section II: Contract Documents and Administration

      practice area 4:   Contract
                             Documents

      practice area 5:   Contract
                             Administration
      practice area 6:   Professional Practice

Section III: Schematics and Design Development Practicum

Because there is so much overlap in the areas of building regulations and sustainable design, chapters on these topics are grouped toward the end of the book.

For additional practice refer to the companion volume titled *Interior Design Practicum Exam Workbook,* by Pamela E. B. Henley.

THE NCIDQ EXAM

The NCIDQ exam measures the minimum level of competence needed to practice in the profession of interior design. Successful completion of the exam is mandatory for certification in those U.S. states and Canadian provinces where licensing, registration, or certification statutes govern the profession of interior design. It is also required for membership in most professional interior design organizations and for advanced professional certification as offered by the

Governing Board for Contract Interior Design Standards.

The NCIDQ exam is developed and administered by the National Council for Interior Design Qualification (NCIDQ). Formed in 1972 and incorporated in 1974, the Council's purpose is to identify to the public those interior designers who have met the minimum standards for professional practice by passing the NCIDQ exam. In addition, the Council defines, researches, and updates bodies of knowledge, conducts field surveys, analyzes candidate performance, evaluates subject areas and question validity, develops and pretests questions and problems, improves scoring, implements grading and jury procedures, reviews education and practice requirements, and identifies public health, safety, and welfare issues. The council also maintains the Interior Design Experience Program (IDEP), which is a structured program to help recent graduates gain a wide range of professional experience by working with mentors and supervisors in professional design firms.

The Council is composed of representatives from professional design organizations and regulatory agencies from those states and provinces having statutory requirements. The professional organizations represented include the American Society of Interior Designers (ASID), Interior Design Educators Council (IDEC), Interior Designers of Canada (IDC), and the International Interior Design Association (IIDA). Passing the NCIDQ exam is a prerequisite for professional membership application in these organizations.

Some states require NCIDQ certification as a prerequisite for using the various titles defined by the legislative acts of those states. These titles include interior designer, certified interior designer, and registered interior designer. In addition, several states, Washington, DC, and Puerto Rico currently require NCIDQ certification to qualify to *practice* in their jurisdictions. Some states require that designers pass the Building and Barrier-Free Codes examination. Until further notice from NCIDQ, this section from the old exam will continue to be offered for those jurisdictions that require it by law.

At the time of this writing, states that have some type of statute governing the profession include Alabama, Arkansas, California, Connecticut, Florida, Georgia, Illinois, Kentucky, Louisiana, Maine, Maryland, Minnesota, Missouri, Nevada, New Jersey, New Mexico, New York, Tennessee, Texas, Virginia, and Wisconsin. Puerto Rico and Washington, DC, also have statutes governing the profession. The Canadian provinces with statutes include Alberta, British Columbia, Manitoba, New Brunswick, Nova Scotia, Ontario, Quebec, and Saskatchewan. Colorado has permitting legislation, which gives qualified interior designers the legal right to provide interior design services for spaces of any size in a building of any type or size in Colorado. Similar legislation is pending in several other locations, and it is likely that more states will require certification in the future.

The NCIDQ exam is designed to reflect the skills and knowledge currently required in the profession. The current revision of the exam was made based on the 2003 study, *Practice Analysis Study for the Profession of Interior Design*, commissioned by NCIDQ. Using the 2003 study, NCIDQ correlated examination content with the tasks interior designers must perform, with the goal of providing the most up-to-date and appropriate exam possible.

The exam is given twice a year, on a Friday and Saturday, in April and October, and is offered at examination sites throughout North America. Candidates accepted to sit for the exam will be notified of the exam location nearest the address given on their application.

The examination is composed of three sections: two multiple-choice sections and one design practicum section. Candidates may take the entire exam at one sitting or individual sections at different times. If one section receives a failing grade, only that section needs to be retaken. Time limits on passing all three sections of the exam may be imposed on candidates at the discretion of individual states or provinces, or by professional membership organizations for regulatory or administrative purposes.

The exam is priced by section. For current costs and the latest information on the application process, refer to the NCIDQ website at www.ncidq.org.

ELIGIBILITY REQUIREMENTS

Candidates must have a certain number of education credit hours and hours of experience to qualify to sit for the exam. For candidates with a baccalaureate degree, there is a maximum number of hours of work experience that can be applied prior to graduation and a certain number of hours of education credit that must be taken before work experience counts toward exam candidacy or participation in the IDEP program.

Refer to the NCIDQ website at www.ncidq.org for current information. In addition, candidates must provide three letters of reference and academic transcripts. All first-time exam candidates apply directly to NCIDQ for determination of eligibility.

Beginning January 1, 2008, candidates must complete their work experience under a qualified professional rather than in independent practice. A qualified professional is defined as an NCIDQ certificate holder or a licensed (registered)

interior designer or architect offering interior design services.

CONTENT OF THE NCIDQ EXAMINATION

The exam's content is based on studies of the profession. Using the 2003 *Practice Analysis Study for the Profession of Interior Design*, NCIDQ determined that six performance domains characterize the work of interior design.

- programming
- schematic design
- design development
- contract documents
- contract administration
- professional practice

The weighting structure of the exam is derived from each domain's relative importance, criticality, and frequency. Questions relating to these six performance domains are distributed throughout one or more parts of the exam.

The current exam places great importance on health, safety, and welfare issues and less emphasis on topics such as history and communication methods.

QUESTION TYPES

The exam uses three question types. The first is multiple choice, which requires that candidates select from three or four options. Questions may be based on written information and graphic materials, such as drawings, pictures, or symbols. Multiple-choice questions are used in Sections I and II of the exam and are machine graded.

The second question type is a written scenario, which puts the candidate in the position of the interior designer for a specific situation and also requires a multiple-choice answer. Scenarios are used in Sections I and II of the exam.

The third type of question requires candidates to complete a graphic presentation. This question type is used in Section III (practicum) of the exam. Candidates are given a program based on a multifunctional facility (a commercial and residential facility of approximately 3500 ft^2) and must produce a design solution. The solution must also address the principles of universal design. Section III is currently jury graded, but NCIDQ is considering converting this section to a computer administered and graded format.

The exam uses three varieties of multiple-choice questions: recall, application, and developmental. A recall question requires candidates to name, identify, or remember the correct term or concept from a list. To solve this question type, candidates must recall, recognize, or discriminate information.

Example:

The units used for the measurement and description of the brightness of a direct glare source are

    (A) footcandles
    (B) footlamberts
    (C) candelas
    (D) lumens

An application question requires candidates to apply a principle, concept, or skill. Comparison and contrast can be tested with this type of question.

Example:

In detailing a door frame for a conference room where acoustical privacy is critical, which of the following is LEAST likely to be required?

    (A) an automatic door bottom
    (B) a heavy duty, silent door closer
    (C) neoprene gasketing
    (D) a solid-core door

A developmental question requires candidates to make a judgment, solve a problem, or apply a skill, principle, or concept to a complex situation. Candidates may be required to integrate many principles or concepts to answer a question or problem in an acceptable way.

Example:

A doorway is installed by the contractor according to the drawings. After viewing the job, a building inspector tells the contractor that the door is not wide enough. Who has financial responsibility for correcting the problem?

    (A) framing subcontractor
    (B) interior designer
    (C) owner
    (D) contractor

This book includes sample questions of each of these types at the end of each chapter, and the solutions are given in Ch. 31. While most questions can be answered based on information given in this book, some require previous knowledge of interior design. Questions of this nature are included to give a feeling for what to expect on the exam, because no one book can possibly provide all the information for all the questions that may be on the actual exam.

EXAM FORMAT

The exam is divided into three sections given over two subsequent days. Section I, Principles and Practices of Interior Design, addresses the domains of programming, schematics design, and design development. Section II, Contract Documents and Administration, addresses the domains of contract documents, contract administration, and professional practice. At the time of this writing, Section I contained 150 multiple-choice questions and Section II contained 125 multiple-choice questions. Of these, 25 questions in each section are included for development purposes and do not count for grading.

Section III, Schematics and Design Development, is the design practicum section. Candidates receive a program based on a multifunctional facility and must produce a graphic design solution. The solution must address the program requirements as well as the principles of universal design. Section III is given in two parts, which are described in Ch. 30. See Table 1 for the time limits of each exam section.

Table 1. Exam Time Limits*

exam section	time limit
Section I	3.5 hours
Section II	3 hours
Section III	
Part I	3 hours
Part II	3 hours

*Note: Exam sittings are preceeded by a half-hour instruction period. Mandatory lunch breaks are also scheduled into both exam days.

HOW TO TAKE THE EXAM

People have a wide variety of responses to tests. Some are comfortable taking them, while others are terrified by any exam, no matter how simple it is or how well prepared they are. Some people review very little, while others spend months studying every piece of material they can find and taking every review course offered. Each person must determine the best approach for his or her experience, needs, time availability, and personality. However, the following time-management suggestions and exam-taking tips may help lessen exam-taking anxiety.

The NCIDQ exam is fair and accurately evaluates minimum competency to practice as an interior designer. Ultimately, it is knowledge of the subject matter and professional experience that provide the confidence to pass the exam.

Time Management

One of the biggest problems many candidates have in taking the NCIDQ exam is simply completing it in the time allowed. This is especially true of the design practicum. For most people who know the material, there is plenty of time to complete Sections I and II as well as Section III.

Section III, the design practicum, requires that candidates assimilate, analyze, and communicate much information in a short time. The key is good time budgeting so all the mandatory drawings can be completed in time. Also remember that highly refined, drafted drawings are not required. They may be drawn freehand and can be rather rough as long as the drawings show the jurors that the problem has been solved and all the program requirements have been met. Ultimately, when Section III is computerized, drawing quality will be less of an issue.

For the design practicum, candidates must read the program quickly and develop a design concept that meets all of the design requirements. Allow time to develop and draw the concept. Do not attempt something that is complicated or unusual or that requires complex construction. Avoid shapes and construction elements that require a lot of drawing time. Remember that the jurors are not looking for innovative, award-winning solutions, just proof that a candidate can respond to a program and integrate design principles, accessible design, and health, safety, and welfare issues into a three-dimensional solution.

Detailed suggestions for completing Section III are given in Ch. 30. For Sections I and II, the portions of the exam that consist of multiple-choice questions, one of two methods can be used. With the first approach, proceed from the first questions to the last, trying to answer each one regardless of its difficulty. Divide the time allotted by the number of questions to give an average time per question. Of course, some will take less than the average, some more. If a question cannot be answered in the allotted time, make a note of it and move on to the next one. Leave some time at the end so difficult, unanswered questions can be reviewed and at least guessed at.

With the second approach, go through the exam twice. During the first pass, read each question, answering the easy ones or the ones that do not require any lengthy calculation or study of the information given. Because this approach requires jumping around, make sure the correct spaces are marked on the answer sheet. If a question does not fit into the first category of "easy to answer," leave it for the second pass. During the second pass, answer the remaining questions. These should be the ones that can be confidently answered after applying some deductive reasoning or performing a familiar calculation. Again, make sure the correct spaces are being marked on the answer sheet.

Using the two-pass method gives a feeling for the difficulty of the exam during the first pass and helps to budget the remaining time for the unanswered questions. One of the tricks to making this method work is to avoid going back and re-reading or re-answering any completed questions. In most cases, the first response (or guess) is the best response.

Regardless of which approach is used, be sure to answer every question. Unanswered questions are counted as wrong, so if necessary, make a best guess among the most likely options.

Test-Taking Tips

Even when a candidate is extremely familiar with the subject matter, taking the NCIDQ exam can be an arduous process simply because of its length and the concentration required to get through it. This is especially true if all three sections are being taken for the first time. As with any activity requiring endurance, it is important to be well rested on exam day. Stop studying a day or two before the first exam day, and relax as much as possible. Get plenty of sleep the night before and between exam days.

Allow plenty of time to get to the exam site, to avoid transportation problems such as getting lost or stuck in traffic jams. Arrive at the exam room early to select a seat with good lighting, as far away from distractions as possible. Once in the room, arrange working materials and other supplies to make it easy to begin as soon as allowed. The proctor will review the exam instructions as well as general rules about breaks, smoking, permitted materials, and other housekeeping matters. Candidates can ask any questions about the rules at this time.

Once the exam begins, quickly review the materials given in the exam booklet. Check the number of questions and decide on your exam-taking approach, as described in the previous section. If the approach is to tackle the questions in sequence, about half the questions should be completed when half of the allotted time is up. In scheduling, leave some time at the end of the period to double-check uncertain answers and to see if any questions have been marked with two responses.

Here are some additional tips.

• Make a notation of the most doubtful answers. If there is time at the end of the exam, go back and recheck these answers. Remember, the first response is usually the best.

• Many times, one or two choices can be easily eliminated. This may result in a guess, but at least the chances are better between two choices than among four.

• Some questions may appear too simple. Although a few very easy and obvious questions are included, it's more likely that a simple question should serve as a red flag. It might be best to reevaluate these questions for exceptions to a rule or special circumstances that would make the obvious, easy response incorrect.

• Watch out for absolute words in a question, such as "always," "never," or "completely." These often indicate some little exception that can turn what reads like a true statement into a false statement, or vice versa.

• Be on the alert for words like "seldom," "usually," "best," or "most reasonable." These indicate that some judgment will be involved in answering the question, so look for two or more options that may be very similar.

• Occasionally, there may be a defective question. This does not happen very often, but if it does, make the best choice possible under the circumstances. Flawed questions are usually discovered. Either they are not counted in the exam or any one of the correct answers is credited instead.

• Try to relax as much as possible during study periods and during the exam itself. Worrying too much is counterproductive. Candidates who have worked diligently in school, have obtained a wide range of work experience, and have started exam review early will be in the best possible position to pass the exam.

Study Guidelines

Each individual's method of studying for the NCIDQ exam should be based on both the content and form of the exam and the individual's school and work experience. Because the exam covers such a broad range of subject matter, it cannot include every area of practice. Rather, the exam focuses on what is considered minimum competency to practice interior design.

Recent work experience should also help determine what subjects to study most. Someone who has been involved with construction documents for several years will probably require less work in that area than in others with which they have not had recent experience.

This review book was prepared to help candidates focus on those topics that will most likely be included in the exam. It is organized according to the sections of the exam and the individual practice areas of each section.

Some subjects may seem familiar or may be easy to recall from memory. Others may seem completely foreign; these are the ones to give particular attention to when using this book. It may be wise to study additional sources on these subjects, take review seminars, or get special help from someone who knows the topic.

The following steps provide a useful structure for organizing an exam study program.

Step 1: Start early. It is not advisable to review for an exam like this by starting a few weeks before the date. This is especially true for candidates taking all portions of the exam for the first time.

Step 2: Go through the review book quickly to get a feeling for the scope of the subject matter. Although this book has been prepared based on the content covered by the exam, it may be best to review the detailed list of tasks and considerations given in the *NCIDQ Examination Study Guide.*

Step 3: Based on this review and a realistic appraisal of personal strong and weak areas, set priorities for study and determine which topics need more study time.

Step 4: Divide review subjects into manageable units, and organize them into a sequence of study. It is generally best to start with less familiar subjects. Based on the exam date and plans for beginning study, assign a time limit to each study unit. Again, a candidate's knowledge of a subject should determine the time devoted to it. For example, a candidate may want to devote an entire week to building and barrier-free codes if it is an unfamiliar subject, and only one day to space planning if it is a familiar subject. In setting up a schedule, be realistic about other life commitments as well as personal ability to concentrate on studying for a given amount of time.

Step 5: Begin studying, and stick with the schedule. This, of course, is the most difficult part of the process and the one that requires the most self-discipline. The job should be easier for candidates who started early and are following a realistic schedule, allowing time for recreation and other personal commitments.

Step 6: Stop studying a day or two before the exam to relax. By this time, no amount of cramming will help.

Here are some additional tips:

• Know concepts first, then learn the details. For example, it is much better to understand the basic ideas governing interior design contracts and agreements than it is to attempt to memorize every word of the standard contracts.

• Do not overstudy any one portion of the exam (for candidates planning to take more than one session at a time). It is generally better to review the concepts than to become an overnight expert in one area.

• When taking the design practicum section, follow the instructions outlined in the criteria. Do not spend time on unnecessary details or minor issues.

• Try to talk with people who have already taken the exam. Although the exam questions are continually changing, it is a good idea to get a general feeling for the types of questions asked, the general emphasis, and areas that previous candidates found difficult. A good resource is the NCIDQ Exam Forum on PPI's website (www.ppi2pass.com/NCIDQforum .html), where examinees discuss the process online.

What to Bring to the Exam Site

For Sections I and II, only number two or HB lead pencils, an eraser, and a nonprogrammabl, battery-operated calculator may be brought into the exam room. Reference materials are not allowed for any of the three sections.

For the design practicum, Section III, consider bringing the following items.

• portable drafting board (no smaller than 24 in × 36 in (610 × 914) with a parallel bar, if drafting boards are not supplied at the exam center. Check before the exam to see if drafting boards and parallel bars are provided. Although all sketching may be done freehand, some candidates feel more comfortable using a parallel bar. Do not use a T-square; it is too difficult to use when rushed.

• architect's scale (imperial or metric depending on what scale is being used and where the exam is being given)

• 30°/60° and 45° triangles

• templates for shapes such as plumbing, furniture, and circles

• pencils and marking pens

• erasers

• nonprogrammable, battery-operated calculator (make sure the batteries are fresh)

• pencil pointer and/or sharpener

• tracing paper

Bring any other drawing tools that will make the work easier. Bring a variety of grades of lead and types and thicknesses of marking pens because the vellum supplied may be of varying quality and it may smear one type of marker and not another.

In addition, consider taking "survival" items like the following.

- watch

- tissues

- small, unobtrusive snacks and bottled water, if allowed in the exam center

- aspirin

- eye drops

HOW SI UNITS ARE USED IN THIS BOOK

This edition of the *Interior Design Reference Manual* includes equivalent measurements, using the Système Internationale (SI), in the text and illustrations. However, the use of SI units for construction and book publishing in the United States is problematic because the building construction industry in the United States (with the exception of federal construction) has generally not adopted the metric system, as it is commonly called. Equivalent measurements of customary U.S. units (also called English or inch-pound units) are usually given as *soft* conversions, whereas customary U.S. measurements are simply converted into SI units using standard conversion factors. This always results in a number with excessive significant digits. When construction is done using SI units, the building is designed and drawn according to *hard* conversions, where planning dimensions and building products are based on a metric module from the beginning. For example, studs are spaced 400 mm on center to accommodate panel products that are manufactured in standard 1200 mm widths.

During the present time of transition to SI units in the United States, code-writing bodies, federal laws (such as the Americans with Disabilities Act, or ADA), product manufacturers, trade associations, and other construction-related industries typically still use the customary U.S. system and make soft conversions to develop SI equivalents. Some manufacturers produce the same product using both measuring systems. Although there are industry standards for developing SI equivalents, there is no consistent method in use for rounding off conversions. For example, the International Building Code (IBC) shows a 152 mm equivalent when a 6 in dimension is required. The Americans with Disabilities Act Accessibility Guidelines (ADAAG) gives a 150 mm equivalent for the same customary U.S. dimension.

To further complicate matters, each book publisher may employ a slightly different house style in handling SI equivalents when customary U.S. units are used as the primary measuring system. The confusion is likely to continue until the United States construction industry adopts the SI system completely, precluding the need for dual dimensioning in publishing.

For the purposes of this book, the following conventions have been adopted.

When dimensions are for informational use, the SI equivalent rounded to the nearest millimeter is used.

When dimensions relate to planning or design guidelines, the SI equivalent is rounded to the nearest 5 mm for numbers over a few inches and to the nearest 10 mm for numbers over a few feet. When the dimension exceeds several feet, the number is rounded to the nearest 100 mm. For example, a given activity requires a space about 10 ft wide, the modular, rounded SI equivalent will be given as 3000 mm. More exact conversions are not required.

When an item is only manufactured to a customary U.S. measurement, the nearest SI equivalent rounded to the nearest millimeter is given, unless the dimension is very small (as for metal gages), in which case a more precise decimal equivalent will be given. Some materials, such as glass, are often manufactured to SI sizes. For example, a nominal $^1/_2$ in thick piece of glass will have an SI equivalent of 13 mm but can be ordered as 12 mm.

When there is a hard conversion in the industry and an SI equivalent item is manufactured, the hard conversion is given. For example, a 24" × 24" ceiling tile would have the hard conversion of 600 × 600 (instead of 610) because these are manufactured and available in the United States.

When an SI conversion is used by a code agency, such as the IBC, or published in another regulation, such as the ADAAG, the SI equivalents used by the issuing agency are printed in this book. For example, the same 10 ft dimension given previously as 3000 mm for a planning guideline would have a building code SI equivalent of 3048 mm because this is what the IBC requires. The ADAAG generally follows the rounding rule of taking SI dimensions to the nearest 10 mm. For example, a 10 ft requirement for accessibility will be shown as 3050 mm. The code requirements for readers outside the United States may be slightly different.

The Sample Design Practicum is shown only in customary U.S. units in order to avoid confusion and minimize clutter on the printed page.

Throughout this book, the customary U.S. measurements are given first and the SI equivalents follow in parentheses. When the measurement is millimeters, no suffix is shown. For example, a dimension will be indicated as 4 ft 8 in (1422). When the SI equivalent is some other unit, such as volume or area, the suffix is indicated. For example, 250 ft^2 (23 m^2).

1

INFORMATION GATHERING

Programming is a process during which information about a problem is collected, analyzed, and clearly stated to provide a basis for design. It defines a problem before a solution is attempted. Programming is problem analysis, whereas design is problem synthesis.

Programming involves gathering information about the client's specific needs as well as identifying broader issues of human factors, environmental responsibility, and social and cultural influences on the design.

Thorough programming includes a wide range of information. In addition to stating the client's goals and objectives, a program should contain an analysis of the existing building, aesthetic considerations, space needs, adjacency requirements, organizing concepts, code review, budget requirements, and scheduling requirements.

THE PROGRAMMING PROCESS

There are several methods of programming, all of which can be used to establish the guidelines and information on which the design process can be based. For residential projects and small commercial jobs, a program may simply consist of a few sentences stating the goals of the project and a list of the required spaces and the furniture to be accommodated. On very large projects, like the headquarters for a corporate office, the program may be a bound volume containing very detailed information about current and future needs of the organization. If a program has not already been completed, it is the responsibility of the interior designer to determine how much information is required before design can begin and to collect and analyze that information.

One popular programming method uses a five-step process in relationship to four major considerations of form, function, economy, and time. This method is described in *Problem Seeking*, by William Pena, et. al.

The Five-Step Process

The five-step process involves establishing goals, collecting and analyzing facts, uncovering and testing concepts, determining needs, and stating the problem.

① *Establishing goals:* Goals indicate what the client wants to achieve and why. They are important to identify because they establish the directions of programmatic concepts that ultimately suggest the physical means of achieving the goals. It is not enough simply to list the types of spaces and required square footages the client needs; it is important to also know the objectives the client is trying to reach with those spaces and square footages. For example, a goal for a restaurant owner might be to increase revenues by increasing turnover, so the owner may want a design that discourages people from lingering over their meals.

② *Collecting and analyzing facts:* Facts describe the existing conditions and requirements of the problem, such as the number of people to be accommodated, space adjacencies, user characteristics, the existing building within which the interiors will be constructed, equipment to be housed, expected growth rate, money available for construction and furnishings, and building code requirements. There are always many facts; part of the programmer's task is not only to collect them but also to organize them so they are useful. Information gathering is discussed at length later in this chapter.

③ *Uncovering amd testing concepts:* The programming process should develop abstract ideas that are functional solutions to the client's performance problems, without defining the physical means that could be used to solve them. These ideas are called programmatic concepts and are the basis for later design concepts. It is important to understand the difference between programmatic concepts and design concepts. A *programmatic concept* is a performance requirement related to methods of solving a problem or satisfying a need. A *design concept* is a specific physical response that attempts to achieve a programmatic concept.

For example, the following might be one of many programmatic concept statements developed for a retail store: *Provide a medium level of security to protect against theft of merchandise without making the security methods obvious.*

This statement identifies and responds to a particular problem (security), narrows the problem focus (security of property from theft, as opposed to security of people or security from fire, for instance), and establishes a way of evaluating how well the goal was reached (are the security methods obvious or not?). There could be many possible design concepts that satisfy this programmatic concept, including the following.

1. Provide a central cash/wrap station at the entry/exit point to the store.

2. Tag all merchandise with concealed electronic identifiers, and incorporate the detection device in the design of the entry.

3. Display only samples of merchandise as a basis for buying, and have purchases delivered to the customer from a storage room.

An example involving the programming and design of a residential project might include the clients telling the designer that they entertain a lot and would like a place to hold parties, but that the children are always in the way. From that need the following programmatic concept could be developed: *Because the parents entertain frequently apart from the children's activities, the design should provide for functional separation of the children's spaces from the entertainment areas.*

If this programmatic concept were approved by the client, the designer would later develop several design concepts for consideration and testing against other requirements of the problem. For example, Fig. 1.1 shows five possible design concepts (diagrams that have actual physical implications) that respond to the programmatic concept. Diagram (a) shows splitting the parents' and children's areas into two wings of the house, each with its own entrance but connected with a corridor. Diagram (b) shows another physical response, with both areas in the same building but separated by some type of buffer zone. Diagrams (c), (d), and (e) show other possibilities. Because the various options are also concepts, there is still much detailed design work to do with whichever concept is selected.

④ *Determining needs:* This step of the programming process balances the desires of the client against the available budget or establishes a budget based on the defined goals and needs. It is during this step that "wants" have to be separated from "needs." Because most clients want more than they can afford, clear statements of true needs at this early stage can help avoid problems later. At this time, one or more of the four elements of cost (quantity, quality, budget, and time) may have to be adjusted to balance needs against available resources.

⑤ *Stating the problem:* The previous four steps are a prelude to succinctly stating the essence of the problem. The problem statements are the bridge between programming and the design process. They are statements, agreed upon by both the client and the programmer, that describe the most important aspects of the problem and serve as the basis for design and as the criteria by which the solution can be evaluated. There should be a minimum of four problem statements—one for each of the major considerations of form, function, economy, and time.

Four Major Considerations During Programming

The four major considerations of any design problem are form, function, economy, and time. *Form* relates to the existing

Figure 1.1
Design Concepts

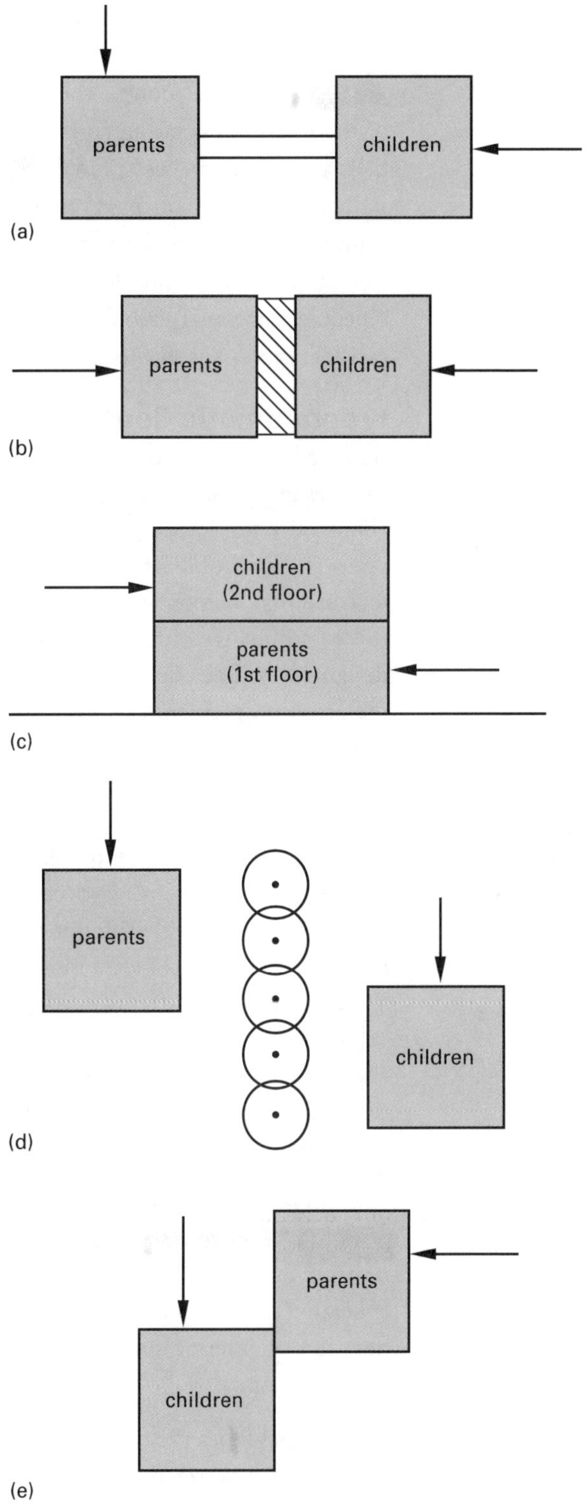

(a)

(b)

(c)

(d)

(e)

conditions in a space, the physical and psychological environment of the interior, and the quality of construction. *Function* relates to the people using a space, the activities to be performed there, and the relationship of spaces to eacher other. *Economy* concerns money: the initial cost of the interior, operating costs (if applicable), and life cycle costs. Finally, *time* describes the ideas of past, present, and future as they affect the other three considerations. For example, the required schedule for construction is often a time consideration, as is the need for expansion.

Programmatic Concepts

As stated in the previous section, the interior designer must develop abstract ideas about how to view and solve the client's performance problems (i.e., programmatic concepts) before attempting to solve those problems with three-dimensional design ideas. Later in the design process, the interior designer develops design concepts, which are physical solutions to the client's problems and which reflect approaches to satisfying the programmatic concepts. For example, expandability is a programmatic concept. Two corresponding design concepts that might be used to respond to this are (1) lease more space in a building than currently required and sublease it until it is required or (2) plan and design the space for low-cost, short-term occupancy, and move the entire business when additional space is required.

The book *Problem Seeking* identifies 24 programmatic concepts that tend to recur in all types of buildings, although they generally do not all occur in the same building or interior space. These include the following.

Priority establishes the order of importance of things such as size, position, or social values. For example, an entrance and reception area may have higher priority than individual offices, to reflect the goal of enhancing a company's image.

Hierarchy relates to the idea of the exercise of authority and is expressed in physical symbols of authority. For example, to reflect the hierarchy of a traditional law firm, senior members may be given larger offices than junior members and may be located in the corners of the building.

Character is a response to the desired image the client wants to project. This may later be expressed in design concepts using materials, lighting, space layout, and other physical responses to project character.

Density—low, medium, or high—may relate to how a space or group of spaces are used to respond to goals such as efficient use of space or the desired amount of interaction in an office.

Service groupings include mechanical services, such as mechanical systems, as well as other functions that support the use of a space. Distribution of supplies, storage space, information, and vending areas are examples of these types of functions. For example, a goal of decentralizing access to information could be accomplished by the physical design concept of using satellite libraries throughout a facility, or by developing an electronic database accessible to all workers through computer terminals.

Activity grouping states whether activities should be integrated (i.e., bundled together) or separated and compartmentalized. For example, compartmentalizing dining areas would respond to a goal of creating an intimate dining atmosphere in a restaurant.

People grouping states the degree of massing of people in a space and is derived from the physical, social, and emotional characteristics of the group. For example, the goal of establishing work teams in an office might suggest a concept of keeping small groups together in the same physical space.

(8) *Home base* is related to the concept of territoriality and is a place where a person can maintain his or her individuality.

(9) *Relationships* include the affinities of people and activities. This is one of the most common programming concepts established in any design problem because it most directly affects the organization of spaces and rooms.

(10) *Communications* as a concept is a response to the goal of promoting the effective exchange of information or ideas. This concept states who communicates with whom and how they do it.

(11) *Neighbors* is a concept that refers to how the project will promote or prevent sociablity and how it will relate to its neighboring spaces. For example, one department in a large organization may share a common entry court with another department to foster interaction and a sense of community.

(12) *Accessibility* relates to the idea of entry to a building or space and to making the facility accessible to the disabled. It answers the question of how people can find the entrance and whether or not there should be multiple entrances.

(13) *Separated flow* relates to segregating the flow of people, service access, and other activities of a building or space. For example, people may need to be separated from service access, or public visitors to a courthouse may need to be separated from prisoners.

(14) *Mixed flow* as a concept is a response to the goal of promoting interaction among people. Conversely, mixed flow may not be a desired programmatic concept in controlled facilities.

(15) *Sequential flow* is often required for both people and objects where a specific series of events or processes is required. For example, a show at an art museum may need to direct people from a starting point to an ending point. In a factory, material must progress from one station to another in a definite sequence.

(16) *Orientation* refers to providing a point of reference within a space or building to help keep people from feeling lost within a larger context. A common example of a physical design concept used to provide orientation is a central atrium or lobby within a large building or suite of offices.

(17) *Flexibility* includes three components. The first, *expandability*, refers to how a space can accommodate growth with expansion. The second, *convertibility*, refers to how a space can allow for changes in function through the conversion of spaces. The third, *versatility*, provides for several different activities with multifunctional spaces.

EXPANDABILITY
CONVERTABILITY
VERSATILITY

(18) *Tolerance* allows for extra space for a dynamic activity (one likely to change) instead of fitting the space precisely to a static activity. For example, an indoor swimming pool area can be sized to accommodate just the pool and circulation around it. Providing for tolerance would give extra room to accommodate future bleachers or extra seating areas.

(19) *Safety* focuses attention on life safety and the conceptual ways to achieve it. Building codes and other safety precautions are closely tied to this concept.

(20) *Security controls* refers to ways that both people and property can be protected based on the value of the potential loss—minimum, medium, or maximum.

(21) *Energy conservation* can be achieved in several ways: by keeping the heated area to a minimum, keeping heat flow to a minimum, using materials produced using low amounts of energy, using recycled materials, and using recyclable materials.

(22) *Environmental controls* explores the kinds of controls necessary to meet human comfort needs, including air temperature, light, sound, and humidity. This concept includes mechanical systems as well as natural means for climate control.

(23) *Phasing* determines if the project must be completed in stages to meet time and cost schedules. It also states whether the project can be based on linear scheduling or must provide for concurrent scheduling to meet urgent occupancy requirements.

(24) *Cost control* explores ways to establish a realistic preview of costs and a balanced budget to meet the client's available funds.

Programming Format

Regardless of what programming method is used or how complex the project is, the programming process should produce some type of written document that records the information gathered and the conclusions drawn from analysis. This document should be reviewed and approved by the client before design begins, because any incorrect programming information will result in a design that may not meet the client's needs.

Although the exact format of the final programming document will vary depending on the size and complexity of the job, every program should include at least the following information.

• A statement of goals and objectives. This may include result-oriented goals, such as "to increase sales by updating the image of the store," and functional goals, such as "to improve circulation and personal interaction among departments."

• A list of client requirements. This should include the number of people who will be using the space as well as information about the kinds of activities they engage in, the required adjacencies between people and activities, and the particular furniture and equipment each person requires.

In addition, special needs for lighting, acoustic separation, flexibility in space use, and electricity should be noted.

• A list of spaces and their square footages. This information is basic and serves as a starting point for space planning. This kind of list should also include allowance for secondary spaces like corridors, closets, and other nonlisted spaces that are necessary to make the space functional.

In addition to these data, a program may also include a survey of existing conditions, budget requirements, scheduling constraints, and expansion requirements. Refer to the section on information gathering later in this chapter for more detail on the kinds of information required and how it is collected. Chapter 2 discusses how the information is analyzed and compiled before beginning design.

HUMAN FACTORS

The field of *human factors* involves the correctness of fit between objects and spaces and the needs of the people using those objects and spaces. It encompasses a number of design disciplines that relate to the physical, psychological, and social needs of people. Because all interior design is based on the physical size of people and their physiological and psychological needs, the designer must have a good understanding of these topics.

Anthropometrics

Anthropometrics is the measurement of the size, proportions, and range of motion of the human body. A large amount of research has been performed that establishes the range of human dimensions from foot length to shoulder width. These dimensions have been established for various population groups and ages, as well as by sex, and include percentile distributions showing what percentage of the population falls within various measurement limits. *Static anthropometrics* measures the human body at rest, while *dynamic anthropometrics* measures the body while performing activities.

Based on anthropometric measurements, there is also a large body of knowledge about the minimum or optimum dimensions required for the average human to perform common activities. Room widths, heights of shelving, and clearances around furniture are examples of dimensions that are set by the interior designer and that must relate to the physical sizes, needs, and limitations of people.

Although there are hundreds of individual dimensions that have been found to be either minimum or optimum in a wide variety of situations, the designer should be generally familiar with some of the more basic ones. These are shown graphically in Figs. 1.2 through 1.9.

Ergonomics

Ergonomics is the study of the relation between human physiology and the physical environment. Ergonomics uses the information developed by anthropometrics, but it goes further by studying exactly how humans interact with physical objects like chairs, control panels, desks, and the like.

Because of the increasing number of office workers, design guidelines for several workstation components, such as chairs, computer terminals, and work surfaces, have been developed based on extensive research. Figure 1.8 shows some of the criteria for chair selection and design.

Figure 1.9 illustrates critical dimensions in computer workstation design. Note that one of the most important aspects of designing a computer station is keyboard height. The keyboard surface should be from 26 in to 28½ in (660 to 725) high and be adjustable. Reducing glare on the screen is also important but is usually accommodated in the design of the lighting or the layout and orientation of the

Figure 1.2
Seating
Dimensions

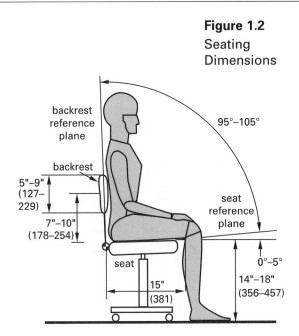

(a) work or secretarial chair

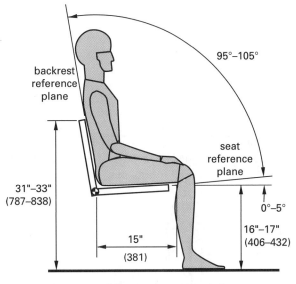

(b) general-purpose chair

workstation. When standup workstations are provided, they should have footrests.

One of the most important factors to include in the design of workstations and the selection of chairs is adjustability. Because there is no such thing as an average person, things like chair height, angle of a VDT (video display terminal), and keyboard position should be adjustable by the person using them. For chairs, the things

Figure 1.3
Office
Workstation

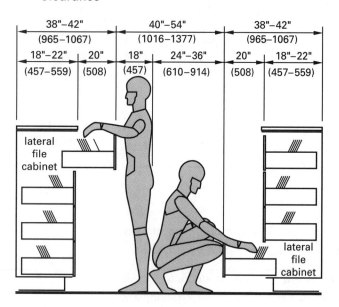

keyboard
surface

60"–72"
(1525–1829)

30"–48"
(762–1220)

30"–36"
(762–914)

work surface

Figure 1.4
Lateral Filing
Access
Clearance

38"–42" (965–1067)		40"–54" (1016–1377)		38"–42" (965–1067)	
18"–22" (457–559)	20" (508)	18" (457)	24"–36" (610–914)	20" (508)	18"–22" (457–559)

lateral
file
cabinet

lateral
file
cabinet

that should be adjustable include the seat height, the angle of the back, the height of the lumbar support in the back, and the distance from the front of the chair to the back support. If armrests are provided,

their height should also be adjustable, if possible.

Human Comfort

Human comfort is based on the quality of the following primary environmental factors: temperature, humidity, air movement, temperature radiation to and from surrounding surfaces, air quality, sound, vibration, and light. For each of these factors there are certain limits within which people are comfortable and can function most efficiently. Acoustics and lighting are reviewed in other chapters. This section discusses human comfort relative to the thermal environment.

Human Metabolism

The human body is a heat-producing machine. It takes in food and water and, through the metabolic process, converts these to mechanical energy and other bodily processes necessary to maintain life. Because the body is not very efficient in this conversion, it must give off excess heat to maintain a stable temperature. At rest, the human body gives off about 400 Btu/hr (117 W). This increases to around 700 Btu/hr to 800 Btu/hr (205 W to 235 W) for moderate activities like walking and work, and up to 2000 Btu/hr (586 W) for strenuous exercise. A *Btu*, or *British thermal unit*, is the amount of heat energy required to raise one pound of water by one degree Fahrenheit. This is approximately the amount of energy released by burning an ordinary wooden match. In SI units, this heat energy is measured in joules. Acting over a period of one hour, the corresponding unit of Btu/hr is watts (W).

The body loses heat in three ways: by convection, evaporation, and radiation. It can also lose heat by conduction, but this accounts for a very small portion of total body heat loss. *Convection* is the transfer of heat through the movement of a fluid, either a gas or liquid. This occurs when the air temperature surrounding a person is less than the body's skin temperature, around 85°F (29°C). Heat loss through *evaporation* occurs when moisture changes to vapor as a person perspires or breathes. *Radiation* is the transfer of heat energy through electromagnetic waves from one surface to a colder surface. The body can lose heat to a cooler atmosphere or to a cooler surface. *Conduction* is the transfer of heat through direct contact between two objects of different temperatures.

The body loses heat (or is prevented from losing heat) through these three processes in various proportions depending on the environmental conditions. If the body cannot lose heat one way it must lose it another. For example, when the air temperature is above the body temperature of 98.6°F (37°C), there can be no convection transfer, because heat always flows from a high level to a low level. The body must then lose heat by evaporation.

The sensation of thermal comfort depends on the interrelationship of air temperature, humidity, air movement, and radiation.

Air temperature: Temperature is the primary determinant of comfort. It is difficult to state precisely a normal range of comfortable temperature limits, because the range depends on factors such as humidity levels, radiant temperatures, air movement, clothing, cultural factors, age, and gender. However, a generally comfortable range is between 69°F and 80°F (21°C and 27°C), and a tolerable range is from 60°F to 85°F (16°C to 29°C). A value called the *effective temperature* (ET) has been developed that combines the effects of air temperature, humidity, and air movement.

Humidity: Relative humidity is the percentage of moisture in the air compared with the maximum amount of moisture the air can hold at a given temperature

Figure 1.5
Conference Tables

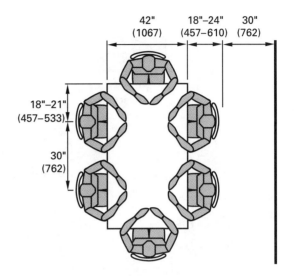

(a) rectangular table dimensions

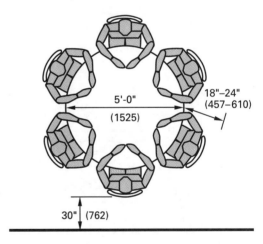

(b) round table dimensions

without condensing. Comfortable relative humidity ranges are between 30% and 65%, and tolerable ranges are between 20% and 70%. Relative humidity is particularly important in the summer because as the air temperature rises, the body loses less heat through convection and must rely mostly on evaporation. However, as the humidity rises, it is more difficult for perspiration to evaporate, and

Figure 1.6
Dining Tables

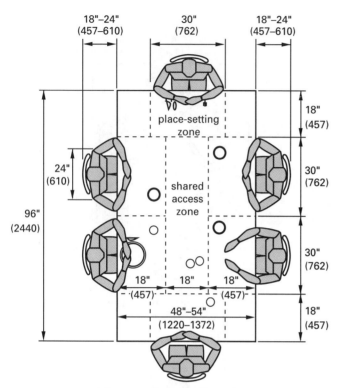

(a) rectangular table dimensions

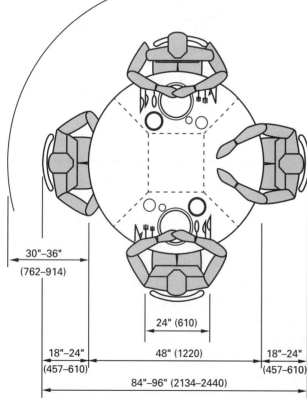

(b) round table dimensions

therefore people feel much hotter than the air temperature might indicate.

Air movement: Air movement tends to increase evaporation and heat loss through convection. This is why a person feels comfortable in high temperatures and humidities if there is a breeze. It also explains the windchill effect when a tolerably cold air temperature becomes unbearable in a wind. Wind speeds of from 50 ft/min to about 200 ft/min (0.25 m/s to 1.02 m/s) are generally acceptable for cooling without causing annoying drafts.

Radiation: Because the body can gain or lose heat through radiation, the temperature of the surrounding surfaces is an important factor in determining human comfort. If the surroundings are colder than the surface temperature of the skin, about 85°F (29°C), the body loses heat through radiation; if they are warmer the body gains heat. For example, if a chair is near a poorly insulated exterior wall in a cold climate, a person sitting in that chair may feel cool because heat is being radiated from the person's warm body to the cooler wall surface.

The *mean radiant temperature* (MRT)—a weighted average of the various surface temperatures in a room, the angle of exposure of the occupant to these surfaces, and any sunlight present—is the value used to determine radiation as an aspect of comfort. The MRT is an important comfort factor in cold rooms or in the winter because as the air temperature decreases, the body loses more heat through radiation than by evaporation. Even a room with an adequate temperature will feel cool if the surfaces are cold. Warming these surfaces by covering them with wall hangings or drapes or providing radiant heating panels are ways to counteract this effect.

Clothing acts as in insulator, moderating the effects of conduction, convection, and radiation. Nearly all measurements and standards for human comfort are based on wearing clothing. To quantify the effects of clothing, the unit of the Clo was developed. One Clo is about equal to the typical American man's business suit, or about 0.15 Clo/lbm (0.35 Clo per/kg) of clothing.

Ventilation

Ventilation is required to provide oxygen and remove carbon dioxide, to remove odors, and to carry away contaminants. The amount of ventilation required in a room depends on the activity in the room, the size of the room, and whether people smoke in the room. For example, a gymnasium needs a higher ventilation rate than a library. Building codes give the minimum requirements for ventilation, either by specifying minimum operable window areas, minimum mechanical ventilation rates, or both.

Building codes specify the minimum amount of fresh, outdoor air that must be circulated and the total circulated air in cubic feet per minute (liters per second). Mechanical systems are designed to filter and recirculate much of the conditioned air, and they also introduce a certain percentage of outdoor air along with the recirculated air.

Where exhausting of air is required, such as in toilet rooms, kitchens, and spaces where noxious fumes are present, additional requirements are given.

Building codes either give minimum exhaust rates in cubic feet per minute per square foot of floor area (liters per second per square meter) or else they specify how often a complete air change within the room must be made. In these situations, the ventilation system must exhaust directly to the outside; none of the exhausted air can be recirculated. A toilet room exhaust fan, for example, will be connected to a duct

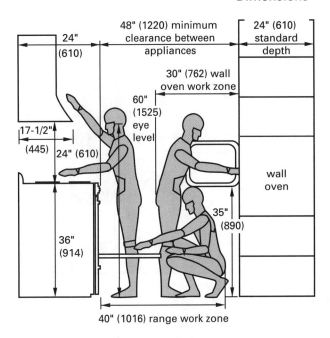

Figure 1.7
Kitchen
Clearance
Dimensions

24" (610)

48" (1220) minimum clearance between appliances

24" (610) standard depth

30" (762) wall oven work zone

60" (1525) eye level

17-1/2" (445)

24" (610)

wall oven

35" (890)

36" (914)

40" (1016) range work zone

that leads to the outside without connecting in any way with the building's ventilating system.

PSYCHOLOGICAL AND SOCIAL INFLUENCES

A well-designed interior should respond to the psychological and social needs of the people using it as well as to the users' physical needs. In many cases a general understanding of these human needs can be applied to any design situation. In other cases the particular needs must be identified during the programming process by determining the exact special needs of the users.

Although there has been much research in the field of environmental psychology, predicting human behavior and designing spaces that enhance people's lives is an inexact process. However, the interior designer must attempt to develop a realistic model of both the people who will be using the designed environment and the

Figure 1.8
Chair Design
Criteria for
Workstations

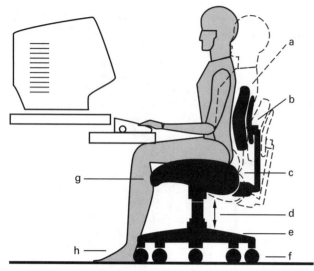

a. thoracic support: contoured backrest adjusts up and down, forward and backward; remains in constant contact with user's back regardless of tilt angle
b. lumbar (lower back) support: the seat's contoured sides support pelvic rotation as the user moves backward and forward, regardless of the tilt angle of the seat. Seat angle adjustment; pivot allows feet to remain on floor.
c. foam construction not too soft; firm enough to cushion and support the body
d. pneumatic height adjustment
e. five-prong base for extra stability, balance
f. casters for smooth, friction-free movement
g. waterfall front edge aids thigh circulation, reduces leg fatigue
h. feet comfortably flat on floor

nature of their activities. This model can then serve as the foundation on which to base many design decisions. The following concepts are some of the more common psychological influences on interior design. For a review of additional social and cultural influences and how they affect design theory, refer to Ch. 3.

Maslow's Hierarchy of Needs

One of the basic theories of human motivation was proposed by Abraham Maslow. His conceptual model was a hierarchy of needs. According to Maslow's theory, humans have a variety of needs, which he divided into two groups: deficiency needs and growth needs. The most basic needs must be met first before a person can move to the next highest level of needs satisfaction. Meeting needs and moving to the next highest level provides the motivation for behavior.

At the most basic level in the deficiency needs group, humans have physiological needs for food, water, and minimal bodily comforts. The next level consists of safety needs, which includes the need for protection and the avoidance of personal harm. The third level is that of belonging and love. Here, a person strives for membership in a group, acceptance, and love. The top level of the first group is self-esteem, which includes the need to achieve, be competent, and gain approval and recognition by others.

Originally, Maslow proposed that the top level of need was that of self-actualization, defined as developing to the fullest potential as a human being, feeling an appreciation of life, and demonstrating the ability to have peak experiences. Later, Maslow added two additional needs in the growth group below self-actualization: the cognitive need to know and understand, and the aesthetic need for order and beauty. The need he added above that of self-actualization was self-transcendence, the need to help others find self-fulfillment and connect to something beyond the ego.

Behavior Settings

A *behavior setting* is a particular place with definable boundaries and objects in which a standing pattern of behavior occurs at a particular time. It is a useful concept for studying the effects of the environment on human activity. For example, a weekly board of directors meeting in a conference room can be considered a behavior setting. The activity of the meeting follows certain procedures, it occurs in the same place (the conference room) and the room is arranged to assist the activity (chairs are arranged around a table, audiovisual facilities are present, lighting is adequate, and so forth).

The behavior setting is useful for the interior designer because it connects the strictly behavioral aspects of human activity with the effects of the physical environment on people. Although a behavior setting is a complex system of activities, human goals, physical objects, and cultural needs, it provides the interior designer with a definable unit of design. By knowing the people involved and the activities taking place, programmatic concepts can be developed that support the setting.

Territoriality

Territoriality is a fundamental aspect of human behavior and refers to people's need to lay claim to the spaces they occupy and the things they own. Although partially based on the biological imperative for protection, territoriality in humans is more related to the needs for self-identity and freedom of choice. When someone personalizes a desk at the office with family pictures, plants, individual coffee mugs, and the like, he or she is staking a claim to a personal territory, as small and temporary as it may be. In a more permanent living environment such as a house or apartment, walls, fences, and property lines provide territorial boundaries. Often, boundaries are subtle. A row of file cabinets or a change in level may serve to define a person's or group's territory.

Territoriality applies to groups as well as to individuals. A study club or school class can claim a physical territory as its own, which helps give both the group and the individuals in the group an identity. Environments should allow people to claim territory and make choices about where to be and what activities to engage in.

Proxemics

The term *proxemics* was created by anthropologist Edward T. Hall to describe

Figure 1.9
Computer
Workstation
Dimensions

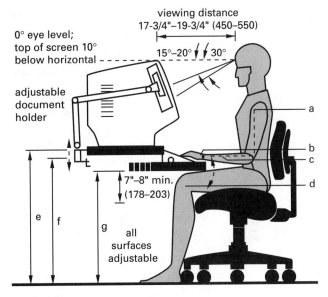

a. vertical upper arm
b. wrist incline no more than 10°
c. horizontal lower arm
d. adequate knee and leg clearance—no structural obstructions
e. work surface height to 30" (762)
f. keyboard surface 26"–28-1/2" (660–725); home row keys 28"–31" (711–787)
g. leg clearance 27" (686)

the interrelated observations and theories of humans' use of space as a specialized elaboration of culture. Proxemics deals with the issues of spacing between people, territoriality, organization of space, and positioning of people in space, all relative to the culture of which they are a part.

For example, proxemics suggests that where strangers will be sitting near each other, single chairs with their own definable spaces are preferable to sofas or benches. People will sit at the two ends of a sofa or bench, leaving the middle empty, rather than sit close to each other or risk physical contact. In other cases, a knowledge of proxemics helps a designer decide the spacing between toilet fixtures or the density of public seating.

As part of the theory of proxemics, Hall observed four basic distances that can be used to study human behavior and serve as a guide for designing environments. The actual dimensions of the four distances vary with the circumstances and with cultural and social differences, but they always exist. The interior designer should be aware of the fact of personal distance needs and design accordingly, because forcing people closer together than the situation warrants can have adverse effects.

The closest of Hall's distances is the *intimate distance*. See Fig. 1.10. This ranges from physical contact to about 6 in (150) for the close phase to 18 in (450) for the far phase. People only allow other people to come within this distance under special conditions. If forced this close together (for example, on a crowded elevator), people have other defense mechanisms, such as avoiding eye contact, to minimize the effects of the physical contact.

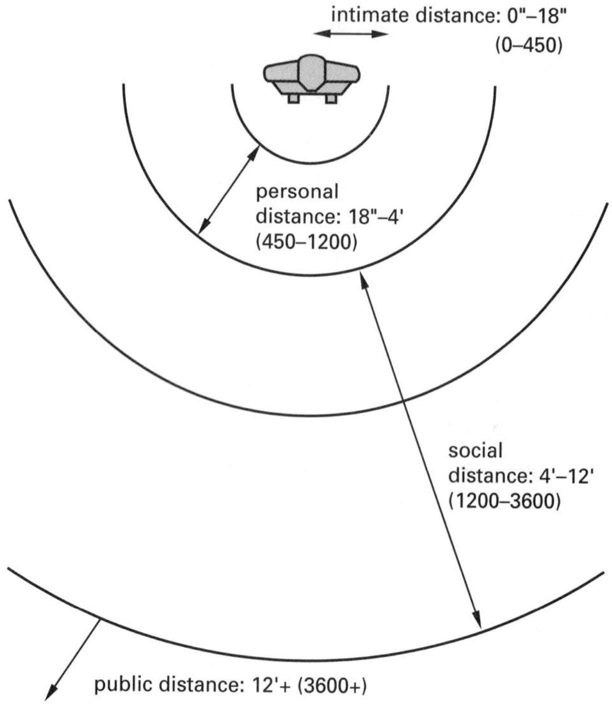

The next distance is the *personal distance*, from about $1^1/_2$ ft to $2^1/_2$ ft (450 to 750) for the close phase and from $2^1/_2$ ft to 4 ft (750 to 1200) for the far phase. If given the choice, people will maintain at least this distance between themselves and others.

Social distance is the next invisible sphere, ranging from about 4 ft to 7 ft (750 to 2100) for the close phase and from 7 ft to 12 ft (2100 to 3600) for the far phase. This is the distance at which most impersonal business, work, and other interaction takes place between strangers or in formal situations. In this area, speech and nonverbal communication are clearly understood, but personal space is maintained. At about 10 ft (3000) it is not considered rude to ignore other people nearby, such as in a reception room or library.

Public distance is the farthest, ranging from about 12 ft (3600) outward. The greatest amount of formality can be achieved at this distance. In addition, this distance allows people to escape if they sense physical danger from another person.

Personalization

One of the ways territoriality manifests itself is with the personalization of space. Whether it happens in one's home, at the office desk, or in a waiting lounge, people will often arrange their environment to reflect their presence and uniqueness. The most successful designs allow this to take place without major adverse effects to other people or to the interior as a whole. At home, people decorate their spaces the way they want. At the office, people bring in personal objects, such as family photographs, to make the space their own. In an airport lounge, people place coats and suitcases around them, not only to stake out a temporary territory, but also to make the waiting time more personal and a little more comfortable.

Figure 1.10
Personal Space

intimate distance: 0"–18"
(0–450)

personal distance: 18"–4'
(450–1200)

social distance: 4'–12'
(1200–3600)

public distance: 12'+ (3600+)

Another way people personalize space is to modify the environment. If a given space is not conducive to the needs of the people using it, the users can either modify their behavior to adapt to the environment, change their relationship to the environment (leave), or try to change the surroundings. The simple act of moving a chair to make viewing a screen easier is an example of modifying and personalizing a space. If the chair is immovable, the design is not as adaptable to the varying needs of the people using the interior space.

Group Interaction

To a certain extent, the environment can either facilitate or hinder human interaction. In most behavior settings, groups are predisposed to act in a particular way. If the setting is not conducive to the activities, the people will try to modify the environment or modify their behavior to make the activity work. In extreme cases, if the setting is totally at odds with the activity, stress, anger, and other adverse reactions can occur.

Seating arrangement is one of the most common ways of facilitating group interaction. Studies have shown that people will seat themselves at a table according to the nature of their relationships with others around them. For intimate conversation, two people will sit across the corner of a table or next to each other on a sofa. For more formal or competitive situations, people will sit across from one another. Where social contact is not desired, two people will take chairs at opposite corners of a table. See Fig. 1.11.

Round tables tend to foster more cooperation and equality among those seated around them. Rectangular tables tend to make cooperation more difficult and establish the person sitting at the end in a more superior position. Strangers do not like to share the same sofa or park bench.

Figure 1.11
Table Seating

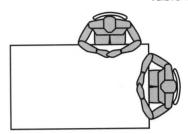

(a) intimate position

(b) competition position

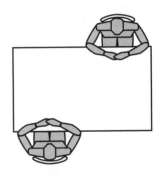

(c) avoidance position

Knowing these basics of group interaction can assist the interior designer in making decisions. For example, individual study carrels in a library will be more efficient than large tables because the tables will seldom be fully occupied by strangers.

In places where informal group interaction takes place, studies have shown that over 97% of groups are comprised of two to four people. Designing to accommodate these group sizes makes more sense than anticipating larger groups of people, although a plan that allows for the possibility of very large groups while preferring small groups would be the best combination. In most cases, providing a variety of spaces for interaction is the best approach.

Status

An individual's location or position within the environment can also communicate status. In the United States, for example, someone with a corner office has more status than someone whose office has only one exterior wall. Office size is also equated with status in many cultures. Tables near the door of an exclusive restaurant are often considered the high-status position. Status can also operate at the scale of an entire interior project. The client may want the interior to symbolize some quality of the organization and give him or her a higher physical and psychological status in the community.

An interior design program should investigate the requirements or implications of status. Some clients may clearly state the status-related goals they want to achieve. If the client does not raise the issue, the interior designer must explore the matter of status with the client and document the response as a programmatic concept.

SUSTAINABLE DESIGN

Sustainable building design (also known as "green building" or "green design") is an increasingly important part of interior design. It includes a wide range of concerns such as the environmental impact of a building, the wise use of both exterior and interior materials, energy conservation, use of alternative energy sources, adaptive reuse, indoor air quality, recycling, reuse, and other strategies to achieve a balance between the consumption of environmental resources and the renewal of those resources. Sustainable design considers the full life cycle of a building and the materials that comprise the building. This includes considering the impact of raw material extraction throughout the cycle of fabrication, installation, operation, maintenance, and disposal.

This section discusses sustainable design as it affects the preliminary interior design

of spaces and the development of project concepts. Subsequent chapters cover daylighting and artificial lighting, new material technologies, material selection, specifying for sustainability, and building systems. Chapter 26 is devoted to the topic of sustainable design.

Leadership in Energy and Environmental Design Certification

The Leadership in Energy and Environmental Design (LEED™) Green Building Rating System is a national, consensus-based building rating system designed to accelerate the development and implementation of green building practices. It was developed by the U.S. Green Building Council, which is a national coalition of leaders from all aspects of the building industry working to promote buildings that are both environmentally responsible and profitable and that provide healthy places to live and work. In addition to developing the rating system, the full LEED program offers training workshops, professional accreditation, resource support, and third-party certification of building performance. In order for a building to be certified, certain prerequisites must be achieved and points must be earned for meeting or exceeding the program's technical requirements. Points add up to a final score that relates to one of four possible certification levels: certified, silver, gold, or platinum. LEED is one of the primary building rating systems in the United States.

The LEED program includes a portfolio of rating systems, one of which is for commercial interiors (LEED-CI), which is also applicable to tenant improvements of new or existing office space. Other rating systems include LEED for new construction and LEED for existing buildings. Additional systems are being developed for homes, neighborhood developments, and core and shell work.

Preliminary Sustainability Decisions During Programming

Although most of the sustainability issues related to interior design are implemented during the schematic design, design development, and contract documents phases of the project delivery process, there are many decisions that are appropriately made by the client during programming. These sustainability decisions include those that affect site selection, or selection of the building in which the tenant or interior design project will be located. Not all suggestions need be implemented for the same tenant space. Some of these include the following and are only briefly stated. Refer to the LEED-CI requirements for a detailed explanation of the technical criteria for receiving points under the LEED system.

• Select a building for the tenant space that is LEED certified.

• Locate the tenant space in a building that has been documented as a brownfield site. A *brownfield site* is, with certain legal exclusions, commercial or industrial property where the development, expansion, or reuse may be complicated by the presence or potential presence of a hazardous substance, pollutant, or contaminant.

• Locate the tenant space in a building where a stormwater management plan has been implemented. There are various technical options for this approach, depending on how the building management has implemented the LEED criteria.

• Locate the tenant space in a building that provides shade and/or uses light-colored/high-albedo materials and/or uses open-grid pavement equal to at least 30% of the site's non-roof impervious surfaces. *Albedo* is the fraction of the radiant energy (in this case the sun's energy) received on a surface that is subsequently reflected back into space.

• Locate the tenant space in a building having a minimum of 50% of parking spaces underground or covered or that uses an open-grid pavement system for 50% of the parking lot area.

• Locate the tenant space in a building with roofing having a high solar reflectance index, a green (vegetated) roof, or a combination of both.

• Locate the tenant space in a building whose exterior lighting does not create light pollution.

• Locate the tenant space in a building that uses high-efficiency irrigation technology or uses captured rain or recycled site water to reduce potable water for irrigation.

• Locate the tenant space in a building that does not have a permanent landscaping irrigation system or that uses only rain or recycled site water.

• Locate the tenant space in a building that reduces the use of municipally provided potable water for building sewage conveyance.

• Locate the tenant space in a building that supplies at least 5% of its total energy use through on-site renewable energy.

• Select space in a building that is located in a established, walkable community with a minimum density of 60,000 ft^2/ac (13 774 m^2/ha).

• Select space in a building that is located within 0.5 mi (0.8 km) of a residential zone and that has pedestrian access to at least 10 of the basic services such as banks, pharmacies, schools, and supermarkets.

• Locate the tenant space in a building within $1/2$ mi (0.8 km) of a commuter rail, light rail, or subway station or within $1/4$ mi (0.4 km) of two or more bus lines.

• Locate the tenant space in a building that provides secure bicycle storage with convenient changing and shower facilities.

• Locate the tenant space in a building where the guaranteed tenant parking does not exceed the minimum number required by zoning or where no parking is provided with the tenant lease, or provide preferred parking for carpools or vanpools capable of serving 5% of the building occupants.

INFORMATION GATHERING

There are four methods of collecting the information required to complete a program and prepare for design. Each has its own advantages and disadvantages. In most cases, two or more methods are used together on any given project. Before these are discussed individually, the following lists provide a comprehensive itemization of the specific information that may be needed for a project. Of course, not every item on the list is required for every project.

Checklist of Required Information

Goals and Objectives:

• purpose for building a new or remodeled interior space

• functional goals (e.g., larger space, more efficient operation, change in workflow)

• aesthetic goals

User Requirements:

• individual users: by name, title, or position

• number and function of groups if not individual users

• whether the user is a specific, full-time user or public user

• number of people: at present, at move in, and in future growth

• job description of the user

• user characteristics: age, sex, special needs (right- or left-handed, physical disabilities, etc.)

• personal preferences: colors, special interests, and so on

• location of user or activity space (e.g., bedrooms on north side, executives in corner offices)

Activity Requirements:

• primary activity

• secondary activities

• nature of the activity: physical movement involved, workflow, and so on.

• when the activity is performed: time of day or night

• how often the activity is performed: number of times per day, week, and so on

• part-time activities such as in conference rooms, reception areas, copy areas, and so on

• if the activity is done alone, in small groups, or in large groups

• visitors involved with the activity

• if the activity shares space with other activities

• special environmental requirements for the activity: lighting, acoustics, heating or cooling, ventilation

• special security requirements

Furnishings and Equipment:

• kinds of furniture or equipment required

• whether existing furnishings will be used or new furnishings will be purchased

• sizes of reused and new equipment

• relationships of equipment or furnishings

- types and requirements of communication equipment: telephones, computers, facsimile machines, modems, and so on

- types and amount of storage: bookcases, shelves, drawers, file cabinets, and so on

- electrical requirements of equipment: voltage, special outlets, dedicated circuits, or special lighting

- mechanical requirements of equipment: cooling, ventilation, and so on

- private or shared furnishings and equipment

- accessories used: reference manuals, staplers, stamps, postage machines, and so on

- future needs

- required style, color, quality level, ergonomic needs, and so on

- display space required: tack boards, marker boards, and so on

- audiovisual equipment requirements

Adjacencies:

- required person-to-person contacts

- required movement of objects, paper, or equipment

- degree of adjacency: mandatory, preferred, or not important

- required zoning of related activities, departments, or functional groups

- required adjacencies with the outside: visitors, service, views, shipping, and so on

Space Requirements Listed by Area and Square Footage:

- space required by activity areas: people and equipment

- space requirements determined primarily by equipment or activity alone rather than by full-time users in an activity area

- nonassigned space needs: corridors, closets, storage rooms, and other circulation space

Time and Money Requirements:

- total budget broken into construction budget, furnishing costs, equipment costs, taxes, contingencies, and others as required by project type

- lifecycle cost analysis

- move-in deadline or phasing requirements

The Client Interview

Interviewing users is one of the most valuable ways of collecting information. It combines observation (actually seeing what the user currently has), a structured process (following a pre-established set of questions), the ability to clarify ambiguous questions or responses (by elaborating or asking follow-up questions), and the opportunity for extemporaneous exploration of needs and ideas of the user not previously considered. If questionnaires have been used, interviews can verify their accuracy. In addition, a good interviewer can pick up on nonverbal clues about what the user may really be thinking or his or her attitudes toward certain aspects of the topics being discussed. The interview technique works with residential design as well as with large corporations.

However, interviewing takes time and requires that the person being interviewed be kept on the subject while still allowing for some open-ended questions and comments. The designer must also have the approval and direction of the management or of the supervisors of the interviewees. It is usually best to have the client send an email or memo to all those being interviewed to explain why the process is being undertaken, what the answers will be used for, and that the interviews are approved and encouraged (or required) by management.

The number and types of people being questioned should be determined ahead of time and should represent a cross section of the organization. An individual worker may have a very different view of his or her needs than a department manager, but both opinions are valuable. The interviewer should prepare a list of specific questions or talking points for which answers are needed. This keeps the process on track and provides a common ground on which to compare interviews and compile results. However, there should be an opportunity for open-ended discussions or questions than can arise only when the interviewer actually sees and talks to an individual.

To conduct the interview, appointments should be made for a specific time and location (preferably the user's workplace or activity area) and limited to a predetermined length. Two interviewers should be present: one to ask the questions and observe, and one to take notes and provide a second opinion on observation. It is usually difficult for one person to do everything well.

The person recording the information from the interview should take down the most important points. A verbatim record is not required. In some cases a sketch or diagram is as useful as words. The person asking the questions may also want to take notes on interviewee responses and later compare them with the information recorded by the other person on the team.

General topics for which questions may be developed include the following.

- number of people involved
- communication needs of people
- workflow
- adjacencies required
- furniture and storage requirements
- equipment requirements
- need for expansion (growth)
- budget requirements
- open versus closed space
- reusing furniture versus buying new furniture
- circulation system
- shared use of space
- amount of time a space is used
- spatial requirements of an activity

All of these topics have physical implications for planning and design related to the number, size, location, quality, and furnishing of activity spaces.

Interviews may be conducted individually or in small or large groups. An individual interview consists of two people from the programming team and one person from the client's organization, for the reasons previously mentioned. Once interviews are conducted in groups, the social dynamics of group interaction come into play.

A small-group interview may include all of the people in one department, with or without the group's supervisor. If a supervisor is present, the others in the group may feel intimidated. Small-group interviews have the advantage of efficient exchange of ideas but can turn into a complaint session if the discussion and questions are not kept on track by the interviewer. Sometimes, a client coordinator sits with the interviewers to monitor and check the validity of the answers and mediate differences of opinion. However, as with having a supervisor in the group of interviewees, the presence of a client coordinator may be intimidating.

A large-group interview may include up to 20 people who may come from several departments or disciplines in the client's organization. As the group gets larger, fewer people tend to participate, unless specifically prompted by the interviewer. In most cases, before interviewing can begin, an initial presentation is given that provides everyone with the project background and outlines what type of information is being sought.

Questionnaires

Questionnaires are written forms that people fill in with requested information. They are useful when a large number of people need to be surveyed and time or resources do not allow for individual interviews. However, to be effective, they must be well designed and their completion should be required by management. Questionnaires may also be distributed through email or through a web server if the client has a company intranet. However, this requires someone knowledgeable in setting up a web-based questionnaire and having the information automatically organized into a database.

No one likes to complete a form, paper or electronic, even if it leads to improvements in the workplace. A questionnaire must be designed to be as short, unambiguous, and easy to fill in as possible. If an item is not clear, people will ignore it or provide questionable information. One of the best ways to develop an effective questionnaire is to design one and try it out on a select sample. Confusing or unnecessary questions can then be revised before the full sample is taken. A questionnaire should be accompanied by a cover letter from management explaining why the form is being distributed and encouraging or requiring that it be completed and returned. In some cases, information from questionnaires is verified by interviews.

Alternatively, a questionnaire may be developed by the designers but administered by someone from the designer's office. The designated administrator can clarify unclear questions and ensure the questionnaire's completion. Unlike an interview, a questionnaire requires only one administrator, and the process usually requires less time.

Observation

One of the most reliable ways to gather information is by observing what people do rather than by listening to what they say. The danger of observation, however, is jumping to conclusions without understanding why people are doing things in a particular way. For example, a person may have numerous small appliances on a kitchen counter not because it is convenient but because there is nowhere else to store them. The client might prefer to have a storage location in a closet out of sight, yet an observer might draw the incorrect conclusion that the client likes having appliances on the counter.

Observation is best used to verify information gathered by interviews or questionnaires or as a way of generating questions to determine the reason behind the observed behavior. Observation is also useful in situations where questionnaires or interviews are not possible—for example, to determine how people use a public space.

Field Surveys

Because interior design is accomplished within an architectural space, an important part of programming is to determine existing conditions. This is true whether the building already exists or is still in the planning stages. An existing building can be field measured and photographed, and special onsite conditions can be noted. If a building is still being designed, the information must be determined from architectural drawings.

A field survey should determine the following.

• the size and configuration of the existing building or space. This involves taking field measurements and drafting a plan to scale that can be used for the final interior plan. The plan should include structural elements such as exterior walls, columns, and interior loadbearing walls. It should also include fixed architectural reference points from which interior dimensions can be made. These may include points like column centerlines, faces of structural walls, or faces of permanent partitions.

• existing nonloadbearing partitions, cabinetry, and built-in items

• locations and sizes (width and height) of doors and windows

• types and heights of ceilings

• locations of electrical and telephone outlets

• locations and sizes of heating diffusers, radiators, and other exposed mechanical equipment

• locations of plumbing fixtures and plumbing pipes

• locations and types of existing artificial lighting

• conditions and capacities of the electrical, plumbing, heating, and other mechanical systems in older buildings. These will need to be determined by engineering consultants.

• general conditions of construction elements. These will help determine what can be reused and what will need to be repaired or replaced.

• location of true north, and notes on the quality and amount of natural light

• views from windows

• potential noise problems, either from within or outside the building

• special architectural features, molding, or unusual elements

• potential environmental problems with asbestos, lead paint, and the like. The interior designer's survey can only suggest the possibility of these types of problems. Actual field testing and verification must be done by companies qualified to perform this type of work.

Methods of Field Measuring and Recording

Traditionally, collecting information on the size and configuration of existing buildings and spaces has required the interior designer to visit the site and make sketches and measurements using a tape measure and traditional surveying equipment. Drawings are then produced from the measurements taken on site. This method is labor intensive and prone to human errors as well as errors generated by the measurement tools. However, it can be a useful, low-cost method to use when measuring spaces of moderate size and complexity. Hand measuring is also well suited for recording small details that cannot be seen by instruments using other techniques.

The development of more precise measuring instruments has augmented the use of the simple tape measure. Low-cost, line-of-site sonic devices can be used by one person and give reasonable accuracy for many uses. However, their range is limited and they cannot precisely differentiate between closely spaced elements.

A more accurate procedure is to use *electro-magnet distance measurement* (EDM). This process uses a laser-based instrument with an onboard computer to measure the distance, horizontal, and vertical angles of the instrument's laser beam to a reflective prism target. EDM instruments are accurate to $\pm^1/_{64}$ in at 1600 ft (± 0.5 at 500 m). As with hand measuring, this method requires a knowledgeable operator to select the points to be measured. Two people are usually required to use an EDM instrument.

A similar technique uses a *reflectorless electromagnetic distance measure* (REDM) device. This type of device does not require the use of a prism reflector; instead, it relies on the return signal bounced from the object being measured. The accuracy is less precise: $\pm^1/_8$ in at 100 ft (±3 at 30 m). The accuracy of REDM is affected by the obliqueness of the laser beam on the targeted point, the distance from the instrument to the targeted point, and the reflective quality and texture of the targeted point.

Several other image-based techniques, other than standard photography, are available to assist in the accurate surveying of existing structures. These include rectified photography, orthophotography, photogrammetry, and laser scanning.

Rectified photography uses large-format, film-based view cameras (the type typically used to do high-quality architectural photography) to photograph façades. The camera's focal plane is set parallel to the façade and gives a flat image with no perspective distortion. Dimensions can be scaled off of the image, but to improve accuracy the building plane should be relatively flat. In addition to providing the ability to scale building elements not readily accessible to hand measuring, the photograph provides an accurate image of the building, as any photograph would.

Orthophotography is similar to rectified photography except that it relies on digital photography and correction of optical distortion through computer software.

Photogrammetry is the surveying of objects or spaces by using photography and associated software.

Stereophotogrammetry uses two overlapping photographs that are loaded into a computer program to produce a digital stereo image. The image can then be used to extract information to make a three-dimensional drawing. In addition to producing accurate three-dimensional drawings, this technique also produces a photographic record. It does require specialized equipment and computer software, as well as trained technicians, to do the work.

Convergent photogrammetry uses multiple, oblique photographic images of an object taken at different angles. Measurements and three-dimensional models are derived by using software that traces the multiple overlapping photographs taken from the different angles. This field measuring technique requires that reference points be established by standard surveying techniques or by measuring distances between the reference points to establish a correctly scaled coordinate system that the software can use. Although relatively inexpensive, it is slower than laser scanning. It has an accuracy of about $\pm0.05\%$.

Laser scanning uses medium-range pulsing laser beams, which systematically sweep over an object or space to obtain three-dimensional coordinates of points on the surfaces of the object or space being scanned. The resulting image is a "point cloud" forming a 3D image. From this image, plans, elevations, sections, and three-dimensional models are developed by computer software. The laser scans from one or more points, depending on the exact system being used. For multiple room interiors, the images can be stitched together to give an overall image of an entire building. Unlike photogrammetry, no surveyed reference points are required; all the information can be gathered from a single point rather than from multiple photographs. Laser scanning has an accuracy ranging from $\pm0.05\%$ to $\pm0.01\%$ or better.

SAMPLE QUESTIONS

1. Which of the following would be the most important consideration in the design of ergonomically correct chairs for air traffic controllers?

  (A) adjustability

  (B) firm cushions

  (C) lumbar support

  (D) tilt and swivel capability

2. When designing a computer workstation, which of the following factors is LEAST important?

  (A) keyboard height

  (B) VDT angle

  (C) screen glare

  (D) work-surface depth

3. Symmetrically positioned identical furnishings in a college dormitory room shared by two people represent an attempt to satisfy which psychological need?

  (A) personal space

  (B) territoriality

  (C) group interaction

  (D) personalization

4. Proxemics might assist a designer in

  (A) deciding on the size of a doctor's examination room

  (B) determining where to locate the office of the president within an office suite

  (C) planning the size and shape of a conference table

  (D) making decisions about the type and spacing of seating in an audiovisual presentation room

5. Most people in the United States typically conduct business and relate to strangers at which distance?

  (A) 1.5 ft to 4 ft (450 to 1200)

  (B) 4 ft to 12 ft (1200 to 3600)

  (C) 7 ft to 12 ft (2100 to 3600)

  (D) 12 ft to 25 ft (3600 to 7500)

6. A client complains that her office is too hot. The interior designer could most easily improve the situation by suggesting an accessory that affects

  (A) convection

  (B) ventilation

  (C) evaporation

  (D) conduction

7. An interior designer would most likely use anthropometric information to

  (A) design countertops for a public rest room

  (B) determine the percentage of children who would be comfortable on custom-designed benches in a puppet theater

  (C) develop the best position for multiple VDT screens in a stock trader's workstation

  (D) evaluate a new chair design that has just come on the market

8. Which type of information regarding a multipurpose room in an apartment building for the elderly would be LEAST important for the interior designer to give to the mechanical engineer?

  (A) the ages of the residents in the apartment building

  (B) the types of activities that commonly occur in the space

  (C) an estimate of the number of people using the room

  (D) a copy of the reflected ceiling plan

9. In addition to being decorative, tapestries in Gothic and Renaissance castles

  (A) reduced the amount of sound reflection within a room

  (B) minimized drafts

  (C) increased the mean radiant temperature

  (D) reduced heat loss by increasing the insulating value of the walls

10. An interior designer would be most likely to suggest to the mechanical engineer that additional ventilation or exhaust be provided in

- (A) a private toilet room
- (B) a commercial kitchen
- (C) a corporation conference room
- (D) an exercise room in a community recreation center

11. A library is being designed to occupy only one portion of a building, and a complete set of drawings is available for the building. What information would be the most important to obtain from the field survey?

- (A) the locations of structural elements
- (B) existing natural light sources
- (C) sources of noise within the building
- (D) the locations and capacities of electrical power

12. Which of the following is a true statement about the difference between a programmatic concept and a design concept?

- (A) A design concept specifies a particular way to achieve the programmatic concept.
- (B) There are as many programmatic concepts for a problem as there are design concepts.
- (C) A design concept is a performance requirement.
- (D) Programmatic concepts are developed concurrently with design concepts.

13. For an interior designer conducting a programming interview with a client for a small clothing boutique, which is the LEAST important question to ask?

- (A) Which items are most frequently purchased on impulse?
- (B) Will rest rooms be available to the customers?
- (C) What amount of merchandise will be on display?

- (D) What is the relationship between the cash/wrap counter and the dressing rooms?

14. Which of the following statements is generally FALSE regarding programming interviews?

- (A) They can verify the accuracy of questionnaires.
- (B) They minimize inaccurate results from ambiguous questions.
- (C) They allow for the revelation of information that the programmer may not have considered.
- (D) They make efficient use of the interviewer's time

15. An interior designer has been hired to redesign a very large Victorian house into a bed and breakfast inn. During an initial interview, the client says that he wants to restore the interior to an original Victorian look as well as enlarge some of the bedrooms into suites so the inn will be the best in town. After hearing these comments, what should be the designer's FIRST course of action?

- (A) Suggest that the client also retain an architect to determine the feasibility of enlarging rooms and removing walls.
- (B) Ask the client if he has a budget, and suggest conducting a preliminary cost estimate to see if he can afford what he wants.
- (C) Tell the client that he needs to define what he means by "the best in town," to give the designer a more definite idea of how to proceed.
- (D) Recommend to the client that field measurements of the house be conducted, and begin research on authentic Victorian furnishings and finishes.

2
INFORMATION ANALYSIS AND PRESENTATION

In many cases, information provided by the client and on-site information gathered during the programming process do not constitute all the information the designer needs to provide thorough design services. The designer generally needs to do additional research and collaborate with the project consultants. After the necessary gathering of facts from the client and additional research, the designer must analyze the information and present the results of the entire programming process. This chapter reviews these processes.

RESEARCHING DESIGN REQUIREMENTS

Projects typically require additional research related to building codes and regulations, construction materials, building systems, and building-type requirements. In addition, the designer may also be interested in understanding the broader social, economic, and design trends influencing the business.

Literature Review

If the interior designer is undertaking a new project type, it may be necessary to research how other designers have completed similar projects. One way to do this is with a literature search of books and journal articles written on the subject. There are many books devoted to specific building and interior types that can be found in most public and university libraries. R. R. Bowker's annual *Books in Print* is one place to find currently published books on any subject.

Journals offer a better way to access current design and technical information on a wide variety of topics. Many printed indexes are still available to help find journal articles by subject, but most have a corresponding electronic database. Although most comprehensive literature search databases, such as the *Avery Index to Architectural Periodicals* or the Compendex® database, are only available on a subscription basis; access to them is often available through university or public libraries.

When researching a particular design type or specialized area of client need, a literature search should not be limited to design- and construction-related journals. The journals published in the client's business area are often an excellent source of information on the latest trends in their business, and on technological and design solutions related to their needs.

Internet Research

The internet provides a convenient way to research almost any topic. Nearly every product manufacturer and trade association has a website. In addition, local, state, and federal websites provide authoritative information on building code requirements, laws, regulations, and permitting procedures.

However, the researcher needs to understand that not all sites provide authoritative information. Many sites are operated by individuals or organizations with a particular bias. Although commercial sites are obviously trying to promote their own product, they do provide current data on the product. However, if unbiased information is needed to compare several manufacturers of the same product type, another source should be selected. Trade associations are often a good source for comparison information.

Trade Associations

Trade associations are one of the best sources of information for design professionals. There is at least one association (often more) for nearly every topic imaginable, ranging from the Architectural Woodwork Institute (AWI) to the Window Covering Manufacturers Association (WCMA). Trade associations produce accurate and often voluminous information on the product type or interest they represent and make it available to designers at no cost or relatively low cost. In some cases, the guidelines and standards developed by trade organizations are adopted as industry standards that become the benchmark against which the quality of manufacture and installation is compared.

Because most associations are promoting only one type of product or interest, they are usually an authoritative information source without being biased toward any one manufacturer or personal point of view. Larger organizations may also have experts on staff who are available for consultation. A complete listing of trade associations can be found in *Encyclopedia of Associations*, published by Thomson Gale. The printed version is usually available in large public libraries and university libraries. Links to trade associations are also often found on internet sites.

Product Information

There are several information sources that can provide a designer with the most current, authoritative data on a particular manufacturer's products. Manufacturers publish catalogs, cut sheets, and brochures fully describing their products through photographs, descriptions of how the products are used, testing information, building code conformance, specifications, suggested details, and use limitations. In addition, most manufacturers have a network of product representatives around the country that can provide current information and consultation on the product and how it can be used in the designer's project. If there is no local representative, information is usually available from the manufacturer's headquarters or factory and from the manufacturer's website.

Many manufacturers also publish at least a portion of their product literature in the multi-volume *Sweets Catalog*, published by McGraw-Hill. Although many of the catalogs included in Sweets are architecturally related, a large percentage of them are applicable to interior design as well. Design centers in large cities around the country have manufacturers' showrooms where the designer can obtain information, talk with product representatives, and see product samples.

Consultant Collaboration

For most medium- to large-size commercial projects, it is necessary to have professional consultants on the project team. In addition to producing the necessary drawings and specifications, these consultants can provide valuable advice in the early stages of a project. Consultants may include an architect, a structural engineer, a mechanical engineer, and an electrical engineer, among other specialized service professionals. Additional specialty consultations may include advice and design contributions on the following subjects.

- acoustical design
- construction specifications
- building code compliance
- fire protection
- hardware
- commercial food service
- security systems
- audio-visual systems
- telecommunication systems

The interior designer must understand the typical scope of the consultant's work. Refer to Chs. 17 and 18 for more information on structural, mechanical, and electrical systems.

If the interior designer is the lead professional on a project, local building department laws and regulations may require that design work related to the building structure—such as fire-rated vertical shafts, exterior walls, life-safety system, elevators, or other building elements—be performed by an architect.

A structural engineer must be retained to design any structural modifications, including the building frame, floors, and loadbearing walls. The engineer will produce any drawings and specifications for the structural portion of the project.

A mechanical engineer designs and produces the drawings and specifications for the heating, ventilating, and air conditioning systems (HVAC) on a project. A mechanical engineer will also provide design of any plumbing systems required. Most mechanical engineers also design the fire protection systems, including the sprinkler systems, although a separate fire-protection consultant may be used. Occasionally, the fire-protection contractor will design the system.

The electrical engineer designs and produces the drawings and specifications for the power system (outlets and equipment) and the lighting system. On most projects the electrical engineer will also design the telephone system, signal systems, and security systems. However, on larger commercial projects, which have more sophisticated security, computer, and signal systems, this job may be completed by security and telecommunications consultants. A separate lighting designer may also be retained.

Refer to the Building Systems Review section later in this chapter for a description of what parts of the building systems should typically be reviewed as part of the analysis of a building.

Observation

One of the best ways to become familiar with a project type is to visit similar projects. Not only can the designer observe how other designers have solved particular problems, mistakes can be viewed and possible solutions noted. Existing public projects—such as a restaurant or retail store—can be visited on an informal basis. Arrangements can usually be made with the client or designer to visit facilities not open to the public. Generally, it is preferable to visit projects with the designer or client so the reasons behind decisions can be questioned and other insights obtained.

INFORMATION ANALYSIS

Once all the information about a problem has been gathered, it must be organized and analyzed before space planning and design can begin. Of all programming data, required area and adjacencies are two of the primary factors that determine the size and configuration of the interior space. In addition to the primary spaces, there are also support spaces that add to the overall space requirements. These include areas such as corridors and other circulation space, closets, toilet rooms, and nonspecified mechanical areas.

Determining Space Needs

Space needs are determined in a number of ways. Often, when programming begins, the client will have a list of the required functional spaces and the corresponding square footages, in addition to any special height requirements. These may be based on the client's experience or on corporate space standards, or they may simply be a list of what currently exists. For example, a corporation's space standards may dictate that a senior manager have a 225 ft^2 (21 m^2) office while a junior manager be allotted 150 ft^2 (14 m^2).

These types of requirements may provide a valid basis for developing space needs, or they may be arbitrary and subject to review during programming. Where square footages are not defined by one of these methods, space for a particular use is determined in one of three ways: by the number of people that must be accommodated, by an object or piece of equipment, or by a specific activity that has its own clearly specified space needs.

The first way to determine space is to multiply the area one person needs by the total number of people in the same area. Through experience and detailed analysis, general guidelines for space requirements for one person en-gaged in various types of activities have been developed and are commonly used. For example, a student sitting in a standard classroom needs about 15 ft^2 to 20 ft^2 (1.4 m^2 to 1.9 m^2). This includes space for sitting in a chair in addition to the space required for circulating within the classroom and space for the teacher's desk and shelving. To find the total square footage for the classroom, the number of students is multiplied by the standard 15 ft^2 to 20 ft^2 (1.4 m^2 to 1.9 m^2) requirement. An office worker needs from 100 ft^2 to 250 ft^2 (9.3 m^2 to 23 m^2), depending on whether the employee is housed in a private office or is part of an open office plan. This space requirement also includes room to circulate around the desk and may include space for visitors' chairs, personal files, and the like. Multiply the number of office workers by the space required by one worker to find the space needs of the office.

Occasionally, space needs can be based on something that is directly related to the occupancy rather than on the number of people. For instance, preliminary planning of a restaurant kitchen may be based on a percentage of the size of the dining room, or library space can be estimated based on the number of books.

For the various parts of the NCIDQ exam, it is not necessary to memorize the general guidelines for space requirements, but it is necessary to know how to apply given space and furnishing requirements to a problem. For example, the practicum portion of the test will give only the furniture and equipment requirements for a user; the total area required must be derived from that information. The program may state that a workstation must include 15 ft^2 (1.4 m^2) of work surface, space for a computer terminal, 12 ft (3600) of filing space, a chair, two visitors' chairs, and space for a calculator and telephone. The space needed for this function would then have to be determined.

The second way space needs are determined is by the size of an object or piece of equipment. The size of the printing press, for example, partially determines the area of a pressroom. Automobile size determines the space needs for an automobile showroom or a parking garage.

The third way space needs are defined is through a built-in set of rules or customs related to the activity itself. Space needs of sports facilities are determined with this method. A racquetball court must be a certain size regardless of the number of spectators present, although the seating capacity would add to the total space required. A courtroom is an example of a place where the procedures and customs of the trial process dictate an arrangement of human activity and spacing of individual areas that only partially depend on the number of people.

For data gathering, forms can be developed to compile the necessary area information. Depending on the client's long-term planning goals, information on the number of people to be accommodated should be collected for the anticipated move-in date as well as some time in the future if the client is planning on having the new facility accommodate planned growth. It is sometimes useful to note the current (at the time of the interview) number of people and the space currently used. The information is gathered by interviewing supervisors and department heads and can be verified by observation. One such data collection form for an office is shown in Fig. 2.1.

Determining Total Required Area

Once the space needs are established using one or more of the methods described previously, the total area required to accommodate the client must be determined. This is done in a number of ways, depending on whether the client will be leasing space or constructing a new building. There are a number of area definitions with which the interior designer must be familiar.

The areas determined with the methods described previously result in the net area of a facility. The *net area* of a building or interior is the actual area required to accommodate specific functions. For example, five offices of 150 ft^2 (14 m^2) each require a total net area of 750 ft^2 (70 m^2). Net area does not include primary and secondary circulation space, closets, electrical and telephone equipment rooms, exterior walls, or the building core. The net area does include interior walls and building columns. Sometimes the net area is referred to as the *net assignable area* and the secondary spaces are referred to as the *unassigned areas.*

For the purposes of analyzing lease space, it is useful to differentiate between primary circulation and secondary circulation space. *Primary circulation space* includes what can be considered the public circulation space of a leased building: the entry lobby, elevator lobbies, main corridors, and exits required for building code egress. *Secondary circulation space* includes the corridors in private leased areas used to connect the net assignable areas to the primary circulation areas of the building.

Useable area is the area available for assignment to a tenant, including the actual net area (where activities are taking place) and the secondary circulation space. In the case of an office tenant leasing space in an office tower, the usable space consists of all the activity areas within the perimeter walls of the leased space, as well as the private corridors, partitions, and columns within the space.

In leased buildings, another area measurement is used as the basis for leasing office and retail space. The *rentable area* is the total amount of usable space available,

Figure 2.1
Data Collection
      Form

Area Tabulation

Division:	Finance and Administration	Date:	6/15
Department:	Accounting	Interviewed by:	BDB

Information provided by:		Reviewed by:	JBW		
Name:	B. Smith				
Title:	Controller				
Telephone					
email:					

Area/Personnel	Number			Space	Area		
	Current	Move	Future	Open/ Closed	Area each	Sub-total	Total
Controller	1	1	1	c	225	225	
Supervisor	1	1	1	c	150	150	
Bookkeeper/Accts.	2	3	4	O	100	400	
Data entry	1	1	2	O	75	150	
Subtotal							925
Files/bookcases/storage							
Files (4-dwr) 3' x 42"	4	6	10	O	10	100	100
Auxiliary areas							
Major equipment							
Copier	1	1	1	c	100		100
Net assignable total							1125
Circulation @ 25%							275
Gross Total							1,400

but it also includes structural columns, the thickness of some partitions, and typically a portion of the exterior wall of the building.

When an office lease space only occupies a portion of a floor, the rentable area is measured from the inside glass surface of exterior walls (if the glass is more than 50% of the wall area) to the finished surface of the tenant side of the public corridor partition and from the centerlines of partitions separating adjacent tenant spaces. See Fig. 2.2. The rentable area also includes a proportionate share of the elevator lobby, public corridor, rest rooms, and mechanical rooms.

When a tenant occupies an entire floor, the rentable area includes all the space taken by the public corridors as well as the elevator lobby and the rest rooms on that floor. The partitions separating adjacent tenant spaces and separating a tenant space from public spaces are often called *demising walls*.

Finally, the *gross area* of a building includes the areas of all floors that are totally enclosed, measured from the outside faces of exterior walls.

When analyzing space needs, it is clear that more floor space is required than simply the total of all the required net areas. For preliminary planning, the total amount of space required is calculated with efficiency factors. An *efficiency factor* is simply the mathematical ratio between one area and another. For a single lease space, the *interior layout* efficiency is the ratio of the net area (or net assignable area) to the usable area. The efficiency factor takes into account the required circulation space. For most office and retail spaces, the interior layout efficiency is about 0.70 to 0.80. This means that about 20% to 30% of the total useable space is devoted to circulation. Efficiency depends on the type of occupancy, the size of individual spaces, and

Figure 2.2
Method of Measuring Rentable Area

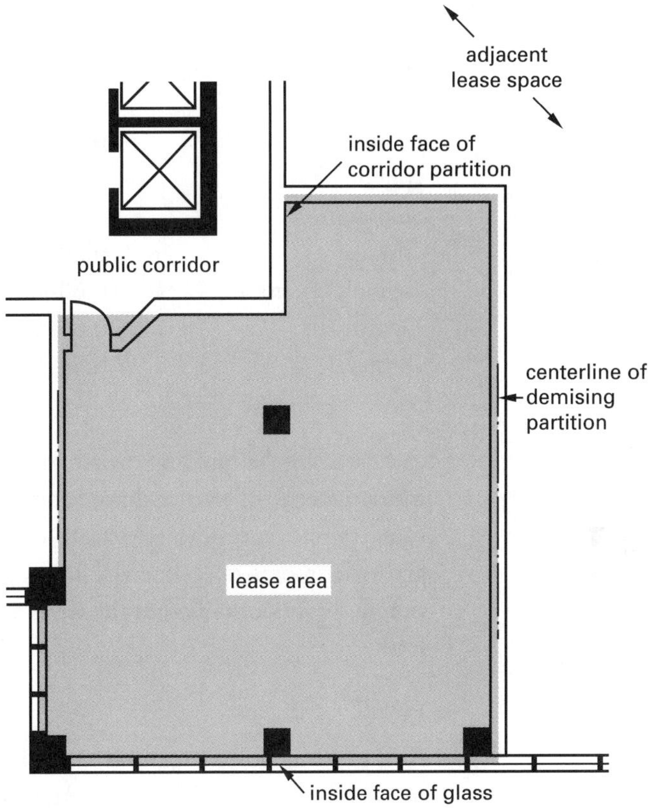

adjacent lease space

inside face of corridor partition

public corridor

centerline of demising partition

lease area

inside face of glass

how well the space is planned. A hospital with many small rooms and a great number of large corridors has a much lower efficiency ratio than a factory where the majority of space is devoted to production areas and very little space is allotted for corridors and other secondary spaces. Generally, efficiency ratios range from 60% to 80%, with some building types more or less efficient than this. Some common efficiency factors are shown in Table 2.1. The required usable area of a space is calculated by dividing the net area by the efficiency factor.

When leasing space, more area is required than is represented by the usable area. This area is calculated by using the *rentable-usable ratio*, which is the rentable area divided by the usable area. This multiplier is

Table 2.1
Net-to-Gross Ratios for Common Building Types

building type	efficiency ratio
office	0.75–0.80
retail	0.75
bank	0.70
restaurant, table service	0.66–0.70
bars, nightclubs	0.70–0.77
hotel	0.62–0.70
public library	0.77–0.80
museum	0.83
theater	0.60–0.77
school, classroom	0.60–0.66
apartment	0.66–0.80
hospital	0.54–0.66

calculated by the building owner based on measurements of the building and allocates public corridors, elevator lobbies, and toilet rooms to each tenant in proportion to the amount of space the tenants are leasing.

Example 2.1

A small insurance company is planning to move to new leased office space. After programming, the designer determines that the client will require approximately 4500 ft^2 (418 m^2) of net assignable space. If the leasing manager for the building tells the client the building rentable-usable ratio is 1.20, about how much space does the client need to consider leasing?

First, the usable area needs to be calculated to account for required circulation space. For an office space, estimate an efficiency factor of 0.75 as shown in Table 2.1.

Customary U.S. units:

$$\text{usable area} = \frac{\text{net assignable space}}{0.75}$$

$$= \frac{4500 \text{ ft}^2}{0.75}$$

$$= 6000 \text{ ft}^2$$

SI units:

$$\text{usable area} = \frac{418 \text{ m}^2}{0.75}$$

$$= 557 \text{ m}^2$$

Next, the rentable area must be calculated. Using the building manager's ratio of 1.20, multiply the usable area by the multiplying factor.

Customary U.S. units:

$$\text{rentable area} = (\text{usable area})(1.20)$$

$$= (6000 \text{ ft}^2)(1.20)$$

$$= 7200 \text{ ft}^2$$

SI units:

$$\text{rentable area} = (557 \text{ m}^2)(1.20)$$

$$= 668 \text{ m}^2$$

In a similar manner, if the rentable area is known, the designer can work backward to determine the usable area available and then the net area and compare this to the net area determined by programming to compare the two figures. If the two numbers were significantly at variance, the client would either have to rent more space or reduce the amount of net space required.

If a client is constructing a new building, even more floor area is required for the building structure, mechanical and electrical equipment, storage, stairways, elevators, and building entrance, as well as other service areas. The ratio of the net assignable area to the gross building area is the *overall building efficiency* and can range from 0.50 to 0.90 depending on the building type and the efficiency of the building's architectural design.

Task and Activity Analysis

In addition to analyzing space needs, the requirements for the client's workflow or business processes should be compared with the space available. Some of the common types of workflow are diagrammed in Fig. 2.3. With a *linear workflow*, the work or business process proceeds from one location to another in a strict sequence. With a *centralized workflow*, the work is controlled from one central position. A departmental flow is hierarchical, typically with one group controlling work divided into separate departments. With a *network workflow* organization, there is no strictly organized method of workflow.

In some cases the connection between points needs to be immediate, with direct contact for either people or exchange of materials. In other cases, it may be possible for the communication to be electronic. Each of these types of business process may fit better in some spaces than others. For example, a linear workflow system may work best in a long, narrow space or in a space where the line can be "folded." A departmental workflow could work in an irregularly shaped building or spread among several floors. Workflow can be analyzed with respect to the existing building using the following criteria.

- points of public entry
- points of service entry
- spaces with views
- spaces without views
- size and shape of space
- locations of plumbing and other building services
- interference with building structure
- available ceiling height

Code Review

To make building code information usable for preliminary design, it is helpful to develop a code checklist. This checklist only needs to contain the code requirements that affect the overall planning of the space. A detailed checklist for use during

Figure 2.3
Workflow Types

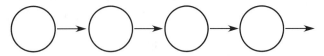
(a) linear

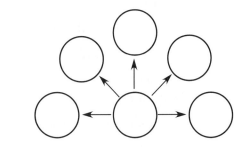
(b) central

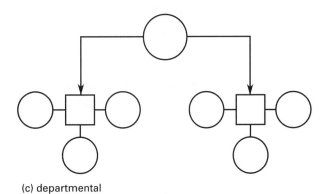
(c) departmental

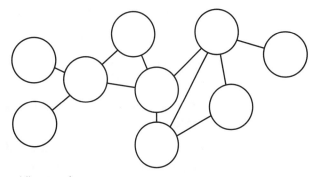
(d) network

schematic design and the contract documents phases can be developed separately. Such a detailed checklist would contain requirements for items such as hardware, toilet room accessories, finishes, handrails, and similar construction elements. Refer to Ch. 7 for more information on these detailed requirements.

To assist with the preliminary design, the following information should be available to the designer before space planning begins.

- occupancy group(s)

- requirements for special occupancies, if any

- gross area of the space

- occupant load(s)

- common path of egress travel requirements

- number of exits required

- maximum distance to exits

- arrangement of exits

- required minimum width of exits

- allowable length of dead-end corridors

- special requirements for exiting from A or R occupancies

- accessibility requirements related to space planning

- required separations for mixed occupancies, if any

- construction requirements forcorridors

- requirements for doors

- requirements for glazing, especially in fire-rated partitions

- requirements for ramps and stairways, if any

Refer to Chs. 27 and 28 for detailed information on building code requirements.

Building Systems Review

The interior designer should review the existing building systems to determine if they are adequate for the client's proposed use. In most cases this review should be made with the assistance of an architect, mechanical engineer, and electrical engineer. If structural changes are anticipated, a structural engineer should also be consulted.

The structural system should be reviewed to determine the adequacy of the existing structure and to locate any loadbearing walls slated for modification. An engineer may also be required for the following reasons.

- to recommend additional structure when floors need to be strengthened for file rooms, libraries, heavy equipment, or other unusually heavy loading

- to advise on where floor penetrations may be made in a reinforced slab for electrical and telephone outlets

- to calculate the amount of floor deflection expected when slip joints are used in slab-to-slab partitions

- to design modifications to a loadbearing wall if the client wants to penetrate one with an opening

Mechanical systems should be reviewed to check the capacity of the central plant, the condition of the distribution system, and the adequacy of the registers, thermostats, and any other equipment that is planned for reuse. The size and location of ductwork should also be noted to see if it would interfere with the proposed ceiling and lighting design of the new space.

Plumbing systems should be reviewed to verify capacity for any new fixtures that are proposed, to review the condition of pipes and fittings, and to determine where existing piping can be tapped for new plumbing fixtures.

The fire protection system should be studied to see if it meets current life safety codes. The extent of the sprinkler system should be studied to determine how much additional work would be required for the new space. In some cases, existing sprinkler heads can be used directly or relocated slightly to conform to code spacing requirements with little additional cost. However, if the designer wants to make significant changes to sprinkler head locations, to conform to a specific reflected ceiling plan, the cost increase could be much greater.

Electrical systems should be reviewed, including the capacity of service to the building, conditions of primary and secondary service, conditions of wiring and devices, and conditions of lighting and other electrical components.

COMMUNICATING THE PROGRAM

Programming and analysis should be summarized into a written report. In most cases the report is accompanied by a presentation to the client. Any feedback received from the client should be incorporated into a revised report and used for subsequent design.

Organizing the Written Program

Written reports vary in content and organization depending on the scope of the programming work, the complexity of the project, and whether the report will need to go through several department level approvals in the client's organization. Generally, a formal approval process requires a more detailed, formal report.

The following topics should be included in a programming report.

- title page
- introduction
- executive summary (optional for shorter, less formal reports)
- goals and objectives of the report (optional)
- summary of space needs
    existing staff and staff projections
    workflow analysis (optional)
    equipment needs
    tabulation of space needs with circulation

- space adjacencies
    adjacency matrices
    bubble diagrams
    stacking diagrams (optional, not needed for one-story projects)
- code requirements
- analysis of existing space
    architectural space configuration
    structural requirements
    mechanical requirements
    electrical requirements
    life safety requirements
- budget and schedule requirements
- programming concepts
- appendices
    detailed space needs tabulation (optional for small projects)
    existing furniture inventory (not required if all new furniture is being used)
    other detailed survey information (optional for small projects)

Presentation Techniques

The method of presenting the programming report will vary with the size and complexity of the project, the size and organization of the client's company, and the original agreement between the interior designer and the client. For small projects with a single decision maker, the presentation may be very informal with a few summary charts and tables showing the area requirements and adjacency needs. With large, corporate clients for whom the programming was a major project in itself, the presentation will require a formal, written programming report as well as one or more formal presentations.

Regardless of the format, the goals of the final programming report and presentation are the same: to elicit client comments on the conclusions and to get approval so design can proceed. If the client was an integral part of the programming process, there should be little disagreement with the final conclusions, and only final approval will be required. In other cases, the final presentation is the last chance to receive any corrections the client may have.

The programming document should make it clear that the report is for the client's approval and work cannot proceed without it. In some cases, signatures of the client or client's representatives may be required. In the presentation, the designer can make a simple statement such as "Our programming report represents how we see your needs and will be used to develop the design. It everything correct?" to give the client the chance to respond. Generally, direct questions are the best.

In most cases, programming presentations are given in simple, face-to-face meetings with the client. For very small, informal presentations, copies of the programming report may be distributed and discussed around a table. For larger groups, the interior designer may want to prepare presentation boards. These should contain summaries of the area requirements as well as diagrams showing the major programming concepts and the required adjacencies.

For larger, more formal presentations, an electronic presentation format may be required. There are three possible methods or venues for conducting electronic presentations: face-to-face, virtual, and internet.

With *face-to-face presentations* the presenter and the audience are in the same place at the same time with electronic devices used to supplement the presentation, through computer projection, interactive monitors, or traditional photographic slides. Most presentations will use the face-to-face method.

With *virtual presentations*, the presenter and the audience may be in different locations but interacting in real time. Teleconferencing is the common method of accomplishing this type of presentation.

Internet presentations separate the presenter and the audience in both location and time. A web-based presentation is developed and made available to the audience whenever it is convenient to view it. Web-based presentations can be constructed so the audience can post their feedback or add additional information.

Whatever meeting method is employed, keeping the following guidelines in mind during preparation should make the electronic presentation clear and easy to follow.

- Be consistent with the format of each slide.

- Put only one idea on each slide.

- Use bold graphics that are easy to understand.

- Be specific with thoughts and suggestions.

- Preview the presentation before giving it.

SAMPLE QUESTIONS

1. Which of the following sources would be the LEAST useful for obtaining current information on a manufacturer's building product?

(A) the internet

(B) the product representative

(C) *Sweets Catalog*

(D) a trade association

2. In calculating lease area for tenant space occupying only a portion of a floor, measurements are taken to the

(A) inside finish faces of the tenant sides of all demising walls

(B) centerlines of the partitions separating tenants from each other, and from the public corridor

(C) inside finish faces of walls separating tenants, and to the centerline of the public corridor wall

(D) centerlines of walls separating tenants, and to the inside finish face of the partition separating the tenant space from the public corridor

3. To begin preliminary space planning, the interior designer would most likely need which of the following two building code requirements first?

(A) occupancy group and total floor area

(B) number of exits and maximum distance to exits

(C) allowable length of dead-end corridors and glazing requirements

(D) occupant load and corridor construction requirements

4. Direct space adjacencies would be LEAST necessary in which business type?

(A) consumer product call center

(B) doctor's office

(C) electronic assembly plant

(D) retail shoe store

5. The initial determination of area required for a client's program gives the

(A) gross area

(B) net area

(C) rentable area

(D) usable area

6. A designer has determined that a client needs about 8000 ft^2 (743 m^2) of usable office space. The leasing agent for the building says that the rentable-usable ratio will be 1.25. Approximately how much area should the interior designer recommend that the client lease?

(A) 7500 ft^2 (700 m^2)

(B) 10,000 ft^2 (930 m^2)

(C) 10,700 ft^2 (990 m^2)

(D) 13,300 ft^2 (1240 m^2)

7. Thermostat locations are determined by the

(A) architect

(B) electrical engineer

(C) HVAC contractor

(D) mechanical engineer

8. At a minimum, a programming report should include all of the following EXCEPT

(A) space adjacencies

(B) budget requirements

(C) area requirements

(D) an executive summary

9. In surveying existing conditions of an older building before beginning space planning, an interior designer would probably need to seek expert consulting assistance to determine the

(A) number of supply air diffusers in the space

(B) existence of floor-mounted electrical outlets in an open space

(C) presence of adequate water pressure to add a sink in a washroom

(D) feasibility of opening a double-wide doorway in an existing wall

10. In which case would the number of people occupying a space NOT be critical to the programming effort?

(A) the dining room of a housing complex for the elderly

(B) the workroom of a commercial laundry

(C) a multipurpose meeting room in a neighborhood recreation center

(D) a waiting area in a hospital

3

DEVELOPING AND PRESENTING DESIGN CONCEPTS

As described in the previous chapters, the process of gathering information and developing a program provides the factual and objective basis for a design project, establishing space needs, budget, building code requirements, the client's desires, among many other factors. However, before space planning and detailed design can begin, the designer must have a theoretical basis for design that, when combined with programmatic requirements and social and cultural influences, contributes to the development of design concepts.

This chapter summarizes the stage of a design project after the necessary information has been collected and a program has been developed. It describes the effects of design theory, the influence of social and cultural factors, how design concepts are developed, and how spatial relationships are represented in order to make them usable for space planning.

DESIGN THEORY

Although there are many definitions for theory, in general terms a theory is a mental construct of how and why things happen, which is often used to predict future events or actions. As the idea relates to interior design and architecture, a *design theory* is a way to direct design based on a system of beliefs or philosophy.

Theory is the most fundamental beginning of design. It is the unique quality each designer brings to the creative and problem-solving process. For example, the theories of Mies van der Rohe, Le Corbusier, and Frank Lloyd Wright produced vastly different buildings, even though all three architects produced similar building types during approximately the same time period. (Differences in countries of birth only accounted for a small portion of the differences among their designs.)

It is important to understand that theory is *not* style. For example, southwestern is a style and includes the use of courtyards as semiprivate space. The belief that enclosed outdoor space should mediate between public and private space is part of a theory of the public/private continuum in architecture. It is also interesting to note that the use of courtyards in southwestern building has a historic and cultural precedence as a way of providing safety and outdoor space within the confines of a walled compound. This approach to public/private space is quite different than the semiprivate front porch and front yard typical of many other parts of the United States.

Theory can be developed in many ways. It can be based on the designer's personal worldview, historic precedent, environmental design research, functional needs, how humans perceive their environment, a particular process of design, or any number of factors. Most designers base their design theories on several of these influences. Some of the more common ones are briefly described below.

Historic Precedent

A common approach to design theory throughout the ages has been to base current design on ideas and styles of the past. In some cases, such as with the classical revival style of the late-18th to mid-19th century in America, the adoption was literal, with new designs being an almost exact duplicate of the past style. In other cases, such as with the post-modern movement of the 1970s, the new design approach was based on a reaction *against* the ideals of the previous age of modernism.

Historic precedent plays a large part in an individual's response to interior design and architecture, regardless of the philosophy of the designer. Many clients will insist that their house look like a New England saltbox or a Victorian cottage because that is their image of what a house should look like or what they grew up in, regardless of any design theory that suggests it should look like something else, with planning, materials, and accessories more appropriate to the current time.

In the best case, history can be a valuable contribution to design theory by suggesting how past designs solved certain problems or represented particular ideals. These

solutions or representations can then be applied to current design problems.

For example, the flowing curves of the art deco style or the organic architecture of Frank Lloyd Wright responded to the human desire for connection with the earth and with natural forms. Although the forms of art deco or Wright do not have to be recreated, the lesson of the importance of the human-nature connection can be used to guide design decisions. For other designs, the strong axial and symmetric organization of religious and governmental buildings used throughout history can still be employed without creating duplicates of cathedrals or Greek temples.

Environmental Design Research

Environmental design research focuses on theories of the interaction between humans and their environment. It attempts to develops an approach to rational design based on scientific research rather than just anecdotal evidence or personal philosophies. The problem with conducting environmental design research and using it directly to make design decisions is the complexity of the interaction between humans and buildings. To be scientifically valid, most research only studies one variable at a time, so the effect of changing that variable can be measured without influence from other variables.

Often, research is conducted in a laboratory to focus on one aspect of a question. For example, seating preferences could be explored by having a large number of people sit in different chairs and then rate the seats according to comfort. The results would probably be statistically valid. However, if the same chairs were placed in a real environment and preferences were measured by observation, the reason for the preference would not be clear. Variables such as the design of the chair, type of environment (library, school, waiting room, etc.), position of the chair in the room, and others would all be factors in a persons' preference for a chair, apart from comfort. A less comfortable chair might even be preferable if other factors such as position near a window, color, or separation from other people were taken into account. If a particular chair was found to be preferable for the research environment, could that information be appropriately used in the decision to use the same chair for another building?

In spite of the inherent problems with easily and accurately adopting environmental design research to a theory of design, environmental design research should not be dismissed. Some concepts, such as territoriality and personal space, described in Ch. 1, have been shown to be useful in most situations. Further, if the design project is especially important and the client's budget allows it, the designer can perform the necessary research to add to his or her store of knowledge before proceeding with design. The research can be as simple as a literature review of past work done on the subject of interest or as complex as performing original investigations specifically targeted to the project. Some of the methods of research are described in Ch. 2.

Functional Needs

Functionalism places emphasis on providing simple, rational solutions to design problems without extraneous decoration. It is best represented by the modernism movement of the early 20th century, which was an outgrowth of the English arts and crafts movement. Developed and nurtured in the Bauhaus school of design, modernism used newly emerging technology to create functional, machine-like objects and architecture. In interior design, spaces were reduced to what was required to meet strict functional needs without unnecessary decoration.

The functionalist approach was clearly stated by the architect Le Corbusier when he said, "a house is a machine for living in." He made this statement to reflect his theory of modernity in which he, and many other architects of the time, distanced themselves from the past and based their designs on functionality without ornament so that buildings would be true to their essential purpose. The quote also reflects design that requires efficiency, simplicity, and elegance with a form consistent with its function.

Although all interior design should meet the functional requirements of the client and the users of the space, the ultimate reaction against the strict functional dogma of modernism suggests that humans require more than just functional space, and that functionalism, like historic precedent, should only be one aspect of a larger theory of design.

Theories of Perception

The elements and principles of design are the basic building blocks of visual perception and are manipulated to create forms, spaces, and interior components that solve programmatic problems. While these are discussed in detail in Chs. 8 and 9, the following theories briefly describe some of the basic processes of perception that scientists, psychologists, artists, and others have discovered to be useful in understanding how people perceive the world. With knowledge of these principles, designers can better understand why some designs do or do not work and can use these principles to help make design decisions.

Gestalt Psychology

Founded in Germany in the early part of the 20th century by Max Wertheimer, *Gestalt psychology* holds that humans innately perceive things as a whole so that what is perceived is complete and comprehensible. This theory asserts that perception is

Figure 3.1
Principles of
Grouping

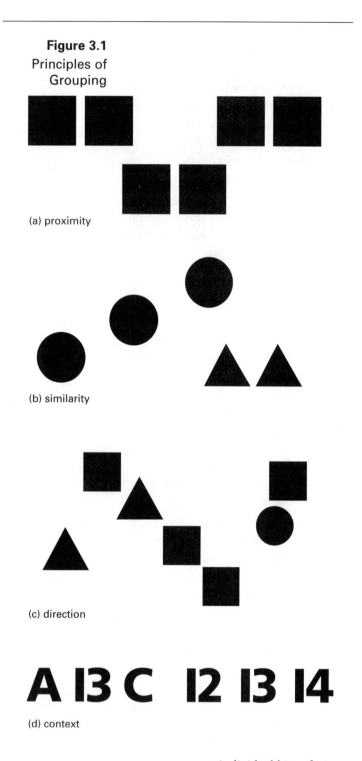

(a) proximity

(b) similarity

(c) direction

A I3 C I2 I3 I4

(d) context

that people will bring to the setting their own ideas about what things are. Among other theories, it explains the phenomenon known as *simultaneous contrast* with color, in which the same color appears to change depending on the background color it is seen against. This is discussed in Ch. 8 in the section on color.

Some of the principles of Gestalt psychology include the following. They are frequently used in developing optical illusions, but more importantly explain how most people see forms in the environment.

The concept of grouping states that humans perceive separate units in the visual field as a group. There are several means by which this can occur, including proximity, similarity, direction, and context. With proximity, the objects closest together are seen as belonging together. In Fig. 3.1(a) the brain sees three pairs of squares instead of six squares. With similarity, the brain groups objects of similar shape, size, or color. In Fig. 3.1(b) the brain sees three circles and a pair of triangles rather than five basic shapes. With direction, objects perceived to be moving simultaneously in the same direction are seen as a group. In Fig. 3.1(c) the four shapes in the middle of the diagram seem to have a diagonal movement. Finally, objects are grouped based on context or past experience, one of the main tenets of Gestalt psychology. In one context, in Fig. 3.1(d), the central figure in the first group reads as the letter B, while in the second group it appears to be the number 13, even though it is exactly the same in both groups.

While simple diagrams can illustrate the principles of grouping, in reality grouping is more complex because two or more grouping principles can operate at the same time. For example, objects can be located in close proximity but have varying shapes or colors that, when seen with

not a response to individual bits of stimulus, but to the whole, and that people actively *add* structure to what they see rather than just reacting to it. For interior designers, Gestalt psychology suggests that individual elements cannot be placed or designed as single entities, but must be seen as part of a larger environment, and other objects in the visual field, set up a different type of grouping.

Closure (sometimes called *form constancy*) is the tendency to perceive incomplete forms as complete. When faced with incomplete information in the visual field, humans tend to want to add information to make sense of what is being seen. Figure 3.2(a) shows several lines of different lengths and directions. However, the brain wants to make sense of these random lines, and most people will perceive a triangle. Figure 3.2(b) shows a figure commonly used to illustrate this phenomenon. If the two shapes are arranged in a certain way, the brain again perceives a triangle, this time where no portions of a triangle exist at all.

Continuity is the tendency to see a line or shape as continuing in a particular direction rather than making a sharp turn. In Fig. 3.3 most people see two straight lines intersecting rather than two acute angles whose vertices meet at a common point.

Simplicity as part of Gestalt psychology states that people prefer the simplest, most stable organization of forms or the overall structure of elements in the visual field rather than complex individual parts. Generally, the brain organizes things into the fewest number of lines or parts. In Fig. 3.4(a) the assembly of lines is seen as a triangle overlapping a rectangle rather than, as shown in Fig. 3.4(b), as three objects—a notched triangle, a trapezoid, and a notched rectangle. Simplicity is often intertwined with other Gestalt principles.

Figure-ground describes the way people distinguish a form from its surroundings. It is fundamental to all perception and can occur with two-dimensional elements as well as with three-dimensional objects. Figure 3.5 shows one of the commonly illustrated examples of figure-ground. In one instance, it appears that the black figure is

Figure 3.2
Closure

(a)

(b)

Figure 3.3
Continuity

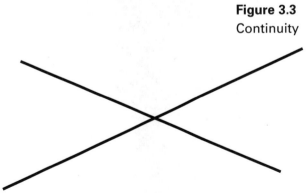

a vase on a white background. Alternately, two profiles can be seen facing each other. The brain can perceive one or the other, but not both at the same time.

Figure 3.4
Simplicity

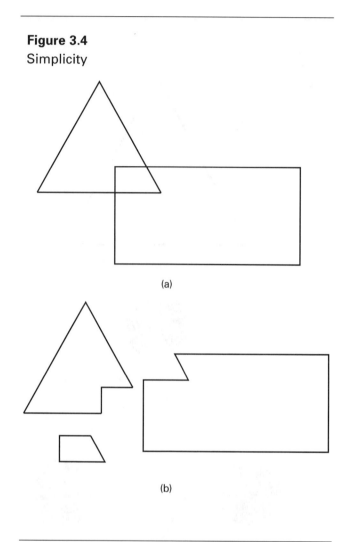

(a)

(b)

Figure 3.5
Figure-
Ground

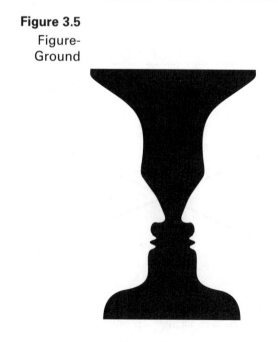

Graphic designers and other artists often call the ground around an object negative space. They frequently use the figure-ground principal for logos in which one or more letters or symbols are shown in the color of the ground, but are defined by surrounding letters or symbols shown as figure. See Fig. 3.6. In this case the negative space between the two arrows becomes the circle "figure."

Interior design and architecture often use the concept of figure-ground as a conceptual way to create space; one designer may view the surrounding walls as the figure on the ground of empty space while another designer may view the space itself as the figure and the surrounding construction elements at the ground. On flat surfaces, openings and wall hangings can be designed as figures while the surface becomes the ground. Alternately, by manipulating size, transparency, color, and position, openings can be viewed as the background for the figure of the walls.

Perceptual Constancy

People seldom view objects or spaces statically. The observer moves closer or farther away, the angle of view changes, lighting changes, or other factors change. Regardless of these constant changes, a person perceives an object or a space as essentially the same regardless of the exact image on the retina of the eye. The mechanism that allows humans to do this is called *perceptual constancy*. Psychologists have identified several types of perceptual constancies. These include shape constancy, size constancy, lightness constancy, and color constancy.

Shape constancy means that people perceive objects as having their original shape regardless of a change in orientation of the object or the point of view of the observer. This constancy of perception occurs because of memory and the fact that the brain takes into account depth of the object as the object's shape changes on the retina.

Size constancy means that people tend to perceive an object as having the same size regardless of the changes in viewing distance to the object. Size constancy occurs because people have memories of how large certain objects are and take into account their distance from the object.

Lightness constancy means that people perceive the lightness or darkness of an object as the same regardless of the illumination of the space in which the object is viewed. When interpreting brightness information on the retina, the brain considers the relative brightness of all objects.

Color constancy means that people perceive the color of an object as the same regardless of the lighting conditions under which the object is viewed. Unlike photographic film, the brain makes adjustments for the color of the lighting as well as its brightness.

Depth Perception

The perception of depth is a basic human ability. Without it, understanding the world and getting about would be nearly impossible. Humans perceive depth through a variety of means. Because the eyes are separated by a slight distance, the left eye and the right eye see slightly different views of the world. The difference in what each eye sees is called *binocular disparity*. The brain interprets the slight difference in view and gives people the ability to perceive distance and see three dimensions. Binocular disparity is most prevalent at distances under about 10 ft (3 m).

Even without binocular disparity, the eye and brain use several clues to perceive depth and distance even when the image on the retina is two-dimensional. These perceptual elements allow artists to give depth to two-dimensional paintings and are the reasons why the *tromp l'oeil*

Figure 3.6
Negative Space

painting technique works to create the illusion of depth.

- *Interposition:* the overlap of a near object by a more distant object

- *Linear perspective:* the common experience of parallel lines appearing to recede toward a point in the distance

- *Atmospheric perspective:* Because there are small particles in the air, more distant objects appear to be hazy and may even change color. For interiors, this effect is seldom of any consequence.

- *Texture perspective:* The density of a texture seems to increase as the distance from the viewer increases. The texture may be fine grain, as on a fabric, or of a larger scale, such as ceiling or floor tiles.

- *Size clues:* When two objects are the same size, the more distant one will make a smaller image on the retina than the closer one.

- *Relative closeness of objects to the horizon line:* For objects below the horizon line (on the ground), the closer objects are to the horizon line, the farther away they are. For objects above the horizon line (in the sky or above the observer), the same holds true, but more distant objects are lower in the visual field than close objects.

Cue Inconsistency/Cooperation of the Senses

Although the visual sense dominates humans' perception of the environment, people gather information about their surroundings through nearly all the senses: sight, sound, smell, and touch. The reception from each sense is used as a cue to provide a message about the environment. In most cases, these messages should be consistent; that is, they should each reinforce the purpose and intent of the environment. For example, the experience of a functional, beautifully designed restaurant can be ruined if the patrons smell a strong cleaning compound instead of the food the restaurant is serving. Similarly, the design of a small, intimate space can be marred if the sound echoes, an effect most people associate with large, formal or religious spaces.

In many cases, cue inconsistency occurs because there are conflicting visual cues. For example, two or more details or finishes may not be compatible with each other, considering the design intent of the space. By understanding the influence of each of the senses on people, the designer can create the most appropriate type of space for the client's needs.

Social and Cultural Influences

In addition to having a theoretical basis, interior design and architecture also represent what the culture and society thinks is important. For example, in the United States, most single-family residential design clings to the agrarian roots of the country, with a house on the farm or estate, surrounded by open space, even though the amount of open space has shrunk greatly as land costs have risen and land has become more scarce. Further, our social idea of status is typically represented by increasing the size of a house as much as possible at the expense of better materials or more detailing. Inside, most

home design reflects our culture's idea of privacy (separate bedrooms), hierarchy (master bedroom larger than the others), and methods of entertaining (the great room or a formal living room separate from the family room).

In commercial design, our cultural ideas about status and hierarchy are often reflected in the design of office space. The highest-ranking company officials get the larger, corner offices or a private office with a view while lower-echelon workers are placed in small cubicles in an open plan.

Some of the social and cultural beliefs that often influence interior design include the following. Many of these are common to all cultures in all time periods, although in each society or culture the physical response may be different. Refer to Ch. 1 for additional social influences on design.

- *Political conditions:* Prevailing political attitudes and policies may affect design thinking. For example, the sustainability and green architecture movement promoted by environmental awareness, and the political recognition of this value, encouraged a response by interior designers and architects.

- *Economic conditions:* The state of the economy is often reflected in architecture and interior design. Prosperous times may promote lavish design (at least within the limits of one's budget). Uncertain or less prosperous conditions may promote austere or inward-looking design. The "cocooning" movement was partially a result of uncertain economic times. The rising cost of energy is a main factor in the trend of sustainable and energy-conserving design.

- *Cultural attitudes:* The prevailing cultural views of the family, shared values, religion, fashion, leisure pursuits, sports, and the like may influence a design response. Current trends in fashion and consumer goods regarding color, material use, and industrial design often reach into the realms of interior design and architecture.

• *Symbolism:* The physical environment holds a great deal of symbolism for people. Some people like houses with early American interiors because such designs symbolize to them the idea of "home." Some people expect banks to be of classical design with large lobbies because that is what they think a bank should look like.

• *Regionalism:* Regionalism is design that reflects the local geographic area. Most designers, architects, and users of interior design believe that each geographic area is unique and design should reflect that fact. A common belief might be that buildings and interior design in Florida should be different than those in the Pacific Northwest.

As with theories of perception, people's cultural and social backgrounds affect their *response* to design. While these factors can be accounted for by interviewing the client in the case of small-scale design, such as a residence, they are difficult to incorporate when designing for a public space, where the users of the space, each with their own likes and dislikes, will come from many cultures and social backgrounds. In most cases the best the designer can do is make a prediction about the most likely cultural forces acting on a design problem. In some cases, environmental design research can assist the designer in making choices, but in many instances the designer must understand the prevailing culture and social norms of the society in which the designer works.

DESIGN CONCEPTS

During programming, general concepts are developed in response to the client's goals and needs. As discussed in Ch. 1, these *programmatic concepts* are statements about functional solutions to the client's performance requirements. They differ from *design concepts*, as discussed in this and the next chapter, because no attempt at an actual physical solution is made during programming. Programmatic concepts guide the later development of design concepts. For example, a programmatic concept might be that a corporate office facility should encourage interaction among all the employees. The physical means to make that happen would be developed as a design concept. One possible design concept might be that the corridors cross near the center of the building at an informal lounge area. This design concept is something that the designer can actually put on paper and that would determine a portion of the space planning for the office. In other words, a design concept is a general or overall idea of how a design problem will be approached. A design concept also takes into account the existing space within which the designer must work, its size, shape, entry points, windows, and other fixed elements.

Although design concepts specify particular physical responses, they are still a broad-brush approach that leaves some flexibility in deciding the details of the design. For example, a design concept for a restaurant located in a scenic area might be to design a neutral background of warm color finishes while maximizing the view to the outside. A statement like this would help determine such things as space planning of the rooms and tables (oriented to the view, possibly on stepped platforms like a theater), location of service spaces away from the primary view, selection of finishes (warm colors primarily), and selection of materials (window coverings that do not obstruct the view, simple neutral forms and shapes, and so forth). The same statement precludes other decisions such as a strong "theme" look or a layout of tables and lounge areas focusing on the interior of the restaurant.

Although a concept statement may be simple or complex depending on the size and complexity of the project, it should be concise and define the essence of the design. Generally, a good concept statement can be made in one to four sentences. As with programmatic concepts, the concept statement should be reviewed with the client before more detailed space planning and material selection begin.

COMPONENTS OF A DESIGN CONCEPT

As with design theories, there are a multitude of ideas about what constitutes the makeup of a design concept. However, the following list includes some common issues of preliminary conceptual ideas that can be shown as sketches, written down, or developed as material samples. A more detailed discussion of space planning is included in Ch. 4 while the basic elements and principles of design are discussed in Chs. 8 and 9.

Plan Arrangement

For interior design and architecture, the configuration of the plan is one of the most basic conceptual ideas even though the user typically does not experience its true organization. A plan takes on particular importance for the interior designer because the existing ceiling or roof plane typically limits the third dimension of height in interior design.

Regardless of the enclosing walls, a plan can be viewed conceptually in one of six ways. The concepts can also be combined. These are illustrated in Fig. 3.7.

Open

With the open configuration there are no space-defining partitions within the existing limits of the building. The only objects are furniture and accessories. Typically, this concept cannot be used by itself because there are usually spaces that must be enclosed for security, privacy, light control, acoustical isolation, or other reasons. However, some enclosure criteria can be satisfied with large expanses of glazing without compromising the open concept.

The open concept is typically used where a display of hierarchy through separate spaces is not wanted, where function requires a free flow of people, materials, or ideas, or where individual functional areas change frequently.

Linear

A linear concept arranges spaces in a row, either connected to each other directly or related to a linear element, such as a corridor. In its simplest form, the linear concept runs in a straight line. Variations include bending the line in an L- or U-shape, forming a circle or other enclosed

Figure 3.7
Conceptual Plan Arrangements

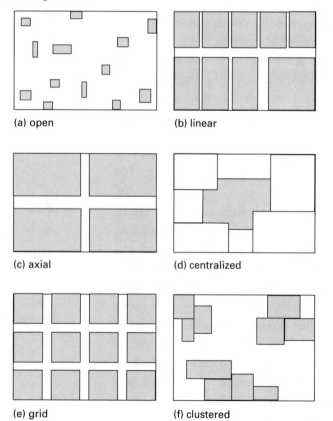

(a) open

(b) linear

(c) axial

(d) centralized

(e) grid

(f) clustered

shape, placing significant spaces at the termination of the line, or using the line to divide two different types of spaces.

Linear concepts are typically used for practical reasons as an efficient way to connect many different types and sizes of spaces with a circulation corridor and to provide for access to exits. The linear concept is often used to separate groups of enclosed spaces with a large open space.

Axial

An axial concept aligns spaces on a significant feature or features. The significant feature may be the entry to the spaces, a view, or an important architectural element, or a formal grouping of spaces can create an axis where otherwise one may not naturally exist or be suggested by existing conditions. Generally, the space creating the axis is important, more than just a corridor.

An axial concept combines some of the features of a centralized concept and a linear concept. The space is significant, either symbolically or functionally, and the direction of the axis focuses attention not on the space but usually on something at one or both ends of the axis. If two axes intersect, the point of intersection takes on special significance, often becoming a centralized space.

Centralized

A centralized concept uses a single, dominant space with secondary spaces grouped around it. In its purest form the central space is a regular shape large enough to accommodate the required number of secondary spaces. However, the central space can also be asymmetrical or irregular in form, as long at it is perceived as a single space and not as a rambling, oversized corridor. The secondary spaces may be similar in size, form, and function or they may be irregular to adapt to the configuration of the base building shape.

As a concept, the centralized plan is nondirectional and focuses attention on the central space. As such, the central space may have symbolic or functional importance.

Grid

A grid concept arranges spaces on a predefined, regular pattern of points or intersecting parallel lines. The pattern may be strictly regular, as with a grid of squares, or less regular, as with a grid of rectangles or a grid in which the spacing of the lines varies in a repeating pattern. The grid may be defined or suggested by the base building, as with a post and beam structure, or the grid may be developed by the designer and overlaid on the existing building.

A grid concept is a useful way to organize many different types and sizes of spaces while maintaining an overall regularity and pattern. Individual grid units can be combined when a larger functional unit is required, and other concepts can be juxtaposed on a grid when appropriate. For example, a linear element can run through the grid, or a symmetric group of grids can be carved out of the entire grid to create a central space.

Clustered

A clustered concept organizes spaces based on proximity to each other. The spaces are usually similar in function, size, or shape and are connected with other clusters by a central space, by a corridor, or about an axis, or may be free standing within a larger open space.

By its very nature, a clustered plan concept can accommodate a variety of sizes and shapes of spaces and is well suited to expansion or change. For very large areas, however, wayfinding in a clustered plan consisting of many shapes and sizes of spaces and clusters can be problematic. This is why most clustered concepts are organized about an axis, central space, or some other strong visual element that helps people maintain their orientation.

The diagrams in Fig. 3.7 indicate very general ideas. As an example of how these concepts could be studied in the context of a real building with a definite shape, definite size, and definite entry points, refer to Fig. 3.8. The concepts were applied based on the program for an advertising agency, which required a combination of closed and open spaces. The lease space was on the upper floor of a mid-rise building in an urban setting with full window exposure

on three sides of the space and partial window exposure on the fourth side.

In some cases, the application of a particular concept may not be appropriate for an existing space due to the shape of the space, the functional requirements of the rooms and spaces that need to be accommodated, or other conceptual ideas. In Fig. 3.8, for example, the existing building does not lend itself to an axial organization; the axis suggested by the elevator lobby is weak and breaks down when it meets the exterior wall. A pure

Figure 3.8
Planning
Concept in
Existing
Building

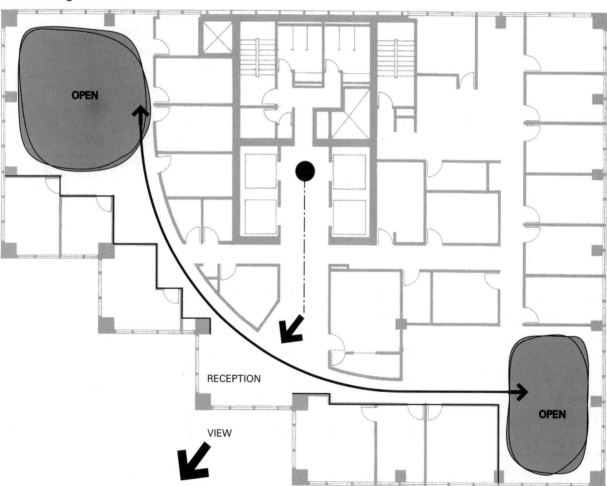

open concept is also not appropriate because of the programmatic needs of the client. The grid concept would also be forced for this particular client's program, although a 5 ft grid was used to design the building. Instead, a linear concept was used, with the main corridor establishing a strong linear element by the nature of its curved shape. Various shaped spaces were then organized on either side of this linear concept. Although there are many angles and types of rooms and spaces, the curved linear element also serves as an orienting device in the complex floor plan.

Space Relationships

In addition to general planning concepts, there are several ways individual spaces can be related to other spaces, which can also become part of the design concept. Spaces can be adjacent, overlap, or share a common space, or one space can be placed within another. See Fig. 3.9.

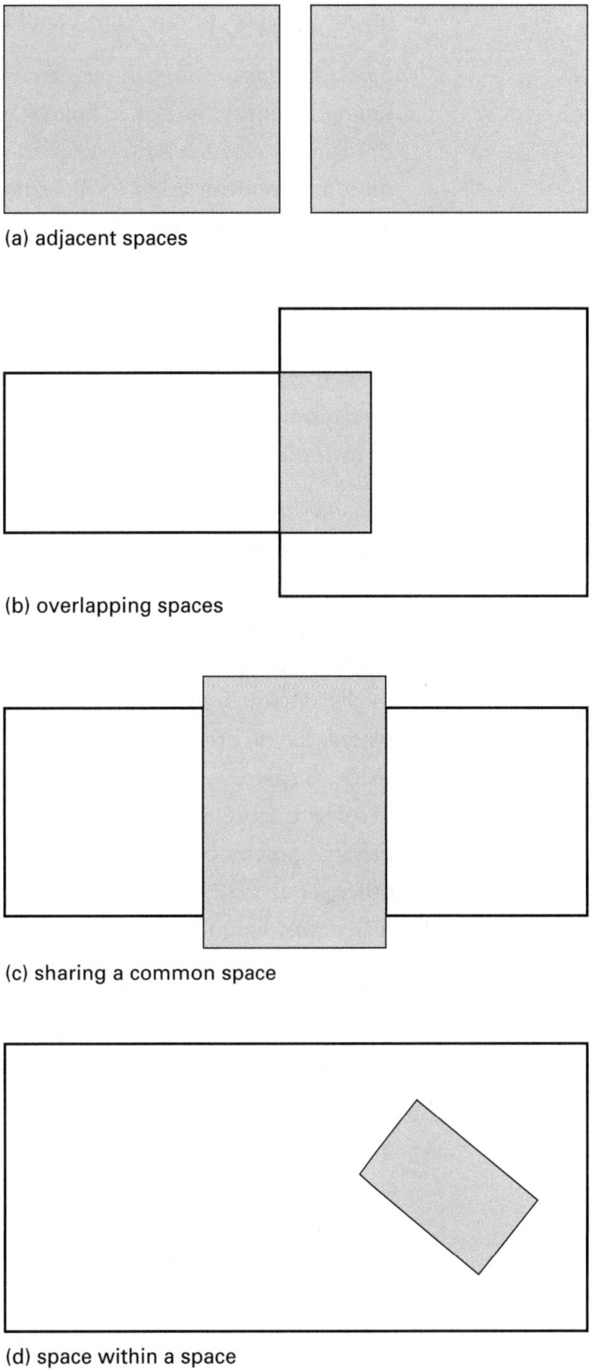

Adjacent spaces are the most common type of interior relationship, in which each space or room has its own use and functional requirements and is separated by a partition or other construction element. The separation may range from a solid wall to the mere suggestion of separation, as with a piece of furniture or a change of level. The amount of transparency between the spaces depends on how much privacy or separate identity each room requires.

Overlapping spaces consist of two spaces whose unique limits can be perceived but that share a common space. The overlapping portion can be used for a function common to both spaces, can serve to visually tie the two spaces together, or can purposely create a unique third space by implication. A thrust stage is an example of an overlapping space, with the performing part of the stage being both a stage, clearly for the actors, and part of

Figure 3.9
Space Relationships

(a) adjacent spaces

(b) overlapping spaces

(c) sharing a common space

(d) space within a space

the larger auditorium, clearly for the audience.

When two spaces are overlapped, it creates a unique tension, with the common space being neither definitely part of one or the other. However, the designer can manipulate the separating partition, levels, materials, lighting, and other physical elements so the common space seems to belong to one of the spaces more than the other.

Spaces sharing a common space retain their unique identity and are linked with a third space that has its own identity. The most common variation of this concept is a corridor being used as the common space. A house with rooms built around a courtyard is another example of this idea. The common space can be larger or smaller than the spaces sharing it, but unlike overlapping spaces, the common space has its own identity.

A *space within another space* is created when a clearly identifiable space or room is placed as an object within a larger open space. In Gestalt terms, it becomes a figure-ground relationship. For example, a totally enclosed conference room can be placed in an otherwise open-plan office space. A space within a space can be used to solve functional requirements, such as a private conference room in an open-plan office, or the concept can be used to signify status, hierarchy, or control.

Components of Interior Design

There are elements common to all interior design and architecture that designers can use to solve clients' functional requirements as well as to create spaces that meet the user's emotional and psychological needs. These elements include walls, ceilings, floors, steps, doors, and glazed openings (windows).

By viewing these elements on a conceptual basis in terms of their performance requirements at the beginning of design, the designer can make better choices about specific construction materials. For example, rather than just accepting that a suspended acoustical ceiling is the only choice for a commercial space, the ceiling

should first be viewed as an enclosing plane with certain functions and opportunities to enhance the overall design concept. Likewise, instead of just using a gypsum wallboard partition, the plane between two rooms or spaces should be viewed as a separating device to be designed to provide certain qualities of privacy, sound isolation, visual control, and so on.

Walls, or vertical planes, are the primary space-defining element in interior design. Because they are viewed straight on, they are also the most prominent structural feature in any room or space. They can be solid, transparent, partially open, decorated, vertical, slanted, partial height, or combined with other materials in an almost infinite number of ways. Even low-cost painted drywall partitions can be manipulated into a variety of forms.

Ceilings are what truly make space interior. Ceilings are often an afterthought of a design, relegated to performing the functional duties of containing lighting, sprinklers, HVAC equipment, and the like. Because of the limitations of existing floor or roof structures, the interior designer often has limited choices in ceiling height, but even minor changes in ceiling height can help define space, direct movement, and affect the scale of a room. Modifications in ceiling finish type can also provide the designer with a tool for manipulating the quality of space.

Floors establish stability and a fixed reference plane. Although often mostly covered with furniture and equipment, floors and flooring material can affect the visual, acoustical, and tactile qualities of a space. Like ceilings, floors can help define space and direct movement.

Steps, or changes in horizontal level, create vertical movement and define space. As such, steps can create excitement in a space and emphasize the third dimension that is often lacking in interiors. Although they are often a limited possibility because of the fixed height of the existing building structure, even a few steps or a single raised platform can create a special space, signal a change in hierarchy, or modify the scale of a room. Due to accessibility requirements, ramps most typically need to be designed along with steps, although ramps in themselves can create a dynamic and interesting form of vertical movement.

Doors are important points of transition between rooms or spaces. Like walls, doors serve a variety of functions: to control movement, vision, sound, light, and weather, and to provide security. However, in addition to serving basic functional needs, doors can celebrate movement and transition, impress, set status, and generally enhance the design intent of the space. For example, in one case a doorway between two spaces that were similar in function might be detailed in the simplest way possible, to de-emphasize the connection. In another case, between adjacent spaces designed to each have their own identity, a doorway could be given special treatment and detailed larger and more ornately to emphasize the transition between one space and another.

Glazing is a unique material in that it can establish separation and connection simultaneously. In addition, interior glazing can help bring daylighting deeper into the interiors while still allowing enclosed rooms along the exterior window wall. With all the glass types on the market, the designer can select glazing to meet nearly any functional and decorative need. The availability of various types of fire-resistive glazing makes it possible to achieve transparency in places where previously it was impossible.

Details

Details are the smaller scale components of interior construction. Details serve three purposes. The first is basic; they are simply a way of fitting the larger components together. In this role, details resolve problems of connection and transition. For example, a ceiling must be connected with a wall in some way. This could be done as simply as the intersection of two surfaces of wallboard or as elaborately as creating a lighting cove, using ornate trim, and supporting the ceiling so it looks like it is floating free of the wall. The second purpose is to solve functional problems, such as providing a horizontal work surface with adequate lighting for reading. The third purpose is to enhance the design intent of the overall design concept. For example, a standard steel doorframe detail would not be appropriate in a space intended to look like a traditional, wood-paneled office. This would be a type of cue inconsistency described in the previous section on theories of perception.

Details can and should use the same basic elements and principles of design, described in Chs. 8 and 9, that would be used in developing the overall look of the space. By doing this, details can be consistent with and reinforce the design intent.

Lighting and Color

Because light makes all things visible, it is one of the most important components of a design concept. Beyond the functional requirement to have enough light to work or play by, lighting can emphasize, obscure, create mood, add interest, shape space, and provide variability in the environment. Lighting can also change the appearance of colors and materials by its type, the color temperature of the lamp, its intensity, and its position.

Color is one of the most emotionally charged components of any design. As discussed in Ch. 8, color has meaning to people and can affect their moods and sometimes even their behavior. During concept development, the designer may select very broad palettes of color for the client's review and approval without selecting specific colors. In this way, undesirable color ranges can be eliminated early, and the designer can focus on refining color choices during the design development phase of a project.

Materials

As with other components of design, materials serve both functional and aesthetic purposes. Functionally, they provide finish, concealment, protection, sound modulation, light reflectance, and fire resistance. Aesthetically, materials can convey meaning, denote status, create style, symbolize ideals, and generally add to the overall look of the space.

During early concept development, material selection can be treated similarly to color; that is, different "palettes" of material types can be selected in broad categories to develop a general direction for later detailed material selection and specification, to come later.

Furniture

Furniture is often considered the primary component of interior design. Although this is not true in all cases, furniture does occupy a significant portion of the visual field in a space. It must be selected to satisfy the client's basic functional needs and budget, but furniture also carries its own meaning and contribution to the overall design intent of the space in which it is used. Furniture concepts can include basic issues of light or heavy, soft or hard, small or large, colorful or neutral, or similar to or contrasted with the architecture of the space.

Accessories

Accessories include art, lamps, vases, pillows, and anything that is not part of the structure or architecture of the space and not a piece of furniture. Like detailing, accessories should enhance the design intent of the space, complementing it while not dominating it.

DETERMINING AND REPRESENTING SPACE RELATIONSHIPS

After a design concept has been developed based on programming information, design theory, and the application of conceptual ideas, the designer must establish the exact relationships between spaces listed in the program.

Spaces must not only be the correct size for the activity they support, but they also must be located near other spaces with which they share some functional relationship. Programming identifies these relationships and assigns them a hierarchy of importance. The relationships are usually recorded in a matrix or graphically as adjacency diagrams. Figure 3.10 shows a

Figure 3.10
Adjacency Matrix

	entry	living room	dining room	kitchen	study	bedroom	bedroom	bath
entry		●		○	●	○	○	○
living room	●		●		○			○
dining room		●		●				
kitchen	○		●					
study	●	○						○
bedroom	○						○	●
bedroom	○					○		●
bath	○	○			○	●	●	

legend
mandatory adjacency ●
secondary adjacency ○
no adjacency required ☐

matrix indicating three levels of adjacency. Figure 3.11 shows the same information in a "folded" version that eliminates duplication of information.

There are three basic types of adjacency needs: people, products, and information. Each type implies a different kind of design response. Two or more spaces may need to be physically adjacent or located very close to one another when people need face-to-face contact or when people move from one area to another as part of their activity. For example, the entries to a theater, the lobby, and the theater space have a particular functional reason for being arranged the way they are. In a house, the kitchen should be adjacent to the dining room but does not have to be adjacent to the bedrooms. With some relationships, two spaces may simply need to be accessible to one another, but this can be accomplished with a corridor or through another intervening space rather than with direct adjacency.

Products, equipment, or other objects may need to be moved between spaces and require another type of adjacency. The spaces themselves may not have to be close to one another, but the movement of objects must be facilitated. Dumbwaiters, pneumatic tubes, assembly lines, and other types of conveying systems can connect spaces of this type without direct adjacency. When objects have to move in a definite sequence, a flow chart with arrows may be used to show adjacencies as well as direction of movement.

Finally, there may be a requirement that people in different spaces merely be able to exchange information. The adjacency may then be entirely electronic or achieved with paper-moving systems. For example, a supervisor electronically monitoring telephone operators would not need to be physically adjacent to (or even in the same building with) the operators, even though

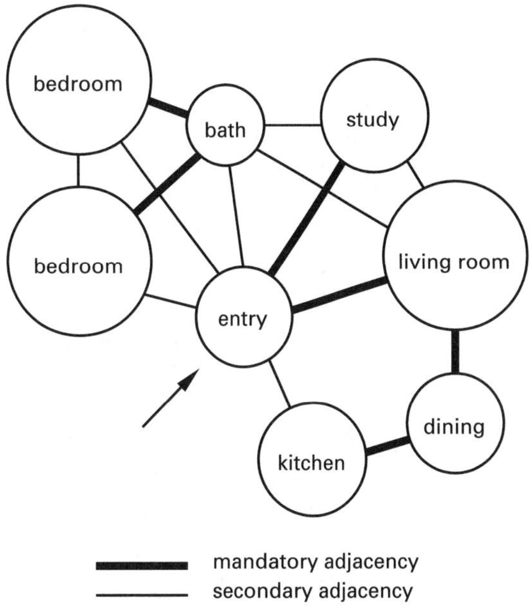

there is a strong relationship between the two functions. Although there are many situations that do not demand physical adjacency, informal human contact may be advantageous for other reasons.

The programmer analyzes various types of adjacency requirements and verifies them

Figure 3.11
Folded Adjacency

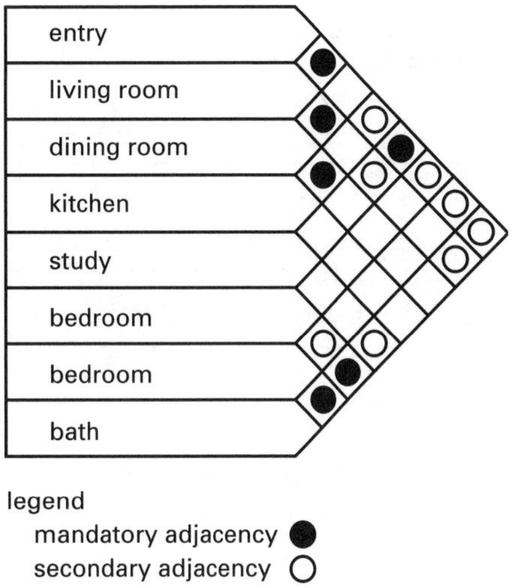

legend
mandatory adjacency ●
secondary adjacency ○

Figure 3.12
Bubble Diagram

━━━ mandatory adjacency
──── secondary adjacency

Figure 3.13

Stacking
Diagram

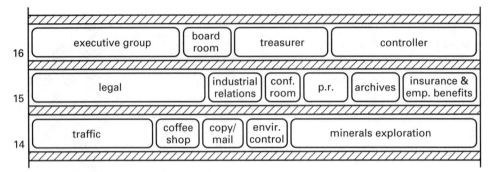

with the client. Because it is a rare case when every desirable relationship can be accommodated, the ones that are mandatory need to be identified separately from the ones that are highly desirable or simply useful. This is often indicated in adjacency diagrams (also called bubble diagrams) with varying weights of connecting lines or with varying numbers of lines: the more lines or the thicker the lines, the stronger the connection should be. Figure 3.12 shows the information given in the matrix of Fig. 3.11 as a bubble diagram.

For the NCIDQ exam, the candidate must be able to complete an adjacency matrix based on programming information. See Ch. 30 for more information.

A special type of adjacency diagram is the stacking diagram. As illustrated in Fig. 3.13, this is a drawing that shows the locations of major spaces or departments when a project occupies more than one floor of a multistory building. A stacking diagram based on departments or major groupings of spaces is usually worked out before each floor area is planned in detail.

SAMPLE QUESTIONS

1. A rational approach to design that emphasizes human-environment interaction would most likely be based on

(A) environmental design research

(B) functional requirements

(C) Gestalt psychology

(D) social influences

2. The most organic, humanistic interior design of houses is best represented by

(A) Frank Lloyd Wright

(B) Le Corbusier

(C) Mies van der Rohe

(D) Walter Gropius

3. The given plan drawing diagrammatically illustrates a built-in seating space within a larger room. The overall shape would be perceived according to which Gestalt principal?

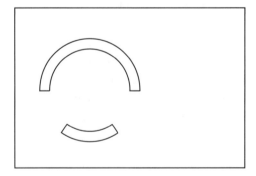

(A) simplicity

(B) grouping

(C) continuity

(D) closure

4. Which of the following plan arrangements would be most appropriate for the entry, nave, altar, and choir of a church moving into an existing rectangular space?

(A) axial

(B) clustered

(C) linear

(D) open

5. The complexity of the human-environment interface makes it difficult to base a design theory only on

(A) environmental design research

(B) functionality

(C) historic precedent

(D) perception theories

6. Overall department relationships of a large company being planned to occupy a multistory building would most likely be shown in

(A) a block diagram

(B) an adjacency matrix

(C) a stacking diagram

(D) a bubble diagram

7. Preliminary space planning shows that it is impossible to satisfy all the programmed adjacencies shown on the adjacency matrix that has been approved by the client. What is the best course of action?

(A) Verify that the adjacencies require physical connection, and then review the problem with the client.

(B) Satisfy as many adjacency connections as possible, and present this information to the client for review and approval.

(C) Ask the client to downgrade the importance of the problematic adjacency.

(D) Develop several alternatives that come as close as possible to the requirements, and have the client select the one that best satisfies the program.

8. Which of the following would provide the most cost-effective space-defining construction element?

(A) a raised platform

(B) gypsum wallboard partitions

(C) oversized doors

(D) a glazed wall

9. A design concept statement for a public gathering area around a fireplace in a ski lodge would probably NOT include the

(A) size of the fireplace

(B) number of individual seating groups

(C) types of finish materials

(D) method of lighting the space

10. Adjacency requirements for the physical movement of goods in a manufacturing plant would best be illustrated with

(A) an adjacency matrix

(B) a bubble diagram

(C) a flow chart

(D) a stacking diagram

4

SPACE PLANNING

As described in Ch. 3, design concepts are based on the space and adjacency needs of the client developed during programming as well as on theoretical, social, cultural, and psychological issues. Once these design concepts are developed and approved by the client, detailed space planning begins. Space planning is the process used to translate programmatic needs and broad design concepts into a physical plan of the space by organizing major rooms and areas, determining circulation systems, and laying out furniture. Space planning deals with the design of the arrangement of spaces and objects, not with the particulars of materials, finishes, colors, or accessories.

SPACE ALLOCATION

Regardless of the complexity of a program, there is a logical method to developing a space plan that satisfies the client's needs and the design concept. The steps involved in this process are outlined as follows. Additional design considerations are discussed in the following section.

Existing Conditions

Because the interior designer always develops a plan within the context of an existing architectural space (or one that is designed but not yet constructed), many preliminary space planning decisions are based on existing conditions. These are determined during the field survey and recorded on plans, elevations, and other sketches as necessary. Photographs can also be used to document things like existing views, lighting, and the condition of any materials and finishes that may be reused. If the building is still in the planning stages or existing drawings are available, copies of the architectural plans can be obtained. However, base building floor plans may not include certain information that is needed for design, such as wall finishes, equipment added by the previous owner, or hardware types.

If an existing floor plan is not available at the scale necessary, a base plan should be drawn to use for subsequent planning and development of construction documents. A *base plan* is a floor plan drawing of the existing space within which the new design will be placed. In most cases, the entire floor of the existing building is used, even if the tenant will use only a portion of the floor. This is done in order to show the position of the tenant on the floor, the extent of the public corridors, the location of the entry or elevator lobby, service entrances, the locations of exits, the locations of the public restrooms, and other public or semipublic spaces. Existing walls and structures are usually drawn with a solid black poché to differentiate them from new construction.

Several aspects of existing conditions can influence the space plan of an interior design project. These are briefly outlined as follows. Of course, depending on the nature of the project, not all will apply in every circumstance.

Relationship to surrounding areas: The surrounding area includes exterior features such as entry doors to the building as well as interior points of connection like stairways and corridors. Obviously, reception areas of an office should be located close to the main entrance or elevator lobby, or the primary furniture grouping of a living room should be near a focal point like a fireplace. In existing commercial buildings, the locations of exits are always one of the primary determinants of how corridors and large spaces are planned. Service access from loading docks or service elevators should be also noted.

Size of existing space: The size of the existing space will also affect planning decisions. Some parts of the existing space may not accommodate some of the larger programmed spaces, so the locations of these will be determined by the available large, unobstructed areas. If ceiling height is important, such as in athletic facilities and auditoriums, this too may influence how the project must be planned.

Views: Views are important to both residential and commercial interior design. Desirable views should be fully utilized, while undesirable views can be blocked or modified with window coverings. Undesirable view areas can also be used for rooms where view is not important. In commercial construction, decisions must be made concerning what spaces are placed at the exterior walls. Guidelines for such decisions should be made during the programming phase. In many cases, offices with windows are a sign of status or hierarchy in an organization. In other cases, windows may be provided in common areas and open work areas for everyone to use and to increase the availability of daylighting.

Special features: Both existing and new buildings often have unique characteristics that can be incorporated into the designer's planning. For instance, older structures may have ornate millwork or vaulted ceilings that can be featured in the primary interior spaces. The locations of these spaces would, in turn, dictate the locations of adjacent spaces. New buildings might have interior atriums or attractive public corridors that could suggest the positioning of certain rooms. For sustainable design, existing partitions should be used whenever possible.

Structural considerations: The locations of columns and loadbearing walls is often one of the most troublesome existing factors for interior design. Columns cannot be moved, and loadbearing walls may only be pierced or partially removed after review and design by a structural engineer, and then only at significant expense. Existing structural elements may affect the spacing of rooms, the positions of new partitions, or the locations of large areas. New partitions can coincide with column locations so that columns do not awkwardly end up in the middle of a room. If a room is required to be of a size that exceeds the column spacing, it should be centered between the columns so that the columns are off to both sides as much as possible. In spaces used for open office planning or restaurant dining rooms, furniture placement can be planned around the columns or service spaces like closets and storage rooms, or space dividers can minimize the effect of the columns.

The existing bearing capacity of a building's floor system can also influence space planning. If heavy loading, such as library shelving, densely packed file cabinets, or heavy equipment, is present, a structural engineer should be hired to review the situation. Some areas of a building may have a greater loadbearing capacity than others. In some instances, additional structural reinforcing may be required.

Plumbing: Kitchens, bar sinks, toilet rooms, and other spaces that require water supply and drainage should be located close to existing building plumbing to minimize cost and simplify construction. For residential projects, the plumbing lines can be easily located by the placement of existing bathrooms and kitchens or by inspecting the basement or crawl space. In commercial construction, the architectural plans may need to be reviewed because plumbing line locations are not always evident. In high-rise buildings, the plumbing is located in vertical stacks at the core of the building near the toilet rooms. Often, however, wet columns are provided. Wet columns are structural columns located away from the core of the building, next to which water supply pipes and drains are located to make it easier to tap into them as required for tenant finish work.

Organization Concepts

After the pertinent existing conditions have been identified and noted, the next determinant of space planning is function. Required adjacencies and the relative sizes of various rooms and areas, in conjunction with existing constraints, dictate much of the organization of a plan. However, even with these objective requirements there are usually many ways the same program can be accommodated

within any given architectural space. One of the designer's tasks is to develop organizing concepts that will satisfy the client's needs and then test them against criteria unique to the situation, to find the best one to develop in more detail.

As described in Ch. 3, there are six general ways plans can be organized. These include open, linear, axial, centralized, grid, and clustered, and their variations. Four of the more common concepts are shown in Fig. 4.1.

Even with an open system, the furniture or other elements are arranged according to one of the four concepts. Clustered concepts also use one of these four basic layouts. These general concepts can be applied to large space planning problems as well as to individual rooms.

Linear organizations consist of a series of spaces or rooms that are placed in a single line. The spaces can be identical or of different sizes and shapes, but they always relate to a unifying line, usually a path of circulation. A linear organization is very adaptable; it can be straight, bent, or curved to work within an existing architectural space. It is easily expandable and can be planned in a modular configuration if desired. The typical layout of office space, with rooms positioned on either side of a corridor that encircles the building's core, is a variation of the linear concept.

Axial organizations have two or more major linear segments about which spaces or rooms are placed. There may be additional, secondary paths growing out of the primary axes, and the major linear segments may be at right angles to each other or at some other angle. Axial plans usually have a featured termination at one or more ends of the axis, or the axis is a major design element in itself.

Grid systems consist of two sets of spaced elements. The grid elements may

Figure 4.1
Organizing
Concepts

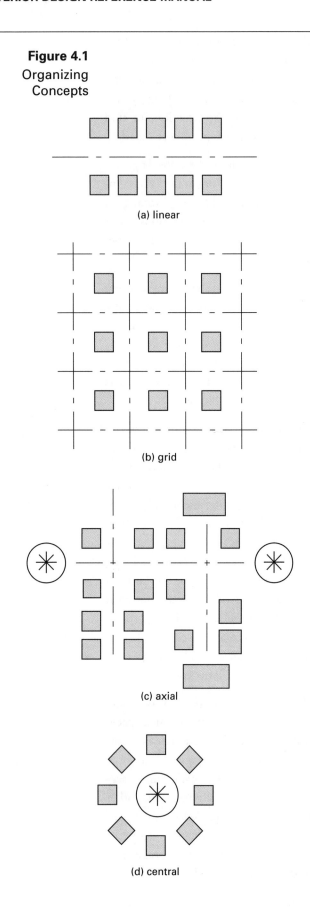

(a) linear

(b) grid

(c) axial

(d) central

be regularly spaced and perpendicular to each other, or irregularly spaced and at angles to each other or to the architectural space. Within a grid, portions can be subtracted, added, or modified. The size of the grid can be changed to create different sizes of spaces or to define special areas. However, a grid can become very monotonous and confusing if not used properly. Because a grid system is usually defined by circulation paths, it is more appropriate for very large spaces or in buildings where a great deal of circulation is required. Open-plan workstations or restaurant tables are two examples where grid organizations are commonly used.

Central organizations are based on one space or point about which secondary elements are placed. This is usually a very formal method of organizing interiors and inherently places the primary emphasis on the central space. A hotel lobby is a common example of this type of concept.

When more than one linear organization extends from a centralized point, it becomes a *radial organization*. Radial plans have a central focus but also extend outward to connect with other spaces or rooms. Radial plans can be circular or assume other shapes as well.

Circulation Patterns

Developing a direct, efficient circulation plan is critical to successfully completing the design practicum portion of the NCIDQ exam. The candidate must demonstrate the ability to allocate space efficiently, use circulation to maintain adjacencies, and provide the required arrangement and widths to satisfy barrier-free and building code exiting requirements.

One of the common mistakes in space planning is to let adjacency requirements dictate the arranging of rooms and spaces in the preliminary planning and then to connect rooms with a circulation path as an afterthought. What often remains is a maze of awkward corridors and circulation routes that decrease efficiency and result in dead-end corridors or other exiting problems.

Circulation patterns are one of the primary ways of organizing a room, an open space, or an entire interior design project. They are vital to the efficient organization of space and provide people with their strongest orientation within an environment.

Circulation is directly related to the organizational pattern of a project, but it does not necessarily have to mimic it. For example, a major circulation path can cut diagonally across a grid pattern. See Fig. 4.2. Normally, there is a hierarchy of paths. Major routes connect major rooms or spaces or are spaces themselves and have secondary paths branching from them. Different sizes and types of circulation are important for accommodating varying capacities and for providing an orientation device for people.

All circulation paths are linear by their very nature, but there are some common variations, many of which are similar to the organizational patterns described in the previous section. Because circulation is such an important part of space planning, it is helpful to have a mental picture of the various circulation concepts and the advantages and disadvantages of each before taking the exam. There are three basic patterns as shown in Figs. 4.3 through 4.5. These can be applied to an individual room when laying out furniture as well as to a group of rooms and spaces when planning a larger facility.

The linear, *dumbbell layout* diagrammed in Fig. 4.3(a) is the simplest and one of the most flexible circulation path patterns. Spaces are laid out along a straight path that connects two major elements at the ends—usually the entrance to the space or

Figure 4.2
Juxtaposed Organizing and Circultion Concepts

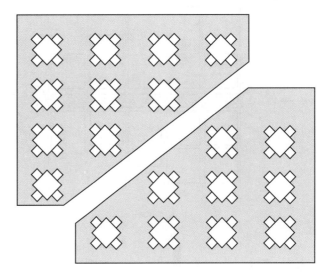

group of rooms at one end and an exit or other access point at the other (although the primary entrance can occur anywhere along the path). Spaces are laid out along the spine as required. The path can be straight, bent, or curved as required to accommodate the fixed architectural space. The typical double-loaded corridor arrangement (rooms on both sides of a common corridor) makes space planning very efficient. Figures 4.3(b) and 4.3(c) show the dumbbell layout applied to rooms of identical area in an efficient and inefficient way.

Making a complete loop results in a *doughnut configuration* as shown in Fig. 4.4. This is also very efficient because it provides a double-loaded corridor and automatically makes a continuous exitway so two exits are always available if required by building codes. Entries, doorways, and exits can be located anywhere along the path. This pattern is only appropriate for larger groups of spaces because the ratio of circulation area to usable area should be kept as low as possible.

Figure 4.3
Circulation
Layouts

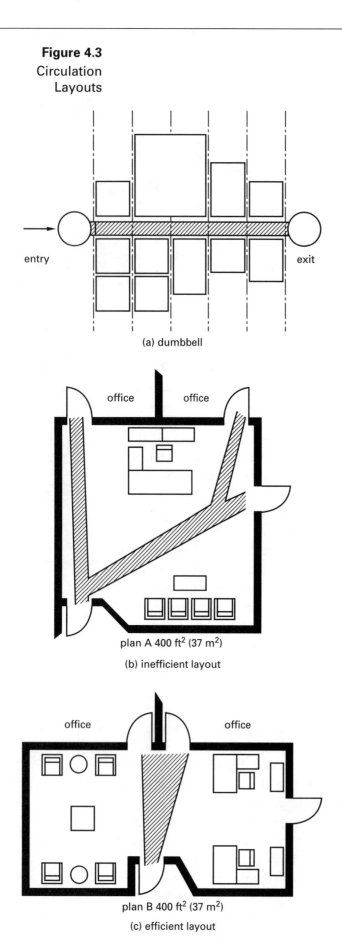

(a) dumbbell

plan A 400 ft² (37 m²)

(b) inefficient layout

plan B 400 ft² (37 m²)

(c) efficient layout

The *radial layout* shown in Fig. 4.5 is oriented on one major space with paths extending from this central area. This configuration is generally used when there is a major space that serves as the focal point for secondary spaces, such as with a hotel lobby. A well-planned house is another example of a radial layout, with the entry hall being the central space from which the other circulation paths radiate. Because of the commercial construction building code requirement for at least two paths to an exit in most situations, the ends of the linear routes extending from the central space must lead to an exit or must loop around to the central space. However, if the building code allows dead-end corridors not exceeding 20 ft (6096), a short corridor does not have to terminate in an exit.

Furnishings Layout

Furniture layout is simply a space planning problem in miniature. Before starting to work on a furnishings layout, however, the overall context of the room or space in which the furniture will be placed should be determined. This includes determining fixed items, such as window locations and structural elements, and planning those things that can be controlled to give as much flexibility as possible for furniture arrangement. For example, if a door can be located anywhere in a new partition, it should be placed so it does not create an awkward circulation path through an area best used for a furniture grouping. The simplest way to avoid problems is to view furniture groupings as "rooms" and the spaces between them as circulation paths, and to follow the organizational and circulation concepts described in the previous two sections.

Nearly all furniture placement, whether in residential or commercial design, can be viewed as part of a furniture grouping. For example, a bedroom consists of a bed, nightstands, and storage cabinets, while an office workstation may consist of a desk, a desk return for placement of a computer terminal, a chair, and possibly a file cabinet or credenza. The grouping creates a planning module consisting of three elements: the individual pieces of furniture, the space around them, and the access points to get to the grouping (the "door" to the grouping). If furniture groupings are thought of in these terms it is easier to plan them efficiently.

The first step is to determine the types and number of individual pieces. Of course, the program defines the function of the grouping and often specifies the individual pieces of furniture. If the program simply specifies a function, such as "lounge seating group," some assumptions will have to be made about the exact number of people to be accommodated, the types of furniture (chairs versus sofas, for example), and other pieces like side tables, lamps, or coffee tables. If existing furniture is being reused, it can be measured to determine how much space is required. If new furniture is planned, an approximate size of the individual pieces has to be assumed if they have not yet been selected.

Next, consider the space between the pieces and their orientations to each other. For example, the space between a desk and a credenza behind should be about $3^1/_2$ ft to 5 ft (1050 to 1500). This allows for a chair and easy access to drawers. A well-planned seating group places chairs and sofas about 4 ft to 10 ft (1200 to 3000) apart for comfortable conversation. Knowledge of typical space planning dimensions and human factors, discussed in Ch. 1, will help determine spacing and orientation.

Finally, think about the general access to the grouping and its relationship to existing elements within the room. For example, a dining table in the middle of a room

with three doors requires more space around it for general circulation than would a table at the end of a room, which would only need enough space near the

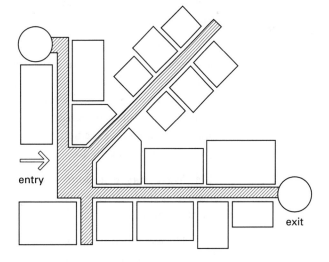

Figure 4.4
Doughnut
Circulation
Layout

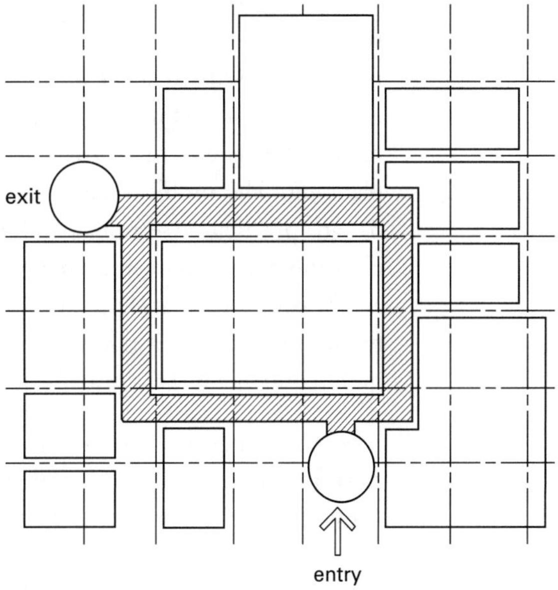

Figure 4.5
Radial
Circulation
Layout

walls to allow for seating and access to each chair.

Code Restrictions

Building code requirements concerning exiting, corridors, and doors affect initial space planning. Building code requirements are discussed in detail in Chs. 27 and 28, but the following guidelines summarize the requirements for preliminary planning. The problem statement of the design practicum section of the exam gives the major code requirements, which are the only ones that should be used. The following checklist gives some of the common requirements that must be followed.

• Verify that the required number of exits from individual rooms and from the entire space are shown. Smaller rooms and nonassembly spaces usually require only one exit door. Spaces with large occupant loads, like auditoriums and classrooms, will require two exits. Normally the practicum problem will require two exits from the commercial space. Even though residential spaces (apartments) do not require two exits in most instances, the problem may specifically state that two are required.

• If two exits are required they must be separated by a distance at least one-half of the diagonal distance of the room or area they serve. See Ch. 28 for more information on this requirement. In many cases the problem statement will give a specific minimum distance.

• Make sure exit doors are a minimum of 3 ft (914) wide and swing in the direction of travel.

• Doors must not encroach more than 7 in (179) into the exit space when fully open.

• Use corridors of adequate exit width. Generally, the minimum is 36 in (914) for residential construction and 44 in (1118) for commercial construction, but school and other occupancies may require wider corridors. In most cases, the problem statement will give the minimum width, usually 44 in (1118). It may be advisable to use 48 in to 60 in (1220 to 1525) wide corridors regardless, to provide adequate width for normal use and to provide for the minimum 60 in (1525) turnaround space for accessibility.

• Although dead-end corridors of less than 20 ft (6096) are acceptable in some circumstances, try to develop the space plan to avoid these completely.

• Plan corridors for efficient layout so the total length is minimized. Refer to Ch. 28 for information on maximum travel distances.

• Verify that corridor widths, turns, and other clearances meet the requirements for accessibility for the physically disabled. This includes adequate clearance in front of and to the sides of door openings. A minimum of 18 in (455) on the pull side of the door on the latch side and 12 in (305) on the push side of the door is required. See Ch. 29 for specific accessibility requirements.

DESIGN CONSIDERATIONS

The design practicum section of the exam requires that the programmed spaces on a given floor plan be fitted with efficient circulation and that the required adjacencies be maintained. Consideration should also be given to public versus private spaces, enclosed or open spaces, daylighting and views, and sustainability.

Maintaining Adjacencies

One of the basic requirements of space planning is to maintain the programmed adjacencies. Bubble diagrams or matrices record these and indicate varying levels of connection such as mandatory, desired, or not important. The plan should place rooms or areas with mandatory adjacencies next to each other. Spaces with less important adjacencies are often separated somewhat if they cannot be abutted. This is usually done with corridors.

During space planning, required adjacencies can be maintained by translating roughly scaled bubble diagrams to scaled, rectangular shapes representing individual rooms and areas in such a way that as many lines of adjacency as possible are maintained. This diagram can then be laid over the base floor plan as a starting point for locating partitions and other area separations.

Public Versus Private

Except for single rooms, almost all interior design projects have a hierarchy of privacy requirements. For example, a residential living room is considered more public than a bedroom or bathroom. The reception area of an office suite can be considered public, while a conference room is semiprivate, and individual offices are private.

A good space plan recognizes the need for different levels of privacy based on the type of occupancy and the function of the space. This need can be met by using barriers (walls and doors), distance, sequencing, and other physical means.

Enclosed Versus Open

As with public and private spaces, different uses require or suggest varying levels of openness. These may be specified in the program or implied based on the type of space and its function. Generally, open spaces are used because they encourage communication, improve the appearance of the space, and reduce cost by making hard construction unnecessary. Open spaces can be created by using low partitions, systems furniture, or freestanding panels.

Daylighting, Views, and Artificial Lighting

Electric lighting and the cooling it requires typically account for 30% to 40% of a commercial building's total energy use and can sometimes range as high as 50%. Using natural light as much as possible can provide significant energy savings in a building as well as help reduce the requirement for power-generating plants that use nonrenewable energy. In addition, natural light and views to the outside have been shown to have physical and psychological benefits to the occupants of a space. For these reasons space planning should try to maximize daylighting.

The efficiency of daylighting depends greatly on the architectural design of the building, but the interior designer can still take several actions to make the best use of a building's existing fenestration. During initial space planning, it is helpful to develop concepts that use open planning as much as possible, leaving the areas near windows available for views as well as to admit as much natural light as possible. Using low partitions and extensive interior glazing can also maximize light penetration and views to the outside.

The interior designer can also select appropriate window coverings to maximize the reflectance of interior surfaces and can coordinate the artificial lighting with the type and quantity of available natural light. Chapters 12, 19 and 26 discuss these design strategies.

In order to effectively employ any design strategy, the interior designer should have a basic understanding of the many variables involved with daylighting. These include the compass orientations of the façades utilizing daylight, the brightness of the sky (which is affected by solar altitude, cloud conditions, and time of day), the area of the glass, the height of the head of the glass, the transmittance of the glass, the reflectance of both room surfaces and nearby outdoor surfaces, and obstructions such as overhangs and trees. Figure 4.6

Figure 4.6
Daylighting
Variables

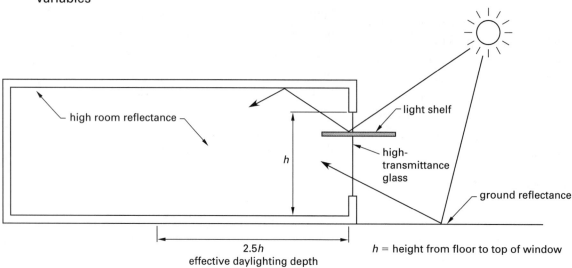

2.5*h*
effective daylighting depth

h = height from floor to top of window

illustrates some of the variables of day-lighting design.

The advantages of daylighting must be balanced by the potential problems. These include unwanted heat gain or loss as glass area is increased, glare, and imbalanced lighting if side lighting is too strong. The issue of control must also be addressed because daylighting does not conserve energy if electric lights are not switched off. Normally, automatic switching is used to overcome this problem.

Of particular note in Fig. 4.6 is the effective daylighting depth, which is approximately two and one-half times the height of the head of the window. While this is generally a given condition for interior designers, knowing that effective daylighting drops off rapidly at this point may suggest where enclosed spaces should be planned.

One of the problems with using daylighting, especially with large, high windows on the south side of a building, is the resultant glare and heat gain of direct sun. One of the most effective ways architects solve this problem is by using a light shelf.

A *light shelf* is simply a horizontal surface placed above eye level that reflects direct daylight onto the ceiling while shading the lower portions of the window and the interior of the room. A light shelf also has the desirable effect of distributing the light more evenly from the window to the back of the room. This is shown diagrammatically in Fig. 4.6.

In most situations, the interior designer has no control over whether a light shelf is used or not. However, in older, existing buildings that have large, high windows, the designer may consider studying the feasibility of adding light shelves. They can be added to the interior of the building with some benefit, although they are most effective when partially inside and partially outside the glass line.

Another term to be familiar with is the daylight factor (DF). The *daylight factor*, expressed as a percentage, is the ratio of the indoor illuminance at a point on a horizontal surface to the unobstructed exterior horizontal illuminance. Direct sunlight is excluded. The daylight factor can be calculated and compared with recommended daylight factors for various tasks. These range from about 1.5% for ordinary visual tasks to about 4% for difficult visual tasks such as drafting.

LEED credits can be gained by providing a daylight factor of 2% for 75% of all space occupied for critical visual tasks. Credits can also be obtained by providing at least 90% of regularly occupied spaces with direct lines of site to perimeter glazing.

Sustainability

During space planning, some aspects of sustainable design can be considered. First, an area for the storage and collection of recyclables should be included in the program. The area needs to be appropriately sized and conveniently located. Before the project can be considered for LEED certification, this requirement must be met.

Second, if feasible, some of the existing building stock may be reused. For example, some existing partitions from a previous tenant might be incorporated into a new space plan. This would reduce the amount of construction waste and reduce the amount of new material required. Other building materials can also be reused. The LEED rating system gives credit for maintaining 40% of nonbuilding shell systems, including walls, flooring, ceilings, and doors. An additional credit is given if this is increased to 60%.

Third, for large tenants or single-tenant occupancies, LEED credit is given for providing secure bicycle storage and changing and shower facilities for 5% or more of the tenants. This additional space could be added to the client's program and made a part of the initial space plan.

SAMPLE QUESTIONS

1. Of the open plan workstations shown, which is most efficient and most appropriate for frequent visitor conferences?

(A)
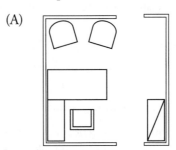

(B)
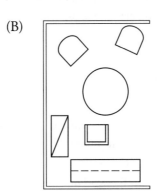

(C)
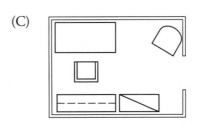

(D)
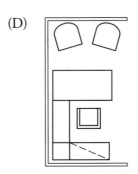

2. Which of the following drawings would be most needed to begin space planning in an existing building?

(A) base plan
(B) circulation plan
(C) exiting plan
(D) reflected ceiling plan

3. For a restaurant in an old building undergoing remodeling, what would have the most influence over the planning of the dining area?

(A) existing structural columns and walls

(B) dimensions of the building

(C) locations of existing plumbing

(D) decorative millwork and existing ornate lighting fixtures

4. Planning an interior in a building with an atrium would suggest which of the following organizational concepts?

(A) axial

(B) grid

(C) radial

(D) central

5. In determining required space for a hospital nurses' station, which is the most important factor?

(A) patient files and number of patient contacts

(B) work surface and storage

(C) movable carts and space for writing reports

(D) electrical requirements and communication equipment

6. Which seating group shown would be best for planning a waiting area to accommodate six people in a health clinic?

(A)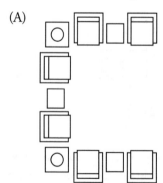

(B)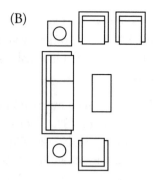

(C)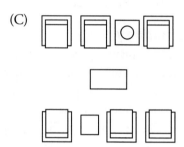

(D)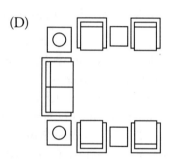

7. The LEAST important consideration in planning exit corridors is

(A) making sure dead ends do not exceed 20 ft (6 m)

(B) providing at least two exits from rooms where they are required

(C) maintaining a minimum width as required by the occupancy type

(D) having the corridors empty into approved exitways or stairways

8. The most efficient type of circulation system for the majority of planning problems is a

(A) radial system

(B) single-loaded corridor

(C) double-loaded corridor

(D) grid system

9. The most effective design strategy an interior designer can use to maximize daylighting involves

(A) changing the type of glazing

(B) increasing the head height of glazing

(C) installing a light shelf

(D) specifying a high-reflectance paint

10. LEED credit is only available when

(A) areas for recyclables are provided

(B) bicycle storage is provided

(C) existing partitions are used

(D) recycled ceiling tile is used

5

COMMUNICATION METHODS

The NCIDQ requires examinees to demonstrate a basic understanding of the common methods of graphic communication and the application of that knowledge when explaining problem solutions. For the design practicum section, the candidate must be able to draw a floor plan and reflected ceiling plan as well as an elevation and section. Although the practicum drawings are not evaluated for drafting techniques, they do need to clearly communicate the solutions.

This chapter discusses using a scale, the four major types of presentation drawings, the format of preliminary presentation drawings, and how models and mockups are used. Refer to Ch. 14 for a more detailed review of construction drawings and the standard graphic symbols used on drawings.

SCALE

Scale in the context of graphic communication is not the same as the design principle of scale discussed in Ch. 8. *Graphic scale* is the ratio of a measuring unit to the full-size item it represents. For example, stating that something is drawn at $^1/_4$ in

scale, or $^1/_4$ in = 1 ft 0 in, means that one quarter of an inch on paper represents exactly one foot of actual size. Scaling makes it possible to represent a very large object on a limited-size piece of paper while showing accurate proportion and the true relationships between objects of different sizes.

A *scale* is a drafting instrument that facilitates making and reading scaled drawings when doing manual drafting. In computer-aided drafting and design (CADD), all drawings are created at full size and only scaled when it is necessary to plot on a piece of paper. There are three types of scales used for architectural, interior design, and engineering drawing. These are the architect's scale, the metric scale, and the engineer's scale.

The *architect's scale* uses fractions of an inch (or multiples of an inch) to represent feet and inches. One of the most common types of architect's scale is the 12 in triangular scale, which contains 12 different scales along six edges (two edges for each vertex of the triangle). Figure 5.1 shows one end of one side of a triangular architect's scale.

Figure 5.1
Architect's Scale

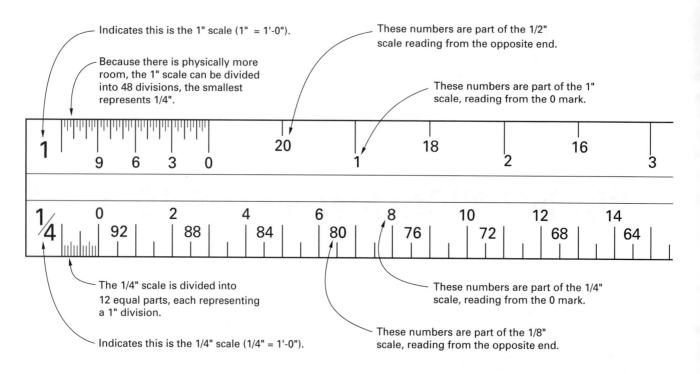

Indicates this is the 1" scale (1" = 1'-0").

Because there is physically more room, the 1" scale can be divided into 48 divisions, the smallest represents 1/4".

These numbers are part of the 1/2" scale reading from the opposite end.

These numbers are part of the 1" scale, reading from the 0 mark.

The 1/4" scale is divided into 12 equal parts, each representing a 1" division.

Indicates this is the 1/4" scale (1/4" = 1'-0").

These numbers are part of the 1/4" scale, reading from the 0 mark.

These numbers are part of the 1/8" scale, reading from the opposite end.

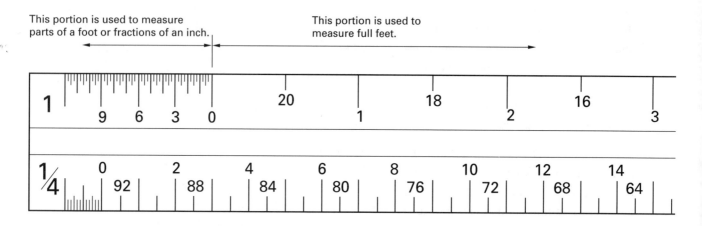

This portion is used to measure parts of a foot or fractions of an inch.

This portion is used to measure full feet.

Each edge contains two scales starting from opposite ends of the scale. Along each edge, one of the scales is always one-half the scale of the other so they can both use the same graduations. As shown in Fig. 5.1, the 1/4 in scale and the 1/8 in scale share the same edge. The numbers for the two scales are differentiated along the scale by locating them in separate rows and by varying the lengths of the graduation lines.

A *metric scale* is used when a project is planned and represented with SI (metric) units. Metric scales are graduated in proportions such as 1:50, 1:10, and 1:5, and individual markings are based on millimeter lengths. For example, on the 1:50 scale, one scale unit equals 50 actual-size units. This is approximately the same scale as 1/4 in = 1 ft 0 in because 1/4 in scale shows objects reduced 1/48 of their actual size, which is very close to a 1:50 reduction. Some metric scales have large-scale proportions appropriate for interior design and architectural work (architect's metric scale), such as 1:5, while other metric scales have small-scale proportions appropriate for site planning and civil engineering work (engineer's metric scale), such as 1:300.

An *engineer's scale* indicates feet and fractions of a foot and uses scales such as 1 in = 40 ft or 1 in = 100 ft. Civil engineers typically use these types of scales. The interior designer seldom sees these scales used except on a set of architectural drawings, where site plans and utility plans use them.

There are two main parts of any scale. With architect's scales, at one end a 1 ft segment is marked off into fine graduations representing inches and fractions of an inch. The remainder of the scale is just marked off in full foot increments. The two portions are separated with a zero marking.

Note that the accuracy with which something can be drawn depends on the scale used. For example, with the 1/4 in scale shown in Fig. 5.1, the 1 ft segment can only be subdivided 12 times, so each mark represents 1 in. This is the smallest distance that can be manufactured in the length of 1/4 in. It also represents the greatest accuracy with which a manually produced drawing can be drafted using this scale. In contrast, the 1 in scale is subdivided 48 times, so each mark represents 1/4 in. This is possible because there is physically more room to make more graduations. Therefore, a manually produced drawing shown at 1 in scale can be drafted with an accuracy of 1/4 in. On some of the larger scales, like the 1 1/2 inch and 3 in scales, the numbers 3, 6, and 9 are placed on the subdivided portion to indicate those lines used for 3, 6, and 9 in, respectively.

Using Scales

To use a scale, measure fractions of a foot in the portion on the end with the subdivisions, and measure full feet with the remainder of the scale. For example, to use the 1 in scale to measure a drawing object that is between 2 ft and 3 ft long, place the 2 ft mark at one end of the item to be measured, and read the fraction of a foot off the portion with the subdivisions. Although visual interpolation can be done, it is best to read off the measurement at an accuracy no greater than the markings on the scale.

Commonly Used Scales

Although there are many scales on an architect's or metric scale, certain ones are used for certain types of drawings. These are listed in Table 5.1. The choice of which scale to use is typically based on the

Table 5.1
Common Scales for Drawing

metric	architectural	typical uses
1:200	1/16 in = 1 ft 0 in	floor plans of very large buildings
1:100	1/8 in = 1 ft 0 in	floor plans
1:50	1/4 in = 1 ft 0 in	floor plans, simple interior elevations, building sections
1:30	3/8 in = 1 ft 0 in	complex interior elevations, complex building sections
1:20	1/2 in = 1 ft 0 in	enlarged floor plans, very complex elevations
1:20	3/4 in = 1 ft 0 in	enlarged floor plans, full wall sections
1:10	1 in = 1 ft 0 in	simple details (not often used)
1:10	1 1/2 in = 1 ft 0 in	ceiling details, simple cabinet details
1:5	3 in = 1 ft 0 in	door, cabinet, furniture, and similar details
1:2	half full size	cabinet details, other complex details
1:1	full size	very complex details

amount of detail, dimensioning, and notation that must be shown and the amount of paper that is available to contain the drawing or drawings. For interior design work, it is not uncommon to draw some details at full size or half full size.

Although they are available on many architect's scales, $3/32$ in and $3/16$ in scales should never be used. They are too close to $1/8$ in and $1/4$ in scales. Anyone looking at one of these uncommon scales would mistake them for the more commonly used $1/8$ in and $1/4$ in scales. Regardless of the scale used, each individual drawing should have its scale listed below the title of the drawing as shown in Fig. 14.14.

With CAD, even though all drawings are produced at full size and later scaled for plotting, the lettering, arrowheads, graphic symbols, and other annotation must be a consistent size on all drawings. Thus, if notes are going to be shown $1/8$ in high on the final plot, the drawing itself must be scaled so that there is sufficient space to fit all the required notes, symbols, and dimensions.

Graphic Scales

When scaled drawings are going to be reproduced at a larger or smaller size than the original numeric scale, a written scale, such as $1/4$ in = 1 ft 0 in, will no longer be accurate. To overcome this problem and still provide an indication of scale, a graphic scale can be used. A *graphic scale* is a band of alternating light and dark portions, each of which represents a given length. See Fig. 5.2. When a graphic scale is used, the measurement of scale is not dependent on having a scale instrument;

the graphic scale changes size in the same proportion as the drawing when reproduced. Although not as accurate as using a standard scale, a graphic scale is very useful when drawings are reproduced at an odd size for presentations or publication. Graphic scales can be used alone, for presentation drawings, or with a numeric scale in case the drawing is resized.

ORTHOGRAPHIC DRAWINGS

Orthographic drawings use orthographic projection to enable a three-dimensional object to be seen in two dimensions. They are ideal for communication in the flat world of paper and computer screens because, by using multiple orthographic views, even the most complex object can be accurately and completely described.

Orthographic projection is a view of an object seen as though the viewer's line of sight were simultaneously perpendicular to every point on the face of the object. Another way to understand it is to imagine that each significant face of an object is projected onto a flat, transparent plane parallel to the face of the object, as shown in Fig. 5.3.

In orthographic projection, all pieces are shown in their true relationship with other pieces, and the scale and proportion are the same for multiple views of the same object. There is no distortion for lines and planes parallel to the plane on which the view is projected. However, when a diagonal line or plane is shown, it is foreshortened. For example, the top view of the building in Fig. 5.3 shows a foreshortened view of the width of the roof while the length is shown true to scale. If the length of the line from the eaves to the peak of the roof is scaled in the top view, the distance is shorter than the true length as scaled on the side view.

Orthographic drawings are most often drawn to scale as described in the previous

Figure 5.2
Graphic Scale

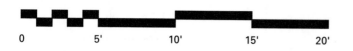

0   5'   10'   15'   20'

PROFESSIONAL PUBLICATIONS, INC.

Figure 5.3
Orthographic
Projection

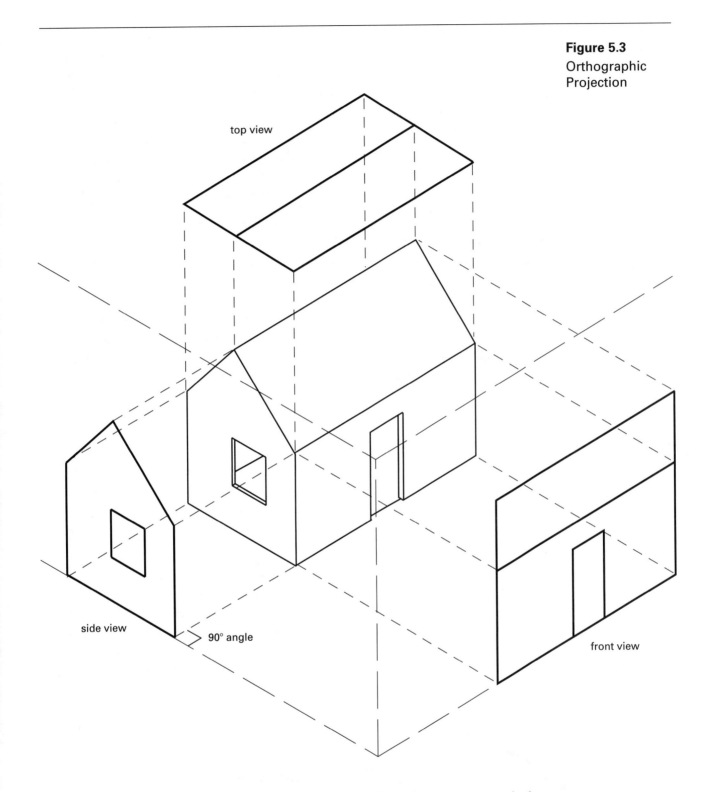

top view

side view

90° angle

front view

section. That is, one unit of measure is used to represent another, larger unit of measure. A floor plan, for instance, is often drawn so that $1/4$ in on the drawing represents 1 ft. This is shown as $1/4$ in = 1 ft 0 in (1:50). Scale is used to accommodate large objects on paper and to regulate the amount of detail shown. Large scales have the effect of bringing the viewer closer to the object so more can be seen. A scale of 3 in = 1 ft 0 in (1:5) is good for showing very complex construction details, while a small scale like $1/8$ in = 1 ft 0 in (1:100) is sufficient for many floor plans.

The most common types of orthographic drawings are floor plans, reflected ceiling plans, elevations, and sections. Orthographic projection is also used as a basis for some types of three-dimensional drawings, including axonometric drawings, elevation obliques, and one-point sectional perspectives.

Plans

A *plan* is an orthographic view of an object as seen from directly above. In architectural and interior design work, the *floor plan* is the most common type of plan, although strictly speaking a floor plan is really a section. The theory behind a floor plan is that a horizontal cut is made through a building (or portion of a building) about 5 ft (1500) above the floor, and the top portion is removed. See Fig. 5.4. What remains is drawn as the

Figure 5.4
Floor Plan
Generation

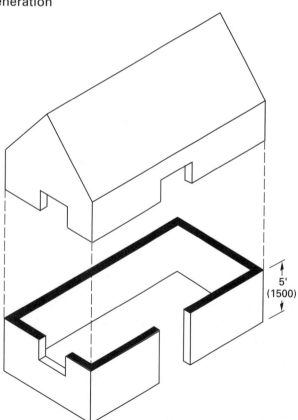

5'
(1500)

plan, including what shows on the floor. Cutting a section at this point makes it possible to show windows, doors, and other openings.

A view of a building seen from above without the section cut is a *roof plan*. If some of the ground on which the building sits, landscaping, walks, drives, and property lines are shown, the drawing is a *site plan*.

Of course, some compromises to the strictly theoretical approach are made with a floor plan. Even though a section would show all the construction materials within the walls, they are more commonly shown as just two parallel lines. In many cases, the walls are drawn with *poché*, which is a graphic pattern or solid black used to make the walls stand out or to indicate the wall construction type. Also, all openings are shown, even if their bottom edges are above the theoretical 5 ft high section cut. Other construction elements that may also be above the 5 ft line are shown as well, such as kitchen cabinets, ceiling breaks, and shelving. Dashed lines are used for these items to indicate that they are above the normal section cut.

Variations of the floor plan are used to communicate different types of information. A floor plan rendered with color and showing furniture, floor materials, and shading may be used for a client presentation. A construction drawing plan shows a very different set of data for the contractor's use. The various types of plan drawings are reviewed in more detail in Ch. 14.

Reflected Ceiling Plans

As shown in Fig. 5.5, a *reflected ceiling plan* is an orthographic view of the ceiling of a room or building as though there were a mirror on the floor and a viewer could see through the roof to the ceiling's reflection. In other words, it is as though all the points on the ceiling could be projected through the roof onto a transparent plane above the building. Awkward as they may be, these views of the ceiling are important so that the orientation of the reflected ceiling plan is identical to the floor plan. That is, if the north side of the building is toward the top of the paper on the floor plan, north must also be toward the top on the reflected ceiling plan.

Reflected ceiling plans are another variation of a section, only the viewer is looking up rather than down. Theoretically, the reflected ceiling plan shows only those construction elements that touch the plane of the ceiling, as well as the ceiling itself and the objects in the ceiling. Therefore, walls that extend to or through the ceiling are drawn, but low walls are not. Likewise, the opening of a 7 ft high door in a room with an 8 ft ceiling does not show. Instead, the wall above the door is drawn continuously, just as the wall touches the ceiling at that point.

In practice, however, liberties are taken with this strictly theoretical approach. Door openings may be shown to provide better orientation for the contractor. Elements that do not actually touch the ceiling, like cabinets, may be indicated to show their relationship to some part of the ceiling construction.

Elevations

Because plans can show only the dimensions of length and width, elevations are

Figure 5.5
Reflected Ceiling
Plan Theory

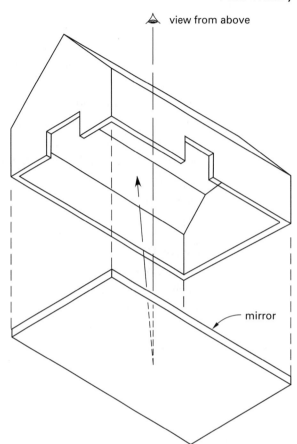

view from above

mirror

usually required. An *elevation* is an orthographic view of the side of an object. Interior elevations show the lengths and heights of walls of a room. Two interior elevations of the building shown in Fig. 5.3 are illustrated in Fig. 5.6. Elevations can show not only vertical dimensions but also the types and extent of materials and

Figure 5.6
Elevations

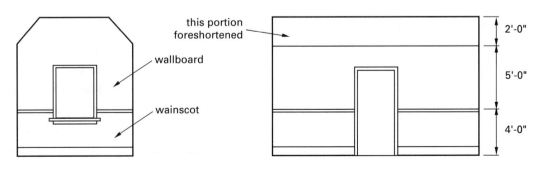

this portion foreshortened

wallboard

wainscot

2'-0"

5'-0"

4'-0"

finishes in a room that cannot be adequately described on other drawings.

Because elevations are often drawn at a slightly larger scale than the floor plans, some horizontal dimensions can also be described if there is not enough room on the plan or if the construction is complex. For these reasons, the spacings of wall panel joints or the widths of cabinets are commonly shown on interior elevations rather than on plans. Notice that on the elevation of the length of the room, the diagonal plane of the ceiling is shown foreshortened because this is an orthographic projection.

Sections

Like a floor plan, a *section* is an orthographic view of an object after the object has been cut and one portion has been removed. A section may be a view through an entire building as shown in Fig. 5.7(a)

Figure 5.7
Sections

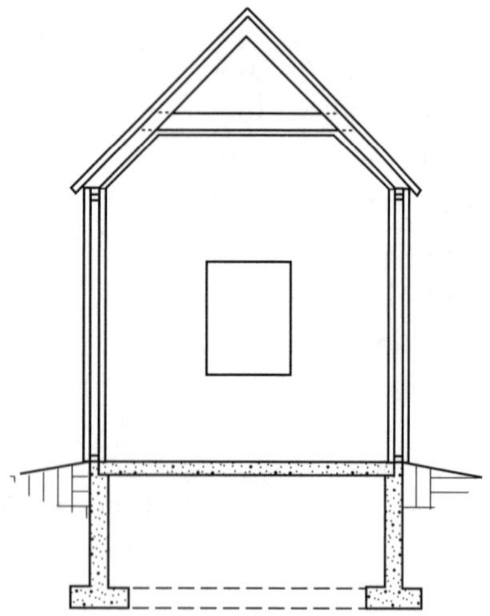

(a) small-scale section

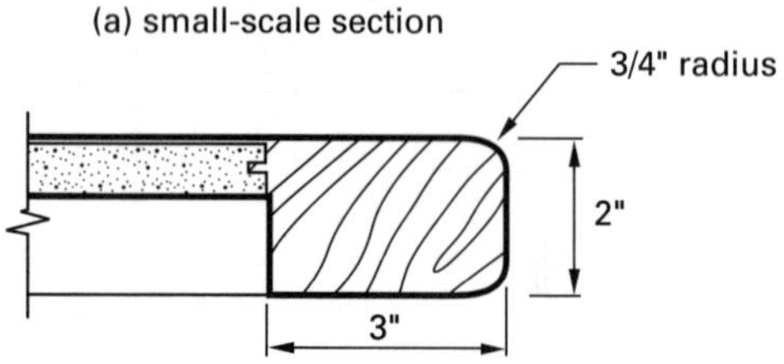

3/4" radius

2"

3"

(b) large-scale section

or through a very small portion of construction, like the front edge of a countertop, as shown in Fig. 5.7(b). Although sections are normally vertical slices through objects, they can be cut horizontally (as with plans) or at any angle that is convenient to show the internal construction of something.

Sections are invaluable drawings. Not only do they show the vertical dimension, but also they show hidden information about construction that cannot be described on plans or elevations. While architects frequently use building sections, as in Fig. 5.7(a), to show the overall configuration of a structure, interior design sections typically illustrate larger scale views through walls, millwork, door frames, and other details. Because sections commonly show complex construction information at a relatively large scale, they are most often simply called details. Most details on a set of construction drawings are section views of one sort or another.

A section drawing shows a cut through both solids and voids. Because sections can be complex, certain graphic techniques are used to avoid confusion. Solid portions are often poché with standard material indications as shown in Fig. 5.7(b). Voids are left blank, and the lines separating solid from void, known as *profile lines*, are drawn very heavy. To show the relationship between the material cut in section and adjacent construction, thin lines are used to indicate elements that occur beyond the section cut.

AXONOMETRIC DRAWINGS

An *axonometric drawing* is a view of an object inclined to the picture plane in such a way that the three principal axes are foreshortened. There are three types of axonometric drawings: isometric, dimetric, and trimetric.

An *isometric drawing* is a three-dimensional view of an object where the object is tilted in relationship to a picture plane (rather than parallel in relationship to a picture plane, as with an orthographic drawing). All lines of projection from the object to the picture plane are parallel, as in an orthographic drawing, but in an isometric drawing these lines are oblique to the picture plane. The three principal axes of the object make equal angles with the picture plane, or the drawing surface. In practice, this makes the vertical axis of an object vertical on the paper and the two horizontal axes form angles of 30° on the paper. The lengths of all three principal axes are drawn at the same scale. These principles are illustrated with a simple cube as shown in Fig. 5.8.

Isometric drawings are quick and easy to draw, and they can be measured at any convenient scale. However, because the horizontal plane is a parallelogram, floor plans and other planes must be redrawn at the 30° angle. Then, the third dimension is shown by simply extending points vertically. See Fig. 5.9(a). Diagonal lines are drawn by projecting their endpoints from the basic three-dimensional grid and connecting them. See Fig. 5.9(b).

Isometrics can be used to draw buildings, interior rooms (by omitting the top and two front sides), details, millwork, furniture, and any other object. Complex details can be shown by drawing a section in one plane and then extending the rest of the object with lines isometrically perpendicular to the section cut.

With isometric drawings, the lines of projection make equal angles with the picture plane. With a *dimetric drawing*, one of the other two types of axonometric drawings, two of the principal axes are equally foreshortened. With a *trimetric drawing*, all three of the principal axes are foreshortened.

Figure 5.8
Principles of
Isometric
Drawing

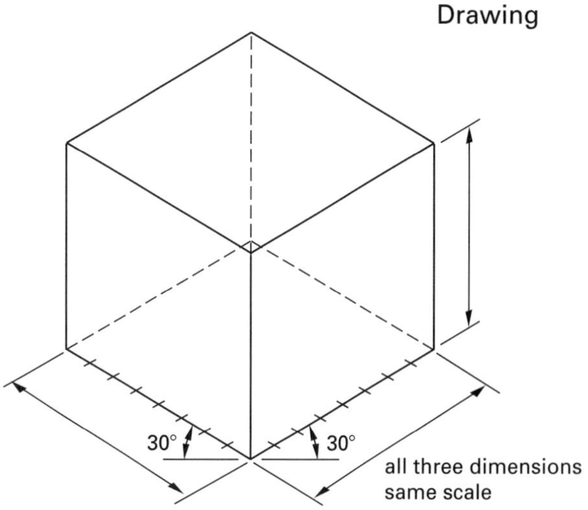

30° 30°

all three dimensions
same scale

While all three axonometric drawings can be created using formal drafting techniques and precise projections, for convenience, shortcuts are used to make drawing easier and faster. For example, a true isometric projection should have foreshortened lines in the three principle axes, but they are scaled equally at true size. Likewise, in a true dimetric projection, the angles and foreshortened lengths are complex to construct exactly, but for convenience a given angle, such as 15°, is used for two of the axes, and the third is drawn vertically on the paper. The vertical lines are drawn at full scale, while the other two foreshortened axes are drawn at an arbitrary three-fourths actual scale.

OBLIQUE DRAWINGS

An *oblique drawing* is a three-dimensional view of an object where one plane of the object is parallel to the picture plane while the third axis is oblique to the picture plane. An oblique drawing shows one plane of an object (two dimensions) in true shape and scale with the third dimension drawn as lines at a fixed angle to the true plane. Figure 5.10 shows a plan oblique and an elevation oblique.

Figure 5.9
Isometric
Drawing

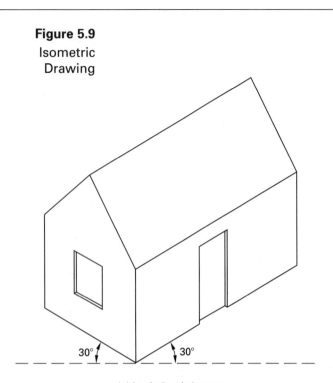

30°   30°

(a) basic 3-axis layout

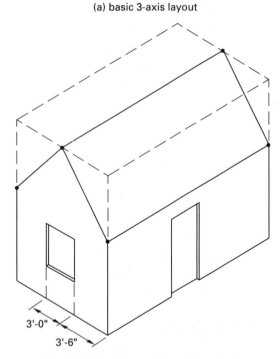

3'-0"

3'-6"

(b) establishing diagonal lines in isometric

The advantage of an oblique drawing is that an existing orthographic floor plan can be used as the starting point without any redrawing. The plan is simply tilted at any desired angle. The third dimension is created by projecting vertical lines. However, if the third dimension is scaled the same as the true shape, the object often looks distorted (i.e., higher or wider than it really is). To compensate for this, the third dimension is usually drawn at one-half to three-fourths of the scale of the true plane. As with isometrics, diagonal lines in the nontrue plane dimension are drawn by determining the locations of their endpoints through projection along one or more of the three main axes. See Fig. 5.11. Interior views are created by omitting the top and two front sides of the room (or just the top), or by selectively cutting away portions of the enclosing planes to show what is inside.

The plan may be tilted at any angle as long as the walls are 90° to each other, but as with isometrics, it is most convenient to set the plan at 30, 60, or 45° (the angle between a horizontal line and the wall).

PERSPECTIVE DRAWINGS

Of all the methods used to draw objects, *perspective drawings* give the most accurate two-dimensional representation of the three-dimensional world. This is because they use the principle of *convergence*, which is the apparent diminishing size of objects as they get farther from the eye. Convergence also explains how parallel lines seem to look nonparallel and point to, or converge on, the same imaginary spot in the distance.

When the point of view is perpendicular to one of the planes of the object, a one-point perspective is created. All vertical lines are drawn vertically, and all lines perpendicular to the line of sight are drawn horizontally. Lines parallel to the line of sight converge at the one vanishing point used to create the drawing. See Fig. 5.12.

A two-point perspective is created when the point of view is at normal eye level and is not perpendicular to any plane of the object. Although the NCIDQ exam does not require the creation of a perspective drawing, candidates should be generally familiar with perspectives in terms of the theory behind them, why they are used, and some of the common terminology associated with them. The following is a very brief description of perspective construction. Other books on the subject may be reviewed for further information.

Figure 5.13 shows some of the basic elements of a two-point perspective construction. To construct a perspective, a plan is placed at a convenient angle on the drawing board. The angle selected determines how much of the two sides of the object will be visible. A horizontal line is then drawn somewhere near the back edge of the plan. This is the *picture plane* (PP), the imaginary vertical plane on which all points of the object are projected to create the two-dimensional image. In plan view, of course, the picture plane appears just as a line.

In Fig. 5.13, this line touches the back corner of the plan, but it can be placed slightly forward or back to decrease or increase the size of the perspective. For example, moving this line farther away from the plan will change the projection of the sight lines from the station point (the point from which the object is being viewed), which widens the perspective when it is plotted.

Next, the *station point* (SP) is selected. Two lines are extended from the station point to the left and right parallel to the two major sets of parallel lines of the object. Because these lines are parallel to the object, they determine the vanishing points, or those imaginary points in the distance where the lines of the object appear to converge. Where these two lines intersect, the picture plane vertical lines are projected downward.

At some convenient point under the plan, a horizontal line is drawn across the paper. This is the *horizon line* (HL) and

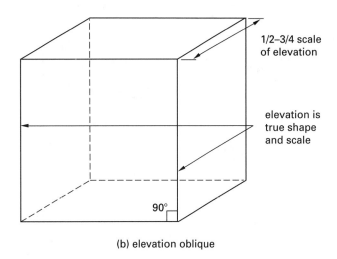

Figure 5.10
Principles of
Oblique Drawing

represents the place where the earth meets the sky, just as in the real three-dimensional world. The points where the horizon line intersects the two vertical lines projected from above become the vanishing points for the actual perspective drawing: the *left vanishing point* (VPL) and the *right vanishing point* (VPR).

Figure 5.11
Oblique Drawing

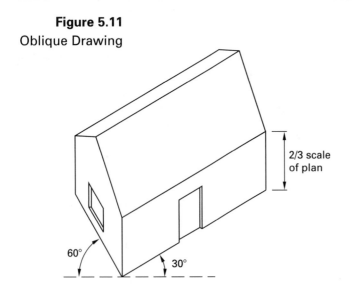

2/3 scale
of plan

60°   30°

Figure 5.12
One-Point
Perspective

horizon line (HL)   VP

Sometimes these two are simply noted as VP or v.p.

Where the picture plane touches the plan drawing, a vertical line is projected down to intersect the horizon line. This becomes the true height line, or simply the *height line* (HL) and is the only line on the perspective drawing where vertical dimensions can be directly scaled. All other vertical dimensions must be developed by using dimensions from this line and one of the vanishing points as two points from which to project a line to other parts of the drawing, to pinpoint the height of something.

At this point, the height of the corner of the building can be scaled on the height line where it crosses the horizon line. In most perspectives, the horizon line is assumed to be at eye level, or about 5 ft 0 in or 5 ft 6 in (1525 or 1675) above the floor level. The bottom point of the height line (floor level of the building) is set by measuring 5 ft down from the horizon line. If the height of the wall is 9 ft, then the top point of the height line is set by measuring 4 ft above the horizon line.

Using the ends of the height line and the vanishing points, the two back edges of the building are drawn. The extent of how far they project is determined by drawing a guideline from the station point through the left and right edges of the building in the plan until they intersect the picture plan. Lines projected vertically downward from these points locate the corners of the building in perspective view. All other points in the horizontal planes are projected in a similar fashion. Vertical dimensions are scaled on the height line and projected from one of the two vanishing points along surfaces of the object until they intersect the appropriate vertical lines projected from the picture plane above.

When perspective drawings are plotted according to the procedure described previously, it is a time-consuming process, although very accurate. To shorten the time required to produce perspective drawings, preprinted *perspective grids* can be used. These have horizon lines, vanishing points, and distances already marked

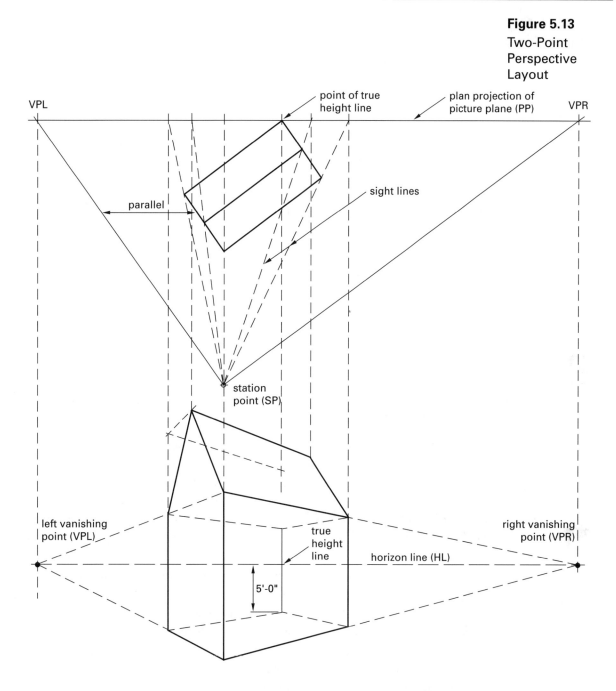

Figure 5.13
Two-Point
Perspective
Layout

off. A sheet of paper is placed over the grid and a drawing is sketched in. Figure 5.14 shows a perspective grid used for an interior drawing.

In most cases, it is more useful to produce several quick sketches of different views of the project for client review than to spend an inordinate amount of time to render one perfect perspective. The drawings can be very simple, black-and-white sketches to simply show the general configuration of a space, or they can show more detail and be quickly colored to indicate materials and conceptual color schemes.

Most three-dimensional CAD programs or other computer drawing programs can be used to model a building or interior space and then automatically show and produce a perspective drawing. Some programs also

Figure 5.14
Perspective
Grid

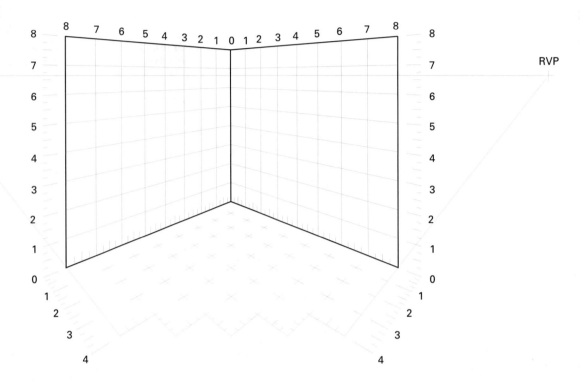

allow the user to switch from orthographic projection to isometric views to perspective views.

FORMAT OF PRELIMINARY DESIGN DRAWINGS

During the schematic design and design development process, drawings can take many forms, depending on the amount of design thinking that has been done and the client's specific requirements. After adjacencies and bubble diagrams have been produced as described in Ch. 3, design drawings may progress from rough block diagrams to design development drawings to final construction drawings. Figure 5.15 shows the progression of drawings for a design showroom in a merchandise mart building.

Figure 5.15(a) shows the bubble diagram developed from an adjacency matrix. Figure 5.15(b) illustrates the major concepts and constraints sketched on a base plan of the lease space. Figure 5.15(c) shows the block diagram combining the requirements of the bubble diagram, the constraints and concepts, and the relative areas required for each of the spaces. Finally, Figure 5.15(d) establishes the final layout of the space plan in preparation for working drawings. In addition to these drawings, furniture could be added to the final space plan, and the entire plan could be rendered to make it suitable for a formal client presentation. Figure 14.1 shows the construction drawing floor plan of this space.

Note that each drawing varies in appearance depending on the stage at which it is developed in the design process. At each point, the client's approval should be obtained before moving to the next stage of the process.

MODELS

Models are an excellent way to communicate the three-dimensional aspects of an interior space, especially to clients who

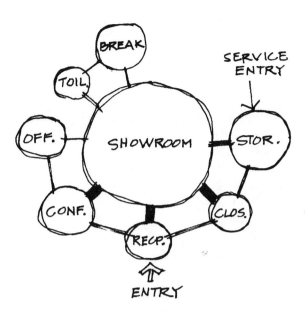

Figure 5.15
Development
of
Presentation
Drawings

(a) bubble diagram

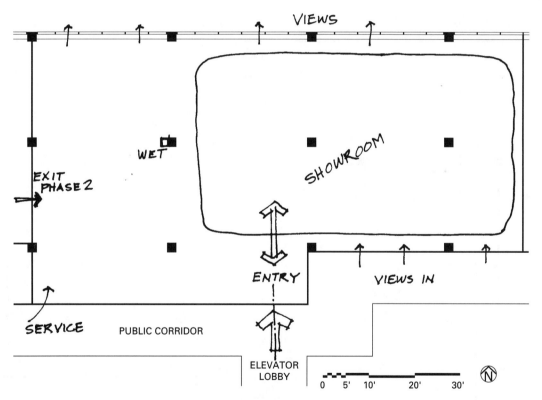

(b) concept diagram

may not be adept at understanding two-dimensional drawings of elevations and rendered floor plans. Models can sometimes show a space even better than can three-dimensional drawings like perspectives or isometrics.

There are two basic types of models: those made for presentation and those used for study. *Presentation models* are very detailed and accurately represent furniture, detail, colors, and finishes. They are most often used for a final, formal client presentation.

**Figure 5.15
(cont.)**
Development
of
Presentation
Drawings

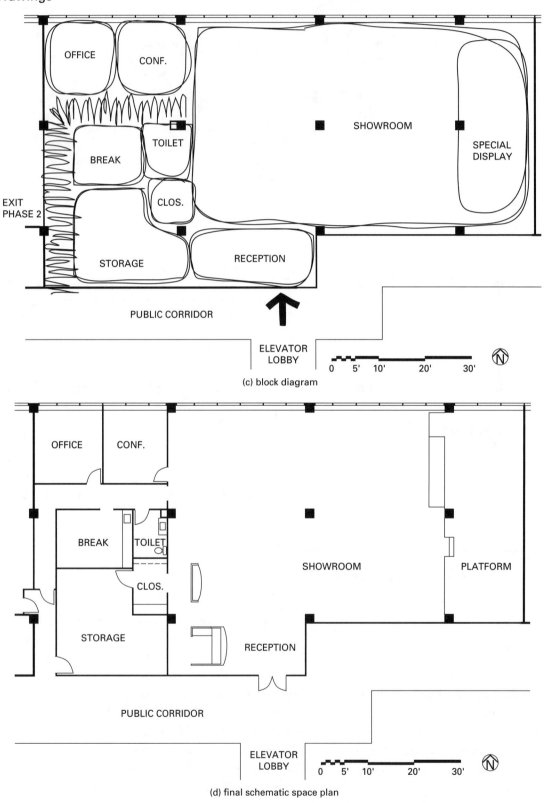

(c) block diagram

(d) final schematic space plan

Because they are difficult to build, presentation models are usually made by a professional model builder. *Study models*, or *working models*, are rough models used by the designer as an aid to understanding the three-dimensional aspects of the space and are constructed in a variety ways, depending on the needs of the designer and the time and budget available.

In its most basic form, a study model may simply be constructed of inexpensive chipboard, foam-core board, illustration board, or other materials to show the major partitions and other space-defining planes. These materials make it easy to cut openings for doors and windows and to glue the model together fairly quickly. A study model may be constructed to any scale, but $1/4$ in or $1/2$ in scale is often used. Rough representations of furniture can also be made if it is important to study the volumetric effect of furniture in a space.

If more detail is required, material patterns can be drawn directly on the cardboard, or prints of drawing elevations can be cut out and glued to the cardboard components. A printed floor plan can be used to help locate partitions. Rough indications of color can be added with colored pencils, markers, or paper.

Three-dimensional computer models can also be constructed. Computer models make it possible to view spaces from any vantage point and do "fly-throughs" as though the viewer were walking through the space. At any time, a hardcopy printout of any view can be made. Most computer programs allow the designer to render the model with accurate representations of finishes and materials. As with presentation models, creating a detailed, fully rendered computer model can be labor intensive and require skill in using a particular computer program.

Mockups are full-size representations of a portion of a design. Mockups can be made of small elements, such as furniture, or of entire rooms. They are a good way to communicate to the client how something will look that has not yet been built, such as a custom-designed workstation or a prototype for a hotel room.

Like a model, a mockup can be constructed in a wide variety of ways. Simple, inexpensive materials, such as corrugated cardboard, can be used to convey how a design component will look in three dimensions and to study things such as clearances, human fit, and overall scale. A more refined mockup can be made of sturdier materials if it must be transported, used for a long time, or used for more rigorous testing. In the most refined condition, a mockup can be built as the actual construction. If the client wants to see what the final product will look like, a mockup is most often built by the contractor or a vendor. Normally, a final mockup is called for in the construction specifications and paid for by the client. If the client accepts the mockup, it is common for it to be used as part of the final construction work.

SAMPLE QUESTIONS

1. What is a drawing that shows a top view of a building and its surroundings?

(A) floor plan

(B) site plan

(C) roof plan

(D) horizontal section

2. What characterizes an isometric drawing?

(A) All axes are drawn to the same scale.

(B) A three-dimensional view can easily be created by tilting a floor plan and extending vertical lines.

(C) Lines of projection are perpendicular to the picture plane.

(D) The view shows a cut about 5 ft above the floor.

3. Orthographic drawings are unreal views of objects primarily because

(A) more than one is required to describe an object

(B) the point of view is directly in front of every location on the object

(C) a transparent plane has to be imagined

(D) some planes may be foreshortened

4. What does SP in a perspective mean?

(A) standard perspective

(B) secondary point

(C) side plane

(D) station point

5. A perspective is the best drawing type to use when presenting to a client because it

(A) is the quickest method of rendering space

(B) most accurately shows vertical dimensions relative to the viewer

(C) is most like the way space and objects are perceived

(D) offers the widest choiceof viewpoints

6. Which of the following scales should NEVER be used for interior design construction drawings?

(A) $1/8$ in = 1 ft 0 in

(B) $3/16$ in = 1 ft 0 in

(C) $3/4$ in = 1 ft 0 in

(D) 1 in = 1 ft 0 in

7. When creating a drawing that will be used for reproduction in a magazine, it is best to use

(A) an architect's scale

(B) an engineer's scale

(C) a graphic scale

(D) a metric scale

8. A quick-sketch perspective drawing could most easily be made by

(A) employing a computer model

(B) plotting the perspective

(C) tracing over a model photograph

(D) using a perspective grid

9. The most accurate representation of materials can best be shown with

(A) computer renderings

(B) full-size mockups

(C) presentation models

(D) study models

10. The primary advantage of an oblique drawing is that

(A) it shows the most realistic view of an object

(B) all three axes are drawn at the same scale

(C) existing orthographic drawings can be used as a starting point

(D) it shows foreshortened lines and planes accurately

6

SELECTION OF MATERIALS, FINISHES, AND FURNISHINGS

This chapter discusses the preliminary selection and evaluation of finishes, materials, and furniture, fixtures, and equipment (FF&E). Various methods of communicating these decisions to the client are also presented. Refer to Ch. 15 for a discussion of how finish and material selections are written into construction specifications. Refer to Ch. 16 for information on how the selection of furniture is formalized into contract documents.

Although the selection of materials and furnishings deals mostly with technical issues as described in this chapter, the designer must also consider the aesthetics of the product. In addition to looking at colors, finishes, and other visual qualities, the basic elements and principles of design should be applied. These are discussed in Chs. 8 and 9.

MATERIAL AND FINISH SELECTION

Material and finish selection involves a rational approach to deciding which products meet the client's aesthetic, functional, and economic needs as well as selecting products that meet the requirements of safety, durability, and sustainability. Because of the legal consequences of poor selection, this process is especially important for the designer.

This section discusses products that are normally considered surface finishes. Closely related to the procedures and criteria described here are design criteria for developing construction details as reviewed in Ch. 13.

Of course, standards for selection vary with the material or product. For example, selecting doors and doorframes involves different types of standards than selecting vinyl wall covering does. The following guidelines and criteria will not apply to every product; the designer should select the ones that are appropriate for the product being evaluated.

General Guidelines for Material and Finish Selection

When selecting materials, finishes, and other products for a project, the interior designer should always follow certain general procedures to help make the best selection and to avoid potential legal problems. Following these procedures is especially important when using a new product or using an existing product in a new way. All of the actions taken by the interior designer should be documented.

• Obtain as much information as possible about the products being reviewed. This includes the manufacturer's promotional literature as well as technical data, suggested details, recommended installation procedures, material safety data sheets (MSDSs), and a list of comparable projects where the product has already been used.

• Inform the client of the products being selected, and notify the client of any potential problems or risks. Obtain client approval for all products being used, especially those that are relatively new or that are being used in unusual ways.

• Ask the manufacturer or manufacturer's representative specifically about any potential problems with the product or any situations where product installation has failed.

• For each item on the list of comparable projects, obtain the owner's name, the name of the design professional responsible, and the installing contractor's name. Contact these people to discuss their experiences with the product.

• Notify the manufacturer, in writing, of the intended use of the product, and ask for confirmation, in writing, that the product is appropriate for its intended use.

• Follow the manufacturer's recommendations for detailing and specifications, and obtain written approval of the specifications from the manufacturer. If appropriate, require that shop drawings be prepared by the manufacturer or the installing contractor, and require that the shop drawings be approved by both parties.

• Although installation supervision is not the responsibility of the interior designer, if proper installation of the product is critical, make at least one visit to the site to verify that correct installation procedures are followed.

• If installation is particularly difficult or specialized, require that the manufacturer provide a field representative to observe the installation and to certify that the product has been installed according to the manufacturer's recommendations. The specifications should require that any installing contractor be approved by the manufacturer.

• Investigate the production capability and financial condition of the manufacturer, distributor, and installing contractor. This is especially important if any of these parties are small or do not have a well-established performance record. In the rush to sell a product or service, the installing contractor or manufacturer may over commit and not be able to complete the job.

Criteria for Selection

Criteria for the selection of materials and finishes can be broadly classified into five groups: function, durability, maintainability, safety/health, and cost. Each of these groups involves dozens of individual selection criteria that should be considered when appropriate for the material or finish being selected. The following is brief description of some of the common criteria with which the interior designer should be familiar. The list is not inclusive, as some criteria are specific to only one type of material.

Function

Acoustic qualities of a material relate to the material's ability to absorb sound or to block the transmission of sound. For most finish materials, sound absorption is the more important criteria and is typically measured in the noise reduction coefficient (NRC). For open-plan office design, the articulation class of ceilings may also be important. Refer to Ch. 20 for more information on acoustics.

Aesthetics are commonly one of the first criteria considered by the designer. However, the appearance of a material must be balanced with all of the other technical and cost criteria. The basic elements and principles of design are discussed in Chs. 8 and 9.

Availability of materials relates to how easily a product can be obtained and if it can be delivered to the job site in time to maintain the overall project schedule. Some specialty products can require six months or more to get. Other products are in stock for immediate delivery but may only be available in a limited choice of colors or finishes. Some products, such as furniture, are specifically available in "quick ship" programs to meet tight schedules.

Choice of color, texture, and other visual characteristics will vary depending on what manufacturers offer. Some manufacturers or product lines may have a wider range of choice than others, and this fact alone my sway the decision to use a particular company or material.

Installation method is the precise sequence of steps needed to place the material or product into the work. Installation method can affect the cost and scheduling of a material and whether skilled workers will be required or not. In most cases, installation methods for the same types of materials will be very similar. However, some specialty items may require a particular method using factory-approved installers.

Durability

Durability relates to the serviceability of the product or material when in use. There are many aspects of durability, and one or more of these may apply to a particular product. The following list gives some of the more common aspects of durability. Most of them have associated ASTM or other recognized standards that describe how they are measured and applied to products. Some standards are specific to a particular type of test while others apply to a particular type of material. For example, durability standards for wall coverings are covered in ASTM F793, Standard Classification of Wallcovering by Durability Characteristics.

Abrasion resistance is the ability of a material or finish to resist being worn away or to maintain its original appearance when rubbed with another object. Abrasion resistance can be measured according to several standard test methods as described later in this chapter.

Attachment is the method by which one material is connected to another. This criterion can have a significant influence on product selection, depending on the substrate. Some products or materials cannot be attached to other materials or can only be attached with significant expense or extra effort. Attachment is one criterion that applies to nearly all materials and that must be reviewed as part of a systematic view of the entire detail of which the material is a part.

Blocking resistance is the capability of a material to resist adhesion or sticking between two surfaces of a wall covering.

Breaking strength refers to the load that, when placed on a material, is just great enough to break the material. In interior design it typically refers to fabrics and other textiles where the load is applied in the plane of the material, with the material laid flat. It may also apply to tile, stone, and other materials subjected to a localized load.

Chemical resistance is a material's resistance to damage, change of finish, or other deleterious changes resulting from exposure to chemicals. Because there are so many possible combinations of chemicals and finishes, most manufacturers specifically state which chemicals their products are resistant to.

Coating adhesion refers to the ability of a thin coating, like wall covering or paint, to adhere to its substrate.

Cold-cracking resistance is the resistance of coated or decorative surfaces to cracking when they are exposed to low temperatures.

Colorfastness is the resistance of a finish to change or loss of color when exposed to light, most commonly the ultraviolet light of the sun.

Corrosion resistance is a product's resistance to deterioration by a chemical or electrochemical reaction resulting from exposure to moisture, chemicals, or other elements. Corrosion is typically a problem when metal products are exposed to moisture.

Crocking resistance is a material's resistance to the transfer of color from a wall covering surface when rubbed.

Fabrication quality is the measure of how well a product is assembled in the factory. Each industry establishes measures of fabrication quality. For example, woodwork is measured according to three grades—economy, custom, and premium—as established by the Architectural Woodwork Institute's (AWI's) Quality Standards.

Heat-aging resistance is a wall covering's resistance to the deterioration caused by high temperatures over an extended time.

Light fastness is the ability of paint or other finishes to resist loss of color when exposed to sunlight. It is similar to colorfastness.

Scrubability is a material's ability to be cleaned repeatedly with a brush and detergent.

Shrinkage is a decrease in dimension when a material is exposed to moisture. This characteristic is most typically applied to fabrics.

Stain resistance is a material's resistance to a change in appearance after the application and removal of another material. As with chemical resistance, all products are resistant to some staining agents more than others, so the manufacturer's literature should be consulted to verify if a material is resistant to staining agents likely to be present in a particular application.

Strength/structure is a general criterion referring to the inherent ability of a product to withstand any loads that may be placed on it. This may be as simple as the ability of one part of a detail to support the weight of another part of a detail, or as complex as the ability of a product or detail to withstand complex gravity and wind loads that may require a structural engineer to calculate.

Tear resistance, or *tear strength*, is the resistance of a thin material, like fabric, to the propagation of an existing tear.

Washability is a material's ability to be cleaned repeatedly with a sponge and detergent solution, to remove surface dirt.

Maintainability

Maintainablity is an important quality for finish materials, products, and details that experience wear and tear through the life cycle of a building. All buildings and interior finishes need to be maintained to preserve their appearance and service life. Many durability criteria directly relate to maintainability; the more durable a material is, the less maintenance is required.

Cleanability refers to the ease with which a material can be cleaned using whatever methods are appropriate for the material. For example, carpet must be easy to vacuum, while wall finishes in a restaurant should be easy to wash. Because all materials in all types of buildings get dirty with time, cleanability is one of the most important criteria to consider when selecting finishes.

Repairability is a product or material's ability to be repaired when damaged. The ability to replace damaged components of a finish or detail may also be evaluated when selecting a product. The designer should avoid details that make it difficult or expensive to repair or replace one of the component parts.

Resilience is a material's capacity to recover its original size and shape after deformation caused by some load. Resilience is typically applied to soft floor covering material, such as vinyl tile, but may also be an important consideration for wall covering materials.

Self-healing quality is a material's ability to return to its original configuration after it has been deformed or temporarily changed. It is similar to resilience but may apply to any type of product. For example, the holes in a corkboard should be self-healing after pins have been removed.

Sustainability as a broad term means meeting the needs and wants of the present generation without harming or compromising the ability of future generations to meet their needs. Sustainable design involves the design, operation, and reuse concepts that together can create functional, healthy, nonpolluting, and environmentally friendly buildings without compromising practical requirements or human comfort. Refer to Ch. 26 for a more detailed discussion of the various components of sustainability. When evaluating products for sustainability, the designer should consider many individual criteria, including recycled content, recyclability, energy consumption, and life-cycle assessment, among others as described in Ch. 26.

Safety/Health

Safety relates to the prevention of accidental harm to people, as well as to security from intentional harm. Health covers a wide variety of topics, from mold resistance to indoor air quality.

Finish safety relates to the surface and edge condition of products. There should be no sharp projections, edges, or surfaces rough enough to cut or abrade when people come in contact with the product.

Flammability, the likelihood that a material will combust, is one of the most important criteria for material and finish selection. For most materials, flammability is rated in terms of flame spread, smoke developed, and fuel contributed. The most common test developed for flame spread and smoke is the Steiner tunnel test, ASTM E 84. Other tests are also available and may be required by the local building department. Refer to Ch. 27 for a full discussion of flammability issues and the various tests that are used.

Mold and mildew resistance of a material is important to prevent the growth of these microscopic organisms. Many materials are inherently susceptible to the growth of mold or mildew because they provide an organic nutrient that, when combined with moisture and a suitable temperature, will provide a growing medium for these biological contaminants. Most materials can be treated to resist the growth of mold and mildew.

Outgassing is the release of toxic gasses from materials, most commonly after the material has been installed. These gasses include formaldehyde, chlorofluorocarbons (CFCs), and others listed on the Environmental Protection Agency's list of hazardous substances. Outgassing is one of the important components of indoor air quality. Refer to Ch. 26 for a detailed discussion of indoor air quality issues.

Security is providing protection against theft, vandalism, intentional physical harm, or a combination of all three. If security is an important aspect of a design, material and product selection can be evaluated in these terms. Doors, glazing, and hardware are common products that are available with various levels of security. Refer to Ch. 13 for more information on security design when reviewing design details.

Slip resistance is the ability of a flooring material to help prevent accidental slipping. It is commonly measured with the coefficient of friction (COF). Although both the International Building Code and the Americans with Disabilities Act require flooring to be slip resistant, there are no specific requirements for the COF or any other measure. Refer to Ch. 12 for more information on slip resistance.

Volatile organic compound (VOC) *emissions* result when chemicals that contain carbon and hydrogen vaporize at room temperature and pressure. VOCs are found in many indoor sources such as paint, sealants, and carpeting. When selecting a material, its VOC content must be limited to the applicable standards. Refer to Ch. 26 for more information on VOCs.

Cost

The cost of a material or product is nearly always an important criterion for selection. However, cost should always be balanced with considerations of value and durability. A low first-cost material may actually cost more than an expensive material over the life of an installation because it has to be replaced several times. There are two aspects of cost: first cost and life-cycle cost. The *first cost* is the initial amount of money required to purchase and install a product. The *life-cycle cost* is the entire cost of a product over its life or the life of the building and includes the initial cost, maintenance costs, energy costs, financing costs, and replacement costs. Refer to Ch. 7 for further discussion of budgeting and costing.

Material and Finishes Resources

In order to make informed decisions regarding materials and finishes, the interior designer must have accurate, complete, and authoritative information. This information is available from a variety of sources.

The best source of information is the product manufacturer. Manufacturers can provide the designer with promotional literature, full product catalogs, and personal advice via manufacturers' representatives, telephone, and email. In addition, nearly all manufacturers have internet websites that provide accurate information on their products.

When comparing similar products, it is helpful to have a resource that shows many manufacturers' products together. One of the best printed sources is *Sweets Catalog*, previously described in Ch. 2. This annual publication is a multivolume catalog of catalogs organized according to the Construction Specification Institute's (CSI's) MasterFormat™ numbering system. It is also available on CD-ROM. Showrooms in merchandise marts or design centers also provide a good way to compare similar materials. Not only is technical information available, but actual samples can also be viewed.

Standards-writing organizations are excellent sources of information for testing and selection standards of nearly all materials. The American Society for Testing and Materials (ASTM) and the American National Standards Institute (ANSI) are two of the leading standards organizations in the United States. The Canadian Standards Association (CSA) is the leading standards organization in that country. Standards may be searched on the ASTM website based on number, title, or keyword. Search results give the standard name, the establishment date, and a brief description of what the standard covers. Standards may be purchased individually or as part of one of the many volumes in the entire collection of ASTM or ANSI standards.

As described in Ch. 2, trade association standards are excellent sources of unbiased, accurate information on a particular material or product type. Many of the standards that trade associations develop become adopted as industry standards and are referenced by building codes and regulatory agencies.

Documenting Evaluation and Selection

It is important to document the decision-making process involved with selecting materials, finishes, and furnishings. This documentation is required for the client's review, as backup information for billing, and to guard against claims of negligence. *Negligence* is the failure to use the care ordinarily exercised in similar cases by other qualified members of the profession and the failure to use reasonable diligence and best professional judgment in the exercise of work. Documentation can provide evidence that the interior designer acted appropriately and professionally, should product problems later develop with a particular project.

Documentation can take any written form, including letters or emails to and from manufacturers or manufacturer's representatives, comparison charts evaluating similar products, product catalogs, personal notes, and other correspondence to anyone involved in the product selection process.

SELECTION OF FURNITURE, FIXTURES, AND EQUIPMENT

Furniture, fixtures, and equipment (FF&E) describes freestanding interior components that are not physically attached to the construction and that are usually purchased under a separate contract. Sometimes things like office equipment, storage shelving, bank teller equipment, and other built-in items that must be coordinated with construction are selected and specified by the interior designer, while the construction itself may be the responsibility of the architect. FF&E is typically a separate line item on a client's budget and is purchased under a separate contract because the methods of specifying, ordering, and installing are different from those used in a standard construction contract. The Uniform Commercial Code, discussed in Ch. 22, governs contracts for FF&E.

There are three basic categories of furniture: ready-made, custom-designed, and built-in. *Ready-made furniture* is purchased from a selection of standard products of a particular manufacturer. The specifier usually has some choice of fabric types, fabric colors, and wood finishes, but the selection is limited to what is available on the market. Even with these limitations, there are thousands of possible variations of style, furniture type, cost range, and quality from which to choose. With ready-made furniture, the designer and client can look at the piece, touch it, sit in it, and have a good knowledge of its appropriateness before it is specified and purchased. Other advantages of selecting ready-made furniture include knowing its cost, having a guarantee, and being able to judge its quality based on a finished piece.

Custom-designed furniture allows the designer and client to get exactly what they want, but the burden of correctly designing the piece, having it manufactured, and being responsible for its ultimate quality is placed on the designer. In most cases, the time investment and cost of a custom-designed piece will be greater than those of a comparable ready-made item. Some furniture pieces, like chairs, are so difficult to design well that they are seldom custom designed for a single job. On the other hand, conference tables, storage units, and the like can be developed and built as millwork.

Built-in furniture is custom designed but, as the name implies, it becomes part of the architectural construction of the project. This type of furniture usually makes more efficient use of space and is often less expensive than ready-made furniture for the same function, and its design is usually more consistent with the architectural appearance of the space. However, it is obviously less flexible and more difficult to change when styles change or the room's function changes.

Types of Furniture

Furniture can be grouped according to the function it serves. The following list describes some of the general considerations of each type.

- *Seating:* Seating must be appropriate for its use, comfortable, adaptable to a wide range of body types and sizes, strong, and have a durable finish. Because no one type of seating can serve all functions, there are thousands of styles of chairs, sofas, stools, and other designs for seating. A desk chair used eight hours a day must be quite different from a waiting-room lounge chair. In addition to comfort and function, furniture must be appropriate for the overall interior design concept of the space in which it is used.

Regardless of the specific purpose of the chair or sofa, there are some criteria common to all seating that must be evaluated when purchasing or designing. These are described in Ch. 1. Of course, not all of the criteria are critical in all situations. A lumbar support on a chair, for example,

may not be necessary if the seating is only for short-term use.

- *Tables:* Common table types include dining, conference, work-surface, and occasional tables. In addition to correct dimensions for their function, several other factors should be considered. These include a sturdy support structure, a durable surface, and a color and texture that will give the correct light reflectivity for the visual tasks performed. For dining and conference tables, plan enough space so that people are not crowded. Generally, this is from 24 in to 30 in (600 to 750) per person along the edge.

- *Workstations:* Workstations are single pieces of furniture or groups of components providing a work surface and storage. The traditional workstation consists of some type of desk with or without drawers in its base. There may also be an attached return at a lower height for a computer and keyboard. A separate credenza and additional file cabinets or bookcases may be part of the workstation. For open plan offices, workstations often consist of systems furniture (see the following description).

- *Storage:* Because storage space is always required, its design must be given the same consideration as any other type of furniture. Basic parameters for designing storage space include the types and sizes of items to be stored, the location of the storage, how often the stored items will need to be accessed, and the visibility desired.

- *Beds:* Most beds consist of a mattress or mattress set and some type of supporting framework, whether it is as simple as a platform base or an elaborate system of bedposts, a footboard, and headboard. Other types of sleeping furniture include simple floor pads, water beds, bunk beds, trundle beds, and sofa beds. The traditional type of Murphy bed that folds into a storage wall is also available for areas where space is at a premium. In addition to the actual sleeping surface, beds may be integrated with storage headboards, canopies, and built-in lighting, or simply used alone with side tables.

• *Systems furniture:* Systems furniture is a collection of modular components designed to fit together in various ways to make up office workstations. It most often consists of panels to divide workstations and define areas, work surfaces, storage units, and lighting and wire management facilities.

Although there are hundreds of different systems available from dozens of manufacturers, there are three basic varieties of systems furniture. The first uses freestanding panels with conventional freestanding furniture. The second type uses panels of various lengths and heights that link and provide support for work surfaces and storage units that are suspended from the panels. The third type consists of self-contained L-shaped or U-shaped workstations that include the work surface, storage, and other required components. The storage portion of this type of system is usually high enough to serve as a privacy barrier. Both the second and third types usually contain task lighting and sometimes ambient lighting.

Systems furniture is used in open-office planning and where flexibility of layout is required. Systems furniture makes more efficient use of space than a private-office layout does, and a wide variety of individual needs can be satisfied by selecting the appropriate components from the manufacturer's catalog.

Selection Criteria

Furniture must satisfy a wide range of needs. It must first satisfy the functional needs of its intended use. Tables for a grade-school classroom, for example, will be quite different in size, appearance, and construction from a corporate boardroom table. Some of the functional considerations include the purpose of the piece of furniture, the type of people who will be using it, the need for adjustability, finish requirements, durability, and size.

Because people come in direct contact with furniture, comfort is another critical consideration. Chairs, especially, should be appropriately selected for their use and their effect on the human body. A chair used for long periods of time by many people should be adjustable. Even tables, storage cabinets, beds, and other pieces should be selected so they are sized correctly, are easy to use, and do not present safety hazards.

Furniture is also a major design element. Not only does each piece of furniture have its own aesthetic characteristics, but it also affects the appearance of its surroundings. It must be selected to be compatible with the size, shape, and visual characteristics of the space in which it is used. Qualities of scale, color, line, form, texture, and touch must all be considered.

Quality is a practical consideration. Balanced against cost, the level of quality selected depends on the furniture's use, the type of users, expected maintenance, and the length of time before replacement is expected.

Finish is a selection criterion that is closely related to several of the others. It affects the furniture's aesthetic impact, durability, maintenance, and flammability.

Finally, furniture selection is always governed by cost considerations, including the life-cycle cost as well as the initial cost. A higher-priced, well-built piece of furniture may have a high initial cost, but it should last much longer and require less maintenance than a less expensive piece.

SELECTION OF FURNITURE FABRICS

The selection of fabric for upholstered furniture has a great influence on the furniture's appearance, durability, and safety. Because the same piece of furniture can be covered with a variety of fabrics, the interior designer must know what is available and the criteria for selecting fabrics and padding for specific uses. This is true whether the designer is selecting from fabric offered by the furniture manufacturer or specifying COM (customer's own material).

Types and Characteristics of Fabrics

Fibers used for furniture fabrics can be broadly classified into natural and synthetic. The natural fibers are further divided into cellulosic and protein. Cellulosic fibers, such as cotton and linen, come from plants, while protein fibers, such as wool, are manufactured from animal sources.

The most commonly used fibers are as follows.

- *Wool:* Obtained from the fleece of sheep, wool is one of the best natural fibers for all types of fabrics, including carpet. Although individual fibers are relatively weak, this is compensated for by the yarn's excellent resilience. Resilience is especially important for drapery and upholstery because creases and crimps fall out easily for a smooth appearance. Wool also has excellent elasticity and wears well. It is resistant to soiling and cleans easily. Although wool will burn when exposed to flame, it is self-extinguishing when the flame is removed. However, wool is expensive, and it can be stretched so it is not as dimensionally stable as some fabrics.

- *Cotton:* Cotton is a cellulosic fiber that comes from the seed hairs of the cotton plant. It is relatively inexpensive and has good tensile strength and moderately good abrasion resistance. However, cotton has poor resilience and recovery properties, and it degrades under prolonged sunlight exposure. It burns readily and is subject to mildew.

- *Linen:* Linen is made from the fibers of the flax plant. It is a *bast fiber*, meaning it is derived from the stalk of a plant, like jute, ramie, and hemp. Linen is seldom used for upholstery because it lacks resilience and flexibility and is susceptible to abrasion. In addition, it does not take printed dyes very well. Most linen is *tow linen*, which means it is made of short-staple fibers. These fibers are dimensionally stable and resistant to fading, making linen usable for draperies and wall coverings.

- *Silk:* Silk is obtained from fibers spun by silkworm larvae. It is very strong and has good resilience and flexibility. The finish and luster of silk are generally highly valued, but silk is very expensive and degrades in sunlight.

- *Rayon:* Rayon is a regenerated cellulosic fiber. It has very poor resistance to sunlight and poor resiliency. It has high absorbency, low resistance to water and moisture, and is flammable. It is seldom used for upholstery.

- *Acetate:* Acetate is a regenerated cellulosic fiber composed of cellulose, acetic acid, and other chemicals. Although low in cost, it is flammable and does not wear well. Like rayon, in its unmodified state it has poor sunlight resistance. A variation, triacetate, has a similar composition, but it has a higher ratio of acetate to cellulose to improve aging, flammability, and resistance to sunlight.

- *Nylon:* Nylon is one of the most popular synthetic fibers. It is exceptionally strong with high resiliency and elasticity. Nylon is resistant to many chemicals, water, and microorganisms. Some of the first nylons were not resistant to sunlight and had a shiny appearance, but these problems can now be compensated for by chemical formulations. Nylon is often combined with other synthetic or natural fibers to obtain the superior advantages of both.

- *Acrylic:* Acrylic is often used as a replacement for wool because of its appearance. It has moderately good strength and resilience and is very resistant to sunlight but can be flammable. Modacrylics have similar properties but have a much greater resistance to heat and flame.

• *Olefin:* Olefin is inexpensive and is highly resistant to chemicals, mildew, and microorganisms. It is highly resilient and nonabsorbent. Its desirable qualities make it useful for carpeting and carpet backing, but its low resistance to sunlight, heat, and flame makes it undesirable for most upholstery fabrics.

• *Polyester:* Polyester has many desirable qualities including good resilience and elasticity, high resistance to solvents and other chemicals, and good resistance to sunlight. Although is has undesirable burning properties, it can be treated to make it more flame resistant. However, it tends to absorb and hold oily materials.

• *Specialty fibers:* Various manufacturers have developed many times of proprietary fibers to meet specific needs. For example, Avora® FR is a polyester yarn that uses a modified polymer so it is permanently flame resistant regardless of wear or the number of washings. In addition, fabrics made with this fiber are easy to clean, abrasion resistant, crease proof, and dimensionally stable, and they do not retain odors or support bacteria.

Another specialty fabric is Crypton®, which is an engineered fabric made by a patented process of immersion in a chemical solution followed by a heat set to form a durable coating on the face. It is then given a polyurethane chemical spray on the back. This fabric is stain, water, flame, and bacteria resistant. It is available in a variety of construction and for upholstery, wall coverings, bedspreads, shower curtains, and other uses. Fabrics like this are a good choice for healthcare facilities and retirement communities, where durability and fire resistance are important qualities.

Gore™ seating protection is an upholstery fabric lamination and treatment process that applies a breathable moisture barrier to the back of a fabric and a topical coating to the front of the fabric.

Selecting Fabrics

Selecting the correct fabric for a piece of furniture is a matter of balancing the functional and aesthetic requirements against cost and availability. The best fabric for a hospital waiting room must be quite different from that used in a private office. Some of the important criteria for fabric selection are listed here.

• *Durability:* The durability of a fabric includes resistance to abrasion, fading, staining, and other mechanical abuses as well as its cleanability. Resistance to abrasion is the most important durability factor. The amount of abrasion-resistance a piece of upholstered furniture has depends on the type of fiber, how the yarn is made and applied to the piece, the fabric's backing, and the undercushion. In most cases, the most durable upholstery is achieved by using strong, smooth fibers like nylon or wool, having the yarn tightly twisted, specifying heavy or thick fabrics, using close-set weaves, and employing relatively soft undercushions to allow the fabric to flex under use.

Some of the problems encountered with fabrics include snagging, fuzzing, and pilling. *Snagging* is catching and pulling a yarn out of the fabric surface. *Fuzzing* occurs when small fibers work out of the yarn onto the surface of the fabric. *Pilling* occurs when fuzzing fibers roll into small balls.

• *Flammability:* Flammability is one of the most important considerations for fabric selection, especially in public areas like waiting rooms, hospitals, or theaters. Some fabrics are inherently more flame resistant than others, but nearly any fabric can be treated with various chemicals to enhance its resistance to ignition and smoldering. Many states and most federal agencies have flammability standards for furniture. These standards are discussed in more detail later in this chapter.

There has been concern about the health effects of some types of chemical flame retardants. Specifically, halogenated flame retardants have been found to cause neurological, developmental, and reproductive damage in laboratory animals and to persist in the environment. This class of flame retardant, known as poly-brominated diphenyl ethers (PBDEs), is used in furniture, textiles, and other building materials and comes in various types. PentaBDE is used in furniture and carpeting while decaBDE is used in textiles and electronics. Some manufacturers have already stopped using these types of retardants even though research is still ongoing. When specifying flame-retardant chemicals, the interior designer must verify which chemicals are being used and avoid those that may create a health or environmental problem.

If no type of flame-retardant treatment is used, various types of fibers have inherent responses to fire. Fabrics perform differently depending on whether they are near a flame, in a flame, or have been removed from a flame. For example, some fibers, such as nylon and wool, will burn when in a flame but are self-extinguishing when removed from the flame. Others, like olefin and cotton, continue to burn when removed from a flame.

The following list gives fabric types from the most resistant to fire to the least resistant to fire when they are untreated.

- wool
- silk
- modacrylic
- nylon
- olefin
- polyester
- acrylic
- acetate
- cellulosic fibers (cotton, linen, rayon)

- *Dimensional stability:* This characteristic is a fabric's ability to retain its shape and fit over cushioning without sagging, wrinkling, stretching, or tearing. A fabric should be resilient enough to return to its original shape after being deformed by use. It is therefore critical that the fabric and cushion be matched. A cushion that allows for more deformation than a certain fabric can resist will cause problems.

A fabric applied over a large area of cushioning may stretch or slip over the cushion if the fabric is not stable by itself. In many cases, fabric is attached to the cushion by buttoning, tufting, or channeling. *Buttoning* secures the fabric to the cushion with a lightly tensioned button and thread. *Tufting* is similar except that the button is pulled tightly against the cushion, resulting in a deeply folded surface. *Channeling* secures the fabric to the cushion in parallel rows.

- *Maintenance:* Because furniture fabric is subjected to much wear, it must be selected with the intended use in mind. (An ongoing program of regular maintenance must also be considered.)

- *Appearance:* An otherwise elegant, appropriately selected piece of furniture can be ruined by choosing a fabric that is the wrong color, texture, or pattern. It is important to consider both the other materials used in the furniture and the materials used in the space and adjacent furniture.

- *Scale:* Scale is the size of the fabric texture and pattern in relationship to the piece of furniture and to the space in which it is used. A large sofa in a large room, for instance, may be covered with large, bold patterns and heavy weaves without seeming out of scale.

- *Comfort:* People come in direct contact with furniture more than any other component of interior space, so comfort must be appropriate for the intended use and for ergonomic requirements. A waiting-room chair does not need to be as comfortable as an office worker's chair. Fabrics and cushioning can affect comfort by their porosity, resilience, surface texture and finish. A highly porous fabric can "breathe" and is more comfortable for long periods of sitting or where the temperature and humidity are high. Similarly, smooth fabrics are more comfortable than those with rough textures or finishes.

- *Touch:* Touch is how the fabric feels to a person's skin. In some cases, it is appropriate to use a smooth fabric, like satin, while in other instances a rough fabric is the correct choice. Sometimes the choice is purely a matter of preference, while other times it can be very practical. For example, a rough, heavily textured surface can make it difficult for people to slide in and out of restaurant banquette seating.

Cushioning and Seaming

Cushioning and seaming affect the comfort, wearability, and flammability of furniture. Some common cushioning materials include cotton batting, poly-ester batting, polyurethane foam, latex foam, rubberized fibers, and shredded fibers. These may be used alone or in cushions placed on coiled or sinuous spring support.

Because cushion material affects the flammability of upholstery as much as the surface fabric, it should be selected carefully. Untreated cellular plastic cushioning presents a particularly high fire hazard. These plastics include the following types of foams: polyurethane, polystyrene, polyethylene, polypropylene, PVC and ABS, cellulose acetate, epoxy, phenolic, urea, silicone, and foamed latex. Untreated cellulosic batting, such as cotton batting, is also dangerous when cigarette ignition resistance is required. When flammability resistance is a high priority, polyester batting is a better choice. The following list gives padding types, from the most resistant to cigarette ignition and small flame to the least resistant.

- neoprene, and combustion modified polyurethane

- polyester batting

- smolder-resistant and flame-resistant polyurethane foam

- smolder-resistant and flame-resistant cellulosic batting

- mixed fiber batting

- untreated polyurethane foam

- cellulosic batting

- latex foam (rarely used)

One of the important considerations in upholstery fire safety is smoldering resistance or, as it is sometimes referred to, cigarette ignition resistance. It is affected by the combination of fabric material, cushioning, and seating construction. Fire hazards are increased if tufting or any type of decorative treatment is used on the seats or arms of upholstery, because dropped cigarettes may lodge in these areas. Avoid using welt cording and similar seaming on surfaces where cigarettes may be dropped. A *welt* is a fabric-covered cord sewn into the seam of upholstery for ornamental purposes or to improve the durability of the covering. Instead, seaming such as railroading can be used. *Railroading* is the application of fabric to furniture so that there are no intermediate seam details. Railroading is also used when vertical stripes on the fabric must run horizontally. In addition to specifying smooth seaming, specify that the backs and seats of booths and other seating be separated by at least 1 in, so cigarettes cannot get lodged in this area.

Upholstery safety can be enhanced in two additional ways. Flammability can be minimized by treating the cushioning material with one of several chemicals. Cotton batting and polyurethane foam can both be treated to increase their resistance to smoldering and flame spread. Liners can also be used between the fabric and cushion to provide a barrier that slows or inhibits the spread of heat and flame from the fabric to the cushion.

Cushioning also affects the comfort and wearability of furniture. For foam cushions there are three performance criteria.

The first criterion is *density*, the mass per unit volume. It is normally expressed in lbm/ft^3 (or kg/m^3). The greater the density, the greater the support. However, a high-density foam does not necessarily provide a firm cushion.

One of the common types of cushioning is flexible polyurethane foam (FPF). FPF is available in densities ranging from as low as 0.8 lbm/ft^3 up to 6.0 lbm/ft^3 (12.8 kg/m^3 to 96.1 kg/m^3). However, most upholstered furniture uses a foam density in the range of 0.9 lbm/ft^3 to 2.5 lbm/ft^3 (14.4 kg/m^3 to 40.0 kg/m^3). Generally, the higher the density, the more durable (and more expensive) the foam is.

The second criterion measure firmness and is called the *indentation load deflection* (ILD). This is also sometimes called the *indentation force deflection* (IFD). To determine a cushion's ILD, a metal plate with an 8 in diameter is pushed against a sample of foam 4 in thick. The number of pounds required to compress the foam down 1 in (or 25%) is the ILD rating. For example, an ILD rating of 35 means that 35 lbm were required to compress the foam sample to 25% of its height. Therefore, a higher ILD rating means a firmer foam. Samples with an ILD of 25 or less are considered soft foams; those with ILDs from 25 to 50 are considered firm; and those with ILDs greater than 50 are considered very firm foams.

The third criterion is the *support ratio* (also called the *support factor* or *compression modulus*). This is the ratio of the force required to compress a foam sample to 65% of its original thickness to the force required to compress the sample to 25% of its original thickness (the normal ILD rating). The higher the support factor is, the better the foam's ability to support weight. Generally, high support ratios (firm seating) from 2.25 to 4.0 should be used for medical, institutional, and assembly seating. Moderate firmness cushioning with support ratios from 2.0 to 2.5 should be used for light- to medium-use seating, while softer cushions with ratios below 2.0 should be used for backs of chairs and booths.

Finally, cushioning affects wearability. While firm cushions give better support and are more appropriate in many situations, soft undercushioning permits fabric to give and resists the grinding action of normal use. Fabric is quickly abraded when it is pulled tightly over sharp corners or welts, so the correctly selected cushion can minimize these problems.

STANDARDS

Flammability Standards

Many test methods, adopted by various local and state governments, have been developed to set standards for the flammability of upholstery and fabrics used for interior applications. Although these standards have not been consistently adopted across the United States, it would be wise to become familiar with them all. These standards define limits on a material's flammability in terms of one or more of the following characteristics: resistance to ignition, resistance to flame spread, resistance to smoldering, prevention of smoke development, prevention of heat contribution to the growth of a fire, and prevention of toxic gas release. The most commonly used standards are listed as follows. Refer to Ch. 27 for a description of other tests for interior finishes, including carpet and flooring, and for a table summarizing tests commonly used for interior design furniture, finishes, and construction.

- *Vertical ignition test*

Full title: Standard Methods of Fire Tests for Flame-Resistant Textiles and Films

Agency and test number: NFPA 701

Summary: This standard establishes two procedures for testing the flammability of draperies, curtains, or other window treatments.

Description: This standard defines two test procedures that are used to assess the propagation of flame beyond the area exposed to an ignition source. Test 1 provides a procedure for assessing the response of fabrics lighter than 21 oz/yd^2 individually and in multilayer composites. Test 2 is for fabrics weighing more than 21 oz/yd^2 such as fabric blackout linings, awnings, tents, and similar architectural fabric structures and banners. The tests are appropriate for testing materials that are exposed to air on both sides. A sample either passes or fails the test. The equivalent test is UL 214, Test for Flame Propagation of Fabrics and Films.

- *Cigarette ignition resistance test of furniture components*

Full title: Standard Methods of Tests and Classification System for Cigarette Ignition Resistance of Components of Upholstered Furniture

Agency and test number: NFPA 260

Summary: This standard tests the resistance of upholstered furniture components, separately, to flame and cigarette ignition.

Description: This standard, also known as CAL TB 117 (State of California Technical Bulletin 117), tests individual *components* (fabric and fillings) of upholstered furniture for resistance to cigarette ignition as well as flame. Separate fill materials, such as expanded polystyrene beads, cellular materials, feathers, nonartificial filling, and artificial fiber filling are tested separately for a variety of characteristics. This test is also similar to ASTM E 1353.

- *Cigarette ignition resistance test of furniture composites*

Full title: Standard Test Method for Cigarette Ignition Resistance of Mock-Up Upholstered Furniture Assemblies

Agency and test number: NFPA 261

Summary: This standard tests the resistance of a seat cushion mock-up (including foam, liner, and fabric) to a lighted cigarette.

Description: This test, similar to CAL TB 116 and the Business and Institutional Manufacturers Association (BIFMA) X5.7, is used to evaluate the cigarette ignition resistance of upholstered furniture by using a mock-up. It determines how the composite material (padding and covering) reacts to a lighted cigarette. The mock-up includes vertical and horizontal surfaces meeting at a 90° angle. The cushion fails the test if it breaks into flames or if a char more than 2 in (50) long develops. It is not intended to measure the performance of upholstered furniture under conditions of exposure to open flame. The BIFMA standard classifies fabrics into class A, B, C, or D, with class A being the most resistant to charring.

- *Full seating test*

Full title: Standard Method of Test for Fire Characteristics of Upholstered Furniture Exposed to Flaming Ignition Source

Agency and test number: NFPA 266

Summary: This test evaluates the effect of an open flame on an actual sample of a chair.

Description: This test, similar to CAL TB 133, evaluates the response of an actual sample of furniture to an open flame. During the test, several measurements are made, including the rate of heat and smoke released, the total amount of heat and smoke released, the concentration of carbon oxides, and others. The most important measurement is the rate of heat release, which quantifies the intensity of the fire generated. This is one of the strictest tests for furniture and is required in many states.

Following are some common definitions related to flammability that are important to know.

Char: material remaining from incomplete combustion

Fire resistance: the property of a material or assembly to withstand fire or give protection from it

Flammable: capable of burning with a flame, and subject to easy ignition and rapid flaming combustion

Flame resistance: the ability to withstand flame impingement or give protection from it

Flame-retardant: (or fire-retardant) as an adjective it should only be used as a modifier with defined compound terms such as flame-retardant treatment. Flame retardant and fire retardant as nouns should not be used unless they are describing a chemical used for that purpose.

Smoldering: combustion without flame that may burn for a relatively long time while generating smoke, toxic gases, and heat

Wearability and Durability Standards

In addition to test methods for the flammability of fabrics and furniture, there are dozens of test methods for specific aspects of fabric wearability and durability. These tests are promulgated by ASTM, the American Association of Textile Chemists and Colorists (AATCC), and the Chemical Fabrics and Film Association (CFFA). Some of the more important tests for fabrics are listed here.

- *Wyzenbeek abrasion resistance test*

Full title: Standard Test Method for Abrasion Resistance of Textile Fabrics (Oscillatory Cylinder Method)

Agency and test number: ASTM D4157

Summary: This test determines the abrasion resistance of woven textile fabrics.

Description: A sample of material about 2 in × 8 in (50 × 200) is secured to the testing machine and rubbed back and forth with various types of abradants: no. 8 cotton duck, no. 220 grit silicon carbide sheet, stainless steel screen, a 14-18 mesh support screen, or other abradants as specified. The sample is abraded at a rate of 5000 double rubs per hour. A fabric is considered good if it withstands 15,000 double rubs. Some manufacturers and specifications consider a fabric that withstands 3000 cycles as light duty, 9000 cycles as medium duty, and 15,000 cycles as heavy duty. Some upholstery fabrics can withstand hundreds of thousands of double rubs. This test is also referred to as CCFA-1, the Wyzenbeek method.

- *Taber abraser test*

Full title: Standard Guide for Abrasion Resistance of Textile Fabrics (Rotary Platform, Double-Head Method)

Agency and test number: ASTM D3884

Summary: This test determines the abrasion resistance of textiles, most commonly of carpet.

Description: A sample of material is cut into a circle about 4 in (100) in diameter and mounted on a platform. The platform is rotated so that the sample rubs against two abrading wheels moving in opposite directions. Different abrasion hardnesses, test weights, and test cycles can be used depending on the type of material being tested. The results of the test are reported in the number of revolutions of the platform (cycles) required to break a yarn or expose the backing material. This test is also referred to as CCFA-1, the Taber abraser method.

- *Martindale abrasion test*

Full title: Standard Test Method for Abrasion Resistance of Textile Fabrics (Martindale Abrasion Tester Method)

Agency and test number: ASTM D4966

Summary: This test determines the abrasion resistance of textile fabrics, generally with a pile depth of less than 0.08 in (2).

Description: The Martindale test is similar to the Wyzenbeek test.

- *Fade-Ometer® test*

Full title: Colorfastness to light

Agency and test number: AATCC Method 16

Summary: This test determines the colorfastness, under light exposure, of textile materials using six different test options. The most common test option uses a xenon-arc lamp with continuous light.

Description: Samples of a textile material are exposed to ultraviolet light in a laboratory testing device at specific humidity levels, and any color change is compared with an unexposed material using the AATCC gray scale for color change or by an instrumental color measurement. For most fabrics, 80 hours of exposure without color loss is considered a minimum rating. A similar test for chemical coated fabrics is CFFA-2 using ASTM G155, Standard Practice for Operating Xenon Arc Light Apparatus for Exposure of Non-Metallic Materials.

- *Crocking resistance test*

Full title: Colorfastness to Crocking: AATCC Crockmeter Method

Agency and test number: AATCC Test Method 8

Summary: This test determines the resistance of a colored textile to transfer its color from its surface to other surfaces by rubbing.

Description: In this test a sample of colored fabric is rubbed with a white test cloth under controlled conditions. The amount of color transferred is assessed by comparing it with a standard gray scale or with a chromatic transference scale. The sample can either be tested dry or wet and before or after washing. The test is generally not recommended for carpet or for prints where the singling out of areas is too small for valid testing. A similar test for coated fabrics is CFFA-7, Crocking Resistance.

- *Tearing strength test, tongue method*

Full title: Standard Test Method for Tearing Strength of Fabrics by the Tongue (Single Rip) Procedure (Constant-Rate-of-Extension Tensile Testing Machine)

Agency and test number: ASTM D2261

Summary: This test measures the tearing resistance of fabrics after an initial cut has been made in the fabric.

Description: This is one of three commonly used tests for tearing strength. In the tongue method test, a test sample 8 in (200) long by 3 in (75) wide is clamped in the testing apparatus, and the load necessary to continue the tear is measured. The tearing strength is the average of five test specimens. A similar test designation is CFFA-16, method b.

- *Bacterial resistance test*

Full title: Antibacterial Activity Assessment of Textile Materials: Parallel Streak Method

Agency and test number: AATCC Test Method 147

Summary: This test detects bacteriostatic activity on textile materials.

Description: Specimens of the test fabric are placed in contact with an agar-growing agent and covered with different types of bacteria. After incubation, the incubated plates are examined for interruption of growth along the streaks of inoculum and for a clear zone of inhibition beyond the specimen edge. A corresponding test method is CFFA-300.

Other test methods evaluate fabrics for qualities such as resistance to fungus, cold-crack resistance, flex resistance, seam strength, shrinkage, and water vapor transmission. There are also other test standards for abrasion resistance in addition to the three listed.

There are other standards that measure the durability of commercial furniture. For example, the Business and Institutional Furniture Manufacturers Association (BIFMA) has developed several standards for office furnishings. These include standards for general-purpose office chairs (ANSI/BIFMA X5.1), lateral files (ANSI/BIFMA X5.2), vertical files (ANSI/BIFMA X5.3), lounge seating (ANSI/BIFMA X5.4), desk products (ANSI/BIFMA X5.5), and panel systems (ANSI/BIFMA X5.6).

COMMUNICATING RECOMMENDATIONS FOR MATERIALS AND FURNISHINGS

In addition to the various types of drawings and models used to communicate the three-dimensional aspects of the design, as described in Ch. 5, the designer must also communicate decisions about finishes and furnishings. Most often, this is done with sample boards showing exact samples of the materials proposed for use. Actual samples are preferred to sketches, renderings, or computer drawings because only a real sample can convey the accurate color, texture, and look of a finish. Some designers assemble one or two large boards with the samples sized in proportion to the amount they will be used. For example, a sample of a wall covering used on two walls will be much larger than a fabric sample for two pillows. The material samples may be keyed to a small-scale floor plan showing where each material is proposed for use.

Furniture decisions are most often communicated with photographs of the furniture accompanied by actual samples of the fabrics proposed for each type of furniture. Furniture may be shown on the same boards as the finish samples or on separate boards. In most cases, separate sample boards are assembled for individual rooms so the client can understand how the finishes and furnishings in a particular room will look. As detailed backup material, manufacturers' product data sheets for finishes or furniture may be assembled on boards or in a separate notebook.

When a design is particularly unusual or important, a full-scale mockup can be constructed to show the client how a furniture group or room will look. The mockup can be constructed with temporary materials, such as cardboard or plywood, or an actual sample can be constructed, complete with finishes and furniture.

SAMPLE QUESTIONS

1. What fabric would have the best appearance for the longest time when used in theater seating?

    (A) vinyl

    (B) wool/nylon blend

    (C) acrylic/acetate blend

    (D) cotton/rayon blend

2. What type of cushioning would be best for a hospital waiting room?

(A) high-density foam

(B) cotton batting

(C) combustion modified foam with a low ILD

(D) low-density polyurethane

3. In what order of importance should tables for a college library be selected?

(A) flammability, design, then comfort

(B) finish, flammability, then design

(C) durability, cost, then design

(D) quality, comfort, then finish

4. Which type of seaming would be LEAST appropriate for seating where cigarettes are likely to be dropped?

(A) channeling

(B) buttoning

(C) railroading

(D) welt cording

5. What performance tests should be specified for a custom-blended fabric to be used in a recreation center reception area?

(A) flammability and Fade-Ometer

(B) Wyzenbeek and fading

(C) Taber and Wyzenbeek

(D) indentation load deflection and Taber

6. How can a drapery treatment be changed to minimize its hazard during a fire?

(A) Shorten the length of the fabric.

(B) Use an open-weave fabric.

(C) Increase the amount of fabric.

(D) Use a composite fabric.

7. A Class A fabric will not

(A) char

(B) ignite

(C) smolder

(D) produce smoke

8. What most affects the flammability of upholstery?

(A) type of chemical retardant used

(B) cushioning and surface fabric

(C) surface fabric and interliner

(D) surface fabric

9. If you were specifying the fabric for sofas in a sunroom, which would be the LEAST desirable choice?

(A) polyester

(B) modacrylic

(C) rayon

(D) acrylic

10. The best way to avoid fabric slippage over a cushion would be to specify

(A) a heavy fabric pulled tightly over the cushion

(B) a high-density foam cushion with an interliner

(C) rounded corners with welts

(D) channeling

11. NFPA 701 relates to which of the following items?

(A) wallcoverings

(B) fabrics

(C) draperies

(D) floor coverings

12. When a fabric has been fire-retardant treated, it will

(A) resist ignition

(B) not burn

(C) contribute to smoke inhibition

(D) have a lower flame spread

13. When selecting paint for a hospital, which of the following criteria is most important?

(A) abrasion resistance

(B) chemical resistance

(C) flammability

(D) VOC emissions

14. Information regarding standard test methods for evaluating a product can be found

(A) through ASTM

(B) on the internet

(C) at CSI

(D) in *Sweets Catalog*

15. The most naturally fire-resistant untreated fabric is

(A) acrylic

(B) cotton

(C) nylon

(D) wool

7

COORDINATION, BUDGETING, AND SCHEDULING

An important part of the schematic design phase of a project is coordinating the work of consultants, integrating the design with the applicable buildings systems, and making sure all the requirements of codes and regulations are met. In addition, the designer needs to begin budgeting the project based on the client's resources and developing design and production schedules for his or her work.

COORDINATION

The interior designer is responsible for coordinating the efforts of the designer's office as well as everyone on the building team who is under a contractual agreement with the designer. Important aspects of coordination during schematic design include consultant coordination, coordinating building systems with the design, and making sure code requirements continue to be satisfied as the design is developed.

Consultant Coordination

The interior designer should involve the consultants in the project as early as possible. Their advice and expertise is vital to determining the scope of the project,

developing broad conceptual approaches to solving the client's problem, and understanding the concerns of the client and other design professionals working on the project.

One of the most important tasks for the interior designer during the early stages of a project is the assembly and coordination of the various consultants on the project. These may include structural, mechanical, and electrical engineers at a minimum. Additional consultants may include fire protection engineers, acousticians, preservation experts, security consultants, and audio-visual consultants. The expected services of each consultant must be determined, with the advice of the consultant and the approval of the client. Client involvement is mandatory if the owner contracts directly with the consultant for services.

The contractual arrangement between the consultant and the interior designer or owner must also be determined. If the owner contracts directly with the consultant, the interior designer avoids any problems with contract provisions and payment but may lose some ability to direct the consultant. If the interior designer writes an agreement directly with the consultant and is responsible for paying the consultant, he or she has more control but may encounter problems with paying the consultant's fees if the client's payment is delayed.

Once the consultants are retained, the interior designer should inform the appropriate consultants about the applicable code requirements. The interior designer is also responsible for informing the consultants of any design decisions that may have code implications. Although the interior designer is responsible for ensuring that the drawings and specifications conform to the applicable codes, the consultants are responsible for code compliance regarding their area of work in the same way the interior designer is responsible to the owner. By signing their drawings, the engineering consultants become responsible for compliance with applicable codes and regulations.

Each consultant is also responsible for accurate production of his or her own drawings and specifications. Further, the consultants are responsible for checking their own various documents for consistency. However, the interior designer is the prime consultant and is liable to the owner for the consultant's work.

Refer to Ch. 2 for a description of the services consultants provide. Refer to Ch. 14 for a discussion of coordination with the consultant's drawings.

Building Systems Coordination

As the project design is developed, it should be reviewed against the existing building's systems: structural, mechanical, plumbing, electrical, lighting, security, and fire-protection. As described in Ch. 2, the preliminary investigation that should have been completed during the programming stage serves as the basis for this review. As the design is developed, the designer and consultants can more accurately compare the existing systems against the needs of the design.

As the space plan and design concepts are finalized, copies of the drawings should be given to the consultants working on the project. At this point the consultants can begin their schematic design work. The interior designer must coordinate this effort and keep the consultants constantly informed of any changes to the client's program or the layout of the plan.

Refer to Chs. 17, 18, and 19 for detailed information on structural, mechanical, electrical, and lighting systems.

Coordination of Code Requirements

The code review and application that begins during programming and early space planning should be continued during schematic design. The development of a code checklist to be used for preliminary design was discussed in Ch. 2. Some of the important code requirements for space planning were listed in Ch. 4.

During schematic design, all of the preliminary information used to do space planning should be verified, especially if changes were made to the space plan, occupancy type, and occupant load. The interior designer should check the basic exiting requirements of number of exits, minimum exit separation, maximum travel distance, common path of egress travel, exit width, dead-end corridors, and door swings. Generally, very detailed code requirements can be verified and applied later, during the design development stage. These requirements are listed in Ch. 13. The exception would be for design elements that could affect the overall space plan or have significant cost implications. For example, the design decision to use expensive fire-rated glazing instead of gypsum wallboard partitions would have a serious budget impact. It would be better for the designer and the client to study the design, building code, and cost implications during schematic design rather than waiting until a later phase.

BUDGETING

Establishing a budget early in the programming or design process is one of the most important aspects of design because it influences many design decisions and can help determine whether a project is even feasible. Once a budget is set, the interior designer must work within it and keep the client advised about any changes that might influence final costs.

Initial budgets can be set in several ways. In most cases, the client has already estimated the amount of money available and simply gives this figure to the interior designer. Corporate clients or organizations with ongoing building programs usually have a good idea of what new or remodeled facilities cost, and their budgets are usually realistic. Residential clients or people who are contracting for interior design services and construction for the first time may have a very poor idea of the costs involved. Occasionally, budgets are set through public funding or legislation. The maximum project costs are set long before the design or construction begins and without the interior designer's involvement. The project, however, must be completed for that cost.

In other cases, the client will describe the extent of work he or she would like and ask the designer to develop an anticipated budget. From this preliminary figure, the client and designer can determine if there is enough money to do the job or whether the budget must be increased or the scope of work must be decreased.

There is always a relationship among quantity, quality, and money. Changing one affects the others. For example, if the client has a fixed budget and must build and furnish a specific amount of space, then the quality of materials or extent of work must reflect the budget and the space. If the client wants a particular level of quality and a given amount of space, then the budget should reflect these two requirements.

Cost Influences

Many factors affect the final project cost. The client must budget for more than construction costs and furnishings expenses. The following sections describe some of the possible expenses that can occur on an interior design project. Of course, not all of them apply on every job.

Construction Costs

Construction costs are the moneys required to build or remodel the interior, including such things as demolition, partitions, ceilings, millwork, finishes, and plumbing, electrical, and mechanical work—generally anything that is attached to and becomes part of the structure.

Furniture, Fixtures, and Equipment

This category can include many things. On most projects, furniture, fixtures, and equipment (FF&E) are separate budget items because the way they are specified, purchased, and installed is different from the way construction items are handled. Furnishings are either purchased directly by the interior designer, who arranges for delivery and installation, or specified by the interior designer for purchase and installation by one or more furniture dealers. They are also a separate budget item because of the various discounts the designer or client receives and the tax that must be paid. In most cases, clients also prefer to allocate money to these items separate from hard construction costs.

On some jobs, there may be a choice concerning whether to place an item in the FF&E budget or the construction budget. For example, a refrigerator and range may be specified by the designer and purchased and installed by the general contractor as part of the construction cost, or they may be purchased directly by the client or interior designer for installation after construction is complete. In the former case, the contractor will purchase the items at wholesale cost and charge the client a retail price in addition to adding fees for overhead and profit, while in the latter case the client may save on these charges by arranging for delivery and installation.

Some of the items that are normally part of the FF&E budget include

- furniture

- appliances

- free-standing equipment such as vending machines and library bookshelves

- window coverings

- rugs and mats

- interior plants and planters

- lamps

- artwork

- accessories

Contractor's Overhead and Profit

This line item includes the general contractor's profit and cost of doing business. For construction projects, overhead can be divided into general overhead and project overhead. *General overhead* is the cost of running a contracting business and includes such things as office rent, secretarial help, utilities, and other recurring costs. *Project overhead* is the money it takes to complete a specific job, not

including labor, materials, or equipment. Temporary offices, project telephones, trash removal, insurance, permits, and temporary utility hookups are examples of project overhead. The total overhead costs can range from about 10% to 20% of the total costs for the contractor's labor, materials, and equipment.

Profit is one of the most highly variable parts of a budget. It depends on the type of project, its size, the amount of risk involved, how much money the contractor wants to make (or thinks he or she can charge), the general market conditions, and of course, whether or not the job is being bid on or negotiated. For construction costs, profit is a percentage of the total of labor, materials, equipment, and overhead to do the job. During extremely difficult economic conditions, a contractor may cut the profit margin to almost nothing, simply to get the job and keep his or her work force employed. If the contract is being negotiated with one contractor rather than with multiple contractors, the profit percentage is usually higher. In most cases, however, profit will range from 5% to 15% of the total cost of the job. Overall, overhead and profit can total about 15% to 25% of construction cost, with most jobs in a competitive market at the lower end of the scale.

Professional Fees

Professional fees include the charges for the interior designer's services as well as fees for other professionals such as architects, mechanical engineers, and electrical engineers. In addition, costs for special consultants, legal fees, and testing may be included here. If an interior designer is working on a retail basis where markups on purchased furniture account for the designer's fee, then this line item may not exist unless other professionals are involved.

Taxes

Taxes include sales tax paid on furniture, accessories, and other purchased items. If the interior designer buys these things, he or she is responsible for collecting tax from the client and paying it to the appropriate taxing jurisdictions. If the client has a total budget for purchased items, the tax must be deducted from the top so the designer knows how much money is actually available for buying the items. If the interior designer is working in a jurisdiction that collects taxes on professional services, such tax is usually included in the professional fees category, although it can be placed under taxes if it needs to appear as a separate line item. Taxes on materials used in construction are paid by the general contractor and subcontractors and are included in the total construction budget.

Moving Costs

Some clients prefer to include moving costs in their total building budget. This includes the money required to physically relocate and may also include things like the cost to reprint stationery and downtime caused by the move. For large companies, moving costs can be substantial.

Telephone and Data System Installation

Because telephone and data systems (computers, local area networks, and the like) are purchased separately and installed by specialty companies, the costs for these systems should be kept separate. In most cases, the client will coordinate these items separately without involving the interior designer. However, the designer may need to coordinate his or her work with the suppliers of these services to provide space for equipment, proper location of outlets and conduits, and other required mechanical and electrical support services.

Contingencies

A contingency should always be added to the budget to account for unforeseen change requests by the client and other conditions that will add to the total cost of the job. For an early project budget, the percentage of the contingency should be higher than contingencies applied to later budgets, because there are more unknowns at the beginning of a project. Normally, from 5% to 10% of the total budget should be included. There may be one contingency to cover everything, or one for construction and one for furniture, fixtures, and equipment.

Other Costs

There are two additional costs that a client may want to include in the budget. The first is financing, which is not only the long-term interest paid on permanent financing but also the immediate costs of loan origination fees, construction loan interest, and other administrative costs. On long-term loans, the cost of financing can easily exceed all of the original building, FF&E, and development costs. In many cases, long-term interest, called debt service, is not included in the project budget because it is an ongoing cost to the owner, as are maintenance costs.

The second cost item is an inflation factor. Because some large interior design projects take a great deal of time, a factor for inflation should be included. Generally, the present budget estimate is escalated to a time in the future at the expected midpoint of construction. Although it is always difficult to predict the future, using past cost index and inflation rates and applying an estimate to the expected conditions of the construction will permit the interior designer to make an educated guess.

Methods of Estimating

There are many methods of developing a budget and estimating the possible cost of a job. As previously stated, the client may already have a certain amount of money available, in which case the interior designer must work backward, subtracting money for fees, taxes, and similar costs to arrive at what is left over for the actual construction and furnishings. In other cases, the designer must determine the scope of the project with the client and assign costs to the various individual elements to arrive at the final figure.

Whichever method is used, the exact procedure for budgeting will vary depending on the time at which a budget is developed. Budgeting is an ongoing activity; it is revised at each phase of the project as more decisions are made. Very early in the project, little is known about the job except its overall size and general quality. Later, when construction documents are complete and furniture specifications are finalized, a very detailed estimate can be calculated.

Square Footage

Budgets based on size are usually the first and most preliminary type of estimate done before much design work has started. The anticipated square footage of the project is multiplied by a cost per square foot to arrive at a number. The square footage costs may be based on the designer's or client's experience with similar projects, or they may come from knowledgeable contractors or commercially available cost books. Other costs, like contingencies, may in turn be generated by estimating them as a percentage of the basic construction cost. When using a square-foot cost, the interior designer must know if it includes additional costs such as contractor's overhead and profit, taxes, and the like.

Units other than square feet can also be used for certain facilities. For example, there are rules of thumb for costs per hotel room when budgeting for hotels, costs per

hospital bed, and similar functional units. Whichever unit is used, it is usually best to develop three budgets based on a low, medium, and high cost per square foot or cost per functional unit. This way, the client can see the probable range of money that will be required.

Parameter

As design progresses and the interior designer and client have a better idea of the exact scope of the work, the budget can be refined. The procedure most often used at this time is the parameter method, which involves an expanded itemization of construction quantities and furnishings and assignment of unit costs to these quantities. See Fig. 7.1.

For example, floor finishes can be broken down into carpeting, vinyl tile, wood-strip flooring, and so forth. The areas are multiplied by an estimated cost per square foot, and the total budget for flooring is developed. If the design has not progressed to the point of selecting individual flooring types, an average cost of flooring can be estimated and assigned to the total area of the project. Furniture can be estimated in a similar way. The final manufacturer and fabric of a seating group may not be decided, but costs for typical sofas, chairs, and coffee tables based on the designer's experience can be totaled to get a working budget number.

With this type of budgeting, it is possible to evaluate the cost implication of each building component and to make decisions concerning both quantity and quality that meet the original budget estimate. If floor finishes are over budget, the interior designer and the client can review the parameter estimate and decide, for example, that some wood flooring must be replaced with less expensive carpeting. Similar decisions can be made concerning any of the budget parameters.

Budget for Headquarters Remodel
Project #330

Figure 7.1

Parameter Cost
Estimate

section	item	quantity/unit	unit price ($)	amount	subtotal ($)
100	demolition				
100.01	partitions	3600 SF	2.00	7200	
100.02	ceilings	3700 SF	0.25	925	
100.03	carpet	3700 SF	0.25	925	
100.04	relocate entry	1 allowance	7200.00	7200	
					16,250
200	partitions				
200.01	full height	225 LF	27.00	6075	
200.02	partial height	24 LF	21.00	504	
200.03	partial glass	44 LF	100.00	4400	
200.04	operable partitions	50 LF	175.00	8750	
200.05	drywall facing	124 LF	20.00	2480	
					22,209
300	doors/frames/hardware				
300.01	entry	5 EA	600.00	3000	
300.02	interior—singles	3 EA	500.00	1500	
300.03	interior—pairs	2 EA	900.00	1800	
300.04	sliding	4 EA	800.00	3200	
300.05	closet—pairs	5 EA	1000.00	5000	
					14,500
400	finishes				
400.01	walls—paint	(included in partitions)		0	
400.02	walls—fabric tack panels	130 SF	6.00	780	
400.03	walls—wall covering	1 allowance	2000.00	2000	
400.04	floor—carpet	450 SY	22.00	9900	
400.05	floor—vinyl tile	140 SF	1.50	210	
400.06	floor—inset carpet	1 allowance	1000.00	1000	
400.07	ceiling	3740 SF	2.25	8415	
400.08	window coverings	342 SF	3.25	1112	
					23,417
500	millwork				
500.01	kitchen cabinets	28 LF	350.00	9800	
500.02	mail counter & boxes	14 LF	400.00	5600	
500.03	office alcoves counters	130 LF	100.00	1300	
500.04	wall storage	86 LF	150.00	12900	
500.05	president's office	9 LF	250.00	2250	
500.06	workroom	30 LF	200.00	6000	
500.07	display	21 LF	300.00	6300	
500.08	shelving	30 LF	50.00	1500	
500.09	admin assistant	35 LF	300.00	10500	
					56,150
600	electrical				
600.01	fluorescent lighting	67 EA	175.00	11725	
600.02	incandescent downlights	7 EA	125.00	875	
600.03	wall outlets	36 EA	150.00	5400	
600.04	dedicated wall outlet	1 EA	250.00	250	
600.05	floor outlets	4 EA	300.00	1200	
600.06	telephone outlets	9 EA	100.00	900	
600.07	fire/security system	1 allowance	10000.00	10000	
600.08	upgrade power panel	1 allowance	3500.00	3500	
600.09	undercounter lights	47 EA	100.00	4700	
600.1	exit lights	6 EA	100.00	600	
					39,150
700	plumbing				
700.01	kitchen sink	1 EA	3000.00	3000	
					3000
800	heating/ventilating/A.C.				
800.01	additional roof unit	1 allowance	5000.00	5000	
800.02	secondary distribution	1 allowance	3000.00	3000	
800.03	controls	1 allowance	500.00	500	
					8500
900	equipment				
900.01	refrigerator	1 EA	600.00	600	
900.02	microwave	1 EA	400.00	400	
900.03	garbage disposal	1 EA	300.00	300	
900.04	water heater (insta-hot)	1 EA	300.00	300	
900.05	dishwasher	1 EA	400.00	400	
900.06	projection screen/motor	1 EA	1600.00	1600	
					3600
			Subtotal $		186,776
			10% for contingency		18,677
			10% contractor's overhead and profit		20,543
			TOTAL $		225,996

Another way to compare and evaluate alternative construction components is with *matrix costing*, a technique in which a matrix is drawn with the various alternatives along one side and the individual elements that combine to make up the total cost of the alternatives along the other side. For example, in evaluating alternatives for workstations, all of the factors that would comprise the final costs could be compared, including the cost of custom-built versus pre-manufactured workstations, task lighting that could be planned with custom-built units versus higher-wattage ambient lighting, and so on.

Parameter line items are based on commonly used units that relate to the construction element or cost item under study. For instance, a gypsum wallboard partition would have an assigned cost per square foot or cost per linear foot (for a given height) of a complete partition of a particular construction type, rather than separate costs for studs, gypsum board, screws, and finishing. This way, it is an easy procedure to calculate the linear footage of partitions (even based on a preliminary space plan) and multiply by a unit cost. Secretarial chairs, however, would be budgeted on a "per each" basis because the number required is easily determined.

Sometimes the parameter cost for an item cannot be estimated using a construction unit. In these situations an allowance can be used. An allowance is a set amount of money estimated by the interior designer to cover a particular material, construction component, furnishing, or piece of equipment when the cost for that material or item cannot be determined precisely at the time of estimating. It is generally a "best guess" estimate or is based on costs from past projects. In Fig. 7.1, for example, there are allowances for two finishes and some electrical work.

Allowances are also used later in the project, although to a lesser extent, for bidding or negotiation of the final costs. At this stage of costing, an allowance is usually applied to a piece of equipment or specialty interior item that has not yet been selected. For example, the interior designer may want a custom-made carpet inset, but the price has not been finalized from the artist. An allowance is, in effect, a placeholder so some amount of money can be reserved for the item. The allowance (or allowances) is stated in the appropriate section (or sections) of the specifications, so all bidders are using the same amount in their bids. The contractor must add to the allowance the costs for unloading, handling, and installing the item as well as costs for the contractor's overhead and profit. If the costs for the allowance are more or less than the original estimate, the contract sum is adjusted accordingly by change order.

Detailed Quantity Takeoffs

The most precise kind of budget is developed by counting actual quantities of materials and furnishings and multiplying these quantities by firm, quoted costs. Such detailed estimates cannot be done until late in the design and construction document phase of a project. At this point, the work of revising the budget to a fairly exact level generally is divided between the interior designer and general contractor.

For furnishing costs, the interior designer develops a list of all the individual pieces of furniture required along with other items like window coverings, accessories, artwork, and anything else that is being specified by the designer. The exact manufacturers and model numbers are known, along with color and fabric selections, applicable discounts, delivery costs, and required taxes. For some small projects, furniture may be supplied by the designer, but for large commercial projects, furniture is often purchased through dealers who develop the purchase orders and finalize exact costs to the client. In either case, the final cost to the client can be easily calculated.

If the project involves construction, detailed quantity takeoffs can be made in several ways. For negotiated jobs, the selected contractor will take the construction documents and specifications and make a precise estimate, including overhead and profit. If the final quotation is too high, the client, interior designer, and contractor can work to change quantities or qualities of materials or the entire scope of the job to meet the budget. With several contractors bidding, the final quoted costs are not known until the bids are in. Before hiring a contractor, the client may also hire an independent cost estimator to develop a reasonably accurate budget.

Cost Information

One of the most difficult aspects of developing project budgets is obtaining current, reliable prices for the kinds of furnishings and construction units being used. Furnishings costs are a little easier to develop than construction costs because items are priced on a unit basis and price quotes and discounts from dealers are available at any time. However, from the early phases of a project until the time when purchase orders are actually written, costs and taxes can increase or the client may change his or her mind and request a more or less expensive item.

For construction costs, several commercially produced cost books are published annually. These books list costs in different ways; some are very detailed, giving the cost for labor and materials for individual construction components, while others list parameter costs and subsystem costs. There are even reference books oriented strictly toward interior design that give parameter costs for construction as well as furnishings.

For interior construction, there are also computerized cost estimating services that only require the interior designer to provide general information about the project, location, size, major materials, and so forth. The computer service then applies its current price database to the information and produces a cost budget. Many interior designers also work closely with general contractors to develop a realistic budget.

Remember, however, that commercially available cost information is the average of many past construction projects from around the country. Local variation and particular conditions may affect the value of its use on a specific project.

Two conditions that must be accounted for in developing any project budget are geographical location and inflation. These variables can be adjusted by using cost indexes that are published in a variety of sources, including the major architectural and construction trade magazines. Using a base year as index 1000, for example, for selected cities around the country, new indexes are developed each year that reflect the increase in costs (both material and labor) that year.

The indexes can be used to apply costs from one part of the country to another and to escalate past costs to the expected midpoint of construction of the project being budgeted.

Example 7.1

The cost index in a designer's city is 1257. The designer will be working on an interior construction project in another city, and the cost index for that city is 1308. If the expected construction cost is $1,250,000 based on prices for the designer's city, what will be the expected cost in the other city?

Divide the higher index by the lower index.

$$\Delta \text{CI} = \frac{\text{CI}_{\text{city B}}}{\text{CI}_{\text{city A}}} = \frac{1308}{1257} = 1.041$$

Multiply this by the base cost.

$$C = C_{\text{cityA}}\Delta \text{CI}$$

$$= (\$1{,}250{,}000)(1.041)$$

$$= \$1{,}300{,}716$$

Life-Cycle Cost Analysis

Life-cycle cost analysis (LCC) is a method for determining the total cost of a building or building component or system. It takes into account the initial costs of the element or system under consideration as well as the cost of financing, operation, maintenance, and disposal. Any residual value of the component value is subtracted from the other costs. The costs are estimated over a length of time called the study period. The duration of the study period varies with the needs of the client and the useful life of the material or system. For example, investors in a building may be interested in comparing various alternate materials over the expected investment time frame, while a city government may be interested in a longer time frame representing the expected life of the building. All future costs are discounted back to a common time, usually the base date, to account for the time value of money. The *discount* rate is used to convert future costs to their equivalent present values.

Using life-cycle cost analysis allows two or more alternatives to be evaluated and their total costs to be compared. This is especially useful when evaluating energy conservation measures where one design alternative may have a higher initial cost than another, but a lower overall cost because of energy savings. Some of the specific costs involved in a LCC of a building element include the following.

- Initial costs, which include the cost of acquiring and installing the element.

- Operational costs for electricity, water, and other utilities.

- Maintenance costs for the element over the length of the study period, including any repair costs.

- Replacement costs, if any, during the length of the study period.

- Finance costs required during the length of the study period.

- Taxes, if any, for initial costs and operating costs.

- Residual value, which is the remaining value of the element at the end of the study period based on resale value, salvage value, value in place, or scrap value.

The first six costs listed are estimated, discounted to their present value, and added together. Any residual value is discounted to its present value and then subtracted from the total to get the final life-cycle cost of the element.

Note that a life-cycle cost analysis is not the same as a life-cycle assessment (LCA). An LCA, as described in Ch. 26, analyzes the environmental impact of a product or building system over the entire life of the product or system.

SCHEDULING

There are two major parts of a project schedule: design time, and construction and installation time. The interior designer is responsible for developing the schedule for the design of the job and the production of contract documents. The designer may also be responsible for scheduling the ordering, delivery, and installation of furniture if that is part of the designer's agreement with the client.

Construction scheduling, on the other hand, is the responsibility of the contractor. However, the design professional must be able to estimate the entire project schedule so the client has a general idea of the total time that may be required to complete the project. For example, if the client must move by a certain date and normal design and construction sequences make this impossible, the interior designer may recommend a fast-track schedule or some other approach to meet the deadline.

At the beginning of a project, the designer must estimate the time required to complete the design and construction drawing production and must apportion this work among the people assigned to the project. The time is based on the scope of work, jointly defined by the client and designer, and is generally divided into phases of work as described in Ch. 20, including programming, schematic design, and so on. To assign an estimated time (usually in hours or days) to individual work tasks, the designer uses time records and experience in completing similar jobs. Ideally, this estimating process is used to establish the fees so there is enough time to do the job properly and still make a profit. The various methods of charging for professional fees are discussed in Ch. 25.

The time required for the various design phases is highly variable and depends on the following factors.

• The size and complexity of the project. Obviously, an 80,000 ft^2 (7430 m^2) office will take much longer to design than a 4000 ft^2 (300 m^2) office.

• The number of people working on the project. While adding more people to the job can shorten the schedule, there is a point of diminishing returns. Having too many people simply creates a management and coordination problem, and for some phases of a project will only require a few people, even for very large jobs.

• The abilities and design methodology of the project team. Younger, less experienced designers will usually require a little longer to do the same amount of work as senior staff.

• The type of client and the decision-making and approval processes of the client. Large corporations or public agencies are likely to have a multilayer decision-making and approval process. The time required for getting the necessary information or approval on one phase may take weeks or even months, whereas a small, single-authority client or residential client can make the same decision in a matter of days or hours.

• Fixed dates such as move-in, agency approval, or lease expiration over which the designer has no control.

Although the construction schedule is established by the contractor, it will usually be estimated by the interior designer during the programming phase so the client has some idea of total project time. When the designer does this, it should be made very clear to the client that it is only an estimate and that the interior designer cannot guarantee any time frame for the construction schedule.

There are several methods used to schedule both design and construction. The most common and easiest is the bar chart, sometimes called a Gantt chart. See Fig. 7.2. The various activities of the schedule are listed along the vertical axis, and a timeline is extended along the horizontal axis. Each activity is given a starting and finishing date, and overlaps are indicated by overlapping bars for each activity. Bar charts are simple to make and understand and are suitable for small to midsize projects. However, they cannot show all the sequences and dependencies of one activity on another.

Another scheduling tool often used is the critical path method, or CPM chart. A *CPM chart* graphically depicts all the tasks

Figure 7.2
Gantt Chart

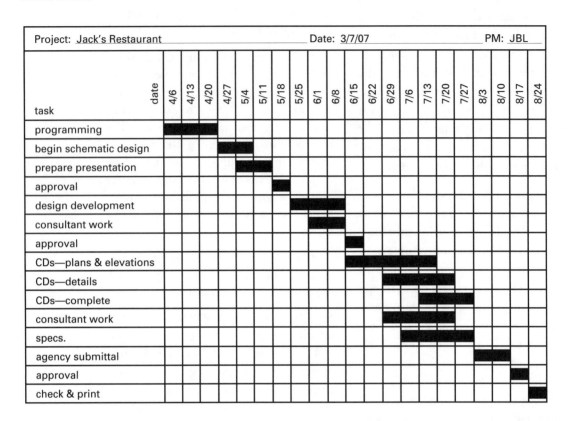

task	date	4/6	4/13	4/20	4/27	5/4	5/11	5/18	5/25	6/1	6/8	6/15	6/22	6/29	7/6	7/13	7/20	7/27	8/3	8/10	8/17	8/24
programming		██																				
begin schematic design				██																		
prepare presentation					██																	
approval						██																
design development								██														
consultant work									██													
approval											██											
CDs—plans & elevations											██	██										
CDs—details														██								
CDs—complete															██	██						
consultant work														██								
specs.														██								
agency submittal																			██			
approval																				██		
check & print																						██

Project: Jack's Restaurant   Date: 3/7/07   PM: JBL

required to complete a project, the sequence in which they must occur, their duration, the earliest or latest possible starting time, and the earliest or latest possible finishing time. It also defines the sequence of critical tasks or tasks that must be started and finished exactly on time if the total schedule is to be met. A CPM chart for a simple design project is shown in Fig. 7.3.

Each arrow in the CPM chart represents an activity with a beginning and end point (represented by the numbered circles). No activity can begin until all activities leading into the circle have been completed. The heavy line in the illustration shows the critical path, or the sequence of events that must happen as scheduled if the deadline is to be met. The numbers under the activities give the duration of the activity in days. The noncritical activities can begin or finish earlier or later (within limits)

without affecting the final completion date. For very large, complex projects using the critical path method, computer programs are often used to develop and update the schedule.

Another technique sometimes used by contractors for large jobs is the program evaluation and review technique, or *PERT chart*. This is similar to the CPM technique but uses different charting methods.

Although schedules using these methods can be produced manually, there are numerous software programs available to simplify the process, especially for complex projects that span a long time period.

One useful technique for developing a schedule while at the same time involving all members of the design and construction team (including the client) is to complete a *full wall schedule*. With this process

Figure 7.3
CPM Chart

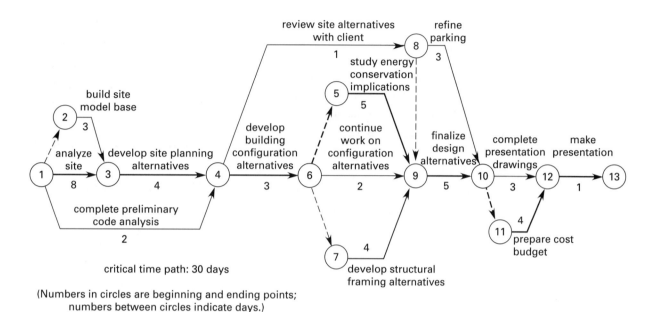

review site alternatives with client
refine parking

build site model base

study energy conservation implications

analyze site

develop building configuration alternatives

continue work on configuration alternatives

finalize design alternatives

complete presentation drawings

make presentation

develop site planning alternatives

complete preliminary code analysis

develop structural framing alternatives

prepare cost budget

critical time path: 30 days

(Numbers in circles are beginning and ending points; numbers between circles indicate days.)

vertical lines are drawn 5 in apart on an entire wall, with the space between each line representing one week. The project manager develops a preliminary list of project tasks and names of individuals who may be responsible for completing the tasks. Each task is written on two 3 in × 5 in index cards with one labeled "start" and one labeled "finish." The names of all the people responsible for tasks are placed along the left edge of the chart. Each person is asked to place the start and finish cards where they think the activity should be placed in the total schedule, to indicate the time they need allotted for the task. This large, interactive schedule serves as a starting point for discussion among everyone on the project team. Cards can be moved around easily, and once everyone agrees, the schedule can be copied in a smaller format and used by everyone on the team.

SAMPLE QUESTIONS

1. An interior designer recommends that a client purchase appliances directly rather than through a general contractor. What would be the primary reason for this recommendation?

(A) The client could avoid the contractor's markup.

(B) The client could not be overcharged for delivery and installation.

(C) The interior designer could provide the client a broader selection by acting as the client's agent.

(D) The client could get a better discount than the contractor.

2. Based on previous projects, it is known that it costs about $45/ft to construct a full-height partition. On the project now being budgeted, there are about 350 ft of this type of partition. If the contractor's overhead and profit are estimated to be 14%, how much should the interior designer budget for this line item?

- (A) $15,120
- (B) $15,750
- (C) $17,950
- (D) $18,900

3. Bids have been submitted by four contractors on a midsize restaurant. The lowest bid is 10% over the client's budget, and the next lowest bid is 12% over budget. What is the interior designer's best course of action?

- (A) Suggest that the client obtain additional financing for the extra 10%, and accept the lowest bid.
- (B) Accept the lowest bid, and tell the contractor that if he wants the job he should reduce his bid by 10%.
- (C) Work with the client to redesign the project to reduce the cost.
- (D) Remind the client that the designer is not responsible for construction costs, and tell the client that additional money must be found.

4. Which of the following is generally NOT considered FF&E?

- (A) a commissioned sculpture bolted to a wall
- (B) vending machines built into an opening
- (C) wall-to-wall carpeting
- (D) vertical blinds

5. When designing a project in an unfamiliar city, what is the best source of cost data?

- (A) the most current cost data book with prices adjusted for geographical location and inflation
- (B) a local contractor who builds projects of a similar type
- (C) a computerized cost database targeted for that city
- (D) interior designers and architects who practice in that city and design projects of a similar type

6. In addition to construction, what are the major cost components of most interior design projects?

- (A) furnishings, taxes, signal systems, and moving
- (B) furnishings, professional fees, taxes, and telephone installation
- (C) fixtures, overhead and profit, moving, and telephone installation
- (D) furniture, fixtures, taxes, and moving

7. Which method provides the most accurate estimate of project cost?

- (A) square footage
- (B) functional unit
- (C) parameter
- (D) quantity takeoff

8. In preparing a budget, which of the following elements would an interior designer most likely ask the client to include?

- (A) legal fees and artwork consulting
- (B) taxes on furniture and computer system installation
- (C) contingencies and an interior designer's fee
- (D) furnishings and furniture delivery

9. A line item included in a budget to account for unknown conditions is called a

- (A) unit price
- (B) parameter
- (C) contingency
- (D) budget adjustment

10. Furniture budgets can be accurately estimated by the

- (A) general contractor and furniture manufacturer
- (B) interior designer and furniture dealers
- (C) furniture representative and client
- (D) furniture manufacturer and interior designer

8

ELEMENTS OF DESIGN

To create spaces that satisfy the functional and aesthetic goals of a problem, interior designers make use of several design elements according to some basic principles. These design elements and principles are the same ones used by painters, graphic designers, sculptors, and other visual artists. Familiarity with these concepts and skill in their use are essential to successful completion of the NCIDQ exam. The examinee's knowledge of these concepts is tested with multiple-choice questions, and these design elements and principles must be properly applied in the three-dimensional exercise. This chapter discusses the individual elements of design, and the next chapter shows how these elements can be combined according to several fundamental principles.

FORM

Form is the basic shape and configuration of an object or space. It is often the way we first distinguish one thing as being different from another. For example, the form of a chair is different from the form of the wall behind it. There are an infinite number of possible forms, but people most often generalize and describe forms with words such as *cylindrical, flat, square,* or *linear*. Although an object or space can be viewed in isolation, their form is usually viewed in relation to other forms according to the principles discussed in Ch. 9. Form gives the interior designer a powerful tool to create order, establish mood, and coordinate the diverse components of a finished space.

However, the form of an object or space can be affected by other factors such as light, color, and the other basic elements discussed in this chapter as well as by the effects of human perception. A circle seen obliquely becomes an ellipse, for example. Optical illusions may also alter the perceived form of an object.

Form or shape is generated with lines, planes, volumes, and to a lesser extent, points. Each has its own characteristics, strengths, and limitations for interior design. Even though geometric points, lines, and planes do not have a third dimension, people perceive a third dimension when the second or third dimension greatly exceeds the theoretically nonexistent dimension. For example, in Fig. 8.1(a) the balusters of the railing read as linear elements because

Figure 8.1
Linear and
Planar
Construction

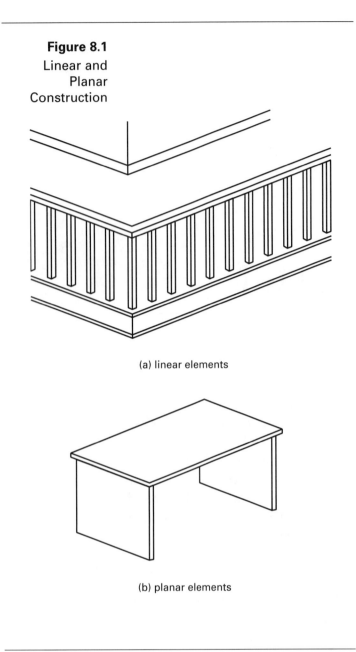

(a) linear elements

(b) planar elements

Figure 8.2
Points
Suggesting
Direction

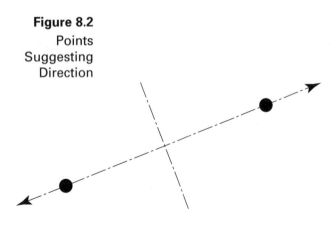

their length is much greater than their width and depth.

Point

Theoretically, a point is a position with no dimension. Practically, a *point* is perceived when a two-dimensionally perceived object appears relatively small in relation to the plane against which it is seen. Although points are typically conceived of as very small dots, a point can be any shape as long as its dimension is very small in relation to its background.

The perception of points in architecture and interior design depends on distance. A painting on a wall is a plane viewed from a few feet away but becomes a point when viewed from a distance of 100 ft. Because viewing on the interior of most buildings occurs at a relatively close range, an object that is to be perceived as a point must be fairly small as a figure in relation to the ground against which it is placed.

A single point creates a location or position. Two points create both a distance between them and an implied direction between the points as well as an implied direction between the points perpendicular to the imaginary line connecting them. See Fig. 8.2. When several points are used close together and in alignment, they can create a line according the principals of Gestalt psychology discussed in Ch. 3.

Points used in groups can create either a static composition or a dynamic one and energize the plane on which they are placed. For example, as shown in Fig. 8.3, small pictures (point figures) can be placed statically or dynamically on a wall. The same effect can be achieved with small window openings in a partition. Because people generally perceive space by looking forward at vertical surfaces, composition with points generally works best on walls, but small point objects can be suspended on the ceiling plane or the floor plane.

Line

A *line* is an object or form whose actual or visual length greatly exceeds any actual width or depth it may have. Lines are also formed and perceived where one plane meets another, where edges occur, and where there is a change in material, texture, or color. Lines convey a very strong directional sense and can affect a person's feeling about a space. Horizontal lines are generally perceived as restful, stable, and related to the plane of the earth. Vertical lines usually connote strength, equilibrium, permanence, and a strong upward movement. Diagonal lines are dynamic and often represent movement, either upward or downward depending on the slope of the line. Curved lines relate more to the natural world and the human body. They are graceful and suggest gentle movement. Curved lines can be either geometric, like circles, arcs, and ellipses, or free form.

Lines can also affect the perception of the space in which they are used. Generally, a vertical line appears longer than a horizontal line of the same length. See Fig. 8.4. Various theories have been offered to explain this phenomenon. One is that vertical lines often represent lines extending away from the observer, so they are seen as being foreshortened and the brain adds length to them. Another explanation is that seeing horizontally is more natural for humans, so looking vertically requires more effort. Whatever the reason, the effect seems to hold true in many cases. Vertical lines tend to make a space appear higher than it is, while horizontal lines tend to make a space appear lower.

Diagonal lines are the most dynamic and exist in interior design and architecture two different ways. First, they may be actual diagonal lines relative to the vertical

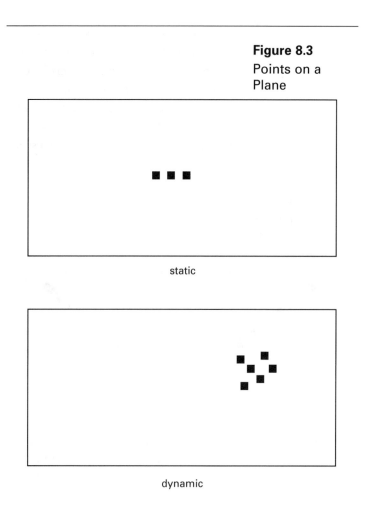

Figure 8.3
Points on a Plane

static

dynamic

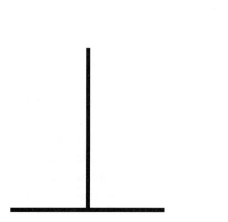

Figure 8.4
Apparent Length Differences

and horizontal. Second, they always exist in the field of vision because of the way people perceive vertical and horizontal lines in perspective. Used appropriately, diagonal lines can enliven a space, direct the eye, and create a sense of movement. As shown in Fig. 8.5, a line sloping from upper left to lower right suggests down-ward movement while the opposite slope suggests upward movement. This is probably due to people's tendency to read shapes from left to right. While diagonal lines can be dynamic, if not used carefully, they can create an imbalance in a space.

Figure 8.5
Movement
Created with
Diagonal Lines

Lines can be introduced into a space by using objects with strong linear forms, by structural elements, by applied decoration, with applied finish materials, and even with lighting. The designer can use line as a basic design element to create the desired effect in concert with other elements.

Plane

A *plane* is a form with two dominant dimensions, length and width. See Fig. 8.1(b). As with lines, all planes in the real world have some depth, but that dimension is not perceived as much as the dominant dimensions. For example, a 3 ft^2 tabletop with a 1 in thickness appears planar, while the same 3 ft top with a 6 in edge appears massive and three dimensional.

Planes are a significant component of interior design because space is typically defined by planar surfaces like walls, ceilings, and floors. Even furniture and other objects are usually constructed of planes. Unlike lines, planes help determine the form of a space with the additional characteristics of shape, texture, color, and pattern. Because of this, planes

are a major factor in determining the character of a space.

A plane can be treated as a single surface with only one color and texture, or it can be subdivided like a painting, with different individual materials, textures, and colors. The planes used to define a space can be harmonized or contrasted with the planar forms of furniture, accessories, and other elements.

Volume

Volume is the true three-dimensional aspect of interior design because an object with volume is clearly perceived as a spatial form having length, width, and depth. Volume can be either solid or void, sometimes referred to as positive or negative space, or figure-ground, as described in Ch. 3. As shown in Fig. 8.6, a *solid* is a form that has mass and appears to occupy space. A *void* is space itself, defined by planes or other elements.

An object with volume has definite shape and is usually perceived and categorized as regular (such as cubic, cylindrical, or the like), as irregular (such as free-form shapes or very complex shapes), or by a dominant characteristic (such as tall, narrow, curvilinear, or pie-shaped). As with other design elements, volume can be employed to enhance the overall desired effect of a spatial composition.

Shape

Shape is the unique characteristic of an object or space that defines it as distinct from adjacent objects or spaces. Shapes are clearly distinguished by planar or volumetric forms and can be geometric (like a square, circle, or cylinder), irregular (like a free-form table), or natural (like a tree). It is also possible to combine these categories. A tree, for example, can have a globular, pyramidal, or ovoid geometrical shape.

          PROFESSIONAL PUBLICATIONS, INC.

Shape can convey powerful symbolic or emotional qualities. The shape of a cross or the outline of an apple, for example, are not just abstract forms but carry definite meanings for some people. That meaning can vary greatly depending on the culture, background, and experience of the person viewing the shape. On a more basic level, some shapes tend to have associative qualities that are similar for large groups of people. For example, a square generally suggests a rational, stable form with no directionality. A circle implies unity and completeness with a definite focus at its center. A triangle is a stable but dynamic shape. Structurally, it is a rigid shape because it cannot change shape unless the length of one of its sides is changed.

SCALE

Scale is the relative size of something as related to another element of known size. *Proportion*, discussed in Ch. 9, is simply the relationship of parts of a composition to each other and to the whole. Human scale is the most common scale, in which objects and spaces are judged relative to the size and form of the human body. This comparison can occur directly or indirectly. For example, the volume of a room can be compared with a person standing in the room, or the same space can be compared with something inanimate that has a direct relationship with a human, like a chair. In either case, the judgment of the room's scale is the same. See Fig. 8.7.

Other judgments of scale occur when one object or space is seen in relationship with the size of another object or space. For example, in Fig. 8.8(a) the smaller openings make the major space onto which they open seem larger than the same space as it appears in (b). However, in neither case is there much of a clue as to the true size of the space, because no relationship to a human or any other known size is shown.

Figure 8.6
Positive and Negative Space

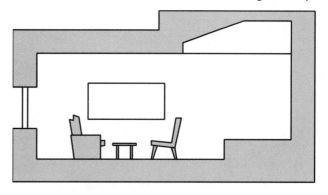

(a) solid—positive space

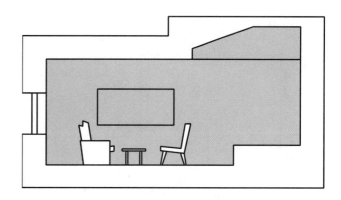

(b) void—negative space

Even though human scale is vitally important for interior design, decisions are often made based on the scale relationships between two or more nonhuman objects. For example, an 8 in × 10 in framed photograph will look hopelessly out of scale on a wall 20 ft long with a 10 ft high ceiling, regardless of how artfully it is positioned.

There are no definite rules for scale relationships. The judgment of scale is always complex because of the multitude of objects within a space, the form of the space itself, and the way the perception of objects and spaces is affected by color, value, texture, lighting, repetition, and other factors. The "correct" scale is also dependent on the design intent. Scale can be used to give

Figure 8.7
Scale Based on
Known Objects

Figure 8.8
Scale
Relationships

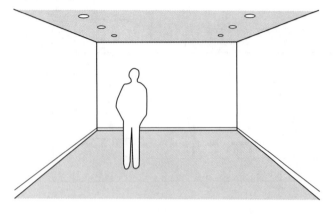

(a) small-scale space

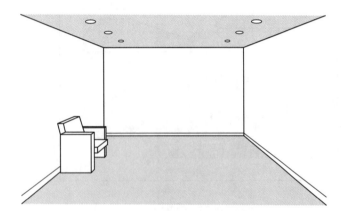

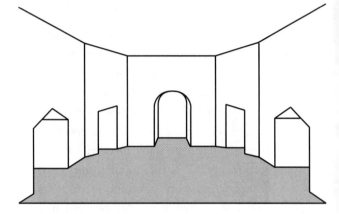

(b) large-scale space

spaces an intimate feeling or a monumental character. It can be used to provide emphasis and contrast or to harmonize otherwise diverse forms.

COLOR

Color is one of the most dominant perceptions of the physical world and one of the most powerful tools for interior design. At the same time, color is one of the most complex physical and psychological phenomenon to understand and use correctly. This section describes some of the fundamentals of color and its use.

Color Basics

Color is a physical property of visible light that is one part of the larger electromagnetic spectrum, which also includes other radiation like X-rays and infrared light. Each color is differentiated from the others by its wavelength. Red has the longest wavelength of the visible spectrum, while violet has the shortest wavelength. The eye and brain perceive variations in wavelengths to give the sensation of color. When all the colors of light are present in equal amounts, we perceive white light. For this reason, colors created with light are called *additive colors*.

The color of an object is conveyed by the color of light the object absorbs and the amount of light it reflects to the eye. For example, a blue object absorbs, or subtracts, most of the colors of light except blue, which is reflected to the eye. For this reason, colors created with pigments are called *subtractive colors*. When all the colors of a pigment are present in equal amounts, the viewer perceives no color, or black. When pigments are mixed in unequal amounts, they absorb various colors of light striking them.

The three primary colors of light are red, green, and blue. In various combinations and quantities, these three colors can create the other colors. They produce white light when combined equally. The three primary colors of pigments are yellow, red, and blue. Theoretically, all other colors can be produced by mixing various proportions of the primaries. This arrangement is typically shown on a circle known as the color wheel, illustrated in Figure 8.9.

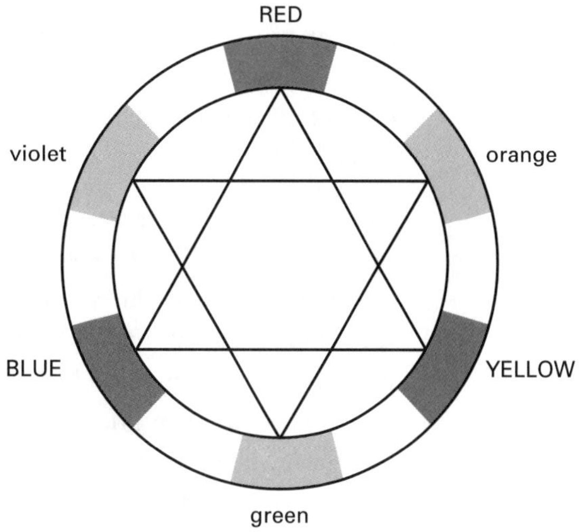

Color has three basic qualities: hue, value, and intensity (or chroma). The *hue* is the basic color, that attribute by which, for example, blue is distinguished from red. The *value* describes the degree of lightness or darkness of color in relation to white and black. The *intensity* (or chroma) of a color is defined by the degree of purity of the hue when compared with a neutral gray of the same value. These basic qualities of color are represented diagrammatically in Figure 8.10. When white is added to a hue, its value is raised and a tint is created. When black is added, its value is lowered and a shade is created. Adding gray of the same value to a hue creates a tone. A tone can also be created by adding its complement, the hue of the color opposite it on the color wheel.

Color Systems

Many systems have been developed to describe and quantify color. Some deal with light and some focus on pigments, while others try to define color strictly in mathematical terms. For most interior design purposes it is necessary to be familiar with at least two of the commonly used

systems: the Brewster system and the Munsell system.

The *Brewster color system*, also known as the *Prang color system*, is the familiar color wheel that organizes color pigments into the three primary colors of red, blue, and yellow. See Fig. 8.9. In this case, "primary"

Figure 8.9
Brewster Color Wheel

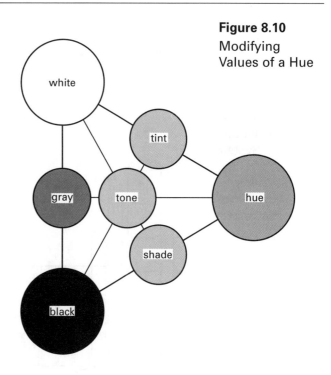

Figure 8.10
Modifying Values of a Hue

means that these colors cannot be mixed from other pigments. When the primary colors are mixed in equal amounts, they produce the secondary colors of violet, orange, and green. In turn, when a primary color is mixed with an adjacent secondary color on the color wheel, a tertiary color is created.

The *Munsell color system* defines color more accurately than the color wheel and uses three scales in three dimensions to specify the values of hue, value, and chroma (intensity). Figure 8.11 shows these scales. There are five principle hues (yellow, green, blue, purple, and red), designated by a single letter, and five intermediate hues, designated by two letters, all arranged in a circle. Each of these ten hues is subdivided into four parts and given the numbers 2.5, 5, 7.5, and 10. Each of the ten basic hues is given the number 5, indicating that they are midway

between the adjacent hues and represent the most saturated color of that particular hue. When necessary, the colors can be further subdivided into 100 different hues.

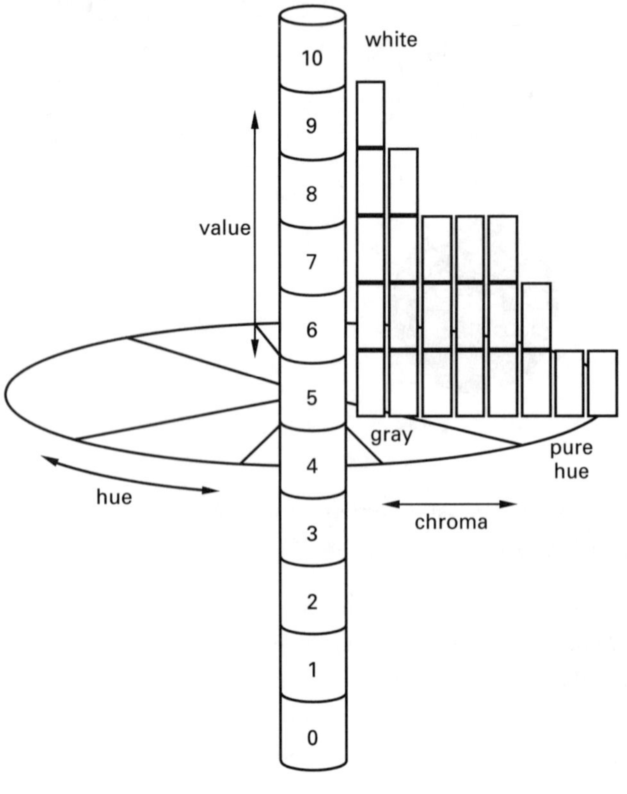

Value (the degree of lightness or darkness) is represented by a scale at the hub of the circle and consists of nine neutral grays plus white and black. White is at the top of the scale and is given the number 10, and black is at the bottom with a value of 0.

Chroma is represented on a scale extending outward from the value axis. At the outside of the chroma scale the color is most saturated; as the color moves toward the center, it comes closer to a neutral gray of the same value. Because different hues have different maximum saturation strengths at different value levels, the number of chroma steps varies with the hue, so the three-dimensional Munsell color solid is not a symmetrical form.

Any color in the Munsell system can be designated with a combination of letters and numbers. For example, G/6/3 is a principle hue of green with a value 6 and a chroma position of 3.

Effects of Adjacent Colors and Light

Like all other aspects of interior design, a single color does not exist in isolation. It affects and is affected by surrounding colors and by the color of the light striking it. There are many specific examples of how two colors affect each other when seen together. Some of the most common examples follow.

• Complementary colors (those opposite each other on the color wheel) re-inforce each other. This phenomenon manifests itself in several ways. For example, when someone stares at one color for some time and then looks at a white surface, an afterimage of the color's complement is seen. In addition, an object's color will induce its complement in the background. When two complementary

Figure 8.11
Munsell Color
System

colors are seen adjacent to each other, each appears to heighten the other's saturation. When a small area of one color is placed on a background of a complementary color, the small area of color becomes more intense.

• When two noncomplementary colors are placed together, each appears to tint the other with its own complement. This means that the two colors will seem farther apart on the color wheel than they are.

• Two primary colors seen together will tend to appear tinted with the third primary.

• A light color placed against a darker background will appear lighter than it is, while a dark color against a lighter background will appear darker than it actually is. Figure 8.12 shows an identical value placed against two contrasting backgrounds. This is known as simultaneous contrast.

• A background color will absorb the same color in a second, noncomplementary color placed over it. For example, an orange spot on a red background will appear more yellow because the red "absorbs" the red in the orange sample.

• A neutral gray will appear warm when placed on a blue background and cool when placed on a red background.

One of the most important aspects of color interaction is how light affects the appearance of a color. Even though the human eye often perceives all light as white, each light source carries some colors more than others. For instance, incandescent light is very yellow while mid-day sunlight is predominantly blue. Cool white fluorescent lamps have a large blue and green component, and warm white fluorescent lamps have a higher yellow and orange spectral distribution.

In general, light that has a particularly strong hue component will intensify colors with similar hues and neutralize colors

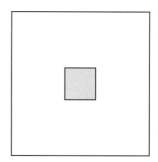

Figure 8.12
Simultaneous Contrast

of complementary hues. For example, a red object seen under incandescent light will appear red and vibrant, while a blue object of the same value will appear washed out and muddy. The same blue object, however, would be rendered closer to its actual color if seen under mid-day light or under a cool white fluorescent light. Because of this fact, color selections should be made under the same type of lighting that is going to exist in the final interior installation.

The amount of light also affects color. Dim lighting reduces a color's value and diminishes its hue. High lighting levels can either intensify the hue or make the color appear washed out.

The Psychology of Color

In addition to its physical effects on the eye and brain, color carries with it many symbolic and associative meanings. For example, in many cultures red means danger or stop. Although there has been a large amount of research on the effects of color on humans, much of it is inconclusive or conflicting. This is partly due to the large number of variables that exist when talking about color, such as the physiology of color perception, the situation under which color is seen, cultural values, the value and chroma of the colors viewed, and the environment, to name just a few.

There are, however, some general statements that seem to hold true for most people. The first is that people distinguish between cool and warm colors. The cool colors are generally considered to be blue, green, and violet, while the warm colors are red, yellow, and orange. Cool colors are considered to be restful and quiet; warm colors are seen as active and stimulating. Reds are often seen as exciting and hot. Yellows are regarded as cheerful. Greens are associated with nature and are sometimes used to connote cool, restful environments. Blues are also cool colors and can be calming and restful while implying dignity in some situations. Of course, much of a color's effect also depends on its value and intensity. A light value of a color will make a room appear larger, while the same hue in a dark value will make the room appear smaller.

Effect of Color on Spatial Perception

Hue, value, and chroma of color can be used in many ways to affect the appearance of a space and the objects in it. Bright, warm colors tend to make an object, such as a piece of furniture, appear larger. A dark color will make an object look smaller and heavier. Light, neutral colors extend the apparent space of a room while dark values make a space feel closed in. Warm colors tend to advance while cool colors recede.

These principles can be used to modify the spatial quality of a room. For example, a long, narrow room can be "widened" by painting the end walls with a bright, warm color and by painting the side walls a lighter, cooler color. A high ceiling can be "lowered" by painting it a darker color. Individual pieces of furniture can be made more prominent if they are much lighter than a background of dark floors and walls. Conversely, a large object can appear

to be smaller if its color is light and similar to its background.

Color Schemes

There are five common methods of using color, and these are applicable regardless of the specific hues employed. These color schemes are monochromatic, analogous, complementary, triad, and tetrad.

A *monochromatic color scheme* employs one hue with variations only in intensity and value. Although monochromatic systems are fairly easy to develop and almost always work, they can become monotonous if used in an area that is occupied continuously. A monotone scheme is a variation of this type, but it consists of only a single hue of low intensity (near gray) in one or a very limited range of values. It is best used where a neutral background is needed for other activities, as in an art gallery where the space should not compete with the artwork.

Analogous color schemes use hues that are close to each other on the color wheel. An analogous color scheme might include such combinations as one primary color, one secondary, and the tertiary between them, or one primary and one secondary with the colors on either side of them. Generally, the colors in an analogous scheme will not extend beyond one 90° segment of the color wheel. In most cases, analogous systems work best if one color is dominant and the others are subordinate.

When hues on opposite sides of the color wheel are used it is called a *complementary color scheme*. Because complementary hues can be harsh when viewed together, large areas of colors are generally of low chroma (grayer) and are a tint or shade of the color. Smaller areas or accents can have a higher chroma. One variation of this scheme is a split complementary in which a color on one side of the color wheel is used with two hues that lie on either side of the complementary color. A similar variation is the double complementary in which four hues are used: a pair on either side of two complements. In either case, one color should be dominant and used at low levels of chroma.

A *triad color scheme* uses colors equally spaced around the color wheel, such as yellow-orange, blue-green, and red-violet. Because of the potential for producing a confusing, glaring appearance, triad schemes, like complementary schemes, employ low-chroma tints or shades except for possibly one intense color that is used as an accent.

Finally, a *tetrad color scheme* uses four colors that are equally spaced around the wheel. Tetrad schemes are difficult to do well because a wide range of color is used. As with triad and complementary schemes, one or two colors should dominate and be of lower chroma.

TEXTURE

Texture is the surface quality of a material. It results from the inherent structure of the material or from the application of some type of coating over the material. Most people think of texture as the relative smoothness or roughness of a surface and associate certain textures with certain materials: metal is smooth while brick is rough.

Although every material has a specific texture, the perception of texture is closely tied to the texture's visual qualities, the relationship of the texture with surrounding textures, the viewing distance, and the lighting. Altering any one of these can affect the final, perceived appearance of the material.

Texture can be either actual or visual. Actual texture is the physical quality that can be sensed by touch: the smoothness of polished marble, the roughness of concrete, or the fuzziness of a wool fabric. Visual texture is what people imagine a surface to be simply by looking at it and based on a memory of similar textures. Viewed close up, the viewer can know concrete is a rough texture without touching it. Every actual texture has an associated visual texture, but visual textures do not necessarily have an actual texture. For example, artificial prints of wood grain or woven mat on a plastic laminate surface look textured but are actually quite smooth. Trompe l'oeil painting can produce a wide variety of apparent textures with very smooth, flat paint.

A texture is also affected by its relationship to nearby textures through scale relationships. Sand finish plaster may seem very rough next to a flat, smooth, shiny metal, but it will be perceived as relatively smooth next to an exposed aggregate concrete wall. It is important to remember this when combining a number of textures within the same space. See Fig. 8.13.

Similarly, texture changes based on viewing distance. Because of the limitations on the resolving powers of the human eye, any given surface appears smoother the farther away it gets. What may appear as a rough texture when selected in a showroom 2 ft away may become very smooth when applied to a wall that most people will see from 20 ft.

Finally, the way a surface is lighted alters the apparent texture. Very diffuse lighting or strong, direct lighting tends to wash out texture, while strong side lighting will emphasize the actual texture. Conversely, texture affects the perception of light. Smooth, glossy surfaces reflect light sharply, often creating glare or showing surface imperfections. Matte or rough textures tend to diffuse and absorb light, reducing the apparent brightness and color of a surface.

Texture can be a powerful design tool if used properly. Texture adds interest to a

Figure 8.13
Perception of
Textures

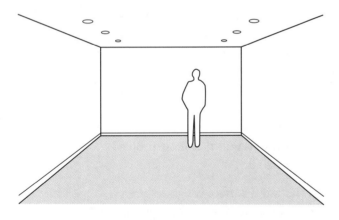

Figure 8.14
Modifying Space
with Texture

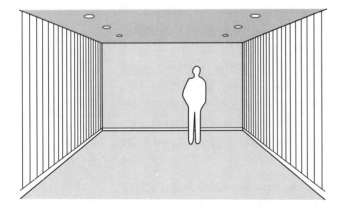

space, reinforces the design concept, helps differentiate objects and surfaces from each other, modulates light, and adds scale. For example, a contemporary interior can be enhanced by using smooth or very finely textured materials. On the other hand, a "traditional" room may look best with heavier fabrics and dark wood textures. In another case, a large room can be made to seem smaller by using heavy textures, which tend to bring surfaces closer, as diagrammed in Fig. 8.14. Texture can also be used to provide emphasis or focus on one part of a space.

PATTERN

Pattern is the repetition of a decorative motif on a surface. It is closely related to texture, but the individual elements of a pattern are usually discernible (at a reasonable viewing distance) as individual items, whereas texture appears as an overall tone. See Fig. 8.15. However, if a pattern becomes very small or is viewed from a distance, it can blend into a visual texture. Texture is also generally considered a two-dimensional quality of plane surfaces, while pattern can be a two-dimensional or linear composition.

Pattern can be built into a material, like ceramic tile or concrete block, or it can be applied with wallpaper or paint. However it is created, pattern can add visual interest to a space, change the scale of a room, and reinforce the design concept. Like texture, though, it should be used carefully. Excessively bold patterns or the juxtaposition of too many patterns in the same space creates a busy and overpowering space.

LIGHT

Light is basic to interior design. It is the means by which all the other aspects of the environment are seen, and it strongly affects *how* space and objects are perceived. The same space can be made to take on many different appearances simply by changing how it is illuminated. Because of this, lighting is a powerful design tool. This section briefly outlines some of the basic design elements of lighting. Chapter 19 describes in more detail the design and technical requirements of lighting.

Good lighting is an art as well as a science. Because light has both a physiological and emotional effect on people, it is not simply enough to provide a sufficient quantity of light. The quality of light must also be considered. For example, excessive contrast can cause the iris to open and close constantly as it tries to compensate for variations in illumination. This leads to physical fatigue, sore eyes, and other physical ailments. At the same time, absolute uniformity in lighting levels can be monotonous and dull.

Both the light source and its effect should be considered as design elements. A light source can be a point, line, plane, or volume and can have the qualities of brightness and color. The illumination the light provides can, in turn, be seen as a point, line, or plane on objects and surfaces, each with its own brightness and color. With these effects, lighting can be used with other design elements to provide emphasis, rhythm, balance, and contrast.

Because lighting is both an art and science, a good lighting scheme requires a combination of technical and aesthetic sensibilities. The general lighting level must, of course, provide sufficient illumination for the activities taking place. Detrimental situations like glare, excessive contrast, and inaccurate color rendition must be avoided. Beyond this, however, a good lighting design can

- set or enhance the mood of the interior space

- add interest to the visual environment

- accent and emphasize objects and areas

- de-emphasize undesirable areas or architectural features

Figure 8.15
Patterns

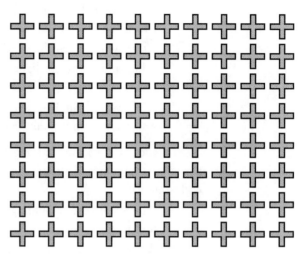

(a) two-dimensional pattern

(b) linear pattern

- highlight surfaces and textures

- enhance color

- affect spatial perception

The methods for achieving these effects and the lighting tools available are discussed in more detail in Ch. 19.

SAMPLE QUESTIONS

1. A client has asked a designer to create an intimate seating area for a hospital waiting room. Which of the following is likely to have the greatest impact on achieving the client's goal?

(A) pattern

(B) scale

(C) texture

(D) color

2. To give a sofa a heavy appearance, the designer should use which of the following color combinations for the sofa and the surrounding walls?

(A) a hue with a dark value for the sofa and a slightly lighter value for the walls

(B) a light colored sofa of any hue and a dark value wall color

(C) a sofa with a warm hue and dark value and a much lighter wall color

(D) a sofa with a light, cool color and a wall color of similar value and hue

3. A good selection for lighting to enhance the appearance of a rough, plastered wall would be

(A) fluorescent cove uplighting on all four sides of the room

(B) decorative chandeliers near the wall

(C) track lighting near the center of the room, aimed at the wall

(D) recessed incandescents close to the wall

4. A Parsons table primarily uses which of the following types of design elements?

(A) plane and volume

(B) line and plane

(C) plane and point

(D) volume and line

5. To create the most vivid and easily perceived color-coding system in an elderly housing facility, the interior designer should use which of the following combinations?

(A) a bright color against a background of a noncomplementary color

(B) complementary colors of high saturation

(C) either highly saturated warm or cool colors next to a neutral gray

(D) the primary colors and white

6. Which design elements could be used to lower the apparent height of a ceiling?

(A) a dark, highly textured ceiling

(B) strong horizontal lines on the walls

(C) fine-grained patterns on the ceiling and dark walls

(D) a light ceiling and textured walls

7. The Prang system organizes colors according to

(A) three scales of hue, value, and chroma in a three-dimensional form

(B) the hue and value in a matrix system

(C) their relationship to the primaries as organized in a circle

(D) five principle hues and their values on a wheel

8. Wallpaper is most useful to a designer in creating

(A) texture

(B) line

(C) scale

(D) pattern

9. When three colors near each other on the standard color wheel are used together, the scheme is called

(A) monochromatic

(B) triad

(C) complementary

(D) analogous

10. When black is added to a color, the result is called a

(A) tint

(B) shade

(C) tone

(D) value

PRINCIPLES OF DESIGN

BALANCE

Balance is the arrangement of elements in a composition to achieve visual equilibrium. Balance is important in interior design because every interior is composed of a wide variety of forms, shapes, colors, lines, patterns, textures, and light. Functional needs may determine much of the way an interior is designed, but the final composition must still be coordinated to establish a comfortable environment.

Balance depends on the idea of visual weight. To the human eye, some elements appear "heavier" than others by the nature of their size, shape, complexity, color, texture, or location in space. These elements can be balanced by other objects in a variety of ways.

A good analogy is that of a balancing scale as diagrammed in Fig. 9.1. Two identical objects are in balance if they weigh exactly the same and are placed an identical distance away from the fulcrum, or balance point. If one object is half as heavy as the other, things will still be balanced if the lighter object is placed twice as far from the fulcrum as the heavier one. Balance

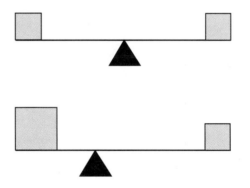

Figure 9.1
Balance of Visual Weight

depends on both object (weight) and placement.

For interior design (as well as architecture, graphics, and other visual arts) balance is not quite as exact or objective as weighing objects on a scale, but the same principles apply. Some of the ways objects or elements vary in visual weight include the following.

• Large objects are heavier than smaller objects with the same form, shape, color, and texture.

• Highly textured or detailed elements are heavier than plain elements.

• Dark elements are heavier than lightly shaded elements.

- Bright colors carry more "weight" than neutral colors.

- Complex or unusual shapes weigh more than simple shapes.

- Several small objects closely grouped can balance a single object with the same area.

Of course, it is possible to modify each of these guidelines by combining them in different ways. A small form can become heavier than a much larger identical form by adding texture, color, or other detail. See Fig. 9.2.

Figure 9.2
Variation in
Visual Weight

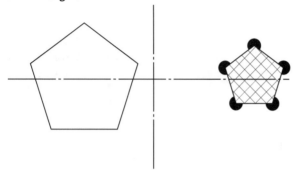

As with the balancing scale analogy, position is important, and all visual compositions have a balance point or axis or a field within which the balancing takes place. For example, in Fig. 9.3(a) two adjacent shapes appear to be balanced about the imaginary vertical axis. If these objects are seen as pictures on the wall of a room (the field), they do not have the same balance if placed so that the physical distances from each of their edges to the ends of the room are identical. See Fig. 9.3(b). Increasing the space between the end of the room and only one object places them even more out of balance. See Figs. 9.3(c) and (d). However, when the center of the room coincides with the imaginary point of balance, the composition appears balanced. See Fig. 9.3(e). In

many cases, the field of the objects, or negative space, also becomes an important part of the composition.

Establishing balance in interior design is a challenge because there are so many variables and because balance must be created in three dimensions, unlike in a painting or graphic. What may appear balanced in a floor plan can be severely imbalanced when the space is viewed normally.

The three types of balance—symmetrical, asymmetrical, and radial—are described in the following sections. In most interior designs they are used together, but one will have dominance.

Symmetrical Balance

Symmetrical balance consists of identical elements arranged equally about a common axis as shown in Fig. 9.4. This is also called bisymmetrical, bilateral, or axial symmetry. The common axis may be an actual object, like the peak of a cathedral ceiling, or an imaginary centerline about which the elements are ordered. This type of balance is very stable and typically connotes formality. Many traditional interior designs are based on this kind of balance. Symmetry can emphasize either the area in the middle of the composition or a focal point at one or both ends of the axis.

In most cases, a purely symmetrical organization is not possible because of existing limitations of architectural space or required functional arrangements. Even if it is possible, absolute symmetry may not be desirable because it can be too static and formal. However, it can be used in combination with other organizational principles. For example, a perfectly symmetrical seating group may be placed asymmetrically within a room and balanced with another symmetrical arrangement of furniture.

The perception of symmetry is most likely to occur when elements are symmetrical about the vertical axis rather than the horizontal axis. See Fig. 9.5. Even though both compositions of squares are symmetrical in this illustration, the arrangement in Fig. 9.5(a) appears immediately symmetrical, while the arrangement in Fig. 9.5(b) first appears out of balance.

Asymmetrical Balance

Asymmetrical balance depends on equalizing the visual, or optical, weights of nonsimilar elements in a composition within a visual field or about a common axis. Figure 9.6 shows a symmetrically balanced seating group at one end of a room. This is balanced with the furniture and plants at the opposite end. Even though there is more furniture in the seating group, it is balanced by the visually more "complex" group of plants as well as the dining table. Some of the ways visual weights are established were outlined at the beginning of this chapter.

Asymmetrical balance is generally considered informal and dynamic. It is capable of organizing a wide diversity of objects, forms, colors, and textures within either symmetrical or asymmetrical architectural spaces. Unlike symmetry, there are no fixed rules; each situation must be composed and arranged by the interior designer by "eye." For instance, a colorful, uniquely shaped chair near the corner of a room may balance the objects in other parts of the room, but placed in a room 50% larger the same chair may be hopelessly overpowered by other elements.

Radial Balance

Radial balance is a type of symmetrical balance in which elements are arranged uniformly about a central point, as shown in Fig. 9.7. By its very nature, radial balance usually focuses attention on the center of the grouping. However, individual elements can be oriented away from the center as well.

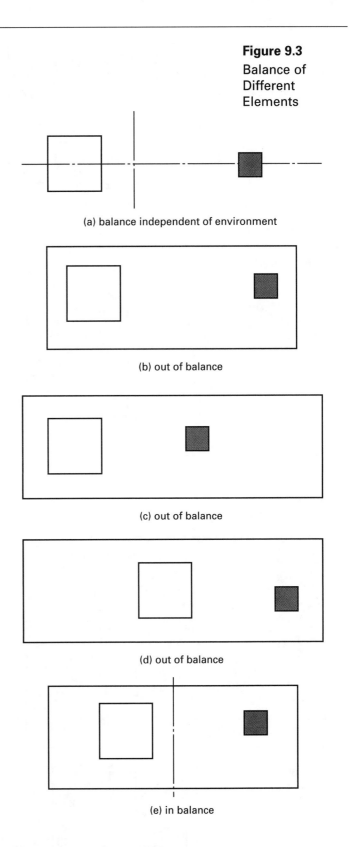

Figure 9.3
Balance of Different Elements

(a) balance independent of environment

(b) out of balance

(c) out of balance

(d) out of balance

(e) in balance

HARMONY AND UNITY

Harmony in a composition is the agreement of the parts to each other and to the whole. It is often one of the most difficult

Figure 9.4
Symmetrical
Balance

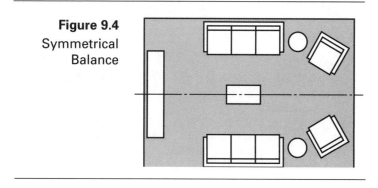

Figure 9.5
Symmetry About
a Vertical and
Horizontal Axis

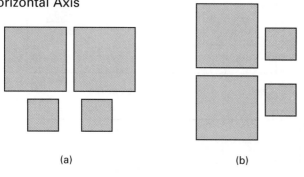

(a)   (b)

Figure 9.6
Asymmetrical
Balance

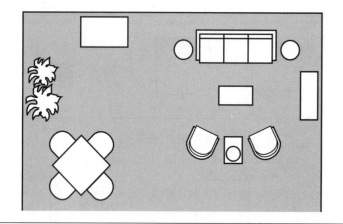

Figure 9.7
Radial Balance

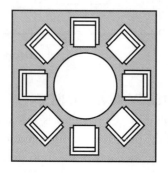

design principles to apply because there are no fixed rules and because it includes the opposing concepts of unity/variety and rhythm/emphasis. Harmony results in a composition in which all the pieces seem to belong together and work to reinforce the overall design theme. Harmony is the way in which the wide variety of forms, shapes, colors, textures, and patterns found in any interior is balanced into a unified, satisfying composition.

Harmony is most often achieved by relating a number of different elements through a common characteristic. For example, a number of different furniture pieces may share the same basic scale and form. If the scale and form are different, they may harmonize by using the same colors. Harmony can be achieved by grouping the elements close together, by relating them to a common architectural element, or by organizing them around a shared design feature. See Fig. 9.8.

Harmony and unity can also be achieved by using a common shape in varying sizes and textures as shown in Fig. 9.9. Harmony achieved by using collections of things together uses the Gestalt principal of grouping discussed in Ch. 3.

While harmony seeks to achieve a unity of appearance in which everything belongs, some variety is required to prevent the composition from becoming dull and monotonous.

RHYTHM

One of the most powerful design principles is *rhythm*, which is the repetition of elements in a regular pattern. Because rhythm sets up a sequence of multiple elements through space, it also includes a time component as the eye or body moves past the individual pieces. In most situations, elements follow a common baseline to which they are related either by physical connection or by an imaginary line that the eye and mind use to tie the elements together.

The simplest kind of rhythm is the uniform repetition of identical objects. More complex compositions include irregular spacing, emphasizing or changing elements and regular intervals, and uniformly increasing or decreasing the size of the elements, much the same way composers use musical rhythms. *Gradation* is an important type of rhythm where the size, color, or value of design elements are gradually modified as the elements repeat. See Fig. 9.10. In more complex compositions, two or more rhythms can be juxtaposed, or the repeating element can be changed slightly as it repeats.

A regular rhythm is often effective when contrasted with a unique element for emphasis. See Fig. 9.11. Rhythm can also be established in the smallest architectural detail or in fabric patterns. Sometimes, the juxtaposition of large-scale and small-scale rhythm provides a subtle contrast and adds interest to a space.

Because interior design is a three-dimensional art, rhythm can occur with shapes, forms, colors, textures, furniture, doors, lighting, and plants, among many others.

EMPHASIS AND FOCUS

Within any interior there are some elements that are more important than others. The important elements may be things like the table in a dining room, a spectacular view from a window, artwork in a museum, or a special merchandise display in a retail shop. The designer needs to understand the various dominant and subordinate parts of a space to create a design that enhances these hierarchies and provides a focus on the important features. A space in which everything is equally important tends to be bland and lifeless.

Emphasis can be created in a number of ways as shown in Fig. 9.12. A part of the

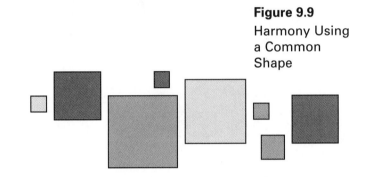

Figure 9.8
Harmony Using a Common Element

Figure 9.9
Harmony Using a Common Shape

interior can be located in an important position. It can be centered, placed at the termination of an axis, or offset from a rhythmic grouping of other elements. An element can also be given emphasis by its size, color, shape, or texture, or in any way that creates a noticeable contrast between it and its surroundings.

In most situations, there are several levels of emphasis and focus. For example, in a living room a seating group around the fireplace could be the main area of focus, while an art collection could be given secondary emphasis. All other furniture, finishes, and objects could be background elements. However, emphasis should be employed judiciously. If everything is emphasized, nothing is emphasized. There must be a clear differentiation between dominant and subordinate elements.

Figure 9.10
Variations of
Rhythm

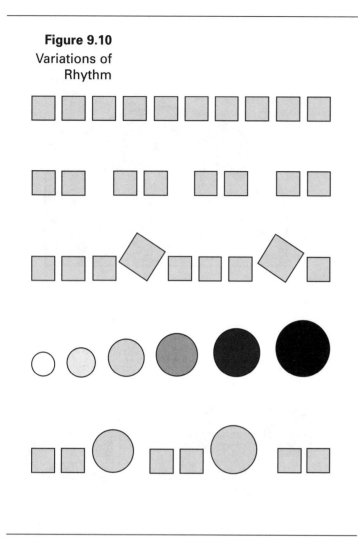

Contrast can be subtle, as between two minor shades of a color, or extreme, where two elements have completely different sizes, shapes, colors, textures, and proportions. The choice must be made by the designer based on the requirements of the space and the design objectives.

One dramatic way of creating contrast is with lighting. By simply varying the amount of artificial light in a space, even objects similar in color, texture, and size can be given contrast. Natural light can be also be used to provide contrast. Depending on the type of fenestration, contrast can change throughout the day as the sun changes position. However, light contrast must be controlled or limited if it involves critical visual tasks, such as reading, writing, or performing other work. Excessive brightness contrast can cause glare and actually make seeing difficult and promote eye fatigue.

For critical visual tasks, a maximum brightness ratio of 3 to 1 between the task surface and its background is recommended. A maximum brightness ratio of 5 to 1 is recommended between the task and the surrounding surfaces of the room; that is, it is not desirable to work on a bright surface in a dark room. To use light contrast as a principle of design and avoid glare and undesirable brightness ratios, limit bright lighting to highlighting painting, sculptures, or other small accent pieces. Refer to Ch. 19 for more information on light quality and controlling glare.

Figure 9.11
Rhythm with
Emphasis

CONTRAST AND VARIETY

Contrast, the juxtoposition of dissimilar elements, is a necessary condition of life. Black does not exist without white, left without right. Contrast is the way we perceive the difference between things, create importance, and add interest and variety to our environment. Good interior design is a balance between harmony, or the unity of a space, and the liveliness and interest created by emphasis and contrast.

PROPORTION

Proportion is the relationship between one part of an object or composition and another part and to the whole, or between one element and another. It is similar to the element of scale discussed in Ch. 8, but it is not dependent on the relationship of one element to another of known size, such as the human body. For example, the parts of a table can be perceived as in or out of proportion to one another without knowing how large the table is. See Fig. 9.13. In another situation, an object can appear out of proportion in one setting and perfectly correct in another. Figure 9.14 shows chairs crowded in one room while the same chairs seem proportionally correct in a room with a higher ceiling.

Proportion, by definition, is relative. It is also a matter of judgment and situation, and for interior designers it is dependent on the three-dimensional relationship of object and space. A tall, thin object may seem too skinny and top heavy if oriented vertically, but the same object might appear correct if laid on its side. See Fig. 9.15. In some cases, something is deliberately made out of proportion to emphasize it or to create extreme contrast. Of course, the final judgment depends on the space in which the object is used, other furniture and accessories, color, lighting, and the other features of the immediate environment.

Because of these factors, most design decisions concerning proportion are made "by eye," adjusting size and shape until the visual relationships seem correct for the situation. However, throughout history, mathematicians, artists, and others have attempted to discover and quantify the

Figure 9.12
Methods of
Emphasis

(a) focus

(b) offset and contrast

Figure 9.13
Proportions of
Parts of an
Object

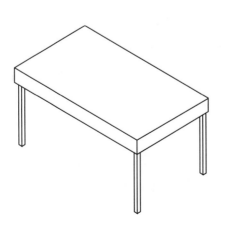

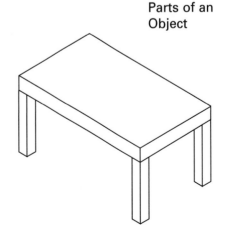

ideal proportioning system. The most well known and studied of these systems is one in which a single line is divided into two unequal segments such that the ratio of the smaller part is to the larger part as the larger part is to the whole. This is the so-called *golden ratio*, and when translated to a rectangle it becomes the *golden section*. In fact, the golden ratio is developed by using a square to geometrically form the golden section. See Fig. 9.16.

The ratio developed by dividing a line according to these proportions is an irrational number designated by the Greek letter phi, φ. It is approximately equal to 1.618. Since the time of the Greeks, the golden section has been believed to be the most pleasing proportion possible and has been found to occur repeatedly in nature as well as in human-formed structures, artwork, and musical harmony.

Related to the golden ratio is the Fibonacci series. The *Fibonacci series* is a sequence of numbers beginning with 0 and 1. Each successive number in the series is the sum of the previous two. It begins as 0, 1, 1, 2, 3, 5, 8, 13, 21, 34, 55, 89.... When any number is divided by the previous term, the quotient approximates the golden ratio, and as the numbers get larger, the quotient gets closer to the value of the golden ratio.

Figure 9.14
Correct Proportion Based on Situation

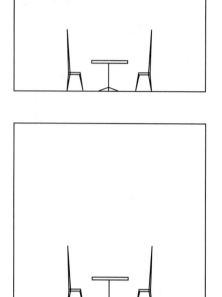

Figure 9.15
Proportion in Three-Dimensional Space

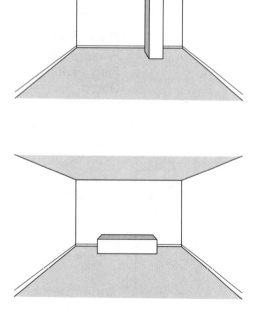

Figure 9.16
Golden Section

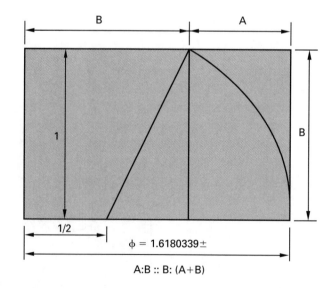

φ = 1.6180339±

A:B :: B: (A+B)

Another well-known proportioning system is the *Modulor system*, developed by the architect Le Corbusier. It is loosely based on the golden section but uses the human body as a starting point. The system begins by dividing the height of a man, averaged to 1829 mm (about 6 ft) at the waistline, or navel. Another proportion is developed by the distance from the top of the head to the fingertips when the arm is naturally raised above the head. From these three dimensions and proportions, all the others are developed. See Fig. 9.17. The distance from the bottom of the feet to the navel, about 44 in (1130), is equal to the distance from the navel to the tip of the raised hand. The dimension from the navel to the raised hand divided by the dimension from the top of the head to the raised hand is approximately equal to the golden section. From these three main dimensions of 44 in (1130), 72 in (1829), and 88 in (2260), Le Corbusier developed two series, the red series and the blue series, each with 10 numbers. Le Corbusier believed that these dimensions could be used to maintain human scale in design and create unity with diversity. He also though his system could be used to facilitate prefabrication of building elements while avoiding the repetitive monotony of a modular system with identical dimensions.

SAMPLE QUESTIONS

1. Which of the following statements is LEAST accurate in describing balance?

(A) A balanced composition drawn in an elevation can appear imbalanced when constructed in three dimensions.

(B) A collection of small elements of various textures appears "heavier" than a very large object with no texture.

(C) Placement is more important than the visual weight of an object when viewing an entire composition.

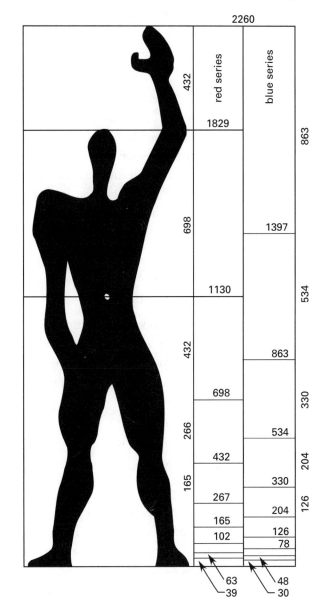

Figure 9.17
The Modulor

(D) Generally, neutral colors appear lighter than bright colors.

2. A designer uses the principle of harmony in order to

(A) develop a visual consistency and equilibrium to the individual elements

(B) establish an agreement of individual elements to each other and to the entire composition

(C) provide interest by developing one or two elements as more important than the other parts of a composition

(D) achieve a variation of the component parts without causing an imbalance in the entire design

3. A series of workstations is arranged in a row. All are identical except that the acoustical panels surrounding each workstation are covered with a fabric that has a color of a lighter tint than the workstation in front of it. This best illustrates an example of which design principle?

(A) gradation

(B) unity

(C) repetition

(D) rhythm

4. A composition of furniture and architectural elements organized around three or more axes intersecting at a common point most likely represents what type of balance?

(A) bilateral

(B) asymmetrical

(C) symmetrical

(D) radial

5. If a designer wanted to emphasize one item in a retail client's store, which of the following design features would best achieve this goal?

(A) Locating the item on a main circulation axis and highlighting it.

(B) Arranging a grouping of several of the items among single pieces of the other items.

(C) Having an oversized model of the item made for display near the entrance.

(D) Putting the item on a brightly colored pedestal in its usual place in the store.

6. A casual restaurant uses dining tables with identical bases but with table tops that are different shapes and colors. The tables are equally spaced and distributed evenly within a square space. This configuration primarily illustrates which design principle?

(A) symmetrical balance

(B) variety

(C) harmony

(D) rhythm

7. Which of the following represents the golden proportion?

(A) A : B :: B : (A + B)

(B) A : B :: A : (A + B)

(C) (A + B) : A :: 2B : A

(D) A : B :: B : 2A

8. Which architect developed the Modulor system?

(A) Frank Lloyd Wright

(B) Mies van der Rohe

(C) Le Corbusier

(D) Walter Gropius

9. If 13 black-and-white photographs, all framed with different styles and colors of frames, were grouped on a wall painted a light, cool gray, which design principle would the designer be using?

(A) variety

(B) rhythm

(C) contrast

(D) focus

10. The given diagram BEST represents which of the following principles?

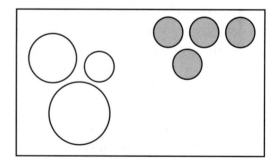

(A) proportion

(B) scale

(C) rhythm

(D) balance

10

INTERIOR CONSTRUCTION

Interior construction consists of those building elements that are assemblies of several components. This is in contrast with finishes, which are single materials surface applied to another substrate. This chapter reviews the major interior construction elements, including partitions, doors and hardware, glazing, ceilings, ornamental metals, and rough and finish carpentry. Because the topic of architectural woodwork is emphasized on the NCIDQ exam, this topic is covered in a separate chapter.

Refer to Ch. 12 for information on finish materials, Ch. 13 for a discussion of designing interior details, Ch. 17 for a review of structural systems, and Ch. 18 for information on mechanical and electrical systems.

PARTITIONS

Partitions are the most common construction element for both residential and commercial interior design. This section discusses three of the most frequently used materials for partitions: gypsum wallboard, lath and plaster, and masonry. Wallboard is the most common type of partition. Lath and plaster construction is seldom used for standard walls but is required for certain conditions. Masonry is least specified by interior designers, but it can be used in special situations.

Gypsum Wallboard

Gypsum wallboard consists of a gypsum core sandwiched between heavy paper or other materials. It is factory formed into standard-size sheets ready for dry application onto framing. Because of its many advantages, it is the most common material used for constructing partitions in both residential and commercial construction.

Advantages of gypsum wallboard include a low installed cost, quick and easy installation, fire resistance, sound control capability, easy availability, versatility (for a variety of uses), ease of finishing and decorating, and ease of installation of doors and other openings.

Gypsum wallboard is commonly available in 4 ft wide (1200) sheets in lengths of 8, 10, 12, and 14 ft (2400, 3000, 3600, and 4200). One manufacturer makes a $4^1/_2$ ft wide (1372) product to reduce the number of joints when finishing a 9 ft high

(2743) ceiling when the boards are placed horizontally. Thicknesses range from $1/4$ in to $5/8$ in (6 to 16). Special 1 in thick (25) core board used for shaft enclosures is manufactured in 2 ft (600) widths. There is also a special $3/4$ in thick (19) product that carries a two-hour fire rating. This allows a two-hour-rated partition to be constructed with a single layer without resorting to a standard two-ply application.

The thickness used depends on the particular application, frame spacing, and building code requirements. For most commercial work, $5/8$ in thick (16) wallboard is used. $1/2$ in is commonly used in residential projects and for some commercial applications, such as furred walls. $1/4$ in (6) wallboard is used for forming curved surfaces and for providing new finishes over old wall and ceiling surfaces. $3/8$ in (10) wallboard is used in some double-layer applications or when wallboard is applied over other finished walls in remodeling work. Double-layer applications are used when additional fire resistance is required or for extra acoustical control between rooms.

Gypsum wallboard is available in a variety of types and edge treatments. The most common wallboard has tapered edges on the face side along the long dimension of the panel and square edges at the ends. The tapered edges allow for application of reinforcing tape and joint compound without causing bulges at the joints. Square-edge panels are used where appearance is not a factor, for base layers of two-layer applications, and for veneer plaster work.

Other available types include Type X for fire-rated partitions, foil-backed for vapor barriers, water-resistant for use behind tile and in other moderately moist conditions, backing board for two-layer applications, and predecorated with vinyl wallcovering already applied. Recycled products are also available.

Gypsum wallboard is applied by nailing or screwing it to wood or metal framing, or with mastic when applying it to smooth, dry concrete or masonry walls or to a base layer of wallboard. The joints are finished by embedding paper or fiberglass tape in a special joint compound and allowing it to dry. Additional layers of joint compound are added and sanded after each application to give a smooth, finished wall surface. Various types of textured finishes can be applied, or the surface can be left smooth for the application of wallpaper, vinyl wallcovering, or other finishes.

The types of finishes on gypsum wallboard have been standardized by the Gypsum Association and published in GA-214-CCD, *Recommended Levels of Gypsum Board Finish*. The levels provide a way to specify the exact requirement for any project. This is important because factors such as lighting conditions and paint type can affect the appearance of a surface that has not been properly finished. For example, strong side lighting from a window perpendicular to a partition can accentuate minor flaws and dents in the wallboard.

Level 0: Requires no taping, finishing, or accessories.

Level 1: Joints and interior angles have tape embedded in joint compound with the surface free of excess joint compound. This level is used for plenums above ceilings and other areas not normally open to view.

Level 2: All joints and interior angles have tape embedded in joint compound, and one separate coat of compound is applied over all joints, angles, fastener heads, and accessories. This level is used where water-resistant backing board is used as a substrate for tile and in other areas where appearance is not critical.

Level 3: Similar to Level 2, except that two coats of joint compound are used and the surface is free of tool marks and ridges. This level is used where the surface will receive heavy- or medium-textured finishes or where heavy-grade wall coverings are to be applied.

Level 4: Similar to Level 3, except that three coats of joint compound are used. This level is used where light textures or wall coverings will be applied or where economy is of concern. Gloss, semigloss, and enamel paints are not recommended over this level of finish.

Level 5: Similar to Level 4 except that a thin skim coat of joint compound is applied over the entire surface. This level is used where gloss, semigloss, enamel, or nontextured flat paints are specified or where severe lighting conditions exist.

Either wood or metal studs are used to form wallboard partitions. 2″ × 4″ and 2″ × 6″ studs are common framing members for residential construction, while metal framing is typically used for commercial construction because it is noncombustible and easier to install. Metal framing consists of light-gauge steel studs set in floor and ceiling runners (C-shaped channels). See Fig. 10.1(a).

Steel studs come in standard depths of $1^5/_8$, $2^1/_2$, $3^5/_8$, 4, and 6 in (41, 64, 92, 102, and 152). Standard studs are very lightweight, but heavier gauges are available for high partitions or where other structural considerations are important. Hat-shaped furring channels are used for ceiling framing and to fur out from concrete or masonry walls if the walls are uneven or if additional depth is needed for electrical outlets or insulation. See Fig. 10.1(b). Wood furring strips of nominal 1″ × 2″ (25 × 51) size can also be used in some situations. Resilient channels are

Figure 10.1
Gypsum
Wallboard
Framing

1-5/8″, 2-1/2″
3-5/8″, 4″, 6″
(41, 64, 92, 102, 152)

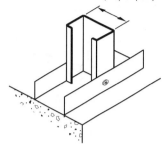

(a) typical stud and runner

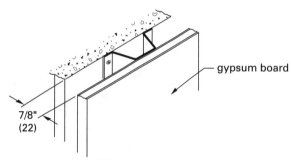

gypsum board

7/8″
(22)

(b) furring channel
(also known as a hat channel)

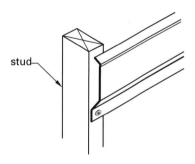

stud

(c) resilient channel

used to improve the acoustical properties of a wall by isolating the wallboard from rigid attachment to the framing. See Fig. 10.1(c). Insulation is also placed in the stud cavities to improve the acoustical quality of the partition. Refer to Ch. 20 for information on how partitions are rated by STC level.

The depth of the stud depends on the height of the partition, the gauge of the stud, the number of layers of wallboard, and the spacing of the studs. The most commonly used size is $2^1/_2$ in (64), which is sufficient for normal ceiling heights

and slab-to-slab partitions and allows enough room for electrical boxes and small pipes. Metal studs are normally spaced 16 in or 24 in (400 to 600 modular) on center—the narrower spacing is used for residential construction and the wider spacing is used for commercial construction. Wallboard with $^1/_2$ in (13) thickness is typically applied in residential construction, and wallboard with $^5/_8$ in (16) thickness is typically applied in commercial construction.

Because its edges are rough, wallboard must have fabricated edging whenever its edges are exposed. This includes a corner-bead, which is used for all exterior corners not otherwise protected, and various types of edge trim. These trim pieces are shown in Fig. 10.2 and include the following.

- *LC bead:* edge trim requiring finishing with joint compound. It has a back flange, so it must be fitted over the edge of the wallboard before the wallboard is fastened to the substrate.

- *L bead:* edge trim without a back flange; good for installation after the wallboard has been installed. It requires finishing with joint compound.

- *LK bead:* edge trim for use with various thicknesses of wallboard in a kerfed jamb (one with a small slot cut in). It requires finishing with joint compound.

- *U bead:* edge trim in which the edge of the metal is noticeable. It is sometimes called J metal by contractors. It does not require finishing with joint compound.

Figure 10.3 illustrates three of the most common types of gypsum wallboard partitions. One is the standard wood frame partition used in residential construction. This is commonly constructed with 2" × 4" studs 16 in (406) on center, covered with one layer of $^1/_2$ in (13) wallboard on each side. The other two types are metal frame partitions commonly used in commercial construction.

Figure 10.2
Gypsum Wallboard Trim

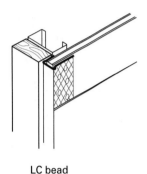

LC bead

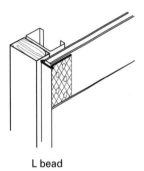

L bead

U bead

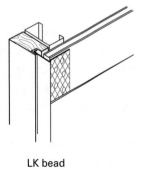

LK bead

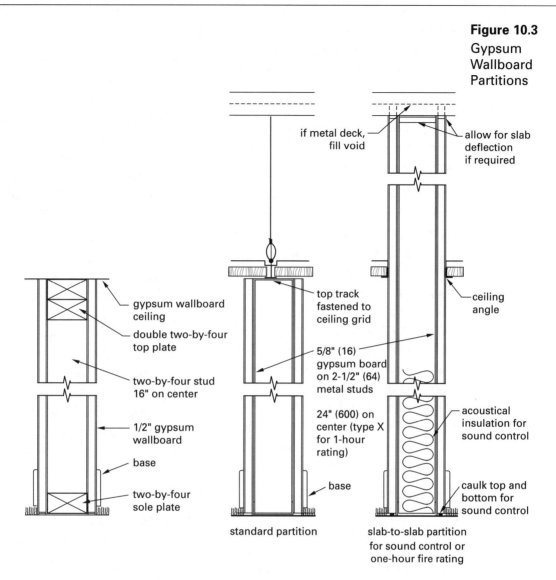

Figure 10.3
Gypsum
Wallboard
Partitions

if metal deck,
fill void

allow for slab
deflection
if required

gypsum wallboard
ceiling

double two-by-four
top plate

two-by-four stud
16" on center

1/2" gypsum
wallboard

base

two-by-four
sole plate

top track
fastened to
ceiling grid

ceiling
angle

5/8" (16)
gypsum board
on 2-1/2" (64)
metal studs

24" (600) on
center (type X
for 1-hour
rating)

acoustical
insulation for
sound control

base

caulk top and
bottom for
sound control

standard partition

slab-to-slab partition
for sound control or
one-hour fire rating

Commercial construction typically uses $2^{1}/_{2}$ in or $3^{5}/_{8}$ in (64 or 92) metal studs spaced 24 in (610) on center. Metric construction uses stud spacing of 400 mm or 600 mm on center to frame drywall manufactured to the metric sizes. In commercial work, the standard partition is only built up to the suspended ceiling, while the slab-to-slab partition is used when a complete fire-rated barrier must be constructed or when sound control is needed. By adding additional layers of Type X wallboard, fire-resistive ratings of two, three, and four hours can be obtained. A slab-to-slab partition with a single layer of $^{5}/_{8}$ in (16) Type X wallboard on each side provides a one-hour

rated partition, while two layers on each side provide a two-hour rating. Gypsum wallboard is also used for ceilings and to provide fire protection for columns, stairways, and elevator shafts.

When partitions extend to the structure above in commercial buildings, the head of the partition needs to be designed with a slip joint to prevent the wall from being damaged if the structural floor above deflects. Refer to Ch. 17 for information on building movement and types of slip joints for partitions.

Because gypsum wallboard is produced in such large quantities, its manufacture, use, and disposal have an effect on the environment. Since the 1950s, gypsum wallboard manufacturers have been using recycled paper to manufacture the surfaces of wallboard. In addition, some manufacturers are using recycled newspaper mixed with gypsum as the core material to yield a product that is more rigid than standard wallboard yet still maintains all the other advantages of the product.

About 7% of the industry's total use of gypsum is synthetic gypsum. Synthetic gypsum is chemically identical to natural, mined gypsum but is a byproduct of various manufacturing, industrial, or chemical processes. The main source of synthetic gypsum in North America is flue-gas desulfurization. This is the process whereby power-generating plants (and similar plants) remove polluting gases from their stacks to reduce emission of harmful materials into the atmosphere. Using this byproduct allows the efficient use of refuse material that would otherwise have to be discarded.

The larger environmental concern involves the disposal of used gypsum wallboard, which cannot be reused for its original purpose when it is ripped out of an old building or a renovation project. Some gypsum wallboard plants around the country are recycling old drywall. The only condition is that the wallboard must be free of screws, nails, asbestos, and lead paint. Currently, the cost of collecting, separating, and transporting the old wallboard is a disincentive for recycling.

Old wallboard can also be pulverized into pieces equal to or smaller than $1/2$ in size and worked into the ground as a soil additive. Farmers in California and parts of Colorado use recycled gypsum as a soil conditioner for grapes, peas, and peanuts. It is also possible to work the gypsum directly into the soil around a job site as long as the land has adequate drainage

and aeration and local and state regulations allow it.

Glass-Reinforced Gypsum

The term *glass-reinforced gypsum* (GRG) refers to a broad class of products manufactured from high-strength, high-density gypsum reinforced with continuous-filament glass fibers or chopped glass fibers. These products are also known as *fiberglass-reinforced gypsum* (FRG) and *glass-fiber-reinforced gypsum* (GFRG).

GRG products are used for decorative elements, such as column covers, arches, coffered ceilings, ornate moldings, light troughs, and trim. They are premanufactured products made by pouring GRG into molds. After setting, the products are shipped to the job site for installation and final finishing. They can be finished with any kind of material that can be put on plaster or gypsum wallboard. An unlimited variety of shapes can be manufactured that would otherwise be too expensive or impossible to achieve with site-fabricated lath and plaster.

Lath and Plaster

Plaster is a finish material made from various types of cementing compounds, fine aggregate, and water. It is applied over several kinds of base materials in one to three coats to form a smooth, level surface. Plaster describes various types of interior finish materials of this type, while stucco is an exterior type of plaster made with portland cement.

Plaster is made from gypsum, lime, water, and aggregates of sand, vermiculite, or perlite. Vermiculite and perlite are used when a lightweight, fire-resistant plaster is needed. For most interior construction, gypsum plaster can be used. However, in certain areas other types are required. Keene's cement, for example, is a plaster that has a high resistance to abrasion and water penetration. It is used in wet areas or on walls subject to scratching or other abuse. Portland cement plaster must be used as the base coat for Keene's cement or as a backing for tile walls.

There are two common types of plaster construction. The first is the traditional method using metal lath that is attached to wood or metal studs and serves as the base for the plaster.

Metal lath is available in several types: expanded diamond mesh, paper, backed diamond mesh, flat-rib lath, and high-rib lath. See Fig. 10.4. The first coat of plaster, called the scratch coat, is applied to the metal lath and runs between and partially around the lath, firmly keying the plaster to the lath. In standard plastering, the scratch coat is followed by the brown coat, which is used to level the surface. The finish coat provides final leveling and the desired texture to the surface. The scratch coat is about $1/4$ in to $1/2$ in (6 to 13) thick, the brown coat is about $1/4$ in (6) thick, and the finish coat is about $1/8$ in (3) thick. Two-coat work combines the scratch and brown coats.

The other method of plastering uses gypsum board lath instead of metal lath. This is a special gypsum product specifically designed for plastering. Gypsum lath is available in 16" × 48" (400 × 1200) boards that are applied horizontally to studs, or as 48" × 96" (1200 × 2400) sheets. One or two coats of thin veneer plaster are applied over the boards. Veneer plastering reduces labor because only one coat is needed, but it still retains some of the advantages of plaster: a hard, durable surface that can be finished with a variety of textures.

Like gypsum wallboard, the edges of plaster must be finished with trim. This provides a termination point for the work and serves as a screed to give the plasterers guides for maintaining the required thickness.

Figure 10.4
Expanded
Metal Lath

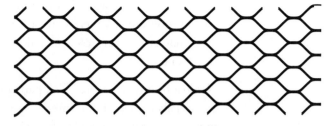

(a) diamond mesh lath

(b) flat rib metal lath

(c) rib metal lath

In general, gypsum wallboard systems have largely supplanted lath and plaster work because of their lower cost and faster construction sequence. However, plaster is still used where curved shapes are required and where a hard, abrasion-resistant surface is needed. Plaster must also be used as a base for ceramic tile in areas subject to continual dampness, like public showers or steam rooms. Ornamental plaster casting and plaster molding are also used in restoration work.

Masonry

Masonry is a general term that includes brick, concrete block, glass block, structural clay tile, terra-cotta, and gypsum block. In most cases, masonry materials are part of the architectural design of a building and are part of the architect's work. Occasionally, however, the interior designer may need to specify a nonload-bearing wall of masonry, most often concrete block or glass block. For example, in a renovation project, there may be a need to match an existing concrete block or brick wall.

Nonloadbearing concrete block partitions are usually specified for interior use to provide a strong, durable, fire-resistant partition. In institutional applications, such as schools or college dormitories, where heavy use is expected, concrete block may be a sensible choice. However, block is very heavy compared with gypsum wallboard and is generally not considered an attractive finish surface. If it will be used, the architect or structural engineer should verify that the existing floor structure can carry its weight.

Concrete block is manufactured with cement, water, and various types of aggregate, including gravel, expanded shale or slate, expanded slag or pumice, or limestone cinders. It is hollow and its size is based on a nominal 4 in (100) module with actual dimensions being $3/8$ in less than the nominal dimension to allow for mortar joints. One of the most common sizes is an $8 \times 8 \times 16$ in unit, which is actually $7\,5/8$ in wide and high and $15\,5/8$ in long. Common nominal thicknesses are 4, 6, 8, and 12 in. Various sizes and shapes are manufactured for particular uses.

Glass block is manufactured as a hollow unit with a clear, textured, or patterned face. It is a popular choice for interior use when a combination of light transmission, privacy, and security is required.

Glass block is manufactured in a nominal thickness of 4 in and in face sizes of 6" $\times$ 6", 8" $\times$ 8", 12" $\times$ 12", and 4" $\times$ 8". Glass block walls are laid in stack bond (with joints aligned rather than staggered) with mortar and horizontal and vertical

reinforcement in the joints. Because of the coefficient of expansion of glass and the possibility of deflection of the floor structure, expansion joints around the perimeter of glass block walls must be provided. Modular concrete block and glass block are also available.

Because glass block cannot be loadbearing, individual panels are limited to 250 ft^2 (23 m^2) or 25 ft (7620) in any dimension. Each panel must be supported with suitable structure both horizontally and vertically and with expansion joints provided at the structural support points.

A typical vertical section through a glass block wall is shown in Fig. 10.5. Normally, a frame overlaps the glass block at the head and jamb sections. However, if the appearance of an overlapping frame is objectionable, the block can be set flush with the steel frame. This requires using vertical reinforcement that is rigidly attached to the bottom and top framing members.

When using a glass block wall, the width and height of the opening should be an even multiple of the size of the glass block used and allow for required expansion and framing. In addition, the deflection of the floors, beams, or other structural members supporting the glass block must not exceed $1/600$ of the span of the structural member. Verification by a structural engineer is necessary.

Demountable Partitions

Demountable Partition Components

Demountable partitions consist of a system of individual components that can be quickly assembled, disassembled, and reused with nearly total salvageability. Demountable partitions differ from operable partitions in that they are intended to remain in place as standard partitions, while operable partitions act as special doors to open and close a space frequently.

Demountable partitions allow space to be reconfigured quickly and easily as needs change. Because the components are prefinished and designed as a system, they can be rearranged and combined with new components, such as doors and glazing panels, without messy demolition and damage to adjacent construction. They can also make initial construction faster because flooring, ceilings, lighting, and mechanical work can be completed first and the partitions can be installed later. Although demountable partitions have higher initial costs than standard partition construction, life-cycle costs are lower because of the savings in material and labor costs in offices where space plans are changed frequently.

Typical Demountable Partition Construction

The configuration and design of individual components varies with each manufacturer, but it generally consist of four components: floor runners, ceiling runners, stud sections with clips to hold the panels, and prefinished gypsum wallboard panels. The panels are typically covered with vinyl wall covering in a range of standard colors and patterns, although custom finishes are possible on large jobs. Panels are usually 24 in or 30 in (600 or 750) wide to work with common building planning modules of 4 ft or 5 ft (1200 or 1500). When a partition is completed, there are small vertical joints between the panels, and the top track is visible as it overlaps the panels at the ceiling. A manufacturer's standard base trim snaps on at the floor line.

In addition to the basic components, all manufacturers' systems have door frames, glazing, bank rails, openings, and similar common components. Some manufacturers also provide for hanging shelves and furniture components in slots between the panels.

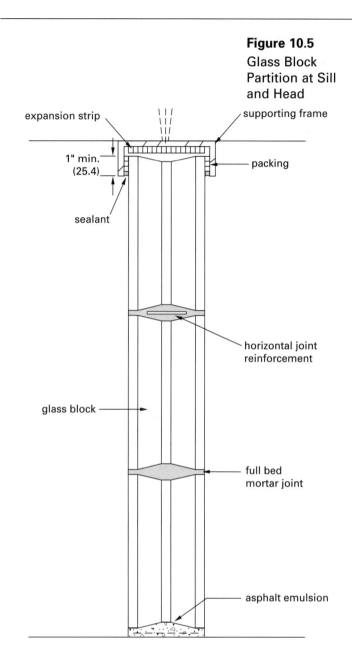

Figure 10.5
Glass Block Partition at Sill and Head

The bottom track can rest directly on the structural floor or finished floor like a standard gypsum wallboard floor runner. As shown in Fig. 10.6, tracks are also available with spikes extending below the runner, allowing the runner to be placed directly over carpeting without crushing it. When the partition is moved, the previous partition's location is less noticeable. The top track is attached directly to the suspended ceiling system, as with standard construction, except that the flange of the

Figure 10.6
Demountable
Partition

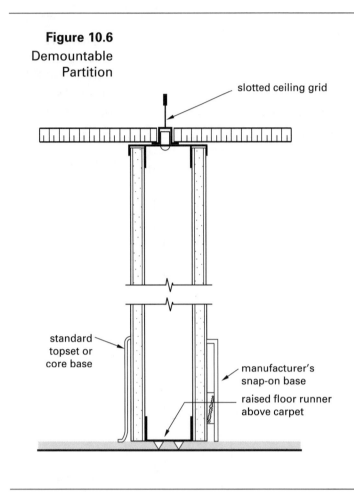

- slotted ceiling grid

standard
topset or
core base

manufacturer's
snap-on base

raised floor runner
above carpet

Figure 10.7
Parts of a Door

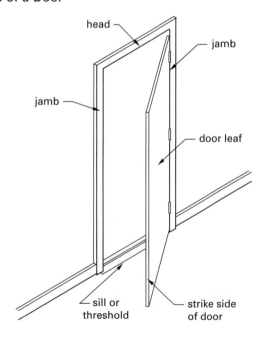

head

jamb

jamb

door leaf

sill or
threshold

strike side
of door

track overlaps the panel and is visible in the final installation.

Partition systems can be either progressive or nonprogressive. In a *progressive system* the first panel must be placed before the second panel, which must be placed before the third panel, and so on. When the partition is taken down, the reverse order must be followed. In a *nonprogressive system* the panels are independent and can be removed or replaced individually. Although progressive systems have a lower initial cost than nonprogressive systems, they are much less flexible.

Coordination with Other Construction Components

Demountable partition systems are only cost-effective if they are coordinated with other building components and systems, including lighting, HVAC (heating, ventilating, and air conditioning), window mullions, and a suspended ceiling system. Space plans should be laid out on the building grid, which should also coincide with the ceiling grid. In this way, the relocation of lights, HVAC diffusers and grilles, and sprinkler heads is minimized when partitions change. Slotted suspended ceiling grids should be used, which allow the top track to be screwed into the grid without damaging its appearance when the track is moved.

DOORS AND INTERIOR GLASS

Doors and glass are two options for selectively controlling openings between rooms. Doors are available in a variety of types and materials to meet various functional needs. Glass can be used to control passage and sound, but it admits light and vision.

There are three major components of a door system: the door itself, the frame, and the hardware. Each must be coordinated with the other and be appropriate for the circumstances and design intent.

The common parts of a door opening are illustrated in Fig. 10.7. To differentiate between the two jambs, the side where the hinge or pivot is installed is called the *hinge jamb* and the jamb where the door closes is called the *strike jamb* or *strike side* of the door.

Wood Doors and Frames

Wood doors are the most common type for both residential and commercial construction. They are available in a variety of styles, methods of operation, sizes, and finishes.

The two styles of wood doors are shown in Fig. 10.8. Which style to select depends on the functional needs of the opening as well as the aesthetic appearance required. For example, a panel door is not appropriate for an opening in a fire-rated partition because wood panel doors do not meet the required fire resistance rating.

Doors are also classified according to their method of operation, or how they open and close. The most common type, the *swinging door*, is attached to its frame with hinges or pivots. Swinging doors are easy to install and can accommodate high traffic volume. In addition, they are the only type acceptable as a required exit door. *Pocket sliding doors* are hung on a top track and can be used where space is limited. However, they are awkward to operate and should only be used where traffic is limited. *Bypass sliding doors* also are hung from a top track and are commonly used for closets only. *Bi-folding doors* are also used for closets. Unlike the bypass sliding door, which can only open half of a doorway, a bi-fold door allows full access. *Accordion folding doors* are often used to divide spaces or close very wide openings. *Flush wood doors* are made of thin, flat veneers laminated to various types of cores. They are either hollow core or solid core.

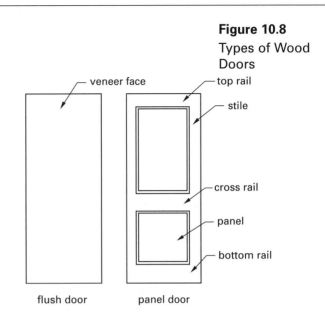

Figure 10.8
Types of Wood Doors

veneer face — top rail — stile — cross rail — panel — bottom rail

flush door   panel door

Hollow-core doors are made of one or three plies of veneer on each side of a cellular interior. The frame is made of solid wood with larger blocks of solid wood where the latching hardware is located. Hollow-core doors are used where only light use is expected and cost is a consideration. They have no fire-resistive capabilities.

Solid-core doors are made with a variety of core types depending on the functional requirements of the door. Cores may be particleboard, stave core (solid blocks of wood), or mineral core for fire-rated doors. Solid-core doors are used for their fire-resistive properties, as acoustical barriers, for security, and for their superior durability. Solid-core doors are available that have fire ratings of 20 minutes, 45 minutes, or 90 minutes.

The face veneers of wood doors are made from any available hardwood species using rotary-cut, plain-sliced, quarter-sliced, or rift-cut methods, as wood paneling (discussed later in this chapter) is made. Veneers of hardboard suitable for painting and plastic laminate are also available.

Panel doors are constructed of solid pieces of wood that frame various types of panels.

Any number of panels can be constructed, and they can be the traditional raised panel style or simple flat panels.

Wood doors can be custom made to any size, but the standard widths are 2 ft 0 in, 2 ft 4 in, 2 ft 6 in, 2 ft 8 in, and 3 ft 0 in (600, 700, 750, 800, and 900). Standard heights are 6 ft 8 in and 7 ft 0 in (2050 or 2100 and 2100), although higher doors, often used in commercial construction, are available. Hollow-core doors are $1^3/8$ in (34.9) thick, and solid-core doors are $1^3/4$ in (44.4) thick.

Frames for wood doors are made from wood, steel (hollow metal, discussed in the next section), and aluminum. A common wood-frame jamb is illustrated in Fig. 10.9. This drawing shows a frame set in a commercial metal stud partition, but the construction is similar for a wood-frame wall. Although the stop and casing trim are shown as rectangular pieces, several different trim profiles are available and frequently used.

The decision concerning the type of frame to use for a wood door depends on the appearance desired, the type of partition the opening is being installed in, the fire-rating requirements, the security needed, and the durability desired. For example, wood frames are available for use in 20-, 30-, and 45-minute fire door assemblies, but a 1-hour door must be installed in a rated steel frame.

Steel Doors and Frames

Metal doors and frames (often referred to as hollow metal) are seldom used for residential construction. They are, however, frequently used in commercial construction because of their durability, security, and fire-resistive qualities.

The three most common types of metal doors are flush, sash, and louvered. *Flush doors* have a single smooth surface on both sides. *Sash doors* contain one or more glass lights. *Louvered doors* have an opening with metal slats to provide ventilation. Paneled steel doors, which resemble wood panel doors, are also available with insulated cores for residential use where energy conservation, durability, and a traditional appearance are required.

Metal doors are available in steel, stainless steel, aluminum, and bronze, but other door materials are available on special order. The most common material is steel with a painted finish. Steel doors are constructed with faces of cold-rolled sheet steel. 18-gauge (1.067) steel is used for light-duty doors, but 16-gauge (1.346) is most common. Heavier gauges are used for special needs. The steel face is attached to cores of honeycomb kraft paper, steel ribs, hardboard, or other materials. The edges are made of steel channels, with the locations for hardware reinforced with heavier gauge steel. Mineral wool or other materials are used to provide sound-deadening qualities, if required.

Although metal doors can be custom made in almost any practical size, standard widths are 2 ft 0 in, 2 ft 4 in, 2 ft 6

Figure 10.9
Standard Wood
Door Frame

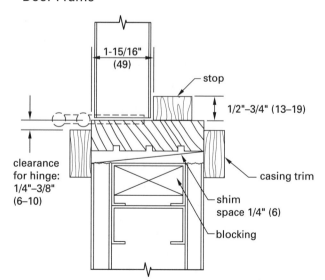

in, 2 ft 8 in, 3 ft 0 in, 3 ft 4 in, 3 ft 6 in, 3 ft 8 in, and 4 ft 0 in (600, 700, 750, 800, 900, 1000, 1050, 1100, and 1200). Standard heights are 6 ft 8 in, 7 ft 0 in, and 8 ft 0 in (2050, 2100, and 2400). The standard thickness is 1³/₄ in (44.4).

Steel door frames are used for either steel doors or wood doors and are made from sheet steel bent into the shape required for the door installation. Two of the most common frame profiles are shown in Fig. 10.10 along with some standard dimensions and the terminology used to describe the parts. Different types of anchoring devices are used inside the frame to attach it to the partition. Where a fire rating over 20 minutes is required, steel frames are used almost exclusively.

Aluminum Doors and Frames

Aluminum is commonly used as stile and rail material for glass doors and as doorframe material for both aluminum glass doors and wood doors. A few manufacturers also offer flush, sash, and louvered doors faced with aluminum. Aluminum doorframes are most commonly used in interior construction to frame wood doors when a lightweight, easily assembled frame is required. Aluminum frames are also used in many demountable partition systems or when a complex frame profile is required. Because aluminum frames are manufactured by extrusion, intricate shapes can be formed easily.

Components

Aluminum frames are constructed of one or more pieces of extruded aluminum. The exact configuration and size of a frame depends on the manufacturer's proprietary system, but most are a double-rabbeted shape with a continuous stop, similar to a steel doorframe. One noticeable difference is that aluminum frames have sharp corners, as opposed to the slightly rounded corners of steel frames. This is because aluminum frames are extruded.

Figure 10.10
Standard Steel
Doorframes

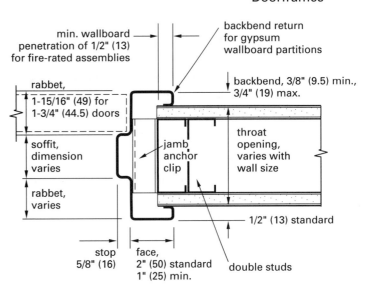

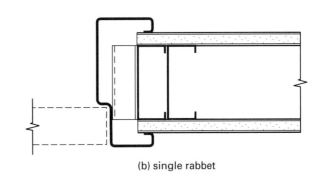

(a) standard double rabbet

(b) single rabbet

Figure 10.11
Typical
Aluminum
Frame

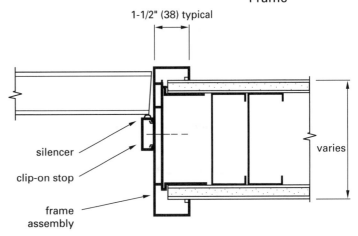

Standard assemblies

Figure 10.11 shows a typical aluminum frame with a separate, continuous anchor member that is attached to the gypsum wallboard partition. The finished jamb and the doorstop are attached to the anchoring subassembly to complete the installation. Other types of aluminum frames have separate jamb pieces and casing trim, similar to wood frames. The doorstops may have individual silencers or a continuous wool pile sealer.

Aluminum frames are available for 20-minute fire-rated opening assemblies. Smoke gaskets, which are sometimes required by code, are also available.

Custom Assemblies

Many proprietary shapes, sizes, and finishes of aluminum frames are available from several manufacturers. If quantities are sufficient, custom extrusion dies can be made to order so that project-specific frame profiles can be manufactured. Curves, angles, and ornate profiles are all possible with custom extrusions.

Coordination

- Most manufacturers offer a complete system of extrusion sizes and shapes for doorframes as well as for glass sidelight framing, bank railing, and partition track.

- Other metals in contact with the frame should be stainless steel or zinc. Contact with dissimilar metals should be prevented by using bituminous paint or nonmetallic gaskets to prevent galvanic action.

- Aluminum framing used with demountable partition systems may substitute prefinished panels of gypsum wallboard for standard wallboard construction.

Glass Doors

Glass doors, or *all-glass doors*, constructed primarily of glass and have fittings to hold the pivots and other hardware. Their strength depends on the glass rather than the framing. They are different from sash doors in that sash doors have a frame around all four sides of the glass.

Components

Glass doors are generally constructed of $1/2$ in (13) or $3/4$ in (19) tempered glass and have fittings and operating hardware as required by the installation. Common door sizes are 36 in (914) wide and 7 ft 0 in (2134) high, although many architects prefer to specify glass doors at the same height as that of the ceiling.

Some of the typical glass door configurations are shown in Fig. 10.12. The minimum configuration requires some type of door pull and a corner fitting at the top and bottom to hold the pivots. In lieu of corner fittings, some manufacturers provide hinge fittings that clamp on the glass and support the door in much the same way as a standard hinged door. If a lock is required, the bottom fitting may be continuous across the door to allow for a dead bolt to be installed. Some architects prefer continuous fittings (sometimes called shoes) on both the top and bottom.

Because a full glass door is a potential hazard and extra strength is required, the glass must be tempered. Any holes, notches, or other modifications to the glass must be made before the glass is tempered.

Standard Assemblies

Glass doors can be used alone and set within a wall opening with or without a frame, or they can be installed between glass sidelights. If glass sidelights are used, the same type of fitting used on the door is generally used to support the sidelights. Although jamb frames of aluminum, wood, or ornamental metal can be used, they are not necessary, and the glass sidelights can be butted directly to the partition or held away a fraction of an inch.

Building Code Requirements for Glass Doors

Because glass doors cannot be fire rated, they cannot be used where a protected opening is required in a fire-rated partition. When they are allowed and serve as exit doors, the type of hardware used must conform to the requirements of the local building code. Some codes and local amendments are more restrictive than others, and most prohibit the use of a simple dead bolt in the bottom rail fitting. Instead, special panic hardware is available for glass doors that allows the door to be locked from the outside (and operated with card keys or keypads, if necessary) but unlatched and opened from the inside in a single operation without any special knowledge or effort. See Fig. 10.13.

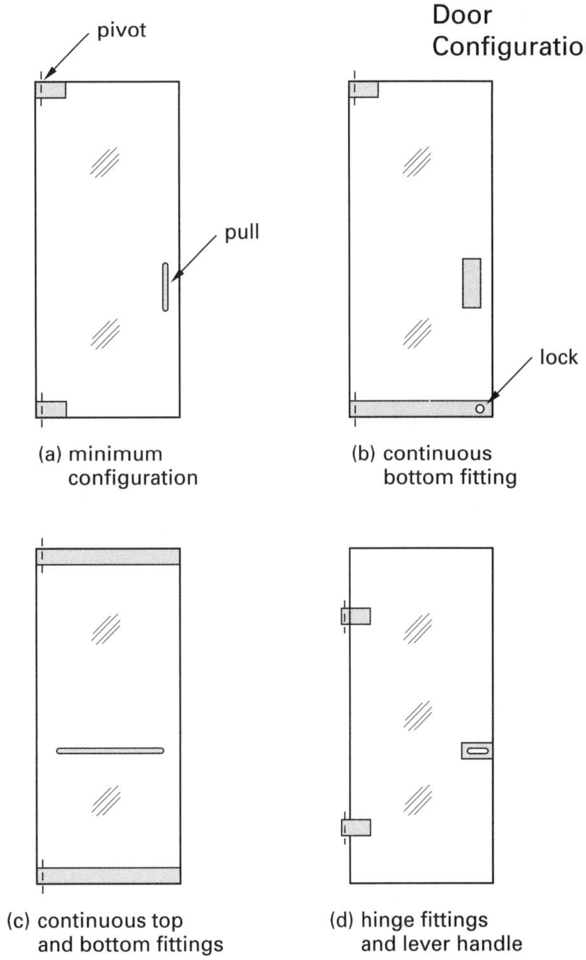

Hardware

• *Hinges:* Hinges are the most common method of attaching a door to its frame. Hinges consist of two leaves with an odd number of knuckles on one leaf and an even number of knuckles on the other. The knuckles are attached with a pin. The knuckles and pin form the barrel of the hinge, which is finished with a tip.

Most manufacturers offer a variety of tip designs for the barrels of hinges. See Figs. 10.14(a)–10.14(f). Typical types are the flat button, hospital, and oval head. Flat button tips are the most common and are furnished if not specified otherwise. Flush tips are concealed within the knuckle. Hospital tips have a sloped end to make cleaning easy and to prevent attachment of ropes or cords in psychiatric wards and jails. Other tips available from some manufacturers include ball tips, steeple tips, and flush tips. Other decorator tips are available for some hinge varieties. Consult individual manufacturer's catalogs for availability.

The full mortise (also called a butt hinge) is the most common hinge type and has both

Figure 10.12
Standard Glass Door Configurations

Figure 10.13
Glass Door Panic Hardware

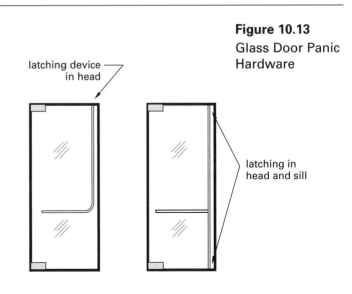

Figure 10.14

Hinge Tip
Designs

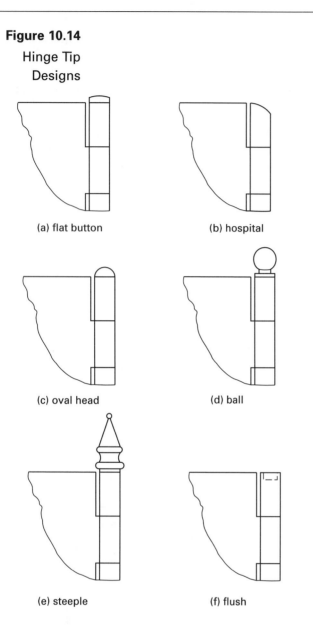

(a) flat button

(b) hospital

(c) oval head

(d) ball

(e) steeple

(f) flush

hinges decrease the opening width by the thickness of the door when it is open 90°.

Hinges are available with or without ball bearings and in three weights. The door weight and frequency of use determine which type to use. Low-frequency doors, like residential doors, use standard-weight plain-bearing hinges. Most commercial applications require standard-weight ball-bearing hinges. High-frequency applications such as office building entrances, theaters, and so forth require heavyweight ball-bearing hinges. In addition, ball-bearing hinges are required for fire-rated assemblies and on all doors with closers.

The number of hinges is determined by the height of the door. Numbers of hinges are commonly equated with pairs; that is, one pair equals two hinges. Doors up to 60 in (1525) high require two hinges (one pair). Doors from 60 in to 90 in (1525 to 2290) require three hinges ($1^1/_2$ pair), and doors 90 in to 120 in (2290 to 3048) require four hinges (two pair).

  • *Latchsets and locksets:* Latchsets and locksets are devices to operate a door, hold it in the closed position, and lock it. A latchset only holds the door in place, with no provision for locking. It has a beveled latch extending from the face of the door edge and automatically engages the strike mounted in the frame when the door is closed. A lockset has a special mechanism that allows the door to be locked with a key or thumbturn. Various types and designs of knobs or lever handles are used with these devices to provide the actual gripping surface used to operate the door.

The most common types of locksets and latchsets are the cylindrical lock (sometimes called a bored lock), the mortise lock, and the unit lock (sometimes called a preassembled lock). These are shown in Fig. 10.15.

leaves fully mortised into the frame and the edge of the door so the hinge is flush with the surface of the frame and door. Other types are available that can be surface applied to the door, the frame, or both.

There are also special types of hinges. Raised barrel hinges are used when there is not room for the barrel to extend past the door trim. The barrel is offset to allow one leaf to be mortised into the frame. Swing-clear hinges have a special shape that allows the door to swing 90° or 95° so the full opening of the doorway is available. Without a swing-clear hinge, standard butt

The *cylindrical lock* is simple to install in holes drilled in the door, and it is relatively inexpensive. It can be purchased in grades of light duty (least expensive), standard duty, and heavy duty. It is the most common lock type for residential construction, but it is also used for commercial projects.

A *mortise lock* is installed in a rectangular area cut out of the door. It is generally more secure than a cylindrical lock and offers a much wider variety of locking options.

With a *preassembled lock*, the mechanism is in a rectangular box that fits within a notch cut in the edge of the door. Because of this, it is easier to install than a mortise lock.

With all types of latches and locks, either a doorknob or lever handle may be used to operate the latching device. In most cases, a lever handle is required to meet code requirements for accessibility.

• *Pivots:* Pivots provide an alternative way to hang doors where the appearance of hinges is objectionable or where a frameless door design may make it impossible to use hinges. Pivots are used in pairs, with the bottom pivot mounted in or on the floor and a corresponding unit mounted in the head frame. They may be center hung or offset. Tall and heavy doors require offset pivots with one or more intermediate pivots. Intermediate pivots are required to keep tall doors from warping or to provide additional support for heavy doors. Center-hung pivots allow the door to swing in either direction and are completely concealed. Offset pivots allow the door to swing 180°, if required. Pivots can be used alone, as shown in Figs. 10.16(a)–10.16(d), or as part of a closer assembly.

Because of the way they operate, center-hung pivots cannot be used with a door stop on the same side of the door on both jambs. This makes it difficult to seal the door against sound or light transmission

Figure 10.15
Types of Locksets

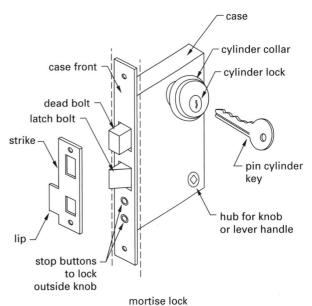

cylindrical lock

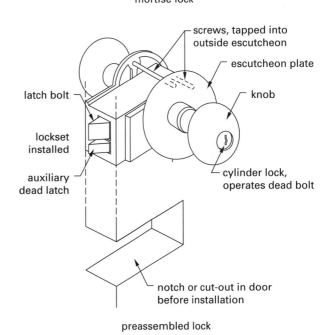

mortise lock

preassembled lock

on the hinge and strike sides, although a flexible strip of wool pile or synthetic stripping can be rabbeted into the edges of the door. The rotation point of a center-hung pivot is typically located $2^3/4$ in (70) from the edge of the frame, but it can be located anywhere along the door.

• *Closers:* Closers are devices that automatically return a door to its closed position after it is opened. They also control the distance a door can be opened and thereby protect the door and surrounding construction from damage. Closers can be surface mounted on either side of the door, or in the head frame, or concealed in the frame or in the door. Closers can also be integral with pivots mounted in the floor or ceiling, either center hung or offset. Closers are required on fire-rated doors.

Figure 10.16

Door Pivots

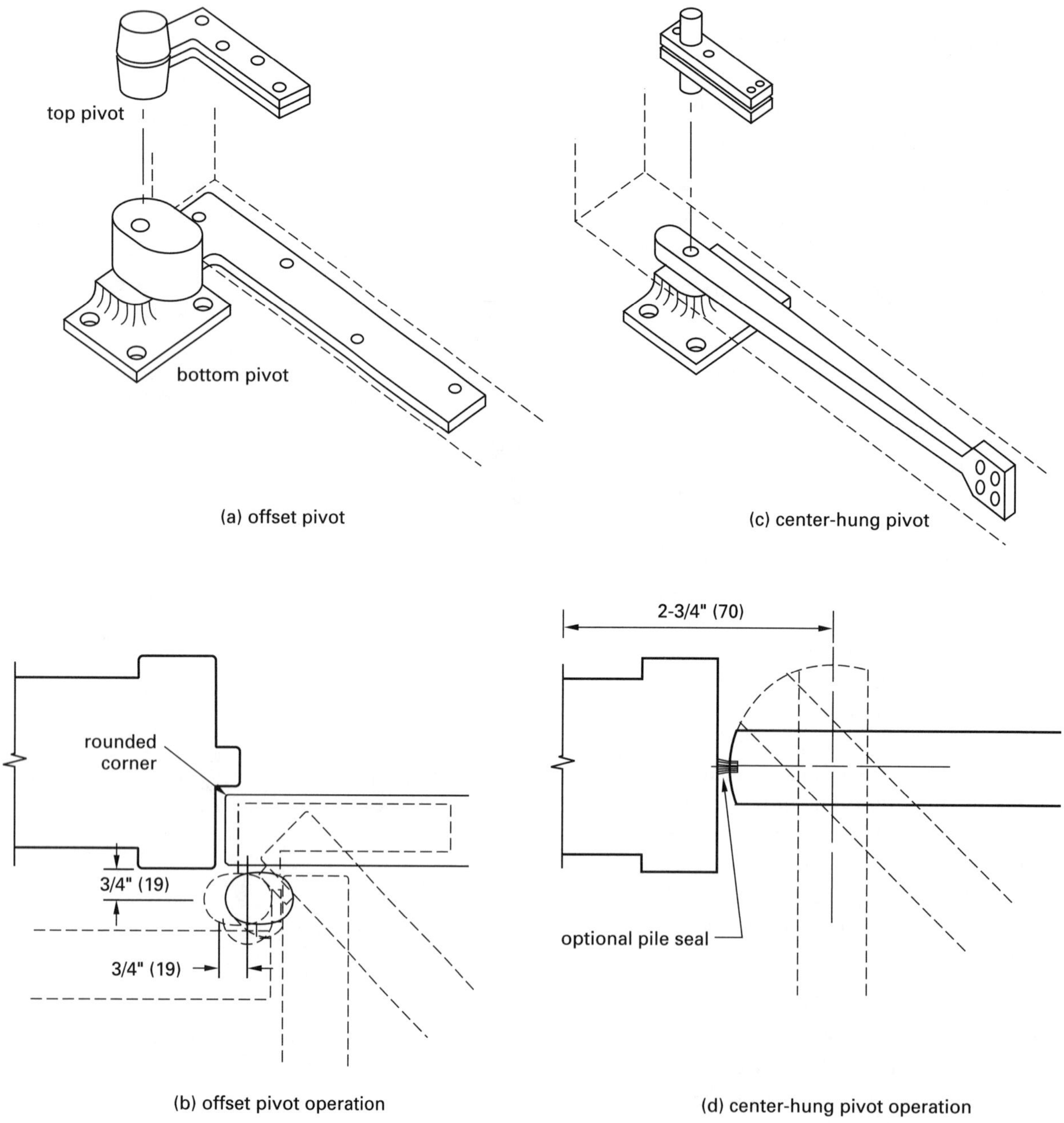

(a) offset pivot

(c) center-hung pivot

(b) offset pivot operation

(d) center-hung pivot operation

• *Panic hardware:* This type of operating hardware is used where required by the building code for safe egress by a large number of people. Push bars extending across the width of the door operate vertical rods that disengage latches at the top and bottom. The vertical rods can be surface mounted or concealed in the door.

• *Door stops and bumpers:* Some method of keeping a door from damaging adjacent construction is required. Closers will do this to some extent, but floor stops or wall bumpers provide more positive protection. These devices are small metal fabrications with rubber bumpers attached. Metal door frames also use silencers, which are small pads of rubber mounted on the door stop to cushion the door when it is closed.

• *Astragals:* Astragals are vertical members used between double doors to seal the opening, act as a door stop, or provide extra security when the doors are closed. An astragal may be attached to one door leaf or may be a separate unit against which both doors close. If the doors are required exit doors and an astragal is attached to one of them, they must have a door coordinator. This is a device that coordinates the closing sequence of the two doors so that they close completely, rather than having the leaf with the astragal close first and preventing the other leaf from closing.

• *Push plates and pull bars:* These are used to operate a door that does not require automatic latching. They are commonly used on doors to toilet rooms and commercial kitchens.

• *Automatic door bottoms:* These are devices that are mortised or surface applied to the bottom of the door to provide a sound or light seal. When the door is open the seal is up; as the door is closed a plunger strikes the jamb and forces the seal down against the floor.

• *Door seals:* Door seals are used along the edges of doors to provide tight seals against smoke, light, and sound. Different types of neoprene, felt, metal, polyurethane, and vinyl are available in many configurations.

Fire-rated seals are required on fire doors to prevent both smoke and drafts from passing through. They are similar to light and sound seals but have been tested by an approved laboratory and certified for use on fire doors. They are used on the head and jamb sections.

As with smoke seals, door seals for blocking the passage of light or sound are available in many configurations for jambs, head, and threshold. The compressible material used most often is neoprene. Double door seals can be used when a high level of sound isolation is needed. This type of construction is usually limited to sound studios, stages, and other occupancies where sound isolation is critical.

When doors must meet the requirements of positive-pressure fire testing, as discussed in the later section on code requirements for doors and frames, intumescent material must be used. Intumescent material expands upon exposure to heat and forms a tight, fire-resistant seal against the passage of smoke, gasses, and heat.

If intumescent gasketing is required, it cannot be used alone. Some type of elastomeric gasketing must also be used for protection below 300°F (149°C), before the intumescent material activates.

• *Thresholds:* Thresholds are used where floor materials change at a door line, where a hard surface is required for an automatic door bottom, or where minor changes in floor level occur.

• *Hardware finishes:* Hardware is available in a wide variety of finishes, and the choice of finish depends primarily on the desired appearance. The finish is either integral to the base metal from which the hardware is made or is a plated finish. There are five basic base metals: steel, stainless steel, bronze, brass, and aluminum. Fire-rated doors must have steel or stainless steel hinges.

Interior Glazing

Glazing is the process of installing glass in framing as well as installing the framing itself. There are a number of types of glass that are available for interior use.

• *Float glass:* Float glass (annealed glass) is the standard type of glass used in common windows and other applications where additional strength or other properties are not required. For interior use, it is employed in small openings or where safety glazing is not required.

• *Tempered glass:* Tempered glass is produced by subjecting annealed glass to a special heat treatment. This glass is about four times stronger than annealed glass of the same thickness. In addition to its extra strength for normal glazing, tempered glass is considered safety glass, so it can be used in hazardous locations (discussed in the next section). If it breaks, it falls into thousands of very small pieces instead of into dangerous shards. Tempered glass for interior use is commonly $1/4$ in (6) thick.

One of the disadvantages of tempered glass is that it must be ordered to the exact size required for the final installation, because once it is tempered it cannot be cut, drilled, or deeply etched. In addition, tempering may produce slight distortions in the field of the glass, as well as near the tong marks for vertically tempered glass.

• *Laminated glass:* Laminated glass consists of two or more layers of glass bonded together by an interlayer of polyvinyl butyral. The glass can be clear or tinted float glass, tempered glass, or heat-strengthened glass. When exceptional impact or ballistic resistance is required, heat-strengthened glass can enclose one or more layers of polycarbonate laminated with interlayers of polyvinyl butyral or polyurethane. Polycarbonates are thermoplastic resins that are dimensionally stable and have high impact strength.

Traditionally, laminated glass used for interior applications has been clear. However, recent developments have provided the interior designer with a wide range of decorative possibilities.

When laminated glass is broken, the interlayer holds the pieces together even though the glass itself may be severely cracked. Laminated glass fabricated with tempered glass or polycarbonate is used where very strong glazing is required. Float glass or tempered glass can be used where acoustical control is needed. It can be bullet resistant and provides high security against breakage (intentional or accidental). Some combinations of glass and plastic thickness qualify as safety glazing and can be used in hazardous locations. Laminated glass is excellent where high strength or acoustical control is required. It qualifies as safety glazing and can be cut in the field. However, its impact resistance is low unless tempered or heat-strengthened glass is used.

• *Wire glass:* Wire glass has a mesh of wire embedded in the middle of the sheet. The surface can be either smooth or patterned. Wire glass is used primarily in fire-rated assemblies where it is required by most building codes. Wire glass cannot be tempered and does not qualify as safety glazing for hazardous locations.

• *Patterned glass:* This specialty glass is made by passing a sheet of molten glass through rollers on which the desired pattern is pressed, which may be on one or both sides. Vision through the panel is diffused but not totally obscured; the degree of diffusion depends on the type and depth of pattern.

• *Fire-rated glazing:* Aside from wire glass, there are four additional types of glazing that can be used in fire-rated openings.

The first is a clear ceramic that has a higher impact resistance than does wire glass and a low expansion coefficient. It is available with a 1-hour rating in sizes up to 1296 in^2 (0.84 m^2) and with a 3-hour rating in sizes up to 100 in^2 (0.0645 m^2). Although some forms of ceramic glass do not meet safety glazing requirements, there are laminated assemblies that are rated up to 2 hours and are impact safety-rated.

The second type is a special, tempered fire-protective glass. It is rated at a maximum of 30 minutes because it cannot pass the hose-stream test, but it does meet the impact safety standards of both ANSI Z97.1 and 16 CFR 1201.

The third type consists of two or three layers of tempered glass with a clear polymer gel between them. Under normal conditions, the glass is transparent, but when subjected to fire, the gel foams and turns opaque, thus retarding the passage of heat. This product is available with 30-minute, 60-minute, and 90-minute ratings, depending on the thickness and number of glass panes used. There are restrictions on the maximum size of lites and the type of permitted framing.

The fourth type of glazing is glass block. However, not all glass block is rated. The glass block must have been specifically tested for use in fire-rated openings and approved by the local authority having jurisdiction.

  • *Electrochromic glazing:* This is a general term for a type of glazing that changes from either a dark tint or milky white opaque to transparent with the application of an electric current. When the current on the glass is transparent, the glass either darkens or turns white (depending on the glazing type) when current is applied. There are three distinct types of this glazing currently on the market, only one of which is technically known as electrochromic glazing. The other two types are suspended particle device (SPD) and polymer-dispersed liquid crystal film. The distinction is important because each of the three types on the market at the time of this writing have slightly different characteristics, although all three depend on the application of a low electric current to keep them clear.

Electrochromic glazing uses an inorganic ceramic thin-film coating on glass and can be manufactured to range from transparent to heavily darkened (tinted). However, it is never opaque, so it cannot be used for privacy glass. It is intended for control of light, ultraviolet energy, and solar heat gain. The amount of tinting is not just an on or off condition; it can be controlled with a simple rheostat switch.

SPD glazing uses a proprietary system in which light-absorbing microscopic particles are dispersed within a liquid suspension film which is then sandwiched between two pieces of transparent conductive material. The appearance of the product can range from clear to partially darkened to totally opaque, so it can be used for privacy as well as for light control and energy conservation. It can also be variably controlled with a rheostat.

Polymer-dispersed liquid crystal film glazing is fabricated by placing the polymer film between two pieces of glass. The transparency can range from transparent to cloudy white. In its translucent state it offers total visual privacy but still allows a significant amount of light to pass through, so it cannot be used for exterior light control. All of the types of electrochromic glazing are very expensive, but the first two types do offer the potential for significant energy savings in the range of 20% to 30%.

Interior glass can be set in wood or metal frames. Figures 10.17 and 10.18 show two common framing methods. When glass is framed conventionally, as in Fig. 10.17, glazing beads are used to hold the glass in place. Glass can also be set in frames at the top and bottom and simply butt-joined on the sides as shown in Fig. 10.19. The gap between adjacent pieces of glass may be left open or filled with silicone sealant.

In addition to wood or metal doors with glass panels, solid glass doors are available. These are tempered glass, typically $^1/_2$ in

Figure 10.17
Standard Glass
Framing

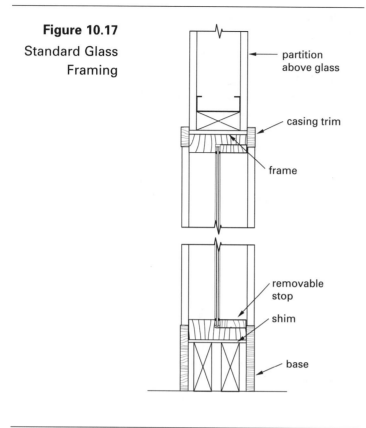

partition
above glass

casing trim

frame

removable
stop

shim

base

Figure 10.18

Frameless
Glazing

metal support braced
to structure

alum.
angles

aluminum angle

ceiling angle

glazing
tape
each side

glass

metal glazing channel

glazing tape

floor finish

setting block

or $3/4$ in (13 or 19) thick with top and bottom metal rails and some type of door pull. There are no vertical framing members on either side of the door. The metal rails allow the door to be set on pivots in the floor and above the door and provide a place for a cylinder lock.

Building Code Requirements for Glazing

The two primary interior glazing situations that are regulated by building codes are limitations on glass in fire-rated assemblies and safety glazing subject to human impact in hazardous locations.

The International Building Code (IBC) (as well as the other model codes in the United States and Canada) places limits on the amount and type of glass in one-hour rated walls. The IBC requires that interior fire window assemblies be protected by $1/4$ in (6) wire glass installed in steel frames or by approved fire-rated glazing. The maximum glazed area cannot exceed 25% of the area of the common wall with any room. Special fire-protection-rated glazing is not subject to this 25% limitation because it is tested as a wall assembly, not as an opening assembly.

To prevent injuries, codes require safety glazing in hazardous locations. Hazardous locations are those subject to human impact such as glass in doors, shower and bath enclosures, and certain locations in walls. A composite drawing of where safety glazing is and is not required according to the IBC is shown in Fig. 10.20. The exact requirements are given in two references, The American National Standards Institute ANSI Z97.1, Performance Specifications and Methods of Test for Safety Glazing Material Used in Buildings, and the Code of Federal Regulations, 16 CFR Part 1201, Safety Standard for Architectural Glazing Materials. Tempered or laminated glass is considered safety glazing. The National Building Code of Canada is a little less prescriptive. It requires tempered or laminated glass in doors, shower enclosures, and glass sidelights greater than 500 mm wide.

Building Code Requirements for Doors and Frames

When a building code requires that a partition be fire-rated, then all openings (such as doors, glazing, ducts, and louvers) in that partition must also be fire-rated. A protected opening is considered an *opening assembly* because it includes all components, but in the case of doors it is usually referred to as simply a fire-rated door, or in the IBC, a *fire door assembly*.

A *fire-rated door* is defined as a door assembly that has been tested by an independent laboratory to determine that it is capable of withstanding a measured temperature, without failure, for a set length of time. The assembly consists of the door itself, the frame, and the hardware used on the door and frame. The classification is stated in hours (or minutes), and some doors are also given a corresponding letter designation. The required rating for a door depends on the rating of the wall or partition in which it is placed and the intended use of the wall or partition. Refer to Table 28.1 for a list of fire door classifications commonly used in interior design work.

Most commercial interior design only requires the use of a 20-minute door in a 1-hour rated exit access corridor or where a smoke and draft assembly is required, or a $^3/_4$-hour rated door in a 1-hour occupancy separation or a 1-hour door in a 1-hour rated exit stair enclosure. For multi-floor projects, a $1^1/_2$-hour rated door must be used in a 2-hour rated exit enclosure (stairway).

Figure 10.19
Butt Glazing

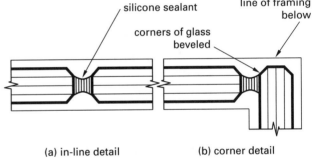

silicone sealant

corners of glass beveled

line of framing below

(a) in-line detail   (b) corner detail

Figure 10.20
Safety Glazing Locations

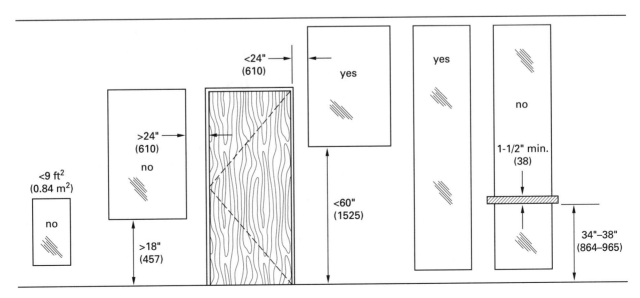

Some codes, such as the UBC and IBC, also require that a 20-minute door ($^1/_3$-hour) be a "tight fitting smoke and draft assembly," which means that listed gasketing must be placed on both jambs and the head to prevent the passage of smoke when the door is closed.

For fire-rated door assemblies, either wood or hollow metal doors may be used. Certain types of wood doors can be labeled up to $1^1/_2$ hours, but standard wood frames can only be used in 20-minute assemblies. For ratings above $1^1/_2$ hours for doors and 30 minutes or more for frames, hollow metal must be used. However, some jurisdictions allow aluminum door frames for 45-minute assemblies.

In recent years, codes have been modified to include a requirement for positive-pressure fire testing. This testing simulates actual fire conditions where there is positive pressure on the fire side of the door above a certain point on the door (called the neutral pressure level) and negative pressure below this point. Under such conditions, there is a greater tendency for smoke and gases to be forced through the crack between the door and frame. There are three standards that provide for this type of testing: UL 10C, NFPA 252, and UBC 7-2. The IBC references UL 10C and NFPA 252 (with the neutral pressure level set at 40 in (1016) above the floor).

When a door must meet the requirements of positive-pressure fire testing, it must have approved gasketing or intumescent material along its edge or frame.

Doors in corridors and smoke barriers must meet the requirements for a smoke- and draft-control door assembly tested in accordance with UL 1784, *Standard for Safety for Air Leakage Tests of Door Assemblies*. Local jurisdiction may require that they carry an S label.

Because exact provisions vary among local building codes, verify the exact requirements with the code having jurisdiction. Refer to Ch. 28 for more information on code requirements for opening assemblies.

Tests for Fire-Rated Doors

There are two primary industry standard tests used in connection with fire-rated doors. NFPA 80, *Standard for Fire Doors and Windows*, deals with the construction and installation of fire doors. NFPA 252, *Standard Methods for Fire Tests of Door Assemblies*, is the standard method for testing fire doors. UL 10B is another designation for essentially the same NFPA test.

Labels and Listing

When a door opening assembly is used, the door, frame, and closer are required to be labeled, and the other hardware must be labeled or listed. A *label* is a permanent identifying mark, attached to the door or frame by a testing organization, that indicates that the component complies with the standard UL tests for fire doors and with the National Fire Protection Association's Standard, NFPA 80, which governs the installation of fire doors. A *listed device* is a product that has been shown to meet applicable standards for use in fire-rated assemblies (including NFPA 80) or that has been tested and found suitable for use in a specific application.

CEILINGS

There are many materials and construction techniques used for ceilings. Most residential ceilings are gypsum wallboard attached directly to the floor joists or ceiling joists. In most commercial construction, the ceiling is usually a system separate from the structure and is usually constructed with some type of suspended system, using acoustical tile, gypsum wallboard, or lath and plaster. This allows a flat ceiling surface for partition attachment, lights, and acoustical treatment while the space above the ceiling, called the *plenum,* can be used for mechanical systems, wiring, and other services.

Gypsum Wallboard

For residential construction, gypsum wallboard ceilings are constructed by screwing or nailing the wallboard directly to the ceiling joists. Any wiring or heating ducts are concealed between the joists. If additional space below the joists is required, it is boxed in with wood framing, and the wallboard is applied over the framing.

Because commercial construction typically requires clear space above the ceiling for piping, electrical conduit, HVAC ductwork, and sprinkler pipes, gypsum wallboard ceilings are applied to a suspended grid of framing members. Figure 10.21 shows the typical construction: $1^1/_2$ in (38) steel channels are located 4 ft 0 in

(1220) on center and suspended from the structural floor above. Metal furring channels are attached to the main runners either 16 in or 24 in on center, with the wallboard screwed to them.

Most commercial construction uses 24 in (610) spacing with $^5/_8$ in (16) wallboard.

Although gypsum wallboard ceilings in commercial construction provide a smooth, uninterrupted finished ceiling, they lack the easy accessibility of suspended acoustical ceilings. Because of this, where access to valves, junction boxes, fire dampers, or other equipment or services is required, access panels must be installed in the ceiling. *Access panels* are prefabricated steel units with hinged doors that allow the wallboard to be framed into them. They are available in several standard sizes, but a 24 in (610) square door or smaller is usually sufficient. Unfortunately, if the design intent is to build a

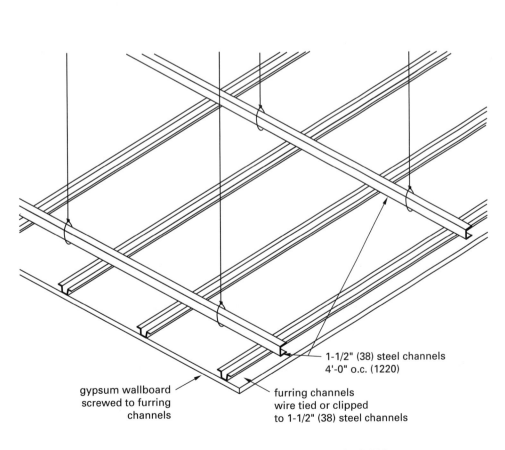

Figure 10.21
Suspended
Gypsum
Wallboard
Ceiling

gypsum wallboard
screwed to furring
channels

1-1/2" (38) steel channels
4'-0" o.c. (1220)

furring channels
wire tied or clipped
to 1-1/2" (38) steel channels

smooth ceiling, access panels interrupt the appearance and become unsightly after they are used a few times. Cracks develop in the joint compound around the frame, and the finish becomes soiled. If possible, wallboard ceilings should be limited to areas not requiring access panels, or the mechanical and electrical engineers should be requested to locate new equipment away from intended wallboard ceilings.

In addition to a flat ceiling, gypsum wallboard can be formed into nearly any configuration. Stepped, sloped, coffered, vaulted, and arched ceilings are all possible using various combinations of suspended framing and studs to form the basic shape. When acoustical control is required in residential construction, resilient channels are attached to the joists, and sound attenuation insulation is placed between the joists.

Suspended Acoustical

Suspended acoustical ceilings consist of thin panels of wood fiber, mineral fiber, or glass fiber set in a support grid of metal framing that is suspended by wires from the structure above. The tiles are perforated or fissured in various ways to absorb sound. These ceilings, though, do not prevent sound transmission to any appreciable extent. See Fig. 10.22

Acoustical ceiling tiles and the metal supporting grid are available in a variety of sizes and configurations. The most common type is the lay-in system in which panels are simply laid on top of an exposed T-shaped grid system. See Fig. 10.23(a). A variation of this is the tegular system which, uses panels with rabbeted edges, as shown in Fig. 10.23(b). Systems are also available in which the grid is completely concealed. Concealed systems typically use $1' \times 1'$ (300×300) tile sizes. See Fig. 10.23(c). Whichever type is used, the tile at the perimeter walls is supported by a ceiling angle. This angle is also used to support light fixtures mounted next to the wall.

Lay-in acoustical ceiling systems are available in sizes of $2' \times 2'$, $1' \times 2'$, $2' \times 4'$ (600×600, 300×600, 600×1200) (the most common), and $20'' \times 60''$ in the United States. The $20'' \times 60''$ system is used in buildings with a 5 ft working module. This allows partitions to be laid out on the 5 ft module lines without interfering with special $20'' \times 48''$ light fixtures located in the center of a module.

Other types of suspended systems that provide acoustical properties are available.

Figure 10.22

Lay-In Suspended Accoustical Ceiling

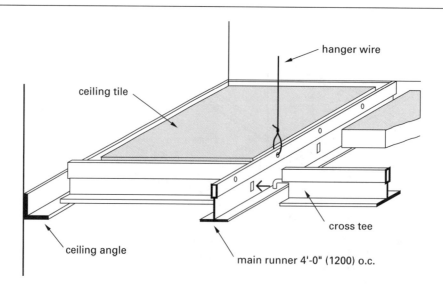

These include metal strip ceilings, wood grids, and fabric-covered acoustical batts. They all serve the same purpose: to provide a finished ceiling with access and to absorb rather than reflect sound (like a gypsum wallboard ceiling does) to reduce the noise level within a space.

Because ceilings serve so many purposes in today's construction in addition to acoustical control, there are many elements that must be coordinated with the selection and detailing of ceiling systems. These elements include recessed lights; duct work; sprinkler piping, fire-alarm speakers, smoke detectors and similar items; and drapery pockets and other recessed fixtures.

In many cases in commercial construction, the space above a suspended ceiling is used as a return-air plenum. Return-air grilles are set in the grid and return-air is simply allowed to pass through the grilles, through the ceiling space, and back to a central return air duct or shaft that connects to the HVAC system. If this is the case, building codes require that no combustible material be placed above the ceiling and that all plastic wiring be run in metal conduit. Some codes allow wiring used for telephone, computer, low-voltage lighting, and signal systems to be exposed if it is approved plenum-rated wiring.

Suspended ceilings may be rated or non-rated. If they are fire-rated, it means that they are part of a complete floor-ceiling or roof-ceiling assembly that is rated. Ceiling systems in themselves cannot prevent the spread of fire from one floor to the next. Rated acoustical ceiling systems consist of rated mineral tiles and rated grid systems, which include hold-down clips to keep the panels in place and expansion slots to allow the grid to expand when subjected to heat. Refer to Ch. 20 for information about the acoustic ratings of ceilings.

Figure 10.23
Acoustical
Ceiling System

(a) lay-in exposed grid

(b) lay-in tegular

(c) concealed spline

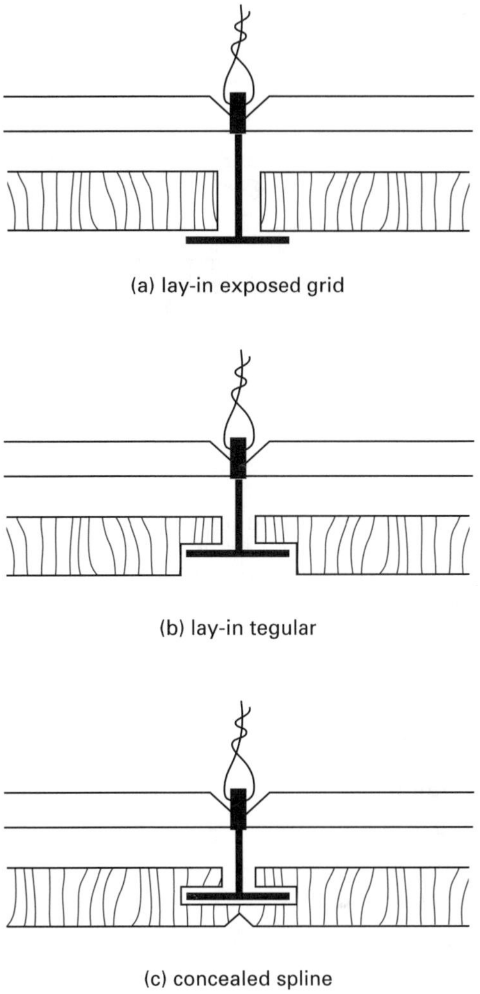

Acoustical ceiling tiles are manufactured with varying degrees of recycled content utilizing newsprint, perlite, and ground-up pieces of old tiles. Recycled content may range from about 50% to nearly 90%.

Seismic Restraint for Suspended Ceilings

In some areas of the United States (including most of California and some portions of Idaho, Montana, Utah, Hawaii, and Alaska), special seismic restraint detailing is required for suspended ceilings. Interior designers working on projects in these areas should verify the exact requirements based on the building code being

Figure 10.24

Partition Bracing
for Zones 3 and 4

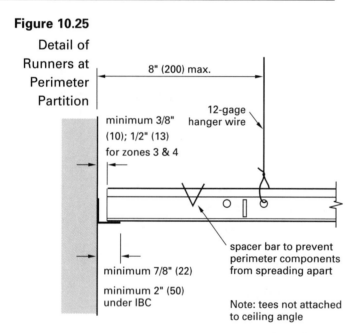

12-gage
wire bracing

ceiling tile shown
cut away for clarity

steel plate bolted
to ceiling tees

ceiling grid

top runner bolted
or riveted to ceiling
tees

Note: All components and connections
must be designed to resist design
loads applied perpendicular to the face
of the partition.

Figure 10.25

Detail of
Runners at
Perimeter
Partition

8" (200) max.

minimum 3/8"
(10); 1/2" (13)
for zones 3 & 4

12-gage
hanger wire

minimum 7/8" (22)

minimum 2" (50)
under IBC

spacer bar to prevent
perimeter components
from spreading apart

Note: tees not attached
to ceiling angle

used and the project's exact geographic location. When seismic restraint for suspended ceilings is required, certain criteria must
be followed. Some of the more common
criteria are listed here.

- Individual light fixtures and other
types of equipment that are normally supported by the ceiling grid must be independently supported with wires.

- The actual weight of the ceiling system, including lights and air terminals,
should be 2.5 lbm/ft^2 (12.2 kg/m^2) or less.

- The ceiling system should not be
used to provide lateral support for partitions. Instead, the partitions should be
braced with detailing similar to that
shown in Fig. 10.24.

- Ceiling angles should provide at
least a $7/8$ in (22) ledge, and there must be
at least a $3/8$ in (10) clearance from the
edge of the tile to the wall. This is shown
in Fig. 10.25.

- The perimeter main runners and
cross runners must be prevented from
spreading without relying on permanent
attachment to the ceiling angle.

- For ceilings in very high-risk seismic
zones, the suspension system must be a
heavy-duty type and must have lateral
force bracing 12 ft (3660) on center in
both directions, with the first point within 6 ft (1830) from each wall. As illustrated in Fig. 10.26, these points of lateral
bracing must provide support in all four
directions and must have rigid struts connected to the structure above to prevent
uplift as well as to support gravity loads.
Additional wire supports are also required
for all runners at the perimeter of the
room within 8 in (200) of the wall. Clearances from the ends of the runners to the
partition must be $1/2$ in (13) instead of $3/8$
in (9.5). The IBC now requires a minimum clearance of $3/4$ in (19) in high-risk
zones and a minimum 2 in (50) wide ceiling angle.

Lath and Plaster

Lath and plaster ceilings are constructed
similarly to lath and plaster partitions.
Like their partition counterparts, lath and
plaster ceilings cost more than gypsum
wallboard ceilings and are more difficult

to construct. However, they can easily be curved in two directions to form complex shapes. Full, three-coat portland-cement plaster ceilings are used most often when ceramic tile must be applied in a continuously wet environment, such as a public shower or a steam room. They are also used in remodeling work when ornate or complex moldings and decorative castings are required.

A typical commercial plaster ceiling assembly consists of a framework suspended from the structure like a gypsum wallboard ceiling. However, instead of using wallboard, expanded metal lath is wired to the framework and the plaster is applied, usually in a three-coat application process. In a traditional plaster ceiling for residential construction, metal lath is attached to the ceiling joists and a two- or three-coat plaster application process is used.

When curved shapes are required, the suspended framing is shaped into the approximate configuration of the ceiling and wire lath is bent to conform to the final profile. The application of the plaster completes the final shape. Large templates are sometimes used to ensure the entire length of a curved shape has a consistent profile. Like plaster partitions, a ceiling can be finished in a variety of textures.

As with partitions, veneer plaster construction can also be used. Gypsum lath is screwed to the framing, and a thin veneer coat of plaster approximately $1/8$ in (3) thick is applied.

For decorative work, complex moldings are formed by cutting a piece of sheet metal or wood to conform to the desired profile. A large amount of plaster is applied in place, and the metal template is run along the length of the molding to shape it. When moldings cannot be formed in place, they can be cast in molds and attached to the walls and ceilings.

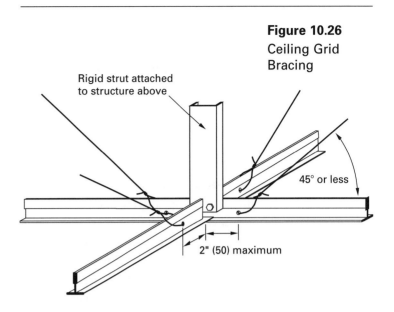

Figure 10.26
Ceiling Grid Bracing

Rigid strut attached to structure above

45° or less

2" (50) maximum

Integrated Ceilings

Integrated ceilings are suspended ceiling systems specifically designed to accommodate acoustical ceiling tile, light fixtures, supply- and return-air grilles, fire sprinklers, and partition attachment in a consistent, unified way. There are many proprietary systems, each with its own characteristics; however, all are intended to be used in commercial applications where the partitions, lights, and other elements connected with the ceiling change frequently. Most of the systems are designed to work with standard building planning grids of 4 ft (1200) or 5 ft (1500).

All of the components are designed for maximum reusability and flexibility. Light fixtures usually have plug-in connectors, and HVAC system air terminals are connected with flexible ducts so all services can be relocated easily. The top tracks of demountable partitions screw or clip onto a specially designed grid.

Integrated ceilings are more expensive than standard acoustical ceilings but can be economical when frequent changes to space plans are made. However, before deciding on an integrated ceiling system, a life-cycle cost analysis should be done to determine if the cost savings of frequent changes offsets the higher initial cost.

ORNAMENTAL METALS

Ornamental metals include a wide variety of both functional and decorative products such as spiral stairs, handrails, guardrails, and elevator interiors. Metal may also be used for custom doors and door facings, partition and millwork facings, building directories and kiosks, signs, custom light fixtures, ceilings, or as part of almost any construction assembly. The decorative options available to the designer are almost limitless. The most commonly used ornamental metals include stainless steel, the copper alloys of bronze and brass, and aluminum. Carbon steel, copper, iron, zinc, and porcelain enamel are used less frequently.

Stainless Steel

Types and Uses

Stainless steel is an alloy of steel containing 12%, or more, of chromium. Most types of stainless steel are supplemented with additional elements, such as nickel, manganese, and molybdenum, to impart particular qualities. Stainless steel is used for its corrosion resistance, strength, and appearance. For interior construction, common uses include wall and door coverings, railings, elevator finishes, lavatory and kitchen equipment, furniture, hardware, and concealed anchors and fasteners.

There are dozens of different types of stainless steels based on the composition of alloys, but two are commonly used for interior design purposes. These are types 304 and 430. The 300 series is chromium-nickel, and the 400 series is straight chromium.

Standard Forms

Stainless steel is available in several stock forms, including sheets, plates, strips, bars, pipes, and tubing. Tubing is much lower in cost than pipe, and ornamental tubing (which is formed by welding) should be specified for most ornamental interior applications. Stainless steel is also available in other common shapes. Angles, channels, tees, and other structural shapes can be used in detailing; however, they are expensive because of their extra weight.

Stainless Steel Finishes

Stainless steel is available in several finishes. These are produced either at the mill or by a metal fabricator and include rolled, polished, and etched finishes.

Rolled finishes are produced on sheet material by passing the steel between rollers under pressure at the mill. The finish of the steel depends on the finish of the rollers and can range from a bright, reflective surface to a deeply embossed pattern. Each manufacturer produces its own set of proprietary rolled finishes and should be consulted concerning availability. Rolled finishes are the least expensive of all the finishes.

Polished finishes are the most common for architectural applications. These are produced by grinding, polishing, and sometimes buffing the metal until the desired surface is obtained. There are five industry-standard polished finishes for sheet and strip stock, ranging from a number 7 finish, which is almost mirrorlike, to a number 3 finish, which has a dull finish. Generally, the more polished the finish is, the higher the cost will be.

Etched finishes are produced by dry or wet methods. *Dry etching* blasts the material with abrasive grit or glass beads to wear away a defined area. Stencils, metal templates, or adhesive materials are used to mask off portions of the metal. *Wet etching* uses acid to wear off some of the finish. Special masking must be used to maintain sharply defined areas and prevent the acid from undercutting the protected area.

Bronze and Brass
Types and Uses

Bronze and brass are the terms commonly used to describe a range of copper alloys. There are three primary groups of copper alloys: those that are almost pure copper, those called architectural bronze or the common brasses, and the nickel–silver and silicon bronze alloys. Technically, *bronze* is an alloy of copper and 2%, or more, of tin. *Brass* is an alloy of copper and zinc. In both metals, the predominant element is copper. In practical use, however, many of the alloys that are really brass are often referred to as bronze. In fact, none of the most common copper alloys used in interior architectural work are true bronzes. To avoid confusion, a copper alloy is referred to by its alloy number.

The choice of which copper alloy to use is usually a matter of the final color and appearance required, along with the cost. For example, alloy 280, also called Muntz metal, is a reddish-yellow, while alloy 200, also called commercial bronze, is a red-gold color.

Because these alloys are true brasses and are the most frequently used for interior applications, the word "brass" will be used for the remainder of this chapter even though the information applies to copper and most of the other alloys as well.

Although the copper alloys are corrosion resistant, they all change color with age and exposure to moisture in the air. After several years of weathering, those exposed to the exterior turn green or brown. For most interior use this is usually not a problem because the metal is protected from atmospheric moisture and chemicals. However, brass will tarnish and may show some color changes after several years, unless protected with some type of coating or refinished periodically.

Standard Forms

Brass is available in the standard forms of sheet, plate, bar stock, tubing, and pipe. As with stainless steel, these basic shapes are used to fabricate custom assemblies by various forming and fastening methods. Brass can also be extruded and cast. Extrusion is common for door and window frames, railings, and trim, while casting is used to manufacture hardware and plumbing fixtures. Brass can be fabricated to any size required; however, it is more economical to design and detail ornamental brass using standard shapes and sizes whenever possible.

Brass Finishes

Brass is available in mechanical, chemical, and coated finishes. Mechanical finishing alters the surface of the metal by rolling or some other mechanical means. Chemical finishes alter the surface with chemical processes. Coatings are applied finishes that are formed from the metal itself through chemical or electrochemical conversion or by adding some other material. Combinations of these three basic finishing methods may be used.

When specifying a brass finish, remember that the more highly polished the finish is, the more difficult it will be to conceal scratches and to refinish. Also keep in mind that large, flat, highly polished surfaces tend to show variations in flatness (oil canning) more than textured or figured surfaces do.

Methods of Fastening

Brass can be joined with mechanical fasteners or adhesives, or by brazing or soldering. Mechanical fasteners include screws, bolts, rivets, and various types of clips in compatible alloys. In most cases, the appearance of interior metal work is improved if mechanical fasteners are concealed. If the installation makes it impossible to conceal fasteners, the types, sizes, and locations of the fasteners should be given careful consideration based on the final installed position.

Adhesives can be used for laminating sheets onto backing material or to join smaller pieces to other materials when exposed fasteners would be objectionable. Unless some additional mechanical fastening device can be incorporated into a detail, adhesive bonding should not be used alone where the metal must support forces other than its own weight. It is usually best to verify the advisability of using adhesives for a particular detail with an ornamental metal fabricator.

Brass can be joined by brazing, soldering, or welding. *Brazing* is the joining of two metals at an intermediate temperature above 800°F (427°C) using a nonferrous filler metal. *Soldering* is the joining of two metals using lead-based or tin-based alloy solder that melts below 500°F (260°C). *Welding* joins two metals by using high temperatures (much higher than brazing)

to heat them above their melting points, either with or without a filler metal. Of the three methods, brazing is most often used to join brass for architectural purposes. If possible, brazed joints should be concealed because the filler metal does not exactly match the brass.

Galvanic Series

Galvanic action is the electrochemical process that occurs when dissimilar metals are in contact in the presence of an electrolyte, such as water. The result is the corrosion of one of the metals. Because most interior applications of metals are in relatively dry environments, galvanic action is not always a problem. However, detailing methods that put dissimilar metals in contact with one another should be avoided, especially in humid climates or where moisture may be present, either in vapor or liquid form. Certain combinations of metals are more susceptible to galvanic action than others. Table 10.1 list some of the metals used for interior applications. The farther apart the metals are from each other in the table, the greater the possibility of corrosion. The metals are listed from the most susceptible to corrosion to the least, from the top of the table down.

Galvanic action can be prevented by using the same, or compatible, metals and fasteners whenever possible. When two or more metals must be combined, they should be separated with isolators made from Teflon®, neoprene, or other suitable material. Teflon-coated screws can also be used when necessary.

FINISH CARPENTRY

Finish carpentry is exposed wood construction assembled at the job site by finish carpenters. It includes such items as installation of doors and windows, door and window trim, standard wood base and other molding, site-built stairways,

Table 10.1
The Galvanic Series

zinc

galvanized steel

aluminum alloys: 5052, 3004, 3003, 1100, 6053

aluminum alloys: 2117, 2017, 2024

low-carbon steel

wrought iron

cast iron

type 410 stainless steel, active

type 304 stainless steel, active

type 316 stainless steel, active

lead

copper alloy 280

copper alloy 675

copper alloys: 270, 230, 110, 651, 655, 923 cast

type 410 stainless steel, passive

type 304 stainless steel, passive

type 316 stainless steel, passive

and handrails. Finish carpentry is commonly used in residential construction and commercial construction where there is a limited amount of woodwork or where cost is a consideration. Finish carpentry is different than architectural woodwork in that the latter is custom, shop-fabricated millwork built of lumber, finished wood, and other materials. Architectural woodwork is reviewed in Ch. 11.

Although finish carpentry cannot be constructed or installed with the same level of quality as factory-built architectural woodwork, it is adequate for a variety of interior finishes in residential and some commercial construction. However, the types of materials used and specification methods are different than those of architectural woodwork.

Materials and Grading

Lumber used for finish carpentry is a regional material, and the available species vary depending on location. Common species include Douglas fir, ponderosa pine, sugar pine, Idaho white pine, southern pine, western red cedar, poplar, oak, and redwood, among others.

For interior construction, one of the most important aspects of specifying finish carpentry is the grade, which determines the type and number of allowable defects. Grading rules vary depending on the species and the trade organization responsible. For most species, B & Better is the highest available grade and is excellent for natural finishes or painted finishes. However, its supply is limited. C Select has only slightly more defects and is usually the best grade to specify for painting and some natural finishes. It is also possible with some species to specify either vertical or flat grain, which describes how the board is cut from the tree. Vertical-grain wood is cut so that the annual growth rings are perpendicular, or almost perpendicular, to the face of the board. Vertical-grain boards

tend to warp less, are more abrasion resistant, and stain more uniformly than flat-grain boards.

Panel Products

Panel products for interior construction include plywood, particleboard, medium-density fiberboard, and medium-density overlay.

Plywood is a panel product made from an odd number of layers of thin veneer glued together under heat and pressure. Each ply is laid in a direction perpendicular to the adjacent ply. Plywood is suitable for natural, stain, and painted finishes and is often used in finish carpentry construction. It is available in several thicknesses, including $^1/_4$, $^3/_8$, $^1/_2$, $^5/_8$, and $^3/_4$ in (6, 10, 13, 16, and 19). Common finished surfaces are softwoods (such as fir), but surfaces of birch and oak veneer are also available where a smooth, finished surface suitable for painting or stain, respectively, is required. Plywood used for finishing is graded by the quality of the face veneer. Veneer grades are classified by the N, A, B, C, and D. N-grade is intended for a natural finish and is made from all heartwood or all sapwood. A-grade is smooth and paintable with a few knots or other defects and is the best grade commonly available. D-grade is the lowest grade and allows for large, unfilled knotholes.

Particleboard is composed of small wood particles, fibers, or chips of various sizes mixed together in a binder and formed under pressure into a panel. It comes in several thicknesses as 4' × 8' sheets and is available in low-, medium-, and high-density forms. Particleboard is commonly used as a substrate for natural and laminate veneers in architectural woodwork construction.

Medium-density fiberboard (MDF) is a panel product made from wood particles reduced to fibers in a moderate-pressure steam vessel and then combined with a resin and bonded together under heat and pressure. It is the most dimensionally stable of the mat-formed panel products. MDF has a smooth, uniform, and dense surface that makes it useful for painting, thin overlay materials, veneers, and high-pressure decorative laminate.

Medium-density overlay is plywood with a thin, smooth veneer, suitable for painting. It has been largely supplanted by MDF.

Molding

Molding is trim used for decorative or functional purposes. For finish carpentry construction, standard profiles of molding are available in softwood and a few species of hardwood. A few representative profiles are shown in Fig. 10.27. In most cases, the standard molding profiles for base molding, casing trim, cornices, chair rails, handrails, and other applications are adequate. When part of architectural woodwork, this product is called standing and running trim. Refer to Ch. 11 for more information on standing and running trim.

For finish carpentry and architectural woodwork, alternatives to solid wood molding are available. Molding can be made from medium-density fiberboard or molded high-density polyurethane foam.

SAMPLE QUESTIONS

1. Under what conditions would a $1^3/_4$ in thick (44.4) hollow metal door be used?

  (A) when a fire rating of over 90 minutes and high security and durability are required

  (B) when a fire rating over 1 hour is required or a steel frame is necessary

  (C) when the door opening is expected to receive heavy use and a smoke-proof opening is required

  (D) when the door will receive minimal maintenance under heavy use

2. What type of locking device is most appropriate for an office building?

  (A) cylindrical lock

  (B) unit lock

  (C) card reader lock

  (D) mortise lock

3. Safety glazing is NOT required in which of the following locations?

  (A) sidelites where the sill is greater than 18 in (457) above the floor

  (B) glass sidelites next to a solid wood door

  (C) shower doors

  (D) full-height glass panels more than 12 in (305) from a door

Figure 10.27
Standard Wood Molding Profiles

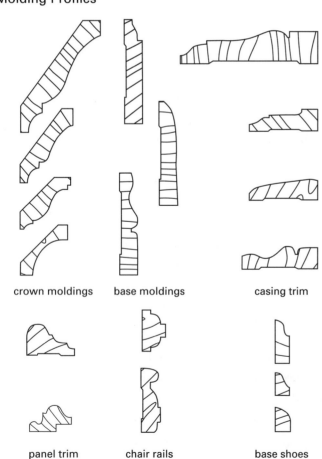

crown moldings   base moldings   casing trim

panel trim   chair rails   base shoes

4. What type of partition does the section shown indicate?

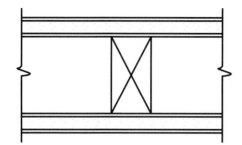

(A) $3^1/_2$ in (89) wood stud with gypsum wallboard

(B) $3^1/_2$ in (89) wood stud with wood paneling

(C) $2^1/_2$ in (64) metal stud with gypsum wallboard

(D) $2^1/_2$ in (64) metal stud with two layers of gypsum wallboard

5. What type of system would be most appropriate in a large commercial remodeling project where a decorative acoustical ceiling and plenum access are required?

(A) integrated

(B) linear metal strip

(C) gypsum wallboard

(D) concealed spline

6. The purpose of a setting block is to

(A) seal the gap between edges of butt glazing

(B) cushion the glass against the frame

(C) hold the glass in place

(D) support the glass' weight and separate its edge from the bottom frame

7. Which of the following metals would undergo the LEAST amount of change in appearance over a period of time?

(A) brass

(B) bronze

(C) copper

(D) stainless steel

8. What is the interior designer's best course of action if a client wants to remove part of a partition thought to be a bearing wall?

(A) have a structural engineer or architect review the problem and make a recommendation

(B) look in the attic to see if the wall supports any beams or joists.

(C) ask the client for the building's structural drawings and review them

(D) check for structural stability by tapping on the wall and determining where it is located in relation to the center of the building

9. To detail a doorframe for a conference room where privacy is critical, which of the following is LEAST likely to be required?

(A) an automatic door bottom

(B) a heavy-duty, silent door closer

(C) neoprene gasketing

(D) a solid-core door

10. In partition construction, the purpose of resilient channels is to

(A) increase the thickness of a partition

(B) increase the acoustical properties of a partition

(C) increase the strength of a partition

(D) provide a suitable base for attaching wallboard over masonry

11. What hourly rated door should be used in a 2-hour-rated stairway enclosure?

(A) 45 minute

(B) 1 hour

(C) $1^1/_2$ hour

(D) 2 hour

12. What is the safest type of glazing to use in a sidelight adjacent to a door?

(A) ceramic

(B) wire

(C) float

(D) tempered

13. What construction should be used to enclose a 1-hour-rated corridor?

  (A) $1/2$ in (13) Type X gypsum wallboard on $3^5/8$ in (92) metal studs

  (B) $5/8$ in Type X gypsum wallboard on $3^5/8$ in (92) metal studs

  (C) two layers of $1/2$ in (13) Type X gypsum wallboard on $2^1/2$ in (64) metal studs

  (D) $3/4$ in (19) gypsum wallboard on $3^5/8$ in (92) metal studs

14. Which of the following must have no less than a Class III (or C) fire rating?

  (A) bookshelves

  (B) wainscoting

  (C) built-in base cabinets

  (D) door and window trim

15. What is NOT required on a 1-hour rated door?

  (A) door closer

  (B) metal frame

  (C) ball-bearing hinges

  (D) panic hardware

11

ARCHITECTURAL WOODWORK

Architectural woodwork is custom, shop-fabricated millwork built primarily of lumber and used for interior finish construction and specialty furnishings. It includes cabinetry, paneling, custom doors and frames, shelving, custom furniture, and special interior trim. In addition to the usual types of millwork items, a wide variety of specialty items can be detailed and constructed. These include such things as conference tables, desks, fabric-wrapped panels, bars, display cases, and counters. In addition to wood, the designer can incorporate other materials into the item, such as ornamental metal, tile, stone, glass, leather, and fabric. Architectural woodwork is sometimes referred to simply as "millwork."

Architectural woodwork makes it possible to produce superior wood items because most of the work is done under carefully controlled factory conditions with machinery and finishing techniques that cannot be duplicated on a job site. In contrast to architectural woodwork, *finish carpentry* is woodwork completed on the job site. Finish carpentry is reviewed in Ch. 10.

Many aspects of the fabrication of cabinets and other millwork items have been standardized by the Architectural Woodwork Institute (AWI) and are described in great detail in *Architectural Woodwork Quality Standards, Guide Specifications and Quality Certification Program.* Three grades of millwork have been established: premium, custom, and economy. Premium grade gives the highest level of quality in materials, workmanship, and installation. It is usually reserved for special projects or special features within a project. Custom is the most common grade and still produces a high-quality job. Economy grade defines the minimum level of quality, materials, and workmanship. Using the AWI standards and grade levels makes if fairly easy to specify architectural woodwork because the exact requirements of the three grades for all types of woodwork construction are detailed in the *Quality Standards* book. They do not have to be redefined by the interior designer.

Another related type of millwork is modular casework. *Modular casework* consists of prefabricated cabinets that are selected from a manufacturer's standard product line. Casework is commonly used in residential kitchens and baths, laboratories, schools, and other areas where quality cabinets are required but custom construction is not required.

Because cabinets, paneling, trim, and similar finish wood pieces are such common interior construction elements, the NCIDQ exam requires extensive knowledge of architectural woodwork and the drawings required to describe its construction.

Figure 11.1
Methods of
Sawing Boards

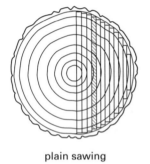
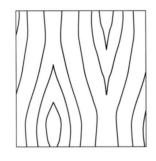

plain sawing

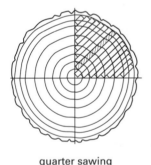
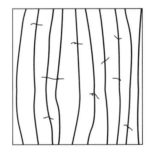

quarter sawing

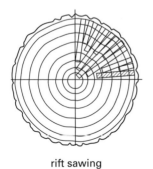
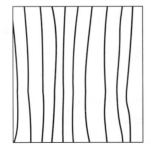

rift sawing

LUMBER AND VENEERS FOR ARCHITECTURAL WOODWORK

The raw material for architectural woodwork is broadly classified as either softwood or hardwood. *Softwood* refers to timber from evergreen trees, such as pine and fir. *Hardwood* refers to timber from deciduous trees, such as oak and maple.

Timber is manufactured into two forms for use in architectural woodwork: solid-stock lumber and veneer. As the name implies, *solid stock* is a thick piece of lumber (generally $1/2$ in (13) or thicker) used alone to form some woodwork component. A *veneer* is a thin piece of wood (usually less than $1/16$ in (1.6) thick) sliced from a log and glued to a backing of particleboard or plywood, normally $3/4$ in (19) thick.

There are many wood species used for both solid stock and veneer. Material comes from domestic and foreign sources and varies widely in availability and cost. Because of the limited availability of many hardwood species, most millwork is made from veneer stock. Because of ecological concerns, rising costs, and limited availability, other types of manufactured lumber products may be used in interior construction. These are reviewed in a later section in this chapter.

TYPES OF SOLID-STOCK LUMBER CUTTING

The way lumber is cut from a log determines the final appearance of the grain pattern. There are three ways solid stock is cut from a log: plain sawing (also called flat sawing), quarter sawing, and rift sawing. These methods are illustrated in Fig. 11.1.

Plain sawing makes the most efficient use of the log and is the least expensive of the three methods. Because the wood is cut with various orientations to the grain of the tree, plain sawing results in a finished surface with the characteristic cathedral pattern shown in Fig. 11.1.

Quarter sawing is produced by cutting the log into quarters and then sawing perpendicular to a diameter line. Because the saw cut is nearly perpendicular to the grain, the resulting grain pattern is more uniformly vertical. Quarter-sawn boards tend to twist and cup less, shrink less in width, hold paint better, and have fewer defects than do plain-sawn boards.

Rift sawing provides an even more consistent vertical grain because the saw cuts are always made radially to the center of the tree. Because the log must be shifted after each cut and because there is much waste, rift sawing is more expensive than quarter sawing and is seldom done.

Because of the limited availability of some species of wood and the expense of making certain cuts, not all types of lumber cutting are available in all species. The availability of cuts in the desired species should be verified before specifications are written.

TYPES OF VENEER CUTS

Just as with solid stock, the way veneer is cut from a log affects its final appearance. There are five principal methods of cutting veneers, as shown in Fig. 11.2. *Plain slicing* and *quarter slicing* are accomplished in the same way as they are when cutting solid stock, except the resulting pieces are much thinner. Quarter slicing produces a more straight-grained pattern than plain slicing because the cutting knife strikes the growth rings at approximately a 90° angle.

With *rotary slicing*, the log is mounted on a lathe and turned against a knife, which peels off a continuous layer of veneer. This produces a very pronounced grain pattern that is often undesirable in fine-quality wood finishes, although it does produce the most veneer with the least waste.

Figure 11.2
Veneer Cuts

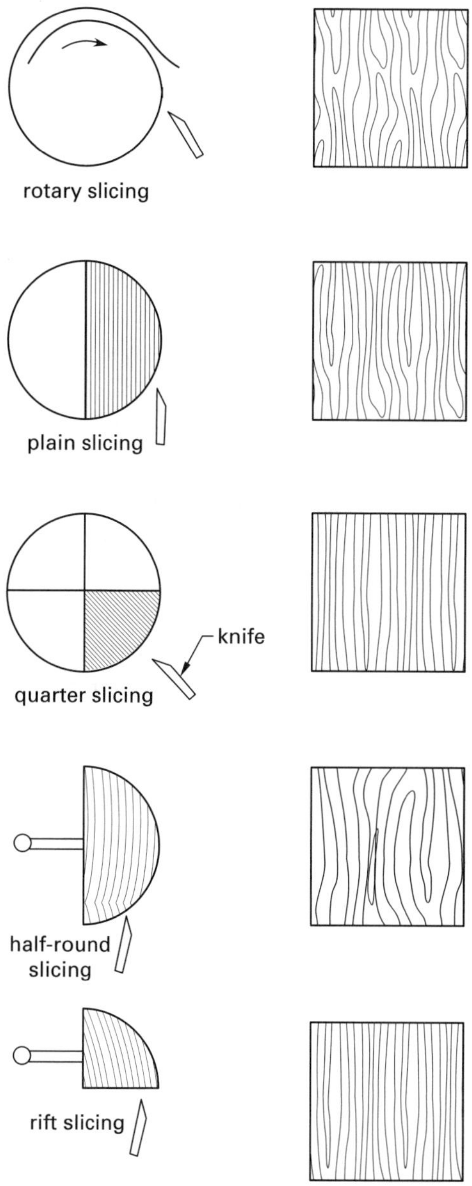

rotary slicing

plain slicing

quarter slicing

knife

half-round slicing

rift slicing

Half-round slicing is similar to rotary slicing, but the log is cut in half, and the veneer is cut slightly across the annular growth rings. This results in a pronounced grain pattern showing characteristics of both rotary-sliced and plain-sliced veneers.

Rift slicing is accomplished by quartering a log and cutting at a 15° angle to the growth rings. Like quarter slicing, it results in a straight-grain pattern and is commonly used with oak to eliminate the appearance of markings perpendicular to the direction of the grain. These markings in oak are caused by medullary rays, which are radial cells extending from the tree's center to its circumference.

Because the width of a piece of veneer is limited by the diameter of the log or the portion of log from which the veneer was cut, several veneers must be put together on a backing panel to achieve the needed size of a finished piece. The individual veneers come from the same piece of log, which is called a *flitch*. The veneer producer gives each flitch a number, which can be used to specifically refer to a set of veneers that the interior designer wants to be used to construct a project. If necessary for a very high-quality project, the interior designer can view all the flitches from a producer and select the ones that give the color and grain pattern desired.

Figure 11.3
Wood Joints

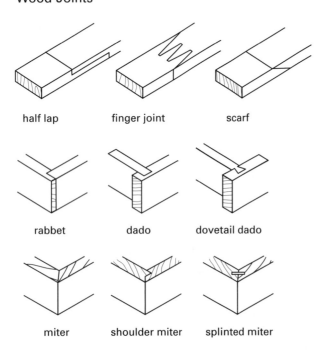

half lap   finger joint   scarf

rabbet   dado   dovetail dado

miter   shoulder miter   splinted miter

JOINERY DETAILS

Various types of joints are used for millwork construction, to increase the joint's strength and improve its appearance by eliminating mechanical fasteners such as screws. With the availability of high-strength adhesives, screws and other visible mechanical fasteners are seldom needed for the majority of work produced in the shop. Field attachment, however, often requires the use of blind nailing or other concealed fastening to maintain the quality look of the work. Some of the common joints used in millwork are shown in Fig. 11.3.

CABINETWORK

Millwork cabinets are built in the shop as complete assemblies and are simply set in place and secured to the surrounding construction at the job site. Cabinets include base cabinets, upper cabinets, open-front storage units, free-standing fixtures, and similar components. Because millwork is a custom-fabricated item, the exact dimensions, configuration, and finishes will vary depending on the design and the client's requirements. When appliances or other built-in equipment is planned, it is critical that the size and clearances required are noted on the millwork drawings. The finish of the exposed drawer and door fronts (as well as the countertop) may be plastic laminate, wood veneer, or other types of finishes such as paint, tile, or stone.

Base Cabinets

Base cabinets are built as a box with a bottom, two sides, a back, a front, and an open top set to receive a countertop. Within this basic box any combination of drawers, shelves, and other accessories can be placed. Figure 11.4 shows the construction of a typical base cabinet.

The sides and bottom of most commercial-grade base cabinets are constructed with a $^3/_4$ in (19) thick panel product, while the back is usually constructed with a $1/4$ in (6) panel. Depending on the quality of the cabinet, the top frame may be a continuous piece of $3/4$ in (19) solid wood or may consist of corner blocks. When the countertop is installed and secured to the cabinet, the countertop provides the additional strength to the cabinet.

Countertop Construction

Countertops are built separately from base cabinets and put in place in the field. This is because countertops are built in single lengths that are much longer than any individual base cabinet. Building and installing countertops separately also gives the installers the ability to precisely fit the countertop to the wall. This is done in one of two ways. The installer may provide a scribe piece on top of the backsplash or at the back of the countertop. A *scribe piece* is an oversized piece of plastic laminate or wood that can be trimmed in the field to follow any minor irregularities of the wall. The installer may also create a template from thin hardboard or cardboard after the base cabinets have been placed. This template is then taken back to the shop and used to precisely cut the countertop, including any out-of-square conditions, wall irregularities, or odd shapes.

Upper Cabinets

Upper cabinets are very similar in construction to base cabinets. The most notable exceptions are that an upper cabinet is not as deep as a base cabinet and some design and detailing consideration must be given to the underside of an upper cabinet because it is visible. In addition, there must be some way to securely anchor the cabinet to the wall. In residential construction, an upper cabinet is attached to the wall by screwing through the cabinet back and wall finish into the wood studs. In commercial construction where metal studs are used, wood *blocking* is required in the stud cavity behind the wall finish. This blocking

is installed as the studs are being erected and is attached to them with screws. The blocking provides a solid base for attaching the cabinets to the wall. Figure 11.5 shows a typical upper cabinet detail.

Figure 11.4
Millwork Base Cabinet

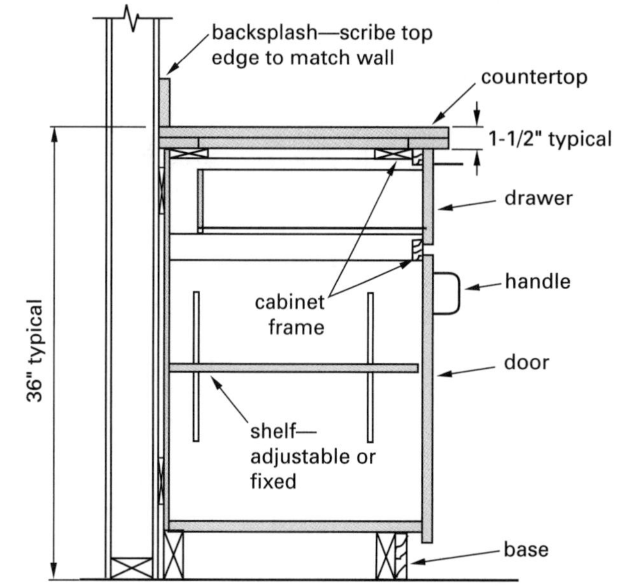

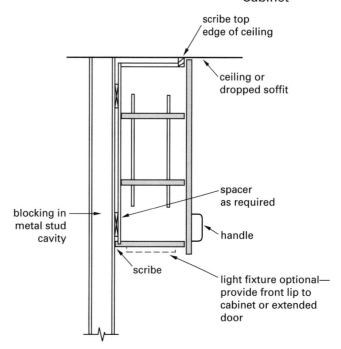

Figure 11.5
Millwork Upper Cabinet

The top of the cabinet may be detailed against the ceiling or, as is common in residential construction, the cabinet may be placed below a dropped soffit. The space between the top of the cabinet and the ceiling may also be left open, or the cabinet may be extended to the ceiling.

Figure 11.6
Types of
Cabinets Door
Framing

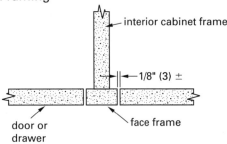

(a) flush construction

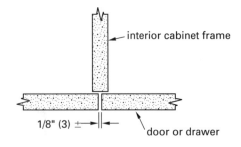

(b) flush overlay construction

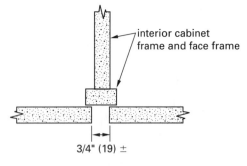

(c) reveal overlay construction

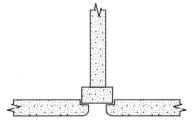

(d) lipped overlay construction

Door and Drawer Front Construction

For both upper base and upper cabinets there are four basic categories of door and drawer front construction: flush, flush overlay, reveal overlay, and lipped overlay. These are shown in Fig. 11.6.

In flush construction (shown in Fig. 11.6(a)), the face of the drawer or door is installed flush with the face frame. Extra care and expense are required to fit and align the doors and drawers within the frame. In many cases, the doors and drawers may sag, resulting in nonuniform spacing between fronts and causing some doors and drawers to bind against the frame.

A variation of flush construction is the lipped overlay construction shown in Fig. 11.6(d). In this version, part of the door or drawer overlaps the frame and covers the joint between the two pieces.

In flush overlay construction, the front of the door or drawer overlaps the face frame of the cabinet. Edges of adjacent door or drawer fronts are separated only enough to allow operation without touching, usually about $1/8$ in (3) or less. Only doors and drawers are visible, and they are all flush with each other. Cabinets using this type of construction are often referred to as European cabinets. See Fig. 11.6(b).

In reveal overlay construction (Fig. 11.6(c)), the edges of adjacent drawer and door fronts are separated enough to reveal the face frame behind. The width of the reveal can be whatever the designer or manufacturer wants, subject to the width of the face frame. This construction is often less expensive than flush overlay construction because minor misalignments and sagging are not as noticeable. Reveal overlay is the more traditional method of constructing cabinets.

In both upper and lower cabinet construction and countertop construction there should be a scribe piece installed, as shown in Figs. 11.4 and 11.5. A scribe allows the cabinet installer to fit the cabinet or countertop edge precisely against a wall that may not be perfectly straight. A scribe may be a separate piece of wood fit between the cabinet or wall. Alternately, the frame next to the wall can be cut slightly oversized to allow for trimming on the job site.

PANELING

There are two basic types of wood paneling: stile and rail, and flush. *Stile and rail paneling*, also called *raised panel*, is the traditional type composed of vertical pieces (stiles) and horizontal pieces (rails) enclosing a paneled area. See Fig. 11.7. *Flush paneling* has a flat, smooth surface with the edges butted together or joined with a

reveal, as shown in Fig. 11.8. Flush paneling is built up of thin wood veneers glued to backing panels of particleboard, plywood, or other suitable panel product.

In addition to the way veneers are cut, as described in the section on veneer cuts, there are several methods of matching adjacent pieces of veneer and veneer panels in a room that affect the final appearance of the job. The veneer matching method is the primary consideration to make when specifying paneling. The three methods, in increasing order of scale, are matching between adjacent veneer leaves, matching veneers within a panel, and matching panels within a room.

Matching adjacent veneer leaves may be done in three ways, as shown in Fig. 11.9.

Figure 11.7
Raised Panel Construction

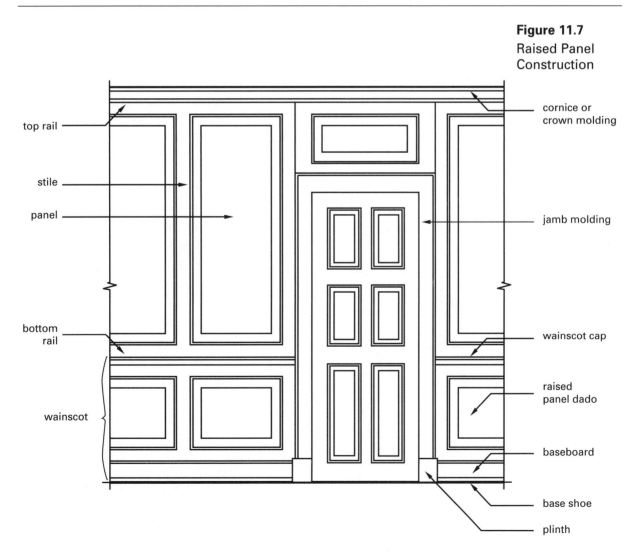

Figure 11.8
Panel Edge
Connections

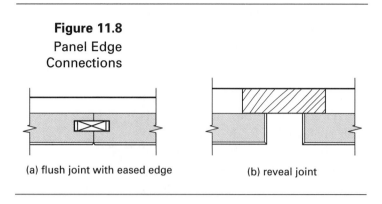

(a) flush joint with eased edge   (b) reveal joint

Figure 11.9
Veneer Matching

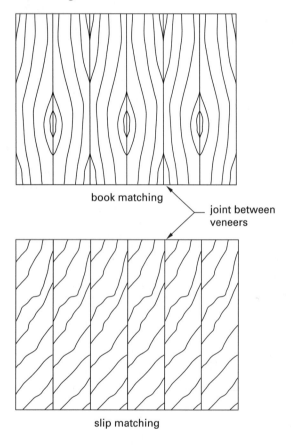

book matching

joint between
veneers

slip matching

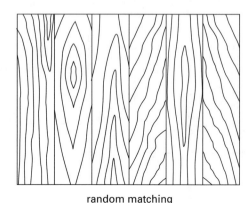

random matching

The most common method is *book matching*, in which the veneers are sliced off the log and every other piece is turned over so that adjacent leaves form a symmetrical grain pattern. With *slip matching*, consecutive pieces are placed side by side and the same face sides are exposed. *Random matching* places veneers in a random sequence, and veneers from different flitches may even be used.

Veneers must be glued to rigid panels for installation. The method of glueing veneers is the next consideration to make when specifying paneling. If the veneers are bookmatched, there are three ways of matching veneers within a panel as shown in Fig. 11.10. A *running match* simply alternates bookmatched veneer pieces regardless of their width or how many pieces must be used to complete a panel. Any portion left over from the last leaf of one panel is used as the starting piece for the next. A *balance match* utilizes veneer pieces trimmed to equal widths in each panel. A *center match* has an even number of veneer leaves of uniform width so that there is a veneer joint in the center of the panel.

There are three ways panels can be assembled within a room to complete a project. Fig. 11.11 shows three sides of a room as if the room were unfolded and the three walls were laid flat. The first, and least expensive, method is called *warehouse match*. Premanufactured panels, normally 4 ft (1200) wide by 8 ft or 10 ft (2400 or 3000) long, are assembled from a single flitch that yields from six to twelve panels. They are field cut to fit around doors, windows, and other obstructions, resulting in some loss of grain continuity.

The second method, called *sequence match*, uses panels of uniform width manufactured for a specific job and with the veneers arranged in sequence. If some panels must be trimmed to fit around doors or other obstructions, there is a moderate loss of grain continuity.

The third, and most expensive, method is *blueprint matching*. Here, the panels are manufactured to precisely fit the room and line up with every obstruction so grain continuity is not interrupted. Veneers from the same flitch are matched over doors, cabinets, and other items covered with paneling.

Joints of paneling may be constructed in a number of ways depending on the finish appearance desired, as shown in Fig. 11.8. Paneling is hung on a wall with either aluminum Z-clips or wood cleats as shown in Fig. 11.12. Using one of these methods of hanging panels allows the panels to move as the wood expands and contracts and obviates the need for exposed fasteners.

LAMINATES

A common finishing material used with millwork is high-pressure decorative laminate (HPDL), often called *plastic laminate*. This is a thin sheet of material made by impregnating several layers of kraft paper with phenolic resins and overlaying the paper with a patterned or colored sheet and a layer of melamine resin. The entire assembly is placed in a hot press under high pressure where the various layers fuse. Plastic laminates are used for countertops, wall paneling, cabinets, shelving, and furniture.

Because laminates are very thin, they must be adhered to panel substrates such as plywood or particleboard. Smaller pieces can be glued to solid pieces of lumber. There are several types of substrates used for plastic laminate construction. These include particleboard, medium-density fiberboard (MDF), hardboard, and veneer core. Among these, 45 lbm density particleboard is one of the most commonly used. It is the most dimensionally stable, provides a smooth surface for laminating, has

Figure 11.10
Panel Matching
Veneers

random widths of veneer
running match

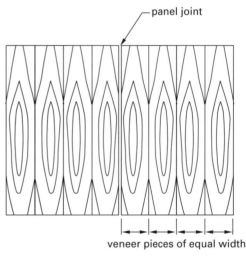

veneer pieces of equal width

balance match

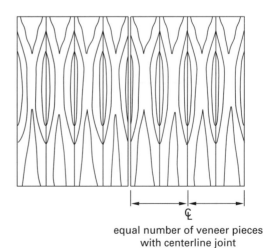

equal number of veneer pieces
with centerline joint

center match

Figure 11.11
Matching Panels
Within a Room

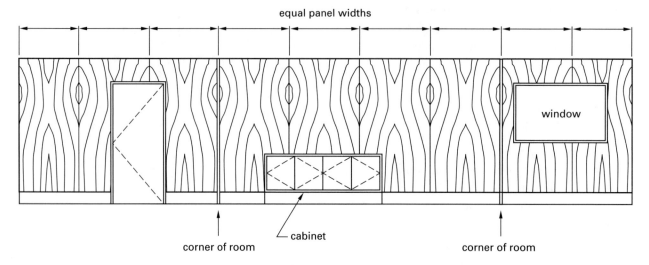

warehouse match

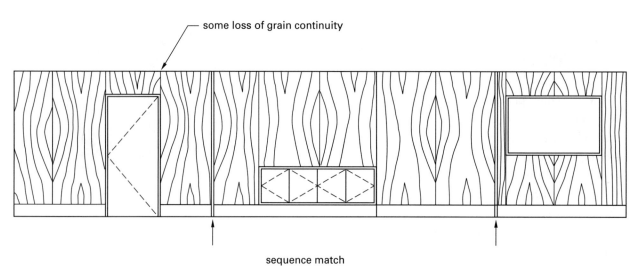

sequence match

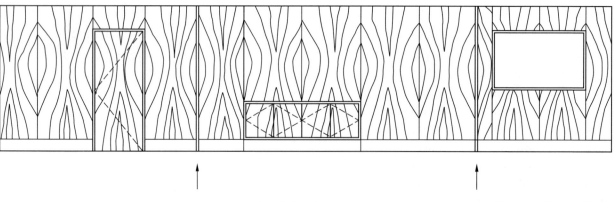

blueprint match

Note: elevations of 3 sides
of room shown "unfolded"

sufficient impact resistance, and provides enough strength for holding screws and for constructing panels and casework. In recent years, some concerns have been raised about the outgassing of formaldehyde from particleboard. With today's particleboard manufacturing techniques, the release of formaldehyde is negligible (0.3 parts per million or less). The laminate also provides a seal on the board, preventing most long-term emissions. If it is a requirement that there be absolutely no emissions, formaldehyde-free particleboard is available.

Medium-density fiberboard (MDF) is also a popular substrate for plastic laminate. MDF is made by breaking down wood fibers into very fine fluff and then mixing them with glue and compressing the mixture under high pressure. The resulting product is normally formed into 4 ft × 8 ft (1200 by 2400) sheets ranging from $^1/_4$ in to $1^1/_4$ in (6 to 32) thick. It can also be formed into molding ranging from 16 ft to 24 ft (4877 to 7315) long.

MDF has a smoother surface than particleboard, which reduces the potential for telegraphing through the laminate and makes it suitable for gloss laminates. However, it is more expensive than particleboard and is not good at holding some types of screws.

In addition to being used as a substrate for laminates, MDF can be used for shelving, molding, and furniture and as part of laminate flooring. Its dense, smooth composition allows routing and a flawless paint finish. It is dimensionally stable, so it does not warp, crack, or cup. Untreated MDF has the same fire rating as plywood, but special fire-resistant MDF is available.

The last two substrates that can be used for plastic laminate, hardboard, and veneer core are not as widely used as particleboard and MDF. Like particleboard, hardboard has a smooth surface, but that

Figure 11.12
Panel Mounting Methods

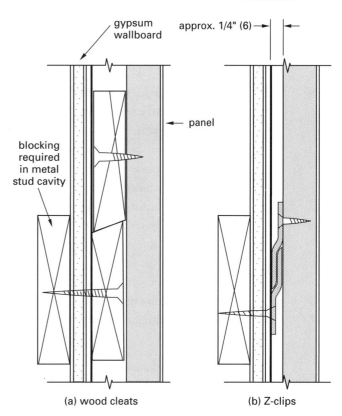

(a) wood cleats   (b) Z-clips

can sometimes cause bonding problems. Veneer core is subject to warpage and other problems; therefore, it is not recommended for interior applications.

There are several types and thicknesses of plastic laminate, the most common being a general-purpose type, which is 0.050 in (1.27) thick. It is used for both vertical and horizontal applications. A post-forming type, 0.040 in (1.0) thick, is manufactured so it can be heated and bent to a small radius. Another common type of laminate is general-purpose laminate for vertical use, which is a thinner material (0.028 in (0.71) thick) for vertical applications that receive less wear and impact than horizontal surfaces do. Other types include backing sheets and cabinet liner, as well as fire-rated, chemical-resistant, static-dissipative, and metal-faced laminates.

When plastic laminate is applied to large surfaces of paneling, it must be balanced with a backing sheet to inhibit moisture absorption and to attain structural balance so the panel does not warp.

STANDING AND RUNNING TRIM

Standing trim is an item of fixed length, such as a door or window casing, that can be installed with a single length of wood. *Running trim* is an item of continuing length, such as a baseboard, chair rail, or cornice. "Standing and running trim" is the term usually applied to wood pieces custom fabricated in a mill shop and then installed at the job site. Wood molding, as described in Ch. 10, is a similar item but comes in standard profiles and sizes; it is ordered by number and installed as a finish carpentry item rather than a millwork item.

Standing and running trim can be custom fabricated in almost any profile and dimension the interior designer wants (subject to limitations in rough wood sizes and fabrication tools) and from any available wood species. If an unusual profile is needed, the mill shop custom-cuts a die that is then used to plane down wood stock to the desired size and profile. Wood molding, on the other hand, is available in only a few wood species (such as pine, oak, and walnut) and is limited to standard profiles. A few of these profiles are shown in Fig. 10.27.

MOISTURE CONTENT AND SHRINKAGE

Because all wood products shrink and swell with changes in air moisture content, all wood construction should be detailed to allow this movement to take place without putting undue stress on the wood joints. Shrinkage and swelling in millwork is not as much of a problem as it is for site-built carpentry because of the improved manufacturing methods available in the shop and the fact that solid stock and veneer can be dried or acclimated to a particular geographical region and its prevailing humidity.

However, there are some general guidelines that should be followed. For most of the United States, Ontario, and Quebec, the optimum moisture content of millwork for interior applications is from 5% to 10% with an average of 8%. The relative humidity necessary to maintain this optimum level is from 25% to 55%. In the more humid southern U.S. coastal areas, Newfoundland, and the Canadian coastal provinces, the optimum moisture content is from 8% to 13% with an average of 11%. The required relative humidity necessary to maintain this level is from 43% to 70%. In the dry southwestern regions of the United States and in the Canadian provinces of Alberta, Saskatchewan, and Manitoba, the corresponding values are from 4% to 9% with an average of 6%. The relative humidity required is from 17% to 50%. See Fig. 11.13. These values should be used when specifying the maximum allowable moisture content in architectural woodwork.

MILLWORK FINISHES

Finishes are used to protect woodwork from moisture, chemicals, and contact, and to enhance the appearance of woodwork. Woodwork can either be field finished or factory finished. A factory finish is the preferred method because the results are easier to control. However, minor cabinet or trim work is often field finished in single-family residential construction. For high-quality woodwork, field finishing is generally limited to minor touchup and repair.

Prior to finishing, the wood must be sanded properly and filled if desired. On many opened-grain woods, such as oak, mahogany, and teak, a filler should be applied

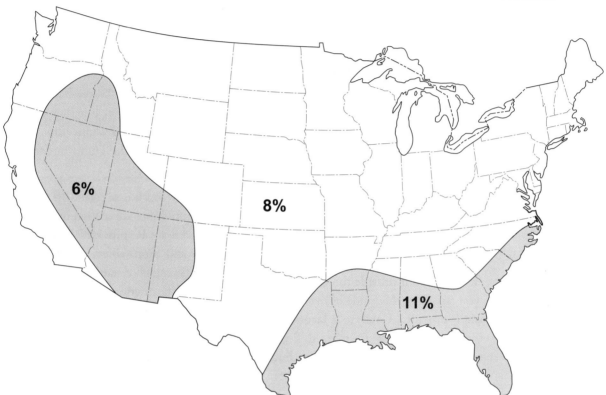

prior to finishing to give a more uniform appearance to the millwork; however, this is not required. Other types of surface preparation are also possible, depending on the aesthetic effect desired. The wood may be bleached to lighten it or to provide uniformity of color. Wood may also be mechanically or physically distressed to give it an antiqued or aged appearance. The color of the wood can also be changed in subsequent finishing operations by using shading or toning compounds.

Opaque Finishes

Opaque finishes include lacquer, varnish, polyurethane, and polyester. They should only be used on closed-grain woods where solid stock is required, and on medium-density fiberboard where sheet materials are required.

Lacquer is a coating material with a high nitrocellulose content modified with resins and plasticizers dissolved in a volatile solvent. Catalyzed lacquers contain an extra ingredient that speeds drying time and gives the finish additional hardness.

Varnish consists of various types of resinous materials dissolved in one of several types of volatile liquids. Conversion varnish is produced with alkyd and urea formaldehyde resins. When a high solids content is specified, the finish becomes opaque.

Polyurethane is a synthetic material that creates a very hard, durable finish. Although difficult to repair or refinish, polyurethane finishes offer superior resistance to abrasion and to penetration or damage from water and many commercial and household chemicals. Opaque polyurethanes are available in sheens from dull satin to full gloss.

Polyesters are another type of synthetic material that give the hardest, most durable finish possible. Opaque polyesters can be colored and are available only in a full gloss sheen. Like polyurethanes, polyester finishes are very difficult to repair or refinish outside the shop, but they create very durable finishes with as much as 80% of the hardness of glass.

Transparent Finishes

Transparent finishes include lacquer, varnish, vinyl, penetrating oils, polyurethane, and polyester.

Standard lacquers are easy to apply, easy to repair, and relatively low in cost. However, they do not provide the chemical and wear resistance that some of the other finishes provide. Catalyzed lacquers for transparent finishes are more difficult to repair and refinish, but are more durable and resistant to commercial and household chemicals. A special water-reducible acrylic lacquer is available if local regulations prohibit the use of other types.

Conversion varnish has many of the same advantages of lacquer but can often be applied with fewer coats.

Catalyzed vinyl yields a surface that has the most chemical resistance of the standard lacquer, varnish, and vinyl finishes. Vinyl is also very resistant to scratching, abrasion, and other mechanical damage.

Oil finishes are one of the traditional wood finishes. They are easily applied and give a rich look to wood, but they require re-oiling periodically and tend to darken with age. The look of an oil finish can be achieved with a catalyzed vinyl.

As with the opaque finishes, both polyurethane and polyester provide the most

durable transparent finishes possible. They are the most expensive of the finishing systems and require skilled applicators. Transparent polyurethanes are available in sheens from dull to full gloss, while polyesters are available only in full gloss.

Stains

Prior to applying the final finish, wood may be stained to modify its color. The two stain types are water-based and solvent-based stains. Water-based stains yield a uniform color, but they raise the grain. Solvent-based stains dry quickly and do not raise the grain, but they are less uniform.

Whichever finish is selected, the specifications should include the requirement that finish samples be provided by the woodworker and approved prior to fabrication. If specific colors of stain or sheen must be matched, the interior designer must supply samples of these to the mill shop so that finish samples can be made for approval.

SOLID SURFACING

Solid surfacing is a generic term for homogeneous, polymer-based surfacing materials. Solid surfacing is a combination of two ingredients—a filler and a clear resin binder, either acrylic, polyester, or a mixture of the two. Various colors and speckles can be added with pigments and small bits of the product itself. Solid surfacing can be formed into thick, flat sheets or into shapes such as kitchen sinks. It is frequently used for kitchen and bath countertops, sinks, toilet partitions, bars, and other areas where high-pressure plastic laminate might otherwise be used.

Solid surfacing is available in a wide variety of colors and patterns. The standard thickness for countertops is $^3/_4$ in (19), but newer, lower-priced products are $^1/_2$ in (13) thick. Because the color is integral throughout the thickness of the material, scratches, dents, stains, and other types of minor damage can be sanded out or cleaned with a household abrasive cleanser. Many of the available patterns resemble stone, so that solid surfacing can be used as a lower-cost, lighter-weight substitute for stone tops.

Solid surfacing materials are easily fabricated and installed with normal woodworking tools. Edges can even be routed for decorative effects. When two pieces must be butted together, a two-part epoxy or liquid form of the material is used for a seamless appearance.

FIRE RATINGS OF ARCHITECTURAL WOODWORK

Although specific building code requirements for woodwork use vary slightly across the United States and in Canada, they also have many similarities. Refer to Ch. 27 for information on model building codes and a more complete discussion of occupancy and use areas.

In general, most model building codes regulate the use of woodwork as wall or ceiling finish material but do not regulate the use of wood in furniture, cabinets, or trim. This includes cabinets attached to a structure.

Interior finish is defined in the International Building Code (and similarly in the Uniform Building Code and other model codes) as wall and ceiling finish, including wainscoting, paneling, or other finish, applied either structurally or for decoration, acoustical correction, surface insulation, or similar purposes. Requirements do not apply to trim, which is defined as picture molds, chair rails, baseboards, handrails, door and window frames, and similar decorative materials used in fixed applications. Nor do they apply to materials that are less than 0.036 in (0.9) thick and are applied directly to the surfaces of walls or ceilings.

As discussed in Ch. 27, the codes limit the class (flame-spread rating) of finish material (either A, B, or C) based on the occupancy, the location in the building, and whether or not the building is sprinklered.

Most wood species without flame-retardant treatment have flame-spread ratings less than 200 (Class C), and some even have ratings less than 75 (Class B). This makes them appropriate for rooms, enclosed spaces, and some corridors without any special considerations.

The model codes do not regulate the use of wood for freestanding furniture or for cabinets and shelves attached to the building because these items are considered fixed furniture. Trim generally must have a minimum Class C flame-spread rating, and combustible trim, excluding handrails and guardrails, cannot exceed 10% of the aggregate wall or ceiling area in which it is located. Trim is not regulated in the National Building Code of Canada if it has a flame-spread rating less than 150 and its area does not exceed 10% of the area of the wall or ceiling on which it occurs.

The strictest regulation on the use of woodwork as an interior finish occurs when paneling is used on walls and ceilings. The paneling must meet the maximum flame-spread rating of the code in force based on occupancy and use area. However, because the codes generally do not regulate finishes less than 0.036 in (0.91) thick, veneer less than this thickness with any flame-spread rating may be used if it is placed on fire-retardant treated material, such as particleboard.

When high-pressure decorative laminate is used on paneling, it is not subject to regulation if it is less than 0.036 in (0.91) thick. However, it should be applied to a substrate (usually particleboard) that is fire-retardant treated. Laminate for vertical use is 0.028 in (0.71) thick, so it does not have to be treated. When thicker laminate is used and the flame-spread rating is critical, fire-rated laminate can be used on a fire-retardant treated substrate with the appropriate adhesive.

Blocking on the outside of the partition on which paneling is applied should also be fire-retardant treated. In addition, some codes may require that blocking within the partition be fire-retardant treated.

ECOLOGICAL CONCERNS

Concern about deforestation of the world's tropical rain forests is causing many interior designers to reevaluate how they design and specify architectural woodwork. Because the problem is very complex and involves the supplying country's economic, political, and cultural milieu as well as worldwide economic factors, simply not specifying endangered species of timber may have very little effect on the problem, especially because such a small percentage of endangered timber is used for architectural woodwork.

One position supported by many design and furniture associations is that conservation, harvesting, and a country's local economic development need not be incompatible if the timber comes from a wisely managed plantation or agroforest that provides sustainable yield production. Unfortunately, less than 1% of the commercial timber trade is currently produced from sustainable-yield forests.

Until more is known about the problem and more countries and timber suppliers begin to produce with sustained-yield management, the designer can either choose to specify woods that can be shown to come from a sustainable-yield forest or select one of the hundreds of alternate domestic species that are in plentiful supply. Various alternate products are also available for use. One example is composite wood veneers, which are manufactured by laminating plain or dyed

veneers from commonly available or fast-growing trees into an artificial "log." The composited log is then sliced to produce a wide variety of decorative veneers. Refer to Ch. 26 for more information on alternative wood products and sustainability issues.

SAMPLE QUESTIONS

1. Commercial-grade cabinets are most often constructed of panel products with a thickness of

(A) $^1/_2$ in (13)

(B) $^5/_8$ in (16)

(C) $^3/_4$ in (19)

(D) $^7/_8$ in (22)

2. If minimizing cost is a concern, which style of cabinet door and drawer construction should be used?

(A) flush

(B) flush overlay

(C) lipped overlay

(D) reveal overlay

3. Composite wood veneers can be used

(A) to improve the appearance of book matching

(B) as a substitute for HPDL

(C) as a "green" alternate to standard wood veneers

(D) to increase the yield of veneer from a log

4. The joint shown is a

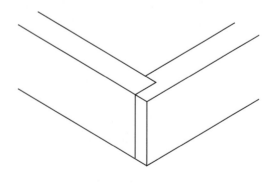

(A) half lap

(B) dado

(C) miter

(D) rabbet

5. In creating drawings for paneling that will be suspended from a wall with cleats, the most important piece of information is the

(A) width of each panel along the wall

(B) dimension between the panel top and ceiling

(C) thickness of the wood cleat

(D) size of the base

6. What should be called out on cabinet drawings to ensure a good fit next to existing construction?

(A) reveals around all edges

(B) spacers at cabinet backs

(C) scribe pieces at cabinet edges

(D) blocking, where necessary

7. Which method of veneer cut results in the straightest grain possible from most species of trees?

(A) half-round slicing

(B) quarter slicing

(C) flat slicing

(D) rotary slicing

8. When specifying the method by which two veneer pieces are to be applied, the most pleasing result is usually obtained with a

(A) balance match

(B) book match

(C) center match

(D) slip match

9. The flame-spread rating of wood panel wainscoting must be

(A) a minimum of class A

(B) class B if the wainscoting takes up more than 10% of the wall area

(C) nothing, because it is not regulated

(D) based on location and occupancy

10. For the most durable wood finish, which of the following finish types should be specified?

(A) lacquer

(B) penetrating oil

(C) polyurethane

(D) varnish

12

FINISHES

FLOORING

This section outlines some of the basic construction methods for flooring that is built with several components above structural floors as well as flooring that is simply applied as a single thin material such as resilient tile or carpet.

Wood Flooring

There are four basic types of wood flooring. *Strip flooring* is one of the most common and consists of thin strips from $^3/_8$ in to $^{25}/_{32}$ in (10 to 20) thick of varying lengths with tongue-and-groove edges. Most strip flooring is $2^1/_4$ in (57) wide, but $1^1/_2$ in (38) wide strips are also available.

Plank flooring comes in the same thicknesses as strip but is from $3^1/_4$ in to 8 in (83 to 203) wide. It is used where a larger scale is desired or to emulate wider, historic planking.

Block flooring is made of preassembled wood flooring in three basic configurations. *Unit block flooring* is standard strip flooring assembled into a unit held together with steel or wood splines. *Laminated block flooring* is flooring made from three to seven plies of cross-laminated wood veneer. Both types of block flooring are from $^3/_8$ in to $^{25}/_{32}$ in (10 to 20) thick. *Parquet flooring* is made of preassembled units of several small, thin slats of wood in a variety of patterns. It may be finished or unfinished. Parquet flooring is usually sold in 12 in (300) squares, $^5/_{16}$ in (8) thick, for mastic application. Parquet flooring is easier and less expensive to install than other types of flooring and can be installed in a wide range of designs.

The fourth type of wood floor is made from solid *end-grain blocks*. These are solid pieces of wood from $2^1/_4$ in to 4 in (57 to 102) thick laid on end. Solid block floors are very durable and resistant to oils, mild chemicals, and indentation. They were often used for industrial floors, but their use has been supplanted by other materials.

Wood flooring is graded differently from other wood products. Grading rules are set by the various trade associations such as the National Oak Flooring Manufacturers' Association and the Maple Flooring Manufacturers' Association. Unfinished oak flooring is graded as clear, select, no. 1 common, and no. 2 common. Clear is the best grade with the most uniform color.

Plain sawn is standard, but quarter sawn is available on special order. Lengths of pieces are $1^1/4$ ft (381) and longer, with the average length being $3^3/4$ ft (1143). Beech, birch, and maple are available in first, second, and third grades along with some combination grades.

Bamboo flooring is an environmentally sensitive alternative to traditional hardwood flooring. This is because it is a fast-growing grass and not a tree and can be obtained from managed forests where other agricultural crops are difficult to grow. Bamboo flooring is available in $1/2$ in (13) and $3/4$ in (19) thick strips about 3 in (76) wide or wider, depending on the manufacturer. It is milled with tongue-and-groove edges, so it can be installed like standard wood flooring or with adhesive.

Another environmentally friendly, alternative wood flooring material is palm wood. This is harvested as a byproduct from plantation-grown coconut palms. Palm wood flooring is available in $3/4''$ × $3''$ wide strips with tongue-and-groove edges. It is harder than oak or maple and comes prefinished in colors ranging from dark- to medium-red mahogany.

Wood flooring must be installed over a suitable nailable base. Because wood swells if it gets damp, provisions must be made to prevent moisture from seeping up from below and to allow for expansion of the completed floor. Strip flooring is installed by blind nailing through the tongue. Figure 12.1 shows two methods of installing wood flooring over a concrete subfloor in commercial construction. In Fig. 12.1(a), a sheet of $3/4$ in (19) plywood is attached to the concrete to provide the nailable base. A layer of polyethylene film is laid down first if moisture may be a problem.

In Fig. 12.1(b), the wood flooring is laid on wood sleepers. This method of installation not only gives a more resilient floor that is more comfortable under foot, but it also provides an air space so any excess moisture can escape. In both instances, a gap of about $3/8$ in to $3/4$ in (10 to 19) is left at the perimeter to allow for expansion and is concealed with the wood base.

Figure 12.2 shows the typical installation over wood framing with a plywood or particleboard subfloor, as is typical in most residential construction. A layer of 15 lbm asphalt felt may be laid to prevent squeaking and act as a vapor barrier. Resilient pads are also available for use in place of sleepers for strip flooring installation.

Figure 12.1
Wood Flooring Installation

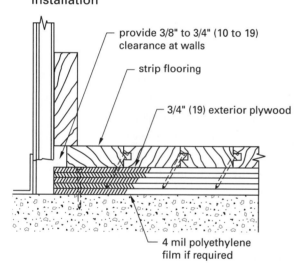

provide 3/8" to 3/4" (10 to 19) clearance at walls

strip flooring

3/4" (19) exterior plywood

4 mil polyethylene film if required

(a) strip flooring over plywood

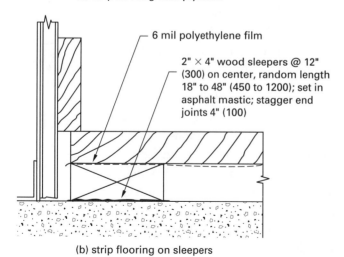

6 mil polyethylene film

2" × 4" wood sleepers @ 12" (300) on center, random length 18" to 48" (450 to 1200); set in asphalt mastic; stagger end joints 4" (100)

(b) strip flooring on sleepers

These provide an even more resilient floor and are often used for dance floors and gymnasium floors.

Engineered wood floors have begun to replace some of the traditional types. Engineered wood floors include the laminated block flooring and parquet flooring described. These are available either unfinished or prefinished. Engineered wood flooring consists of three, five, or seven layers of wood veneer, each oriented at 90° to the adjacent ones, like plywood. The top layer is the actual finished wood species. Because engineered wood floors are more dimensionally stable than solid wood, they shrink and swell less with changes in moisture. Some types of engineered floors are glued directly to a stable wood subfloor; others are laid loose over thin foam padding so they can move independently of the subfloor.

In addition to the commonly used maple, oak, birch, and beech, there are many wood species, both domestic and imported, that can be used for flooring. Of the many available, two qualify as sustainable products: bamboo and palm wood.

Bamboo is not a tree, but a fast-growing grass that reaches maturity in three to four years. It can be used for flooring as well as for veneer and paneling. It can be obtained from managed forests where it is grown on steep slopes and hill lands where other forms of agriculture are difficult to propagate.

Bamboo flooring is available in $1/2$ in (13) and $3/4$ in (19) thick strips about 3 in (76) wide or wider, depending on the manufacturer. It is milled with tongue-and-groove edges, so it can be installed like standard wood strip flooring—by nailing or with adhesive. Bamboo is almost as hard and twice as stable as red oak and maple. It is available in a natural color or a darker, amber color and comes prefinished with a durable polyurethane coating.

Figure 12.2
Wood Flooring on Wood Framing

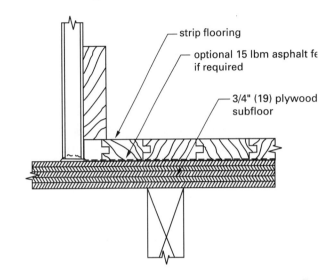

- strip flooring
- optional 15 lbm asphalt fe if required
- 3/4" (19) plywood subfloor

Palm wood comes from coconut palms and is a byproduct of commercial coconut plantations. Palm wood flooring is available in $3/4$" × 3" (19 by 76) wide strips with tongue-and-groove edges like those of standard strip flooring. It is harder and more stable than maple, red oak, and white oak. The flooring ranges from dark- to medium-red mahogany in color and is prefinished with polyurethane.

Stone Flooring

Five types of stone are commonly used in interior construction for flooring as well as for walls: granite, marble, limestone, slate, and sandstone.

- *Granite* is an igneous rock with visible grains. It is available in a wide variety of colors, including gray, beige, white, pink, red, blue, green, and black. For interior use, there are five common finishes. A polished finish has a mirror gloss with sharp reflections. A honed finish has a dull sheen, without reflections. Fine-rubbed finishes produce a smooth surface that is free from scratches, with no sheen. A rubbed finish has a surface with occasional slight "trails" or scratches. Finally, a thermal, or flame, finish has a coarse surface, which varies depending on the granite's grain structure.

• *Marble* is a metamorphic rock formed by layers of shells that, under heat and pressure, form into a composition of crystalline grains of calcite and/or dolomite. Like granite, marble is available in a range of colors and patterns from uniform, pure white to vivid greens and reds with wild streaked patterns. The smoothest finish for marble is a polished finish, which produces a glossy surface bringing out the full color and character of the marble. A honed finish has a satin-smooth surface, with little or no gloss. An abrasive finish has a flat, nonreflective surface suitable for stair treads and other nonslip surfaces. A wet-sand finish yields a smooth surface that is also suitable for nonslip floors.

• *Limestone* is most commonly used for exterior surfaces, but a type of limestone called travertine is frequently used for interior flooring. Because of the way it is formed, travertine has a network of holes in it. These must be filled with an epoxy resin (which can be colored to be compatible with the stone) to make a smooth surface. Travertine is a light, creamy color and is usually finished with a polished surface.

• *Slate* is a fine-grain metamorphic rock that is easily split into thin slabs, making it ideal for flooring as well as roofing. Slate is available in ranges of gray, black, green, brown, and deep red. A natural cleft finish shows the surface as it is cleaved from the rock, so it is rough and the surface level varies by about $1/8$ in (3). A sand-rubbed finish gives an even plane showing a slight grain. A honed finish is semipolished, without a sheen.

• *Sandstone* is a sedimentary rock made of sand and other substances. When cleaved from the original rock, it is called flagstone and has a naturally rough surface. It can be used with irregular edges as it comes from the rock, or it can be saw-cut into rectangular or square shapes.

Stone flooring can be installed in a number of ways; the two primary methods are a thin-set or a thick-set installation. With the first type, a uniform thickness of stone is set on the subfloor with a special thin-set mortar (about $1/8$ in (3) or less in thickness) or with adhesive. A thick-set installation requires that a layer of mortar from $3/4$ in to $1 1/4$ in (19 to 32) thick be applied to a suitably prepared, structurally sound subfloor. Either the stone is then set in the semiwet mortar or the mortar is allowed to cure and the stone is set with another thin layer of dry-set mortar on top of the first.

Thick-set applications are generally the best and must be used when the subfloor is uneven or when the stone varies in thickness, as with slate or sandstone. Thin-set applications are less expensive, add much less weight to the floor, and are faster to install. They are suitable for thin stone floors cut in uniform thicknesses in either residential or commercial construction.

The various types of stone flooring installation methods are shown in Fig. 12.3. With thick-set methods, the mortar bed can be bonded to the subfloor or separated from it with a cleavage membrane. Used with steel reinforcing mesh in the mortar bed, this method allows the finish floor to be structurally separate from the subfloor. If the subfloor deflects or moves slightly, the stone flooring is protected from cracking because it is not bonded to the structural floor. Thin-set floors can be placed on either concrete or wood subfloors.

Stone floors can be set with the joints tightly butted together or with a space between the individual pieces. If there is a gap in the joint, it must be filled with grout or a portland cement/sand mixture that can be colored to be compatible with the color of the stone. Several special types of grout are available that are resistant to chemicals, fungus, and mildew. Another type of grout is latex grout, which provides some flexibility when slight movement in the floor is expected.

Whatever type of stone is used, the weight the stone and mortar will add to the floor, the extra thickness required, and the finish that will be most appropriate must be considered. Most thin stones ($^1/_4$ in to $^3/_8$ in (6 to 10)) that are applied with a thin-set mortar or adhesive do not add significant weight to the floor. Thick-set stone floors are very heavy and require an extra $1^1/_2$ in to $2^1/_2$ in (38 to 64) above the subfloor. Structural capacities should be verified with a structural engineer.

Polished finishes should not be used in areas where the stone might get wet or on stairs because of the potential slippage problems. Flamed finishes with granite, or an abrasive finish with marble, are better choices in these applications and, in fact, are required by code in some applications.

Terrazzo

Terrazzo is a composite material poured in place or precast that is used for floors, walls, and stairs. It consists of marble, quartz, granite, or other suitable chips, in a matrix that is cementitious, chemical, or a combination of both. Terrazzo is poured, cured, ground, and polished to produce a smooth surface.

The advantages of terrazzo include durability, water resistance, ease of cleaning, fire resistance, and the availability of a wide choice of patterns and colors. An unlimited number of terrazzo finishes can be achieved by specifying various combinations of chips and matrix colors.

There are four basic types of terrazzo. *Standard terrazzo* is the most common type, using small chips no larger than $^3/_8$ in (10). *Venetian terrazzo* uses chips larger than $^3/_8$ in. *Palladian terrazzo* uses

Figure 12.3
Stone Flooring Installation Methods

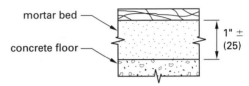

(a) mortar bed bonded to concrete subfloor

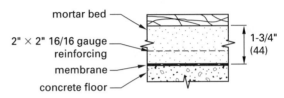

(b) mortar bed separated from concrete subfloor

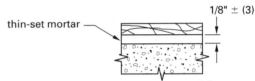

(c) thin-set mortar on concrete subfloor

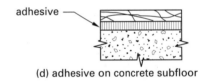

(d) adhesive on concrete subfloor

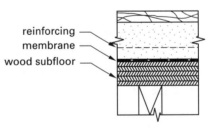

(e) mortar bed separated from wood subfloor

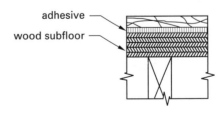

(f) adhesive on wood subfloor

Figure 12.4
Methods of
Terrazzo
Installation

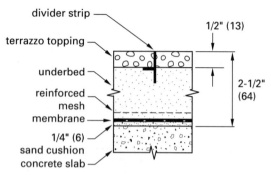

(a) sand cushion terrazzo

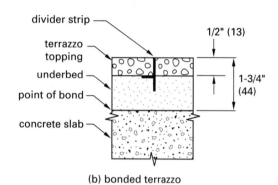

(b) bonded terrazzo

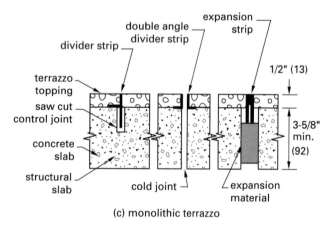

(c) monolithic terrazzo

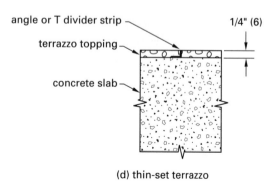

(d) thin-set terrazzo

thin random-fractured slabs of marble with standard terrazzo between. *Rustic terrazzo* has the matrix depressed to expose the chips.

Terrazzo can be installed on walls as well as floors. Several common floor installations are shown in Fig. 12.4. The sand cushion method (a) is the best way to avoid cracking of the terrazzo because the finish system is physically separated from the structural slab with a membrane, much the same as in one of the thick-set stone floor installation methods. Because the underbed is reinforced, the terrazzo system can move independently of the structure. If floor movement or deflection is not anticipated, the bonded method (b) can be used. Where the thickness of the installation is a problem, a monolithic (c) or thin-set (d) method can be used.

Terrazzo is generally finished to a smooth surface with an 80-grit stone grinder, but it can be ground with a rough, 24-grit to achieve a more textured surface. Rustic terrazzo exposes some of the stone when the matrix is washed before it has set, but this finish is usually not appropriate for interior flooring.

Resilient Flooring

Resilient flooring is a generic term describing several types of composition materials made from various resins, fibers, plasticizers, and fillers. It is formed under heat and pressure to produce a thin material, either sheets or tiles. Resilient flooring is applied with mastic to a subfloor of concrete, plywood, or other smooth underlayment. Some resilient floorings may be installed only on floors above grade, while others may be placed below, on, or above grade. The common types of resilient flooring used today include vinyl, rubber, and cork.

• *Vinyl flooring* includes pure vinyl, vinyl composition, vinyl tiles, and sheet vinyl. It is a good, durable resilient flooring that is resistant to indentation, abrasion, grease, water, alkalis, and some acids. Vinyl comes in a variety of colors and patterns and is inexpensive and easy to install. It can be used below grade, on grade, or above grade. It must be installed over a clean, dry, smooth surface. Vinyl tiles are generally 12 in (300) square, although some are available in 9 in (225) squares. Either $^1/_{16}$ in or $^1/_8$ in (2 or 3) thicknesses is available, but for commercial use and better residential floors, the $^1/_8$ in thickness is preferred. Sheet vinyl comes in 6, 9, or 12 ft (1800, 2700, or 3600) wide rolls. Although slightly more difficult to install, it results in a floor with fewer seams.

Vinyl composition tile is similar to vinyl tile but includes various types of fillers that decrease the percentage of polyvinylchloride. While composition tile costs less than homogenous vinyl, it has less flexibility and abrasion resistance. Because of this, through-grain types should be specified. These are tiles where the color and pattern extend uniformly through the tile thickness. Normally, this tile is applied with mastic; however, peel-and-stick types are available for residential applications. Tile is also available with attached foam backing for greater resilience.

• *Rubber flooring* is made from synthetic rubber and offers excellent resistance to deformation under loads, providing a very comfortable, quiet, resilient floor. Rubber, however, is not very resistant to oils or grease. This flooring is available with a smooth surface or with a patterned, raised surface that allows water and dirt to lie below the wearing surface, helping to prevent slipping or excessive abrasion. Rubber flooring is available in tiles or sheets in several thicknesses.

• *Cork flooring* is made from granulated pieces of bark from the cork oak tree that are bonded together under heat and pressure. By varying the heat or adding dyes, a variety of colors and patterns can be produced—some with the characteristic straw color of cork and others as dark as walnut. Patterns range from standard, uniform flakes to alternating strips of dark and light material.

Cork is a renewable resource because after it is harvested, the tree grows a new skin in approximately nine years, and then it can be harvested again. In addition, the cork industry helps preserve forests. Portugal, which produces about half of the world's cork, regulates harvesting and has made it illegal to cut down cork-producing trees.

Cork is available in tile and plank forms and is used where acoustical control or a high degree of resilience is desired. Tiles are commonly 12 in (305) square and $^1/_8$ in to $^1/_4$ in (3 to 6) thick. Planks are 12 in (305) wide and 3 ft (914) long and consist of cork laminated to tongue-and-groove medium-density fiberboard.

Cork tile is installed using adhesive, while the plank form is edge-glued without being adhered to the subfloor. The entire floor then "floats" on the subfloor. In either case, the subfloor must be perfectly smooth so any unevenness does not telegraph through.

Cork flooring is available either unfinished or prefinished. Finishes include acrylic, polyurethane, and carnauba wax. Acrylic requires frequent reapplication—every four to six months. Polyurethane must be reapplied every three to seven years, and the old finish must be completely sanded off to ensure the new application will stick. Wax must be reapplied about once a year.

• *Linoleum* is composed of oxidized linseed oil, wood flour, pigments, and fillers applied over a backing of burlap or asphalt-saturated felt. Linoleum is available in solid colors or with multicolored patterns that extend through the thickness to the backing. Linoleum has very good abrasion and grease resistance but has limited resistance to alkalis. It is commonly available in 0.10 in (2.5) thickness, but other thicknesses are available depending on the manufacturer. Because it is composed of natural materials it is popular as a sustainable material.

Testing Concrete for Moisture Content and Alkalinity

Whatever type of resilient flooring is selected, it is critical that the substrate be free of excess moisture and alkalinity. This is usually problematic when tile or other flooring materials are being placed on concrete floors.

Concrete should be tested for moisture level prior to applying any critical finishes such as vinyl, rubber, linoleum, urethane, and wood. The flooring industry generally recommends that these types of flooring not be installed until the moisture emission from the concrete has reached a certain level. This maximum limit for moisture emission is 3.0 lbm/1000 ft^2/24 h (1.4 kg/42 m^2/24 h) when exposed to a 73°F (23°C) temperature and 50% relative humidity. There are several tests by which moisture level can be determined. The interior designer should state the requirements in the specifications.

The *calcium chloride test* (sometimes called the *moisture dome test*) is one of the most common and is inexpensive and easy to complete. It also gives results in the form that many flooring manufacturers use to determine if their product can be successfully installed. This test is made by placing a standard mass of calcium chloride below a plastic cover and sealing it to the concrete floor. After 60 to 72 hours the calcium chloride is weighed to compare it with its pre-test weight. Through a mathematical formula the amount of moisture the calcium chloride absorbed is converted to the standard measure of pounds per 1000 ft^2 per 24-hour period. One test should be conducted for every 500 ft^2 to 1000 ft^2 (46 m^2 to 93 m^2) of slab area.

The *hygrometer test* (sometimes called the *relative humidity test*) determines the moisture emission by measuring relative humidity (RH) of the atmosphere confined adjacent to the concrete floor. In this test a pocket of air is trapped below a vapor-impermeable box, and a probe in the device measures the RH. Test standards recommend that moisture-sensitive flooring not be installed unless the RH is 75% or less.

The *polyethylene sheet test* is a qualitative test conducted by sealing an 18" × 18" (460 × 460) sheet of plastic to the floor to trap excessive moisture. After a minimum of 16 hours a visual inspection is made of the floor and the sheet. The presence of visible water indicates the concrete is insufficiently dry for the application of finishes.

Similar to the sheet test is the *mat test*. This is also a qualitative method that uses a 24" × 24" (600 × 600) sample of vapor-retardant floor finish. The sample is applied with adhesive, and the edges are sealed with tape. After 72 hours a visual inspection is made. If the mat is firmly bonded or removal of the mat is difficult, then the level of moisture present is considered to be sufficiently low for installation of the flooring material.

The *electrical impedance test* uses proprietary meters to determine the moisture content of the concrete by measuring conductance and capacitance. Probes of the meter are placed on the concrete, and the percentage of moisture content in the slab is read out directly.

In addition to moisture, the slab should be tested for pH level and alkalinity. pH level is a measure of the acidity or alkalinity of a material rated on a scale from 0 to 14, with 7 being neutral. Materials with a pH less than 7 are considered acidic while those with a pH above 7 are considered alkaline. The scale is logarithmic, so a material with a pH of 12 is actually 10 times more alkaline than one with a pH of 11. Concrete normally has a pH of about 12.0 to 13.3. In addition to the alkalis within the concrete, excess alkalinity can also be carried from the soil below a slab-on-grade through the migration of water vapor. Although pH level is an indication of the presence of alkalinity, pH and alkalinity are not the same. Two slabs can have the same pH level, but one can have a much higher alkalinity. Alkalinity cannot exist without moisture, because the moisture causes the soluble alkalis in the concrete to enter into solution.

Alkalinity in concrete can cause two types of problems. High alkalinity on the surface of a slab can damage a tile installation by causing the adhesive to re-emulsify, or return to its original liquid state. It can also cause problems with other coatings. At a level of about 9 or 10, most tile adhesives may begin to experience problems, although professional-grade adhesives can sometimes be used with a pH of 11. Surface alkalinity can be controlled with various proprietary coatings.

Alkalinity is also responsible for the phenomenon known as *alkali-silica reaction* (ASR). In this process strongly alkaline cement begins to dissolve sand and rock within the concrete. The chemical reaction creates a gel-like material that causes tremendous pressure in the pores of the concrete surface. This pressure, in turn, can buckle or blister floor finishes. The risk for ASR can be reduced by specifying aggregates that are not susceptible to ASR, using low-lime cement, proper curing, and not finishing the concrete with a hard trowel surface.

A *pH test* is used to test the surface of concrete that will come in contact with flooring adhesives or other critical floor coatings. It is a simple test that uses a coated paper strip or a small pH meter. Once the pH level is known, it can be compared with the maximum pH recommended by the flooring manufacturer. A pH of 8.5 is considered ideal and about the minimum that concrete can have, with values up to 9.0 being acceptable.

In addition to the pH test, a *titration test* can be used to determine the level of alkalinity in concrete. This involves grinding portions of the concrete, mixing those portions with demineralized water, and performing laboratory chemical analysis. A testing laboratory must perform this test.

Carpet

Carpet is one of the most commonly specified flooring materials. If properly selected it is attractive, durable, quiet, easy to install, and requires less maintenance than many other types of flooring. There are three basic forms of carpet: rugs, sheet carpet, and carpet tiles.

A *rug* is a soft floor covering laid on the floor but not fastened to it. It does not cover the entire floor.

Sheet carpet comes in long rolls, commonly 12 ft (3.66 m) wide and is installed so no seams are visible.

Carpet tiles are individual pieces of carpet, typically 18 in (450) square, that are applied to the floor with pressure-sensitive adhesive. Because of their modular design, damaged or worn pieces can be replaced without removing the entire floor covering. They are generally specified for commercial installations where frequent changes in room layout are expected, where maintenance may be a problem, or where flat, undercarpet electrical and telephone cabling is used.

Fibers

Carpet is made from several fibers and combinations of fibers, including wool, nylon, acrylic, modacrylic, polyester, and olefin.

Wool is a natural material and overall one of the best for carpet. It is very durable and resilient, wears well, has a superior appearance, is flame resistant, and is relatively easy to clean and maintain. Unfortunately, it is also one of the most expensive fibers for initial cost.

Nylon is an economical carpet material that is very strong and wear resistant. It has a high stain resistance and excellent crush resistance, it can be dyed with a wide variety of colors, and it cleans easily. Some nylons have static problems and a glossy sheen, but these problems have generally been alleviated with improved fiber construction and by blending nylon with other fibers. Because of its many advantages, including cost, nylon is the most widely used fiber for residential and commercial carpet.

Acrylic has moderate abrasion resistance, but it has a more wool-like appearance than nylon. Like nylon, it can be dyed with a variety of colors, has good crush resistance, and is easy to maintain. Modacrylic is a modified version of acrylic.

Polyester carpet fiber is made from synthetic polymers and is highly abrasion resistant, has good crush resistance, cleans well, is mildew resistant, and is low in cost. It is sometimes blended with nylon.

Olefin (polypropylene) is used primarily for indoor-outdoor carpet and as an alternative to jute for carpet backing. It is very durable, stain resistant, and cleans easily. However, it is the least attractive of the artificial fibers and has a low melting point.

Manufacturing Processes

Carpet is manufactured by weaving, tufting, needle punching, fusion bonding, and less frequently, by knitting and custom tufting.

Weaving is the traditional method of making carpet by interlacing warp and weft yarns. It is a method that produces a very attractive, durable carpet, but it is the most expensive method of manufacturing

carpet by machine. As shown in Fig. 12.5, there are three primary weaving methods.

Wilton carpet is produced on a Jacquard loom that allows complex patterns to be woven into the carpet and can create several types of surface textures, including level cut pile, level loop, cut/uncut, and multilevel loop. See Fig. 12.5 (a). Because different colors of yarn run beneath the surface of the carpet and are pulled up only when they are needed for the pattern, Wiltons are generally heavier and more expensive than the other woven types for the same total weight.

Velvet carpet is the simplest form of weaving and places all the pile yarn on the face of the carpet. See Fig. 12.5(b). Velvet carpets are generally solid colors, but multicolored yarns can also be used in a variety of surface textures including plushes, loop pile, cut-pile, multilevel loop, and cut-and-loop styles.

Axminster carpets© are made on a modified Jacquard loom that delivers different colors of yarn at different times according to the pattern desired. See Fig. 12.5(c). Because of the weaving process, Axminster carpets can be produced in a range of patterns and colors, from geometric to floral. Unlike the Wilton process, most of the pile yarn is placed on the surface. The carpet has an even, cut-pile surface with a heavily ribbed backing.

Tufting is a process in which the pile yarn is punched through the backing with rows of needles, much like the method employed by a sewing machine. As the needle goes through the backing, the yarn is caught and held while the needle makes the next pass. The loop of yarn can be left as is for loop carpet or cut for cut-pile carpet. Because of the speed and relative low cost of tufting, this process accounts for the majority of the carpet manufactured.

Needle punching is similar to tufting except the fiber is pulled through a backing with barbed needles. It produces a carpet of limited variation in texture and accounts for a very small percentage of the total carpet market.

Fusion bonding embeds the pile yarn in a backing of liquid vinyl. When the vinyl hardens, the tufts are permanently locked in the backing. It is used primarily for carpet tiles.

The appearance and durability of a carpet are affected by the amount of yarn in a given area, how tightly that yarn is packed, and the height of the yarn. The pitch of a woven carpet is the number of ends of surface yarn in a 27 in (686) width. For tufted carpet, this measurement is called the *gauge*, which is the spacing in fractions of an inch between needles across the width of the carpet. Gauges of $5/64$, $1/10$, and $1/8$ in (2.0, 2.5, and 3.2) are common for contract carpet. The *stitch* (or stitch rate) is the number of lengthwise tufts in 1 in. The higher the pitch or gauge number and stitch numbers are, the denser the carpet is. The *pile height* is the height of the fibers from the surface of the backing to the top of the pile. Generally, shorter and more tightly packed fibers result in a more durable but more expensive carpet.

Carpet Backing and Cushion

Carpet backing provides support for the pile yarn and gives added strength and dimensional stability to the carpet. With woven and knitted carpet, the pile yarns and backing yarns are combined during the manufacturing process. Polypropylene backing yarn is the most common for woven carpet, but others include jute, cotton, and polyester. Tufted carpet is manufactured by punching the yarns through a primary backing of woven or nonwoven polypropylene or woven jute. A secondary backing, usually of latex, is then applied.

Figure 12.5
Woven Carpet Types

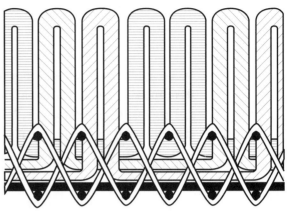

(a) Wilton

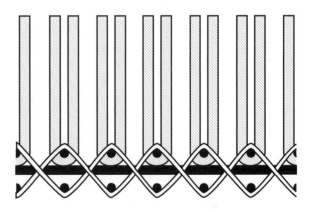

(b) velvet

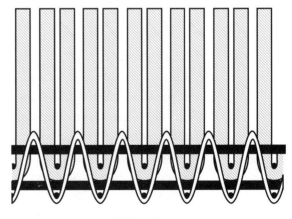

(c) Axminster

An important part of carpet installation is the carpet cushion, sometimes called padding. A cushion is not required for all carpet (such as with direct glue-down), but cushions do increase the life of the carpet, provide better resiliency and comfort, help sound absorption, and lessen impact noise. Common cushion materials include sponge rubber, felt, urethane, and foam rubber.

Sponge rubber is made from natural or synthetic rubber and other chemicals and fillers and has a facing on the top side. It is available in flat sheets or a waffled configuration.

Felt is available in four forms: hair, combination, fiber, and rubberized. Hair felt is composed of 100% animal hair. Combination felt is a mixture of animal hair and other fibers. Fiber felt is composed entirely of felt. Rubberized felt is any of the other three types with a rubberized coating on one side.

Urethane is manufactured in three different ways to produce prime, densified, or bonded sheets, each of which has a different range of densities. Thickness ranges from $1/4$ in to $3/4$ in (6 to 19).

Foam rubber is commonly applied as an integral backing to some carpet. It is natural or synthetic latex rubber with additives, and it has a backing on one side.

Installation

Carpet is installed in one of two ways: direct glue-down or stretched-in installation. With direct glue-down, the carpet is attached to the floor with adhesive. The carpet may have an attached cushion or be installed without a cushion. A stretched-in installation uses tackless strips attached around the perimeter of the room. These strips have embedded sharp points that face toward the walls. The carpet is stretched against these strips, which hold the carpet in place. A carpet cushion is either stapled to wood floors or glued to concrete floors after the tackless strips are in place.

Flammability

All carpet sold in the United States must meet the requirements of ASTM D2859, more commonly known as the methenamine pill test or simply the pill test. This test measures the response of a carpet sample to a burning methenamine tablet. Carpet that does not pass the test cannot be sold in the United States. The test was previously known as DOC FF-1 and is sometimes referred to by its Code of Federal Regulations number, 16 CFR 1630. Refer to Ch. 27 for a description of the test.

In the International Building Code (IBC), carpet must also meet the requirements of the Flooring Radiant Panel Test, ASTM E648, under certain conditions. This test is also described in more detail in Ch. 27. In the IBC, when carpet is not required to be either a Class I or Class II material according to the Flooring Radiant Panel Test, it must meet the requirements of the pill test.

Tile

Tiles are small, flat finishing units made of clay or clay mixtures. The two primary types are ceramic tile and quarry tile. The advantages of tile include durability; water resistance (if glazed); ease of installation and cleaning; a wide choice of colors, sizes, and patterns; fire resistance; fade resistance; and the ability to store heat for passive solar collection.

Ceramic tile is a surfacing unit, usually relatively thin in relation to facial area, made from clay or a mixture of clay and other ceramic materials, having either a glazed or unglazed face. It is fired above red heat during manufacture to a temperature high enough to produce specific physical properties and characteristics. *Quarry tile* is glazed or unglazed tile, usually with 6 in^2 or more of facial area, and is made by the extrusion process from natural clay or shale.

Some of the common types of tile include glazed wall tile, unglazed tile, ceramic mosaic tile, paver tile, quarry tile (glazed or unglazed), abrasive tile, and antistatic tile.

Ceramic mosaic tile is formed by either the dust-pressed or extrusion method, is $1/4$ in to $3/8$ in (6 to 10) thick, and has a facial area of less than 6 in^2 (3870 mm^2). Dust pressing uses large presses to shape the tile out of relatively dry clay, while the extrusion process uses machines to cut tiles from a wetter and more malleable clay extruded through a die.

The United States tile industry classifies tile based on size: under 6 in^2 is mosaic tile, over 6 in^2 is wall tile. Glazed and unglazed nonmosaic tile made by the extrusion method is called quarry tile. Glazed and unglazed tile over 6 in^2 made by the dust-pressed method is called *paver tile.*

Tile is also classified according to its resistance to water absorption. *Nonvitreous tile* has a water absorption rate of more than 7.0%. *Impervious tile* has a water absorption rate of 0.5% or less. *Semivitreous tile* and *vitreous tile* are classified between nonvitreous and impervious tile.

Imported tile is not classified like tile produced in the United States. European manufacturers classify tile according to its production method (either the dust-pressed or extrusion method), degree of water absorption, finish, and whether it is glazed or unglazed.

The classifications of abrasion resistance are Group I, light residential; Group II, moderate residential; Group III, maximum residential; and Group IV, commercial (having the highest abrasion resistance).

Laminate Flooring

Laminate flooring, a variation of plastic laminate material, is composed of a clear wearing sheet over a melamine-impregnated decorative printed sheet with core layers of phenolic-impregnated kraft paper. These sheets are laminated to a high-density fiberboard core under heat and pressure and covered with a water-resistant backing sheet.

The decorative printed sheet can be made to resemble natural wood, tile, or stone, or it can be printed in solid colors or even have photographic quality images in it. Laminate flooring is available in planks (similar to wood strip flooring but a little wider), square tiles, or rectangular blocks. It is about $5/16$ in (8) thick. It is normally laid on a cushioned foam underlayment with the tongue-and-groove edges glued together. A vapor barrier is normally required when it is laid over a concrete floor.

Laminate flooring is hard, durable, resistant to staining, and relatively easy to install. It is gaining popularity where a less-expensive alternative to wood or other types of flooring is required. It can be used in most locations but is not recommended for rest rooms or other potentially wet areas.

Seamless Flooring

Seamless flooring is a mixture of a resinous matrix, fillers, and decorative materials applied in a liquid or viscous form that cures to a hard, seamless surface. Depending on the type of matrix and the specific mixture, the flooring is either poured or troweled on a subfloor. Some products are self-leveling, while others must be worked to a level surface. Some products, such as epoxy terrazzo, are surface ground after they are cured, to produce a smooth surface.

Seamless flooring is high-performance flooring that is used where special characteristics are required, such as extreme hardness, severe stain and chemical resistance, or excellent water resistance, or where cleanliness and ease of cleaning are required. It is used for industrial floors, commercial kitchens and food preparation plants, factories, clean rooms, laboratories, hospitals, correctional facilities, and parking garages.

The many materials used for seamless flooring are generally divided into thermosetting and thermoplastic products. Some of the more common thermosetting matrices are two-part epoxy, two-part polyurethane, polychloroprene (neoprene), and two-part polyester. One-part mixtures are also available but are not as good as two-part mixtures.

Common thermoplastic flooring includes acrylic and mastic products. Mastics are composed of asphalt emulsion, portland cement, and various types of sand or stone filler. Various proprietary mixtures are also on the market.

Seamless flooring is applied in thicknesses from $1/16$ in to $1/2$ in (2 to 13), depending on the type of product. Mastics may be applied in thicknesses up to $1^1/2$ in (38). Seamless flooring is applied over a suitable base of concrete or wood subflooring, with the material turned up at the walls to form an integrated cove base.

Safety Factors

Tile, terrazzo, stone, and other smooth surfaces can be potentially dangerous flooring surfaces, especially when wet or covered with grease or other slippery materials. To evaluate and specify the slip resistance of floor surfaces, the *coefficient of friction* (COF) is used. This is a measurement of the degree of slip resistance of a floor surface and ranges from 0 to 1. The higher the COF, the less slippery the surface. There are two basic measures of friction: the static coefficient of friction, and the dynamic coefficient of friction. The static coefficient of friction is measured

from a resting position, while the dynamic coefficient is measured when the two surfaces are in relative motion. It is difficult to measure the dynamic COF; the measurement must be done in a laboratory for accurate results. Most tests, in the laboratory and in the field, measure static coefficient of friction.

Many variables affect slip resistance, including wet versus dry conditions, shoe material, a person's weight, the angle of impact, stride length, and floor contamination. Numerous tests have been developed to measure the COF accurately and consistently while accounting for the slip-resistance variables. These tests include the following.

• ASTM D2047, *Standard Test Method for Static Coefficient of Friction of Polish-Coated Floor Surfaces as Measured by the James Machine.* This is one of the most common tests used and is considered by many to be the most accurate and reliable measurement of slip resistance. However, it can only be performed in the laboratory on smooth, dry surfaces. It should not be used for wet or rough surfaces.

• ASTM C1028, *Standard Test Method for Determining the Static Coefficient of Friction of Ceramic Tile and Other Like Surfaces by the Horizontal Dynamometer Pull-Meter Method.* This test measures COF in the field. It uses a Neolite heel assembly and can test both dry and wet surfaces, as well as smooth and rough floor surfaces. However, this test method produces inconsistent results from one surface to the next. The coefficients developed from this test cannot be compared with those from other tests.

• ASTM F1679, *Standard Test Method for Using a Variable Incidence Tribometer.* This test can be used either in the laboratory or in the field and can measure wet surfaces or surfaces contaminated with grease, oil, or similar substances.

- ASTM F1677, *Standard Test Method for Using a Portable Inclineable Articulated Strut Slip Tester.* Like the ASTM F1679 test, this test can be used either in the laboratory or in the field to measure wet surfaces or surfaces contaminated with grease, oil, or similar substances.

- ASTM F609, *Standard Test Method for Using a Horizontal Pull Slipmeter.* This test is also widely used in addition to the ASTM C1028 test. It measures static COF of footwear soles, heels, or related materials on walkway surfaces.

- ASTM F462, *Consumer Safety Specification for Slip-Resistant Bathing Facilities.* This test is used with soapy water for bathtubs and shower structures.

When using ASTM D2047, the James Machine test, a COF of 0.5 has generally been considered the minimum required for a slip-resistant floor. Underwriters Laboratories requires a level of 0.5 or higher as a minimum safety level based on the ASTM C1028 standard. The Occupational Safety and Health Administration (OSHA) also recommends a COF of 0.5 as a minimum. Some have suggested a level of 0.6 for a good slip-resistant floor. In any case, when specifying slip resistance, the designer must refer to the specific test being used.

The Americans with Disabilities Act requires that a floor surface be slip resistant, but it does not give any specific test values. However, an appendix in a handbook to the ADA recommends a static coefficient of friction of 0.6 for accessible routes and 0.8 for ramps. This is based on a research project sponsored by the Architectural and Transportation Barriers Compliance Board (Access Board).

Until specific, uniform criteria are established, the designer should take into account the conditions under which floor tile and other flooring materials will be used before selecting a particular type of floor and specifying the minimum coefficient of friction. For example, a public lobby where snow and rain may be tracked may need to be more slip resistant than a residential bathroom, where people are taking smaller strides without slippery shoe material.

WALL FINISHES
Paint

Painting is a generic term for the application of thin coatings of various materials to protect and decorate the surfaces to which they are applied. Coatings are composed of a vehicle, which is the liquid part of the coating, and the body and pigments if the coating is opaque. The vehicle has a nonvolatile part called the binder and a volatile part called the solvent. The binder, along with the body, forms the actual film of the coating, while the solvent dissolves the binder to allow for application of the coating. The solvent evaporates or dries, leaving the final finish. The body of most quality paints is titanium dioxide, which is white. Pigments give paint its color.

Paints are broadly classified into solvent-based and water-based types. Solvent-based coatings have binders dissolved in or containing organic solvents, while the water-based type has binders that are soluble or dispersed in water.

Clear, solvent-based coatings include varnishes, shellac, silicone, and urethane. When a small amount of pigment is added, the coating becomes a stain, which gives color to the surface but allows the appearance of the underlying material to show through. Stains are most often used on wood. For interior applications, clear coatings can be used. It is not necessary to have a pigment to protect an interior surface as is usually required for exterior surfaces.

Oil paints use a drying, or curing, oil as a binder. Linseed oil was the traditional oil, but other organic oils have been used. Today, synthetic alkyd resin is used as the drying oil. Oil paints are durable but have a strong odor when being applied and must be cleaned up with solvents such as mineral spirits. In addition, they cannot be painted on damp surfaces or on surfaces that may become damp from behind.

Latex paints are water based, with vinyl chloride or acrylic resins as binders. Acrylic latex is better than vinyl latex. Both can be used indoors as well as outdoors and can be thinned with water.

For more durable finishes, epoxy is used as a binder for resistance to corrosion and chemicals. Epoxies also resist abrasion and strongly adhere to concrete, metal, and wood.

Urethanes are used for superior resistance to abrasion, grease, alcohol, water, and fuels. They are often used for wood floors and for antigraffiti coatings.

Successful application of coatings depends not only on the correct selection for the intended use but also on the surface preparation of the substrate, the primer used, and the method of application. Surfaces should be clean, dry, and free from grease, oils, and other foreign material. Application can be done by brushing, rolling, or spraying. The amount of coating material to be applied is normally specified as either wet or dry film thickness in mils (thousandths of an inch) for each coat needed. The coating should be applied under dry conditions when the temperature is between 55°F and 85°F (13°C and 29°C).

Most water- and solvent-based paints are available in several surface finishes, which are referred to as glosses. Gloss and semigloss paints are used for their washability and shiny appearance. However, gloss paints tend to show defects in the surfaces on which they are applied. Satin finish paints provide a dull luster while still retaining some washability. The type of gloss is determined by the amount of light reflected from a surface according to a standard test method.

The interior designer should be aware of two important environmental and safety considerations when recommending paint removal and specifying paint: lead-based paint and volatile organic compounds.

Lead-based paint can be a problem in older homes and child-occupied facilities. In many remodeling projects, existing paint must be removed. If the building was built before 1978 it may have lead-based paint. Such paint is dangerous if it flakes off, is chewed on, or is released as dust during construction activities and ingested by children or other occupants.

Federal law requires that anyone conducting lead-based paint activities be certified and that lead-based paint be removed from some types of residential occupancies and child-occupied facilities by a certified company using approved methods for removal and disposal. This can increase the cost of repainting considerably. Sometimes, covering the wall with a new layer of gypsum wallboard or simply repainting is an acceptable alternative. If a client lives in an older house and the presence of lead paint is suspected, the interior designer should inform the client and suggest that a qualified consultant test the paint for lead content and recommend removal methods, if required.

Volatile organic compounds (VOCs) are hydrocarbon solvents used in paints, stains, and other products. They are released into the air during the application of coatings and react with nitrous oxides and sunlight to form ozone, the same product caused by automotive exhaust and other pollutants. As required by the Clean Air Act of 1972, the Environmental Protection Agency (EPA) issued a regulation in 1999 that requires the amount of VOCs in paint and other coatings to be reduced from previous levels. The amount of reduction depends on the type of coating and gloss type. For example, nonflat interior and exterior coatings must now have no more than 380 g per liter of volatile organic compounds. The EPA regulation is applicable to all 50 states, the District of Columbia, and all United States territories. Some state and local jurisdictions, such as California, have VOC regulations even stricter than the federal rule.

For most interior projects, specifying VOC-compliant paint is not a problem because interior designers can require water-based products, which are generally environmentally friendly. Manufacturers now offer water-based flat, nonflat, and multicolor wall paints as well as many floor coverings, stains, and sealers. Refer to Ch. 26 for more information on VOCs.

Wallpaper

Wallpaper is available in a range of colors, patterns, textures, and materials for direct application to plaster or gypsum wallboard partitions. Wallpaper is generally packaged in rolls $20\frac{1}{2}$ in (520) wide by 21 ft (6.4 m) long (about 36 ft^2 or 3.3 m^2) and may be all paper or paper backed with cotton fabric or some other material. Double and triple rolls are also available. Some wallpaper is available with a thin vinyl coating. Before application, a liquid sizing must be applied to the wall to seal the surface against alkali, reduce the absorption of the paste or adhesive used, and provide the proper surface for the wallpaper.

Most wallpaper is manufactured with a short *pattern repeat*—the distance between one point to the next repeated same point. When one length of wallpaper is aligned with the next piece in a direct horizontal line it is called a *straight match*. If the next piece must be lowered to continue the pattern it is called a *drop match*. Some

wallpapers have no repeat pattern because they are strictly for texture. However, some specialty mural or trompe l'oeil wallpapers are available that have no repeats because they are designed to be applied to form an overall image.

Vinyl Wall Covering

Vinyl wall covering provides a durable, abrasion-resistant finish that is easy to clean and can satisfy most code requirements for flammability. It is available in a wide range of colors and patterns. Vinyl wall covering typically comes in rolls 52 in or 54 in (1320 or 1372) wide and 30 yd (27.4 m) long. It can be specified either with or without an additional coating of polyvinylfluoride film, which provides added stain resistance and extra protection for the vinyl. Other types of protective films are also available, but they are not as stain resistant.

There are three grades of vinyl wall covering: Type I is light duty, Type II is medium duty, and Type III is heavy duty. Type I has a total weight of 7 oz/yd^2 to 13 oz/yd^2 (237 g/m^2 to 440 g/m^2), Type II has a total weight of between 13 oz/yd^2 and 22 oz/yd^2 (440 g/m^2 to 745 g/m^2), and Type III has a weight of over 22 oz/yd (745 g/m^2). Type I is used for residential and commercial applications where little or no abuse is expected. The vinyl serves as a substitute for paint while adding texture. Type II is used for residential, commercial, and institutional applications where a moderate amount of traffic and abrasion is expected, such as in offices, dining rooms, classrooms, and some corridors. Type III is used where extra heavy use is expected, such as public corridors, food-service areas, and hospitals.

Vinyl wall covering is applied with mastic to properly prepared gypsum wallboard or smooth plaster walls. Primer should be used on new wallboard to prevent damage to the partition if the wall covering is removed. Stripable adhesive is also available for use over unprimed gypsum wallboard. Two methods of seaming are used: double-cutting and butting. Double-cutting involves overlapping adjacent strips and then cutting through and removing both. This results in a very tight butt joint. Butting must be used for patterned wall covering where matching is critical, or with dark-colored or deeply embossed material where removal of adhesive is difficult.

Fabric Wall Covering

Several types of fabrics can be used for wall covering, including wool, silk, and synthetics, subject to flame-spread restrictions. If the fabric is heavy enough, it can be applied directly to the wall with adhesives. Seams are butted together to give the appearance of a continuous wall surface. In most instances, the fabric must be backed with paper or some other material to prevent the adhesive from damaging the fabric and to give the fabric additional dimensional stability.

When fabric is applied as a single layer of material, the terminating edges are carefully cut against the ceiling, floor base, door molding, and other trim. The adhesive is usually sufficient to hold the fabric in place. In the following situations a tuck joint should be provided: where fabric abuts other finishes, where there is a danger of people brushing against the fabric edge, or where a neat and precise line is needed. This provides a small recess where the fabric can be tucked into a small crack, giving a neater edge and concealing any minor delamination of the fabric edges from the partition should it occur. Tuck joints can be used for both vinyl wall covering and fabric wall covering.

An alternate installation method is an upholstered wall, which is fabric stretched over a frame and secured into place. Various proprietary stretch-fabric wall systems are available that allow fabric to be placed over inside and outside curved partitions as well as flat partitions. The edges can be straight or curved, and the fabric can be placed on doors as well. Some systems provide a fiberglass batting under the fabric for nominal sound absorption.

When the fabric is placed over a thick fiberglass batting, the assembly becomes an acoustic panel, as described in the following section. In whatever way fabric wall covering is applied, it must conform to the required fire rating for finishes either by being fire resistant itself or by being fire-retardant treated. Refer to Ch. 27 for flame-spread requirements of wall finishes.

Acoustic Panels

When a high degree of sound absorption is required, acoustic panels must be used. Although upholstered walls do provide some sound-absorbing qualities and can be designed to provide a high degree of sound absorption, acoustic panels differ in that they are designed as individual panels and have at least 1 in (25) of sound-absorbing material. In addition, they are covered with a permeable material, such as a loose-weave fabric, so that the sound energy can pass through the fabric and be dissipated in the material underneath.

Acoustic panels can be purchased with a manufacturer's standard fabric or a customer's own material (COM), or they can be custom fabricated. Refer to Ch. 20 for information on the fundamentals of acoustic control. When sound control is critical or when very high or low frequencies are involved, an acoustical engineer should be consulted.

Two important decisions have to be made with acoustic panels. The first concerns fabric type, and the second concerns core material. As mentioned, the fabric must be permeable to allow for sound energy to pass through. This also means that the fabric should not be backed. In addition, fabrics should be hydrophobic; that is, they should not absorb and hold moisture that could cause sagging and distortion. Hydrophobic fabrics include modacrylics, polyesters, cotton, linen, olefin, and wool. Hydrophilic fabrics (those that absorb and retain moisture) should be avoided or be limited to 25% of the fabric's contents. These include silk, rayon, nylon, and acetate. Balanced weaves, such as jacquards and damasks, should he used; unbalanced weaves, such as satin, taffetas, and basket weaves, should be avoided.

Core material can be a loose material such as fiberglass or polyester batting, or a tackable material such as mineral fiberboard or tackable, acoustic fiberglass. *Mineral fiberboard* is a dimensionally stable composite of inorganic mineral fibers with a microperforated surface. *Tackable acoustic fiberglass* is noncombustible fibrous glass mat bonded with a resinous binder and formed into a rigid board with a finish face of thin, rigid fiberglass mesh. Avoid pressed, recycled paper products because these tend to absorb moisture and do not have good dimensional stability.

Stone

Stone can be used as a wall finish, in thick slabs or in thin veneer sheets. With the traditional, standard-set method of applying stone, slabs about $3/4$ in (19) thick are attached to wall substrates (either masonry or gypsum wallboard) with stainless steel wires or ties. See Fig. 12.6. These are anchored to the substrate and hold the stone by being set in holes or slots cut into the back or sides of the stone panel. Lumps of plaster of Paris, called spots, are placed between the substrate and the back of the stone panel at each anchor to hold the slab in place and allow for precise alignment before they harden. For rooms with normal ceiling heights, the stone rests on the

floor with the anchors simply serving to hold each panel in place. The joints can be filled with nonstaining portland cement mortar, filled with sealant, or left open.

With new technology in cutting and laminating stone to various types of reinforcing backing, thin stone tiles are largely replacing the traditional thick-slab construction. These tiles are about $3/8$ in (10) thick and come in sizes of $1' \times 1'$ and $1' \times 2'$ (305 × 305 and 305 × 610), although other sizes and thicknesses are

Figure 12.6
Thick-Set Stone Veneer

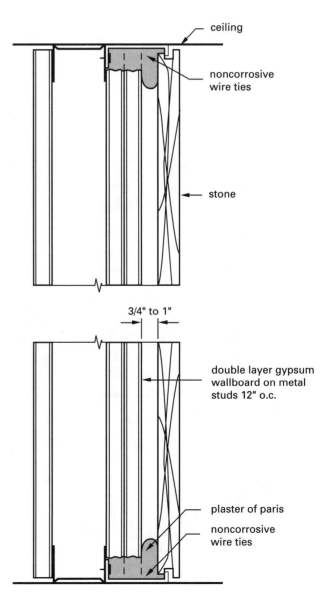

available depending on the manufacturer. In many cases, the stone is simply mastic-applied to a suitable substrate. Some manufacturers provide special clips that hold the stone in place against the backup wall.

Refer to Ch. 27 for flammability requirements of wall finishes.

WINDOW TREATMENTS

Window treatments are used to enhance the appearance of windows, control light, provide privacy, reduce heat gain and heat loss, block undesirable views, and reduce sound reflections within a space. They can also be used to unify or disguise an awkward or undesirable grouping of openings. Because they are such a dominant part of an interior space, they should be selected and designed to be suitable to the type of

window they are covering as well as the overall design theme of the space.

Window coverings can be broadly classified into four categories: shades, blinds, soft coverings, and fixed. Within each of these categories are several variations, as shown in Fig. 12.7.

- *Roller shades and inverted roller shades:* These coverings consist of a piece of cloth wound around a spring roller. They are normally pulled closed from the top but can also be mounted so a pulley-mounted cord unwinds them from the bottom up. They are inexpensive and can be covered with decorative fabric. These coverings, however, block off all the view when closed and can interfere with ventilation. They also block light unless made from a translucent material.

- *Roman shades:* Roman shades pull up with a cord into accordion folds.

- *Austrian shades:* These operate in a way similar to Roman shades but are made of several rows of fabric seamed in such a way that they fold into scallops when opened.

- *Venetian blinds:* Traditional Venetian blinds consist of horizontal slats of wood, aluminum, or plastic whose angle can be adjusted with a control cord. The blinds can also be pulled up to varying levels with another cord.

- *Mini blinds:* Mini blinds are horizontal slats of aluminum like Venetian blinds, but they are only $1/2$ in to 1 in (13 to 25) wide. The angle of the slats is controlled with a plastic rod. They can be pulled up to expose the entire window area.

- *Vertical blinds:* Vertical blinds hang from a track and adjust only in the vertical direction. They can be pulled to the side to expose the window. They are available in several materials (primarily plastic), widths, and colors.

Figure 12.7

Window Coverings

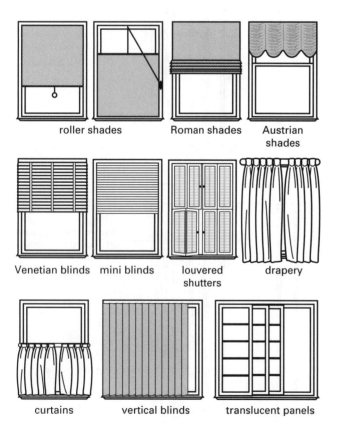

roller shades Roman shades Austrian shades

Venetian blinds mini blinds louvered shutters drapery

curtains vertical blinds translucent panels

- *Louvered shutters:* Shutters are rigid panels, usually of wood, that are hinged so they can be opened or closed. Individual panels have thin, adjustable horizontal louvers to control the view and light. Plantation shutters are similar in design but feature much wider louvers.

- *Drapery:* Drapery is one of the most common types of window covering in residential and commercial interiors. Generally, drapery is any loosely hung fabric that covers the window. Most commonly, the fabric is attached to a traverse rod that allows the drapery to be drawn open and closed, but many styles of hanging are possible including fixed, tieback, and loose-hung swags. Drapery can be made from a variety of fabrics using several pleating methods. Four common methods of pleating include pinch pleat, stack pleat, roll pleat, and accordion pleat.

Drapery can be hung to cover just the window or can be sized to extend to the floor or so the drapery stacks clear of the window opening. When special light control is required, blackout drapery lining or linings for solar control can be specified. When selecting drapery for commercial, institutional, and public residential applications, one of the most important considerations is flammability. This takes precedence over other criteria such as durability, fading resistance, and style.

- *Curtains:* Like draperies, curtains use fabric, but they are usually hung within the window frame and close to the glass. In most instances, curtains are not intended to be opened, but are meant to remain fixed across all or a portion of the window.

- *Translucent panels:* When a clear view is not required or desired, translucent panels can be used to admit diffused light. These can be constructed of various types of plastic, sheer fabric, frosted glass, or even paper using fixed or sliding Shoji screens.

- *Grilles:* Grilles can be used to modify strong light or minimize an undesirable view while still providing some visual connection between the inside and outside. Grilles can be constructed of any durable material such as wood or metal and can be fixed or movable. Decorative metal grilles can also be used when security is required.

One unusual architectural window type that the interior designer sometimes has to deal with is the *jalousie* window. A jalousie window consists of individual horizontal pieces of glass, about 3 in to 4 in (76 to 102) wide, that all pivot outward at once for ventilation. When closed, the lower edge of each piece of glass overlaps the piece below it to prevent water from entering. Because it is impossible to get a good seal on the joints between windows and because single panes of glass are used, these types of windows are seldom used anymore and when they are, they are appropriate only for warm climates.

SAMPLE QUESTIONS

1. Which vinyl wall covering should be recommended for the family room in a single-family dwelling?

(A) Type I
(B) Type II
(C) Type III
(D) Type IV

2. Which carpet type allows a complex, custom-patterned carpet with varying pile heights?

(A) tufted
(B) Axminster
(C) Wilton
(D) velvet

3. Which of the following types of stone flooring would be the most functional choice for an entry lobby to a restaurant?

(A) granite with a flame finish
(B) marble with a honed finish
(C) travertine
(D) granite with a polished finish

4. Which type of wood flooring could be installed easily and LEAST expensively in a residential living room?

    (A) block

    (B) strip

    (C) parquet

    (D) plank

5. Which of the following would be the LEAST desirable choice for a carpet installation for hotel rooms that have concrete subfloors?

    (A) nylon carpet stretched in over a foam cushion

    (B) polyester carpet stretched in over a felt cushion

    (C) acrylic carpet direct-glued

    (D) wool carpet direct-glued

6. A window covering that is made from fabric and generally not intended to be opened is called

    (A) a curtain

    (B) an Austrian shade

    (C) a vertical blind

    (D) drapery

7. What is the purpose of construction element A in the following diagram of a wood floor?

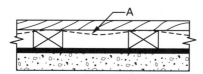

    (A) to minimize squeaking

    (B) to prevent chemicals from the sub-floor from contaminating the wood

    (C) to act as a vapor barrier

    (D) to provide added resiliency

8. An interior designer has been retained for a building project that is currently being planned by an architect. On the second floor of the building, slate flooring over a concrete subfloor is being used. What type of installation should ideally be designed for?

    (A) a thick-set application using a cleavage membrane

    (B) a bonded thick-set installation

    (C) a $1/2$ in (12) layer of mortar with the stone dry-set on top

    (D) a standard thin-set installation

9. What type of resilient flooring would be the best choice for a commercial kitchen?

    (A) $1/8$ in (3) commercial-grade vinyl tile

    (B) sheet vinyl

    (C) heavy-duty cork flooring

    (D) sheet rubber

10. A 216 pitch carpet has

    (A) a pile height that is almost $1/4$ in (6) high

    (B) 8 surface yarns per inch

    (C) an equivalent gauge of $1/6$

    (D) a commercial-grade stitch rate

13

FINALIZING DESIGN DEVELOPMENT AND PRESENTATION TO THE CLIENT

Prior to moving into construction document production, the concluding stages of design development should include a last check of design decisions to verify that they satisfy the design intent of the project, meet good practice standards for construction, meet the requirements of codes and building systems, and meet the rules of the base building. A concluding presentation to the client is also required to communicate the final decisions regarding space planning, materials, furnishings, and costs. This chapter reviews some of these individual design development issues.

DEVELOPING AND REVIEWING DESIGN DETAILS

During schematic design and the early stages of design development, the interior designer refines early design concepts into a more detailed scheme. Much of this work does not include deciding the specifics of the actual construction other than how the designer wants it to look. The process of working out the technical requirements of how individual components fit together is called *detailing*.

The manner in which an assembly of several parts is organized and connected is commonly referred to as a *detail*. A detail may be as simple as two sheets of wallboard covered with joint compound or as complex as a custom stair consisting of structural framing, treads and risers, a glass railing, a metal handrail, and soffit finish.

Detailing serves to meet one or more of three objectives. First, detailing must resolve how to physically connect the various components of a design. Doors must fit into partitions, ceilings must attach to walls, and so on. Second, detailing solves functional problems, such as providing a durable work surface, resisting moisture penetration, or simply covering base building construction. Third, detailing is a way to enhance the design intent of the project and contribute to the overall look or style of the project design.

The process of developing or reviewing a detail is a way of satisfying the requirements in the four categories of design intent, constraints, function, and constructability. See Fig. 13.1. The first three categories are used to develop alternative detail concepts for an individual component that can be reviewed by the interior designer, client, and consultants. These concepts can be evaluated in much the same way as design or space planning concepts are reviewed, to select the best one. When a final detail concept is selected for refinement, constructability requirements are then applied to develop the final detail, ready for construction document drafting. There may be dozens or hundreds of individual details used on a project.

The following categories cover most of the common characteristics that must be considered in a construction assembly's design or evaluation. Of course, not all of them relate to every detail, but combined with the specific information on materials given in other chapters, they should help candidates to make rational evaluations during the examination.

Design Intent

The *design intent* is the approach the designer and owner decide to take to satisfy the program requirements and specific needs arising from these requirements. It also includes the overall appearance that the owner and designer are striving for. While these needs and requirements must be balanced against practical considerations such as codes, cost, and material limitations, the design intent is the basic starting point for developing and reviewing a detail. Sometimes, during the long process of design and detailing, the original design intent gets lost in the practicalities of solving functional problems and making changes. A detail may work but may not look like what the client and designer originally intended.

The interior designer should constantly check the development of a detail against the detail's original purpose and desired appearance. For example, a client might have originally requested a simple, unobtrusive demountable partition system. Through material selection, cost analysis, and integration with other building systems, the final product may satisfy the requirements of demountability, sound transmission, cost, and finish, but may not have the clean, simple look the client wanted.

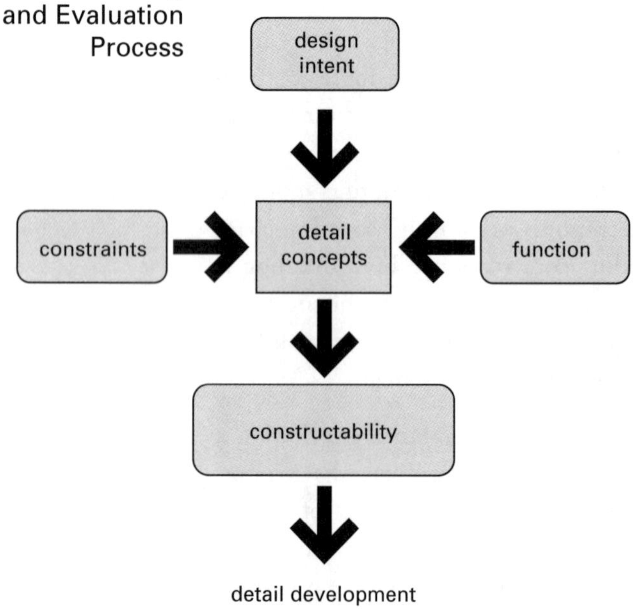

There are two major aspects of design intent. First, details should contribute to the overall design concept. This includes the various elements and principles of design as described in Chs. 8 and 9. For example, if a strong vertical line is used in the overall design of a space, that element can be repeated in the details, reinforcing the concept. Second, details must resolve problems of connection or transition. This includes determining how connections of major construction elements are made and how individual elements are placed on, or become part of, other construction components. For example, the transition between a partition and a ceiling can be made in dozens of different ways: by butting the two surfaces together at a 90° angle, by making a curved transition, by using a reveal so the ceiling looks

Figure 13.1
The Detailing and Evaluation Process

design intent → detail concepts ← function

constraints → detail concepts

detail concepts → constructability → detail development

separated from the wall, or in countless other ways.

Constraints

Constraints are the given conditions within which a detail must perform and over which the designer has little or no control. Some of the common constraints encountered in interior design detailing include the following.

Code Requirements

Of course, all details must satisfy the requirements of the local building code and other statutory regulations. Checking for compliance should be an automatic reaction when developing or reviewing details and construction drawings. Many of these requirements are discussed in other chapters, with reference to specific materials and areas of construction. Refer to Ch. 27 for a general discussion of building codes.

Substrates

Interior design details are always built on or as part of other construction—either the base building construction or other interior design elements. Details must take into account the conditions and limitations of the construction of which they are a part. Detailing a floor closer for a door is quite different on a concrete slab than on a wood-framed floor.

Costs

During the late design development stage of a project, the budget for the job will have been well established. Any design and detailing work the interior designer does must fit within the overall cost limitations.

Cost control in detailing involves striking the proper balance between client needs, initial costs, and life-cycle costs. The client or designer may want more than is affordable, or the client may ask for the lowest initial costs without realizing that inexpensive materials and details will cost more in the long run. If the building is a speculative venture, low initial costs may be acceptable to the developer regardless of the consequences. It is up to the interior designer to make sure the client understands all the choices and ramifications of detailing decisions.

The cost of a portion of a project in proportion to the total cost is another important concept to understand. If the entire project is going to cost $2 million, it does not make sense to spend a great deal of time and worry over saving $100 on one detail. On the other hand, if extensive research and study on a typical wall detail of the same building can save $30,000, then it is reasonable to make the effort. In another situation, saving a little money on quantity items is desirable. If just $100 can be trimmed from the construction cost of one door detail that occurs 300 times, then saving this amount will add up to $30,000.

Of course, cost is directly related to the choice of materials, which is a function of the detail's intended use, durability, strength, and maintainability, and all the other considerations involved with designing a detail. Labor cost is largely determined by the effort required to build a detail so that, in general, construction costs can be minimized by developing simple details that still satisfy all the other criteria.

Industry Standards

Certain common methods of building are considered industry standards. These methods have been developed through practice and experience, from the recommendations of trade associations, and from building codes. All gypsum wallboard partitions should be built in a similar manner regardless of the designer, the builder, or the use. The only things that may change to suit the particular needs of the project are the stud size, wallboard thickness, finish, and similar variables.

Conforming to these types of industry standards not only increases the likelihood that the detail will work, but also minimizes potential liability if something goes wrong. This is not to say that the interior designer should not try new design approaches or be creative in solving unusual technical problems. But he or she should only do so when necessary and when a standard method will not work.

Industry standards should be deviated from only after performance requirements specified for the building assembly have been precisely defined, the materials and construction techniques being proposed to meet the requirements have been thoroughly researched, and the construction's potential actual performance has been carefully analyzed. Then, the client should make the final decision based on information and recommendations provided by the interior designer.

Material Availability

Construction is a geographically localized industry. Not only does labor availability vary with location, but material availability also varies with location. Of course, any material can be shipped anywhere else, but the cost may not be justified. Specifying stone from Italy will probably be more expensive and time consuming than specifying stone from a United States quarry.

Climate

Climate can affect interior design detailing as it relates to weather and sunlight. For example, near the entrance to a building located in a wet or snowy climate, the interior designer may want to detail and specify a flooring material that can withstand water and is slip resistant. The choice of window coverings and furnishings may be affected by how sunlight enters a building. If the base building was built to use passive solar design, the choice of interior materials and construction should not compromise this intent.

Labor and Construction Practices

All construction details should be developed and reviewed to ensure they conform to the standard methods of construction, both generally and in the project's specific geographic location. Of course, some custom interior detailing may require specialized labor, but in general, cost and time can be minimized if standard labor practices are followed. For example, in some parts of the country it is standard practice to use a veneer plaster over gypsum lath rather than simply to use textured gypsum wallboard. As another example, installing a door frame in an opening requires shim space to compensate for possible deviations in plumb of the rough door opening, so details should be developed to allow for this.

Function

Function includes the requirements the detail must meet based on the basic purpose of the detail. For example, the functional requirements of a stairway include safety, durability, and a good anthropometric fit to the human body. Some of the common functional elements of a detail include the following.

Concealment and Finish

The simplest functional purpose of a detail is to conceal other rough construction or to simply provide a finish. For example, a base not only provides protection from maintenance work but also conceals the gap between the floor and the bottom edge of gypsum wallboard.

Human Fit

In many instances, humans come in direct contact with interior details. When this occurs, the detail must be designed accordingly. A clerical work surface may be designed with a large drawer under the counter, but if there is insufficient knee space the detail will not work. Refer to

Ch. 1 for more information on anthropometrics and ergonomics.

Safety

There are many aspects to safety, which is one of the most important elements of detailing, because the interior designer is responsible for protecting the health, safety, and welfare of the public. Be aware of safety concerns such as the following.

- *Structural safety:* Will the material or detail physically collapse or otherwise fail, causing harm?

- *Fire safety:* Is the material fire resistant enough for its intended use? Will it produce smoke or toxic fumes if burned? If it burns, will its failure lead to the failure of adjacent construction?

- *Safety with human contact:* Is there a potential for harm when people come in contact with the material or detail? For example, will sharp edges cut people, wet floors promote slipping, or poorly designed stairs cause falls?

Security

Security is an important aspect of design today. Security can be viewed as providing protection against theft, vandalism, intentional physical harm, or a combination of all three. Common security concerns include residential and commercial burglary, employee pilferage, vandalism, sabotage or theft of company records and property, confinement of prisoners, protection of personnel, safety and confinement in psychiatric wards, abduction, and in extreme instances, terrorism.

In addition to physical barriers, security systems include methods for preventing entry, detecting intruders, controlling access to secure areas, and notifying authorities in the event of unauthorized entry or other emergencies. Refer to Ch. 18 for more information on security.

Although the security consultant, equipment vendor, electrical engineering consultant, and contractor are responsible for designing and installing security systems and the power these systems need to operate, the interior designer is the person who must coordinate the design team's efforts so their work fits within the overall design and construction of the project. Some of the important elements of security system coordination that may be included on the drawings and in the specifications include the following.

- Lighting that is required for surveillance and deterrence should be compatible with the general ambient lighting whenever possible. The electrical engineer or lighting designer should know what types of cameras are being used in order to select the best lighting types. Lighting positions and details are shown on the interior design drawings, but the electrical engineer will produce detailed circuiting drawings.

- The interior designer must show on the drawings adequate space and support for video cameras, monitors, access devices, controls, and other equipment. The actual electrical and signal circuiting will be shown on the electrical drawings.

- Conduit must be shown on the electrical consultant's drawings to accommodate signal system wiring, electric lock wiring, telecommunication wiring, and other wiring that may be provided by a separate contractor.

- Audio speakers that are required for public address and communication within secured areas should be shown on the interior design drawings and coordinated with other elements on the reflected ceiling plan.

- Power transfers for doors should be specified to met the necessary level of security, but should be concealed whenever possible. A power transfer is a flexible cable or other device that transmits power between a door and its frame while allowing the door to operate normally.

Durability and Maintainability

Most building materials and details are subject to a wide range of intentional and nonintentional abuse from human use. To the greatest extent possible, they must be able to withstand this abuse and be maintained and repaired throughout their lifetimes. Materials and details within human reach should be resistant to scratching, abrasion, impact, and marking.

Maintainability includes the ability to easily clean a material as well as the ability to make adjustments and repairs. A detail should also allow damaged components to be replaced easily.

Fire Resistance

As previously mentioned, materials and details must provide the required degree of fire resistance. For interior materials, this generally includes resistance to flame spread. For construction assemblies, a fire-resistance rating may also be required. The likelihood of a burning material producing excess smoke or toxic fumes should be investigated as well. Refer to Ch. 27 for more information on fire ratings.

Acoustics

Acoustics is not always a concern with details, but partition detailing and room finishes may need to provide a certain level of sound absorption or reduce the transmission of sound. Refer to Ch. 20 for more information on acoustics.

Resistance to Moisture and Weathering

Controlling moisture is one of the most troublesome areas of construction design and detailing and one of the most error-prone. Whenever water might be a problem, the detail should be carefully reviewed. These situations include areas under and around showers and tubs, kitchens, mechanical rooms, pools, and any other interior space where excess moisture is present. Some of the considerations are as follows.

- *Material permeability:* Can it resist moisture, or must it be protected with a coating or by some other mechanical means?

- *Material durability:* Will aging, building movement, and other forms of deterioration cause the material to crack or break up, allowing water to penetrate?

- *Aggravating circumstances:* Will other conditions, such as pressure, puncture, or abuse, cause a normally water-resistant detail to leak?

- *Joints:* Are joints constructed, flashed, and sealed so that water cannot enter? Will building movement damage the integrity of the joints?

- *Capillary action:* Does the material have tiny joints or holes that can admit water?

- *Sealants:* Have the proper types of sealants been selected for the type of material used and for the expected movement of the joint? Is the backup material correct, and is the sealant installed with the correct dimensions?

Sustainability

Given the increased interest in the sustainability of buildings, interior designers must review details with an eye toward the environmental impact of details and how buildings are put together. Some of the same criteria for evaluating building materials that are discussed in Ch. 26 can be used as detailing guidelines for sustainability. These include the following.

- The embodied energy of the materials used in the detail should be as low as possible. This includes materials that are hidden, like blocking or bracing, as well as the obvious finish materials.

- As many of the materials and components as possible should be made from renewable materials or have recycled content.

- Details should reduce energy consumption in the building. Something as simple as adding insulation in a small gap in a detail can yield significant energy savings, especially if the detail is repeated dozens or hundreds of times in a building.

- As many of the materials and components as possible should come from local sources.

- Adhesives, cleaning compounds, and finishes should have low VOC content. For example, in some cases, mechanical fasteners can be used instead of construction mastics.

- If possible, the detail should be designed to allow for easy deconstruction so the individual components can be recycled.

Constructability

Constructability includes the requirements produced by the detail itself, regardless of its design intent or functional needs. For example, a detail may add to the design intent of the project, meet all of the constraints, and solve the functional problems, but may be impossible to build because it is impossible to make a good connection to the existing building or because required tolerances are too tight to be built economically. Some of the common constructability elements of a detail include the following.

Connection

Connection refers to the way the various parts of the detail are attached to one another and to the substrate. This attachment may be done in one of three ways. The first is rigid, such as plaster fixed to lath. In a rigid connection, if one material moves, both move. The second is rigid but adjustable for installation. A ledger screwed to a wall is one example. The third is flexible to allow for movement. An expansion joint is a typical example of this attachment.

Within each detail there must be space for the attaching device as well as clearance for workers. Problems with incompatible materials must also be considered, such as possible galvanic action or deterioration of one material from water leakage through another. If the materials are chemically bonded, joined, or covered with sealants, mastics, paint, or other coatings, the base material must be compatible with the coating or the joining material.

Structure

Structure refers to the strength required by the detail to resist the forces applied to it as well as its own weight and loading. Details need to withstand the obvious natural forces of gravity, wind, and seismic loading, as well as other forces such as impact. The particular type of detail will determine what kinds of forces the detail must resist, and each force should be reviewed. Some possible common forces on a detail are the following.

- live and dead loads
- wind loads
- seismic loads
- hydrostatic pressure
- forces induced by building movement
- loads induced by normal human use
- loads created by one material acting as the substrate for another
- forces caused by accidental or intentional abuse
- strength properties of a material or assembly that may be necessary to resist various forces, including compression, tension, shear, torsion, rupture, hardness, and impact

Movement

Movement as a constructability element of detailing includes making provisions for both movement of the detail (if any) and of the building that the detail must accommodate. Movement is inevitable, whether it is from live, dead, or lateral loading; temperature changes; water absorption; or other forces. The amount of movement that will occur on a given detail varies, but some degree of movement is always present. For example, a partition that extends to the structure above must allow for deflection of the floor above, or else a buckled partition or cracked finish may result.

Tolerances

All elements of construction are built to a different closeness to perfection. The lines and dimensions on the construction drawings typically represent this level of perfection. The amount of allowable variance from a given line, dimension, or size is known as *tolerance* and must be accounted for in detailing. Some construction items, such as woodwork, have a very small tolerance—sometimes as small as $1/16$ in (0.4) or less—whereas other elements, such as poured concrete footings, may be oversized by as much as 2 in (51) and still be acceptable.

Tolerances for a great many construction components have been established by various trade organizations and are the accepted norms unless the interior designer specifies otherwise. However, requiring tighter tolerances than is industry standard usually requires better materials, more time, more labor, or a combination of all three, which also results in a higher cost.

Details should allow for expected tolerances. For example, a finished wood-panel wall installed over cast concrete must have enough space for shimming and blocking so that the final wall surface can be plumb, whereas the rough structural wall may be out of plumb by as much as $1/4$ in or more in a 10 ft height (6 or more in a 3050 height).

Clearances

A *clearance* is a gap or space designed to allow for the construction or installation of a material, construction element, or piece of equipment. Details must provide enough clearance to make construction possible. For example, the shim space around doors and windows is provided so the door or window unit can be slipped into the rough opening and leveled and plumbed before being attached to the framing.

Construction Trade Sequence

Because all building requires the involvement of many trades and material suppliers, the best details are those that allow for construction to proceed directly from one trade to another in a timely fashion. Because labor is one of the biggest expenses of a building project, anything that can be done to minimize it saves money (within the bounds of adequate craftsmanship, of course). Designing details to allow for a clear division of the labor trades can minimize interference and potential conflicts.

Each detail should be reviewed to see if its construction can proceed from one trade to another with the least amount of overlap. For example, in building a standard partition, the drywallers can install the metal framing. Then the electricians and plumbers can install conduit and piping. Then the drywall finishers can finish the wall and leave, making way for the painters. Partition details that deviate from this standard sequence will take more time to complete and will be more costly.

Designer Liability

Designer liability involves looking at details from the standpoint of the designer and then detailing to minimize exposure to liability. This is especially important for custom details or details that use new, untried materials.

Other Properties

There are many other properties of materials and construction details to review when developing or evaluating drawings, such as (when applicable) acoustical properties, light reflection, abrasion resistance, resistance to termites and other insects, holding power of fasteners, resistance to fading, mildew resistance, color, and finish. Of course, no material will completely satisfy all criteria, but the interior designer must find the best balance.

EVALUATING MATERIALS AND PRODUCTS

During the final stages of design development, materials and products should first be reviewed to verify that they still meet the basic design and aesthetic needs of the client. Often, during the schematic design and development process, other factors cause the designer to change materials, and with the effort to meet functional, code, and cost constraints, the original reason for selecting a material is lost. If changes have been made, the client should be informed, and the interior designer should get the client's written approval on any changes.

As described in Ch. 6, individual finishes and materials should also be evaluated according to a rational process including the criteria of function, durability, maintainability, safety, health, cost, and sustainability. Refer to Ch. 6 for a detailed discussion of the individual factors involved with each of these criteria.

The material safety data sheets for products and materials should also be reviewed, especially those for materials that are unfamiliar to the interior designer. A *material safety data sheet* (MSDS) is a printed sheet or sheets containing information about the physical makeup of a substance, proper procedures for storage and handling, and what to do in case of a spill. The Occupational Safety and Health Administration (OSHA) requires manufacturers to provide MSDSs for potentially hazardous substances. Although MSDSs are intended to be used by workers and emergency personnel and not consumers, they do provide valuable information on the potential toxicity of a material. Specifically, they contain the name and address of the manufacturer; an identification of the substance, including trade names; physical data; fire and explosion data; and information on toxicity, health effects, first aid for exposure, reactivity with other substances, storage and disposal, conditions to avoid, spill and leak procedures, and protective equipment required, if any.

However, remember that MSDSs do not describe potential long-term effects of a chemical product and are not available for most of the finish materials used by interior designers. Other sources, such as the Environmental Protection Agency (EPA) or the product manufacturer, should consulted for information on other materials.

EVALUATING OTHER DESIGN AND CONSTRUCTION ISSUES

Codes

The development of a code checklist to be used for preliminary design is discussed in Ch. 2. Some of the important code requirements for space planning are listed in Ch. 4.

The following detailed code components should be reviewed during the design development phase. Some of them are the responsibility of the consulting engineers, but the interior designer should be aware of those elements that need to be checked. Refer to Chs. 27 and 28 for detailed information on building code requirements.

- construction of fire-rated corridors

- construction of other fire-rated partitions, including occupancy separations and shaft enclosures

- requirements for fire ratings based on construction type

- detailed requirements for stairs, including risers, treads, and handrails

- detailed requirements for ramps, including slope, landings, and handrails

- construction of glazing where safety glazing is required

- glazing details where fire-rated glazing is used

- detailed requirements for doors, door ratings, and door hardware

- requirements for flame-spread ratings of finishes

- requirements for toilet room planning for accessibility, including accessories

- requirements for penetrations of fire-rated assemblies

- limitations on the use of plastics

- locations of exit signs

- locations of required fire extinguishers

- ventilation requirements, including separate exhaust systems

- requirements for emergency lighting

- sprinkler requirements

- smoke detector requirements

- signage accessibility and egress notification

Accessibility

At the conclusion of design development, all accessibility issues that relate to the broad issues of space planning should have been incorporated into the design. These issues include such things as the widths of accessible routes, door sizes and maneuvering clearances, ramp locations and sizes, and toilet room layout. Prior to moving into the construction documents phase, accessibility issues should be evaluated one last time to make sure all requirements are met.

In addition, the following detailed aspects of barrier-free design should be evaluated at this time.

- surfaces of accessible routes, including thresholds and level changes

- details of toilet room design, including grab bars, mirrors, faucets, and accessories

- drinking fountain mounting

- bathtub and shower design, if used

- details of stair design, including treads, risers, and handrails

- protruding objects

- requirements for reach ranges

- detectable warnings, if needed

- locations and design of visual and audio alarms

- public telephone access and mounting height

- amount of seating and other elements governed by scoping provisions

Refer to Ch. 29 for detailed requirements for barrier-free design.

Rules, Regulations, and Standards of the Building

If an interior design is being completed in a leased building, there are usually rules, regulations, and standards that the building owner or manager imposes on all tenants. These rules, regulations, and standards must be incorporated into the designer's plan. The exact requirements will vary with the building and the type of lease, but some of the typical regulations and standards the interior designer should be aware of include the following.

- the rentable-usable ratio. This is a standard that can affect how much rent a tenant pays based on the amount of actual space they require for their business. Refer to Ch. 2 for a discussion of how building area is measured and the various terms involved.

• building standard allowances for things such as partitions, doors, light fixtures, and electrical outlets. In some cases, a certain number of building standard items are provided to the tenant based on the amount of spaced leased. In other cases, a lump sum amount of money may be given to the tenant, also based on the area leased.

• limitations on the design and finishes of the public corridor side of partitions

• limitations on the design of the main entrance to the lease space

• regulations for corridor and lobby signage

• requirements for security, including locks, security codes, and check-in and check-out procedures for employees as well as visitors

• regulations for service access and use of freight elevator

• availability of mechanical and electrical systems, including availability for after-hours use and special equipment

• capacity of the structural system to carry unusually heavy loads like libraries, file rooms, and heavy equipment

• provisions for expansion in case the tenant requires additional space. This is typically written into the lease and is based on the length of the lease, the location in the building, and the terms of the leases of adjacent tenants.

• requirements on window coverings. Some buildings demand that the building standard window covering be used instead of the tenant's choice.

• regulations on the type of lighting that can be used. Certain types of lights may be required to achieve a consistent image from the building and to minimize maintenance problems.

• hours that the building is open to the public

CLIENT PRESENTATIONS

At the end of the design development phase, the interior designer again needs to communicate to the client the status of the project and what the final decisions are regarding the space plan, materials and finishes, and furnishings. In addition, an updated budget is usually presented. Client approval is required before the designer begins the construction documents portion of the project.

The various types of drawings and models that can be used to communicate the design are reviewed in Ch. 5. Specific presentation techniques are reviewed in Chs. 2 and 6.

The main difference between a design development presentation and earlier presentations is that the former is very specific. At this stage, the exact dimensions of the floor plan are set, specific products and materials have been selected, furniture selection is finalized, and for most products, exact colors and finishes have been determined. This is the last chance for the client to make changes without adversely affecting the project's cost and schedule.

SAMPLE QUESTIONS

1. Before preparing construction documents, the interior designer should verify if any particular types of lighting fixtures are required by coordinating with the

(A) architect

(B) building owner

(C) contractor

(D) electrical engineer

2. When reviewing a detail of a gypsum wallboard niche to receive a built-in millwork cabinet, the interior designer should be most concerned with

(A) clearance

(B) connection

(C) movement

(D) tolerance

3. When coordinating with a security consultant, the interior designer's drawings should show

(A) a schedule of all security devices

(B) the emergency backup power supply

(C) the positioning of required lighting

(D) the wiring of the security devices

4. The determination of exact requirements for grab bars in toilet rooms is most appropriately made during

(A) programming

(B) schematic design

(C) design development

(D) construction drawing development

5. Which of the following is NOT an effective tool for controlling moisture when detailing the area around a spa pool?

(A) adhesives

(B) drainage

(C) flashing

(D) sealants

6. The interior designer's best source concerning the limitations on the use of a product can be obtained from the

(A) building code official who inspects the product

(B) specialty contractor who installs the product

(C) manufacturer who makes the product

(D) trade association representing the product type

7. The use of particleboard as part of a construction detail should be carefully evaluated in terms of the particleboard's

(A) availability

(B) permeability

(C) strength

(D) VOC content

8. A slip joint at the top of a partition is required to account for

(A) clearance

(B) movement

(C) tolerance

(D) structure

9. Important criteria for designing a lighting cove detail would include all of the following EXCEPT

(A) cost

(B) design intent

(C) ergonomics

(D) substrates

10. When specifying a specialty flooring material, the interior designer can obtain unbiased information on the hazards of a cleaning agent, required for maintenance, from the

(A) cleaning agent manufacturer

(B) Environmental Protection Agency

(C) flooring manufacturer

(D) material safety data sheet

14

CONSTRUCTION DRAWINGS

One of the most important parts of the contract documents is the set of construction drawings (sometimes called working drawings) that describe, in detail, the extent of the work and the locations, dimensions, and relationships of the various construction elements. Construction drawings represent the interior designer's final decisions concerning design, building methods, and construction technology. As such, they must show the technically correct ways of meeting the functional requirements of the design, such as constructing partitions, building architectural woodwork, distributing electricity, providing safe finishes, and satisfying thousands of other concerns.

Because they are used to build the project, the construction drawings must clearly communicate the information to the contractor, material suppliers, and other people involved with the project. In addition to being accurate, they must be coordinated with the specifications and the consultant's drawings. The drawings form part of the contract and are legal documents. To pass the NCIDQ exam, the candidate must be able to read and interpret construction drawings as well as have the knowledge to produce them.

ORGANIZATION OF CONSTRUCTION DRAWINGS

Construction drawings are organized in a generally standardized sequence based on the normal sequence of construction and through many years of use. For interior design projects, the sequence may vary slightly depending on the size of the project and whether the interior drawings are part of a larger architectural set of drawings. For instance, a small residential project may include the floor plan, a finish schedule, and some interior elevations on the first sheet in a set of drawings, while these individual drawing elements may be shown on separate sheets as part of a set of drawings for a larger project.

For a set of construction drawings produced and coordinated by the interior designer, the drawings are usually organized in the following sequence:

- *Title and index sheet* (if used): On large projects, the first sheet often contains a large title and sometimes a graphic identifying the project. In addition, this sheet may contain an index to the set of drawings, a list of standard abbreviations and symbols used on the job, project data required by the building department (square footage, occupancy category, building type, and the like), and general notes that apply to the entire job. On small projects, this information, if included, is placed on the first sheet of the set, which is usually the floor plan.

• *Floor plans:* The number and types of plan drawings depend on the project. Small, residential designs may only have one floor plan that includes all the necessary information. Large projects may have several plans of the same area, each showing a particular type of information. Some of the types of plans commonly used on midsize to large projects include demolition plans, construction floor plans, finish plans, telephone and power plans, and furniture plans. When the project is very complex, additional large-scale construction plans may also be required of certain portions of the small-scale floor plan.

• *Reflected ceiling plan(s)*

• *Elevations*

• *Details:* Details may include construction elements such as wall types, doors, glazing, ceilings, millwork, stairways, flooring, and any other special construction. The number of details depends on the size and complexity of the project and whether the job is being bid or negotiated. If the project is competitively bid, the details must be very complete and fully describe the extent of the work so the client will get a valid cost quote. On smaller, negotiated contract jobs where the majority of details are somewhat standard, there may be fewer details because some of the final decisions may be made during construction.

• *Mechanical drawings* (if required): If the project requires the services of a mechanical engineering consultant, the engineers prepare their own drawings with their professional seal. These drawings include (as necessary) information about the

heating, ventilating, and air conditioning (HVAC) systems as well as any plumbing systems. Refer to the section on coordination later in this chapter for information on what is included on the consultant's drawings.

• *Electrical drawings* (if required): Electrical drawings are prepared by an electrical engineering consultant if the project includes new or revised power and lighting circuiting and specialty wiring such as fire alarms, communications systems, security systems, and the like. On most residential projects, light fixture and switch locations may be shown schematically by the interior designer. It is the electrical contractor's responsibility to show the correct gauge of wire and to circuit the system properly and according to local building codes.

• *Fire protection drawings* (if required): When a sprinkler system is required for commercial construction, fire protection plans must be completed by a mechanical engineer and are usually included with the complete set of construction drawings.

Occasionally, structural drawings are needed if work is being performed that requires the services of a structural engineer. If these are included, they are produced by the structural engineer and placed after the interior drawings and before the mechanical drawings. Drawing sets also include schedules (discussed in more detail in the following section). The locations of schedules may vary depending on the size and procedures of individual offices. However, they are generally located on the sheet where they most logically apply. For example, the room finish schedule and door schedule should be on the same sheet as the floor plan (assuming a separate finish plan is not used).

CONTENTS OF CONSTRUCTION DRAWINGS

Drawings should show the general configuration, size, shape, and location of the components of construction with general notes to explain materials, construction requirements, dimensions, and other graphic material. Detailed requirements for material quality, workmanship, and other items are contained in the technical specifications of the project manual, discussed in Ch. 15. The following is a brief description of some of the more common items that should be included with the interior design drawings. This list is by no means inclusive.

Floor Plans

Construction Plan

Construction plans, also called floor plans or partition plans, are the most common type of floor plan and are required for every project regardless of size or complexity. *Construction plans* are views seen as though a building were cut horizontally about 4 ft (1.2 m) above the floor with the top section removed. The construction plan shows the building configuration, including all walls, dimensions, existing construction to remain, references to elevations and details drawn elsewhere, room names (and numbers, if used), floor material indications, millwork, plumbing fixtures, built-in fixtures, stairs, special equipment, and notes as required to explain items on the plan. See Fig. 14.1. Construction plans are usually drawn at the scale of $1/8$ in = 1 ft 0 in (1:100) or $1/4$ in = 1 ft 0 in (1:50). If large-scale plans are required for very complex areas, they are typically drawn at a $1/2$ in scale (1:25). If there are other plans in the set of drawings, they should be drawn at the same scale as the primary construction plan.

Demolition Plans

If required by the complexity of the project, *demolition plans* show which existing construction is to remain and which is to be removed. A separate construction plan is then drawn to show new construction. If the extent of demolition work is minor,

the portions of the building to be removed can be shown with dashed lines on the construction plan. A contractor needs some type of demolition plan before partitions on a remodeling project can be removed.

Power and Telephone Plan

For large or complex projects, the interior designer sometimes draws a separate *power plan* or *telephone plan* showing the locations of electrical outlets, telephone outlets, and other signal systems like the locations of computer terminals and intercommunication systems. See Fig. 14.2. A separate plan is usually required for large projects because there is not enough room on the construction plan to show the outlets and include dimension lines to precisely locate each one. The interior designer's plan only shows the outlet locations. The electrical circuiting, conduit size, and other technical information are included on the plans prepared by the electrical engineer. If the interior designer does not produce a power plan, then the power plan drawn by the electrical engineer shows electrical outlets, telephone outlets, security systems, and fire alarm devices. Compare the power plan in Fig. 14.3 with the designer's outlet plan in Fig. 14.2.

Finish Schedule

There are a number of ways to communicate what finishes are required. Most commonly, a *finish schedule* is developed by the interior designer that lists, in tabular format, each room and the types and specifics of finishes for the floor, base, walls, and sometimes ceilings. Figure 14.4 shows a typical finish schedule. This method works well for fairly simple projects with only a single finish on each wall. However, when there are several finish types on each wall and other complex finish configurations, a separate finish plan can be used, as shown in the partial plan

Figure 14.1
Construction
Drawing

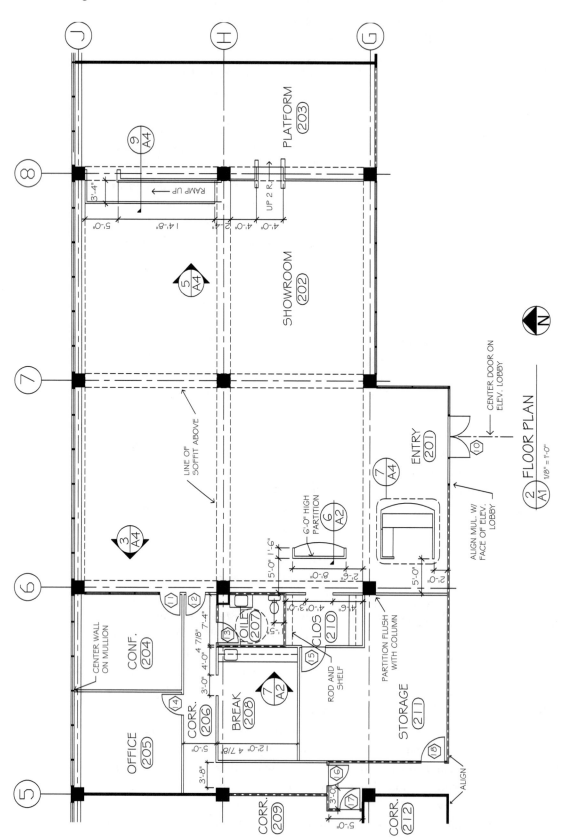

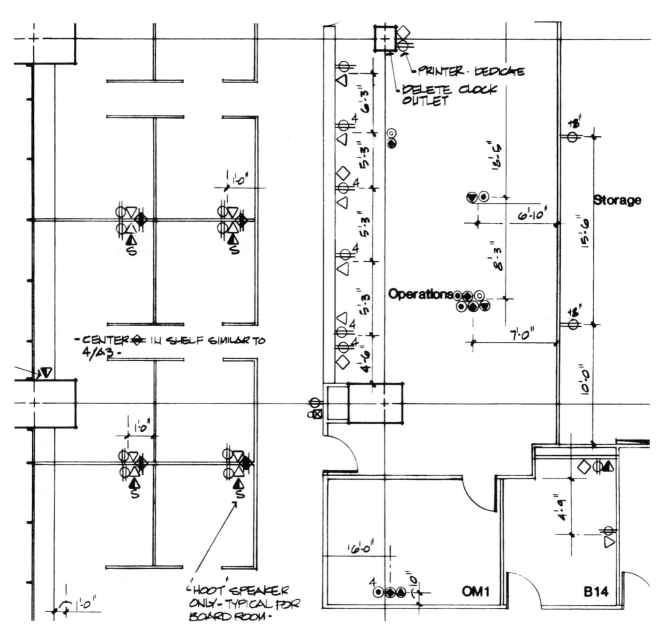

Figure 14.2
Interior
Designer's
Power Plan

of Fig. 14.5. Here, each finish is given a code number that is listed in a legend specifying the exact manufacturer, catalog number, and color. For example, all wall fabric notations could be preceded with a WP and then given numerical designations such as WP1, WP2, and so on.

However, specification items, such as installation instructions, are not included on the plan but are in the specifications.

Furniture Plan

Because the exact locations of furniture are important to an interior design project,

Figure 14.3
Electrical
Engineer's
Power Plan

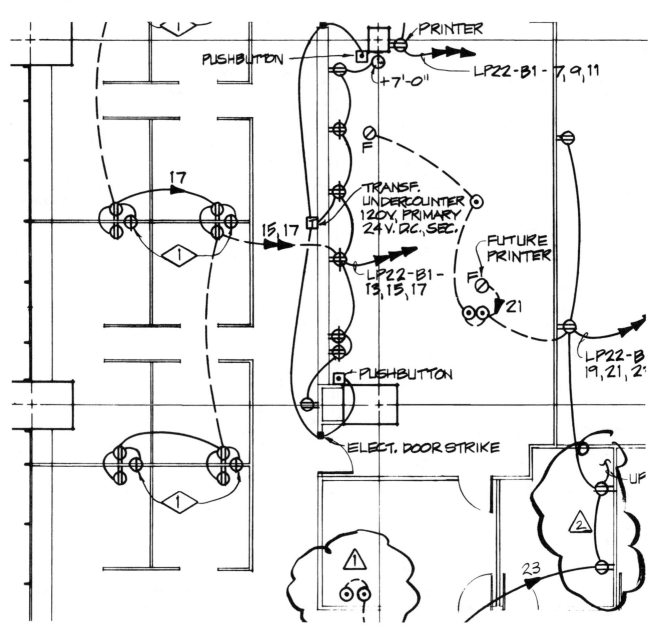

separate furniture plans are often drawn. See Fig. 14.6. A *furniture plan* shows the location of each piece of furniture on a floor plan with corresponding code numbers that identify each piece. The plans are used to itemize the furniture for pricing and ordering as well as to show the installers where to put each piece during move-in. The furniture plan is sometimes doubled up with a power and telephone plan because the exact locations of outlets can be directly related to the locations and

Figure 14.4
Finish Schedule

				east wall		north wall		west wall		south wall		ceiling		
no	room	floor	base	mat.	color	mat.	color	mat.	color	mat.	color	ht.	mtl.	remarks
201	lobby	F1	B2	–		W2		–		W2		10'–0"	C1	
202	east corridor	F1	B2	W2		W2		W2		W2		12'–0"	C2	W1 above trim
203	vending	F1	B2	W2		W2		W2		W2		10'–0"	C3	base surface applied
204	north corridor	F1	B2	W2		W2		W2		W2		12'–0"	C2	W1 above trim
205	west corridor	F1	B2	W2		W2		W2		W2		12'–0"	C2	W1 above trim
206	south corridor	F1	B2	W2		W2		W2		W2		10'–0"	C1	
207	service	exist.	exist.	W3		W3		W3		W3		exist.	exist.	
208	corridor	F2	B3	W1		W3		W1&3		W1		exist.	exist.	
209	not used													
210	closet	F1	B1	W1		W1		W1		W1		10'–0"	C2	
211	conference	F1	B1	W1		W1		–		W1		12'–0"	C1	
212	conference	F1	B1	W1		W1		W1		W1		10'–0"	C2	
213	cf fice	F1	B1	W1		W1		W1		W1		10'–0"	C2	
214	lexis	F1	B1	W1		W1		W1		W1		10'–0"	C2	
215	closet	F1	B1	W1		W1		W1		W1		10'–0"	C2	
216	law library	F1	B1	W1		W1		*		W1		10'–0"	C1&2	* paint furred columns
217	telephone	F1	B1	W1		W1		W1		W1		9'–0"	C2	
218	telephone	F1	B1	W1		W1		W1		W1		9'–0"	C2	

FINISH SCHEDULE

orientations of furniture. For example, telephone and electrical outlets are best placed directly to the side of a desk.

Site plan

A *site plan* is a view of a building as seen from directly above, showing the roof of the building as well as the surrounding yards, walks, driveways, and other features within the property line. It also usually shows the streets and property immediately adjacent to the site. (The interior designer does not draw a site plan, but the NCIDQ exam may ask examinees to be able to identify the characteristics of a site plan.)

Reflected Ceiling Plans

Reflected ceiling plans show a view of the ceiling as though it were reflected onto a mirror on the floor, or as though the ceiling were transparent and it was possible to see through it. This view is necessary to ensure that the ceiling has the same orientation as the floor plan. That is, if north is toward the top of the sheet on the floor plan, north will also be toward the top of the sheet on the reflected ceiling plan.

Reflected ceiling plans should be drawn at the same scale as the construction plan.

Reflected ceiling plans show partitions that extend to the ceiling and those that extend through the ceiling (as on commercial projects that use a suspended ceiling). They also show ceiling materials, building grid lines (if used), notes calling out ceiling heights, changes in ceiling heights, locations of all lights (including exit lights), sprinkler heads, air diffusers and vents, access panels, speakers, and any other item that is part of (or touches) the plane of the ceiling. In addition, dimensions are included where necessary to precisely locate elements that cannot be reasonably inferred by their relationship to something else. For example, recessed light troffers placed in a suspended ceiling can be located by the contractor by simply counting the number of tiles, but the position of a downlight in a gypsum wallboard ceiling must be dimensioned to its center point so the electrical contractor knows where to install it.

Figure 14.5
Finish Plan

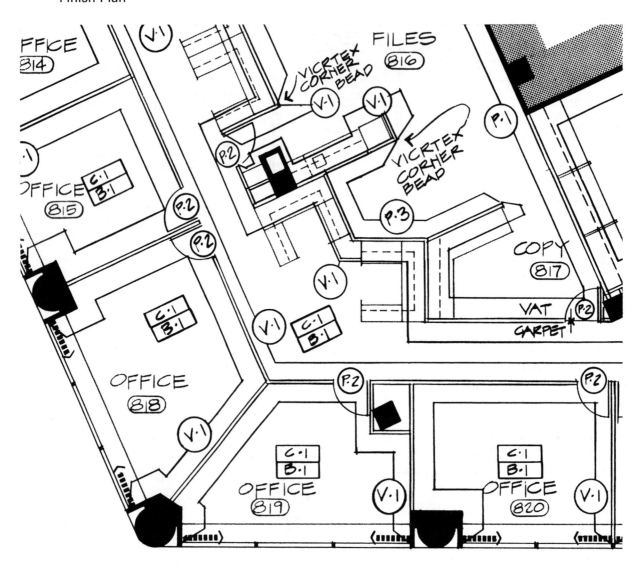

Although some items like lights and air diffusers will also be indicated on the engineering consultant's drawings, everything should be shown on the interior designer's reflected ceiling plan. This way, all items can be coordinated so the designer has a full understanding of what the final ceiling will look like.

The reflected ceiling plan will also have section cut reference marks and other notations referring to details drawn elsewhere in the set. One example is shown in Fig. 14.7.

Elevations

An *elevation* is a drawing showing a vertical surface from a point of view perpendicular to the surface. Elevations are straight-on views, so there is no distortion as with perspective or isometric drawings. All portions of the drawing are done at the

Figure 14.6
Furniture Plan

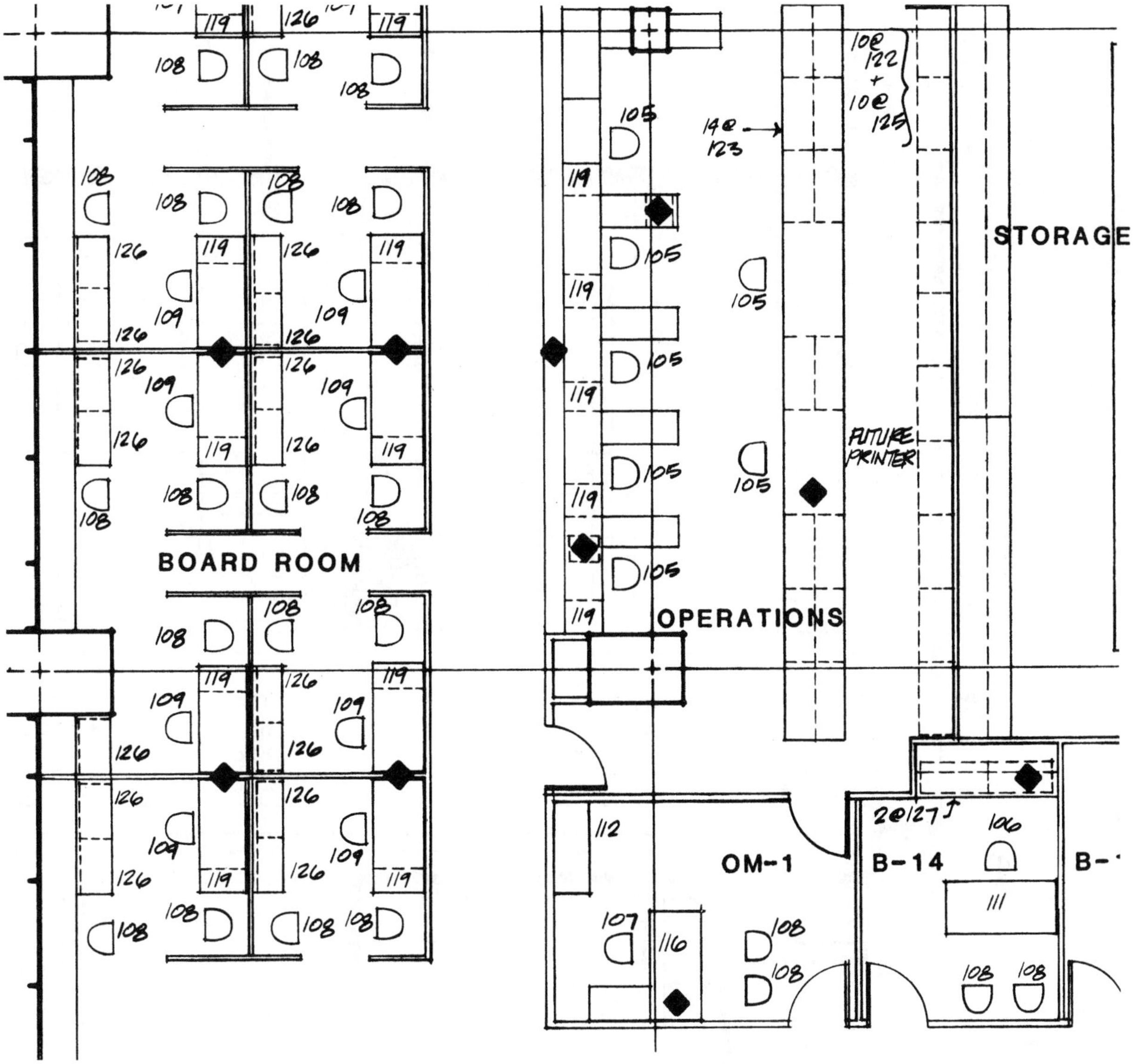

same scale, and if curves or angled surfaces are included, these are projected onto the flat plane of the elevation drawing. See Fig. 14.8.

Elevations are drawn for interior design projects to indicate the configuration and finish of wall surfaces—something that is difficult, if not impossible, to do with a plan drawing. Elevations are also used

to show the vertical dimensions and design of millwork and other freestanding construction.

Elevations are useful for showing the configuration of a surface, vertical dimensions, openings in walls, built-in items, materials and finishes on a wall, and the locations of switches, thermostats, and other wall-mounted equipment. When

Figure 14.7
Reflected Ceiling Plan

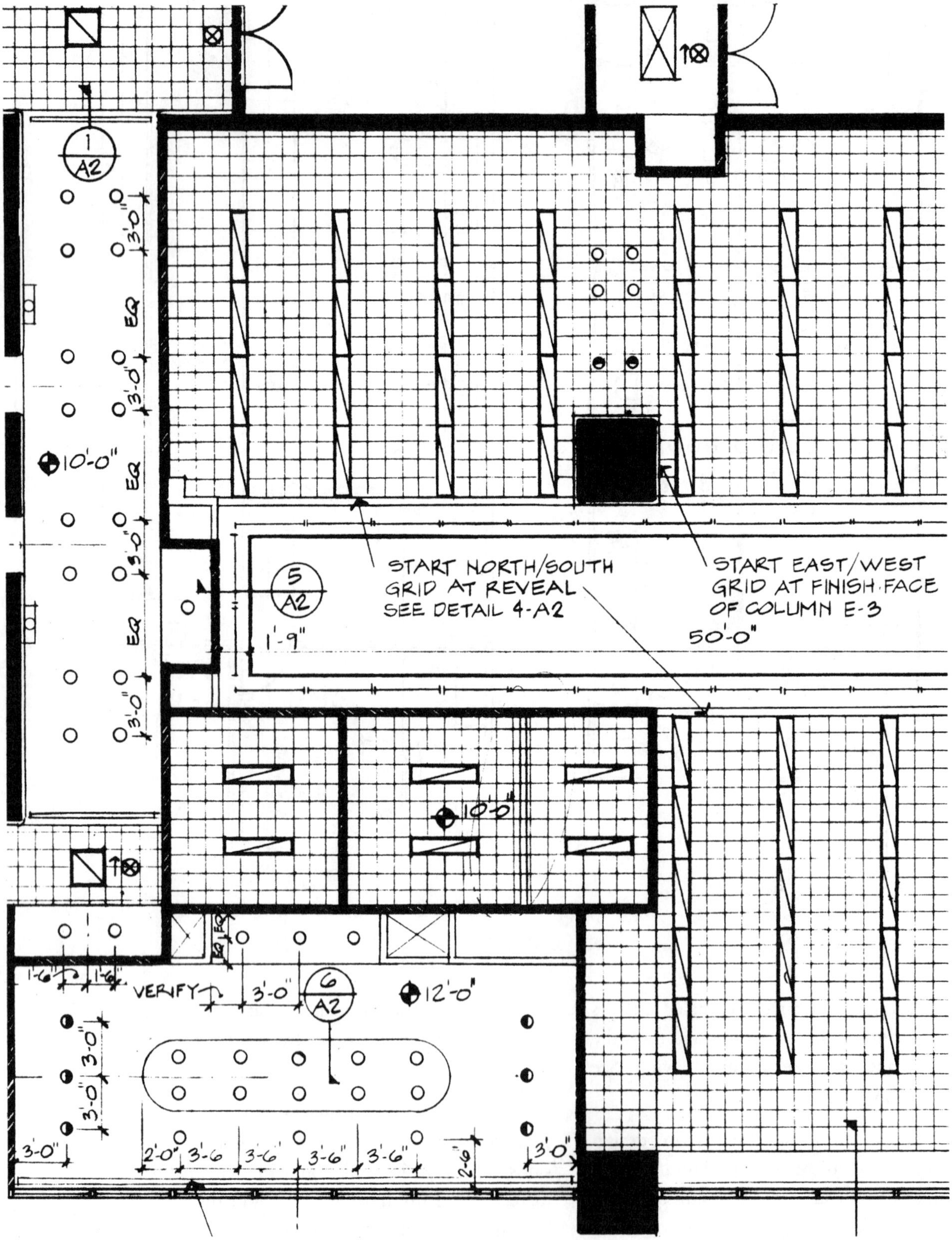
1
A2
3'-0"
EQ
3'-0"
10'-0"
EQ
3'-0"
EQ
3'-0"
5
A2
1'-9"
START NORTH/SOUTH
GRID AT REVEAL
SEE DETAIL 4-A2
START EAST/WEST
GRID AT FINISH FACE
OF COLUMN E-3
50'-0"
10'-0"
EQ
EQ
1'-6"
1'-6"
VERIFY
3'-0"
6
A2
12'-0"
3'-0"
3'-0"
3'-0"
2'-0"
3'-6
3'-6
3'-6"
3'-6"
2'-6"
3'-0"

Figure 14.8
Interior Elevation

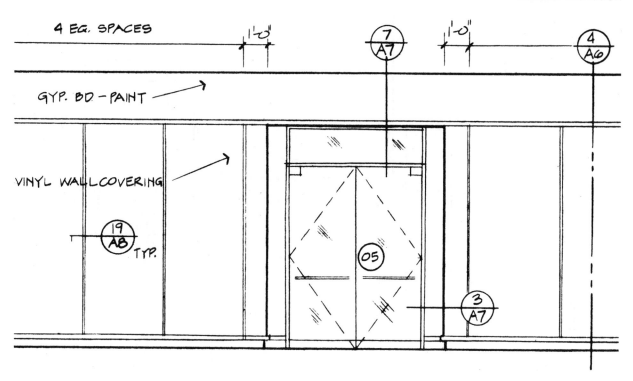

there are numerous or complex horizontal dimensions, such as with wall panels or cabinet units, elevations can include horizontal dimensioning that would not fit on a floor plan. They are also used to indicate references to other sections and details with the use of section cut lines. See Fig. 14.8. The scale of elevations depends on the complexity of the surface to be shown, but common scales are $1/4$ in = 1 ft 0 in (1:50) for simple wall planes to $3/8$ in (1:40) or $1/2$ in = 1 ft 0 in (1:25) for more complex surfaces.

Sections

A *section* is a drawing showing what a part of the construction would look like if there was a cut straight through it. Because of this, it shows a view that does not really exist but one that is very useful for showing the relationships between materials. Figure 14.9 shows the section referenced in Fig. 14.8. A section can be cut horizontally, as with a plan, or vertically, to show partition construction, for example. In either case, the section cut is perpendicular to the plane of construction that will be exposed in the detail.

Strictly speaking, an interior elevation is also a section cut because the outline of the elevation (the floor, side walls, and ceiling) is a portion of construction that is cut through to show the face of the wall. Generally, only the outline of the section is shown because the actual construction of the floor, walls, and ceiling is not the important element of an elevation drawing. See Fig. 14.10. The details of these construction elements are shown elsewhere in the drawings, if needed.

The terms *section* and *detail*, as used in interior construction drawings, are sometimes confused. This is because the majority of details are section cuts through small

Figure 14.9

Section

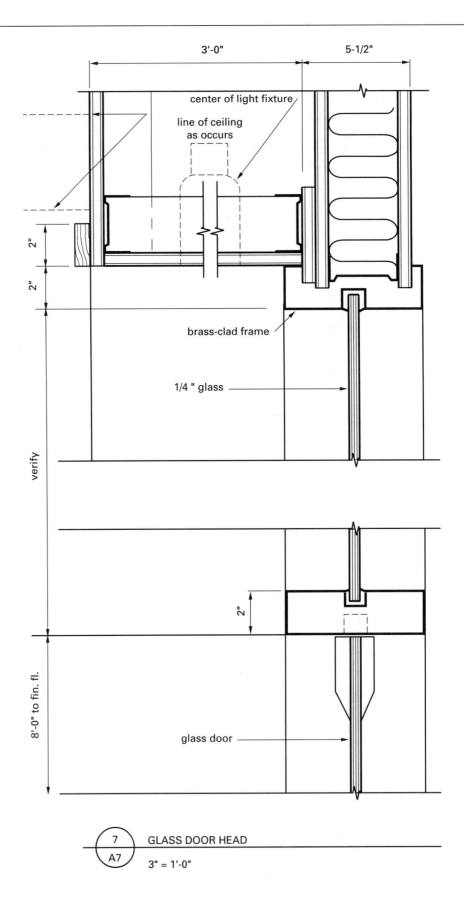

3'-0"

5-1/2"

center of light fixture

line of ceiling
as occurs

2"

2"

2"

verify

brass-clad frame

1/4 " glass

2"

8'-0" to fin. fl.

glass door

7
A7
GLASS DOOR HEAD
3" = 1'-0"

portions of construction, as described in the following text about details. In addition, the term "section" is used on architectural drawings to refer to sections through entire buildings. However, not all details are sections. A detail can also be a very large-scale plan view, an isometric view, or a large-scale partial elevation. Normally, a detail section is simply called a detail.

Details

A building or interior design project is a complex collection of component parts, all of which are connected to other parts in various ways. The manner in which an assembly of several parts is organized and connected is commonly referred to as a *detail.* The construction drawing showing such a part is called a *detail drawing* or simply a detail, for short. A detail may be as simple as nailing wallboard to a stud or as complex as the intersection of the structural steel of a stairway and floor with the finish flooring, ceiling below, handrail, and concealed lighting, all of which might include dozens of different materials and connection techniques.

Because details show complex information, they are usually large-scale drawings of sections cut through a portion of construction as shown in Fig. 14.11. However, it is also possible to have a detail plan or detail elevation if a large-scale view of something complex is required. In Fig. 14.11, notice that in addition to showing the materials cut by the section, the detail also shows what is beyond the section cut. In effect, it is a small elevation of the portion of construction near the object through which the section is cut.

Details are commonly drawn at scales of 1 in = 1 ft 0 in (1:10), $1^1/_2$ in = 1 ft 0 in (1:8), or 3 in = 1 ft 0 in (1:4). For very small and complex construction elements, half-size or even full-size drawings can be produced.

Figure 14.10
Elevation

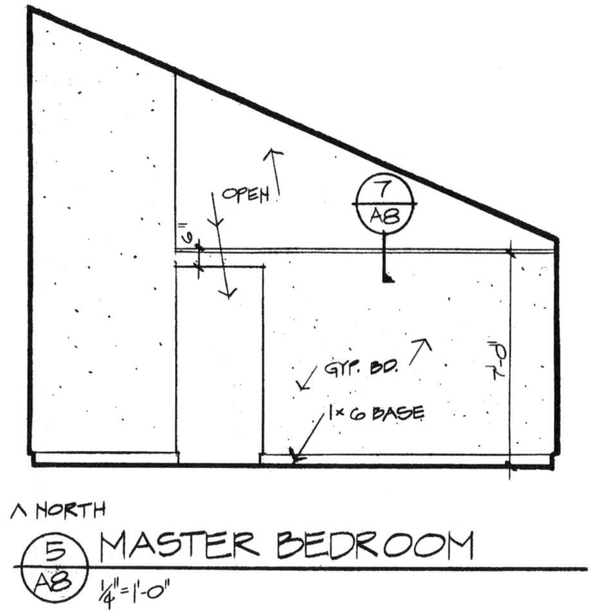

Schedules

Schedules show information in tabular format with rows and columns of data. They are used because they are a very efficient way to communicate a large amount of complex information in a small space. Common schedules for interior design construction drawings include room finish, door, kitchen equipment, millwork, and hardware schedules. Figure 14.12 shows a typical door schedule. Notice that there is a list of unique entities (in this case, door numbers), and each occupies one row of the table. Each entity has a number of attributes associated with it, such as type, size, material, and so on. These attributes are common for each of the rooms (entities) regardless of how many doors there are. This is typical of all construction schedules.

In addition to providing their own information, schedules may also refer to other parts of the drawings, if necessary. For example, the door schedule in Fig. 14.12 has a column that lists the numbers and sheets on which details for the doors are drawn.

Figure 14.11
Detail

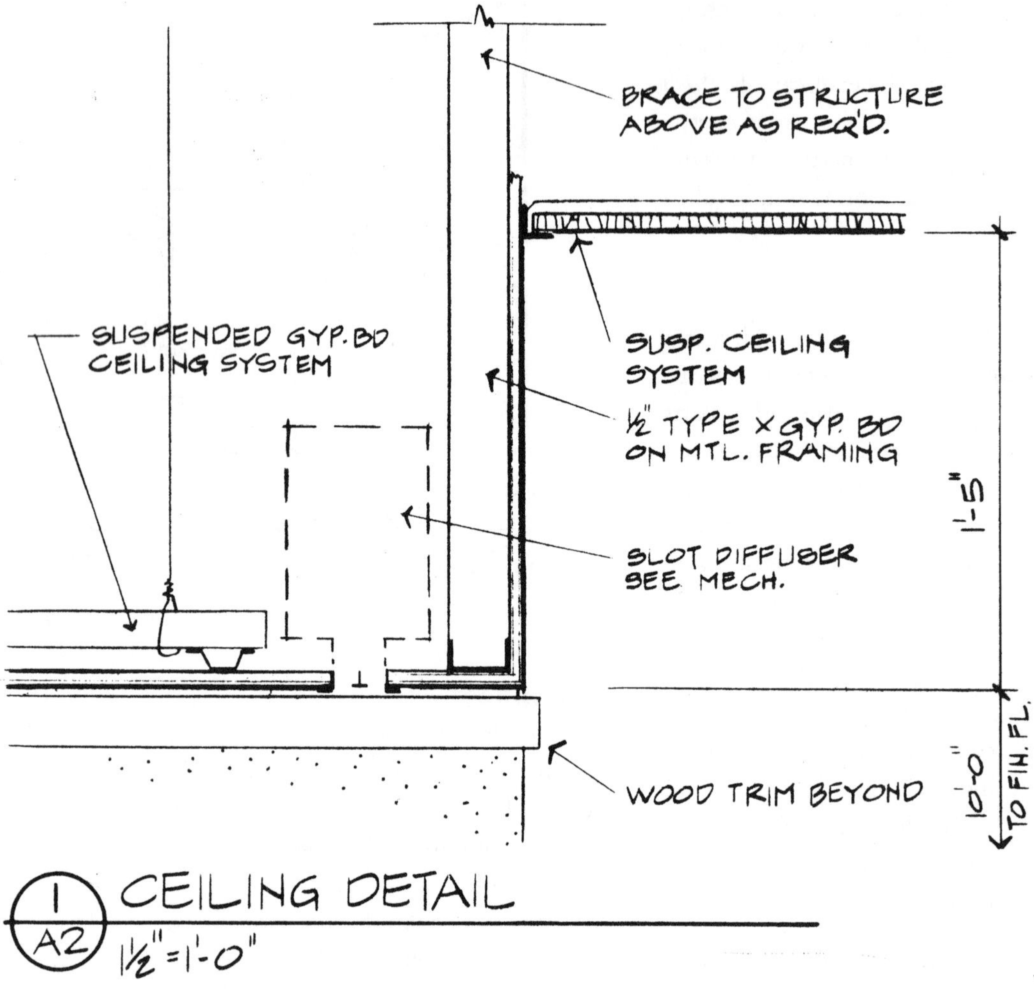

BRACE TO STRUCTURE
ABOVE AS REQ'D.

SUSPENDED GYP. BD
CEILING SYSTEM

SUSP. CEILING
SYSTEM

½" TYPE X GYP. BD
ON MTL. FRAMING

SLOT DIFFUSER
SEE MECH.

1'-5"

WOOD TRIM BEYOND

10'-0" TO FIN. FL.

CEILING DETAIL
1
A2
1½"=1'-0"

Another column refers to the hardware groups listed in the specifications.

DRAFTING OF CONSTRUCTION DRAWINGS

Regardless of the size or configuration of an individual project, there are common drafting concerns that must be addressed with any project, whether the project is manually drafted or completed with computer-aided design (CAD). These concerns include the sheet size to use, the makeup of the title block, and how individual sheets are organized. Layering is a consideration only with CAD.

Sheet Sizes

The size of a drawing sheet used for interior design projects depends on several factors. Typically, an office will use one or two standard sizes for all the projects it does. Sheet size depends on the typical size of the office's projects, the filing system used, the capabilities of reproduction and plotting equipment, and client requirements. Sheet size is most typically determined by the size needed to draw a floor plan on one sheet without dividing the plan into sections.

For either manual drafting or CAD, standard sheet sizes are used in the interior

Figure 14.12

Door Schedule

no.	type	mat.	width	height	thk.	type	mat.	head	jamb	jamb	sill	fire rate.	hwd gp.	remarks
DOOR SCHEDULE															
	door					frame								
01	A	HM	3'-0"	7'-0"	1 3/4	1	HM	1-A7	5-A7	5-A7		3/4	B	
02	B	HM	2-3'-0"	7'-0"	1 3/4	2	HM	1-A7	5-A7	5-A7		3/4	C	relocate existing to new fm.
03	C	SC WD	3'-0"	7'-0"	1 3/4	1	HM	8-A7	11-A7	11-A7		1/3	D	
04	B	SC WD	2-3'-0"	7'-0"	1 3/4	*	exist.	exist.	exist.	exist.			E	reuse existing frame
05	D	glass	2-3'-0"	8'-0"	1/2	3	brass	7-A7	3-A7	3-A7	10-A7		G	glass transom above
06	exist.						exist.	10-A8	15-A8	16-A8			F	existing door and frame
07	exist.						exist.	6-A8	1-A8	1-A8			F	existing door and frame
08	C	SC WD	3'-0"	8'-0"	1 3/4	4	HM	2-A7	6-A7	6-A7		1/3	G	use exist. bldg. std.
09	exist.						exist.	7-A8	3-A8	3-A8			F	existing door and frame
10	D	glass	2-3'-0"	8'-0"	1/2	3	brass	7-A7	3-A7	3-A7	10-A7		G	glass transom above
11	not	used												
12	D	glass	2-3'-0"	8'-0"	1/2	3	brass	7-A7	3-A7	3-A7	10-A7		G	glass transom above
13	not	used												
14	C	SC WD	1'-10"	8'-0"	1 3/4	5	WD	9-A7	13-A7	13-A7			H	
15	C	SC WD	3'-0"	8'-0"	1 3/4	5	WD	9-A7	12-A7	13-A7			I	
16	C	SC WD	3'-0"	8'-0"	1 3/4	5	WD	9-A7	12-A7	13-A7			I	
17	C	SC WD	3'-0"	8'-0"	1 3/4	5	WD	9-A7	12-A7	13-A7			I	
18	C	SC WD	2-3'-0"	8'-0"	1 3/4	5	WD	9-A7	13-A7	13-A7			H	
19	F	SC WD	2'-6"	8'-0"	1 3/4	–	WD	12-A8	17-A8	17-A8			J	glass panel in door
20	F	SC WD	2'-6"	8'-0"	1 3/4	–	WD	12-A8	17-A8	17-A8			J	glass panel in door
21	E	SC WD	3'-0"	7'-0"	1 3/4	–	exist.	6-A8 SIM	7-A6	7-A6			L	dutch door, match existing

design, architectural, and engineering industries. These standard sizes are based on one of three systems: architectural, ANSI (American National Standards Institute), and ISO (International Standards Organization). Each size is given a letter designation. These are shown in Table 14.1.

The ISO sizes are based on the SI system of measurement, commonly called metric. Although most offices in the United States use the architectural sizes, the U.S. federal government requires projects to use the ANSI sizes. Other countries use the ISO sizes.

Title Blocks

Title blocks contain identifying information about the project on each sheet of the drawing set. In addition, they contain information specific to each sheet, such as the sheet number, sheet name, revision

dates, and so on. Title blocks may also contain general notes and keynoting information. A *keynote* is a note placed in the title block or elsewhere on the drawing sheet with an identifying number that is used in the field of the drawing itself. Instead of making a lengthy note next to the item it annotates, it uses a number that refers to the list of keyotes. This system minimizes the space required on the drawing and can save time when repetitious notes are required in several places. The keynote number can also be coordinated with specification numbers.

Title block layouts for every office are standardized so the same information will appear in the same place on every job. When drawings are being produced with CAD, title blocks and borderlines are usually drawn as part of a reference file. This

Table 14.1
Drawing Sheet
Sizes

| | sytem and sheet sizes | | | | |
| architectural | | ANSI | | ISO | |
size (in (mm))	mark	size (in (mm))	mark	size (in (mm))	mark
9 × 12 (229 × 305)	A	8.5 × 11 (216 × 279)	A	210 × 297 (8.3 × 11.7)	A4
12 × 18 (305 × 457)	B	11 × 17 (279 × 432)	B	297 × 420 (11.7 × 16.5)	A3
18 × 24 (457 × 610)	C	17 × 22 (432 × 559)	C	420 × 594 (16.5 × 23.4)	A2
24 × 36 (610 × 914)	D	22 × 34 (559 × 864)	D	594 × 841 (23.4 × 33.1)	A1
36 × 48 (914 × 1219)	E	34 × 44 (864 × 1118)	E	841 × 1189 (33.1 × 46.8)	A0
30 × 42 (762 × 1067)	F	–	–	–	–

way, only one file has to be drawn, and the same file can be referenced into drawing files, saving computer memory and allowing individual project drawings to be updated if the title block changes.

In offices using manual drafting, standard title block sheets with border lines are preprinted on vellum or polyester with the line work and information that does not change from job to job, such as the designer's name and address, printed on each sheet. When a new sheet is needed, a preprinted one can be used and the necessary information filled in.

The design and placement of title blocks varies with each office. Most offices design their own with the type of information they want and maybe their company logo and have blank sheets printed in two or three standard drawing sizes the office uses. Title blocks are usually placed along the full length of the right side of the sheet. The information may either be placed the way the sheet is normally viewed, or widthwise, along the short dimension of the sheet.

The following is a list of the information that should be on every title block. Optional information is noted.

• designer's name, address, phone number, and fax number (a logo or some special design is optional, as is a listing of email and website address)

• consultants' names, addresses, and phone numbers (fax and email sometimes included)

• project title and address

• owner's name and address, if the owner desires it (some owners don't want to be identified; some do and want their logo to appear as well)

• project number (optional if the project is simple and single phase; most designers have project numbers for accounting reasons)

- space for professional stamps, if required (provide a 2" × 2" (51 × 51) space for each stamp)

- revisions column (should include space for the revision number, date, and a brief note; leave space for at least 10 revisions, more is not uncommon)

- sheet title (keep it short, like Details, or First Floor Plan)

- sheet number (place in the lower right-hand corner, and make it large so it is easy to see)

- drawn by (a small space for the initials of whoever drew the sheet)

- checked by (a small space for the initials of whoever checked the drawing)

- approved by (optional, but good to have a space for the client to sign off on the drawings)

- copyright notice (optional, but a good idea)

- space for a key plan (optional for interior work, but useful for very large projects)

- file number (optional; large offices develop their own filing systems to make it easy to index and retrieve drawings)

- scale (Some offices make this mandatory, but it is more flexible to indicate scale as part of the title of each individual drawing on the sheet, to avoid confusion if there are several drawings with different scales.)

- north arrow (Optional on sheets used for elevations or details. Some offices provide space for it, if necessary.)

- space for notes, legends, or keynotes (an option if the office uses these systems consistently and the drawing sheet is large enough that extra space can be provided)

Sheet Organization

In most offices, individual sheets used for drawings are organized in a consistent manner, sometimes in conformance with the Uniform Drawing System (UDS) of the Construction Specifications Institute (CSI). Whatever specific method is used, offices use standard sheet sizes and generally locate the title block along the right side of the drawing sheet. See Fig. 14.13.

Borderlines are typically used on drawings to confine the actual drawing within a set area. Borderlines were originally needed to allow for imperfections in reproducing drawings from originals. Today, borderlines are required to account for the fact that most plotters cannot plot to the extreme edges of paper. Borderline width varies with each office and the limitations of plotting devices. Typically, the right, top, and bottom edges are $1/2$ in or $3/4$ in (13 or 19) wide and the left, binding edge is about $1^1/2$ in (38) wide.

After the borderlines and title block are drawn, the remaining drawing area is commonly organized on a module system as shown in Fig. 14.13. The exact size of the module depends on office standards, the size of the drawing sheet, and how much of the sheet is allotted for the borderline width and the title block (usually drawn along the right side of the sheet). The typical drawing module is about 6 in square (150), but this dimension varies slightly so there is an even division of modules within the confines of the borderline. Drawings are developed to fit within one or more modules. For example, a small detail may require only one module. A wall section may require a space one module wide and three modules high. A floor plan may require an entire sheet of modules.

Using such a system allows for the development and easy use of standard or master details that are drawn to fit within the module. This system works with either manual drafting or CAD. A standard numbering system for the modules also makes it possible for individual drawings

Figure 14.13
Drafting Sheet
Layout

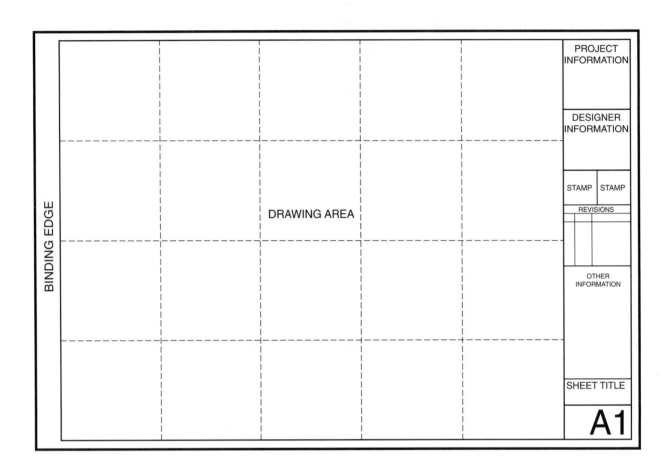

to be numbered early in the development of the construction drawings.

Layering

Layering of drawings refers to the system of placing particular information on separate layers (or levels) in a CAD system. Layering allows information to be shown or hidden so that several drawings can be developed from one computer file of information. For example, the same partition layout layer can be used for the floor plan as well as the reflected ceiling plan of a building. Individual offices may have their own layering systems or use the CAD layering system of the American Institute of Architects.

COORDINATION WITH THE CONSULTANT'S DRAWINGS

On nearly all projects, there are several consultants working with the interior designer. Small- to medium-size jobs may only require a mechanical and an electrical engineer. Larger projects may have additional consultants in architectural design, structural design, fire protection, food service, security systems, and acoustics, among others.

Each consulting firm develops its own drawings, so coordination among everyone on the team is critical. Someone must make sure that a recessed light fixture is not placed where it is in conflict with an air duct, for example. Although all consultants must be diligent in their efforts to work with others and produce complete and correct documents, the primary responsibility for overall coordination should rest with one design professional. The specific terms of the client's contracts with the various professionals will ultimately determine who coordinates the team. On large projects, there may be an architect who coordinates the others, including the interior design consultant. On projects where the interior designer is the primary design consultant, he or she is responsible for coordination.

If the interior designer is responsible for retaining the services of other consultants, then the designer is usually responsible for directing and coordinating the consultants' work so the final set of construction documents (both drawings and specifications) represents a complete set of coordinated information. This does not mean that the interior designer is directly responsible for the work of any of the consultants; it means only that he or she is managing the efforts of the team. If the client hires the interior designer and other consultants separately, then someone other than the designer may be responsible for coordination.

A typical example of the coordination required between the consultants and, ultimately, the various subcontractors on the job is that of electrical design. The interior designer may develop the furniture plan and show the locations of many of the electrical and telephone outlets and the basic lighting design. The electrical

engineer is responsible for taking this information and developing the required electrical drawings, including circuiting and other technical information. The designer's outlet plan must coordinate with the electrical power plan, and if one professional makes a change, everyone needs to know about it.

The following list includes the information typically found on interior design consultants' drawings.

- *Structural drawings:* framing plans (if needed), major structural sections, detail sections, and connection details. Based on information from the structural engineer, the interior designer incorporates the exact sizes of structural members in the interior design details, to coordinate construction details and make sure that sufficient space is provided for construction, clearances, tolerances, and finishes. Generally, only the overall outline of structural walls and framing is shown on the interior design drawings. Elevations for tops of beams, structural walls, and floors are shown on both sets of drawings.

- *Mechanical and plumbing drawings:* locations of mechanical equipment; layout of ductwork, pipes, fixtures, and other major components; plumbing isometrics; details of mechanical room layout; details, such as ductwork connections and pipe support; and equipment schedules. Generally, mechanical and plumbing items are only shown on the interior design drawings where they interface with other construction. Examples include the locations of grilles and registers on the reflected ceiling plan, the locations of sprinkler heads on the reflected ceiling plan, plumbing fixtures, ducts and piping when part of an interior design section or detail, and other situations where coordination with other construction elements is important. Because of the obvious potential for conflicts when different offices complete different drawings, coordination between the interior designer and the consulting engineers is critical.

- *Electrical drawings:* power plans, lighting plans, telecommunication plans, signal and security systems, one-line diagrams, and transformer, equipment, and fixture schedules. The number of plans will vary depending on the complexity of the project. For example, for simple projects all telecommunications and signal work may be shown on the power plan. In other cases a separate plan is developed for each system.

The electrical drawings contain information concerning the exact circuiting of lighting and power outlets, including the number and sizes of conductors in each conduit, the sizes of conduits, and home runs to panel boxes. A *home run* is a graphic indication (using an arrowhead and the numbers of the circuits) that the line on the drawing connecting lights or outlets is connected to particular circuit breakers in a particular electrical panel box. Figure 14.3 shows home run indications. This graphic device is used so that the entire line does not have to be drawn to the panel box, thereby avoiding clutter on the drawing. As with mechanical and plumbing work, electrical elements shown on the interior design drawings are for coordination and location only. For example, where the locations of power outlets are critical, the interior design drawings may include a separate power and telephone plan with exact dimensions. The locations of luminaires are also shown on the interior designer's reflected ceiling plan so the luminaires can be coordinated with other ceiling-mounted equipment and architectural features. Usually, no other electrical information is given on these drawings. However, in some cases, the interior designer may want to show the locations of switches on the reflected ceiling plan.

In most interior design offices (and other consultants' offices), the responsibility for coordination usually falls on the project manager, although in smaller firms or on small jobs the project designer may take on this task.

There are a number of ways to accomplish coordination during the design and production of contract documents. First, regularly scheduled meetings should be held to exchange information and alert everyone to the progress of the job. At these meetings, everyone should feel free to ask questions and raise issues that may affect the work of the others. Second, progress prints should be exchanged between the interior designer and the consultants for ongoing comparison of work being produced. Third, the project manager (or whoever is directing the job) must be responsible for notifying all consultants, in writing, of changes made as they occur. If overlay drafting or CAD is being used, base sheets or electronic information can be exchanged according to the particular methods being employed. Finally, the interior designer must have a thorough method for checking and coordinating the entire drawing set before issue for bidding or negotiation of a construction contract.

REFERENCE SYSTEMS

A complete set of construction drawings is a carefully coordinated and interrelated grouping of individual graphic components. To refer someone looking at the drawings from one element (an elevation, for example) to another (a detail section of a portion of that section), standard graphic symbols are used.

To make any referencing system work, each drawing element, whether plan, elevation, or detail, must have a unique number. This is usually a combination of a sequential number starting with 1 on each separate sheet, and the number of the sheet on which the drawing element occurs. Drawing numbers are always combined with the title of the drawing. Some examples of these drawing titles are shown in Fig. 14.14. For example, in the first example shown, the number 6 indicates that this is the sixth detail on drawing sheet A8.

Various reference symbols are used with these unique drawing title numbers to direct someone to the correct, related drawing. Figures 14.15 through 14.17 show examples of the three commonly used reference symbols. These symbols are also used in Figs. 14.7 and 14.8.

Figure 14.15 shows several examples of elevation reference marks. Although these examples differ slightly, they all do the same job. An *elevation reference mark*, often called an *elevation bubble*, is placed on a floor plan to indicate that an elevation of the wall (or walls) is drawn somewhere in the set. The number on top of the line indicates the unique sequential number of the elevation drawing, and the number below the line indicates the sheet on which the drawing is placed. As shown, there can be a separate mark for each elevation drawn, or there can be only one symbol with arrows pointing to the elevations within a room that are drawn elsewhere in the set.

Figure 14.16 shows two examples of section reference marks. A *section reference mark* is used to indicate where a section is cut through a portion of the construction. These can be used vertically or horizontally on plans, elevations, or even other sections to indicate that the drawing referred to shows a view that is 90° to the plane in which the mark is made. For example, one of these marks oriented vertically on an elevation of a door indicates that there is a detailed drawing of a vertical section through the door. See Figs. 14.8 and 14.9.

Figure 14.17 shows two examples of a detail reference mark. A *detail reference mark* is used to show that a detail of the portion circled is drawn. Unlike the section reference mark, this symbol indicates that the detail is drawn in the same plane of the circled part of the plan, rather than being a view 90° to the cut line. The detail differs from the portion that references it

Figure 14.14
Drawing Titles

Figure 14.15
Elevation
Reference Marks

Figure 14.16
Section
Reference Marks

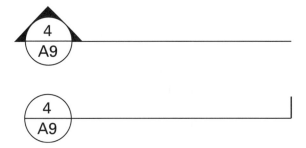

only in that it is drawn at a larger scale. One way to remember the difference is that this symbol looks like a magnifying glass. As with the other marks, the top number is the detail identification while

Figure 14.17
Detail Reference
Marks

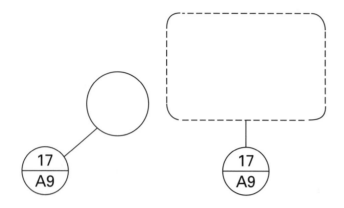

the bottom number is the sheet where the detail is drawn. If the circle around the detail is replaced with a larger rectangle with rounded corners, the meaning of the symbol does not change: it indicates an enlarged floor plan or other detail of the area highlighted.

DRAWING SYMBOLS

Standard drawing symbols are used to efficiently communicate various types of graphic information. In addition to the reference symbols discussed in the previous section, the candidate must be familiar with some of the more common drafting conventions used to indicate materials, architectural features, electrical items, and miscellaneous drawing features. These are shown in Figs. 14.18 through 14.21. Note that the symbols shown may not be the same as those that are required to be used on the practicum part of the exam.

PERMITTING AND CONTRACTING PROCESS

In addition to knowing the specific requirements of building codes as described in Chs. 27, 28, and 29, the interior designer must also understand how the code review and permitting process works. This is the process whereby the designer's plans

and specifications are submitted to the local building department and reviewed, a permit is issued, and inspections are performed during the construction of the project.

However, before the formal permitting process starts, the designer may work formally or informally with the local building department during design of the project. This is most often done when there are unusual aspects of the project that are not clearly defined by the building code or when alternate designs or materials are being proposed. The interior designer can present a proposed design with specific questions, and the building official can provide opinions or likely requirements that the designer's plans must meet to be acceptable to the building department when they are formally submitted for review.

Plan Submittal and Review

The formal permitting process begins after the interior designer has completed the drawings and specifications. These are given to the contractor who has been selected through a bidding process or through negotiation. The contractor is responsible for submitting the documents to the local building department, or as it is often called, the authority having jurisdiction (AHJ). Although in some instances the building owner or registered design professional may submit a permit application, this submittal is usually done by a licensed contractor. The contractor submits a specific number of copies of the construction documents, a permit application, and a permit fee to the AHJ.

When the AHJ has received the documents, they are reviewed by one or more plan examiners. For small projects, only one person may review the documents. For larger projects, the duties are usually split between a building plan examiner and plan examiners for electrical, mechanical, and

Figure 14.18
Architectural
Plan Symbols

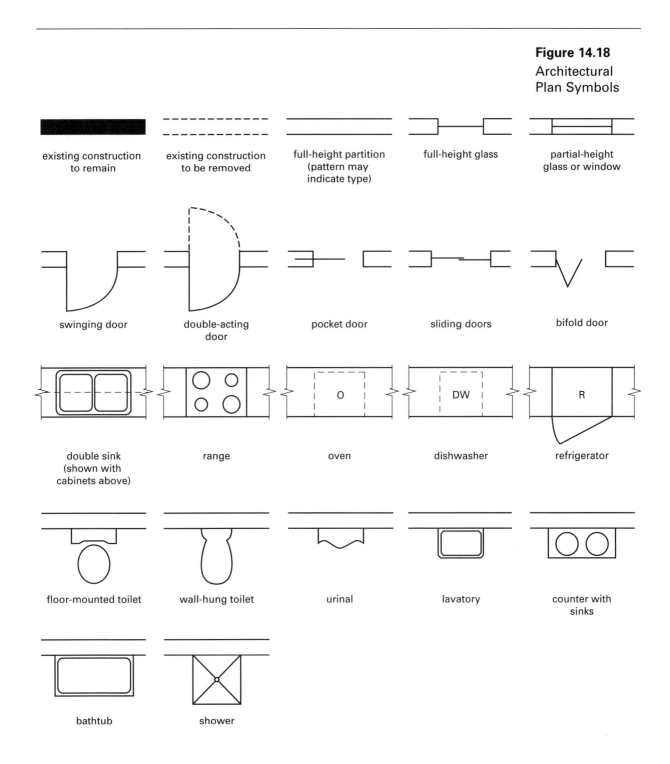

structural. The local fire marshal may also review the plans. If the documents are found to be acceptable they are stamped by the AHJ and one set is issued back to the contractor, who must keep a copy at the building site. If problems are found, the necessary changes must be made and resubmitted. It is usually the responsibility of the interior designer to make the changes to the documents.

Information Required by Building Departments

Although the contractor typically submits the construction documents, the interior designer is responsible for making sure

Figure 14.19
Electrical and
Lighting
Symbols

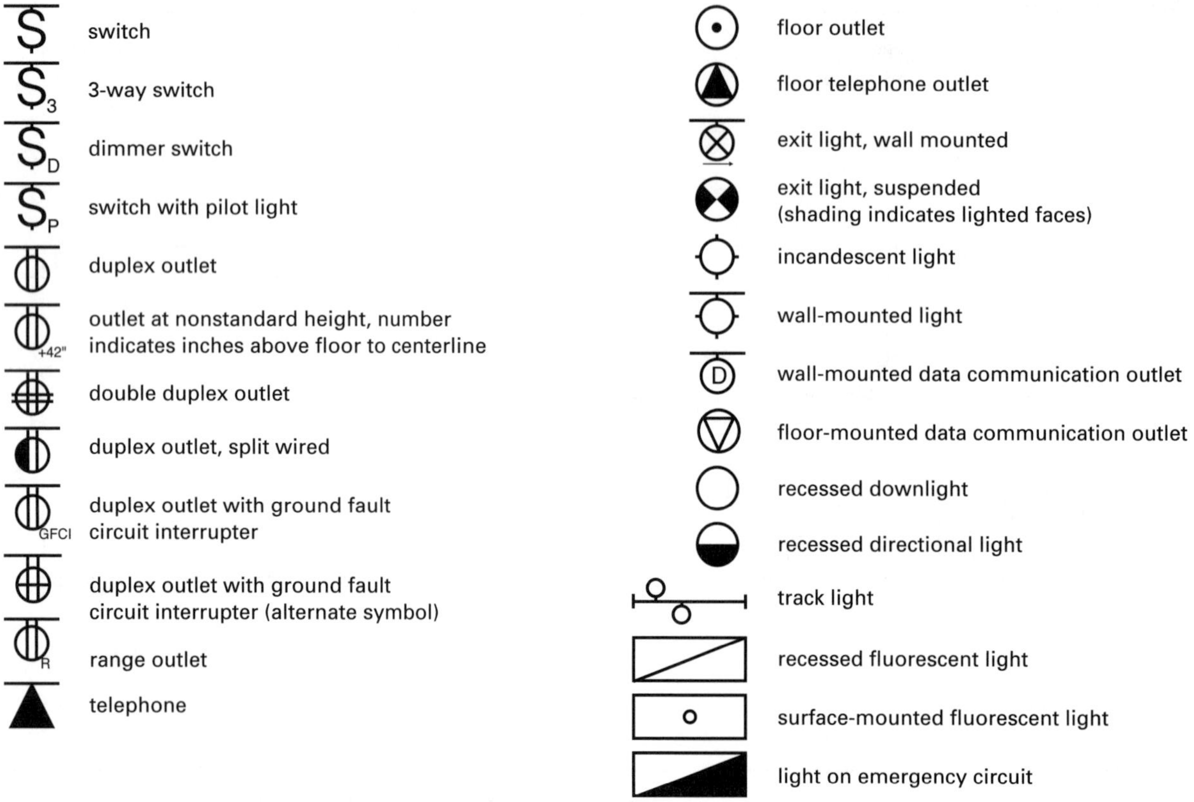

S	switch
S₃	3-way switch
S_D	dimmer switch
S_P	switch with pilot light
	duplex outlet
	outlet at nonstandard height, number indicates inches above floor to centerline
	double duplex outlet
	duplex outlet, split wired
	duplex outlet with ground fault circuit interrupter
	duplex outlet with ground fault circuit interrupter (alternate symbol)
	range outlet
	telephone
	floor outlet
	floor telephone outlet
	exit light, wall mounted
	exit light, suspended (shading indicates lighted faces)
	incandescent light
	wall-mounted light
	wall-mounted data communication outlet
	floor-mounted data communication outlet
	recessed downlight
	recessed directional light
	track light
	recessed fluorescent light
	surface-mounted fluorescent light
	light on emergency circuit

that the project design complies with all applicable codes and regulations. Compliance must be reflected in the documents. Building codes require that certain information appear on the set of construction documents submitted for plan review. Although the exact list of required information will vary from one jurisdiction to another, the following is required by the IBC and is typical of most codes.

• In general, construction documents must be of sufficient clarity to indicate the location, nature, and extent of the proposed work and how it will conform to the code. This normally includes the standard types of drawings of floor plans, elevations, sections, and details for architectural, structural, mechanical, electrical, and other specialty construction as well as applicable schedules and written specifications.

• A location plan must be included, showing the position of the interior space being designed in relation to the entire floor or building.

• The drawings must show all portions of the means of egress. The number of occupants to be accommodated on every floor and in all rooms and spaces must be indicated.

• Fire-rated partitions, doors, and other openings must be shown, along with construction details.

• The locations of exit signs and fire extinguishers must be shown.

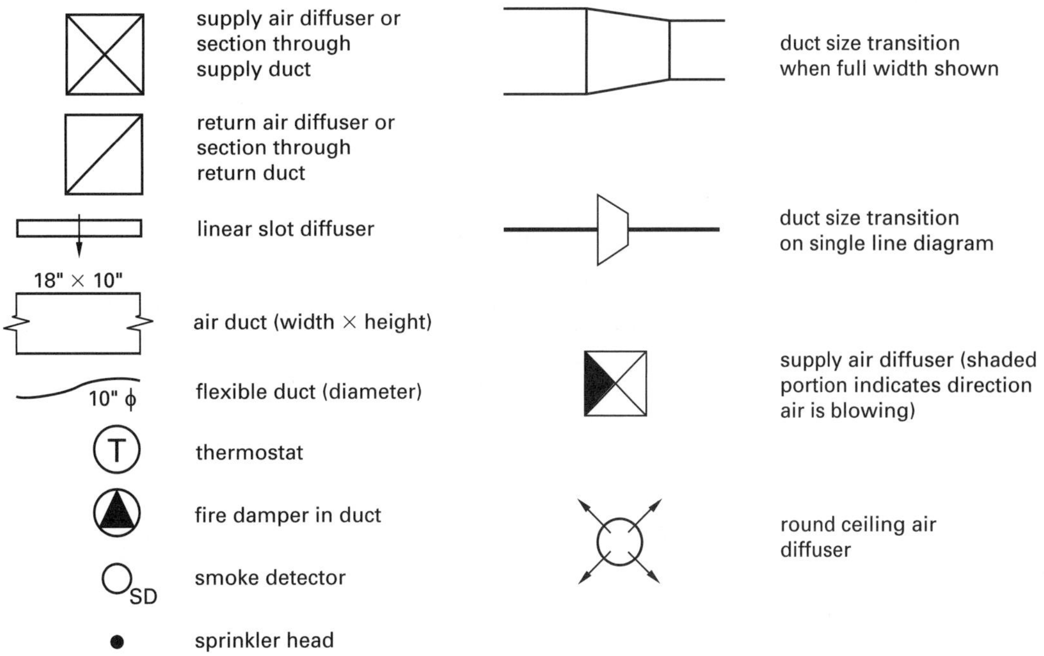

Figure 14.20
Mechanical
Symbols

supply air diffuser or section through supply duct

return air diffuser or section through return duct

linear slot diffuser

18" × 10" — air duct (width × height)

10" φ — flexible duct (diameter)

T — thermostat

fire damper in duct

SD — smoke detector

sprinkler head

duct size transition when full width shown

duct size transition on single line diagram

supply air diffuser (shaded portion indicates direction air is blowing)

round ceiling air diffuser

• Fire protection shop drawings may have to be submitted to show conformance with the code.

• Structural calculations (if necessary) may have to be submitted.

• Mechanical and electrical drawings prepared by the consultant must also be submitted, showing conformance to the mechanical and electrical portions of the code.

• The construction specifications must include the necessary details of products, materials, finishes, and the test standards used.

In addition, the local AHJ may want to see listed on the first sheet of the drawings some or all of the following information.

• names and addresses of all design professionals responsible for the work

• street address or legal description of the property

• codes being used

• area of the space designed

• construction type and occupancy group or groups

• occupant load calculations

• an indication of whether the space is sprinklered or not

• the valuation of new construction represented by the plans and specifications

Issuance of Permit and Construction Inspection

After all requirements are met, the AHJ will issue a building permit, which must be displayed at the job site. Only then can construction begin. As construction proceeds, the AHJ makes on-site inspections to ensure that the project is being built according to the code requirements of the construction documents and complies with the applicable building code. The building inspector is typically someone different from the plans examiner.

Inspections are made at specific times during construction. For interior design

Figure 14.21
Material
Indications in
Section

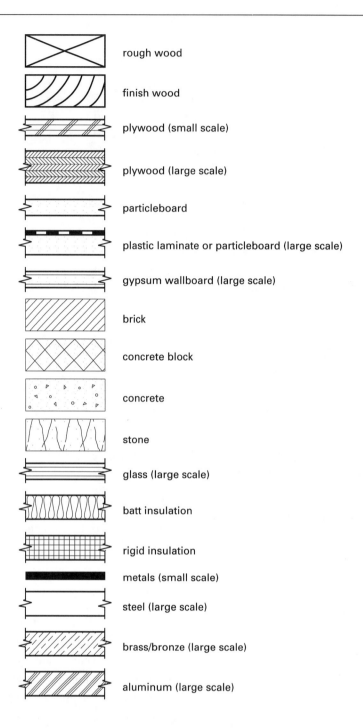

rough wood

finish wood

plywood (small scale)

plywood (large scale)

particleboard

plastic laminate or particleboard (large scale)

gypsum wallboard (large scale)

brick

concrete block

concrete

stone

glass (large scale)

batt insulation

rigid insulation

metals (small scale)

steel (large scale)

brass/bronze (large scale)

aluminum (large scale)

projects there are framing inspections; gypsum wallboard inspections; plumbing, mechanical, and electrical inspections; and a final inspection. The contractor is responsible for calling for inspections at the appropriate times in order not to delay the work.

The framing inspection is done before both sides of partitions are covered and verifies that partitions are built correctly. At this time, rough electrical and rough plumbing inspections are also done to confirm that all work inside the partitions was correctly performed. Mechanical inspections are also done when the equipment is roughed in. A wallboard inspection is done after all the wallboard is up, but before finishing, to verify that all walls and fire-rated partitions are constructed correctly.

Final Inspection and Occupancy

A final inspection is made for finishes, final electrical, and final plumbing. Other items are also inspected. These can include things such as glazing, handrails, door installation, and other elements governed by the code. The final inspection may also include testing the fire alarm and sprinkler system, with the involvement of the fire marshal or fire department.

When the final inspection has been successfully completed, a Certificate of Occupancy (CO) is issued by the AHJ. This is sometimes called a letter of occupancy or a use and occupancy (U and O) letter. This document allows the client to occupy the space. In some cases, especially on large projects or when some problem has arisen, a Temporary Certificate of Occupancy (TCO) may be issued. This allows the client to occupy a portion of the space while the remainder is completed. It may also be called a Partial Certificate of Occupancy. The building official will only issue a TCO if there is no danger with partial occupancy.

The Appeals Process

Sometimes the AHJ will deny a permit for any number of reasons. The designer may be using a new material, or certain aspects of the code may be impossible or prohibitively expensive to satisfy in an older building. If an agreement cannot be reached with the local official, an appeal can be made to the Board of Appeals. This is a formal process by which a request is made in writing stating the reasons why the designer feels the proposed design meets the intent of the code. The Board of Appeals may consult with other professionals and issue a ruling, either denying the application or issuing a variance.

SAMPLE QUESTIONS

1. The full extent of slab-to-slab partitions on a project is best shown on

(A) the reflected ceiling plan

(B) the interior elevations

(C) wall section details

(D) the finish plan

2. Which of the following symbols should be used to indicate that an interior glazing jamb shown on a floor plan is detailed on another drawing sheet?

(A)

(B)

(C)

(D)

3. Who is responsible for verifying that recessed downlights do not interfere with ductwork shown on the mechanical plans?

(A) mechanical engineer

(B) electrical engineer

(C) interior designer

(D) architect

4. Who would be LEAST involved in the selection of an underfloor raceway system?

(A) electrical consultant

(B) structural engineer

(C) architect

(D) mechanical consultant

5. The locations of return air grilles are shown on drawings provided by

(A) the architect

(B) the interior designer

(C) the mechanical engineer

(D) both the interior designer and the mechanical engineer

6. In most situations, the application for a building permit is made by the

(A) building owner

(B) client

(C) contractor

(D) interior designer

7. The symbol shown is used to indicate what type of control?

$$\overline{S}_3$$

(A) a light controlled from two locations

(B) a light controlled from three locations

(C) a light and a fan controlled from the same switch

(D) a three-position switch

8. What type of schedule would be LEAST likely to be found in a set of interior design drawings?

(A) finish schedule

(B) millwork schedule

(C) window schedule

(D) equipment schedule

9. What symbol is used to indicate a floor-mounted telephone outlet?

(A) ▲$_F$

(B) ⧗

(C) ⬤

(D) ◼

10. Where is information about electrical outlets for portable lamps most like to be found?

(A) furniture plan

(B) partition plan

(C) power plan

(D) reflected ceiling plan

15

CONSTRUCTION SPECIFICATIONS

Any interior design project that involves construction requires written specifications as well as construction drawings. The drawings show the general configuration and layout of the interior space as well as the size, shape, and dimensions of the construction. The technical specifications describe the quality of materials and workmanship, along with general requirements for the execution of the work, standards, and other items that are more appropriately described in written, rather than graphic, form. Construction specifications differ from furniture specifications in their content, scope, and form. Furniture specifications are discussed in Ch. 16.

For small, simple projects, specifications may be placed on the drawings for convenience. On most projects, however, the specifications are included in a project manual and issued with the drawings and contract agreements as part of the complete package of contract documents.

ORGANIZATION OF THE PROJECT MANUAL

The project manual is a bound book containing all the contract and noncontract documents for a construction project except the drawings and the agreements. The project manual contains the technical specifications, and it includes several other types of documents. The manual is divided into four major parts: (1) bidding requirements (if needed); (2) parts of the contract itself, which may contain the agreement between owner and contractor, bond forms, and the like; (3) general and supplementary conditions of the contract; and (4) technical specifications.

A more detailed list of possible contents of the project manual includes the following.

- *Bidding requirements*
  invitation to bid
  prequalification forms
  instructions to bidders
  information available to bidders
  bid forms

- *Supplements to bid forms*
  bid security form
  subcontractor list
  substitution list

- *Contract forms*
  agreement (contract between owner and contractor)

performance bond
labor and materials payment bond
certificates of insurance

- *General and supplementary conditions*
general conditions of the contract
(such as AIA Form A201 or similar preprinted forms)
supplementary conditions (anything not covered in the general conditions)

- *Technical specifications*

Contracts, bidding documents, and general conditions of the contract are discussed in more detail in Chs. 21 and 22.

TYPES OF SPECIFICATIONS

There are two broad categories of construction specifications: prescriptive and performance. Prescriptive specifications are sometimes called closed, while performance specifications are known as open.

Prescriptive specifications tell exactly what product or material the contractor must use by using brand names. *Performance specifications* tell what results the final construction assembly must achieve, but they give the contractor some choice in how they will be achieved. Most interior design specifications fall somewhere between these two extremes.

The type selected depends on several factors. Public projects usually require open specifications to encourage competitive bidding. Some private clients may require this as well. In other cases, a closed specification ensures that only one particular product is used. This is often the case with interior design projects because many finish materials and products are so unique that an equal substitute is not possible. Whether the job is bid or negotiated may also affect the choice. With bidding, the contractor should have as much choice as possible so he or she can find the lowest

price within the context of the specification requirements.

There are several types of prescriptive and performance specifications. Proprietary and base-bid are two common variations of prescriptive specifications while descriptive, reference standard, and pure performance are types of performance specifications.

Proprietary Specifications

Proprietary specifications are the most restrictive specifications in that they call out a specific manufacturer's product. These give the interior designer complete control over what is installed. They are easier to write than other types and are generally shorter. However, they do not allow for competitive bidding and may force the contractor to use materials or products that may be difficult or expensive to procure or that require a long delivery time.

Base-Bid Specifications

A *base-bid specification,* or *equal specification,* calls out a proprietary material or product but allows the substitution of other products that the contractor thinks are equal to the one stated. This is a risky method of specifying because the contractor may substitute a less expensive item that he or she thinks is equal, but which may not be equal.

Two variations of a base-bid specification give the interior designer more control over possible substitutions. The first lists several approved manufacturers of a product. The contractor is free to bid on any one listed. This type satisfies the requirements for public work where at least three different manufacturers must be listed, but it puts the burden on the interior designer to make sure that every one of the approved products or manufacturers listed is equal.

The second variation is a base-bid specification with "approved equal" language.

This type of specification states that one product or an approved equal must be used. This means that the contractor may submit a substitution, but the substitution would be subject to review and approval by the designer before it could be incorporated into the bid. This gives the contractor some freedom in looking for lower-priced alternates, and it puts the burden of finding them on the contractor. However, the responsibility for fairly and accurately evaluating the proposed alternates is placed on the interior designer. During a hectic bidding period, this can be a large burden, so the specification should clearly state how much lead time the contractor must give the interior designer and how alternates will be evaluated.

Descriptive Specifications

A *descriptive specification* is a type of performance (open) specification that gives detailed written requirements for the material or product and the workmanship required for its fabrication and installation. It does not mention trade names. In its purest form, a descriptive specification is difficult to write because all the pertinent requirements for the construction and installation of the product must be included.

Reference Standard Specifications

A *reference standard specification* is a variation of the descriptive specification type that describes a material, product, or process based on requirements (reference standards) set by an accepted authority or test method. For example, a product type can be required to meet the testing standards produced by such organizations as the American Society for Testing and Materials (ASTM), the American National Standards Institute (ANSI), or Underwriters Laboratories (UL). Reference can also be made to specific trade associations, such as the Architectural Woodwork Institute or the Gypsum Association.

For example, in specifying gypsum wallboard it can be stated that all gypsum wallboard products must meet the requirements of ASTM C1396. This particular document describes in great detail the requirements for this product. Requirements do not have to be repeated; they are set by a recognized industry standard.

Reference standard specifications are fairly easy to write and are generally short. Chances for errors are reduced and liability is minimized because industry standards and generally recognized methods of building are being used. However, the designer must know what is in the standard and how to refer to the appropriate part of the standard if it includes more provisions than are needed for the job.

Performance Specifications

A *pure performance specification* is a statement setting criteria and results required of the item being specified. The results can be verified by measurement, tests, or other types of evaluation. The means of achieving the required results are not specified; this is left up to the contractor or vendor.

A true performance specification is often used for construction components when the specifier wants to encourage new ways of achieving a particular result. For example, a movable partition system could be specified by stating its required fire rating, acoustical properties, finish, maximum thickness, tolerances, required size, and all other required properties. It would then be up to the contractor and manufacturer to design and develop a system to meet the criteria.

Performance specifications are difficult to write because the specifier must know all the criteria, state the methods for testing compliance, and write an unambiguous document. Specifications of this type are rarely used for interior construction.

Master Specifications

Regardless of what type of construction specification the designer uses, there is a separate specification for each product or activity used on a project. These separate specifications are called *sections*. The standard organization of sections is discussed in the next section.

Because it is difficult to write a complete, accurate, up-to-date specification of any type and most projects require many specifications, the majority of offices use master specifications. *Master specifications*, or *guide specifications* are prewritten specifications that cover nearly all types of products, methods of installation, and other variables that relate to a specific product or construction activity. They also include comments or notes to the specifier providing guidance in editing the section. These are not printed out with the final specification. The specifier or designer uses the master specification to edit out the inapplicable portions and fill in any information that is unique to the project. A sample of one page of a master specification is shown in Fig. 15.1. The boldface, heavily indented text passages are notes to the specifier.

Guide specifications are similar to master specifications, except they are usually not as complete. They simply assist the specification writer in organizing the information and showing what decisions need to be made and where things should be placed in the correct location in the document.

Using some type of master specification is preferred to the old "cut-and-paste" method (still often used, unfortunately) in which the specifier uses portions from previous specifications to paste together a new one using either paper or word processing software. The danger in this approach is that important clauses or conditions may be lost or inappropriately used, especially by an inexperienced designer.

Master specifications are produced in one of three ways (not including cut-and-paste).

First, there are several commercial products available that a design office can buy or subscribe to and that enable them to simply select and edit the required sections to fit the needs of each project. The company providing the specification performs the tasks of writing and coordinating, and most importantly, keeping each section current.

Second, some large offices write and maintain their own master specifications and may even have a separate specification writer.

A third choice is to hire a specification consultant who uses their own or a commercial product. The advantage to using a specification consultant is that this person is experienced and knows what questions to ask, how to select and evaluate materials, how to coordinate all the sections, and how to customize each section for a specific project. If a consultant is hired, it is important to realize that the design office is still responsible for errors and omissions in the specifications, as they are for any consultant working under an agreement with the designer.

ORGANIZATION OF THE TECHNICAL SECTIONS

The organization of the technical sections has been standardized through the general adoption of the *MasterFormat™ system* developed by the Construction Specifications Institute (CSI) and Construction Specifications Canada (CSC) to standardize the numbering and format of project-related information for use in specifying, cost estimating, and data filing.

The most recent version is MasterFormat 04 and is a significant change from the previous 16-division organization that had been in use for several decades. The CSI

Figure 15.1

Page from a
Master
Specification

2.01 FLUSH, SOLID-CORE DOORS

    A. General: Doors shall be of the types, sizes, and configurations as indicated on the drawings and on the door schedule. Flush wood doors shall conform to WDMA I.S. 1-A.

> **Coordinate with local code requirments. Note: NFPA 252, Fire Tests of Door Assemblies, and UL 10B, are the same as former ASTM E 152, which has been discontinued. Select one of the lock block options.**

    B. Fire-rated doors: Fire-rated doors shall comply with test requirements of NFPA 252 and shall bear certifying labels of Underwriters Laboratories, Warnock Hersey, or an independent testing agency approved by the building official. Fire-rated doors shall be provided, as required, with hardware reinforcement blocking and top, bottom, and intermediate rail blocking. Lock blocks shall be manufacturer's standard [not less than 5 inches by 18 inches].

> **Verify local code requirements regarding the applicability of UBC Standard 7-2, including positive pressure fire testing of doors and the "S" label. There are two components, UBC 7-2, Part I (same as UL 10C), which is the positive pressure test, and the "S" rating requirement for air leakage, which is UBC 7-2, Part II (same as UL 1784). If required, include the following language in the paragraph above. Select below as required. Most wood doors require gaskets to meet test requirements.**

In addition, fire-rated door assemblies shall conform to the requirements of UBC Standard 7-2, Part I (UL 10C) for positive pressure fire testing. [20-minute smoke and draft control assemblies shall carry the S label as determined by UBC Standard 7-2, Part II (UL 1784).]

> **Select one of the grades below. Generally, Custom grade is good enough for most work if veneer matching is not critical. Select Premium grade when you want the highest quality veneers, want veneers to match at the transoms, and want vertical edges to be the same species as the veneer. For opaque finishes, Premium grade provides medium density overlay for the best paintable surface. Don't specify Economy grade.**

    C. Doors shall be Premium [Custom] [Economy] grade in accordance with WDMA 1.S. 1-A.

    D. Veneer face doors for transparent finish:

        1. Core type: Particleboard [Mineral core] [Lumber core] [Particleboard or mineral core as required for fire rating]

> **Fill in the desired species. Common choices are red oak, white oak, cherry, walnut, maple, Honduras mahongany, birch, ash, or others. Verify availability of veneers.**

        2. Face veneer species: _____

> **Select slicing method below. Generally plain sliced or quarter sliced is used depending on the amount of grain pattern you want to see. Specify rift sliced for red or white oak if you don't want flaking. Not all species may be available in some cuts.**

        3. Veneer cut: [rotary] [plain sliced] [quarter sliced] [rift sliced].

> **Select one of the following. Book match is the most common and usually looks the best.**

        4. Matching between individual veneer leaves: Book match [Slip match] [Random match].

> **Select one of the following. Center match usually looks the best but is the most costly and is available in Premium grade only. Balance match is a lower cost alternative that still looks good. Running match is the least expensive.**

undertook the revision recognizing that the previous 16 divisions made it difficult to incorporate the increased use of building automation, signal systems, and electronic security and that the numbering system was not particularly well-suited for transportation, utility, marine, industrial, and process engineering construction.

The most recent MasterFormat division organization is shown in Fig. 15.2. There are major subgroups and individual divisions within each subgroup. Many of the divisions are reserved for future use to allow the system to grow as new materials and technologies emerge. Most of the divisions in the Facility Construction Subgroup are essentially the same, with the same numbers, as they were in the previous version. These include Divisions 03 through 14. Divisions 31 and 32, Earthwork and Exterior Improvements, respectively, are typically used on architectural projects. The significant changes in the most recent version that may be used for interior design include the following.

- Much of Division 01, General Requirements, covers the same material, but it has been expanded to allow for writing performance specifications for elements that overlap several specific work sections (the building envelope, for example).

- Division 11, Equipment, is about the same except that equipment related to process engineering is now in the Process Equipment Subgroup and equipment related to infrastructure is now in the Site and Infrastructure Subgroup. Most of the elements that are common to standard interior design work, such as library, audiovisual, and medical equipment, are still in Division 11.

- In Division 13, Special Construction, the work groups that deal with security access, building automation, detection and alarm, and fire suppression are now in various divisions of the Facility Services Subgroup. Special construction

related to process engineering is now in the Process Equipment Subgroup.

- Division 15 is now reserved for future expansion, and all the mechanical and plumbing work groups are now in Division 22, Plumbing, and Division 23, Heating, Ventilating and Air Conditioning of the Facility Services Subgroup. See Fig. 15.2.

- Division 16 is now reserved for future expansion, and all the electrical work groups are now in Division 26, Electrical, and Division 27, Communications of the Facility Services Subgroup. See Fig. 15.2.

Another change in the new MasterFormat system is the use of six-digit numbering for individual specification sections instead of the previous five-digit numbers. In the new system the first two numbers represent the division numbers, with a leading zero used for the single-digit divisions (02, 03, 04, etc.). The next pair of numbers (digits three and four) represents the level-two hierarchy, and the last pair of numbers represents level three in the hierarchy. This change to a six-digit format allows for flexibility and room for expansion as new materials or technologies are added.

Questions on the exam sometimes ask in which CSI MasterFormat section information on a particular material will be found. The candidate should know the names of the divisions, or at least those in the facility construction subgroup and the facility services subgroup, and generally what is included in each subdivision. The following list is a brief summary of what is included in each division. Study this list along with the more detailed level-two divisions, to be thoroughly familiar with the correct locations in the specifications for particular construction elements.

- *Division 00, Procurement and Contracting Requirements:* This division covers requirements for bidding and contracting, including bid solicitation, instructions to bidders, information available to bidders,

Figure 15.2
MasterFormat™
04 Divisions

Procurement and Contracting Requirements Group:
Division 00 – Procurement and Contracting
                          Requirements

Specifications Group:

General Requirements Subgroup:
Division 01 – General Requirements

Facility Construction Subgroup:
Division 02 – Existing Conditions
Division 03 – Concrete
Division 04 – Masonry
Division 05 – Metals
Division 06 – Wood, Plastics, and Composites
Division 07 – Thermal and Moisture Protection
Division 08 – Openings
Division 09 – Finishes
Division 10 – Specialties
Division 11 – Equipment
Division 12 – Furnishings
Division 13 – Special Construction
Division 14 – Conveying Equipment
Division 15 – Reserved for future expansion
Division 16 – Reserved for future expansion
Division 17 – Reserved for future expansion
Division 18 – Reserved for future expansion
Division 19 – Reserved for future expansion

Facility Services Subgroup:
Division 20 – Reserved for future expansion
Division 21 – Fire Suppression
Division 22 – Plumbing

Division 23 – Heating, Ventilating and Air Conditioning
Division 24 – Reserved for future expansion
Division 25 – Integrated Automation
Division 26 – Electrical
Division 27 – Communications
Division 28 – Electronic Safety and Security
Division 29 – Reserved for future expansion

Site and Infrastructure Subgroup:
Division 30 – Reserved for future expansion
Division 31 – Earthwork
Division 32 – Exterior Improvements
Division 33 – Utilities
Division 34 – Transportation
Division 35 – Waterway and Marine
Division 36 – Reserved for future expansion
Division 37 – Reserved for future expansion
Division 38 – Reserved for future expansion
Division 39 – Reserved for future expansion

Process Equipment Subgroup:
Division 40 – Reserved for future expansion
Division 41 – Material Processing and Handling Equipment
Division 42 – Process Heating, Cooling, and Drying
                          Equipment
Division 43 – Process Gas and Liquid Handling, Purification
                          and Storage Equipment
Division 44 – Pollution Control Equipment
Division 45 – Industry-Specific Manufacturing
Equipment
Division 46 – Reserved for future expansion
Division 47 – Reserved for future expansion
Division 48 – Electrical Power Generation
Division 49 – Reserved for future expansion

The Division Numbers and Titles used in this product are from MasterFormat™ 2004 Edition and the three part SectionFormat™ (1997 edition) outline, published by the Construction Specifications Institute (CSI) and Construction Specifications Canada (CSC), and are used with permission from CSI, 2005. For those interested in a more in-depth explanation of MasterFormat™ 2004 Edition and SectionFormat™ and their use in the construction industry contact:

The Construction Specifications Institute (CSI)
99 Canal Center Plaza, Suite 300
Alexandria, VA 22314
800-689-2900; 703-684-0300
CSINet URL: http://www.csinet.org

bid forms, the agreement (contract), bonds and certificates, general conditions of the contract, supplementary conditions, addenda, and modifications. These parts of the contract documents are discussed in Chs. 21 and 22.

• *Division 01, General Requirements:* This division includes requirements that are applicable to the entire project or all the individual technical sections. These include a summary of the work, how pricing and payment will be handled, alternates, value analysis, contract modification procedures, unit prices, construction progress documentation, submittal procedures (for samples, shop drawings, etc.), quality control, temporary facilities at the job site, product substitution procedures, owner-furnished items, special execution requirements, and final cleaning and protection of the work.

The term *General Requirements* should not be confused with *General Conditions* of the Contract for Construction, as discussed in Ch. 22.

- *Division 02, Existing Conditions:* This division is now used to specify site remediation, site decontamination, subsurface investigation, surveying, and selective demolition, among other items related to existing conditions on a job site.

- *Division 03, Concrete:* This division covers all aspects of concrete including forms, reinforcement, cast-in-place concrete, precast concrete, cementitious decks and underlayment, grouts, and concrete restoration and cleaning.

- *Division 04, Masonry:* Masonry covers all aspects of masonry, including brick, concrete block, stone, terra cotta, simulated masonry, glass block, and masonry restoration and cleaning.

- *Division 05, Metals:* The metals division includes all types of structural steel and other structural metals, ornamental metals, and metal fabrications (metal stairs, ornamental iron work, handrails, gratings, metal castings, and stair treads and nosings), as well as expansion joint covers and metal restoration and cleaning. Light-gage metal framing for partitions is located in Division 9.

- *Division 06, Wood, Plastics, and Composites:* This division covers the typical structural wood framing, rough carpentry, finish carpentry, and architectural woodwork. It also includes structural plastics, plastic fabrications, wood and plastic restoration and cleaning, and the newer plastic wood and other specialty composite materials. Note that manufactured casework is in Divisions 12, Furnishings.

- *Division 07, Thermal and Moisture Protection:* This is the same as the previous edition of MasterFormat and includes dampproofing and waterproofing, insulation, vapor retarders, air barriers, shingles, roof tiles, siding, membrane roofing, flashing, joint sealers, fire and smoke protection, and roofing specialties such as roof hatches, smoke vents, roof pavers, scuppers, and gravel stops.

- *Division 08, Openings:* This was formerly called Doors and Windows but contains the same elements as in the previous edition of MasterFormat, including metal doors and frames, wood doors and frames, specialty doors, storefronts, all types of windows, skylights, hardware, curtain walls, and glazing.

- *Division 09, Finishes:* Finishes covers all types of finish materials, including plaster, gypsum wallboard (including metal framing), all types of floor and wall tile, terrazzo, all types of flooring materials, acoustical ceilings and other types of decorative ceilings, wall coverings, acoustical treatment, paints, and other coatings.

- *Division 10, Specialties:* The specialties division covers a long list of items, including visual display boards, toilet compartments, louvers, grilles, wall and corner guards, access flooring, pre-built fireplaces, flagpoles, signage, lockers, awnings, demountable partitions, storage shelving, exterior protection (sun screens, storm panels, etc.), and toilet and bath accessories.

- *Division 11, Equipment:* This division contains information for architectural equipment, including vaults and security items, teller and security equipment, church-related equipment, library equipment, theater and stage equipment, musical equipment, mercantile equipment, checkroom equipment, vending machines, audio-visual equipment, loading dock equipment, detention equipment, athletic equipment, medical equipment, mortuary equipment, and equipment for laboratories, planetariums, observatories, and offices.

- *Division 12, Furnishings:* Division 12 includes furniture, systems furniture, art, window treatments, accessories, multiple seating, and interior plants. Note especially that this division includes manufactured casework, whereas custom casework would be in Division 06.

- *Division 13, Special Construction:* Special construction includes air-supported structures, special-purpose rooms (clean rooms, saunas, planetariums, etc.), seismic control, radiation protection, lightning protection, pre-engineered structures, hot tubs, and kennels.

- *Division 14, Conveying Equipment:* Division 14 includes elevators, escalators, dumbwaiters, moving walks, and lifts.

- *Division 21, Fire Suppression:* This division contains specifications that were previously in Division 13 and includes detection and alarms, and all types of fire suppression systems, such as wet-pipe, dry-pipe, deluge, carbon dioxide, foam, pre-action, and dry chemical systems as well as standpipes and hoses. Note that fire-related materials (doors, fire-stopping, etc.) are in their respective divisions.

- *Division 22, Plumbing:* Plumbing for buildings has been relocated from the previous Division 15. Processing piping is now in the Process Equipment subgroup.

- *Division 23, Heating, Ventilating and Air Conditioning:* HVAC now has its own division, relocated from the previous Division 15.

- *Division 25, Integrated Automation:* This division contains specifications for this expanding technology, including energy monitoring and control, environmental control, lighting control, and similar topics.

- *Division 26, Electrical:* Electrical now has its own division. Specifications for communication, sound, and video have been moved to Division 27.

- *Division 27, Communications:* This division has been established for the expanding technologies and specialized nature of computer networks and all types of communications systems (cable, telephone, internet, sound systems, etc.).

- *Division 28, Electronic Safety and Security:* This division has also been established for the expanding technologies and specialized nature of security systems, including intrusion detection, security access, video surveillance, and related topics.

Questions tend to be especially difficult when they involve Divisions 10, 11, and 13. Use the following suggestions to help remember what item is in which division. Although there are exceptions, these suggestions may assist in categorizing the information. Generally, only the first two numbers (division) have to be remembered if the answer choices give the full six-digit CSI number.

Division 10, Specialties, includes items that are not standard materials (like wallboard, flooring, finishes, and ceilings), are typically small scale, and are usually placed in a building in multiples. For example, visual display boards, lockers, wall and corner guards, and access flooring are typically not found in every building (they are "special"). They are small relative to the building and the spaces in the building. There is also usually more than one of them installed (more than one display board, more than one locker, and more than one corner guard).

Division 11, Equipment, includes items that are generally larger and more expensive than those in Division 10.

Division 13, Special Construction, includes much larger elements that can almost be thought of as a building within a building. Examples include air-supported structures, seismic control, and animal kennels.

The MasterFormat system also establishes a standard way of organizing any particular specification section. The first level of division within a section is the three-part format. This includes Part 1, General; Part 2, Products; and Part 3, Execution.

All sections include three parts, while the specific articles within the parts vary with the type of material or product being specified.

Part 1 gives the general requirements for the section, such as the scope of the section, submittals required, quality assurance requirements, warranties, project conditions, and specifications for the delivery, storage, and handling of materials.

Part 2 details the specifications for the materials and products themselves, including acceptable manufacturer (if applicable), what standards and test methods the materials must conform to, how items are to be fabricated, and similar concerns.

Part 3 tells how the products and materials are to be installed, applied, or otherwise put into place. This part also describes the examination and preparation required before installation, how quality control should be maintained in the field, and the requirements for the adjusting, cleaning, and protection of the finished work.

Figure 15.3 shows the SectionFormat™ outline listing all the possible articles of each part. The specifier selects which ones are appropriate for the item being specified.

SPECIFICATION WRITING GUIDELINES

Because specifications are legal documents as well as a way of communicating technical information, they must be complete, accurate, and unambiguous. The language must be precise. Some of the important things to remember include the following.

• Know what the standards and test methods referred to include and what parts of them are applicable to the project. They must also be the most current editions.

• Do not specify together the results and the methods proposed to achieve those results, as the two may conflict. For instance, if a carpet is specified that must meet certain ASTM test criteria and then a particular carpet is specified that does not meet the stated requirements, the specification will be impossible to comply with.

• Do not include standards that cannot be measured. For example, saying that the work should be done in "a first-class manner" is subject to wide interpretation.

• Avoid exculpatory clauses. These are phrases that try to shift responsibility to the contractor or someone else in a very broad, general way. An example is something like "contractor shall be totally responsible for all . . ." Unless the clause is generally accepted wording or makes sense in the context of the specification, current legal opinion disapproves of such clauses, especially when they favor the person who wrote them.

• Avoid words or phrases that are ambiguous. The combination *and/or*, for example, is unclear and should be replaced with one word or the other. The abbreviation *etc.* is also vague, implies that a list can go on forever, and may include something not wanted. The word *any* implies the contractor has a choice. This is acceptable if allowing a choice is desired, but most often the specifier does not want to allow a choice.

• Keep specifications as short as possible. Specifications can be terse; words such as *all, the, an,* and *a* can be omitted.

• Describe only one major idea in each paragraph. This makes reading easier and improves comprehension. It also makes it easier to change the specifications.

Specifying for Sustainability

There are two main areas of a project's specifications where sustainability issues are addressed. The first is in Division 01, General Requirements, and the second is in all of the individual technical sections that cover specific materials and construction elements.

Figure 15.3
SectionFormat
Outline

PART 1 GENERAL

SUMMARY
Section Includes
Product Supplied But Not Installed
   Under This Section
Products Installed But Not Supplied
   Under This Section
Related Sections
Allowances
Unit Prices
Measurement Procedures
Payment Procedures
Alternates
REFERENCES
DEFINITIONS
SYSTEM DESCRIPTION
Design Requirements,
   Performance Requirements
SUBMITTALS
Product Data
Shop Drawings
Samples
Quality Assurance/Control Submittals
   Design Data, Test Reports,
   Certificates,
   Manufacturers' Instructions,
   Manufacturers' Field Reports,
   Qualification Statements
Closeout Submittals
QUALITY ASSURANCE
Qualifications
Regulatory Requirements
Certifications
Field Samples
Mock-ups
Pre-installation Meetings
**DELIVERY, STORAGE,
AND HANDLING**
Packing, Shipping, Handling,
   and Unloading
Acceptance at Site
Storage and Protection
Waste Management and Disposal
PROJECT/SITE*CONDITIONS
Project/Site*Environmental
   Requirements
Existing Conditions

SEQUENCING
SCHEDULING
WARRANTY
Special Warranty
SYSTEM STARTUP
OWNER'S INSTRUCTIONS
COMMISSIONING
MAINTENANCE
Extra Materials
Maintenance Service

PART 2 PRODUCTS

MANUFACTURERS
EXISTING PRODUCTS
MATERIALS
MANUFACTURED UNITS
EQUIPMENT
COMPONENTS
ACCESSORIES
MIXES
FABRICATION
Shop Assembly
   Fabrication Tolerances
FINISHES
Shop Priming, Shop Finishing
SOURCE QUALITY CONTROL
Tests, Inspection
Verification of Performance

PART 3 EXECUTION

INSTALLERS
EXAMINATION
Site Verification of Conditions
PREPARATION
Protection
Surface Preparation
ERECTION
INSTALLATION
APPLICATION
CONSTRUCTION
Special Techniques
Interface with Other Work
Sequences of Operation
Site Tolerances
REPAIR/RESTORATION
RE-INSTALLATION
FIELD QUALITY CONTROL
Site Tests, Inspection
Manufacturers' Field Services
ADJUSTING
CLEANING
DEMONSTRATION
PROTECTION
SCHEDULES

*Project Conditions is the preferred term in the U.S.,
Site Conditions is the preferred term in Canada

The Division Numbers and Titles used in this product are from MasterFormat™ 2004 Edition and the three part SectionFormat™ (1997 edition) outline, published by the Construction Specifications Institute (CSI) and Construction Specifications Canada (CSC), and are used with permission from CSI, 2005. For those interested in a more in-depth explanation of MasterFormat™ 2004 Edition and SectionFormat™ and their use in the construction industry contact:

The Construction Specifications Institute (CSI)
99 Canal Center Plaza, Suite 300
Alexandria, VA 22314
800-689-2900; 703-684-0300
CSINet URL: http://www.csinet.org

Division 1, General Requirements

In Division 1, there should be a separate specification section that applies to all the other specification sections and sets the goals and general direction of the project for sustainability and environmental quality. It is in this section that the contractor should be advised of the design requirements used by the architect and the rest of the design team in the preparation of the contract documents. These criteria can then be used if the contractor wants to propose substitutions or make enhancements.

Some of the specification articles in the general Division 01 specification section may include the following.

• A summary of the environmental goals of the project and the special requirements required of the contractor. This summary generally includes requirements addressing three areas: resource efficient materials and systems, energy conservation, and indoor air quality. These goals may be a simple or as complex as warranted by the project or the goals of the client. If LEED™ certification is being sought, the individual credits required by LEED may be used to develop a list of requirements. Refer to Ch. 26 for information on LEED certification.

• Required submittals from the contractor. These may include manufacturer's certificates of recycled content, certification of wood products as coming from an accredited certifier (refer to Ch. 26 for information on wood certification), material emission testing reports, cleaning product information, and other documentation as may be required for LEED certification.

The interior designer should request that the contractor submit material safety data sheets for all products that may contain hazardous materials. A *material safety data sheet* (MSDS) is a listing of product safety information prepared by manufacturers and marketers of products containing toxic chemicals. In addition to giving the basic product components, an MSDS is required to list the health effects of the material, first aid, safe storage and disposal guidelines, protective equipment required for handling, and procedures for handling leaks and spills. It is intended for use by employers and emergency responders rather than by consumers.

• Required tests and procedures for testing materials to verify that they comply with the requirements.

• A list of hazardous materials and chemicals.

• A list of definitions with which the contractor may not be familiar. These may be included in this section or in individual sections if they only apply to one material, such as "certified wood product."

• A list of sources of information for product certification or sustainability that the contractor can use. This may also include trade associations and specific regulatory agencies' names and addresses.

• Requirements for the packaging of materials with recycled products.

• Requirements for construction activities to minimize pollution, dust, erosion, chemical emissions, spills, and water and moisture leaks. This could include a "no smoking" provision for the job site.

Individual Technical Sections

The individual technical sections of the specification should contain the sustainability requirements unique to each product, such as use of local products, recycled content, requirements for VOCs, energy efficiency, cleaning and maintenance requirements, certification by a third party, and the other material criteria mentioned in Ch. 26. Generally, the sections affected will include concrete, rough carpentry, architectural woodwork, plastic products, doors, windows, gypsum wallboard, acoustical ceilings, carpeting, resilient flooring, ceramic tile, wood flooring, paints and coatings, and toilet partitions. Others should be included as required.

For actual specifying in Part 2, Products, of each specification section, the interior designer can use several approaches.

First, the interior designer can write a performance specification giving the requirements for recycled content, maximum emissions of chemicals, and other criteria and the testing standard by which products must be evaluated. As stated previously in this chapter, true performance specifications are difficult to write.

Another approach is to give a list of three to five approved products that the interior designer knows will satisfy the requirements of the specification section. This list can contain products that have the desired recycled content or are capable of being recycled, products that have low emissions of VOCs and other hazardous chemicals, and equipment that is low polluting. Along with this, a provision can permit the contractor to submit a proposed substitution if the contractor can prove that the substitution meets all of the requirements. This puts an additional burden on the interior designer during the bidding or negotiation phases when time may be short for full consideration of such substitution proposals.

Finally, if there is only one product that meets both the sustainability and aesthetic and functional requirements of the project, a proprietary specification can be written. This is typically only possible for private work where requirements for competitive bidding are not as strict as they are for public work. Even for private work, the number of proprietary specifications should be kept to a minimum.

COORDINATION WITH THE CONSTRUCTION DRAWINGS

The technical specifications and the drawings are complementary. They must be written and checked to avoid conflicting requirements, duplication, omissions, and errors. There are several areas of particular concern.

First, the specifications should contain requirements for all the materials and construction indicated on the drawings. A common checklist used by both the specifications writer and the project manager or senior designer is one way to accomplish this.

Second, the terminology used in both documents should be the same. If the term "gypsum board" is used in the specifications, the same term should be shown on the drawings.

Third, dimensions and thicknesses should be indicated only on one document. Generally, sizes are shown on the drawings, and the standards for the materials and components that those sizes refer to are stated in the specifications.

Fourth, in most cases, notes on the drawings should not describe methods of installation or material qualities; these belong in the specifications. However, if the project is a small one with a limited amount of construction and a separate project manual is not produced, some designers describe materials and installation procedures in detail on the drawings.

Although the specifications and drawings are complementary, the specifier must give careful attention to the written word. When there is a conflict between the drawings and specifications, the courts have held that the specifications are more binding and take precedence over the drawings.

SAMPLE QUESTIONS

1. What would be the best way to ensure that the finish on new millwork matches the finish on existing millwork on a remodeling project?

(A) Indicate on the drawings and in the specifications that the new work should match the existing work.

(B) Ask the client to find out what was used on the old job, and include that information in the specifications.

(C) Research the manufacturer and color of the existing finish, and include that information in the specifications.

(D) Ask the painting contractor to investigate what finish was previously used, and include that information in the finish schedule.

2. If a client wanted to obtain the most competitive bid price possible while still being assured that the product was acceptable, what type of specification should be written?

(A) open

(B) reference

(C) performance

(D) base bid with approved equal

3. Which item in the following excerpt from a specification is a performance specification?

Part 2—Products

2.01 Metal Support Material

General: To the extent not otherwise indicated, comply with ASTM C754 for metal system supporting gypsum wallboard.

Ceiling suspension main runners: $1^1/_2$ in steel channels, cold rolled.

Hanger wire: ASTM A641, soft, Class 1 galvanized, prestretched; sized in accordance with ASTM C754.

Hanger anchorage devices: Size for 3 times calculated loads, except size direct-pull concrete inserts for 5 times calculated loads.

Studs: ASTM C645; 25 gage, $2^1/_2$ in deep, except as otherwise indicated.

Runners: Match studs; type recommended by stud manufacturer for vertical abutment of drywall work at other work.

(A) ceiling suspension main runners

(B) hanger wire

(C) hanger anchorage devices

(D) runners

4. Where would application instructions for vinyl wall covering be found?

(A) in Part 1 of Section 097200, Wall Covering

(B) in Part 2 of Section 097200, Wall Covering

(C) in Part 3 of Section 097200, Wall Covering

(D) in a finish schedule at the end of Section 097200, Wall Covering

5. Which of the following is more legally binding?

(A) drawings

(B) specifications

(C) schedules

(D) all of the above

6. To minimize conflicts in the contract documents, what is the LEAST important action the interior designer can take?

(A) Show only dimensions on the drawings.

(B) Have someone check the drawings before they are issued.

(C) Write the specifications after the drawings are essentially complete.

(D) Make sure terminology in the specifications is the same as in the drawings.

7. Specifications can be made most concise by

(A) using reference standard specifications

(B) avoiding the use of words like a, the, and all

(C) using phrases instead of complete sentences

(D) using descriptive specifications

8. Which of the following would NOT be found in the project manual?

(A) performance bond

(B) testing requirements

(C) cost estimate

(D) instructions to bidders

9. What is the best way for an interior designer to ensure that the exact product desired will be used in the final design?

(A) Show the configuration of the product on the drawings, and call it out specifically.

(B) Write a closed, descriptive specification.

(C) Require that the contractor submit samples of all items before purchasing.

(D) List the information in a proprietary specification.

10. What does the phrase "or approved equal" mean in a specification?

(A) The client must agree to the use of a product selected by the contractor.

(B) The contractor may propose a substitution, but it must be approved by the interior designer.

(C) An alternate product may be bid on by the contractor if he or she is sure it provides the same quality as the product specified.

(D) The interior designer and client can permit the substitution of an alternate product if they feel it is better than the one specified.

16
FURNITURE AND FURNISHINGS DOCUMENTS AND PROCUREMENT

As with construction, furniture drawings and specifications are required to completely and accurately communicate the design intent and individual furniture selections of the interior designer. Refer to Ch. 6 for a discussion of furniture selection criteria. Dealerships, showrooms, and manufacturers use the furniture and furnishings documents to supply the necessary goods and complete the installation.

The furniture and furnishings documents are typically not a part of the construction contract because of the different way furniture is procured and the laws under which merchandise is bought and sold. Refer to Ch. 22 for a discussion of the Uniform Commercial Code, which governs the buying and selling of goods in the United States.

This part of an interior design project is often called furniture, fixtures, and equipment (FF&E). This chapter discusses the FF&E documents, furniture standards, the various trade sources in the industry, and how furniture and furnishings are procured.

FURNITURE DRAWINGS

As stated in Ch. 14, furniture drawings (typically plans) are required to show the extent and locations of furniture. If existing furniture is being reused, the furniture plans also show what existing furniture is being used and where it should be placed. For large installations it may even be necessary to have separate plans for new and reused furniture because the installation company requires one set of plans and the moving company requires another. Furniture plans may also include equipment such as copy machines, printers, or microwaves. Drawings for custom-built furniture may be grouped with the other furniture drawings.

For projects with interior construction, a furniture plan must be separate from the construction plans or other plans due to lack of space and the confusion it would cause to mix furniture and construction on the same plan. Even placing furniture on the interior designer's telephone and electrical plan, as is sometimes done, can be confusing if not done carefully. If no interior construction is involved, the furniture plan may be the only floor plan drawn.

On the furniture plan, each piece of furniture is given a code that identifies it and refers either to a schedule or to the furniture specifications. See Fig. 16.1. The coding may be set up so that every piece of furniture has a unique number, or so that the same number can be assigned to identical pieces. If a database system will be used, however, each piece of furniture should be given a unique identifying number.

If CAD is used, the object representing the furniture can be tagged with various types of attribute information, and this information can be used to develop anything from a complex database to a simple schedule listing.

For large, complex installations of systems furniture, there may be additional assembly drawings showing the installed spacing between units and partitions and how the pieces should be connected.

FURNITURE AND FURNISHINGS STANDARDS

Many of the standards for commercial office furniture have been promulgated by the Business and Institutional Furniture Manufacturer's Association (BIFMA). The American National Standards Institute has approved these standards. The following are the standards applicable to construction and durability of commercial office furniture. The BIFMA standards define the specific tests to be used for each standard, the laboratory equipment that can be used, the conditions of the tests, and the recommended minimum acceptance levels. Refer to Ch. 6 for information on flammability and fabric standards for furniture.

- *ANSI/BIFMA X5.1, American National Standard for Office Furnishings— General Purpose Office Chairs:* This standard provides manufacturers, specifiers, and users with a common basis for evaluating the safety, durability, and structural adequacy of office chairs, including criteria for factors such as swivel/tilt mechanisms, seating impact, front and rear stability, back durability, and footring durability.

- *ANSI/BIFMA X5.2, American National Standard for Office Furnishings— Lateral Files:* This standard provides manufacturers, specifiers, and users with a common basis for evaluating the safety, durability, and structural adequacy of free-standing lateral files.

- *ANSI/BIFMA X5.3, American National Standard for Office Furnishings— Vertical Files:* This standard provides manufacturers, specifiers, and users with a common basis for evaluating the safety, durability, and structural adequacy of vertical files. The test includes evaluation of unit stability, lock mechanisms, drawer cycle, case racking, unit strength, and the interlock system, among other criteria.

- *ANSI/BIFMA X5.4, American National Standard for Office Furnishings— Lounge Seating:* This standard provides manufacturers, specifiers, and users with a common basis for evaluating the safety, durability, and structural adequacy of free-standing lounge seating. It describes the means of evaluating the function and safety, independent of construction.

- *ANSI/BIFMA X5.5, American National Standard for Office Furnishings— Desk Products:* This standard provides manufacturers, specifiers, and users with a common basis for evaluating the safety, durability, and structural adequacy of desk and table products, including table tipping. The acceptance levels are based on actual field and test experience of BIFMA members.

- *ANSI/BIFMA X5.6, American National Standard for Office Furnishings— Panel Systems:* This standard provides manufacturers, specifiers, and users with a common basis for evaluating the performance and safety requirements of panel-supported office furniture systems as well

Figure 16.1
Furniture Plan

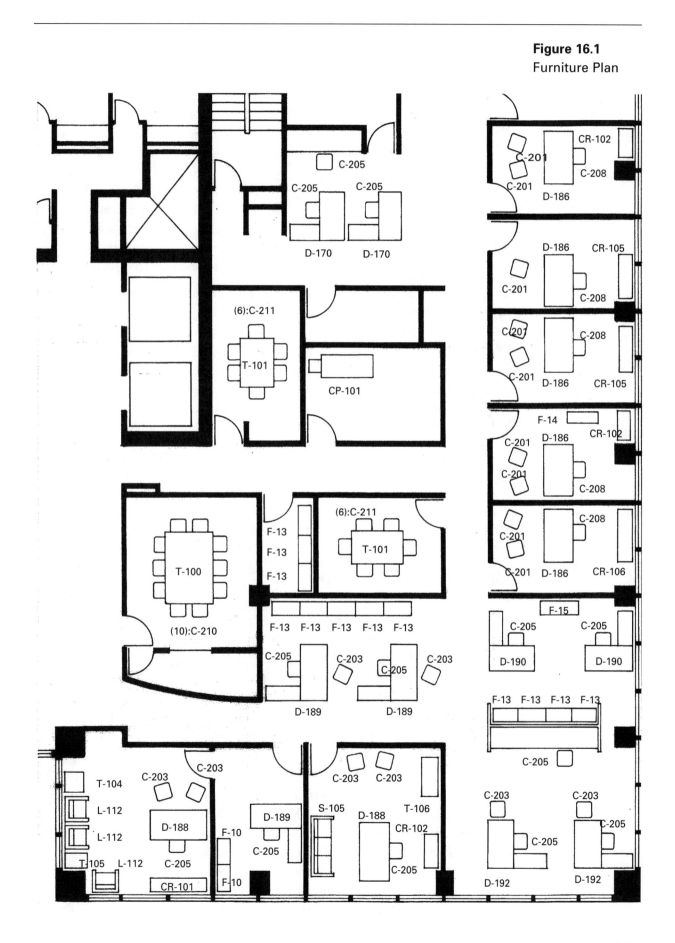

as nonloadbearing screen panels. It includes tests on modular systems and panel-supported components such as work surfaces and storage units.

• *ANSI/BIFMA X5.9, American National Standard for Office Furnishings—Storage Units:* This standard provides manufacturers, specifiers, and users with a common basis for evaluating the performance requirements for freestanding, mobile, and wall-mounted storage units.

• *ANSI/BIFMA/SOHO S6.5, American National Standard for Office Furnishings—Small Office/Home Office:* This standard provides performance and safety requirements for storage and desk furniture intended for use in the small office and home office.

• *BIFMA G1, Ergonomics Guideline for VDT (Visual Display Terminal) Furniture Used in Office Work Spaces:* This standard provides guidelines for furniture intended for computer use by applying the measurable principles and design requirements of ISO 9241 parts 3 and 5, which are, respectively, "Visual display requirements" and "Ergonomic requirements for office work with visual display units."

FURNITURE SPECIFICATIONS

Although the MasterFormat system provides a place to specify furnishings (Division 12), most interior design projects have separate specifications for construction and for furniture and accessories. This is because the procedure for specifying, contracting for, and building construction items is different from that for specifying, purchasing, delivering, and installing furniture.

The exact method of specifying and ordering furniture varies with the size of the project and the particular working methods of the interior design office. The responsibilities of the client, interior designer, furniture dealer, and others are described in the formal contract between the interior designer and the client. These contracts and responsibilities are discussed in more detail in Chs. 22 and 25.

For example, many interior designers select furniture for the client and assume the responsibility of writing purchase orders and coordinating delivery and installation. In this case, furniture specifications are not written. The selections that are approved by the client are directly listed on the purchase order that is sent to the furniture dealer. This is the procedure most commonly used for residential work.

For commercial work and some residential projects, the interior designer may select the furniture but turn the job of ordering, installing, and billing over to one or more furniture dealers who supply the specific brands of furniture needed. The dealer contracts directly with the client and assumes all responsibilities.

On larger commercial projects where a quoted price is requested from one or more dealers bidding on the same work, furniture specifications must be written to clearly state the client's requirements. These specifications not only list in detail all the individual items required but also state bidding requirements, responsibilities, installation procedures, and methods of invoicing. Figures 16.2 and 16.3 show one page of the general conditions of a furniture specification and one specified item.

COORDINATION WITH INDUSTRY

The interior designer is only one part of a rich and complex mix of design professionals, consultants, and trade sources. The designer must understand the role of each of the members of the industry in order to practice effectively and professionally. Design professionals include other interior designers, architects, and engineers, all of whom may contribute to

Figure 16.2
Page from the
General
Conditions of a
Furniture
Specification

d. If within one month after issuing a purchase order, the dealer has not received a written acknowledgment from the factory, he must contact the factory to obtain a written acknowledgment.

e. If requested by the interior designer one month prior to delivery and/or move-in, the dealer must contact all manufacturers confirming all scheduled shipping and delivery dates. Further, this checking with the factory is to continue on a no less than weekly basis until the installation of the goods. The intention of the above is to insure complete knowledge of the furniture status.

f. The dealer shall indicate time allotment that is required to install, assuming all merchandise is in his hands at one time to meet client occupancy schedule.

g. If it is necessary for the interior designer to carry out any undue installation procedures that are already a part of the contractor's agreement of work performance, this work will be computed at the hourly billing rate and the amount spent deducted from the final invoice submitted.

2.07 DAMAGED FURNITURE

a. In cases of merchandise damaged in shipment, bidder will be responsible for immediate repairs acceptable to the interior designer or, if necessary, replacement of such item with new merchandise from manufacturer on time for installation due date. If this is not possible because of delivery date from manufacturer, the interior designer must be informed immediately.

b. The successful bidder or bidders shall be responsible for all claims against the manufacturer for manufacturing defects and against the carrier for all freight and/or drayage damage.

2.08 CLEAN UP

No accumulation of packaging or crating materials permitted at the site. Remove debris daily. Upon completion of work within an area ready for inspection, remove temporary protection and leave area clean and ready for use by Owner.

---

the design of a project. Consultants may include specialized service providers such as acoustical engineers, preservation consultants, or code experts. Trade sources include the manufacturers, dealers, representatives, suppliers, contractors, and craftworkers who provide the goods and services necessary to complete an interior design project. This section describes the various trade sources involved with the furniture and furnishings industry and explains how the interior designer works with them to procure the necessary items. Refer to Ch. 24 for a description of other types of trade sources.

Trade Sources

There are several sources from which interior designers typically procure furniture and furnishings. They can also serve as excellent sources of information.

• *Sales representatives:* Sales representatives, or *reps* as they are commonly called, represent a manufacturer to the interior design and architectural community. They are commonly the designer's primary source of information about the products they represent. Reps also provide product samples, make price quotes, give out catalogs and other information, keep catalogs up to date, help with specification writing,

Figure 16.3
Page from a
Furniture
Specification

code on plans	item description		quantity	unit cost	total cost
LO-1	B & B AMERICA		2		
	Item:	Three Seat Sofa Coronado #05-103 OOY			
	Size:	83-1/8" W × 36-5/8" D × 30-3/4" H			
	Upholstery:	Jack Lenor Larsen Doria 1 I Henna Wool 54" W			
	Tag for:	Reception			
	Delivery Time:				

and can contact the manufacturer directly if special help is required or custom manufacturing is requested by the designer. However, they do not typically order products, handle delivery, or take care of installation. They may have a showroom but many times do not. These functions are usually provided by a dealership.

There are two types of reps: factory reps and independent reps. *Factory reps,* or *manufacturers' reps,* work directly for one company as an employee of the company. They often cover a wide geographical area, and the nearest factory rep may actually be headquartered in a nearby state. *Independent reps* work for themselves or for a small sales group. They often represent several products. The products may be related, like wall finishes, or they may be different. In most cases, manufacturers do not let an independent rep handle competing products. A designer should request a line chart from the independent reps in his or her area. A *line chart* lists all the manufacturers and/or products that the rep handles.

Reps are a vital part of the design industry. An interior designer who is acquainted with the reps in the area where he or she works will have sources to rely on for the most current information about a particular product.

• *Dealerships:* Dealerships take on several forms. They may represent one or more manufacturers and provide any number of services. Manufacturers' dealers carry only the products of one manufacturer. Independent dealers, like independent reps, carry a variety of manufacturers' products and, in some cases, have the exclusive right within a geographic region to represent and display a manufacturer's products. Full-service dealerships maintain a showroom, provide design services, assist with purchasing, handle delivery, and install the furniture at the job site. Full-service dealerships may even carry a significant inventory of commonly ordered items for immediate shipment so these items do not have to be ordered from the factory. Other dealerships may just have a showroom and perform the ordering and purchasing functions. They rely on others to perform design and installation services.

In some cases, a dealership may work directly with corporate clients. For example, a dealership may provide space planning services for an office tenant who is going to use a particular manufacturer's open-plan office system. The dealership will provide a turnkey service from design to installation, completely bypassing the involvement of a separate interior designer. In other situations, there may be several dealerships in the same area who may bid on providing the furniture and related purchasing and installation services the interior designer specifies.

Most dealerships are open only to the trade—interior designers, architects, and others who work for end users. A dealership typically offers a trade discount to interior designers. The designer may have to establish credit with the dealership and have a resale license if he or she will be reselling directly to the client.

• *Showrooms:* Showrooms are established for the primary purpose of displaying samples of the wares a particular manufacturer makes. Some showrooms are restricted to one manufacturer's product while others are more like wholesale stores. For example, an independent showroom, like an independent rep, may display related products, such as tile or lamps, from several different manufacturers.

Designers may purchase directly through some showrooms for items like furniture or lamps. In this situation, the interior designer will probably have to establish credit with the showroom and have a resale license. In other cases, the showroom is for viewing samples and getting product information only; the actual ordering is done through a contractor, tradesperson, or dealership. For example, a wallcovering showroom will have samples of all items in the manufacturer's latest product line, but these products will be specified as part of the construction specifications and purchased by the installing subcontractor as part of the construction contract.

Showrooms may be separate buildings or leased spaces, or they may be part of a larger building. A *mart* is a building that contains many different showrooms for the design trade. One of the best known and largest is the Merchandise Mart in Chicago. There are other, smaller design marts in large metropolitan areas in the United States as well as in other countries.

Trade showrooms, like some dealerships, are open to the trade only. A variation of the trade showroom is the retail furniture dealer, which is available to the general public as well as design professionals. These stores often carry a large stock and have interior designers on staff to assist retail clients. In most cases they sell merchandise at retail cost to the public but offer trade discounts to interior designers buying for their clients.

• *Specialty shops:* Specialty shops are similar to furniture dealers in that they are open to the public, but they specialize in one or a small number of goods. A lamp store or art gallery are examples of specialty shops. Like retail furniture dealers, they generally give interior designers and other professionals trade discounts.

• *Manufacturers:* Manufacturers actually produce the products the interior designer specifies. Most often, the designer does not deal with the manufacturer or factory directly, but rather works through dealers, reps, or showrooms. However, for smaller or specialty manufacturers without a network of reps and dealers, requests for information, catalogs, samples, and pricing need to be made directly with the of the manufacturer's sales staff.

In addition to the trade sources noted previously, there is a wealth of information available electronically, either on the internet or on CD-ROM. All manufacturers have websites that make product information available. There are also catalog-type websites that list products and furniture, making it easy to search for a particular type of furniture. In most cases, these sites provide links, making it easy for the designer to connect directly to a manufacturer once a particular product is found. Many furniture manufacturers also provide their catalog information on CD-ROM or DVD.

Procurement Process

Depending on the agreement with the client and the type of design business, the interior designer can proceed in one of three ways after furniture and other purchased items have been selected and specified.

In the first case, the designer can simply give the furniture specifications to a dealer (or dealers) or furniture manufacturing representative who then assumes the responsibility for writing purchase orders, arranging delivery, troubleshooting problems, and billing the client directly.

In the second case, the interior designer acts as a purchasing agent for the client, writing purchase orders to send to dealers, manufacturers, and vendors, and following up on the other paperwork, in addition to coordinating delivery and installation and then handling any problems that occur.

In the third situation, the designer acts as a reseller of goods. He or she writes purchase orders, accepts delivery, arranges for installation, collects money from the client (including any applicable taxes), and pays the manufacturers or vendors.

In most situations, the interior designer is responsible for the following sequence of activities related to ordering furniture, fixtures, and accessories. These usually occur whether the designer is acting as the client's purchasing agent or as a reseller.

The first step after the furniture and other goods have been selected is to receive a *sales agreement* or contract proposal signed by the client. This obligates the client to

pay for the items listed in the agreement. Such forms typically list the client's name and address, the items to be purchased, the item prices, and any labor, delivery, and taxes to be charged. If such an agreement is not signed by the client and the interior designer orders the goods, the designer is obligated to pay for them if the client does not.

Once the client has signed the agreement, a *purchase order* (PO) is written. See Fig. 16.4. This is a form, sent to the manufacturer or vendor, that lists the items to be purchased, their exact catalog numbers, prices, shipping information, and other data. If more than one manufacturer or vender is supplying goods to the project, a separate purchase order is sent to each. In addition to providing the means to order goods, the purchase order serves as an internal record for the design firm, since it can be used to keep track of outstanding orders. It is also used as the basis for billing the client if payment is made by the client to the interior design firm rather than directly to the manufacturer.

In no case should telephone orders be made. The potential for mistakes, misunderstandings, and misinterpretations is too great. Most vendors do not even accept telephone orders unless they are followed up by a written purchase order.

Some manufacturers may allow electronic or faxed orders. If this is the case, the interior designer should understand and follow the manufacturer's specific requirements. Paper copies of electronic forms should be printed for a record. If orders are faxed, a fax log should also be printed as proof that a PO was sent on a particular date.

Purchase orders can be prepared electronically with a database management program or printed in multiple-copy paper forms. In either case, they should contain the following information.

Figure 16.4
Purchase Order

Elegant Interiors, Inc.

4356 E. Stout Place
Sacramento, CA 95610
(916) 555-7649
(916) 555-4553 (Fax)

PURCHASE ORDER

P.O. # _____

Date: _____

Page: _____ of _____

Vendor:

Name: _____

Address _____

_____

City, ST, Zip _____

Ship to:

Name: _____

Address _____

_____

City, ST, Zip _____

Terms:

Vendor must provide acknowledgment within 5 days of receipt.
Vendor must provide shipping and confirm all prices.
No changes or substitutions may be made without prior approval.
This order may be cancelled without penalty if vendor is not
    able to ship by date specified or fails to notify of any delay.
Vendor agrees that acceptance of this order supersedes any other
    terms and conditions set forth.

Ship by: _____

Ship via: _____

Other instructions: _____

_____

Line	Quantity	Description	Each	Total
1				
2				
3				
4				
5				
6				
7				
8				
9				
10				
11				
12				

Special instructions:

Subtotal: _____

Freight: _____

Other charges: _____

TOTAL: _____

Authorization:

By: _____ **Date:** _____

- the designers name, billing address, phone number, fax number, and email address

- space for the vendor's name and address

- space for where the merchandise is to be shipped, which is typically different from the designer's address. When an order is to be shipped to a different address it is called a *drop ship* order.

- a unique, sequential identifying number so each PO can be identified, even if several are sent to the same vendor

- the date of the PO preparation

- space for shipping instructions, such as ship date or the preferred shipping company

- "tag for" information that may include where the item should be placed on the job site, the client's name, or other identifying information

- space for describing the merchandise, including the quantity, catalog number, description, and price. There may also be a sequential number known as a *line item*, to identify individual pieces of merchandise on one purchase order.

- space for the total price, shipping charges, any other charges, and a grand total

- space for an authorization signature by the design firm owner or some other authorized person and the date of signature

In addition to this information, which will vary for each purchase order, the PO may also contain boilerplate information about the terms of the order, canceling information, limitations on substitutions, and requirements for sending acknowledgement.

One copy of the PO (the original) is sent to the vendor, one copy is placed in a purchase order file in sequential order, for tracking of orders and acknowledgments, and another copy can be placed in the client file. If a warehousing service is being used, an additional copy can be sent there. If a database management system is used, the only copies that need to be printed are those being sent outside of the office.

After a manufacturer receives the PO, they send the designer an *acknowledgment* (sometimes called a *confirmation*) to confirm that they received it and to indicate how they interpreted it. The acknowledgment repeats the PO items, quantities, and costs and indicates a scheduled shipping date and how the consignment will be shipped. It is the designer's responsibility to check the acknowledgment against the PO to make sure the order is correct. One of the most important things to check is the expected shipping date. If this is not what the designer wanted or if delivery by a certain date is critical, the problem must be dealt with immediately. Often, the manufacturer may first tell the designer or the dealer that something is in stock or can be available by a certain time, but later finds a problem that delays shipment.

When the manufacturer ships the merchandise, they normally also send an invoice to the designer (or whoever ordered the goods) at the same time. The designer (or whoever is responsible) pays from this invoice. If the client is paying, the invoice should be sent to the client within 10 days after the merchandise has been received and accepted by the client. If the interior designer is purchasing at a trade discount and reselling to the client at list price, a separate invoice from the designer must be sent to the client.

As the merchandise is shipped, the carrier (usually a trucker) also transports a *bill of lading* that lists the contents of the shipment. When the truck arrives at the final destination, the number of items should be checked against the bill of lading to make sure they match. A *packing list*, which is a detailed list of the number and description of items in the shipment, will be sealed in an envelope attached to one of the items shipped. The packing list should also be checked against the items and the bill of lading. Any discrepancies between what is actually delivered and what is stated on the packing list or the bill of lading should be noted on the bill of lading. The *freight bill* is an invoice from the shipping company for the cost of shipping.

When the merchandise is delivered to a warehouse before shipping to the job site, it should be inspected for any damage that may have occurred in transit. This should be done by the designer or the designer's representative. Any damage should be shown to the driver and noted on the bill of lading. Some people also take photographs of the damaged merchandise to further back up their claims. Damage must be reported to the shipper as soon as possible.

When merchandise is delivered to the job site and the AIA A275/ID General Conditions of the Contract for Furniture, Furnishings and Equipment is being used, the owner is responsible for inspecting delivered goods, but only for the purposes of identifying the merchandise and verifying quantities. Such inspections are not considered final or as constituting acceptance of or taking control over the merchandise. If damage is found, the owner must notify the contractor, who then has the opportunity to correct the situation.

SAMPLE QUESTIONS

1. What interior design service is normally performed during the contract document phase of a project?

(A) coordinate the consultant contracts

(B) perform code review

(C) prepare furniture drawings

(D) review shop drawings

2. An interior designer could determine what products an independent representative handled by consulting

(A) the manufacturer's website

(B) a showroom directory

(C) *Sweets Catalog*

(D) a line chart

3. The client is most typically involved with procurement of furniture through

(A) the acknowledgment

(B) the freight bill

(C) a purchase order

(D) a sales agreement

4. What testing standard should be specified for the durability of office chair construction?

(A) ANSI/BIFMA X5.1

(B) ASTM D 4157

(C) CAL 133

(D) NFPA 701

5. When the interior designer does not want furniture to be delivered to the designer's office, the designer should complete a

(A) customized purchase order

(B) drop ship order

(C) letter of intent

(D) tag for label

6. Under the AIA A275/ID, General Conditions of the Contract for Furniture, Furnishings and Equipment, the inspection and acceptance of furniture upon delivery to the job site is the responsibility of the

(A) dealership

(B) furniture rep

(C) interior designer

(D) owner

7. Detailed information about furniture is commonly found on

(A) the furniture plan

(B) a furniture schedule

(C) a schedule or the specifications

(D) the specifications only

8. Which document provides the designer with verification that an item was ordered correctly?

(A) acknowledgment

(B) bill of lading

(C) packing slip

(D) purchase order

9. A client has requested that she be able to look at a sofa the interior designer is proposing to use. What is the best course of action for the designer?

(A) accompany the client to the nearest designer's showroom

(B) tell the client to visit the local dealership

(C) suggest that the client visit the manufacturer

(D) request that the manufacturer's rep have a sample delivered

10. An interior designer has written furniture specifications for a project and has put the job out for bid to several dealerships. In this situation, purchase orders are most likely to be written by the

(A) owner

(B) dealership

(C) furniture rep

(D) interior designer

17

STRUCTURAL SYSTEMS

Although the interior designer does not design or modify structural elements in a building, the designer should have a basic working knowledge of building structure and be able to read architects' and engineers' plans in order to make informed decisions about a variety of questions. These questions include the following.

• Is an element structural, and is it feasible to modify it?

• Can floor penetrations be made?

• Is building movement expected, and how can it be accommodated?

• Is a structural review necessary for the proposed new floor loading?

• How should new interior construction elements interface with existing structural elements?

• Will fire protection of structural elements need to be repaired, or should new protection be included in the design?

In addition to providing answers to these kinds of questions, this chapter reviews some of the common structural systems and structural issues with which the interior designer should be familiar. This chapter also includes some basic vocabulary and the graphic representation of structural elements the interior designer should know when reviewing drawings and working on the job site.

STRUCTURAL SYSTEMS

This section briefly describes the most common types of structural systems. The interior designer will most likely encounter these systems when modifications are proposed or required because of interior design decisions.

Steel

Two of the most common steel structural systems are the beam-and-girder system and the open-web steel joist system. See Figs. 17.1(a) and 17.1(b).

In the *beam-and-girder system*, large members span between columns, and smaller beams are framed into them. The girders span the shorter distance, while the beams span the longer distances. Typical spans for this system are from 25 ft to 40 ft (7.6 m to 12 m), with the beams spaced about 8 ft to 10 ft on center (2440 to 3050). The steel framing is usually covered with

Figure 17.1
Common Steel
Structural
Systems

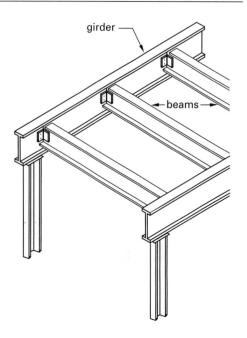

(a) beam-and-girder system

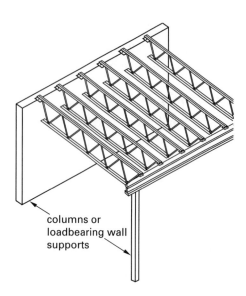

(b) open-web steel joist system

steel decking, which spans between the beams. A concrete topping is poured over the decking to complete the floor slab. This type of construction is commonly found in mid- to high-rise office buildings.

When this type of structural system is encountered, there is usually limited space between the bottom of the girders and the suspended ceiling. The possibility of adding new mechanical ductwork or installing large recessed light fixtures should be reviewed before final decisions are made about the reflected ceiling plan.

In an *open-web steel joist system*, joists span between beams or bearing walls as shown in Fig. 17.1(b). The various types of open-web joists can span from 20 ft (6.1 m) up to 144 ft (44 m). Depths range from 8 in to 72 in (200 to 1830). Open-web joists are typically spaced 2 ft to 6 ft on center (600 to 1800). As with the beam-and-girder system, steel decking spans between the joists, and a concrete slab is poured on top of the decking. A detailed view of one end of an open-web steel joist is shown in Fig. 17.2.

Interior designers usually encounter open-web steel joists in one-story or low-rise buildings with wide column spacing. Because the webs are open, mechanical and electrical service ducts, pipes, and conduit can easily be run between the web members. Suspended ceilings and other lightweight interior elements can also easily be hung from the bottoms of the joists.

Concrete

There are many variations of concrete structural systems, but the two primary types are cast-in-place and precast. With buildings made of *cast-in-place concrete*, concrete is poured into forms where it hardens before the forms are removed. *Precast contract* components are usually formed in a plant and shipped to the job site where they are set in place and rigidly connected to form the structure.

The majority of cast-in-place concrete systems utilize only mild steel reinforcing set in the formwork before the concrete is placed. However, in some instances with long-span structures, cast-in-place concrete is post-tensioned. This means that steel cables within the concrete are tightened after the concrete sets, creating extra compression forces in the beam or slab. If a slab is post-tensioned, it should not be penetrated for pipes or conduit.

There are five basic types of cast-in-place systems. These are shown in Fig. 17.3.

The *beam-and-girder system* shown in Fig. 17.3(a) functions in a manner similar to a steel system in which the slab is supported by intermediate beams, which are carried by larger girders. Typical spans are in the range of 15 ft to 30 ft (4.6 m to 9.1 m). The slab is poured integrally with the beams.

A *concrete joist system*, Fig. 17.3(b), is comprised of concrete members spaced 24 in or 36 in (610 or 914) apart, running in one direction, which frame into larger beams. The slab is also poured integrally with the joists. Because the joists are close together, it is more difficult to drill holes for small pipes and conduit.

With *flat plate construction*, shown in Fig. 17.3(c), the floor slab is designed and reinforced to transfer loads directly to the columns, which generally do not exceed 25 ft (7.6 m) spacing. Flat plate construction is commonly used in situations where floor-to-floor height must be kept to a minimum. Because of the closely spaced reinforcing required, it is often difficult, but not impossible, to drill these types of floors for electrical service or small pipes.

Flat slab construction, as shown in Fig. 17.3(d), is similar to flat plate, except that drop panels (increased slab thickness around the columns) are used to increase strength. Sometimes the truncated pyramids or cones are used instead of drop panels.

A *waffle slab system* (more technically, a two-way joist system), as shown in Fig. 17.3(e), can provide support for heavier loads at slightly longer spans than the flat

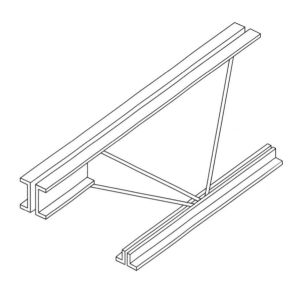

Figure 17.2
Open-Web Steel Joist

slab system. Waffle slabs are often left unexposed, with lighting integrated into the coffers.

Precast concrete consists of factory-made pieces. High-strength steel cables are stretched in the precasting forms before the concrete is poured. After the concrete attains a certain minimum strength, the cables are released and they transfer compressive stresses to the concrete. The members are then shipped to the construction site and set in place. Precast concrete floors include single tees, double tees, and hollow-core slabs as shown in Fig. 17.4. Columns and beams can also be precast.

Single- and double-tee members are a popular form of precast construction because they can simultaneously serve as beam and floor decking and are easy and fast to erect. A topping of concrete (usually about 2 in (50) thick) is placed over the tees to provide a uniform, smooth floor surface. Double-tee construction is commonly found in industrial buildings, one- and two-story commercial buildings, and parking garages.

Figure 17.3
Concrete
Structural
Systems

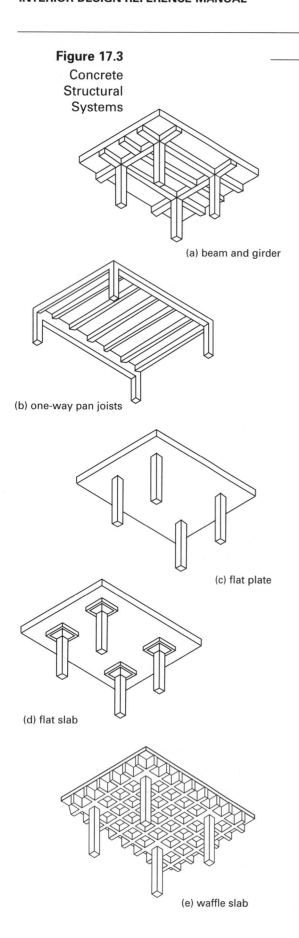

(a) beam and girder

(b) one-way pan joists

(c) flat plate

(d) flat slab

(e) waffle slab

Figure 17.4
Precast Concrete
Shapes

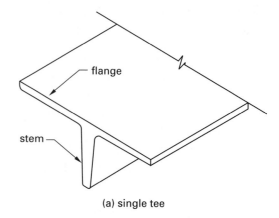

(a) single tee

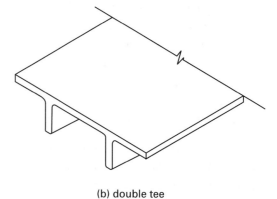

(b) double tee

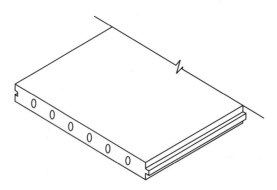

(c) hollow-core slab

Masonry

As a structural system in contemporary construction, masonry is generally limited to loadbearing walls, discussed in the following section. Masonry includes brick and concrete block, but due to the high cost of brick, nearly all masonry structural walls are built of concrete block. Brick is generally limited to use as a veneer over wood stud walls or over concrete block walls. Technically, glass block is defined as unit masonry. Refer to Ch. 10 for information on glass block.

Concrete block is the common term for concrete unit masonry, also known as *concrete masonry units* (CMU). This building product is manufactured with cement, water, and various types of aggregate, including gravel, expanded shale or slate, expanded slag or pumice, and limestone cinders.

CMU dimensions are based on a nominal 4 in (100) module, with actual dimensions being $3/8$ in (10) less than the nominal dimension, to allow for mortar joints. Unit dimensions are referred to by width, height, and then length. One of the most common sizes is an 8" × 8" × 16" unit, which is actually $7\,5/8$ in wide and high and $15\,5/8$ in long. (A metric block is 190 × 190 × 390 with 10 mm joints.) Concrete block is manufactured in a wide variety of shapes to suit particular applications.

Concrete block is manufactured with two open cells on either side of an intermediate rib. The cells in the block may be left open when loading is light, or they may be reinforced and filled with grout if more strength is needed. If an opening is required in a concrete block or brick wall, a structural engineer should be consulted to design the required support for the opening. Creating a small opening for a door or small window is usually not a difficult procedure. Interior design elements can be suspended from masonry walls by using the appropriate type of fastener.

Loadbearing Walls

Loadbearing walls (often simply called bearing walls) support loads from above. These include *live loads*, such as people and furniture, and *dead loads*, such as the weight of the structure itself. A loadbearing wall may be concrete, masonry, or wood framing. Because of their nature as structural supports, loadbearing walls cannot be removed and can only be pierced for doors and other openings if the top of the opening is framed with an adequately engineered lintel or beam.

Interior designers should be able to recognize common instances of loadbearing walls, either from the architects' drawings or from field observations. When it is not clear if a wall is loadbearing or not, an architect or structural engineer should be consulted if any modifications are contemplated.

In residential construction, exterior walls (the walls under the eaves of a roof) are usually loadbearing, and some interior partitions may also be loadbearing. The first-story exterior walls of a two-story house are nearly always loadbearing. If a wall needs to be cut for a moderately sized opening (a doorway, for example), it is a relatively simple matter to have additional studs installed with a double header or other type of lintel.

In commercial construction, fewer loadbearing walls are used than in residential construction; most structures are some form of column-and-beam system with nonloadbearing infill. The core walls of high-rise buildings are nearly always structural and cannot be pierced except for small openings for pipes. In smaller commercial buildings, concrete walls and many masonry walls are loadbearing.

In all cases, a structural engineer should be consulted if the interior designer is not sure whether a wall is loadbearing or not and when an opening needs to be created in the wall.

LOADS ON BUILDINGS

A building load is a force acting on a building element. There are three major load types: gravity, lateral, and dynamic. This section discusses these loads and how they affect interior design.

Gravity Loads

Gravity loads include dead loads and live loads.

Dead loads are the vertical loads due to the weight of the building and any permanent equipment. These include such things as columns, beams, exterior and interior walls, floors, and mechanical equipment. Building structures are designed initially to support all the dead loads. Even though the interior designer will plan interior partitioning and other construction elements that change the dead loads, the original design of the building considers these normal dead loads on an average square-foot basis; that is, in the initial design, an allowance is made for interior partitioning. The only time an interior designer needs to consult a structural engineer relative to dead loading is if plans call for the installation of unusually heavy partitioning (such as a masonry wall) or heavy equipment.

Live loads include the weight of people, furniture, and other moveable equipment. Buildings are originally designed to accommodate a particular amount of uniform live load, which is established by building codes for different occupancies. For example, the structure of residential floors is designed for a live load of 40 lbm/ft^2 (0.18 kN/m^2), while offices are designed for 50 lbm/ft^2 (0.22 kN/m^2).

Codes also require that floors be designed to support concentrated loads if the specified load on an otherwise unloaded floor would produce stresses greater than those caused by the uniform load. The concentrated load is assumed to be located on any space $2^1/_2$ ft^2 (0.232 m^2).

If a space is being designed for a use other than its original purpose and the floor loading will be increased (for heavy equipment, book stacks, or files, for example), the designer should consult with a structural engineer to determine if the floor is capable of carrying the additional load and, if not, to have additional structural reinforcement engineered. In some highrise buildings, the structural bays near the center of the building are designed for heavier loading, so file rooms and book stacks should be located in these areas in the early planning stages.

Lateral Loads

Lateral loads include wind loads and earthquake loads. As with dead loads, these are provided for in the original design of the building. However, they may need to be taken into account if interior construction elements will be attached to the structure of the building or are required by code to resist earthquake loads.

The instances when the interior designer needs to consider the effects of wind on a building are discussed in the section on building movement.

For earthquake loading, the International Building Code and other model codes divide the United States into different zones, representing the potential severity of seismic activity. In the least severe zones, no special detailing needs to be included by the interior designer. In highrisk areas, the designer must ascertain the requirements for the particular geographical area in which the project is located.

Interior construction elements that may need to be detailed to resist earthquake forces include partitions that are tied to the ceiling or are over 6 ft (1829) high, suspended ceilings, HVAC ductwork, light fixtures, sprinkler and other piping, bookcases, storage cabinets and laboratory equipment, and access floors. Some common details for ceiling bracing are shown in Ch. 10.

Dynamic Loads

When a force is only applied suddenly, it is often called an *impact load*.

When a load is applied suddenly or changes rapidly, it is called a *dynamic load*. Examples of dynamic loads are automobiles moving in a parking garage, elevators traveling in a shaft, or a helicopter landing on the roof of a building. An impact load would be created by a large industrial punch press. Interior designers seldom encounter situations where dynamic loads are imposed by the interior use of the building. However, if such a condition may exist, the designer should consult with a structural engineer.

BUILDING MOVEMENT

All buildings move to some extent. Movement can be caused by shrinkage of materials (like wood), compression of materials over time, deflection of materials under load (like floors), ground settling or heaving, earthquakes, swaying caused by wind, and expansion and contraction caused by temperature differentials.

Interior construction must take into account the possible movement of the building structure. For example, interior partitions in commercial construction that attach to the structural floors above and to the perimeter of the building should be designed with slip joints to allow the building to move slightly without putting pressure on the partitions.

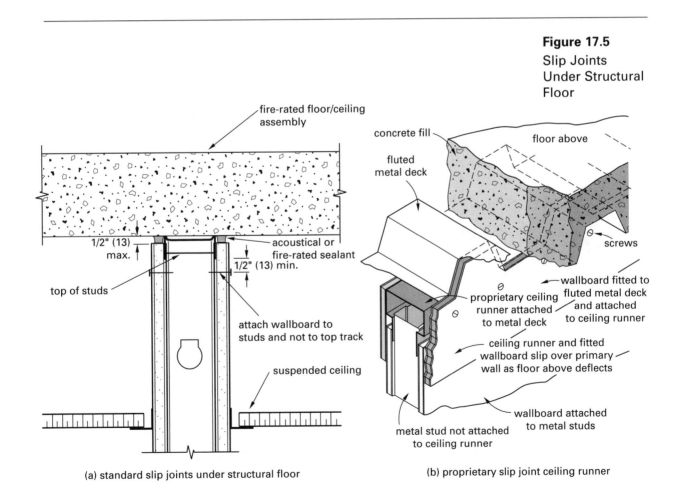

Figure 17.5
Slip Joints
Under Structural
Floor

(a) standard slip joints under structural floor

(b) proprietary slip joint ceiling runner

Figure 17.6
Relief Joint at
Mullion

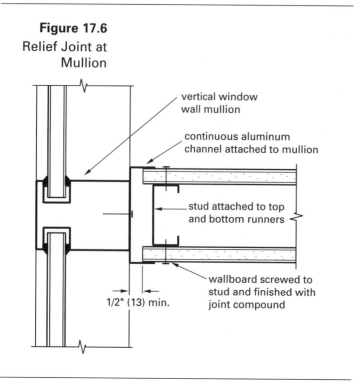

vertical window
wall mullion

continuous aluminum
channel attached to mullion

stud attached to top
and bottom runners

wallboard screwed to
stud and finished with
joint compound

1/2" (13) min.

Figure 17.7
Relief Joint at
Structural Wall
or Column

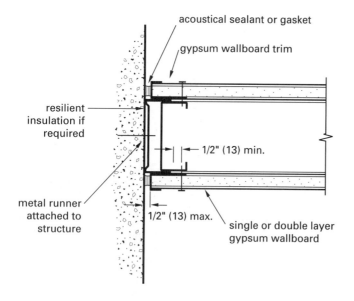

acoustical sealant or gasket

gypsum wallboard trim

resilient
insulation if
required

1/2" (13) min.

metal runner
attached to
structure

1/2" (13) max.

single or double layer
gypsum wallboard

Movement at the top of the partition can be caused by structural deflection of the floor above, and movement at the perimeter can be caused by wind sway. Partitions rigidly attached to the structure may buckle and crack if slip joints are not used.

Figures 17.5, 17.6, and 17.7 illustrate some common methods of detailing slip joints and relief joints. Similar types of slip joints should be used whenever minor building movement is expected. Large movements are accommodated by building expansion joints, but these are usually already in place as part of the design of the building.

In large buildings, provisions have to be made to allow parts of the building to move separately. To enable this movement, the structure of each part is entirely separated during design and construction. The large joints are covered inside the building with expansion joint covers (from 2 in to 8 in (51 to 203) wide) that can slide back and forth as the building moves. Two of the common conditions are shown in Fig. 17.8. If these conditions are encountered during interior design, they cannot be covered up with other finish materials, nor should partitions or furniture be placed over them. In seismically active areas, the interior designer may also encounter similar joints to allow for significant movement of the building. These joints, too, must not be covered.

FLOOR PENETRATIONS

In addition to determining the maximum allowable loads, floor construction may limit the number and types of floor penetrations, if any are possible at all. Floor penetrations range from small holes for an electrical conduit, to major reconstructions, such as for stairways. For minor electrical or telephone conduit, a core drill penetration is used. A *core drill* is a 2 in to 4 in (51 to 102) round hole drilled through the concrete with a special hollow drill bit.

Floors in commercial buildings are constructed primarily of cast-in-place concrete, precast concrete, or concrete on metal decking.

PROFESSIONAL PUBLICATIONS, INC.

Cast-in-place concrete framing types include those shown in Fig. 17.3. All of the cast-in-place concrete structural systems are difficult to cut through, but of the five types shown in Fig. 17.3, the beam-and-girder system and one-way pan joist system are the easiest to penetrate with small core drilling for pipes and poke-through electrical outlets. This is because there is less reinforcing in these systems.

Cast-in-place concrete floor systems can be pierced for small openings such as a floor-mounted electrical box. However, holes cannot be cut near where the columns intersect the floor or where beams are located. For larger openings, the easiest types of concrete floors to cut are flat plates and flat slabs. However, large openings require additional structural support around the opening, which must be designed by a structural engineer. The ribs of waffle slabs can be cut for large openings, such as stairways, but this task is difficult and expensive and also requires additional support around the cut.

Because the stems of tee sections are deep and contain prestressed cable, they cannot be cut, so openings are limited to the areas between the tee sections. For hollow-core slabs, small openings can be cut through the existing cores but should not be cut through the solid portion where the prestressing cables are located.

Post-tensioned concrete is another concrete structural system that is sometimes found in buildings. In this system, the post-tensioning steel strands (called *tendons*) are stressed after the concrete has been poured in place and cured. Because they are stressed under high pressure and keep this stress during the life of the building, the slabs in which they are located cannot be cut.

One of the most common types of floor and roof construction is concrete on metal decking. See Fig. 17.9. Corrugated sheet steel is supported by steel beams and columns and serves as a working platform, the form for the concrete, and part of the structural system. Concrete is poured over the decking and leveled to create the final rough floor. Because of the nature of this structural system, it is easy to have small and moderately sized holes cut for conduit, ductwork, and the like. If larger penetrations are required for stairways or elevators, steel angles or beams can be placed around the perimeter of the cut to provide the necessary support.

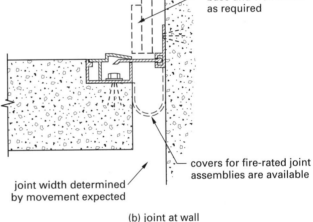

Figure 17.8
Expansion Joint Cover Assemblies

(a) joint in floor

(b) joint at wall

Figure 17.9
Steel Decking

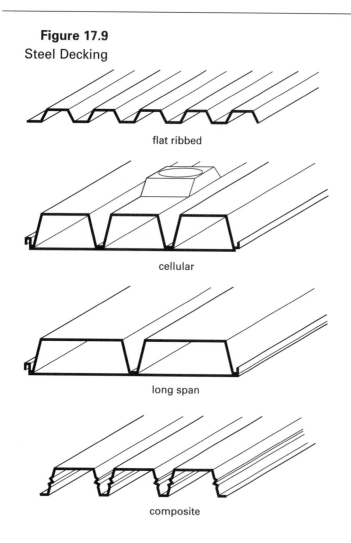

flat ribbed

cellular

long span

composite

Whenever a cut in a concrete floor is proposed, reinforcing bars and other embedded items can be located by having the floor X-rayed near the proposed cut.

FIRE-RESISTIVE RATINGS

As described in Ch. 27, all buildings are classified by the building code as a certain type based on the fire-resistance ratings of various major components such as structure, exterior walls, and shaft enclosures. In commercial construction, the structural frame of a building may be protected with fire-resistant construction rated from 1 hour to 3 hours. The rating and method of protection is part of the original architect's building design. However, there are instances where the interior designer may want to remove the existing covering and

replace it with something else. The new covering must provide the same amount of fire protection as the existing covering. Common examples of this include replacing a column or beam cover with another size or shape of cover, or enclosing a new vertical shaft (such as a stairway or dumbwaiter).

If steel is protected with spray-on fireproofing, there may be some damage when other construction elements are attached. However, the fireproofing can easily be repaired to maintain the fire-resistant rating of the member.

Most laws regulating construction and the interior design profession do not allow interior designers to design, specify, or modify fire protection of structural systems as part of their work. If this is the case, the interior designer should retain the services of an architect to conduct this part of the design.

RESIDENTIAL AND SMALL COMMERCIAL STRUCTURAL SYSTEMS

Structural systems for single-family residential construction and small commercial construction typically use wood and wood products as the primary material.

Wood is one of the oldest and most common structural materials. It is plentiful, inexpensive, relatively strong in both compression and tension, and easy to work with and fasten. In contemporary construction, wood may be used either directly as it is cut from a tree or as a hybrid wood product where pieces of wood are manufactured into a larger structural element.

Figure 17.10 shows typical residential construction. In addition to showing how the joists and exterior stud wall are constructed, this drawing shows how the joists are set on a sill plate, which is anchored to the concrete foundation wall.

In this type of construction, loadbearing walls are typically made with small, repetitive elements called *studs*. For residential construction, the most common type of stud wall consists of 2" × 4" (actual size of $1^1/_2$" × $3^1/_2$" (38 × 89)) studs placed 16 in (406) on center. Occasionally, 6 in (152) deep studs will be used. Studs of this size are adequate to support a one-story or two-story house. The same stud size and spacing are used for nonloadbearing walls and interior partitions.

Joists are horizontal repetitive members used to support the floor. They are made from nominal 2 in thick wood, and their depth is determined by the distance they are required to span. Common depths are 8, 10, and 12 in. The actual size of an 8 in joist is $7^1/_4$ in (184). The actual sizes of 10 in and 12 in joists are $9^1/_4$ in and $11^1/_4$ in (235 and 286), respectively.

The space between joists is spanned with plywood or particleboard subflooring on which underlayment is placed in preparation for finish flooring. Sometimes, a single sheet of $^3/_4$ in (19) subfloor/underlayment is used, but this approach is not as desirable.

Sheathing is nailed to the outside of the stud wall to stiffen the wall and provide a nailing base for the exterior finish material. If brick veneer is used, the brick is held to the sheathing with corrugated metal strips. On the inside of the wall, $^1/_2$ in gypsum wallboard is nailed or screwed to the studs. Insulation is placed between the studs and joists in thicknesses as required by the climate of the region.

When openings for doors and small windows are required, they are framed at the top with lintels (also called *headers*). These are usually double 2" × 4", 2" × 6", or 2" × 8" members oriented vertically to act as a beam to carry the loads. See Fig. 17.11.

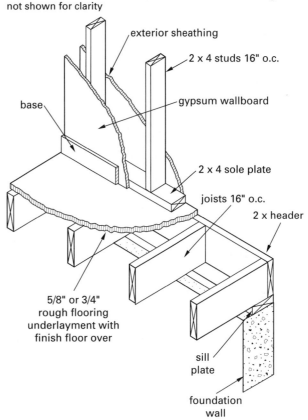

Figure 17.10
Residential Framing

Note: exterior siding and insulation not shown for clarity

exterior sheathing

2 x 4 studs 16" o.c.

gypsum wallboard

base

2 x 4 sole plate

joists 16" o.c.

2 x header

5/8" or 3/4" rough flooring underlayment with finish floor over

sill plate

foundation wall

When large openings are required, methods other than using double two-by members must be used. These may include using stronger laminated veneer lumber (as described in the next section), glued-laminated beams, or small steel beams.

Joists can normally span up to about 20 ft (6.1 m). When longer spans are required or a beam is needed to support several joists, steel or manufactured wood products must be used.

For two-story construction, a technique called *platform framing* is used, as illustrated in Fig. 17.12. With this method, wood studs one story high are placed on a sole plate at the bottom and spanned with a double top plate at the ceiling level. The second-floor joists bear on the top plate and, when the second-floor sheathing is in

Figure 17.11
Open Framing

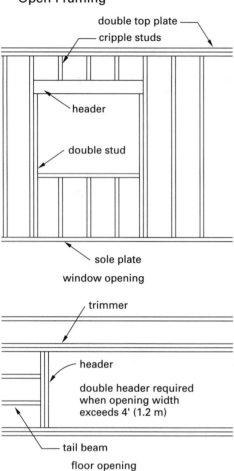

Figure 17.12
Platform
Construction

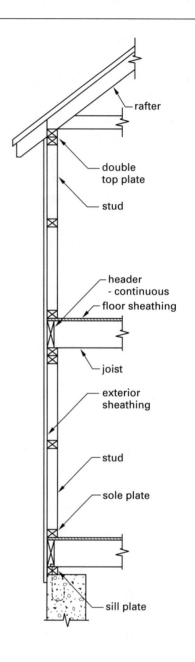

place, serve as a platform on which to erect the second-story stud walls and roof.

When stronger members are required in small commercial construction and some residential construction, glued-laminated members may be used. See Fig. 17.13. *Glued-laminated wood members,* or *glulams,* are built up from a number of individual pieces of lumber, which are glued together and finished under factory conditions for use as beams, columns, purlins, and other structural components. Glulams are used where larger wood members are required for heavy loads or long spans and simple sawn timber pieces are not available or cannot meet the strength requirements. Glulam construction is also

used where unusual structural shapes are required and appearance is a consideration. In addition to being fabricated in simple, linear rectangular shapes, glulam members can be formed into arches, tapered forms, and pitched shapes.

Glulam members are manufactured in standard widths and depths as shown in Fig. 17.13. If necessary, interior design components may be framed into glulam beams using simple wood fasteners.

Alternative Structural Materials

In an effort to employ the many structural advantages of wood and increase utilization of forest products while minimizing the problems of defects and limited strength in solid wood members, several manufactured products have been developed.

One is a lightweight, I-shaped joist consisting of a top and bottom chord of solid or laminated construction separated by a plywood web. See Fig. 17.14(a). This type of joist is used in residential and light commercial construction and allows longer spans than are possible with a solid wood joist system. It has a very efficient structural shape, like a steel wide-flange beam, and because it is manufactured in a factory, problems such as warping, splits, checks, and other common wood defects are eliminated. This product is stronger and stiffer than a standard wood joist. Its use is increasing because straight, good-quality, solid joists are becoming more expensive and difficult to find. Within limits, holes can be drilled in the web to accommodate small pipes and electrical wiring.

Another manufactured product is a wood member manufactured with individual layers of thin veneer glued together. See Fig. 17.14(b). Often referred to as *laminated veneer lumber* (LVL), it is used primarily for headers over large openings, and singly or built-up for beams. It is stronger than solid lumber of the same dimensions.

GRAPHIC REPRESENTATION OF STRUCTURAL ELEMENTS

Existing structural supports generally cannot be removed and can only be relocated with great effort and expense. The interior designer must know how to identify structural elements on plans and sections in order to plan spaces and locate other

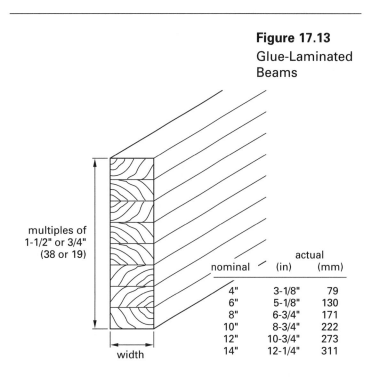

Figure 17.13
Glue-Laminated Beams

multiples of
1-1/2" or 3/4"
(38 or 19)

width

nominal	actual (in)	(mm)
4"	3-1/8"	79
6"	5-1/8"	130
8"	6-3/4"	171
10"	8-3/4"	222
12"	10-3/4"	273
14"	12-1/4"	311

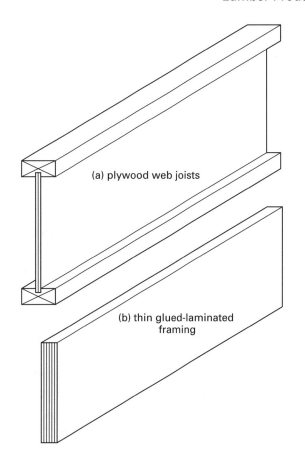

Figure 17.14
Manufactured Lumber Products

(a) plywood web joists

(b) thin glued-laminated framing

Figure 17.15
Structural
Symbols

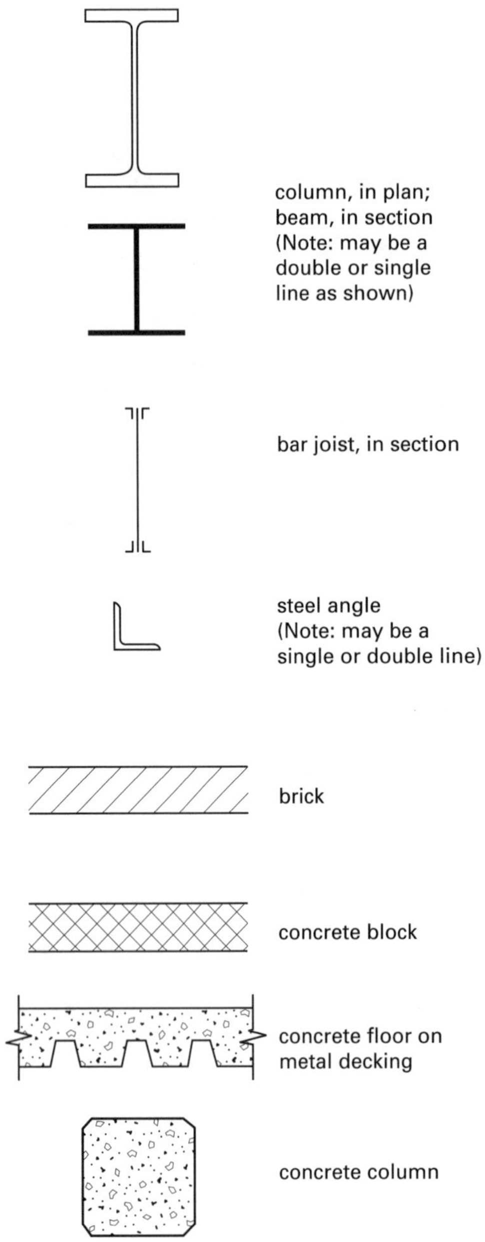

column, in plan;
beam, in section
(Note: may be a
double or single
line as shown)

bar joist, in section

steel angle
(Note: may be a
single or double line)

brick

concrete block

concrete floor on
metal decking

concrete column

DEFINITIONS

Core drill: a machine used to cut a small opening in a concrete floor for conduit or poke-through electrical outlets

Core wall: in a high-rise building, the wall generally used as part of the structure of the building and surrounding the common building services such as elevator and stairway shafts, toilet rooms, mechanical rooms, and the like

Cripple stud: a stud above a door opening or below a windowsill

Decking: light-gage sheets of steel that are ribbed, fluted, or otherwise stiffened by shape for use in constructing a floor or roof (see Fig. 17.9)

Grout: a mixture of portland cement, water, and sand, containing enough water to allow it to be poured or pumped into joints, spaces, and cracks within masonry walls

Header: a framing member that crosses and supports the ends of joists, transferring the weight of the joist to parallel joists. Headers are used to form openings in wood-framed floors.

Lintel: a horizontal structural member over an opening that carries the weight of the wall above it

Purlin: a piece of timber laid horizontally

Sheathing: the plywood or particleboard covering placed over exterior studding or rafters of a building that provides strength and a base for the application of wall or roof cladding

Sole plate: a horizontal wood member that serves as the base for the studs in a stud partition

Trimmer: a wood member in a floor or roof used to support a header

Wide-flange beam: a structural beam of steel having a shape whose cross section resembles the letter H. A wide-flange beam has wider flanges than an I-beam. Wide-flange beams are used for beams as well as columns because

interior elements intelligently. Figure 17.15 shows some common symbols and drafting conventions that indicate various types of structural elements.

Sometimes the same symbol represents different elements depending on whether the view of the drawing is a plan or section. For example, the H-shaped section in Fig. 17.15 represents a steel column if seen on a floor plan, but it (or a similar H-shaped section) represents a wide-flange beam if viewed in a vertical cross section.

their shape gives them approximately equal strength in both directions.

SAMPLE QUESTIONS

1. Small ductwork could most easily be placed within which of the following types of structural systems?

(A) beam-and-girder steel

(B) flat plate concrete

(C) open-web steel joists

(D) twin T concrete

2. A compact filing system is an example of a

(A) dead load

(B) dynamic load

(C) lateral load

(D) live load

3. The interior designer can design details to accommodate building movement caused by all of the following EXCEPT

(A) building expansion

(B) floor deflection

(C) seismic events

(D) wind sway

4. A residential client with a one-story house wants to remove an 8 ft section of a loadbearing wall to make an opening between two existing rooms. What is the most appropriate advice the interior designer can give?

(A) The opening can be framed, but a structural engineer will be needed.

(B) An architect will have to be retained to sign the drawings for the building department.

(C) The opening can be framed with a double 2" × 8" header.

(D) The proposed opening cannot be made, because the wall is a loadbearing wall.

5. When advising a client on where to attach fasteners to support wall-hung bookshelves in a residence, the interior designer should recommend that they be placed

(A) 12 in (305) on center

(B) 16 in (406) on center

(C) 24 in (610) on center

(D) across the double top plate

6. Core drilling would be most difficult in which type of structural system?

(A) concrete over steel deck

(B) flat slab concrete

(C) one-way pan joist concrete

(D) post-tensioned concrete

7. The structure above a small opening cut in a masonry loadbearing wall would be supported with a

(A) beam

(B) header

(C) lintel

(D) trimmer

8. What does the symbol shown indicate on a floor plan?

(A) column

(B) truss

(C) beam

(D) joist

9. What type of slab CANNOT be penetrated for a stair opening?

(A) reinforced concrete

(B) post and beam

(C) waffle slab

(D) post tensioned

10. With whom should the interior designer consult to determine where put stacks in libraries?

(A) mechanical engineer

(B) library planner

(C) structural engineer

(D) fire protection designer

18

MECHANICAL AND ELECTRICAL SYSTEMS

This chapter reviews some of the mechanical and electrical systems with which NCIDQ candidates should be familiar. Mechanical systems include heating and cooling, plumbing, and fire protection. Electrical systems include power, lighting, telephone, and other communication systems. (Refer to Ch. 19 for more information on lighting design.) Stairway design is also included in this chapter. The NCIDQ exam often refers to stairways as vertical transportation.

Although the interior designer is not responsible for designing or producing construction drawings for structural, mechanical, and electrical systems, he or she must know when and how to coordinate with consulting engineers, how to read consultants' drawings, and how to make design decisions based on these systems. For example, the existing location of a soil stack may limit the area within which the designer can plan for a new rest room. In another instance, an interior designer may be able to recommend cutting a hole in a floor to provide for a new stairway if the structural system can accommodate it.

HVAC

HVAC is the acronym for *heating, ventilating, and air conditioning* and includes all the systems used for these purposes. One system may combine all three, or there may be two or more systems to heat and cool a building.

Types of Systems

HVAC systems are often classified by the medium used to heat or cool the building. The two primary methods of heating and cooling use air or water. In some parts of the country, electricity is also used for heating. Some systems use a combination of media.

All-air systems cool or heat spaces by conditioned air alone. Heat is transported to the space with supply and return air ducts. A common example of an all-air system is a residential forced hot-air furnace. A boiler powered by oil or gas heats air that is distributed throughout the house in ductwork. Return air ducts in each room collect the cooled air and return it to the furnace for reheating. If necessary, an air conditioning unit is connected to the same ductwork to provide cooled and de-humidified air.

For commercial buildings, there are several variations of systems, including variable air volume (VAV), high-velocity dual duct, constant volume with reheat, and multizone systems. All types require supply air ductwork, registers, and return air grilles in all spaces. Registers are connected to the supply air ductwork and can be adjusted to control the direction of air flow and the volume of air coming through them. In many instances, separate ductwork is not used for return air, but grilles are simply placed in the suspended ceiling to collect return air. The mechanical system draws the return air back to a central collecting point where it is then returned through ducts to the building's heating plant.

The space between the suspended ceiling and the structural floor above is called the *plenum*. If fire-rated partitions extend above the suspended ceiling, then supply air ducts and openings for return air must be provided. At the locations where the fire wall is penetrated, fire dampers are required that automatically close in the event of a fire.

Supply air registers are often connected to the main ductwork with flexible ducting. This allows some adjustability in the exact location of an air register if its location is in conflict with some other ceiling-mounted item. Because return air grilles are generally not connected to ducts in commercial construction, they may also be relocated if overall circulation is maintained. The mechanical engineer should be consulted to determine how much the registers can be moved.

All-water heating systems use some type of coil unit called a *convector* in each space through which hot water is circulated. The hot water heats the fins of the coil unit, and air is heated as it is drawn over the fins. The air may be circulated by convection, as with most baseboard residential fin-tube radiators, or by forced circulation created with a fan.

There are also combination systems that use ductwork for supplying fresh air but use water to heat or cool the air before it is introduced into the conditioned space. These are called terminal reheat systems. Other installations use an all-water system for heating and a separate duct system for ventilation and cooling. In geographical areas where electric heat is economical, radiant panels can be mounted in the walls or created by running cables in the ceiling. Sometimes electric panels are used where it is necessary to avoid drafts.

System Requirements

There are several things an interior designer should understand about HVAC systems in order to make informed decisions regarding space planning, ceiling design and layout, and remodeling. These considerations are discussed as follows.

Space for Ducts, Pipes, and Mixing Boxes

Small ducts and plumbing pipes are typically run within the walls and floor joists in residential construction. Occasionally, horizontal ducts in a house must be run below the floor joists and a dropped ceiling, or furred down space must be built to conceal them.

In commercial construction, horizontal ducts are normally run in the plenum and vertical ducts are normally run within their own chases. Large, horizontal ducts may occupy most of the vertical distance between a suspended ceiling and the structure above, making it difficult, if not impossible, to recess light fixtures. This is particularly true with standard line-voltage recessed incandescent downlights, which can be fairly deep. Sometimes, it is possible to substitute smaller, low-voltage or low-clearance light fixtures to fit within the low space below a duct. Refer to Ch. 19 for some typical clearances required of various types of recessed luminaires.

Another consideration when planning ceiling layout is the locations of mixing boxes, which are also located in the plenum. A *mixing box* adjusts the quantity or temperature of air going into a space from the main air supply line(s), reduces the velocity of air, and attenuates noise. Lines from thermostats are connected to the mixing boxes. With variable air volume systems, the VAV box, as it is called, varies the quantity of air. One duct leads in and one or several lead out and are attached to registers mounted in the ceiling. A VAV box is typically placed above the ceiling, within or near the space it serves. With dual-duct systems the mixing box actually mixes cool and hot air, coming into it from two separate ducts, and distributes the mixed air to ducts serving individual rooms or spaces. With terminal reheat systems the box contains a hot-water coil that provides additional heat to the air stream. These can easily be identified by air ducts and copper pipes leading into them.

Depending on the type and capacity of the system, mixing boxes can range in size from 6 in to 18 in high, 24 in to 60 in long, and 14 in to 66 in wide (152 to 457 high, 610 to 1525 long, and 356 to 1676 wide). Although they may interfere with light fixture placement and other recessed ceiling items, because of their size and connection with ductwork and thermostats, mixing boxes are often expensive and difficult to move.

The sizes and locations of ductwork, mixing boxes, and piping should be verified before locating light fixtures and other recessed ceiling items. This information can be found on HVAC plans (as shown in Fig. 18.4), by consulting with the mechanical engineer on a job, or by visual inspection on the job site. However, remember that actual construction seldom exactly follows the drawings, so on-site viewing of the space above the ceiling is the best way to confirm the location of existing HVAC, plumbing, electrical, and fire protection services. If the relocation of HVAC equipment or piping is contemplated, the cost, time, and heating and cooling implications should be discussed with the mechanical engineer, contractor, and client.

Some commercial construction uses access flooring, which is a false floor of individual panels raised above the structural floor with pedestals. Although access flooring is most commonly used to run electrical, communication, and computer wiring, it can be used for some types of HVAC ductwork that serves individual workstations.

Small pipes can be run within standard partitions in commercial construction, but larger pipes need to be placed in deeper walls or in chase walls. A *chase wall* consists of two runs of studs separated by several inches, the exact dimension being determined by the largest pipe or duct that has to be concealed. Only the finish side of each run of studs is covered with wallboard. Chase walls are commonly used between back-to-back commercial toilet rooms where extensive plumbing work and toilet carriers are required. A *toilet carrier* is a steel framework that is bolted to the floor inside a pipe chase and carries the weight of wall-hung toilets.

Plenum Requirements

In commercial construction when the plenum is used as a return air space, building codes prohibit the use of combustible materials such as wood or exposed wire within the space. However, some types of telephone and communication wiring are plenum-rated (Teflon coated, for example) for use in such a location, and these may be used in place of running the wires in steel conduits. If required by the local authority having jurisdiction, fire-rated dividers must be installed to limit the spread of fire and smoke horizontally. Normally, such dividers are simply an extension of a fire-rated partition.

Access

Building codes (and common sense) require that access be provided to certain components of mechanical and electrical systems. These include such things as valves, fire dampers, heating coils, mechanical equipment, electrical junction boxes, communication junction boxes, and similar devices. If these components are located above a suspended acoustical ceiling, access is provided by simply removing a ceiling tile. In other locations, such as gypsum wallboard ceilings or partitions, access doors are required for anything that might need to be inspected, adjusted, or repaired. *Access doors* are typically small steel doors with frames that are opened by using a thumb turn or a key. If required, access doors are available as a fire-rated assembly.

Thermostats

The locations of thermostats are normally determined by the mechanical engineer so they are away from exterior walls, heat sources, or other areas that may adversely affect their operation. They are normally located 48 in (1220) above the floor, but this should be coordinated with light switches and other nearby wall-mounted control devices. The mounting height must also be coordinated with the maximum allowable reach distances for accessibility, which may lower the thermostat heights to 44 in (1118) for an obstructed forward reach.

Coordination with Other Ceiling Items

The interior designer should coordinate the locations of supply air diffusers and return air grilles with other ceiling items such as lights, sprinkler heads, smoke detectors, speakers, and the like, so the ceiling is as functional and well planned as possible. However, the mechanical engineer must be consulted to verify that the desired types and locations of supply air and return air devices do not adversely affect the operation of the HVAC system.

Window Coverings

Window covering can affect the heating and air conditioning load in a space and may interfere with supply air diffusers or other heating units near the window. Therefore, in commercial construction the interior designer should have the mechanical engineer or architect check the designer's proposed type, size, and mounting to verify that they will not create a problem with the HVAC system. For example, in commercial construction, there should be at least 2 in (51) between the glass and any window covering to avoid excessive heat buildup, which might cause the glass to crack or break. Other minimum clearances are shown in Fig. 18.1.

Space Planning and Furniture Placement

In residential construction, the existing locations of ductwork and air registers may not work if remodeling is extensive. A mechanical contractor or mechanical engineer should be consulted to determine if the existing furnace has adequate capacity to change or add onto a residence, and also to determine how ducts and registers may need to be relocated, if necessary.

In commercial construction, most HVAC systems are designed to work independently of partition relocation and furniture placement. However, in some cases HVAC zones are designed for one layout and may not work with the desired zoning of a new plan. For furniture placement, the interior designer may want to consider the locations of floor registers, fin-tube baseboard radiators, and other equipment as they affect the placement of furniture and built-in woodwork.

Acoustic Separation

Mechanical and electrical services often pose problems with maintaining acoustic separation, especially in office spaces where ducts, convectors, and piping run continuously along an exterior wall while partitions intersect the exterior wall at regular intervals. Special detailing or construction may be required to create a continuous sound seal around the floor, around the ceiling, above the ceiling, and along the perimeter wall. For example, the cracks between the wallboard and all pipe and duct penetrations must be sealed with acoustic sealant.

A common problem is when an office wall intersects an exterior wall with a convector running near the floor. The openings in the convector that allow warm air to circulate also allow sound to penetrate and travel inside the convector, past the partition, and out the openings on the other side. The convector must be modified in some way to prevent this, either by cutting the convector and piping (a difficult and expensive option) or by sealing inside the convector while still allowing the hot water pipe to run continuously. One of many ways of doing this is shown in Fig. 18.2.

Air-Supply Options

There are several types of air-supply diffusers available, depending on the requirements of the HVAC system, the type of wall or ceiling in which they are mounted, and the appearance desired. Some of the more common types are shown in Figs. 18.3(a) through 18.3(c).

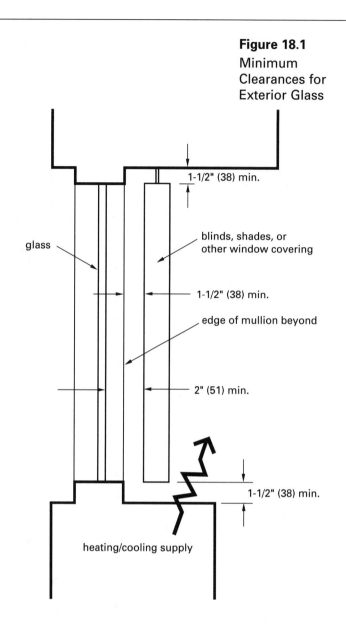

Figure 18.1
Minimum Clearances for Exterior Glass

Air diffusers 1 ft or 2 ft (300 or 600) square are commonly used in suspended acoustical ceilings because they fit within standard ceiling grids, are easy to install, and are inexpensive. They simply lay onto the grid like ceiling tile, as shown in Fig. 18.3(a). Similar types are available for gypsum wallboard and plaster ceilings. These usually have a trim flange that snaps onto the diffuser and covers the rough cut opening in the ceiling, as shown in Fig. 18.3(b).

Slot air diffusers can be used when the appearance of the air distribution device

Figure 18.2
Acoustic Seal
Detail for
Convector Cover

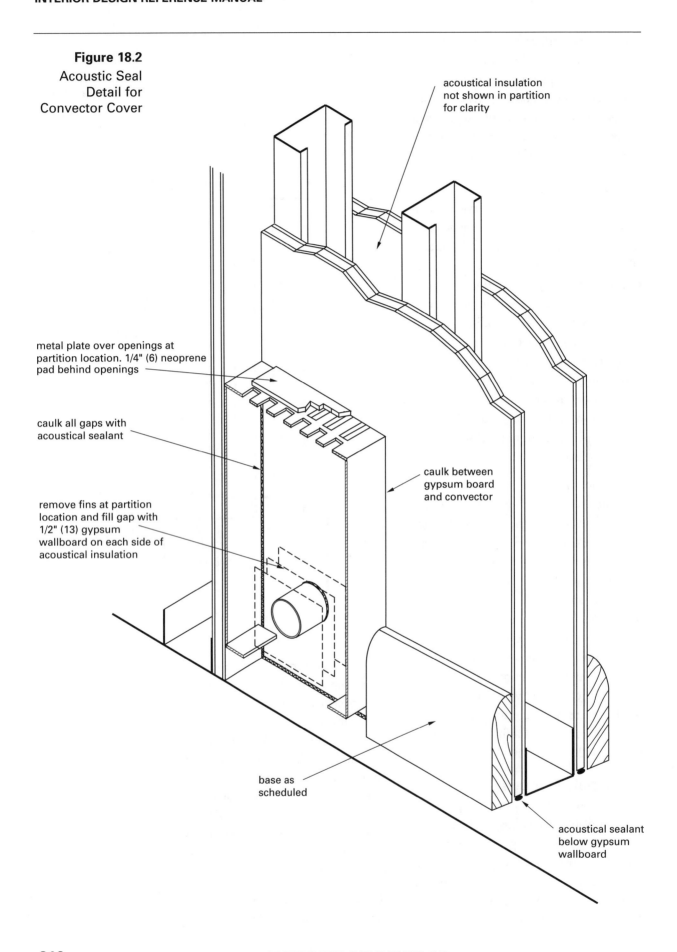

acoustical insulation
not shown in partition
for clarity

metal plate over openings at
partition location. 1/4" (6) neoprene
pad behind openings

caulk all gaps with
acoustical sealant

remove fins at partition
location and fill gap with
1/2" (13) gypsum
wallboard on each side of
acoustical insulation

caulk between
gypsum board
and convector

base as
scheduled

acoustical sealant
below gypsum
wallboard

needs to be minimized or when the available space does not allow a square diffuser. As shown in Fig. 18.3(c), these diffusers are long and narrow and contain from two to eight slots, resulting in a finished opening of about 3 in to 8 in (75 to 200) in width. They can be purchased in any length and used for either supply or return air. There is a box above the slots that is as long as the slots. Air is supplied by a flexible round duct attached to the side of the box. Slot air diffusers are available for either suspended acoustical ceilings or gypsum wallboard and plaster ceilings. However, they are usually used with wallboard ceilings to provide a trim, unobtrusive method of distributing air.

Energy Conservation with HVAC

Most of the energy conservation features related to heating, ventilating, and air conditioning are established by the architect and mechanical engineer in the original design of the building. However, there are some steps the interior designer can take to minimize energy use and improve indoor air quality. For example, the designer may plan a space to utilize daylighting as much as possible or may propose to use a displacement ventilation system. This type of system and other energy conservation techniques and issues are discussed in Ch. 26.

Reading HVAC Plans

Designers should know the basics of reading HVAC plans so they can review drawings to verify existing conditions and coordinate the interior design work with the mechanical engineer's work. HVAC drawings are normally drawn with single lines representing piping and ductwork. Figure 18.4 shows a portion of a typical commercial mechanical plan. Note that ducts are indicated with a line and a number such as 18 × 12. The first number indicates the width of the duct in inches,

Figure 18.3
Ceiling Details for Air Distribution

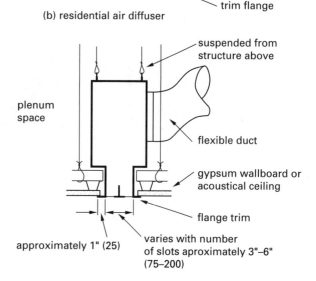

(a) lay-in air diffuser

(b) residential air diffuser

(c) slot air diffuser

and the second number indicates its height in inches.

Figure 14.20 shows some common mechanical drafting symbols with which candidates should also be familiar.

Figure 18.4
Partial HVAC Plan

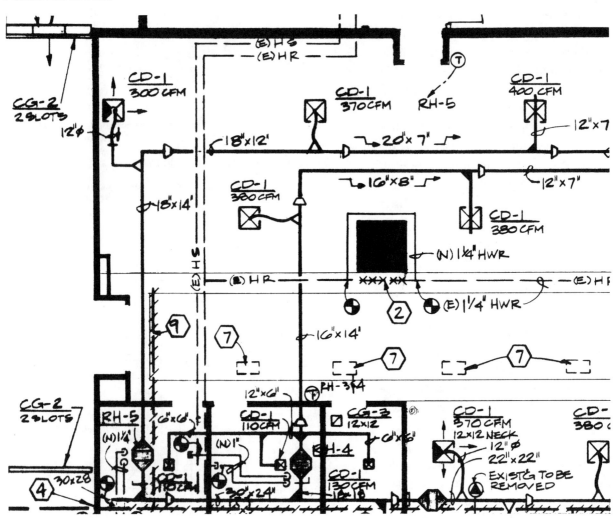

ELECTRICAL
Power System Requirements

Electrical systems include power for lighting (discussed in the next chapter), convenience outlets, and fixed equipment. As with lighting, the electrical engineer or electrical contractor designs and specifies the exact type of circuiting, wire sizes, and other technical aspects of the electrical systems. The interior designer, however, is often responsible for schematically showing the desired locations of outlets and switches, where power is required for special built-in equipment, and the appearance of cover plates and other visible electrical devices. The interior designer should also be familiar with the rudiments of power supply.

There are several types of conductors that supply power throughout a building. These extend from circuit breaker boxes to the individual switches, lights, and outlets. Nonmetallic (NM) sheathed cable, also known by the trade name *Romex®*, consists of two or more plastic-insulated conductors and ground wire surrounded by a moisture-resistant plastic jacket. This type of cable can be used in wood stud residential buildings and buildings not exceeding three floors, as long as it is used with wood studs and protected from damage by being concealed behind walls and ceilings.

Flexible metal-clad cable, or armored cable (AC), also known by the trade name *BX* (or the common term *flex*), consists of two or more plastic-insulated conductors encased in a continuous spiral-wound strip of steel tape. It is often used in remodeling work because it can be pulled through existing spaces within a building. It is also used to connect commercial light fixtures so they can be relocated in a suspended acoustical ceiling.

For commercial construction and large multifamily residential construction, individual plastic-insulated conductors must be placed in metal conduit or other approved carriers. Conduit supports and protects the wiring, serves as a system ground, and protects surrounding construction from fire if the wire overheats or shorts.

Another type of cabling is *under-carpet wiring*, thin, flat, protected wire that can be laid under carpet without protruding. Cable for both 120 V circuits and telephone lines is available, but it must be used with carpet tiles so that it is readily accessible.

Outlets and other types of connections to the power supply must be made in *junction boxes*, steel or approved plastic boxes to which the conduit or other cable system is attached. For single switches and duplex outlets, they measure about 2" × 4" (51 × 102). Larger boxes are 4 in (102) square, and several can be connected if there are more than two switches or two duplex outlets. Junction boxes are also required where light fixtures are connected to the electrical system.

Building codes specify requirements for all aspects of electrical systems, including the locations of outlets. In residential construction, outlets must be spaced no farther than 12 ft (3658) apart, and there must be a duplex outlet on each wall surface where furniture might be placed so lamp cords and the like do not have to be stretched across door openings.

In many commercial projects, special power outlets must be placed on their own circuit. These are called *dedicated circuits* and prevent various types of electrical interference from disturbing sensitive electrical equipment (such as computers) connected to them. These circuits should be clearly differentiated on the plan, and the exact electrical requirements of the equipment should be given to the electrical engineer. Circuits that require voltages greater than 120 V must also be identified. These include outlets for electric ranges, clothes dryers, large copy machines, and other special equipment.

In addition to the protection provided by circuit breakers in the panel boxes that trip off if the circuit is overloaded, there are two other types of protection provided in electrical wiring. The first is *grounding*, which is a separate wire in addition to the two that provide power. The grounding of an electrical system prevents a dangerous shock if someone touches an appliance with a short circuit and simultaneously touches a ground path such as a water pipe. The ground provides a path for the fault.

A ground fault, however, can create other problems, because the current required to trip a circuit breaker is high and small leaks of current can continue unnoticed until someone receives a dangerous shock or a fire develops. *Ground fault interrupters* (GFIs) are devices that detect small current leaks and disconnect the power to the circuit or appliance. GFIs can be a part of a circuit breaker or installed as an outlet. They are required for outdoor outlets and in bathrooms, basements, and kitchens as well as other locations specified in the National Electrical Code.

Telephone and Communication System Requirements

Telephone and communication systems are usually shown on the same plan as the power outlets. The interior designer is responsible for showing the locations of items like telephones, intercommunication systems, public address speakers, buzzers, and computer terminals. As with power outlets, the actual circuiting, wire sizes, and connections to central equipment are usually determined by the electrical engineer or the contractor responsible for installing the equipment.

Because telephone and communication systems are low-voltage systems, the requirements for conduit and other protection are not quite as stringent as for high-voltage power. In many cases, an outlet box is provided at the connection in the wall, and the wire is run within the walls and ceiling spaces without conduit. However, in some commercial construction all cable is required to be protected in conduit to avoid having it catch fire or release toxic fumes in case of a fire. Special plenum-rated cable is available that does not require conduit, but it is more expensive than standard cable.

Electrical System Plans

The interior designer can locate electrical, telephone, and communication outlets on one of several plans. For residential construction, they are often shown on the construction floor plan because the installation is fairly simple. On commercial projects where the floor plan may be crowded with other information, a separate power plan is often used. In addition to showing the outlets themselves, exact dimensions are given if their locations are critical. Outlets can also be shown on the furniture plan because they most often

directly relate to the placement of desks, seating groups, and other furniture. The power plans developed by the interior designer are then used by the electrical engineer to draw the electrical plan. This contains all the detailed information concerning circuiting, wire size, conduit size, panel boxes, and other data required by the electrical contractor. A typical power plan drawn by an interior designer is shown in Fig. 14.2. The corresponding electrical engineer's plan is shown in Fig. 14.3. As with mechanical plans, standard symbols are used to indicate common electrical items. Some of the more common ones are shown in Fig. 14.19.

PLUMBING

Interior designers are often required to locate plumbing fixtures in both new construction and remodeling work. Because plumbing can be a significant cost item and imposes limitations on space planning, the designer should have a good understanding of plumbing basics and how to coordinate the design with existing building services.

Plumbing System Requirements

Plumbing systems consist of two major components: water supply and drainage. Water supply includes cold and hot water. In all plumbing installation, residential or commercial, water is supplied under pressure to individual plumbing fixtures. Because of this and because the pipes are generally small, it is relatively easy to locate pipes within wall cavities, ceiling structure, and other areas to supply a fixture, even if it is some distance from the main source of water. Figure 18.5 shows a schematic representation of a small water supply system.

Drainage systems present a more difficult problem because they work by gravity; drain pipes must be sloped downward to

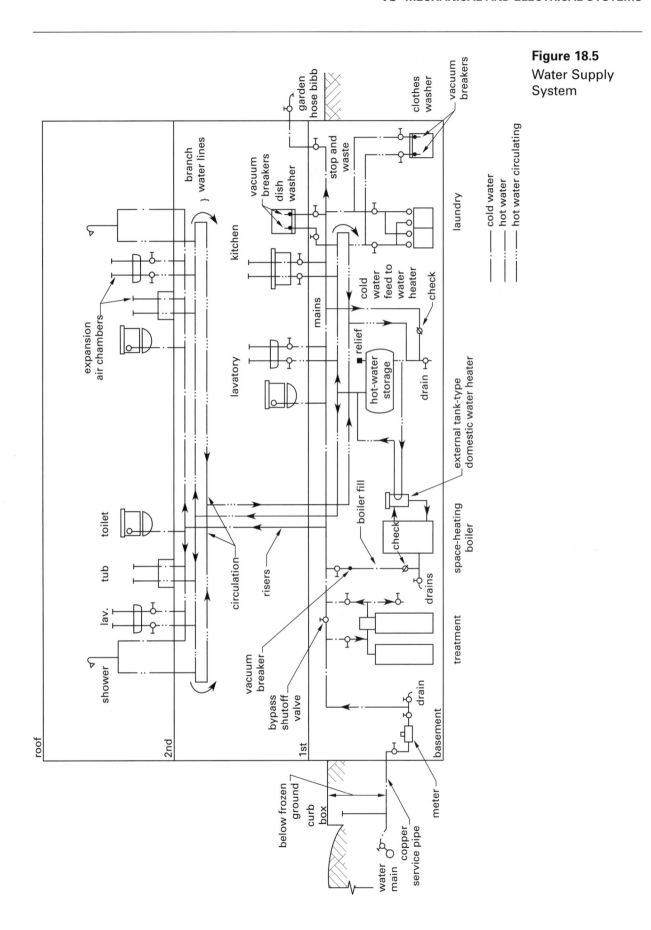

Figure 18.5
Water Supply
System

carry away wastes. In addition, vent pipes are required. Figure 18.6 shows a simplified diagram of a typical drainage and vent system. Beginning with the individual fixture, there are a number of components with which the designer should be familiar.

The first component attached to the fixture is the *trap*. With a few exceptions, traps are located at every fixture and are designed to catch and hold a quantity of water to provide a seal that prevents gases from the sewage system from entering the building. The locations where traps are not installed include fixtures that have traps as an integral part of their design, such as toilets, and where two or three adjacent fixtures are connected, such as a double kitchen sink.

Traps are connected to the actual drainage piping, but they must also be connected to vents. *Vents* are pipes connected to the drainage system at various locations, open

to outside air, and designed to serve two purposes. First, they allow built-up sewage gases to escape instead of bubble through the water in the traps. Second, they allow pressure in the system to equalize so discharging waste does not create a siphon that would drain the water out of the traps.

From the trap, sewage travels in fixture branch lines to a vertical stack. If the stack carries human waste from toilets, it is called a *soil stack*. If the stack carries wastes other than human waste, it is known as a *waste stack*.

Vents from individual fixtures are connected above the fixtures in two ways. If a vent connects to a soil or waste stack above the highest fixture in the system, the portion of the stack above this point is known as a *stack vent*. The stack vent extends through the roof. In multistory buildings, a separate pipe is used for venting. This is called a *vent stack* and either extends through the roof or connects with the stack vent above the highest fixture as shown in Fig. 18.6.

Locating Plumbing Fixtures

Because of the cost of plumbing and the necessity of sloping drainage pipes, plumbing fixtures should be located close to existing plumbing lines. These include horizontal lines or vertical risers that run continuously through a multistory building. Drains must be sloped a minimum of $1/4$ in/ft (6 mm/300 mm) (or $1/8$ in/ft (3 mm/300 mm) for pipes larger than 3 in (76.2)). If a pipe must be concealed within a floor space, then the slope and size of the pipe itself will limit the distance from the fixture to a connection with a riser.

In commercial buildings, most plumbing is concentrated in one area near the core; from this location, it serves the toilet rooms, drinking fountains, and similar facilities. To provide service to sinks, private

Figure 18.6
Drainage and
Vent System

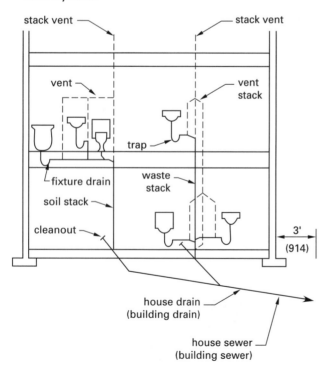

toilets, and the like, wet columns are sometimes included in the building. These are areas, usually at a structural column location, where hot and cold supply and drainage risers are located. Individual tenants can easily tap into these lines, if desired, without having to connect to more remote plumbing at the core of the building.

If extensive plumbing work is required, the necessary pipes may not fit within the space provided by standard partitions. Soil stacks from toilets, for example, require 4 in (102) diameter pipes that have an actual outside diameter somewhat larger than 4 in. In this case, plumbing chases are required. These are constructed with two sets of studs having a space between that is large enough for the pipes.

Plumbing Plans

Like HVAC plans, plumbing plans are drafted by the mechanical engineer and represent piping and other components with single line diagrams and standard drafting symbols. Plumbing plan symbols with which the designer should be familiar with are shown in Fig. 14.18.

FIRE PROTECTION AND LIFE SAFETY

Fire protection and life safety in buildings addresses three major objectives: the protection of life, the protection of property, and the restoration and continued use of the building after a fire. Life safety also involves the protection of people during emergencies other than fire, such as earthquakes, floods, terrorist threats, and similar disasters. However, this section only deals with life safety during fires.

Fire protection in buildings is accomplished by

- preventing fires
- early fire detection and alarm
- providing for quick exiting of building occupants
- containing the fire
- suppressing the fire

Fire prevention includes limiting the products of combustion and other hazardous situations that could lead to starting a fire. Building codes address these concerns in a number of ways that include setting forth minimum flame-spread ratings and establishing flammability standards and similar constraints. These issues and exiting are discussed in Chs. 27 and 28.

Fire detection systems and alarms are critical, to provide sufficient warning for occupants to leave the building and to alert firefighters so that extinguishing efforts can begin before the fire spreads. Fire containment is achieved through building materials, compartmentation, and smoke control. Fire suppression is achieved through fire detection and alarms, sprinkler systems, standpipes, and other methods. These topics are reviewed in the following sections.

Compartmentation

Compartmentation is a critical concept in fire and life safety. The basic idea is to contain a fire and limit its spread, both to allow building occupants to escape and to protect other parts of the building that are not initially subject to the fire. In high-rise buildings, where it may not be practical to evacuate the building immediately, compartmentation can provide places of refuge where occupants can wait until the fire is extinguished or until they can exit safely. Compartmentation provides time for fire suppression, either by automatic sprinklers or by fire fighting personnel.

Compartmentation has been integral to building codes for a long time. Codes require fire separation between different occupancies, between use areas and exits, and between parts of a building when the maximum allowable area is exceeded. Separation is required both vertically, with fire-resistive floor-ceiling assemblies, and horizontally, with fire-rated walls. Any openings through fire assemblies must also provide protection from the spread of fire and smoke. These topics are covered in Ch. 27.

On a smaller scale, structural members are isolated, to protect them from the effects of fire and prevent structural collapse. In addition, the sizes of concealed areas above ceilings, in attics, in pipe chases, and under floors are limited, to prevent the spread of fire, since a fire in these parts of a building would be especially difficult to extinguish. Fire stops in stud spaces between the first and second floors of a house are one important example of this kind of small-scale compartmentation.

Although a building's architect designs much of the building's compartmentation during the initial design, interior designers should understand the concept of compartmentation and be able to recognize the various building elements that function to compartmentalize a building. In some cases, the designer is responsible for maintaining compartmentation by designing components such as corridors and occupancy separations.

Smoke Control

Because more deaths and injuries occur in fires due to inhalation of smoke and other gases rather than due to flame and heat exposure, *smoke control* is one of the most important aspects of fire protection. Smoke is particularly troublesome because many factors cause it to move rapidly through a building, well beyond the location of the fire. Smoke moves by the natural convection forces caused by differential air pressure between cool and warm air. In multistoried buildings, especially tall ones, the stack effect also pulls smoke through any vertical penetration such as stairways,

elevator shafts, mechanical shafts, and atriums. Smoke spread is exacerbated by HVAC systems that can potentially distribute smoke a great distance from the original source.

There are several elements to smoke control. These include containment, exhaust, and to a lesser degree, dilution. The same compartmentation that is used to contain fires is also used to contain the spread of smoke. Devices such as fire dampers, gaskets on fire doors, and automatic closing fire doors seal openings in fire walls. Containing smoke to one area of the building allows places of refuge to be established. However, containment alone is not enough. This is why mechanical systems for high-rise buildings and other structures are designed to exhaust smoke from a structure.

The architect and mechanical engineer of a building are responsible for designing the basic elements of a smoke control system, which include building elements as well as mechanical system components. The interior designer should be aware of the methods used for smoke control in a building and do nothing to compromise either the passive or active methods of smoke control.

Fire Detection and Alarms

In most structures, both commercial and residential, life safety codes require some type of fire or smoke detection device. Although the mechanical engineer is responsible for specifying and locating the devices required, the interior designer must understand the types of detectors and the coordination of their locations on the reflected ceiling plan within the parameters of life safety and building codes.

There are four basic types of fire detection devices. The first is the *ionization detector*, which responds to products of combustion-ionized particles rather than to smoke. Ionization detectors are not appropriate where fires may produce a lot of smoke but few particles. Because they can detect particles from a smoldering fire before the fire bursts into flames, these devices are considered early warning detectors.

Photoelectric detectors respond to smoke, which obscures a light beam in the device. These are useful where potential fires may produce a great deal of smoke before bursting into flames.

Rise-of-temperature detectors sense the presence of heat and can be set to trip an alarm when a particular temperature is reached in the room. The major disadvantage is that flames must usually be present before the alarm temperature is reached. By that time it may be too late, because a fire can smolder and produce deadly smoke long before it reaches the flame stage.

There are also *flame detectors* that respond to infrared or ultraviolet radiation given off by flames. However, like rise-of-temperature detectors, they do not give an early warning of smoldering fires.

In many buildings, a combination of fire detection devices must be used depending on the particular type of space in which the devices are placed. For example, an ionization device would not operate properly where air currents or other circumstances would prevent the products of combustion from entering the device.

The building code states the required types and locations of fire detectors. Detectors are required near fire doors, in exit corridors, in individual hotel rooms, in bedrooms, and in places of public assembly. They are also often required in main-supply and return-air ducts. Codes usually require them in other spaces based on a given area coverage.

When activated, fire detectors can be wired to trigger a general audible alarm as well as visual alarm lights for the deaf. They can also activate a central monitoring station or a municipal fire station. In large buildings with a central station, the detection of a fire also activates fire dampers, exhaust systems, the closing of fire doors, and other preventive measures as the alarm is being signaled to fire officials.

Sprinkler Systems

The most common type of suppression system is a sprinkler system. Fire sprinkler systems are becoming more prevalent in construction because of increasingly more stringent building code regulations and because of the awareness of owners and insurance companies of the systems' ability to minimize property damage and improve life safety. For example, the IBC requires sprinklers in buildings over 75 ft (22 860) high.

In most construction, only the sprinkler heads are visible and a variety of styles are available, including recessed, upright, pendent, and sidewall. Recessed types have a smooth cover that is flush with the ceiling. When there is a fire, the cover falls away and the sprinkler head lowers and activates. Upright heads are used with exposed plumbing and high, unfinished ceilings. Pendent sprinklers are the traditional types for finished ceilings, but their heads extend a few inches below the ceiling. Sidewall heads are used for corridors and small rooms when one row of sprinklers will provide adequate coverage for narrow spaces. Horizontal sidewall sprinklers also can be plumbed from the walls instead of from the ceiling, which makes them good for remodeling work.

Although the interior designer does not design sprinkler systems, the designer should recognize that the required locations of sprinkler heads must be coordinated with other ceiling-mounted items. In addition, sprinkler pipes above the ceiling require additional space that may interfere with recessed lighting and other ceiling construction.

The design and installation of fire sprinkler systems is governed by each local building code, but most codes refer to NFPA 13, Standard for the Installation of Sprinkler Systems, published by the National Fire Protection Association. This standard classifies the relative fire hazard of buildings into three groups: light, ordinary, and extra hazard. Each hazard classification is further divided into groups. The hazard classification determines the required spacing of sprinklers and other regulations.

For example, light hazard includes occupancies such as residences, offices, hospitals, schools, and restaurants. In these occupancies there must be one sprinkler for each 200 ft^2 (18.6 m^2), or 225 ft^2 (20.9 m^2) if the design of the system is hydraulically calculated. For open-wood joist ceilings, the area drops to 130 ft^2 (12.1 m^2). Maximum spacing between sprinkler heads is 15 ft (4.6 m) for the 225 ft^2 coverage requirement, with the maximum distance from a wall being one-half the required spacing.

Standpipes

Standpipes are pipes that run the height of a building and provide water outlets at each floor to which fire fighting hoses can be connected. They are located within the stairway or, in the case of pressurized enclosures, within the vestibule. The interior designer does not design these portions of the fire protection system. However, if they are encountered, they cannot be covered or otherwise modified.

Other Extinguishing Agents

Although sprinkler systems are the most common type of automatic extinguishing system, others are available.

Portable fire extinguishers are helpful for stopping small fires in the early stages of development. There are four general classes of extinguisher: A, B, C, and D. These classes correspond to the four fire types. Fires of type A involve ordinary combustibles of paper, wood, and cloth. Fire extinguishers for these fires contain water or water-based agents. B fires involve flammable liquids such as gasoline, solvents, and paints. B extinguishers contain smothering types of chemicals like carbon dioxide, foam, and halogenated agents. C fires involve electrical equipment, and the corresponding extinguisher contains nonconductive agents. Finally, class D fires involve combustible metals. Each type of fire must be fought with a suitable extinguisher. Combination extinguishers are also available for type A, B, and C fires.

Halogenated agents, commonly referred to as *halon,* are used where water might damage the contents of a room, like in computer installations. Halon is a gas that chemically inhibits the spread of fire. However, halon is a CFC gas that can damage the ozone layer, so alternate extinguishing agents will be used in the future.

Various types of foam can also be used to smother fires. Foam is commonly used where flammable liquid fires might occur, for example, in industrial plants or aircraft hangars.

Another type of extinguishing agent is actually a building material and acts passively in reaction to a fire. *Intumescent materials* respond to fire by expanding rapidly, insulating the surfaces they protect or filling gaps to prevent the passage of fire, heat, and smoke. They are available in the form of strips, caulk, paint, and spreadable putty. For example, a strip of intumescent material placed along the edge of one of a pair of fire doors will expand and seal the crack, substituting for an astragal (moulding) that would otherwise be required. Intumescent paints can be applied to protect normally flammable wood.

SECURITY

In addition to physical barriers, mechanical and electrical security systems include methods for preventing entry, detecting intruders, controlling access to secure areas, and notification in the event of unauthorized entry or other emergencies. The types of hardware and electronic devices that are used depend on the nature of the threat, the level of security desired, and the amount of money that can be devoted to the system. This section outlines some of the more common devices with which interior designers should be familiar.

Intrusion Detection

Security derived from intrusion detection devices can be classified into three types: perimeter protection, area or room protection, and object protection.

Perimeter Protection

Perimeter protection secures the entry points to a space or building. Devices in this category include doors, windows, and skylights, and can also include ducts, tunnels, and other service entrances. Some of the more common types of perimeter protection include the following.

- *Magnetic contacts:* These are used on doors and windows to either sound an alarm when the contact is broken (the door or window is opened) or send a signal to a central monitoring and control station. These can be surface mounted, recessed into the door and frame, or concealed in special hinges. The hinges may only be available in certain sizes and finishes; therefore, the other hardware used on the job must be coordinated with them.

- *Glass break detectors:* These sense when a window has been broken or cut, either by using metallic foil or with a small vibration detector mounted on the glass.

- *Window screens:* These screens have fine wires embedded in them that can be used to set off an alarm when they are cut or broken.

- *Photoelectric cells:* These cells detect when the beam has been broken, either by a door opening or by someone passing through an opening. These can be surface mounted but are more secure and look better if provisions are made to recess them in the partition or other construction.

Area or Room Protection

Area or room protection devices sense when someone is in a room or an area within the field of coverage. These devices have the advantage of warning of unauthorized entry when perimeter sensors have not been activated. Area intrusion devices include the following.

- *Photoelectric beams:* These beams warn of intrusion by sending a pulsed infrared beam across a space. If the beam is broken, the device either sounds an alarm or sends a signal to a monitoring station. Photoelectric beams can be focused in both large and small areas. The equipment is small and usually can be recessed or concealed.

- *Infrared detectors:* These detectors sense sources of infrared radiation, such as the human body, compared with the normal room radiation. They are unobtrusive but must have a clear field of view of the area they are protecting.

- *Audio detectors:* These detectors listen for unusual sounds in a space at levels above what is normally encountered. When that level is exceeded, an alarm is sounded. Microphones can also be used to continuously monitor all sounds in a space through a speaker at a central monitoring station.

- *Pressure sensors:* These sensors detect weight on a floor or on other surfaces. Sensor mats can be separate fixtures laid over the existing floor finish or placed under carpet or other building materials.

- *Ultrasonic detectors:* These detectors emit a very high-frequency sound wave. When an intruder interrupts this wave, an alarm signal is activated. The range of ultrasonic detectors is limited to a space about 12 ft (3.7 m) high and 20' × 30' in area (6.1 m × 9.1 m).

• *Microwave detectors:* These detectors emit a field of microwave radiation and sense interruptions in that field. Their use is limited in interior construction, however, because the microwave radiation can penetrate most building materials and can be reflected by metal.

Object Protection

Object protection is used to sense movement or tampering with individual objects, such as safes, artwork, file cabinets, or other equipment. *Capacitance proximity detectors* detect when metal objects are touched. *Vibration detectors* sense a disturbance of the object. *Infrared motion detectors* determine if the space around an object is violated.

Electronic Surveillance

Electronic surveillance is the interception of sound and electromagnetic signals with remote sensing devices. For example, with readily obtainable, relatively inexpensive technology, it is possible to listen in on conversations from outside a building or pick up signals being emitted from a computer screen at a remote distance. For organizations that require security from this type of intrusion, special rooms are required that have electromagnetic or radio frequency shielding.

Sensitive government installations have used such shielding for some time. It is just recently that many private companies are realizing they must protect themselves from corporate espionage as well as from other types of theft.

The basic principle behind electronic shielding involves building a "cage" of continuously conductive material that catches signals and conducts them to the ground. The type of cage depends on the amount of protection required and the

bandwidth that must be shielded. The rating of protection is measured in decibels (dB) of attenuation. Many government and military facilities are designed for 100 dB attenuation across a broad bandwidth of signals. Theoretically, this level provides 100% protection. However, this level of protection requires heavy steel plate and expensive special construction. For most corporate needs, an attenuation of 60 dB stops more than 99.9% of the electronic signals coming from office computers and other sources.

To achieve acceptable levels of protection for most corporate uses, there are several products available. Copper foils can be used, but these are difficult to install and require soldered connections. There is also nonwoven fabric that is covered with an electronically conductive metallic coating. As with copper foil, this is placed behind the finished wall surface so it is not obtrusive. Other types of fabric material are also available, as is metallic shielding paint. For windows, fine metal screens can be used, but special shielded glass that looks like normal glass is also available. Doors designed for radio frequency or electromagnetic shielding are also required. In addition to the conductive cage, filters must be provided for electrical, telephone, and computer cabling where they penetrate the shielding membrane.

In most cases, detailing rooms protected from electronic surveillance is straightforward and unobtrusive, but a security expert should be consulted for specific product specifications and detailing requirements.

Access Control

Access Control Devices

Access to secure areas can be controlled with a number of devices. The simplest is the traditional mechanical lock. The various types of locksets are described in Ch. 10. High-security locksets are available that provide an additional level of security through the use of key types that are difficult to duplicate, special tumbler mechanisms, and long-throw dead bolts. There are also interlocking dead bolts that secure the door bolt to the strike so that the door jamb cannot be spread to disengage the bolt from the frame. To prevent knobs or lever handles from being torqued apart or otherwise opened by brute force or jimmying, most lock manufacturers provide security strikes, cover plates, cylinder guards, and other devices to make it more difficult to open a locked door.

Because access and duplication of keys can be a problem even for the most secure mechanical lock, various types of electronic locks are available. Not only can these selectively control access better than keys, but they can also monitor who enters and exits a door and can record the date and time of the access.

Card readers are common electronic access control devices. A plastic card containing a coded magnetic strip is used to unlock the door when a valid card is passed through the reader. Card readers can be connected to a central monitoring computer that keeps a log of which person's card was used to open which door and when that door was opened. The computer can be programmed to only allow certain cards to operate certain doors.

Operation can be further limited to specific hours during the day and specific days of the week. If a card is lost or stolen, its access code can be quickly and easily removed from the system.

In most instances, a card reader is mounted on the partition adjacent to the door. Proximity readers are also available that can be completely concealed behind a wall to prevent tampering and minimize the visual impact of the reader. To operate the reader, the user simply has to place the card near the reader. Some readers will sense the card in a person's wallet or purse when it is within a few feet from the device.

Numbered keyboards operate in the same way, by unlocking a door when the user enters the correct numerical code. However, numbered keyboards do not provide the same flexibility as magnetic cards. Numbered keypads can also be purchased integrated with a knob or lever handle. These are not connected to a central station, but they do eliminate the problem with key control of standard locksets.

A variation on the magnetic card reader is the punched card access system used by many hotels. The key code can be changed each time a new person checks into a room; therefore, a previous occupant cannot copy or reuse a key.

New biometric devices are now available that can read individual biological features, such as the retina of the eye or a hand print, providing a counterfeit-proof method of identification. Although expensive, these devices are feasible when a very high level of security is required. Work is continuing on developing commercially available devices that can recognize voiceprints and fingerprints.

Locking Mechanisms

Card readers and other devices control the operation of one of several types of locking mechanisms. One type is the electric lock, which retracts the bolt when activated from the secure side of the door. Unlatching from the inside is done by a button or switch or by mechanical retraction of the bolt with the lever handle. Electric locks require an electric hinge or other power-transfer device to carry the low-voltage wiring from the control device to the door and then to the lock.

Electric strikes are also used. These replace the standard door strike and consist of a movable mechanism that is mortised into the frame. The latch bolt is fixed from the secure side of the door. Upon activation, the electric strike retracts, allowing the door to be opened. On the inside, the latch bolt can be retracted by mechanical means with the lever handle.

Electric bolts are available that drop into a mortised fitting in the top or side of a door. Upon activation, the bolt retracts, allowing normal operation of the door. A fail-safe feature retracts the bolt if there is a power failure or upon activation of a fire alarm. Electric bolts are limited to use on non-exit doors because most building codes now require electronically controlled exit doors to be operable from the inside by purely mechanical means.

Doors can also be secured with electromagnetic locks. When activated, the lock holds the door closed with a powerful magnetic force. Card readers, keypads, buttons, or other devices deactivate the electromagnet. These can be designed to open upon activation of a fire alarm or in case of a power failure.

Notification Systems

When intrusion is detected, an alarm signal is triggered. This signal can activate an alarm, such as a bell or horn, turn on lights, alert an attendant at a central control station, or be relayed over phone lines to a central security service. Combinations of all three notifications are also possible. If an office building has a central station, a building tenant may be able to connect special lease-space security with the central station. When a central station is notified, the alarms are automatically recorded in the system.

Coordination with Electrical and Signal Systems

Although the security consultant, equipment vendor, electrical engineering consultant, and contractor are responsible for designing and installing security systems and providing the power these systems need to operate, the interior designer is often the person who must coordinate the efforts of these team members so that their work fits within the overall interior design and construction of the project. In most cases this involves making sure necessary information is transmitted between the members of the team and that all required data and details are shown on the final set of drawings. It also requires that the interior designer design and detail portions of the construction to accommodate the security equipment. Some of the important elements of electrical and signal system coordination include the following.

• Lighting required for surveillance and deterrence should be compatible with the general ambient lighting whenever possible.

• The closed circuit television (CCTV) vendor needs to know what type of lighting will be used to select the best type of camera tube. Conversely, the electrical engineer may need to provide a particular type of lighting for specific types of cameras.

• The interior designer must provide adequate space and support for video cameras, monitors, access devices, and control equipment. The electrical engineer needs to design power supplies to these devices as well.

• Speakers may be required for public address and communication within secured areas and near doors. These should be coordinated with the other elements of the designer's reflected ceiling plan or partition detailing.

• Conduit must be shown on the electrical consultant's drawings, to accommodate signal system wiring for CCTV, remote-controlled locks, and other security equipment.

• Power transfers for doors should be specified to meet the necessary level of security but should be concealed whenever possible.

VERTICAL TRANSPORTATION

Vertical transportation includes stairs, elevators, and escalators, but the NCIDQ exam only covers stairways. The design of stairs is usually the responsibility of the architect, but there are times when the interior designer must design them. Residential projects may require new or remodeled stairways, and the interior designer should be familiar with their basic requirements. If elevators are being installed or remodeled, the interior designer may be concerned with the interior finishes of the cab, the elevator entrances, and the signal system of call buttons and up/down lanterns.

Although there are many ways a stairway can be designed, there are certain basic elements that each must share to be safe and comfortable to use. These are shown in Fig. 18.7. Building codes set certain restrictions on the rise and run of exit stairs (the vertical and horizontal portions) as well as on handrail design and landings. These are discussed in more detail in Ch. 28.

In addition to the terms shown in Fig. 18.7, there are some other definitions with which the designer should be familiar. A *step* is that portion of egress achieving a change in elevation by means of a single riser. A *stairway* is a change in elevation having two or more risers. A *flight* is a series of two or more risers between one floor or landing and the next. A *landing* is the flat portion immediately adjacent to either the bottom or top of a flight of stairs. A landing must be as wide as the stairway serves.

Note that the International Building Code (IBC) does not have a definition for

Figure 18.7
Parts of a Stairway

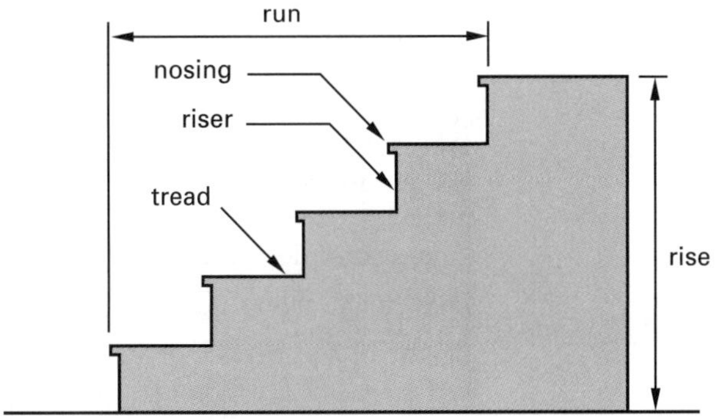

"step" and defines a stair as one or more risers. This will require future design changes in those jurisdictions that adopt the IBC. For example, a single step will require handrails on both sides, unlike the requirements under the current Uniform Building Code. Refer to Chs. 27 and 28 for more information about building code requirements.

The first decision the interior designer must make when designing a stair is the basic configuration; that is, how the steps are arranged to get from one level to the next. The most common configurations of stairways are straight runs, either in a single line, L-shape, or U-shape. The exact layout of a stair depends on the space available, where people have to start on one floor and end on the other, the floor-to-floor distance, aesthetic concerns, and code requirements.

There are three special types of stairways shown in Fig. 18.8: winding, circular, and spiral. *Winding stairways* have tapered treads that are wider at one end than the other. *Circular stairways* have sides whose shape is a circular arc. The inside, or smaller arc, cannot be less than twice the width of the stair. If it is, it is considered a winding stairway. *Spiral stairways* use wedge-shaped treads that radiate from a center support column. Winding, circular, and spiral stairways can only be used as exit stairs in private homes and in private stairways of apartments, condominiums, and the like, and only if they meet specific requirements as discussed in Ch. 28. In the IBC they are also allowed if they are *not* a required stair.

The second decision the interior designer must make when designing a stair is the height of the riser and the length of the tread. For comfort and safety, these dimensions are interrelated and are based on the normal adult stride. As the riser gets lower, the tread increases to maintain a certain relationship. Generally, the height of the riser must be determined first so each riser between the floors is identical within minimum and maximum code limitations. Then the appropriate tread

dimension is calculated. There are several formulas for this, but the most common is

$$2R + T = 25 \text{ in} \quad (635 \text{ mm})$$

R is the riser height in inches, and T is the tread width in inches. For example, if the riser is $6^1/_2$ in, the tread should be

$$(2)(6.5) + T = 25$$
$$T = 25 - (2)(6.5)$$
$$= 12 \text{ in}$$

For most stairs, a 7 in (178) riser and an 11 in (279) tread is a good combination and satisfies the IBC, which limits risers to 7 in (178) in most stairways (7.75 in (197) in residential stairways). The minimum tread width by code is 11 in (or 10 in (254) in residential stairways). If the riser height must be modified to equalize the stairs between a fixed floor height, a dimension between 6 in and 7 in (152 and 178) should be used.

Additional considerations in stair design are the nosing, which normally extends about an inch from the back of the tread, and the handrail as shown in Fig. 28.10. To be accessible for the physically disabled, both the nosing and the handrail must be designed according to certain requirements as specified in Chs. 28 and 29.

Wood stairs are typically used for residential construction and can be constructed in an almost unlimited number of styles and details. Figure 18.9 illustrates a typical site-built wood stairway and the common construction components. Wood carriages are cut out of 2" × 12" (51 × 305) members to form the supports for the treads and risers. If carpeting is used, the treads and risers are finished with plywood or particleboard. If exposed hardwood is used, either the treads can be finished with prebuilt treads with rounded nosings or strip flooring can be applied over an underlayment of particleboard.

Figure 18.8
Non-Straight
Stair Types

winding

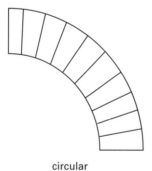

circular

spiral

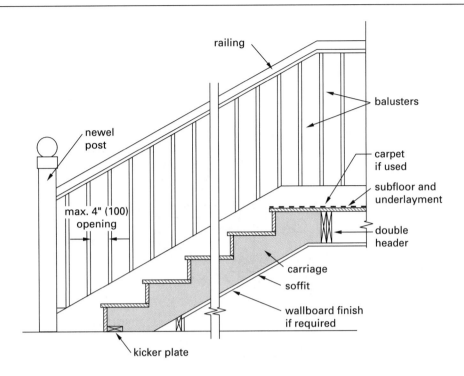

Figure 18.9
Wood Stair
Construction

For commercial construction, metal stairs are typically used. Although there are several variations on the type and detailing, a common method of building steel stairs uses preformed steel risers and treads welded to a supporting framework of steel channels and angles. See Fig. 18.10. For utility stairs, the stringers are normally steel channels with the flanges of the channel on each side pointing away from the stairs. Landings are constructed of steel plate supported on channels and stiffening angles. The treads and landings are filled with 1^1/$_2$" to 2" (38 to 50) of concrete. Any finish material used is applied over this supporting framework. If the underside of the stair needs to be finished, metal studs may be attached to the steel framework and covered with gypsum wallboard or other material.

More decorative steel or ornamental metal stairs are fabricated using similar techniques. The railing is made from ornamental metal or wood, and the railing support can be metal, tempered glass, or some other type of custom-designed assembly.

DEFINITIONS

chase: an enclosed vertical area for pipes or ductwork that runs from one floor to another

convector: a unit or device that radiates heat from water to the surrounding air, usually through closely spaced fins. Convectors are usually placed against a wall under a window.

fire damper: a device placed in a duct that is designed to automatically close when subjected to a certain increase in temperature or with the detection of smoke

flight: a series of two or more risers between one floor or landing and the next

HVAC: acronym for heating, ventilating, and air conditioning

lintel: a horizontal structural member over an opening that carries the weight of the wall above it

Figure 18.10
Steel Stair
Construction

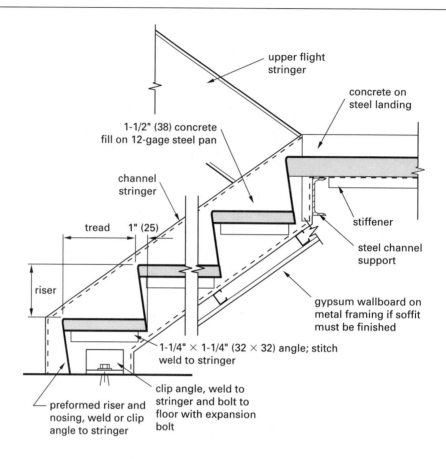

upper flight stringer

concrete on steel landing

1-1/2" (38) concrete fill on 12-gage steel pan

channel stringer

tread   1" (25)

riser

stiffener

steel channel support

gypsum wallboard on metal framing if soffit must be finished

1-1/4" × 1-1/4" (32 × 32) angle; stitch weld to stringer

clip angle, weld to stringer and bolt to floor with expansion bolt

preformed riser and nosing, weld or clip angle to stringer

plenum: the space between a suspended ceiling and the main structure above

stairway: a change in elevation having two or more risers. (In the IBC, a stairway is a change in elevation of one or more risers.)

step: that portion of egress achieving a change in elevation by means of a single riser

SAMPLE QUESTIONS

1. The device that controls the volume of air and its distribution in an HVAC system is called a

(A) convector

(B) grille

(C) register

(D) duct

2. What type of system would be best for an open office plan so the heating and cooling for each workstation could be individually controlled?

(A) all-air

(B) all-water

(C) radiant panel

(D) air-water

3. What is NOT allowed in a return-air plenum?

(A) fire dampers

(B) electrical cable

(C) water supply pipes

(D) wood blocking

4. In working with an electrical engineer on a project, what information would the designer most likely put on the interior design power plan?

(A) switch locations

(B) dedicated outlets

(C) conduit sizing

(D) speaker locations

5. What type of sprinkler head should be used for a decorative, open-grid, wood-slat ceiling suspended from the structural floor above?

(A) upright

(B) pendent

(C) sidewall

(D) recessed

6. In the following diagram, what is the name for the portion of stair identified by A?

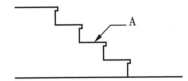

(A) riser

(B) tread

(C) nosing

(D) run

7. In specifying new window coverings and track to replace building standard window coverings, what coordination is LEAST important for the interior designer to undertake?

(A) asking the electrical engineer if the new light reflectance is detrimental

(B) verifying that the building owner does not care about the change in the building's exterior appearance

(C) determining if the mechanical engineer objects to the replacement plans

(D) checking with the architect to see that the new coverings do not adversely affect the heating of the glass

8. What does the symbol shown indicate?

(A) recessed directional light

(B) suspended exit light

(C) floor telephone outlet

(D) fire alarm horn

9. What would be the best combination of dimensions for a stair serving a sleeping loft in a condominium where space was at a premium and the floor-to-floor dimension was 9 ft 4 in?

(A) 7 in riser, 11 in tread

(B) 7 in riser, 9 in tread

(C) 8 in riser, 9 in tread

(D) 8 in riser, 10 in tread

10. What would NOT be allowed in an access floor with removable panels?

(A) computer cable

(B) plumbing

(C) HVAC

(D) electrical conduit

11. In a plenum, how can a fire be prevented from spreading horizontally?

(A) install sprinkler systems

(B) use fire-rated dividers

(C) use fiberglass material

(D) install fire dampers

12. A client has requested that special security protection be provided for critical paper files containing corporate trade secrets, but at a reasonable cost. In designing the file room, the interior designer should suggest

(A) card readers at the doors leading to the file room

(B) photoelectric beams within the room

(C) magnetic contacts on all doors leading to the file room

(D) electronic shielding of the file room

13. In a nonresidential building, how many stair risers equals a flight?

(A) 1

(B) 2

(C) 3

(D) 12

14. What term is used to denote the member supporting the treads in a wood stairway?

(A) carriage

(B) header

(C) saddle

(D) stringer

15. In designing a new space, the interior designer can influence life safety the most by coordinating with consultants concerning

(A) compartmentation

(B) fire detection

(C) smoke control

(D) sprinklers

16. If all of the following are present, what must be modified to achieve acoustic separation in a perimeter office?

(A) acoustical tiles

(B) gypsum wallboard

(C) convector

(D) batt insulation

19

LIGHTING

LIGHTING FUNDAMENTALS

Light is defined as visually evaluated radiant energy. Visible light is a form of electromagnetic radiation with wavelengths that range from about 400 nm (4×10^{-9} m) for violet light to about 700 nm (7×10^{-9} m) for red light. White light is produced when a source emits approximately equal quantities of energy over the entire visible spectrum.

Definitions

There is a relationship among several illumination definitions. Figure 19.1 shows these units of light.

Candlepower (cp) is the unit of luminous intensity approximately equal to the horizontal light output from an ordinary wax candle. In the SI (metric) system of measurement, this unit is the candela (cd).

Lumen (lm) is the unit of luminous flux equal to the flux in a unit solid angle of one steradian (1 sr) from a uniform point source of one candlepower (1 cp). On a unit sphere (1 ft radius), an area of 1 ft^2 will subtend an angle of 1 sr. Because the area of a unit sphere is 4π, a source of 1 cp produces 12.57 lm.

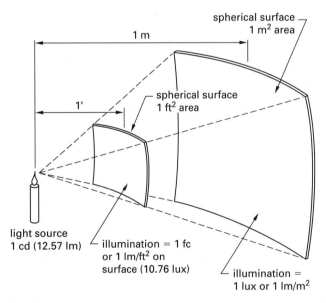

Figure 19.1
Relationship of Light Source and Illumination

If surface has a reflectance of 50%, then its reflected brightness is 1/2 ftL (1.7 cd/m^2).

Illuminance is the density of luminous flux incident on a surface in lumens per unit area. 1 lm uniformly incident on 1 ft^2 of area produces an illuminance of 1 fc. In SI units, the measurement is lux (lx), or lumens per square meter ($1m/m^2$).

Luminance is the luminous flux per unit of projected (apparent) area and unit solid angle leaving a surface, either reflected or transmitted. By definition, the unit (in SI measurements now commonly used) is the candela per square meter (cd/m^2), also called the *nit*. In the older inch-pound system, the unit is the *footlambert* (ftL), where 1 ftL is $1/\pi$ cp/ft^2. Luminance takes into account the reflectance and transmittance properties of materials and the direction in which they are viewed. Thus, 100 lx striking a 1 m^2 surface with 50% reflectance would result in a luminance of 50 cd/m^2. (In customary U.S. units, 100 fc striking a surface with 50% reflectance would result in a luminance of 50 ftL.) Luminance is sometimes called *brightness*, although brightness includes the physiological sensation of the adaptation of the eye, whereas luminance is the measurable state of object luminosity.

Luminous intensity is the solid angular flux density in a given direction measured in candlepower or candelas.

Light Levels

Good lighting design involves providing both the proper quantity and quality of light to perform a task. This section discusses quantity; the next discusses quality. Different visual tasks under different conditions require varying levels of illumination. The variables involved include the nature of the task itself, the age of the person performing the task, the reflectances of the room, and the demand for speed and accuracy in performing the task.

The Illuminating Engineering Society of North America (IESNA) has established a method for determining a range of illumination levels, in footcandles, appropriate to particular design conditions. Various areas and activities are assigned an illuminance category from A to I (A represents the lowest values for general lighting in noncritical areas, and I represents requirements for specialized and difficult visual tasks). These categories are used with other variables of age, surface reflectances, and importance of the task to establish the recommended task and background illuminances.

To conserve energy, most codes require designers to develop a power budget for a project based on the building type and to design lighting systems within that budget. This most often requires that the recommended illumination level be provided for task areas only and that general background illumination (ambient light) be less, about one-third of the task level. Further, noncritical areas such as corridors are usually provided with less light than are the background levels.

Light Quality

The quality of light is just as important as the quantity. Important considerations are glare, contrast, uniformity, and color.

There are two types of glare: direct and reflected. *Direct glare* results when a light source in the field of vision causes discomfort and interference with the visual task. Not all visible light sources cause direct glare problems. The extent of the problem depends on the brightness of the source, its position, the background illumination, and the adaptation of the eye to the environment.

To evaluate direct glare, the *visual comfort probability* (VCP) *factor* was developed. This factor is the percentage of people who, when viewing from a specified location and in a specified direction, will find the situation acceptable in terms of discomfort glare. Although the calculations are complex, some simplifications are made, and many manufacturers publish the VCP rating for their light fixtures when used under certain conditions.

For most situations, the critical zone for direct glare is in the area above a 45° angle from the light source. See Fig. 19.2. This is because when a person is looking straight ahead, their field of vision includes an area approximately 45° above the horizontal. Many direct glare problems can be solved by using a luminaire with a 45° cutoff angle or by moving the luminaire out of the offending field of view. One way to determine the amount of light being emitted by a luminaire at any given angle is to look at a footcandle distribution diagram. Figure 19.3 shows one such diagram that plots light output at various angles to the luminaire.

Reflected glare occurs when a light source is reflected from a viewed surface into the eye. If the light source interferes with the viewing task, it is also called *veiling reflection*. The effect of reflected glare is to decrease the contrast between the task and its background. For example, a strong light on paper with pencil writing can bounce off the relatively reflective graphite, making the graphite almost as bright as the paper and effectively obliterate the writing.

Veiling reflections are a complex interaction of light source and brightness, position of the task, reflectivity of the task, and position of the eye. One of the simplest ways to correct veiling reflections is to move the position of the task or the light source. This relationship is easy to calculate because, for light, the angle of incidence is equal to the angle of reflection. It is not always possible to correct veiling reflections, however, because the exact use of the room and its furniture position are not always known. One way to avoid the problem is to provide general background illumination and specific task lighting that can be moved around by the user.

Contrast is the difference in illumination level between one point and nearby points. Because people see by contrast, it is vitally

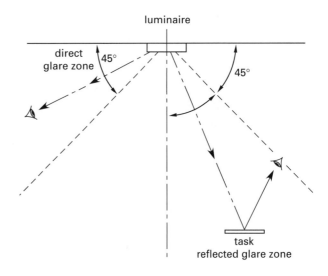

Figure 19.2
Glare Zones

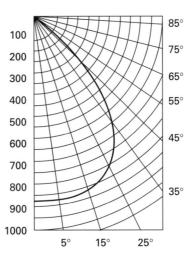

Figure 19.3
Candlepower
Distribution
Diagram

important to the quality of an environment. A printed word on a page is visible only because it contrasts with the brightness of the surrounding paper. However, too much contrast can be detrimental. It is difficult to see fine detail on a small, dark object when viewed against a bright background because the eye adapts to the brighter background and cannot admit enough light to see the darker object. The eye adapts by opening and closing the iris, but too much of this causes eyestrain and fatigue.

In most situations, brightness ratios should be limited to 3:1 between the task and immediate surroundings (for example, between a piece of paper and the desktop), to 5:1 between the task and nearby general surroundings, and to 10:1 between the task and more remote surroundings.

Uniformity of lighting affects a person's perception of a space as being comfortable and pleasant to be in. Complete uniformity is usually not desirable except for certain tasks like drafting or machine shop work. Some amount of shade and shadow provides highlight and interest to a space.

Color in lighting is an interaction between the color of the light source (lamp or daylighting) and the color of the objects that reflect the light. Color in lighting is a complex subject but it can affect people's comfort and their impression of an environment. Colors of light sources are discussed in the next section, and the use of color in lighting design is covered later in this chapter.

LIGHT SOURCES

In addition to daylight, there are three types of light sources: incandescent, fluorescent, and high-intensity discharge. Some of the considerations that influence the selection of a light source include color rendition characteristics, initial cost, operating cost, efficacy, size, operating life, and the ability to control output from a luminaire. *Efficacy* is the ratio of luminous flux emitted to the total power input of the source and is measured in lumens per watt. It is an important measure of the energy efficiency of a light source. The amount of heat generated by a light source is also an important consideration because waste heat usually needs to be removed or compensated for with the air conditioning system, which can add to the total energy load of a building. A summary of some of the more common light sources is shown in Table 19.1. The color temperature and the CRI value shown in the table are explained in a later section of this chapter.

Table 19.1
Characteristics of
Some Common
Light Sources

lamp description	efficacy	color temp. (°K)	CRI	approx. lamp life (hours)
incandescent	5–20	2700–2800	100	750–4000
tungsten-halogen	18–22	3000–3100	100	1000–4000
fluorescent (T12 and T8)	65–105	2700–7500	55–98	6000–24,000
fluorescent (T5)	95–105	3000–4100	75–95	6000–16,000
compact fluorescent	25–48	2700–4100	82	10,000
mercury-vapor	20–60	5500–5900	15–52	14,000–25,000
metal-halide	35–95	3200–4300	65–85	5000–20,000
high-pressure sodium	80–140	1800–2800	22–70	10,000–24,000

Note: The values listed in the table are approximate and representative only. Individual manufacturers and lamps may provide different values.

Incandescent

An *incandescent* lamp consists of a tungsten filament placed within a sealed bulb containing an inert gas. When electricity is passed through the lamp, the filament glows, producing light. Incandescent lamps are produced in a variety of shapes, sizes, and wattages for different applications. Some of the more common shapes are shown in Fig. 19.4. Incandescent lamps are designated by their shape followed by a number that indicates the diameter in eighths of an inch at the widest point. Thus, an R-38 is a reflector lamp with a diameter of $4^3/4$ in ($^{38}/8 = 4^3/4$).

Designers should be familiar with the distribution characteristics of the various reflector lamps: types R, ER, PAR, and MR-16. A standard *reflector lamp* (R lamp) has a wide beam spread. An *elliptical reflector lamp* (ER lamp) provides a more efficient throw of light from a fixture by focusing the light beam at a point slightly in front of the lamp before it spreads out. Its spread is slightly smaller than that of the R lamp. A parabolic aluminized reflector lamp (PAR lamp) focuses light in a tighter spread, with the light rays more parallel because its reflector is a parabola with the filament at the focus of the parabola. PAR lamps, as well as R lamps, are available in both "flood" spreads and "spotlights." An MR-16 lamp is a low-voltage, multifaceted mirror reflector. Several angles of beam spread are available, from a very narrow spot to a medium-wide spread. Generally, however, MR-16 lamps have the narrowest beam spread of the four types of lamps, the next narrowest being a PAR.

Incandescent lamps are inexpensive, compact, easy to dim, can be repeatedly started without a decrease in lamp life, and have a warm color rendition. In addition, their light output can be easily controlled with reflectors and lenses. Their disadvantages include low efficacy, short lamp life,

Figure 19.4
Incandecent Lamp Shapes

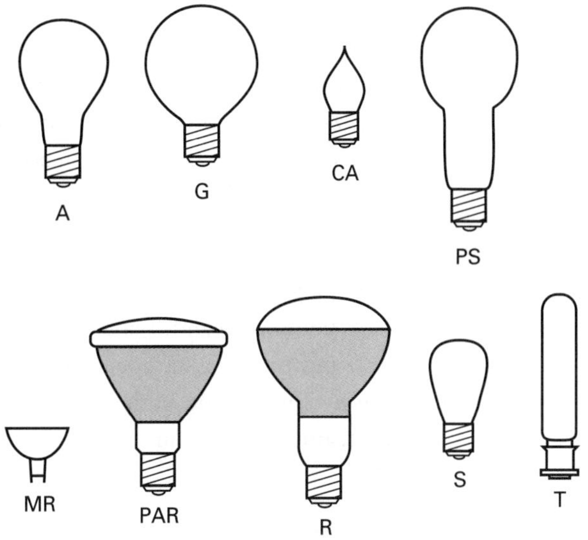

A   arbitrary
G   globular
CA   candleshape
PS   pear shaped
MR   multifaceted mirror reflector
PAR parabolic aluminized reflector
R   reflector
S   straight
T   tubular

and high heat output. The combination of heat production and low efficacy makes incandescent lamps undesirable for large, energy-efficient installations. For example, a 150 W lamp produces less than 20 lm/W, while a 40 W cool-white fluorescent lamp has an efficacy of about 80 lm/W with much less heat output.

Tungsten-halogen is one type of incandescent lamp. Light is produced by the incandescence of the filament, but there is a small amount of a halogen, such as iodine or bromine, in the bulb with the inert gas. Through a recurring cycle, part of the tungsten filament is burned off as the lamp operates, but it mixes with the halogen and is redeposited on the filament instead of on the wall of the bulb as in standard incandescent lamps. This results in longer lamp life, low lumen depreciation over the life of the lamp, and a more uniform light color. Because the filament burns under higher pressure and temperature, the bulb is made from quartz and is much smaller than those of standard incandescent lamps. These lamps are often referred to as quartz-halogen. Both standard voltage (120 V) and low-voltage tungsten-halogen lamps are available.

In addition to their other advantages, tungsten-halogen lamps have a greater efficacy than standard incandescents and are compact, and their higher operating temperature gives more light in the blue end of the spectrum, resulting in a light that looks whiter.

However, because they operate at high temperatures and pressures, failures result in an explosive shattering of the lamp. For this reason, halogen lamps are enclosed in another bulb or are covered with a piece of glass or a screen.

Low-voltage lamps are another class of incandescent. In addition to tungsten-halogen lamps, standard filament types are available. As the name implies, these lamps operate at a lower voltage than 120 V, usually 12 V. However, they operate at higher current (amperage), so their filaments have to be thicker to carry the added current. Because the filaments are thicker, they are also more compact, resulting in smaller lamps and lamps with better beam control.

Due to smaller filaments and better beam control, low-voltage lamps are often used where small luminaires are required or where narrow beam spreads are needed. The narrow beam spread makes low-voltage lamps energy efficient when lighting small objects or larger objects at a distance. The main disadvantage to these lamps is that a transformer is required to step down the line voltage. This results in a bulkier luminaire and higher initial cost.

Fluorescent

Fluorescent lamps contain a mixture of an inert gas and low-pressure mercury vapor. When the lamp is energized, a mercury arc is formed that creates ultraviolet light. This invisible light, in turn, strikes the phosphor-coated bulb, causing it to fluoresce and produce visible light. The three types of fluorescent lamps are preheat, rapid start, and instant start, according to their circuitry. Preheat lamps have been supplanted by rapid start types. All fluorescent lamps have a ballast, a device that supplies the proper starting and operating voltages to the lamp as well as limiting the current.

Lamps are produced in tubular shapes, normally straight, but U-shaped and circular lamps are also available. They are designated according to their type, wattage, diameter, color, and type of starting circuitry. Thus, an F40T12WW/RS describes a fluorescent lamp that is 40 W and tubular, with a $^{12}/_8$ inch diameter ($1^1/_2$ in), warm white color, and a rapid start circuit. Size is designated in eighths of an inch, so a T8 lamp has a 1 in diameter. Fluorescent lamps come in a variety of lengths, with 4 ft being the most common. Lengths of 2, 3, and 8 ft are also available, as well as special U-shaped sizes and compact shapes that are designed to be screwed into normal incandescent sockets.

In the past, one of the objections to fluorescent lighting was that it was too "cold." Actually, lamps are available in a wide range of color temperatures, from a "cool" FL/D (daylight) lamp of 6500K color temperature to a WWD (warm-white deluxe) with a color temperature of 2800K, which has a large percentage of red in its spectral output. Color temperature designations are discussed in a later section.

Standard fluorescent lamps have a high efficacy (from 55 lm/W to 80 lm/W), relatively low initial cost, and long life, and are available in a variety of color temperatures. They can also be dimmed, although fluorescent dimmers are more expensive than their incandescent counterparts. Because fluorescent lamps are larger than incandescent ones, it is more difficult to control them precisely, so they are usually more suitable for general illumination. Today, many of the standard T12, straight fluorescent lamps are being replaced by smaller and lower wattage T8 and T5 lamps, and incandescent lamps are being replaced by compact fluorescent lamps. The primary advantage to both is the energy savings realized by getting the same light level for less power input (wattage). In fact, many of the popular, older T12 lamps are no longer manufactured as mandated by the Energy Policy Act of 1992 (EPACT).

The T8 and T5 lamps (with 1 in and $^5/_8$ in diameters, respectively) have become more popular because of their higher efficacy and better color rendition. Both of these advantages are achieved by using rare earth phosphors. T8 lamps yield up to 80 lm/W on magnetic ballasts and up to 105 lm/W with electronic ballasts. T5 lamps provide from 95 lm/W to 105 lm/W. Color rendering indexes (see a later section of this chapter) from 70 to 98 are possible with the T8 lamps. The smaller diameter lamps also make it possible to design smaller luminaires and more efficiently control the light.

Compact fluorescent (CF) lamps consist of T4 or T5 tubes bent in a U-shape with the pins in one end of the lamp. Various configurations are available using tubes clustered in two, three, or four bends. In addition to providing energy savings, these lamps have a much longer life (10,000 hr) than the standard incandescent lamps they can replace. Most compact fluorescent lamps are designed to work in a fixture specifically designed for them, although some have a built-in ballast and a medium screw base so they can be used in older fixtures and floor and table lamps.

High-Intensity Discharge

High-intensity discharge (HID) lamps produce light by passing an electric current through a gas or vapor under high pressure. HID lamps include mercury-vapor, metal-halide, and high-pressure sodium.

In the mercury-vapor lamp, an electric arc is passed through high-pressure mercury vapor, which causes the lamp to produce both ultraviolet light and visible light, primarily in the blue-green spectral band. For improved color rendition, various phosphors can be applied to the inside of the lamp to produce more light in the yellow and red bands. Mercury-vapor lamps have a long lamp life but poor color rendering. Their use is generally limited to outdoor lighting and industrial applications such as warehouses.

Metal-halide lamps are similar to mercury except that halides of metals are added to the arc tube. This increases the efficacy and improves color rendition but decreases lamp life. Metal-halide lamps provide the best combination of features of the high-intensity discharge lamps. They have color rendering indexes between 60 and 90, high efficacy, and relatively long life. The main disadvantage is that halide lamps experience a large shift in apparent color temperature over their life (see the section on lighting design for a discussion of color temperature). Like all HID lamps, metal-halide lights have an outer bulb to protect the arc tube and to protect people from dangerous ultraviolet light. There are three types of outer bulbs: clear, phosphor-coated, and diffuse. Clear bulbs are used when optical control is required. Phosphor-coated lamps are used for better color rendition. Diffuse bulbs are specified in recessed downlight fixtures installed in low ceilings.

High-pressure sodium (HPS) lamps produce light by passing an electric arc through hot sodium vapor. The arc tube must be made of a special ceramic material to resist attack by the hot sodium. High-pressure sodium lamps have efficacies from 80 lm/W to 140 lm/W, making them among the most efficient lamps available. They also have an extremely long life, about 10,000 hr for the improved-color lamps and up to 24,000 hr for other types. Unfortunately, standard high-pressure sodium lamps produce a very yellow light. However, with available color correction versions, color rendition is acceptable for some interior applications. It is possible to get HPS lamps with color rendering indexes of up to 70.

HID lamps provide many advantages, but all of them require time to restart after being shut off or in case of a power failure. The lamp must first cool, and then it takes time to warm up. Mercury-vapor lamps need about 3 min to 10 min to relight; metal-halide lamps need about 10 min to 20 min; and high-pressure sodium lamps need about 1 minute.

In addition to the three basic types of lamps, there are neon and cold-cathode lamps. Neon lamps can be formed into an unlimited number of shapes and are used for signs and specialty accent lighting. By varying the gases within the tube, a variety of colors can be produced. Cold-cathode lamps are similar to neon in that they can be produced in long runs of thin tubing bent to shape, but they have a higher efficacy, are slightly larger (with about a 1 in diameter), and can produce several shades of white as well as many colors.

Light-Emitting Diodes (LEDs)

A *light-emitting diode* (LED) is a semiconductor device that uses solid-state electronics to create light. LEDs are a class of solid-state lighting that also includes organic light-emitting diodes and light-emitting polymers. LEDs have been used for many years as indicator panel lights and in other small electronic devices. Recent technological developments have made it feasible to use LEDs in traffic signal lights, signage lights, and railroad and automotive applications.

The advantages of LEDs include brightness, long life, and low power consumption. LED lamp life exceeds 100,000 hr. Furthermore, LEDs produce no heat and can be directly controlled by a digital interface. They can be manufactured to produce a number of colors or white light. Their main disadvantages are their low efficacy (lumens/watt) and high cost. However, as the technology improves, LEDs will be used in an increasing number of interior design and architectural applications. Currently, this type of lighting can be used for decorative purposes, exit lights, emergency lighting, and anywhere a life-cycle cost analysis would show that their low power consumption and long life would justify the higher initial cost.

LIGHTING TYPES

Lighting installations are broadly categorized by the overall system used to introduce light into the space and by how individual fixtures (luminaires) are mounted.

Lighting Systems

The types of systems can refer to individual luminaires or to an entire lighting installation and are described as direct, semidirect, direct-indirect, general diffuse, semi-indirect, and indirect. See Fig. 19.5.

Direct lighting systems provide all light output on the task. A recessed fluorescent luminaire is an example of direct lighting. Semidirect systems put a majority of the light down and a small percentage toward the ceiling. Obviously, fixtures for this type of system must be surface mounted or suspended. Direct-indirect systems distribute light up and down about equally.

Indirect systems direct all the light toward a reflective ceiling, where the light illuminates the room by reflection.

A task-ambient system is a common commercial lighting system. This system provides a general background illumination level with separate light fixtures used at individual workstations or wherever light is needed. This is done with desk lamps or directed spotlights, or by locating more fixtures near the tasks requiring more illumination. In addition to being energy efficient and responding to individual lighting needs, task-ambient systems create more pleasant work environments.

Surface-Mounted Fixtures

Surface-mounted fixtures are among the most commonly used types for residential and some commercial interior design. As the name implies, the luminaire is directly attached to the finished surface of the ceiling, directing all or a majority of the light into the space. These fixtures are used where there is not sufficient space above the ceiling to recess a fixture or where fixtures are added after the ceiling has been constructed. Surface-mounted fixtures include incandescent, fluorescent, or HID lights, as well as the various types of track lighting systems.

Recessed Fixtures

Recessed fixtures are widely used in residential and commercial installations. Residential recessed lighting is usually limited to incandescent downlights because these can be located in the limited space between floor or ceiling joists. Commercial installations utilize recessed incandescent lighting as well as recessed troffers that fit within suspended acoustical ceiling systems. When the entire ceiling is made up of lighting, a luminous ceiling is formed. Recessed incandescents can be general downlights for overall illumination or wallwashers, which direct light in one direction only. Continuous, narrow strips of

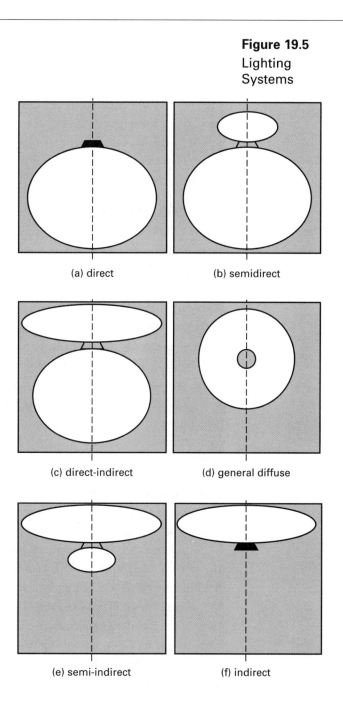

Figure 19.5
Lighting
Systems

(a) direct

(b) semidirect

(c) direct-indirect

(d) general diffuse

(e) semi-indirect

(f) indirect

fluorescent luminaires can also be recessed next to a wall to wash the wall uniformly with light.

Suspended Fixtures

Luminaires dropped below the level of the ceiling are called *suspended fixtures*. These can include direct incandescent or fluorescent fixtures, track lighting, indirect systems, chandeliers, and other types of specialty lights. Suspended mounting is required for indirect lighting systems. The fixture must be located far enough below the ceiling to allow for the proper spread of light to bounce off the surface. Suspended mounting is also used when the designer needs to get the source of light closer to the task area in a high-ceilinged room. Sometimes, suspended specialty fixtures are used for strictly aesthetic reasons.

Wall-Mounted Fixtures

Wall-mounted fixtures can provide indirect, direct-indirect, or direct lighting. For general illumination, sconces direct most or all of the light toward the ceiling. They are often used as decorative elements as well as light sources. Various types of adjustable and nonadjustable direct lighting fixtures are available that serve as task lighting, like bed lamps. Cove lighting can also be mounted on a wall near the ceiling and will indirectly light either the ceiling or the wall depending on how it is shielded.

Furniture-Mounted Fixtures

Furniture-mounted lighting is common with task-ambient systems. Individual lights are built into the furniture above the worksurface to provide sufficient task illumination, while uplighting is provided by lights either built into the upper portions of the furniture or as freestanding elements. Furniture-mounted lighting is also used on items like library bookshelves and study carrels.

Freestanding Fixtures

Floor lamps are the most common type of *freestanding* light fixture. These are available in thousands of different styles and sizes and can be custom designed and manufactured if needed. Freestanding lights that direct most of their output to the ceiling are called *torchères*. For taskambient lighting systems, freestanding kiosks contain high-wattage lights that illuminate the ceiling, providing indirect lighting.

Accessory Lighting

Accessory lighting includes table lights, reading lamps, and fixtures that are intended for strictly decorative lighting rather than for task or ambient lighting. Like floor lamps, these are available from hundreds of manufacturers in an almost unlimited number of styles.

LIGHTING DESIGN

Lighting is both an art and a science. There must be a sufficient amount of light to perform a task without glare and other discomfort, but the lighting also enhances the interior design. Lighting must also be designed to minimize energy use and protect the health of the occupants.

Color of Light

In addition to the issues of glare and contrast discussed in a previous section, the color of light sources is an important factor in the overall quality of any lighting design. The color of any object people see is dependent on both the color of the object as well as the color of the light striking it. For example, incandescent light striking a blue object will tend to gray out the object, while daylight will enhance it.

Every lamp has a characteristic spectral energy distribution. This is a measure of the energy output at different wavelengths, or colors. One such energy distribution curve is shown in Fig. 19.6. This energy distribution curve shows a discontinuous curve, typical of fluorescent and HID lights, with a continuous curve and with peaks at certain points. Daylight and incandescent light have continuous spectrum light without any sharp peaks.

Light sources are given a single number rating of their dominant color based on the temperature in degrees Kelvin to which a blackbody radiator would have to be heated to produce that color. Technically, only incandescent sources can have a color temperature designation, but an apparent color temperature is often used to describe the degree of whiteness of fluorescent lamps and other sources. However, even though a source with a discontinuous spectrum may have the same apparent color temperature as a continuous-spectrum source, the two may render colors quite differently. Table 19.2 gives correlated color temperatures of some common light sources. Notice that the lower the color temperature is, the "warmer" the light will be. As the temperature increases, the light becomes more blue and white.

Another method used to rate the color rendering of light sources is the color rendering index (CRI). This is a measure of how well one source renders the color of an object when compared with the same object lighted with a reference source of similar chromaticity whose CRI is 100. The index is a number between 1 and 100, and in many cases the reference source closely resembles a common incandescent lamp. For most interior applications, color temperatures range from about 2700K to 5000K. Color temperature should be based on the overall appearance desired and the colors of the finishes and furniture. For most office applications, lamps operating at about 3500K are often specified. In most cases, the designer should specify that all lamps in a space have about the same color temperature.

The designer must know the color characteristics of a light source when designing a lighting system because the light color affects the color of finishes, furniture, and other objects in the space. For example, using a lamp with a high complement of blue and violet will make finishes and furniture with the warmer colors of red appear dull, gray, and washed out. Where color appearance is important, finishes and materials should be selected under the same lighting used in the finished space.

Figure 19.6
Spectral Energy Distribution Curve

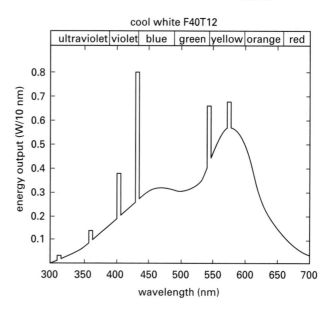

Table 19.2
Correlated Color Temperature of Common Sources

source	color temperature (K)
hazy blue sky	9000
overcast sky	7500
60 W incandescent	2790
150 W incandescent	2800
tungsten-halogen	3000
cool-white fluorescent	4300
warm-white fluorescent	3100
cool-white deluxe fluorescent	4100
daylight fluorescent	6500
metal-halide HID	3600–4200

Design Process

Although there is no one process for designing a lighting installation, this section summarizes the more important considerations and outlines a sequence of steps for completing a lighting design.

The first step is to determine the function of the space and the visual tasks to be performed. This includes determining the light levels needed (footcandle level), whether the space will be single or multiple use, and any special conditions that might dictate a particular kind of lighting solution. For example, a room with computer terminals will require particular care to avoid glare on the screens. An indirect lighting system with local, adjustable task lighting may be appropriate. Existing conditions that might affect the design should also be studied, such as daylighting contribution, ceiling height, ceiling construction, the size of the room, and other physical limitations.

Lighting should also enhance the character and function of the space. A lighting design for a library reading room will be quite different from a lighting design for a nightclub lounge. The character of a space includes not only the lighting level but also the types and styles of luminaires selected. Additional considerations include the degree of uniformity of lighting, light control, fixed lighting versus portable lamps, and the visibility of the light sources.

Next, lamp types are selected, whether they are incandescent, fluorescent, high-intensity discharge, or some combination thereof. The decision is based on the color rendition required, overall economy (both initial cost and life cycle costs), and the type of control required. If spotlighting is required, for example, incandescent lamps will probably have to be used.

Concurrent with lamp selection is luminaire selection. This involves both technical knowledge and aesthetic sensibility. Of course, luminaires must be selected that control glare, are cost effective, provide adjustability if required, and fit into the structure of the room. They must also complement the design of the space and provide the quality of light required for the visual tasks. Most lighting designs require a variety of luminaires. For example, a retail store might use direct or indirect fluorescent lights for general illumination, incandescent wallwashers to highlight vertical surfaces, track lighting for adjustability and for highlighting special areas, and portable lamps for providing task illumination.

Finally, the number and location of the luminaires are determined. These decisions are primarily based on the light level required and the tasks to be performed. For residential design and some commercial design, the number of fixtures can be estimated based on experience or rules of thumb that relate the number of fixtures to a given amount of floor space.

For larger installations, the number and location should be calculated according to the zonal cavity method developed by the IES. In brief, this system determines the number of luminaires required to provide a given footcandle level by using the efficacy of the lamp (lumens per watt), the number of lamps in the luminaire, the coefficient of utilization of the luminaire, the gradual loss of light output of the lamps over time (called the *lamp lumen depreciation factor*), and the conditions under which the luminaire will be used, which affects the amount of dirt collected on the lamps over time (called the *luminaire dirt depreciation factor*). The *coefficient of utilization* (CU) is a number used in these calculations that represents how efficiently the luminaire distributes the light from the lamps under various degrees of finish reflectivity of the floor, walls, and ceiling. Manufacturers test each of their luminaires and publish individual CU tables for each fixture. All of these factors are used in formulas to calculate the number of luminaires, but it is unlikely that the NCIDQ exam will require such calculations. Nevertheless, candidates should know the factors that influence light level.

However, providing the number of fixtures to achieve a certain footcandle level on the task is not enough. Additional lighting may be required to minimize dark wall surfaces, highlight certain areas, and provide interest and contrast to the overall design. Fixtures must also be located to avoid direct and indirect glare and to provide the recommended contrast ratios discussed previously.

Reflected Ceiling Plans

The final lighting design is documented on a reflected ceiling plan. As defined in Ch. 14, this is a technical drawing located in the same orientation as the floor plan and drawn at the same scale. In addition to showing the construction of the ceiling and the locations of air diffusers, smoke detectors, and other objects in the ceiling, it shows the locations of all the built-in lighting. For residential construction and some commercial construction, the switching may also be indicated as shown in Fig. 19.7. On larger commercial projects, the interior designer may develop a reflected ceiling plan showing only the luminaire locations, while the electrical engineering consultant develops a lighting plan that includes switching and circuiting. See Fig. 14.7. Refer to Ch. 14 for more information about reflected ceiling plans.

Circuiting

The interior designer should decide how the lights in a space will be switched. This decision is based on the function of the lighting, how much individual control is required, where the switches would be best located, energy conservation needs, and the maximum electrical load requirements on any one circuit.

The function of a space may simply require one on/off switch for all the lights in the space. In other cases, like a lecture room, it may be necessary to provide several circuits and switches so some lights can be turned off while some are on. Multiple switching also gives the users the flexibility of saving energy by not using all the lights when they are not required.

Switches generally should be located at the door into a space so they can easily be turned on and off as people enter or leave the room. If there are two doors or the space is very large, three-way or four-way switches can be used. These allow a light to be switched at two or three different locations, respectively.

The terms "three-way switch" and "four-way switch" are often confusing because the numbers do not refer to the number of locations from which control is possible. Rather, the numbers refer to the number of conductors required to make the switching possible. For example, a three-way switch requires three conductors (not including the ground) to make it possible to control a light from two different switches.

The circuiting of lights is also dependent on the type of control required. Many lights connected to a dimmer switch must be on their own circuit. Both incandescent and fluorescent lights can be dimmed, but fluorescent dimmers are more expensive, and special fixtures are required to minimize flicker as they are dimmed. Incandescent lights should generally be on a circuit separate from fluorescent lights. In commercial installations this is often mandatory because incandescent lights are on 120 V circuits and fluorescent lights are connected to 277 V circuits. Because they are more efficient, 277 V circuits are often used in large commercial installations. Lights can also be switched by low-voltage relay switching, automatic time clocks, or proximity devices that sense when people enter or leave a room.

Figure 19.7

Switching on
Reflected Ceiling
Plan

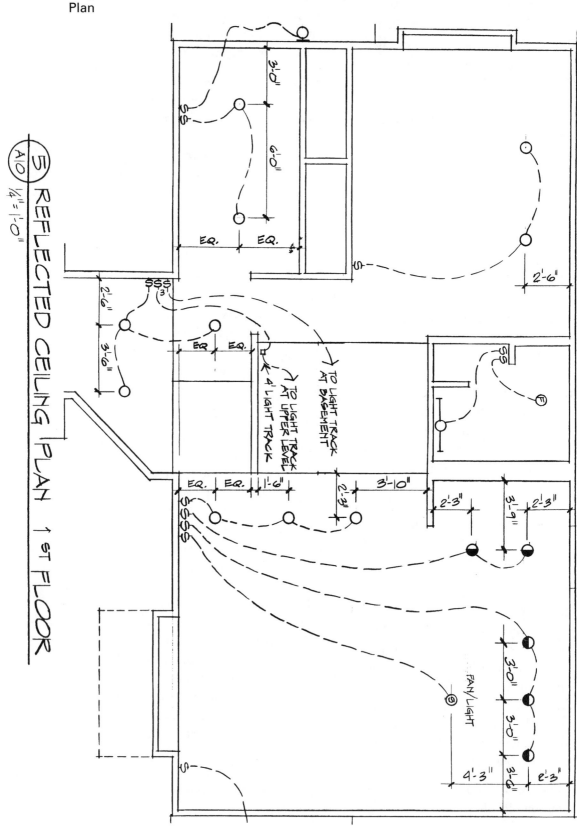

Finally, the number of switches depends on electrical load limitations. This is determined by the electrical engineering consultant or, on small projects, by the electrical contractor. Electrical building codes limit the total wattage that can be connected to any one circuit, so a large space with a great deal of lighting will have several switches.

Daylighting

In many cases, daylighting is used to supplement or replace artificial lighting during certain times. Although the architectural design of a building determines the type of general success of daylighting, the interior designer must be sensitive to locating partitions, specifying office systems, and selecting colors and finishes that do not undermine the methods of the building's daylighting system. For example, in a space with clerestory lighting, partitions and office systems should be kept as low as possible to allow the light to flood the entire space. (A *clerestory* is a vertically glazed area placed between two different roof levels to admit light.)

As discussed in Ch. 26, if daylighting provides adequate illumination during most of the day in some portions of a space, the interior designer should make sure that the electrical engineer incorporates photocell controls to dim the electric lighting when it is not needed. It has been estimated that this type of light control can reduce perimeter energy use from 50% to 60%.

Energy Conservation

In commercial buildings, lighting accounts for a large part of the total energy consumed. The interior designer can help minimize energy use with a variety of strategies: by using daylight as much as possible, selecting high-efficacy lamps, using efficient luminaires, minimizing unneeded ambient illumination, providing task lighting only where it is needed, and selecting high-reflectance ceiling, wall, and floor surfaces to reduce the total number of fixtures required to light a space. In addition, by working with a competent lighting designer or electrical engineer, other technical solutions can be used, such as automatic switching and return-air luminaires. Automatic switching shuts off lights in an unoccupied room after a certain amount of time, and return-air fixtures move exhaust air over the lamps, keeping them cooler and helping them to operate more efficiently.

Most jurisdictions have code requirements for commercial construction concerning the maximum amount of power that can be consumed in a building for lighting. This amount for a particular building type is determined according to certain procedures developed by the IES, and the designer must work within the guidelines so the total power budget is not exceeded. This allows for flexibility in design while conserving energy. Although the total power budget will vary with building type, a figure of approximately 2.3 W/ft^2 for many types of commercial buildings is often considered a maximum.

Another energy conservation measure is *lighting system tuning*. This is the adjustment of the lighting installation after construction is complete. It is common for many changes to have taken place between the time the lighting design was initially completed and when the client is ready to move in. During tuning, lamps are replaced with lower (or higher if really necessary) wattage units, adjustable luminaries are aimed for their optimal position, ballasts are adjusted for maximum efficiency, and switches are replaced with dimmer controls or time-out units.

Emergency Lighting

The International Building Code, National Electrical Code, Life Safety Code, and Canadian codes all include provisions for emergency lighting in commercial buildings. Because each jurisdiction differs slightly in its requirements, the local codes in force must be reviewed. Generally, however, all codes require that in the event of a power failure, sufficient lighting must be available to safely evacuate building occupants.

Emergency and standby power systems are required to provide electricity for emergency egress illumination, exit signs, voice communication systems in some occupancies, smoke control systems, horizontal sliding doors, means of egress elevators, and certain other occupancies. The power systems may include batteries and/or generators. Emergency power circuits are usually a part of the architectural design of a building, and for interior design projects they are designed by the electrical engineer. Any new work or extensive remodeling must include proper connection to the emergency circuits.

Building codes require that the means of egress be illuminated at all times the building is occupied. In the event of a power failure, the emergency power system must provide illumination to the following areas.

• exit access corridors and aisles in rooms and spaces required to have two or more exits

• exit access corridors and exit stairways in buildings required to have two or more exits

• interior exit discharge elements when permitted, such as building lobbies where 50% of the exit capacity may egress through the ground-floor lobby

Refer to Ch. 28 for a description of the means of egress system.

The means of egress illumination level must be a minimum of 1 fc (11 lux) measured at the floor level and must be maintained for not less than 90 minutes.

With some exceptions, exit signs are required at exits and exit access doors such that no point in an exit access corridor is more than 100 ft (30 480) from an exit sign. Directional exit signs are required at corridor intersections or where a corridor changes direction so that it is always evident to the occupants where the exits are. Exit signs may be either externally or internally illuminated. If the sign is externally illuminated, the minimum light level cannot be less than 5 fc (54 lux). Internally illuminated signs must be lit at all times and be listed and labeled. Illuminated exit signs, whether illuminated internally or externally, must be connected to an emergency power circuit.

SAMPLE QUESTIONS

1. Who is responsible for the final design of the lighting and switching system in a commercial interior design project?

   (A) interior designer

   (B) architect

   (C) electrical engineer

   (D) electrical contractor

2. For a jewelry store in an exclusive shopping mall, what type of lamp would be best to use in the display cases?

   (A) 75 W PAR quartz

   (B) 150 W R quartz

   (C) 15 W T

   (D) 90 W MR-16

3. What is the commonly used designation for the lamp labeled *X* below?

   (A) CA

   (B) G

   (C) A

   (D) T

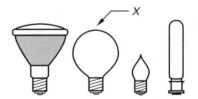

4. The units used for the measurement and description of the brightness of a direct glare source are

(A) footcandles

(B) footlamberts

(C) candelas

(D) lumens

5. One of the most frequent lighting problems in traditional drafting rooms is

(A) veiling reflection

(B) direct glare

(C) visual comfort

(D) excessive brightness ratio

6. An interior designer has just finished reviewing the plans for a large office suite when the building department states that the lighting budget has been exceeded. If the design is composed of 80% fluorescent lighting and 20% incandescent lighting, what is the best course of action to begin redesign?

(A) Reduce the number of luminaires by spacing them farther apart.

(B) Substitute all incandescent lights with fluorescent lights.

(C) Change to a task-ambient lighting system.

(D) Investigate whether lamps with higher efficacies will bring the design within the budget.

7. Which of the following sources would be most appropriate for the warehouse portion of a large furniture dealership?

(A) high-pressure sodium

(B) cool-white deluxe fluorescent

(C) metal-halide

(D) mercury-vapor

8. Surface-mounted luminaires are most often used for which of the following reasons?

(A) Some side and uplighting is desired.

(B) There is not enough space above the ceiling.

(C) They are easier and less expensive to install.

(D) They are used as a design feature.

9. What is the most important criterion for lighting a fabric showroom?

(A) visual comfort probability

(B) color rendering index

(C) coefficient of utilization

(D) apparent color temperature rating

10. In designing a room in which work will take place both at video display terminals and at standard work surfaces at each individual workstation, what approach to lighting design would be most appropriate?

(A) Use indirect ambient lighting, and use individual task lights at each workstation.

(B) Locate downlights over work surfaces, and use indirect lighting fixtures over the terminals.

(C) Use low-brightness troffers controlled by dimmers, and use task lighting on the work surfaces.

(D) Specify a direct-indirect system that is locally controlled at each workstation.

20

ACOUSTICS

Acoustics can greatly influence the overall quality of interior design. Spaces that are too noisy or reverberant are distracting at best and unusable at worst. Likewise, auditoriums or classrooms in which sounds are not audible are equally unsuitable. The interior designer can control the acoustic quality of a room with space planning, the design of walls and ceilings, and the selection of finishes. For many common situations, a basic knowledge of acoustics can help the interior designer make the best decisions. With more complex designs like concert halls or recording studios, the services of a qualified acoustical consultant should be used.

FUNDAMENTALS OF SOUND
Qualities of Sound

Sound has three basic qualities: velocity, frequency, and power. *Velocity* depends on the medium in which the sound is traveling and the temperature of the medium. *Frequency* is the number of cycles completed per second and is measured in Hertz (Hz): 1 Hz equals 1 cycle/sec. The sounds that we call high notes or high-pitched sounds have higher frequencies;

bass notes have lower frequencies. *Power* is the quality of acoustic energy as measured in watts. It is this power that people perceive as loudness.

Loudness

The human ear is sensitive to a vast range of sound power, from about 10^{-16} W/cm^2 to 10^{-3} W/cm^2. Because of this and the fact that the sensation of hearing is proportional to the logarithm of the source intensity, the decibel (dB) is used in acoustic descriptions and calculations. The decibel conveniently relates actual sound intensity to the way humans experience sound. By definition, 0 dB is the threshold of human hearing, and 130 dB is the threshold of pain. Some common sound intensity levels and their subjective evaluations are shown in Table 20.1.

The change in loudness is subjective, but some common guidelines are shown in Table 20.2. These are useful for evaluating the effects of increased or decreased decibel levels in design situations. For example, spending money to modify a partition to increase its sound transmission class (defined later in this chapter) by 3 dB

Table 20.1

Common Sound
Intensity Levels

intensity level (dB)	example	subjective evaluation	intensity (W/cm^2)
140	jet plane takeoff		
130	gunfire	threshold of pain	10^{-3}
120	hard rock band, siren at 100 ft	deafening	10^{-4}
110	accelerating motorcycle	sound can be felt	10^{-5}
100	auto horn at 10 ft	conversation difficult to hear	10^{-6}
90	loud street noise, kitchen blender	very loud	10^{-7}
80	noisy office, average factory	difficult to use phone	10^{-8}
70	average street noise, quiet typewriter, average radio	loud	10^{-9}
60	average office, noisy home	usual background	10^{-10}
50	average conversation, quiet radio	moderate	10^{-11}
40	quiet home, private office	noticeably quiet	10^{-12}
30	quiet conversation	faint	10^{-13}
20	whisper		10^{-14}
10	rustling leaves, soundproof room	very faint	10^{-15}
0	threshold of hearing		10^{-16}

Table 20.2

Subjective Change in Loudness Based on Decibel Level Change

change in intensity level (dB)	change in apparent loudness
1	almost imperceptible
3	just perceptible
5	clearly noticeable
6	change when distance to source in a free field is doubled or halved
10	twice or half as loud
18	very much louder or quieter
20	four times or one-fourth as loud

probably would not be worth the expense because it would hardly be noticeable.

Human Sensitivity to Sound

Although human response to sound is subjective and varies with age, physical condition of the ear, background, and other factors, the following guidelines are useful to know.

• A healthy young person can hear sounds in the range of about 20 Hz to 20,000 Hz and is most sensitive to frequencies in the 3000 Hz to 4000 Hz range. Speech is composed of sounds primarily in the range of 125 Hz to 8000 Hz, with most in the range of 200 Hz to 5000 Hz.

• The human ear is less sensitive to low frequencies than to middle and high frequencies for sounds of equal energy.

• Most common sound sources contain energy over a wide range of frequencies. Because frequency is an important variable in how a sound is transmitted or absorbed, it must be taken into account in building acoustics. For convenience, measurement and analysis is often divided into eight octave frequency bands as identified by their center frequency.

SOUND TRANSMISSION

There are two basic problems in controlling *noise* (defined as any unwanted sound): preventing or minimizing the transmission of sound from one space to another and reducing the noise within a space. This section discusses sound transmission; the next section outlines the basics of sound absorption as the primary means of reducing noise in a space.

Transmission Loss and Noise Reduction

A common problem is unwanted sound transmission from one space to another. Transmission of sound is primarily retarded by the mass of the partition. The stiffness, or rigidity, of the partition is also important. Given two partitions of the same weight per square foot, the one with less stiffness will perform better than the other.

There are two important concepts in noise reduction: transmission loss and actual noise reduction between two spaces. *Transmission loss* takes into account only the loss through the partition. *Noise reduction* is dependent not only on the transmission loss but also on the area of the partition separating the two spaces and the absorption of the surfaces in the "quiet" room (the one not producing the noise). Noise reduction can be increased by increasing the transmission loss of the partition, by increasing the absorption in the "quiet" room, by decreasing the area of the common wall between the rooms, or by some combination of all three.

To simplify the selection of wall construction and other building components, a single-number rating called the *sound transmission class* (STC) is often used to rate the transmission loss of construction. The higher the STC rating, the better the barrier is (theoretically) in stopping sound. Table 20.3 shows some STC ratings and their effects on hearing.

STC ratings represent the ideal loss through a barrier under laboratory conditions. Partitions, floors, and other construction components built in the field are seldom constructed as well as those in the laboratory. Also, breaks in the barrier such as cracks, electrical outlets, doors, and the like will significantly lessen overall noise reduction.

In critical situations, transmission loss and selection of barriers should be calculated using the values for various frequencies rather than the single STC average value. Some materials may allow an acoustic "hole," stopping most frequencies but allowing transmission of a certain range of frequencies. However, for preliminary design purposes the STC value is adequate.

Noise Criteria Curves

All normally occupied spaces have some amount of background noise. This is not undesirable, because some noise is necessary to avoid the feeling of a "dead" space and to help mask other sounds. However,

the acceptable amount of background noise varies with the type of space and the frequency of sound. For example, people are generally less tolerant of background noise in bedrooms than they are in public lobbies, and they are generally more tolerant of higher levels of low-frequency sound than of high-frequency sound.

These variables have been consolidated into a set of noise criteria curves relating frequency in eight octave bands to noise level. See Fig. 20.1. Accompanying these curves are noise criteria ratings for various types of spaces and listening requirements. A representative sampling is shown in Table 20.4. Noise criteria curves can be used to specify the maximum amount of continuous background noise allowable in a space, to establish a minimum amount of

Table 20.3
Effect of Barrier STC on Hearing

STC	effect on hearing
25	normal speech can clearly be heard through barrier
30	loud speech can be heard and understood fairly well; normal speech can be heard but barely understood
35	loud speech is not intelligible but can be heard
42–45	loud speech can only be faintly heard; normal speech cannot be heard
46–50	loud speech not audible; loud sounds other than speech can only be heard faintly, if at all

Table 20.4
Some Representative Noise Criteria

type of space	preferred noise criteria (dB)
concert halls, opera houses, recording studios	15–20
bedrooms, apartments, hospitals	20–30
private offices, small conference rooms	30–35
large offices, retail stores, restaurants	35–40
lobbies, drafting rooms, laboratory work spaces	40–45
kitchens, computer rooms, light maintenance shops	45–55

Figure 20.1
NC (Noise
Criteria)
Curves

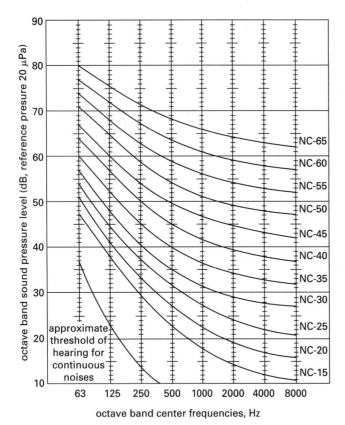

Table 20.5
Noise Reduction
Coefficients

material	NRC
vinyl tile on concrete	0.05
wood strip flooring	0.10
carpet, $1/2$ in pile on concrete	0.50
gypsumboard walls	0.05
1 in fiberglass wall panel with fabric cover	0.80
plywood paneling	0.15
$5/8$ in suspended acoustic tile	0.60
1 in suspended acoustic tile	0.90

noise desired to help mask sounds, and to evaluate an existing condition.

SOUND ABSORPTION

Controlling sound transmission is only part of good acoustic design. The proper amount of sound absorption must also be included to minimize noise within a space. Of course, the source of the noise may be reduced, but this is not always possible. Sound absorption, then, is used to control unwanted sound reflections (noise), improve speech privacy, and decrease or increase reverberation.

Fundamentals

The absorption of a material is defined by the coefficient of absorption, *a*, which is the ratio of the sound intensity absorbed by the material to the total intensity reaching the material. The maximum absorption possible, therefore, is 1, that of free space. Generally, a material with a coefficient below 0.2 is considered to be reflective and one with a coefficient above 0.2 is considered sound absorbing. These coefficients are published in manufacturers' technical literature.

The coefficient of absorption varies with the frequency of the sound, and some materials are better at absorbing some frequencies than others. For critical applications, all frequencies should be checked, but for convenience the single-number *noise reduction coefficient* (NRC) is used. The NRC is the average of a material's absorption coefficients at the four frequencies of 250, 500, 1000, and 2000 Hz, rounded to the nearest multiple of 0.05. Some typical NRC ratings are shown in Table 20.5.

Noise Reduction Within a Space

A material's total absorption is dependent on its coefficient of absorption and area. Because most rooms have several materials with different areas, the total absorption in a room is the sum of the various individual material absorptions. Although noise reduction can be calculated with complex formulas in critical situations, for most interior design the following rules of thumb may suffice.

• Avoid designing rooms with hard, reflective surfaces on the walls, floor, and ceiling. The space will be too "live" and noisy.

• The average absorption coefficient of a room should be at least 0.20. An average absorption above 0.50 is usually not desirable, nor is it economically justified. A lower value is suitable for large rooms, while larger values are suitable for small or noisy rooms.

• Each doubling of the amount of absorption in a room results in a noise reduction of only 3 dB—hardly noticeable. To make any difference, the total absorption must be increased by at least three times to change the reduction by 5 dB, which is noticeable.

• Although absorptive materials can be placed anywhere, ceiling treatment for sound absorption is more effective in large rooms, while wall treatment is more effective in small rooms.

Reverberation

Reverberation is the prolongation of sound as it repeatedly bounces off hard surfaces. It is an important part of the acoustic environment of a space because it affects the intelligibility of speech and the quality of music. Technically, reverberation time is the time it takes the sound level to decrease 60 dB after the source has stopped producing the sound. It is a desirable quality if the reverberation time is appropriate for the use of the space. For example, the recommended time for speech in offices and small rooms is 0.3 sec to 0.6 sec, while for auditoriums it is 1.5 sec to 1.8 sec. Reverberation can be controlled by modifying the amount of absorptive or reflective finishes in a space.

SOUND CONTROL

This section reviews some of the specific strategies that can be used to control sound and noise in various circumstances.

Control of Room Noise

There are three primary ways sound can be controlled within a space: by reducing the level of loudness of the sound source, by modifying the absorption in the space, and by introducing nonintrusive background sound to mask the unwanted sound.

Reducing the level of the sound source is not always possible if the sound is created by a fixed piece of machinery, people, or some similar situation. However, if the source is noise from the outside or an adjacent room, the transmission loss of the enclosing walls can be improved. If a machine is producing the noise, it can often be enclosed or modified to reduce its noise output.

Modifying the absorption of the space can achieve some noise reduction, but there are practical limits to adding absorptive materials. This approach is most useful when the problem room has a large percentage of hard, reflective surfaces.

In most cases, introducing nonintrusive background sound is desirable because such sound can mask unwanted noise. Some amount of background noise is always present. It may come from the steady hum of HVAC systems, from business machines, from traffic, from conversation, or from other sources. For example, in an office, if the sound level on one side of a partition with an STC rating of 45 is 75 dB and the background noise on the other side of the partition is 35 dB, the noise coming through the partition will not be heard (theoretically) on the "quiet" side of the wall. See Fig. 20.2. If the background noise level is decreased to 25 dB, then sounds will be heard.

This phenomenon often called white sound, random noise, or acoustic perfume, is used to purposely introduce carefully controlled sound into a space rather than rely only on random background noise. Speakers are placed in the ceiling of a space and connected to a sound generator, which produces a continuous, unnoticeable sound at particular levels across the frequency spectrum. The sound generator can be tuned to produce the frequencies and sound levels appropriate to mask the desired sounds. White sound is often used in open offices to provide speech privacy and to help mask office machine noise.

Control of Sound Transmission

The control of sound transmission through a barrier is dependent primarily on the barrier's mass and to a lesser extent on the barrier's stiffness. Walls and floors are generally rated with their STC value;

Figure 20.2

Noise Reduction

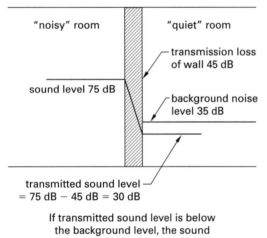

If transmitted sound level is below the background level, the sound is not perceptible.

Figure 20.3

Sound-Resistant Partition

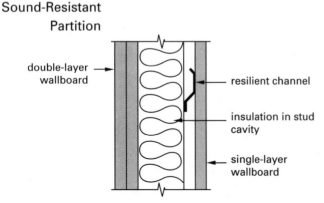

the higher the STC rating, the better the barrier is at reducing transmitted sound. Manufacturers' literature, testing laboratories, and reference literature typically give the transmission loss at different frequencies.

Several methods can be used to build a sound-resistant partition. These are shown diagrammatically in Figure 20.3. The first technique simply adds mass to the wall. This can be done by using a heavy material for the partition (such as masonry) or by using more than one layer of gypsum wallboard. Partitions with high STC ratings commonly have a double layer of wallboard on one or both sides of the stud. The second technique is to place insulation within the stud cavity. This absorbs sound (reduces its energy) that is transmitted through one layer of the wall before it reaches the other. Finally, resilient channels can be used as furring strips on one side of the partition. Because of their design, only one leg of the channel touches the stud so the wallboard "floats" and dampens sound striking it rather than transmitting it to the stud.

In addition to the construction of the barrier itself, other variables are critical to the control of sound transmission. Gaps in the barrier must be sealed. Edges at the floor, ceiling, and intersecting walls must be caulked. Penetrations of the barrier should be avoided, but if absolutely necessary they should be sealed as well. For example, electrical outlets should not be placed back to back but should be staggered in separate stud spaces and caulked. Pipes, ducts, and similar penetrations provide a path for both airborne sound and mechanical vibration and should not be rigidly connected to the barrier. Any gaps between ducts, pipes, and a partition should be sealed and caulked.

Construction with a lower STC rating than that of the barrier itself should be avoided or given special treatment because it will decrease the overall rating of the barrier. Doors placed in an otherwise well-built sound wall are a common problem and can be dealt with in several ways. The perimeter should be completely sealed with weather stripping specifically designed for sound sealing at the jamb and head and with a threshold or automatic door bottom at the sill. An *automatic door bottom* is a piece of hardware that drops a seal from the door to the floor or threshold as the door closes. The door itself should be as heavy as possible, preferably a solid-core wood door. Often, two doors are used, separated by a small air gap.

Interior glass lights can be designed with laminated glass set in resilient framing. Laminated glass provides more mass, and the plastic interlayer improves the damping characteristics of the barrier. If additional transmission loss is required, two or more layers can be installed with an air gap between them.

Flanking paths for sound to travel, including air conditioning ducts, plenums, and hallways, should be eliminated or treated appropriately.

Speech Privacy

In many spaces, the critical acoustic concern is not eliminating all noise or designing a room for music, but providing for a certain level of privacy while still allowing people to talk at a normal level. In many cases, speech privacy is regarded as a condition in which talking may be heard as a general background sound but not easily understood. This is most often required in open-plan offices.

Speech privacy in areas divided by full-height partitions is usually achieved by sound loss through the partitions and, to a lesser extent, by the proper use of sound-absorbing surfaces. In open areas, such as an open-plan office, speech privacy is more difficult to achieve. There are five important factors in designing for speech privacy in an open area. All of these must be present to achieve the optimum acoustic environment.

1. The ceiling must be highly absorptive. The ideal is to create a "clear sky" condition so that sounds are not reflected from their source to other parts of the space.

2. The area must include space dividers that reduce the transmission of sound from one space to the adjacent spaces. The dividers should have a combination of absorptive surfaces to minimize sound reflections placed over a solid liner called a *septum*.

3. Other surfaces, such as the floor, furniture, windows, and light fixtures, must be designed or arranged to minimize sound reflections. A window, for example, can provide a clear path for reflected noise around a partial-height partition.

4. If possible, activities should be distanced to take advantage of the normal attenuation of sound with distance.

5. The area should have a properly designed background masking system. If the right amount of sound-absorbing surfaces is provided, the masking system will absorb all sounds in the space, not just the unwanted sounds. Background sound must then be reintroduced to maintain the right balance between speech sound and the background masking noise.

Control of Impact Noise

Impact noise, or sound resulting from direct contact of an object with a sound barrier, can occur on any surface, but it generally occurs on a floor and ceiling assembly. It is usually caused by footfall, shuffled furniture, and dropped objects.

Impact noise is quantified by the *impact insulation class* (IIC) number, a single-number rating of a floor/ceiling's impact sound performance. The higher the IIC rating, the better the floor performs in reducing impact sounds in the test frequency range.

The IIC value of a floor can most easily be increased by adding carpet. It can also be improved by providing a resiliently suspended ceiling below, floating a finished floor on resilient pads over the structural floor, or providing sound-absorbing material (insulation) in the air space between the floor and the finished ceiling below.

Room Geometry and Planning Concepts

There are many ways the acoustic performance of a group of spaces or an individual room can be affected by floor plan layout and the size and shape of the room itself. In addition to designing walls and floors to retard sound transmission and making proper use of sound absorption, the following ideas can be used to help minimize acoustic problems in interior space planning.

• Plan similar use areas next to each other. For example, placing bedrooms next to each other is better than placing a bedroom next to a noisy space like the kitchen.

• Use buffer spaces such as closets and hallways to separate noise-producing spaces whenever possible. Using closets between bedrooms at a common wall is one example of this technique.

• Stagger doorways in halls and other areas to avoid providing a straight-line path for noise.

• If possible, try to locate furniture and other potential noise-producing objects away from the wall that is separating spaces.

• Minimize the area of the common wall between two rooms where a reduction in sound transmission is desired.

• Avoid room shapes that reflect or focus sound. Barrel-vaulted hallways and circular rooms, for example, produce undesirable focused sounds. Rooms that focus sound may also deprive some listeners of useful reflections.

Acoustic Ratings of Ceilings

Because ceilings play such an important role in room acoustics, several rating methods have been developed to quantify their acoustical properties. Three methods can be used for all ceilings, and two are used to measure the level of speech privacy in open-plan offices, where ceilings are only one part of the acoustic system.

One of the most important ceiling ratings is the *noise reduction coefficient* (NRC), which was briefly described in the previous section. The NRC is a single-number rating of the average sound absorption of a material over a limited frequency range, including 250, 500, 1000, and 2000 Hz, rounded to the nearest multiple of 0.05. NRC ratings can range from 0 (no sound absorption) to 1.0 (total absorption). Acoustical ceiling tiles are generally in the range of 0.65 to 0.90. In open-plan offices, values of 0.85 or higher are recommended.

A rating similar to the NRC is the *speech range absorption* (SRA). This is also a single-number rating, but the frequency range includes 500, 1000, 2000, and 4000 Hz. This range more closely represents the frequencies of speech and may be a better rating to use in evaluating and selecting ceiling tiles.

The third rating method is the *ceiling attenuation class* (CAC). This is a single-number measure of the transmission loss through ceiling tiles between two closed rooms where there is no wall or other barrier above the suspended ceiling. It is given in units of decibels and is similar to sound transmission class (STC) values described in the previous section on sound transmission. Most acoustical ceiling tiles have CAC ratings in the range of 30 dB to 35 dB, which is minimally effective at blocking sound. Refer to Table 20.3 for a subjective description of barrier STC on hearing. The CAC rating of a tile can be improved by using composite tiles that have a gypsum wallboard backing.

The two methods used to measure speech privacy in open offices are the articulation class (AC) and the articulation index (AI). These methods attempt to take into account factors other than just the ceiling tile and address a wider range of frequencies.

The *articulation class* is a single-number summation of how effective a ceiling is in absorbing sound reaching it from over low partitions. The rating is a summation of weighted sound attenuations in 15 test-band frequencies from 200 Hz to 5000 Hz, with higher weighted factors in the frequencies representing most human speech. The test used to determine this rating uses a 9 ft high ceiling and standard 60 in high partitions.

A better method of rating speech privacy is the *articulation index*, which measures the performance of all the elements of a particular configuration working together, including ceiling absorption, space dividers, furniture, light fixtures, partitions, background masking systems (white noise), and HVAC system sound. The AI predicts the intelligibility of speech for a group of talkers and listeners. The result of the test is a single-number rating, which can range from 0.00 to 1.00, with 0.00 being complete privacy and 1.00 being absolutely no privacy, where all individual spoken words can be understood. Confidential speech privacy exists when speech cannot be understood and occurs when the AI is below about 0.05. Normal speech privacy means concentrated effort is required to understand intruding speech and exists when the AI is between

0.05 and 0.20. Unacceptable privacy exists when the AI is above 0.30.

SAMPLE QUESTIONS

1. What ratings are the most important in evaluating the acoustic quality of a floor and ceiling assembly?

  I. STC
 II. NRC
III. IIC
 IV. NC

  (A) I and II
  (B) I and III
  (C) II and III
  (D) III and IV

2. If a material supplier says that adding his product to a wall assembly in a critical acoustic situation would increase the noise reduction (STC rating) between two rooms by slightly more than 3 dB, what should the designer's reaction be?

  (A) Determine what the additional cost would be and then decide whether or not to use the product.
  (B) Thank him for stopping by but explain that the amount of noise reduction his product provides does not make it worth the effort or cost.
  (C) Specify the product as long as it does not affect the construction cost by more than 5%.
  (D) Inquire whether some modification can be made to the product to increase its rating to 6 dB.

3. During the design development phase of design, what method would NOT be used to reduce potential noise problems in a room whose exact size and shape had not yet been determined?

  (A) Design the room to have the largest ceiling surface area possible.
  (B) Plan for sound-absorbent material on the walls of the room.

(C) Study ways to increase the transmission loss of the room's partitions.

(D) Minimize the length of the wall separating the room from noisier areas.

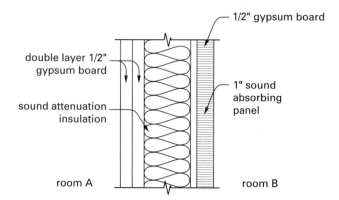

double layer 1/2" gypsum board

sound attenuation insulation

1/2" gypsum board

1" sound absorbing panel

room A

room B

4. The construction assembly shown would be best for controlling which of the following kinds of acoustic situations?

(A) impact noise

(B) transmission from room A to room B

(C) transmission from room B to room A

(D) mechanical vibration

5. Which is the most accurate statement about sound?

(A) A sound of 50 dB is twice as loud as a sound of 25 dB.

(B) A desirable goal of acoustic design is to eliminate all background noise.

(C) A 7 dB reduction of the noise within a room would be clearly noticeable.

(D) A good acoustic material absorbs all frequencies equally.

6. To detail a doorframe for a conference room where privacy is critical, which of the following is LEAST likely to be required?

(A) an automatic door bottom

(B) a heavy-duty, silent door closer

(C) neoprene gasketing

(D) a solid-core door

7. Insulation is used in interior walls to

(A) prevent heat transmission from one side to the other

(B) improve the strength of the wall

(C) improve the acoustic characteristics of the wall

(D) increase the fire resistance of the wall

8. Changing a ceiling from gypsum wallboard to acoustic tile would most affect the room's

(A) reverberation

(B) sound transmission

(C) decibel loss

(D) impact insulation class

9. In a small lecture hall, it would be best to avoid

(A) a sound amplification system

(B) a vaulted ceiling

(C) carpet

(D) parallel walls

10. Which of the following is NOT true about noise reduction between two rooms?

(A) Noise reduction increases with an increase in the transmission loss of the wall separating the two rooms.

(B) The stiffness of the wall can affect noise reduction.

(C) To improve noise reduction, the designer should place absorptive materials on both sides of the wall.

(D) An increase in wall area separating the two rooms is detrimental.

21

BIDDING AND NEGOTIATION OF CONTRACTS

After the interior designer has completed a design and produced the necessary construction drawings, specifications, and furniture, fixtures, and equipment (FF&E) documents, the contract administration phase begins. This includes establishing a contract between the owner and contractor (and others, as required), managing the project in the designer's office, and providing the necessary administrative services that are the responsibility of the interior designer. In addition, the interior designer must understand the roles and obligations of the contractor, owner, and others during the administration of the project. These topics are discussed in the following chapters. The methods of producing FF&E documents and procuring furniture and furnishings are discussed in Ch. 16.

The first step in starting the contract administration phase is finding a contractor and establishing an agreement between the owner and the contractor. Contracts between the owner and the contractor are established in one of two ways. With a *negotiated contract*, the owner (with the possible assistance of the interior designer) selects a contractor to do the work. The contractor and owner then negotiate a price and other terms of their agreement. The contractor may be selected based on a previous working relationship, on the recommendations of others, or both. Negotiation is discussed later in this chapter.

With a *bid contract* (or *tendered contract*, in Canada), the drawings and specifications are completed by the interior designer (and other consultants, if necessary) and then sent to several general contractors who bid on the work defined by the contract documents. The owner (again, with the assistance of the interior designer) can then select the contractor based on cost as well as experience, schedule, and other criteria.

BIDDING PROCEDURES

Competitive bidding for construction and, when feasible, furniture and furnishings, is popular with many owners because it usually results in the lowest cost. For most public agencies, bidding is mandatory. However, bidding must be conducted within clearly defined guidelines to protect the owner from disreputable contractors and unethical bidding practices. Through many years of practice, bidding procedures have generally been standardized and codified in various industry association documents. Everyone involved with the process knows the rules and what is expected. This section describes the typical procedures and documents for bidding. These are described in more detail in the American Institute of Architect's (AIA) document A771, Instructions to Interiors Bidders, which is often used by both architects and interior designers.

Prequalification of Bidders

Bidding may be open to any contractor or restricted to a list of contractors who have been prequalified by the owner. The purpose of prequalification is to select only those contractors who meet certain standards of reliability, experience, financial stability, and performance. For example, an owner contemplating the construction of a million-dollar corporate office headquarters would not be comfortable reviewing the bid of a small home contractor. Once these standards have been met, the owner will be better able to review bids based primarily on price, personnel, and completion time.

Prequalification is usually based on information submitted by contractors concerning their financial qualifications, personnel, experience, references, size, bonding capability, and any special qualities that make them particularly suited for the project under consideration. For public work, when prequalification is allowed, it is usually based on financial assets and the size of the firm.

Advertising for Bids

There are two ways to notify prospective bidders of a project. The first is by advertising in newspapers and trade journals, and the second is with an invitation to bid. With an *advertisement for bids*, the following information is published in one or more newspapers.

- the fact that a call for bids is being made

- the project name and location

- the name and address of the owner and interior designer

- a brief description of the project, including building type and size, principal construction materials and systems, and other pertinent information

- the date, time, and location the bids are due

- how and where bidding documents can be obtained, and deposit required, if any

- the locations where bid documents may be viewed

- the type and amount of bid bonds required

- the procedures for submitting bids

- whether or not the bids will be opened publicly

- other information as required, such as the owner's right to waive irregularities of the bidding process or to accept bids other than the lowest

Advertising for bids is usually required for public work, although much private work is also advertised in the case of open bidding.

For prequalified bidders, an *invitation to bid* is sent to the prospective bidders. The invitation contains the same information listed above for bid advertisements. Even with a prequalified list, there should be enough bidders to encourage price competition. If furniture and fixtures are being bid on private work, the work is usually done on a prequalified basis because there are usually only a few dealers (often only one) that can bid on the same furniture. These dealers are known ahead of time by the interior designer.

Availability of Bid Documents

Bid documents are generally made available through the interior designer's office. Each bidder receives the required documents, including prints of the drawings, specifications, bidding documents, bid forms, and other required items. It is general practice to require that each bidder put down a deposit on each set of documents taken. The deposit may be returned when the documents are returned in usable condition after bidding. In some cases, the documents are loaned with no deposit required. Extra sets of documents over a certain number can be purchased by the contractor. In most large cities, documents are also put on file in a central plan room where subcontractors and material suppliers can review them. There are also electronic document services that make the documents available online.

Substitutions

During bidding, many contractors request that substitutions be considered for some of the materials specified. This most often happens when there are proprietary specifications or a very limited list of acceptable manufacturers. The conditions under which substitutions will be considered and the procedures for reviewing submissions should be clearly defined in the instructions to bidders.

Generally, bidders are required to submit requests for approval at least 10 days before the bid opening. The requests must include the name of the material or equipment for which the substitution is being submitted along with complete backup information about the proposed substitution. The burden of proof of the substitution's merit rests with the bidder. The interior designer then reviews the submission and may either reject it or approve it. If the submission is approved, the interior designer issues an addendum stating this fact and sends it to all the bidders.

Addenda

During the bidding process, there are always questions that need answers, errors that are discovered, and changes that the owner or interior designer decides to make. An *addendum* is a written or graphic document issued by the interior designer before the execution of the contract that modifies or interprets the bidding documents by additions, deletions, clarifications, or corrections. Addenda are issued during the bidding process before bids are submitted. An example of an addendum is shown in Fig. 21.1. When an addendum is issued, it is sent to all bidders no later than four days before receipt of bids to give all the bidders ample opportunity to study the document and modify their proposals accordingly.

Prebid Conference

On some projects, it is advantageous to hold a prebid conference. This is a meeting with the interior designer, owner, architect (if one is involved), engineering consultants, and bidders during which the bidders can ask questions and the interior designer and owner can emphasize particularly important conditions of the project. On very large projects, there may be a separate conference for mechanical subcontract bidders, electrical bidders, and so on. During these conferences, the interior designer should have someone take complete notes concerning the items discussed. A copy of the notes should be sent to all bidders, whether or not they were in attendance.

Bid Opening

In the instructions to bidders, the date, time, and place of the bid opening are included. Unless modified by addenda, the bid opening time and method of submitting the bids should be strictly observed. Bids received after the opening time should not be accepted unless none of the

Figure 21.1 **ADDENDUM #2**
Addendum

Project: Global Transportation Headquarters
Project #:   9042
Date: July 27, 2010

Interiors by ABC, Inc.
2776 N. Ashley

To all general contract bidders of record on the project referenced above:

The contract document are modified as follows:

1. Instructions to bidders, Page 1: Bid due date is changed to 4:00 pm, Thursday, August 12, 2010.

2. Specification section 06400, Page 06400-3: Veneer cut is changed from quarter sliced oak to plain sliced oak.

3. Detail 5, Sheet A-6: Width of storage cabinet should be 1'-9", not 2'-0".

bids has been opened and there are no objections from those bidders present.

Most public bid openings are conducted by the interior designer, with the owner and bidders present. The bids are read aloud, and the presence or absence of any required supporting documentation is noted. The interior designer usually prepares a bid log to note the base bid amount, amounts of alternates (if any), whether receipt of any addenda was acknowledged, and other pertinent information. The bid log should be made available to the bidders in either open or private bidding.

There should be no announcement of the apparent low bid at the bid opening; the interior designer should thank everyone for submitting and state that the submissions will be evaluated and a decision of award will be made within a certain time, usually 10 days. The decision should be sent to all the bidders.

If, after the bids have been opened, a bidder discovers and can support the claim that a clerical or mathematical error has been made, the bidder is usually allowed to withdraw the bid. If it was the low bid, the next lowest bidder is accepted.

Evaluation and Awarding of the Bid

The interior designer may assist the owner in evaluating the bids. This process includes not only looking for the lowest proposed contract sum but also reviewing prices for alternates, substitutions, lists of proposed subcontractors, qualification statements, and other documentation required by the instructions to bidders. The owner has the right to reject any or all bids, to reject bids not accompanied by the required bid bond or other documentation, or to reject a bid that is in any way incomplete or irregular.

If all the bids exceed the project budget and the owner-designer agreement fixes a limit on construction costs, the owner has four options.

    1. to rebid (or renegotiate if it is a negotiated contract)

    2. to authorize an increase in the construction cost and proceed with the project

    3. to work with the interior designer in revising the scope of the project to reduce costs

    4. to abandon the project

Rebidding seldom results in any significant reduction in cost unless the bidding marketplace is changing rapidly. If the project is revised, the extra cost of having the interior designer modify the documents may be borne by the owner unless there are contract provisions specifying responsibility for changing the drawings or specifications if the project comes in over budget. One of the advantages of including alternates in the bid is having a flexible method of deleting or substituting materials or construction elements to reduce the project cost if the bid is too high.

BIDDING DOCUMENTS

Bidding documents are usually prepared by the interior designer using standard forms or forms provided by the owner. Many commercial clients who engage in much building have developed their own forms and procedures, but these forms are typically similar in content to standard forms. The bidding documents are usually bound into the project manual, but these forms are not a legal part of the contract documents.

The bidding documents usually include

- the advertisement or invitation to bid
- instructions to bidders
- bid forms
- bid security information
- requirements for a performance bond, if required
- requirements for a labor and material payment bond, if required

Other documents that are sometimes added include qualification forms, a subcontractor list form, requirements for certificates of insurance and compliance with applicable laws and regulations (such as equal employment opportunity laws), and information available to bidders, such as drawings of existing construction.

In addition to the bidding documents that are not part of the contract documents, the bidding package also includes the drawings, specifications, general and supplementary conditions of the contract, addenda issued before the receipt of bids, and a form of agreement between owner and contractor.

Advertisement to Bid

As previously mentioned, public bidding requires that bidding for the proposed project be advertised in one or more newspapers or trade publications. If a list of prequalified bidders is being used, an invitation to bid is sent to those contractors. On some private projects, the interior designer may simply telephone the contractors on the prequalified list to ask if they would like to bid. The advertisement or invitation to bid is also printed and bound into the project manual with the other bidding documents.

Instructions to Bidders

The instructions to bidders outlines the procedures and requirements that the bidders must follow in submitting bids, how the bids will be considered, submittals required of the successful bids, and how the bids should be physically submitted. Bids are normally submitted in sealed envelopes with the name of the party receiving the bid on the outside along with the project name and the name of the company submitting it.

The AIA document A771, Instructions to Interiors Bidders, is often used. Other organizations also produce similar forms. Instructions to bidders normally include the following items.

- *Consideration of bids:* The procedure for opening bids and reviewing them is stated, including under what conditions bids may be rejected, how they will be evaluated, and conditions for award of the contract. Bids may be opened publicly or privately, although government projects require a public opening. The owner has the right to reject any or all bids. The owner also has the right to accept alternates in any order or combination and to determine the low bidder on the basis of the sum of the base bid and alternates accepted.

- *Bidders' representation:* In making a bid, the bidder represents that he or she has read and understood the documents, reviewed the plans and specifications, and visited the site to become familiar with the conditions under which the work will take place, and that the bid is based on the materials, equipment, and systems required by the bidding documents, without exception.

- *Bidding documents:* This article states where the documents may be obtained, how many sets of documents the bidder may obtain, and the amount of deposit, if any, for the documents. If the documents are returned within 10 days after receipt of bids, the deposit is returned. The cost of replacing any missing or damaged documents is deducted from the deposit. The bidder winning the contract may keep the documents, and their deposit will be returned. Normally, bidding documents are not issued directly to sub-bidders unless specifically stated in the advertisement or invitation to bid. The documents also state what the contractor and subcontractors should do if they discover an error or inconsistency. In such a case, bidders should make a written request to the interior designer for clarification at least seven days before bid opening. The interior designer then issues an addendum to all bidders, answering the questions.

- *Substitutions:* The materials and products described on the drawings and specifications establish a standard for the work. If the bidder wants to propose a substitution, the sustitution must meet these standards. A bidder is required to submit a request for approval at least 10 days prior to the bid opening date. The request must include the name of the material or equipment for which the substitution is being submitted, along with complete backup information about the proposed substitution. The burden of proof of the merit of the substitution rests with the bidder. The interior designer then reviews the submission and may either reject it or approve it. If the submission is approved, the interior designer issues an addendum stating this fact and sends it to all the bidders. No substitutions should be considered after the contract award unless there is a valid reason.

- *Bonds:* The required bonds and the time during which they must be delivered are outlined. Normally the costs of the bonds are included in the bid amount unless they are specifically required to be furnished after the receipt of bids and before execution of the contract. Performance and payment bonds are described in more detail in the following sections.

- *Interpretation or correction of bidding documents:* This article requires the contractor to carefully study the documents, examine the site and local conditions, and report to the interior designer any errors, inconsistencies, or ambiguities discovered. If the bidders or sub-bidders need clarification or interpretation of the bidding documents, they must make a written request that must reach the interior designer at least seven days prior to the bid date. The interior designer must then issue any interpretations or corrections by addendum, which is sent to all bidders. Bidders must acknowledge receipt of all addenda on the bid form.

• *Addenda:* Addenda were discussed previously. The instructions to bidders states that addenda must be transmitted to all bidders and made available for inspection wherever bidding documents are on file for that purpose. Addenda must be issued no later than four days prior to the date of bid opening.

• *Modification or withdrawal of bid:* Bids may not be modified after the designated bid time and date. However, prior to that time, a bid may be modified or withdrawn by making notice in writing over the signature of the bidder. The person receiving bids must date- and time-stamp the request. Withdrawn bids can be resubmitted if they are in full conformance with the instructions to bidders.

• *Post-bid information:* In some cases, the owner may want the contractor to submit to the interior designer a contractor's qualification statement, unless it has already been submitted as part of the bidding process. The contractor must also furnish to the owner the following.

- a designation of the work to be performed with the contractor's own forces

- the names of the manufacturers and suppliers of the principal products proposed for use on the project

- the names of persons or companies proposed to perform major portions of the work

If the successful bidder requests it, the owner must furnish to the bidder reasonable evidence that the financial arrangements have been made to fulfill the owner's obligations.

This must be done no later than seven days prior to the expiration of the time for withdrawal of bids.

Bid Forms

To ensure that all bids will be identical in format, there should be a standard form on which all the bidders enter the required information. This will also make it easier to compare and evaluate the bids. One such form is illustrated in Fig. 21.2. The bid form should contain space for the amount of the base bid, the price for the alternates (if any), unit prices (if any), and the number of calendar or work days in which the bidder proposes to complete the work. Space should be provided for the bidder to acknowledge receipt of any addenda. The bid form must be signed by someone legally empowered to bind the contractor to the owner in a contract.

Bid Security

Bid security is used to ensure that the successful bidder will enter into a contract with the owner. The owner may not require it on small interior design contracts, and it is sometimes waived on larger projects. The final decision concerning the requirement for bid security is the owner's. The form of the bid security maybe a certified check, cashier's check, or bid bond. If the successful bidder does not enter into an agreement, the bid security may be retained to compensate for the difference between the low bid and the next lowest bid. The amount of the bid security is set either as a fixed price or as a percentage of the bid; it is usually about 5% of the estimated cost of the work or of the bid price.

Performance Bonds

A *performance bond* is a statement by a surety company that obligates the surety company to complete construction of the project should the contractor default on his or her obligations. If this happens, the surety company may complete construction by

Figure 21.2
Bid Form

BID FORM

We have received the documents titled

☐ _____ ,☐

dated _____, as prepared by Interiors by ABC, Inc.

We have also received Addenda number _____

and have included their provisions in this bid. We have examined both the documents and the site and hereby propose to furnish all labor, materials, equipment, and transportation in strict accordance with the documents for the full completion of the project for the sum of:

_____ dollars,

($ _____), which sum is hereby designated as BASE BID.

Overhead, profit, taxes, and freight costs are to be included in the BASE BID sum.

ALTERNATES

ALTERNATE #1, add/deduct: $ _____.

ALTERNATE #2, add/deduct: $ _____.

ALTERNATE #3, add/deduct: $ _____.

ALTERNATE #4, add/deduct: $ _____.

Circle add or deduct as appropriate.

Alternates are itemized in Section 01005 of the Specifications.

Unit prices will be required at the time of bid and shall be attached to the bid form. Unit price is defined as the price per unit of measurement for materials and labor to provide the item, plus overhead and profit. Break out labor and material for each case.

If the undersigned is notified of the acceptance of this bid, within thirty (30) days after the date set for opening thereof, or any time thereafter before this bid is withdrawn, he or she agrees to execute a Contract in the form of these documents and to furnish the necessary bonds together with certificate of Insurance as required by the Contract Documents and to provide the required work for compensation as computed from the bids sums included in this bid.

Time of completion: The undersigned agrees, if awarded the Contract, to commence work immediately after receiving official Notice to Proceed and to complete the Work not later than:

_____.

Name of Firm: _____

Telephone: _____ Date: _____

Signed: _____

Printed: _____

Title: _____

hiring another contractor, or it may simply supply additional money to the defaulting contractor to allow construction to proceed.

Performance bonds are usually mandatory on public work and advisable on private work. The cost of the performance bond is a percentage of the construction cost (around 3%) and is ultimately paid by the owner because it is included in the total amount of the contract price. The interior designer or owner should verify that the bond is written by a surety able to issue bonds in the particular state where the work will take place.

Labor and Material Payment Bonds

Although a performance bond ensures the completion of the contract, it does not guarantee payment for labor and materials by a defaulting contractor. The result of nonpayment could be liens against the property or litigation by subcontractors and material suppliers. Accordingly, a *labor and material payment bond* is usually required along with a performance bond to protect the owner against both types of problems.

COST CONTROL

Throughout the design process and up to completion of contract documents, the construction cost is only an estimate by the interior designer. It is only with bidding or final negotiation that the owner finally receives a firm price on the project. If the interior designer has been doing a reasonable job of tracking design changes and has a good idea of component costs, the bid price should be fairly close to the estimated amount.

Although the interior designer does not (and cannot) guarantee that the final construction cost will not vary from the estimate, there are several variables that can affect the final bid price.

Bidding in the Marketplace

By its very definition, bidding is a competitive activity. The price a contractor is willing to submit to an owner is dependent on the actual cost of subcontractor bids, the cost of the contractor's own labor and materials, the cost of equipment rental, and the contractor's indirect costs, overhead, and profit.

Bidding is also affected by the construction marketplace, which is itself competitive. For example, if the local economy is depressed, contractors, subcontractors, and material suppliers may be willing to lower prices or reduce profit margins in order to get work and simply stay in business. In good times when work is plentiful, contractors are more selective about what jobs to bid on and what profit allowance to put in their bids. They are not as concerned about reducing prices to get jobs.

Both the interior designer and owner should be sensitive to these types of market conditions. If there is some flexibility in the owner's schedule, it can be advantageous to either delay or accelerate design and bidding to match favorable market conditions.

Effects of Documents on Bids

One of the variables over which the interior designer and owner have control is the set of contract documents. These can affect the amount of bids by what they contain and how they are put together, beyond just the amount and quality of construction they represent.

Poorly prepared drawings and specifications can raise questions in the mind of the contractor about what is specifically required, what may simply be implied, and what is omitted. To cover possible unforeseen items, the contractor may add extra money in the bid. On the other hand, a complete and clearly coordinated set of documents gives the contractor confidence in the scope and quality of the specified materials and extent of work required. The contractor can then include, with more confidence, only those items shown in the documents.

Alternates

An *alternate* is a request included in the bidding documents asking the contractor to supply a price for some type of variation from the base bid. This variation may be a change in materials or level of quality of a material, a deletion of some component, or the addition of some construction element. For example, the base bid may include carpet as a floor covering in a room, while an alternate may be to substitute wood flooring for the carpet.

Alternates allow the owner some flexibility in modifying the cost of a project when the bids are submitted, by varying the quantity or quality of portions of the job. They also allow the owner to select certain options based on firm prices rather than preliminary estimates.

Alternates are called *add-alternates* if they add to the base bid, or *deduct-alternates* if they reduce the base amount. Because both the interior designer and bidders will need more time to prepare them, alternates should be used carefully and should not be viewed as a substitute for conscientious cost estimating and reasonable design for the base-bid amount.

When evaluating the bids, the selected alternates should be used to arrive at the lowest overall bid, but alternates should not be manipulated to favor one bidder over another.

Unit Prices

Unit prices are set costs for certain portions of the work based on individual quantities, such as linear feet or square yards, of installed material. When required, they are listed on the bid form and provide a basis for determining changes to the contract. For example, a cost per square foot for adding parquet flooring may be requested if the full extent of this type of flooring is unknown when bids are received. Even though the total cost may not be known, the unit costs of the bidders can be compared.

If unit prices are used when work is deleted from the contract, the amount of credit is usually less than the price for an additional quantity of the same item. Spaces should be provided in the bid form for both add- and deduct-amounts when applicable.

Allowances

As described in Ch. 7, an *allowance* is a set amount of money estimated by the interior designer to cover a particular material or piece of equipment when the cost for that material or equipment cannot be determined precisely at the time of the bid or negotiated proposal. For bidding, an allowance provides a way to allocate some amount of money for an item in the bid, even if the exact quantity or quality of the item is not known. The allowance (or allowances) is stated in the appropriate section (or sections) of the specifications, so all bidders are using the same amount in their bids. The contractor must add to the allowance the cost for unloading, handling, and installing the item as well as costs for the contractor's overhead and profit. If the costs for the allowance are more or less than the original estimate, the contract sum is adjusted accordingly by change order.

NEGOTIATION

With a negotiated contract, the owner, with the assistance of the interior designer, works out the final contract price and conditions with one contractor. The contractor with which the owner negotiates may be selected in one of two ways. In the first, the owner may know precisely which contractor he or she wants to complete the project. This knowledge may come from having worked with the contractor before, through a referral, or by reputation. In the second method, the owner may select several possible contractors to be interviewed. Each of the contractors is interviewed, and one is selected based on qualifications and possibly a fee proposal. If requested by the owner, the interior designer may assist in organizing and participating in the selection interviews and the negotiation process. During the negotiation process, the contractor may point out problems, make suggestions, or propose changes in the design or specifications to reduce the cost of the project. If the agreement is negotiated with a general contractor, the subcontracts may be open to competitive bidding.

SAMPLE QUESTIONS

1. Which of the following is a FALSE statement about addenda?

  (A) An addendum is sent only to the contractor requesting the clarification.

  (B) Addenda are only issued before the construction contract is signed.

  (C) Addenda are used to modify or interpret the contract documents.

  (D) An addendum must be issued four or five days before bid opening.

2. Two weeks before the bids are due on a large restaurant project, one of the contractors asks if he can price a type of ceiling tile that was not listed in the specifications. What action should the interior designer take?

  (A) Advise the contractor that he should submit backup proof with the bid that the proposed change is equal to what was specified.

  (B) Refer the contractor to the owner, who will make the final determination, and then notify the other bidders that this has been done.

  (C) Tell the contractor to request approval in writing.

  (D) Issue an addendum stating that one of the contractors has asked for permission to price an alternate and that all contractors may do this.

3. What contractor selection method would be best for a client who wants to get the lowest price for remodeling a complex data-processing facility?

  (A) State the requirements of the project in an advertisement for bidders in local trade journals and newspapers.

  (B) Select a qualified contractor, and negotiate a fixed cost based on detailed drawings and specifications.

  (C) Negotiate the lowest possible price with one contractor, and then bid the project if the first cost is over the client's budget.

  (D) Develop a list of contractors who have experience in the project type, and then ask them to bid on the job.

4. Bid openings are typically attended by the contractors and the

  (A) owner

  (B) interior designer

  (C) owner and interior designer

  (D) subcontractors, owner, and interior designer

5. For a client who wants to hire the best contractor for a project at the best price and limit potentially nonqualified companies, the interior designer should suggest

  (A) an invitation to bid

  (B) an advertisement to bid

  (C) prequalification of bidders

  (D) a negotiated contract

6. To avoid liens against a project, the interior designer should suggest that the owner require the contractor to submit a

(A) bid bond

(B) bid security

(C) performance bond

(D) labor and material payment bond

7. The designer for the interior furnishings of a large public hospital project financed with bond money has assisted the city government in preparing the bidding documents. When the bids from five qualified contractors are opened, they are all over budget, ranging from 4% to 10% over the approved costs. What should the designer do?

(A) Recommend that the city accept the lowest bid and obtain the extra 4% from other sources.

(B) Begin to study ways to reduce the projects scope so it meets the budget.

(C) Suggest that the project be rebid because the lowest bid is so close to the budget.

(D) Wait for the city to tell the designer how it wants to proceed.

8. The requirements for how bidders should propose a substitution is found in the

(A) advertisement to bid

(B) bidding procedures

(C) instructions to bidders

(D) general conditions

9. When the owner wants to make sure some amount of money is included in the bid for as-yet known materials, the interior designer should use

(A) an allowance

(B) an add-alternate

(C) a material bond

(D) a unit price

10. The final responsibility of awarding a contract rests with the

(A) interior designer

(B) construction manager

(C) owner

(D) owner's legal counsel

22
CONSTRUCTION AND FF&E CONTRACTS

Contract documents consist of the Owner-Contractor (or Vendor) Agreement; the General Conditions of the Contract; the Supplementary Conditions of the Contract (if any); the drawings, specifications, and addenda issued before execution of the contract; any other documents specifically listed in the agreement; and modifications issued after execution of the contract. A *modification* is a change order, a written amendment to the contract signed by both parties, a written interpretation issued by the interior designer, or a written order for a minor change in the work. The contract documents are complementary, and what is required by one is as binding as if required by all of them.

This chapter outlines the major provisions of the contractual agreements between the owner and the construction contractor or furniture, fixtures, and equipment (FF&E) vendor and the documents that set forth what are known as the General Conditions of the Contract. These General Conditions can apply to either or both the construction of the project and the supplying of the furniture, fixtures, and equipment for the project.

Drawings and specifications are discussed in Chs. 14 and 15. Change orders and other modification are discussed in Ch. 23. Bidding documents and bidding procedures are outlined in Ch. 21. However, bidding documents are not part of the contract, although they are often bound into the project manual. Refer to Ch. 25 for information on owner-designer agreements.

Because the range of interior design services is wide, from selection of furnishings and accessories for a single residential living room to interior construction and furnishings installation for large corporate headquarters, the type and complexity of contract documents varies. This chapter describes the documents that define the contractual agreement between the owner and the contractor for mid- to large-scale projects.

Various professional organizations publish standard documents that can be used by the interior designer. The American Society of Interior Designers (ASID) has a group of documents for residential design and, at the time of this writing, was working on a similar set of documents for commercial design.

The American Institute of Architects (AIA) has a set of five documents that relate to interior design work. These include the following.

- A175™ID, Standard Form of Agreement Between Owner and Vendor for Furniture, Furnishings, and Equipment where the basis of payment is a Stipulated Sum

- A275™ID, General Conditions of the Contract for Furniture, Furnishings, and Equipment

- A775™ID, Invitation and Instructions for Quotation for Furniture, Furnishings and Equipment

- B171™ID, Standard Form of Agreement Between Owner and Architect for Architectural Interior Design Services

- B175™ID, Standard Form of Agreement Between Owner and Architect for Furniture, Furnishings, and Equipment Design Services

In addition, AIA form A201, General Conditions of the Contract for Construction, can be used for interior construction projects.

METHODS OF COMPLETING INTERIOR DESIGN PROJECTS

The completion of an interior design project can occur in several ways. How it is accomplished, its size and complexity, and the specific responsibilities of the interior designer determine the types of contract documents that should be used.

In the simplest case, the owner hires the interior designer to perform a limited scope of work, such as selecting finishes and furniture. The designer works under a letter of agreement with the owner, completing the design work and preparing furniture and finish specifications, which are then given to various vendors and contractors. The owner contracts with these vendors directly to have the work completed. In some situations, the designer may purchase furniture directly for the client. This is the method commonly used for residential work.

For larger, more complex projects, the interior designer may be the owner's primary consultant, contracting with other consultants such as architects, structural engineers, electrical engineers, and mechanical engineers to develop the drawings and specifications for the job. Larger projects may consist of both interior construction and FF&E. The interior designer completes the design and preparation of drawings and specifications within the limits of state laws and local building code regulations and has other consultants do the design work in their particular area of expertise. This method is commonly used for commercial projects.

In other cases, the interior designer works as a consultant to the architect on the project or with an architect but under separate contract to the owner. In these instances, the architect is responsible for interior construction and the interior designer is responsible for only FF&E. This approach is also common for commercial projects where the extent of the structural work and local laws require that certain drawings be prepared and stamped by a licensed architect.

Regardless of whether the interior designer is working alone or with an architect, interior design projects that involve both construction and furnishings are typically completed under two contracts, one for construction and one for FF&E. The following sections describe commonly used FF&E contract documents produced by the AIA. There are similar provisions in other organizations' standard documents.

Although the owner enters into agreements directly with the contractor (or contractors) for construction and with vendors for FF&E, the interior designer must be familiar with the various provisions of these agreements. The Owner-Vendor Agreement and Owner-Contractor Agreement can be written by the designer's attorney or provided by the owner, or standard professional association forms may be used.

If there are two contracts on larger jobs, one for construction and one for FF&E, there are two contractors. One is the construction contractor, who completes the interior construction, such as partitions, doors, lighting, finishes, and whatever else is specifically included. The other is the FF&E vendor, who is typically a furniture dealer, but may, in some instances, be a furniture manufacturer or other design professional. There are two different contracts because construction contracts are governed by common law that regulates services, and FF&E contracts are governed by statutory law that regulates the sale of goods.

FF&E contracts typically cover only movable items such as furniture, appliances, rugs, lamps, and accessories. There may be more than one FF&E contract. For small projects or projects with furniture as well as specialty finishes, FF&E contracts may cover some applied finishes, but these are typically included as part of the construction contract.

OWNER-VENDOR AGREEMENT

One standard association agreement form is the Standard Form of Agreement Between Owner and Vendor for Furniture, Furnishings, and Equipment where the basis of payment is a stipulated sum, AIA document A175 ID. This section discusses the major provisions in this document.

Identification of Contract Documents

The first article specifies that the contract documents include the agreement, the conditions of the contract (general, supplementary, and other conditions), the drawings, the schedules and specifications, all addenda, and all modifications issued after the execution of the agreement. It refers to a later article in which all the documents are listed in detail. The purpose of this article is to include all the other documents by reference.

Basic Provisions

Some provisions are common to all contracts, such as to include a description of the work, the time of commencement and substantial completion, and the contract sum. These provisions are included in several articles in the AIA documents.

The work normally includes what is described in the contract documents, primarily the drawings and specifications. Any exclusions can be described in the Owner-Vendor Agreement as well as in the other contract documents when they are identified as being the responsibility of other parties.

The date of commencement is important because it is from this date that construction completion time is measured. The date can be the date of the agreement, a specific calendar date specified in the agreement, or the date when the contractor is given a notice-to-proceed letter by the owner.

The date of completion is in the same article as the date of commencement and is expressed with a specific calendar date. The contract sum states the compensation the vendor will receive for doing the work.

Progress Payments

Article 4 lists the requirements for payment, including net days from approval of application for payment, criteria for deposits, discounts, special orders, cancellation, restocking, and final payment.

Based on applications for payment submitted by the contractor, the owner makes periodic payments, usually monthly, to the contractor. The Owner-Contractor Agreement defines how these payments are to be made.

In the standard AIA agreement forms, the amount due in any period is based on the percentage of completed work and any materials purchased and stored but not yet incorporated into the work, less any moneys already paid. To protect the owner against incomplete or defective work on the part of the vendor, a certain percentage of each payment, usually 10%, is often withheld until final completion of the work. This percentage is called the *retainage* (or *holdback* in Canada).

To receive payment, the vendor must submit an application for payment to the interior designer listing the completed work and stored materials. The interior designer then reviews the application, verifies that it is correct, and recommends payment to the owner, who then makes payment. If there is work in dispute, the interior designer may choose not to certify payment of all or a portion of the amount until the problem is resolved.

OWNER-CONTRACTOR AGREEMENT

One standard association agreement form is the Standard Form of Agreement Between Owner and Contractor where the basis of payment is a stipulated sum, AIA document A101. This section discusses the major provisions in this document. Other professional interior design association documents have similar provisions.

Identification of Contract Documents

The first article specifies that the contract documents include the agreement, the conditions of the contract (general, supplementary, and other conditions), the drawings, the schedules and specifications, all addenda, and all modifications issued after the execution of the agreement. It refers to a later article in which all the documents are listed in detail. The purpose of this article is to include all the other documents by reference.

Basic Provisions

Some of the basic provisions include a description of the work, the time of commencement and substantial completion, and the contract sum. These are included in several articles in the AIA documents as well as other professional interior design association documents.

The work normally includes what is described in the contract documents, primarily the drawings and specifications. Any exclusions can be described in the Owner-Contractor Agreement as well as in the other contract documents when they are identified as being the responsibility of other parties.

The date of commencement is important because it is from this date that construction completion time is measured. The date can be a specific calendar date specified in the agreement or can be the date when the contractor is given a notice-to-proceed letter by the owner.

The time of substantial completion is expressed with a specific calendar date or by a number of calendar days from the date of commencement. *Substantial completion* is defined as the stage in the progress of the work when the work or a designated portion thereof is sufficiently complete according to the contract documents so the owner can occupy or utilize the site, though a few minor items may remain to be completed or corrected. Completion time may be extended as provided for in the General Conditions when circumstances are beyond the control of the contractor. If a particular completion date is important to the owner, provisions for liquidated damages may be included. *Liquidated damages* are moneys paid by the contractor to the owner for every day the project is late. They represent actual anticipated losses the owner will incur if the project is not completed on time. For example, if an owner cannot move and must pay double rent, the liquidated damages may be the amount of the extra rent.

In many cases, a liquidated damage provision is accompanied by a bonus provision so the contractor receives a payment for early completion. This, too, is usually based on a realistic cost savings the owner will realize for early completion. If a penalty clause is included (which is different from liquidated damages), an equal bonus provision must also be included. As simply an incentive to complete the project on time, a bonus/penalty clause may have no relationship to actual monetary losses the owner may incur in the project is not completed on time.

The contract sum states the compensation the contractor will receive for doing the work.

Progress Payments

Based on applications for payment submitted by the contractor, the owner makes periodic payments, usually monthly, to the contractor. The Owner-Contractor Agreement defines how these payments are to be made. These are discussed in the next section.

GENERAL CONDITIONS OF THE CONTRACT FOR FURNISHINGS, AND EQUIPMENT

The General Conditions of the Contract for Furniture, Furnishings, and Equipment (AIA Form A275 ID) is one of the most important parts in the entire set of contract documents for FF&E. It is incorporated by specific reference into the Owner-Designer Agreement (B171 ID) as well as the Owner-Vendor Agreement (A175 ID). Candidates should obtain a copy of the General Conditions for Furniture, Furnishings, and Equipment and read the entire document before taking the NCIDQ exam. This section discusses the major articles in this AIA document. Other professional association documents contain similar provisions. If the AIA document is used, the words "interior designer" must be substituted for the word "architect." Some of the topics included in the General Conditions but not discussed here include definitions and execution of the contract, related activities by the owner or separate vendors, protection of persons and property, insurance, and miscellaneous provisions.

The General Conditions of the Contract for Furniture, Furnishings, and Equipment is coordinated with the Uniform Commercial Code (UCC), specifically Article 2, which governs the sale of goods. This is especially important for the interior designer selling furniture and accessories to clients rather than just specifying them. The UCC is applicable in all states except Louisiana, which has only adopted certain sections of the code. AIA Form A275 ID recognizes the commercial standards set forth in the UCC and uses certain standard UCC terminology.

The Uniform Commercial Code

The UCC was written to provide consistent rules for commerce in the United States. It establishes regulations for the buying and selling, along with other types of transactions, of goods that are defined as tangible and movable items. The UCC covers such things as sales contracts, product liability, warranties, ownership (title), and risk.

The provisions of the UCC govern the buying and selling of furniture and other goods for an interior design project if specific written provisions are not otherwise included in the contract. The General Conditions of the Contract for Furniture, Furnishings, and Equipment has been written to recognize the commercial standards of the UCC. In some cases, the UCC may take precedence over the contract. In other cases, state laws may override some provisions of the UCC. The interior designer must know the provisions of the UCC and his or her own state's laws if the designer is acting as a reseller of furniture and furnishings.

The delivery of goods is regulated by the UCC as well as the Interstate Commerce Commission (ICC). Furniture and accessories may be shipped by common carriers, contract carriers, or private carriers. Common carriers are those who offer services to the public. Contract carriers provide service only to certain companies they choose to do business with. Private carriers are companies who own and operate their own trucks to move their own merchandise. If a common carrier is used, the carrier company is responsible for the goods they ship. If a private carrier is used, the responsibility for the furniture during shipment depends on who owns the goods. Generally, whoever has title to the furniture bears the responsibility of damage or loss.

There are several ways furniture and accessories are shipped, and risk to either the seller or buyer is assigned by the UCC. They all use the term FOB, or *free on board*. FOB means the manufacturer pays for loading the goods onto a truck or train. FOB is followed by either the word factory or destination. "FOB factory" means that title is transferred at the factory, the buyer (FF&E vendor) pays the transportation costs, and the manufacturer is not responsible for loss or damage during shipping. This is often referred to as a shipment contract. "FOB destination" means the seller (manufacturer) is

responsible for shipping and for recovering any damage or loss during shipment. This is often referred to as a destination contract. "FOB factory-freight prepaid" means the FF&E vendor owns the furniture, but the supplier pays the shipping charges.

Generally, the FF&E vendor or furniture dealer takes care of all the shipping details, but the interior designer should be aware of these terms to be able to verify that the designer's client is protected from loss during shipment and storage and that all costs are included in the budget.

Duties and Responsibilities of the Owner

Unless otherwise provided for in the contract, the owner must provide each of the following.

- areas on the project premises that the vendor can use to do the work

- access to the premises at reasonable times

- space for the receipt, inspection, and staging of materials and furnishings

- temporary utilities, facilities, and vertical transportation necessary for the execution of the work

- normal security for the project premises

The FF&E General Conditions state that the owner is responsible for a preliminary inspection of the furniture and other goods at the job site, but this inspection does not constitute acceptance. When installation is complete, the owner must conduct an acceptance inspection, and if any problems or deficiencies are found, the owner must notify the vendor in writing.

Duties and Responsibilities of the Vendor

The vendor in an FF&E agreement is responsible for ordering, delivering, and installing the goods described in the contract. The vendor also frequently warehouses the goods between the time they are delivered and when they are actually installed. The vendor must visit the project site and review the contract documents to become familiar with the conditions under which the work will be performed and to correlate personal observations with requirements of the contract documents.

Based on the furniture specifications developed by the interior designer, the FF&E vendor prepares purchase orders. There are separate purchase orders for each manufacturer or supplier providing goods for the project. Based on the purchase orders, the manufacturer prepares acknowledgments that are reviewed by the FF&E vendor prior to manufacture or order filling.

The vendor must supervise the work and pay for labor, materials, FF&E, and other facilities necessary for the completion of the work. The vendor, in turn, sends payment requests to the owner for the moneys paid out by the vendor. The vendor must also prepare a work schedule for review by the owner and the interior designer and provide for final clean up of the work.

Title and Risk of Loss
The vendor takes on the risk of loss of the furniture and fixtures until the owner accepts it after final inspection or upon payment in full to the vendor, whichever occurs first. The owner has no obligation to insure furniture and fixtures that do not conform to the contract documents or that have been rejected by the owner.

Delivery and Installation
The vendor is responsible for delivery and installation and must work according to the vendor's progress schedule or at a time agreed upon by the owner and interior designer. The owner and vendor must consult with each other to identify a route to be used to move the material from the point of initial delivery at the project premises to the place of final placement. Installation includes testing as required by the contract documents.

Acceptance
The owner may conduct a preliminary inspection upon delivery to verify delivery and correct quantities, but this initial inspection does not constitute acceptance. Later, the owner, with the assistance of the interior designer, must conduct an acceptance inspection. If any furniture or fixtures are found to be nonconforming, the owner must notify the vendor in writing. The vendor then has 30 days to provide evidence of arrangement to remedy the basis for rejection.

Payments
In much the same way construction payments are made, the vendor must submit to the owner a quotation schedule showing the values allocated to each quotation for portions of the work. When a payment is due, the vendor submits to the owner this quotation schedule with an itemized application for payment along with any supporting data, such as copies of bills of lading or requisitions from sub-vendors. The owner then pays the vendor.

Duties and Responsibilities of the Interior Designer
The interior designer is the owner's representative and is responsible for the administration of the contract as provided for in the Owner-Designer Agreement and other contract documents. For FF&E contracts, the designer provides similar services as described in the next section regarding general conditions for construction. Refer to Ch. 25 on owner-designer contracts for additional duties and responsibilities of the interior designer.

Time
Time is of the essence in the completion of the contract. The vendor is responsible for

completing the work by the date agreed to in the contract documents and must provide adequate work forces to do the job. However, the owner must cooperate and coordinate his or her activities with agreed-to critical dates identified in the vendor's progress schedule. If the owner fails to do this, the owner is responsible for the costs the vendor incurs for warehousing, demurrage, storage, and delivery charges. *Demurrage* is the detention of a ship in port by the ship owner, or of a railroad car or truck by its owner, beyond the time normally allowed or agreed upon. The vendor is due an extension in completion time for negligence on the part of the owner, for changes in the work, or because of labor disputes, fire, or other causes beyond the vendor's control.

GENERAL CONDITIONS OF THE CONTRACT FOR CONSTRUCTION

AIA document A201, General Conditions of the Contract for Construction, is often used for interior construction, changing the words "interior designer" for the word "architect."

Duties and Responsibilities of the Interior Designer

Article 4 of the General Conditions of the Contract for Construction states the interior designer's roles and responsibilities in contract administration. Some of these are discussed in more detail in Chs. 23 and 25, but the typical duties the interior designer performs are described here.

The interior designer acts as the owner's representative, advises and consults with the owner, and may act on behalf of the owner to the extent provided in the contract documents. The designer assists the owner in coordinating schedules for delivery and installation but is *not* responsible for malfeasance of the contractor or any supplier in performing their duties.

The interior designer visits the project premises as necessary to become familiar with the progress of the work and to determine, in general, if the work is proceeding according to the contract documents. The designer keeps the owner informed of the progress and work quality but is not required to make exhaustive or continuous inspections. One paragraph of the contract documents reiterates that the interior designer does not have control over the means, methods, or procedures of construction, procurement, shipment, delivery, or installation. The designer is also not responsible for safety precautions or acts of omission of the contractor, subcontractors, or suppliers.

The interior designer can recommend that the owner reject work that does not conform to the contract documents. The designer also has authority to require special inspections or testing of the work. The interior designer does not have authority to reject nonconforming work, stop the work, or terminate the contract on behalf of the owner. In any case, the actions or authority of the interior designer do not create any duty or responsibility to the contractor, subcontractors, or others.

The designer reviews shop drawings and other submittals for the limited purpose of checking for conformance with the design concept expressed in the contract documents.

The interior designer prepares change orders and may authorize minor changes in the work that do not involve adjusting either the contract sum or contract time and that are not inconsistent with the intent of the contract documents.

The interior designer interprets and decides on matters concerning the requirements of the contract documents and the performance of work if requested by either the owner or contractor. If the designer's interpretation is not acceptable, there are provisions in the General Conditions for arbitration. The designer's decisions concerning matters related to aesthetic effect are final if consistent with the intent shown in the documents.

The interior designer also conducts a final inspection to determine the dates of substantial completion and final completion, and issues a final certificate for payment.

Duties and Responsibilities of the Owner

Article 2 specifies the duties, rights, and responsibilities of the owner. Among these is the responsibility to furnish evidence, at the request of the contractor, that financial arrangements have been made to fulfill the owner's obligations under the contract—in other words, that the owner will pay the contractor.

The owner must also, if necessary, provide surveys describing the physical characteristics and utility locations for the site and a legal description of the site. Normally, these are not critical clauses for interior work. Additionally, the owner must provide to the contractor the number of copies of the drawings and project manuals that are necessary for the execution of the work.

If the contractor fails to correct work not in conformance with the contract documents or persistently fails to carry out such work, the owner may order the contractor to stop the work until the cause for the order is eliminated.

The owner has the right to carry out the work if the contractor fails in his or her duties to correctly do so. The contractor has seven days from receiving written notice from the owner to commence corrections. If no action is taken by the contractor, the owner must give a second notice, and if no corrective actions have been taken by the contractor after this time the owner may take other actions to complete the work, deducting the cost to do this from the contractor's agreement.

Duties and Responsibilities of the Contractor

The contractor is solely responsible for all fabrication, delivery, and installation means, methods, techniques, and procedures, and for coordinating all portions of the work. This includes visiting the site and taking any field measurements required to perform the work. The contractor must report any problems to the owner. The contractor is also responsible to the owner for the acts and omissions of all subcontractors and other people performing work under him or her.

It is not the contractor's responsibility to ascertain that the contract documents conform to building codes, ordinances, and other regulations. However, if the contractor notices some variance, he or she must notify the interior designer in writing. If the contractor does not give this notice and proceeds to perform work knowingly in variance with some regulation, the contractor assumes full responsibility for such work and must bear all costs to correct the situation.

The contractor is also obligated to provide a schedule for the owner's and designer's information, to keep it current, and to conform to it. The contractor must cooperate with the owner and designer in coordinating the schedule with the schedules of other contractors doing work.

The General Conditions includes a section on indemnification. To *indemnify* is to secure against loss or damage, and the indemnification clause is intended to protect the owner and designer against situations where a person is injured due to the negligence of the contractor or the contractor's agents. The clause also is intended to protect the owner and architect against claims from property damage other than to the work itself. Under the section on indemnification, it is stated that, to the extent provided by law, the contractor shall indemnify and hold harmless the owner and interior designer, and their agents and employees, against claims, damages, and expenses arising out of performance of the work. However, this clause does not relieve the interior designer of his or her liability for errors in the drawings, specifications, or administration of the contract.

Work by Owner or Separate Contractors

The owner has the right to perform work related to the project with the owner's own forces and to award separate contracts for certain work. However, exercising this right does require the owner to provide for coordination of his or her own forces and to act with the same obligations and rights as any contractor would have. This clause is especially important for interior work because there are usually separate contracts for FF&E and construction.

Contract Time

The *contract time* is the period from the starting date established in the agreement to the time of substantial completion, including any authorized adjustments. The contractor is expected to proceed expeditiously with adequate work forces and complete the work within the allotted time. The contract time may be extended by change order if delays occur beyond the contractor's control, such as acts or omissions of the owner or interior designer, labor disputes, fire, unavoidable casualties, or transportation delays.

Payments and Completion

The article on payments and completion specifies the procedures for paying the contractor. The contractor makes monthly applications for payment based on the percentage of work completed. The interior designer reviews these applications and issues to the owner a certificate for payment or decides to withhold issuance if there is a valid reason. The General Conditions clearly states that the contractor warrants that title to all work, materials, furniture, and equipment covered by an application for payment will pass to the owner and that these items are free of liens or other encumbrances.

In the standard AIA agreement forms, the amount due in any period is based on the percentage of completed work and any materials purchased and stored but not yet incorporated into the work, less any moneys already paid. As mentioned previously, a retainage is withheld until final completion of the work. The process for submitting applications for payment was described previously in this chapter.

To receive payment, the contractor must submit an application for payment to the interior designer, listing the completed work and stored materials. The interior designer reviews the application, verifies that it is correct, and recommends payment to the owner, who then makes the payment. If any work is in dispute, the interior designer may choose not to certify payment of all or a portion of the amount until the problem is resolved.

The exact procedures the designer must follow are described in more detail in Ch. 23.

Protection of Persons and Property

The contractor is exclusively responsible for onsite safety and precautions against damage to persons and property. This includes the contractor's employees, other people affected by the work, the work itself, FF&E, and adjacent property. If any damage to the work is sustained due to inadequate protection, the contractor must repair or correct it. However, this does not include damages caused by acts of the owner or interior designer.

Changes in the Work

The General Conditions allow for changes to be made in the work after execution of the contract. If changes are required, they are usually due to unforeseen conditions or requests by the owner. These changes are made by a *change order*, which is based on a written agreement among the owner, contractor, and interior designer concerning the extent of the change and its cost and schedule implications. A change order is always required whenever there is a modification of contract cost or time, and it must be signed by the owner, the contractor, and the interior designer. The interior designer has the authority to make minor changes if they do not involve an adjustment in contract sum or contract time. Change order procedures and other types of documents used to make changes in the work are discussed in more detail in Ch. 23, and a sample change order is shown in Fig. 23.3.

Uncovering and Correction of Work

If the contract documents state that certain portions of the work are to be observed by the interior designer before being covered or enclosed, and if the contractor proceeds with covering the work before the designer has inspected it, then the contractor must uncover the work at no additional charge on request by the designer. If there is no specific mention of an item to be observed before covering and if the work is in accordance with the contract documents, the interior designer may ask that it be uncovered, but the cost is borne by the owner through a change order. If it is found that there is nonconforming work, then the contractor is responsible for the additional cost.

The contractor must correct work recommended for rejection by the interior designer for failing to conform to the requirements of the contract documents. The contractor must bear the cost of such corrections, including testing, inspections, and compensation for the designer's services connected with the correction.

If the owner so chooses, he or she can accept nonconforming work. Because this entails a change in the contract, it must be done by written change order and, if appropriate, the contract sum may be reduced.

SUPPLEMENTARY CONDITIONS OF THE CONTRACT

Because of the unique nature of interior design construction and furnishings projects, not every condition can be covered in a standard document such as the General Conditions of the Contract for Construction and the General Conditions of the Contract for Furniture, Furnishings, and Equipment. Each job must be customized to accommodate different clients, governmental regulations, and local laws. Information that is unique to each project can be included in one of four areas: in the bidding requirements if related to bidding, in the Owner-Contractor (or Vendor) Agreement if it relates to contractual matters, in the Supplementary Conditions if it modifies the General Conditions, or in Division 01 (General Requirements) of the specifications in the project manual. For example, limits of insurance and other bonding and insurance requirements are very specific to each client and project type. These are often placed in the Supplementary General Conditions.

Some of the additional items that may be included in the Supplementary Conditions are

- permission for the architect to furnish the contractor with instruments of service in electronic form

- additional information and services provided by the owner

- cost for the architect to review the contractor's requests for substitutions

- provisions for the owner, instead of the contractor, to pay for utilities

- requirement that the contractor employ a superintendent to coordinate mechanical and electrical work

- provisions for fast-track scheduling

- reimbursement by the contractor for extra site visits by the architect, made necessary by the fault of the contractor

- additional protection for the owner against claims for additional time or for consequential damages

- requirements for more detailed information on costs and overhead

- additional requirements for payment procedures

- requirements for liquidated damages and bonuses

- additional requirements for bonding and insurance

There are additional items that can be included as part of the Supplementary Conditions, but the above list suggests what kinds of things are often included.

Standard forms from professional associations are available to assist with writing the Supplementary Conditions. However, just as many clients may have their own standard forms for the General Conditions, they may also have their own requirements for modifications. The interior designer should use whichever form is most appropriate. In any case, modification to the General Conditions or Supplementary Conditions (as with any contract) should only be done with the advice of legal counsel.

SAMPLE QUESTIONS

1. Which of the following is NOT a part of the contract documents?

(A) addenda

(B) bid form

(C) specifications

(D) Owner-Contractor Agreement

2. The owner is protected from incomplete work by the contractor by the use of

(A) indemnification

(B) liquidated damages

(C) retainage

(D) standard contract forms

3. The risk for furniture being damaged during shipment is assigned by the

(A) FF&E General Conditions

(B) Owner-Designer Agreement

(C) Owner-Vendor Agreement

(D) Uniform Commercial Code

4. If, during construction of a project, the contractor notices that a handrail does not meet the local building codes, what action could the designer reasonably expect the contractor to take?

(A) The contractor should notify the designer of the discrepancy in writing.

(B) The contractor should correct the situation and submit a change order for the extra work.

(C) The contractor should build the handrail according to the contract documents because conformance to building codes is the designer's responsibility.

(D) The contractor should notify the designer of the problem and suggest a remedy.

5. Which of the following is the interior designer prohibited from doing under terms of the General Conditions of the Contract for Furniture, Furnishings, and Equipment?

(A) Prepare change orders and authorize minor changes in the work.

(B) Determine the date of substantial completion.

(C) Reject work that does not meet the requirements of the drawings.

(D) Demand that a special inspection be made to determine if the work conforms to the specifications.

6. During furniture delivery to the fifth floor of a building, elevator transportation is the responsibility of the

(A) building manager

(B) FF&E vendor

(C) general contractor

(D) owner

7. Final acceptance of furniture and fixtures is the responsibility of the

(A) architect

(B) interior designer

(C) owner

(D) vendor

8. Which standard form includes contract information about the owner's right to perform work separate from the main construction contract?

(A) instructions to bidders

(B) Owner-Contractor Agreement

(C) General Conditions of the Contract

(D) Supplementary Conditions of the Contract

9. Under what circumstances does the owner have to provide the contractor with evidence of the owner's financial resources to complete the project according the AIA General Conditions of the Contract for Construction?

(A) whenever the contractor asks for such evidence

(B) if the project is a public project

(C) on request of the contractor if the job is being competitively bid

(D) the owner does not have to offer any such proof

10. What type of agreement would a designer be advised NOT to work under when doing a residential project?

(A) a letter of agreement

(B) a series of purchase orders with terms printed on the back

(C) a standard form of AIA or ASID agreement

(D) a contract prepared by the designer's attorney

23

PROJECT MANAGEMENT AND CONTRACT ADMINISTRATION

PROJECT MANAGEMENT

Project management is one of the most important activities of an interior designer. A project manager coordinates the entire process of a job, from its inception to final move-in and post-occupancy follow-up. Project management consists of planning, monitoring, coordinating and directing, documenting, and closing out the job.

Planning

The project manager should be involved from the first determination of the scope of work and estimating fees to the final follow-up. Planning involves setting requirements in three critical areas: time, fees, and quality. *Time planning* is scheduling the work required and making sure there are enough fees and staff to complete it. Methods of scheduling are discussed in Ch. 7.

A fee projection is one of the earliest and most important tasks that a project manager must complete. A *fee projection* takes the total fee the designer will receive for the project and allocates it to the schedule and staff members who will work on the project, after deducting amounts for profit, overhead, and other expenses that will not be used for professional time.

Ideally, fee projections should be developed from a careful projection of the scope of work, its associated costs (direct personnel expense, indirect expenses, and overhead), consultant fees, reimbursables, and profit desired. These should be determined as a basis for setting the final fee agreement with the client. If this is done correctly, there should be enough money to complete the project within the allotted time.

There are several methods for estimating and allocating fees, including several computer programs. Figure 23.1 shows one simple form that combines time scheduling with fee projections. In this example, the total working fee, that is, the fee available to pay people to do the job after subtracting for profit, consultants, and other expenses, is listed in the lower right corner of the chart. The various phases or work tasks needed to complete the job are listed in the lefthand column, and the time periods (most commonly weeks) are listed across the top of the chart.

Figure 23.1
Fee Projection
Chart

Project: Mini-mall						Project No.: 9274					Date: 10/18/10		
Completed by: JBL						Project Manager: JBL					Total Fee: $26,400		

Phase or Task	Period Date	1 11/3–19	2 11/20	3 11/27	4 12/4	5 12/11	6 12/18	7 12/25	8 1/4	9 1/11	% of Total fee	fee allocation by phase or task	person-hrs. est.
SD-design		1320	1320								10	2640	
SD presentation			1320								5	1320	
DD—arch. work				1980	1980						15	3960	
DD—consultant coord.				530	790						5	1320	
DD—approvals					1320						5	1320	
CD—plans/elevs.						1056	1056	1056	1056	1056	20	5280	
CD—details								2640	2640		20	5280	
CD—consultant coord.						440		440	440		5	1320	
CD—specs.									1320	1320	10	2640	
CD—material sel.						660	660				5	1320	

budgeted fees /period	1320	2640	2510	4090	2156	1716	4136	5456	2376	100%	$26,400	
person–weeks or hours	53 / 1.3	106 / 2.6	100 / 2.5	164 / 4	108 / 2.7	86 / 2.2	207 / 5	273 / 6.8	119 / 3			
staff assigned	JLK	JLK AST JBC	JLK AST EMW-(1/2)	JLK AST JBC EMW	JLK AST EMW	JLK AST	JLK AST EMW →	JLK SBS BFD	JLK AST EMW			
actual fees expended												

The project manager estimates the percentage of the total amount of work or fee that he or she thinks each phase will require. This estimate is based on experience and common rules of thumb the design office may use. The percentages are placed in the third column from the right and multiplied by the total working fee to get the allotted fee for each phase (the figure in the second column from the right). This allotted fee is then divided among the number of time periods in the schedule and placed in the individual columns under each time period.

If phases or tasks overlap (as they do in the example in Fig. 23.1), the estimator can total the fees in each period and place this figure at the bottom of the chart. This dollar amount can then be divided by an average billing rate for the people working on the project to determine an approximate budgeted number of hours the office can afford to spend on the project each week and still make a profit. Of course, if the number of hours exceeds about 40, then more than one person will be needed to do the work.

By monitoring time sheets weekly, the project manager can compare the actual hours (or fees) expended against the budgeted time (or fees) and take corrective action if actual time exceeds budgeted time.

Quality planning involves determining with the client what the expectations are concerning design, cost, and other aspects of the project. Quality does not simply mean high-cost finishes but rather the requirements of the client based on his or her needs. These needs should be clearly defined in the programming phase of a project and written down and approved by the client before design work begins.

Monitoring

Monitoring is keeping track of the progress of the job to see if the planned aspects of time, fee, and quality are being accomplished. The original fee projections can be monitored by comparing weekly time sheets with the original estimate. One way of doing this is shown in Fig. 23.2, which uses the information from the same example project estimated in Fig. 23.1.

In this chart, the budgeted weekly fees are placed in the table under the appropriate time period column and work-phase row. The actual amounts of fees expended are written below them. At the bottom of the chart, a simple graph is plotted that shows the actual money expended against the budgeted fees. The project manager can also plot his or her estimate of the percentage of work completed to compare with money expended. If either line begins to vary too much above the estimate, the project manager must find the problem and correct it.

Monitoring quality is sometimes more difficult. At regular times during a project, the project manager, designers, and office principles should review the progress of the job to determine if the original

Figure 23.2
Project Monitoring Chart

Project: Mini-mall		time												
Phase/People/Departments		1	2	3	4	5	6	7	8	9	10	11	12	total
schematic design	budgeted	1320	2640											
	actual	2000	2900											
design development	budgeted			2510	4090									
	actual			3200										
construction docs.	budgeted					2156	1716	4136	5456	2376				
	actual													
	budgeted													
	actual													
	budgeted													
	actual													
	budgeted													
	actual													
	budgeted													
	actual													
total (cumulative)	budgeted	1320	3960	6470	10,560	12,716	14,432	18,568	24,024	26,400				
	actual	2000	4900	8110										

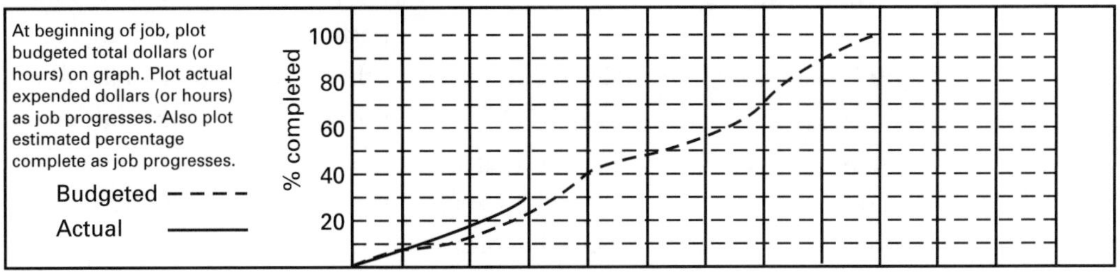

At beginning of job, plot budgeted total dollars (or hours) on graph. Plot actual expended dollars (or hours) as job progresses. Also plot estimated percentage complete as job progresses.

Budgeted – – – –
Actual ———

problems are being solved and if the job is being produced according to the client's and design firm's expectations. The work in progress can also be reviewed to see whether it is technically correct and if all the contractual obligations are being met.

Coordinating and Directing

During the job, the project manager (or whoever is responsible for managing the job) must constantly coordinate the various people involved: the design firm's staff, the consultants, the client, the building code officials, and the firm management. The individual efforts of the staff must also be directed on a weekly or even daily basis to make sure the schedule is being maintained and the necessary work is getting done.

Documenting

Everything that is done on a project must be documented electronically and in writing. This is to provide a record in case legal problems develop as well as to create a project history to use for future jobs. Documentation is also a vital part of communication. An email or written memo is more accurate, communicates more clearly, and is more difficult to forget than a simple phone call, for example.

Most design firms have standard forms or project management software to keep track of things such as transmittals, job observation reports, time sheets, and the like. These forms make it easy to record the necessary information. In addition, all meetings should be documented with meeting notes, and phone calls, emails, personal daily logs, and formal communications such as letters and memos should be documented.

CONTRACT ADMINISTRATION

Contract administration consists of all the activities performed by the interior designer during the time the contract between the owner and the contractor is in force.

The duties of the interior designer are itemized in the AIA General Conditions of the Contract for Furniture, Furnishings, and Equipment (A275™ID) and the General Conditions of the Contract for Construction (A201), if these documents are used. The following sections outline some of the more important provisions of these documents with which candidates should be familiar. Additional information on the duties of the designer is discussed in Ch. 25.

Submittals

After the contract is awarded, the contractor is responsible for providing submittals called for in the contract documents. These include shop drawings, samples, and product data. The submittals are sometimes prepared by the contractor, but most often they are prepared by the subcontractors, vendors, and material suppliers.

Shop drawings are drawings, diagrams, schedules, and other data prepared to show how a subcontractor or supplier proposes to supply and install work to conform to the requirements of the contract documents. As such, they are usually very detailed drawings or product data that show how a portion of the work will be constructed.

Samples are physical examples of a portion of the work intended to show exactly how a material, finish, or piece of equipment will look in the completed job. They become the standards of appearance and workmanship by which the final work will be judged.

Product data includes brochures, charts, performance data, catalog pages, and other information that illustrate some portion of the work. Although all submittals show in detail how much of the work is going to be built and installed, they are not contract documents.

When shop drawings and other submittals are prepared by the subcontractors and material suppliers, they are sent to the general contractor, who is responsible for reviewing and approving them. By reviewing them, the contractor represents that field measurements have been verified, materials have been checked, and other construction criteria have been coordinated. Only after this review should the contractor send the submittals to the interior designer. If they are not checked and signed by the contractor, the interior designer should immediately return them without review.

The interior designer's review of submittals is only for the limited purpose of checking for conformance with information given and to see if they follow the design intent. The interior designer is not responsible for determining the accuracy of measurements or completeness of details, verifying quantities, or checking fabrication or installation procedures. The interior designer's review does not relieve the contractor of his or her responsibilities under the contract documents. This means, for example, that if the designer does not catch a mistake on the shop drawings, the contractor is still responsible for building according to the contract documents and making sure the shop drawings conform to them.

If the submittals require the review of one of the interior designer's consultants, such as an electrical consultant, they are forwarded by the designer to the consultant, who returns them to the interior designer after review. The designer then reviews them and returns them to the contractor who, in turn, returns them to the subcontractor or material supplier who prepared them. The interior designer may indicate on the drawings that no exceptions are taken, that marked corrections should be made, that the drawings should be revised and resubmitted, or that the drawings are rejected.

The interior designer must review submittals with reasonable promptness so as to cause no delay in the work, but neither the Owner-Designer Agreement nor the General Conditions of the Contract for Construction states a specific amount of time except that the interior designer must act with reasonable promptness while allowing sufficient time in the interior designer's professional judgment to permit adequate review. The issue of time is generally dealt with in two ways. First, the General Conditions of the Contract for Construction requires that the contractor prepare a construction schedule for the project, and this schedule must include a schedule of submittals, which must allow the interior designer reasonable time to review the submittals. Second, the interior designer may, and should, indicate in the section on submittals in Division 01 of the specifications the procedure for making submittals, including the time that the contractor must allow for the interior designer's review. The contractor generally includes this time to establish the construction schedule.

According to the Owner-Designer Agreement, the interior designer must keep a log of submittals and copies of the submittals. The log should include the submittal name or other identification and several dates documenting the submittal's movement: when it was received by the interior designer, when the interior designer sent it to the consultant (if necessary), when it was returned to the interior designer, and when the interior designer returned it to the contractor. The action taken should also be noted.

Shop drawings are not a way for the interior designer to make changes in the design or refine details. Although minor corrections and changes can be made, the contractor may request, and is entitled to, a change order if the interior designer's modification of the shop drawings or samples results in an increase in cost or time spent on the project.

Field Administration

Once construction begins, the interior designer has a number of responsibilities under the Owner-Designer Agreement and in accordance with the General Conditions of the Contract for Construction and the General Conditions of the Contract for Furniture, Furnishings, and Equipment.

Construction Observation

If made part of the interior designer's services in the Owner-Designer Agreement, the interior designer visits the site at intervals appropriate to the stage of construction or as agreed to in writing.

The purpose of the interior designer's observation is (1) to become generally familiar with the progress and quality of the work and to keep the owner informed, (2) to endeavor to guard the owner against defects and deficiencies in the work, and (3) to determine, in general, if the work is progressing in such a way that, when completed, it will be in accordance with the contract documents.

During construction observation, definite lines of communication among the parties are established by the General Conditions of the Contract for Construction. During this time, the owner and contractor must communicate through the interior designer, unless otherwise provided in the Owner-Designer Agreement and the General Conditions. Communications between the contractor and consultants should also be through the interior designer. Communications between the interior designer and the subcontractors and material suppliers should be through the contractor.

The number and timing of visits to a job site are left to the judgment of the interior designer based on the size and complexity of the project, the type of construction contract being used, and the exact schedule of construction operations.

During each site visit, the interior designer should make complete notes of the observations and include these in appropriate field reports.

A field report should include the following items.

- the report name and the interior designer's project number

- the field report number

- the date and time of the observation and, if appropriate, the weather conditions at the site

- the work currently in progress

- the number of workers present at the site or an estimate of the number, if the project is large

- observations made, including any problems

- an estimate of the conformance with the schedule and the estimated percent of completion

- items to verify and action or information required

- a list of any attachments, and the name of the person making the report

Copies of the field reports are sent to the owner to keep him or her informed of the progress of the work, and to the contractor. Unless otherwise agreed to in writing in the Owner-Designer Agreement, the interior designer is not responsible for exhaustive or continuous on-site inspections, nor is the interior designer responsible for the contractor's failure to carry out the work or for the means, methods, or techniques of construction, or for safety precautions on the job.

Rejecting Work

The General Conditions of the Contract for Construction gives the interior designer the authority to reject construction work that does not conform to the contract documents. Because rejecting work means extra time and expense for the contractor, the reasons for rejection should be carefully documented, and the owner should be kept informed of the situation. The interior designer has the authority to require inspection or testing of work, whether or not such work is fabricated, installed, or completed. However, this action does not give rise to any duty or responsibility of the interior designer to the contractor, subcontractors, or anyone else performing portions of the work. The contractor must promptly correct work rejected by the interior designer or work not conforming to the contract documents, whether discovered before or after substantial completion. The contractor pays for the cost of correcting such work.

Under the terms of the General Conditions of the Contract for Furniture, Furnishings, and Equipment, the interior designer does not have the right to reject furniture and equipment. Only the owner may reject nonconforming work and must do so in writing to the vendor. However, the interior designer may assist the owner in determining if work should be accepted or not.

Safety

The contractor is solely responsible for safety on the job site. If the interior designer volunteers suggestions or directions concerning construction means and techniques in regard to safety issues, the interior designer may also assume legal responsibility and be held liable for accidents or other problems.

If the interior designer observes an obvious safety violation, he or she should call it to the attention of both the contractor

(but not suggest how it can be corrected) and owner and should follow up with a notice in writing. If the safety problem is not corrected, the interior designer should notify both the contractor and the owner in writing.

Field Tests

When tests and inspections are required by the contract documents or by laws, regulations, or orders of public authorities (building departments), the contractor is responsible for making arrangements with testing agencies acceptable to the owner or with the appropriate public authorities. The contractor pays for the tests and must give the interior designer timely notice of when and where the test is to be made so that the interior designer can observe the procedure.

If the interior designer, owner, or public authorities require additional testing beyond what is required in the contract documents, the interior designer should instruct the contractor to make arrangements, but only after written authorization from the owner. In this case, the owner pays for the tests.

Regardless of whether the tests were required originally by the contract documents or later by the interior designer or public authorities, if a test shows that a portion of the work does not conform to the contract documents (including violating building codes or other laws), then the contractor must pay all costs required to correct the problem, including those of additional testing and compensation for the interior designer's services.

Documentation

During the entire construction administration phase (as well as all phases of the interior designer's service), the interior designer should keep complete documentation of the progress of the job. This includes not only the standard forms used, such as change orders, certificates of payment, and the like, but also all correspondence, meeting notes, emails, telephone logs, and similar written material that records the who, what, why, when, and how of the project. This kind of documentation is critical if disputes arise or the client objects to fee payments for extra services of the interior designer.

Claims

There are usually disputes and claims on any construction project, and these typically occur during the construction phase. The General Conditions of the Contract for Construction as well as for furniture, furnishings, and equipment specifically outline the procedures to be followed if a claim or dispute arises.

A *claim* is a demand or assertion by the contractor or owner seeking payment of money, an extension of time, an adjustment or interpretation of the contract terms, or other relief from terms of the contract. Claims must be made by written notice to the other party and to the interior designer and must be initiated within 21 days from the occurrence of what prompted the claim or 21 days after the person making the claim first recognized the problem. Whoever makes the claim must substantiate it with documentation or other evidence.

The interior designer is responsible for reviewing claims and making decisions, such decisions being final but first subject to mediation, then arbitration. In the worst of cases, a claim may have to be decided by litigation.

Under the General Conditions of the Contract for Construction, if the owner or contractor has a dispute or makes a claim, the interior designer must take certain preliminary action within 10 days of receipt of the claim. Such action may include requesting additional supporting data from the claimant, suggesting a compromise, accepting the claim, rejecting the claim, or advising the parties that the interior designer is unable to resolve the claim because of a lack of sufficient information, or that it would be inappropriate for the interior designer to resolve the claim.

Under the General Conditions of the Contract for Furniture, Furnishings, and Equipment, claims are initially referred to the interior designer. The interior designer makes an initial recommendation in writing, followed by negotiation of the parties. This negotiation is required as a condition precedent to mediation, arbitration, or litigation between the owner and vendor.

In evaluating construction claims, the interior designer may consult with or seek information from either party or from anyone with special knowledge or expertise. The interior designer can ask the owner to authorize the retention of experts at the owner's expense. If the interior designer asks either the owner or the contractor to respond to a claim or provide additional information, that person must respond within 10 days and must give the response or information, tell the interior designer when the response will be furnished, or tell the interior designer that no supporting data will be provided.

The approval or rejection of a claim by the interior designer is final and binding on the parties but is subject to mediation and arbitration. A demand for mediation and arbitration must be made by the claiming party within 30 days from the date on which the party making the demand receives the final written decision from the interior designer on the claim. Mediation is a condition precedent to arbitration or the institution of other legal proceedings.

Although construction claims can arise from a multitude of conditions, there are two types that are especially common.

- *Claims for additional time:* If the contractor feels that extra time is needed, he or she must submit the reasons for the request and include an estimate of the cost.

- *Claims for concealed or unknown conditions:* Sometimes there are surprises on the job site once construction begins. When this happens the contractor may make a claim for additional time or money. However, to be valid, the unknown conditions must meet two criteria: they must be physically concealed, causing the site conditions to differ from what is shown on the contract documents, or they must be of an unusual nature that is different from what would ordinarily be found as part of construction activities for the project type. Claims of this type must be made within 21 days from first discovery.

Mediation and Arbitration

The General Conditions of the Contract requires mediation and arbitration as the method of resolving claims between the owner and contractor or vendor if they are not resolved by the interior designer in the procedures outlined in the previous section. When there is a claim or dispute, the standard agreement requires that mediation be undertaken before arbitration or litigation. *Mediation* is a process by which a neutral third party facilitates and assists the disputing parties to negotiate a settlement using preset rules established by the American Arbitration Association. If an agreement cannot be reached, the Owner-Designer Agreement requires that the dispute advance to arbitration.

Arbitration is a formal, legally binding process for resolving disputes without litigation in a court of law. One or more arbitrators with experience in the construction industry hear the disputing parties' arguments and render a decision, which is binding. The arbitrator is knowledgeable in the construction industry and listens to evidence, reviews documents,

and hears witnesses before making a decision. The arbitration proceedings must be conducted under the Construction Industry Arbitration Rules of the American Arbitration Association and any applicable state laws. Arbitration has the advantages over litigation of speed, economy, and privacy. However, unlike a trial, arbitration involves no rules of evidence and the decision cannot be appealed.

Changes in the Work

During construction, changes in the work are usually required. They may be necessitated by errors discovered in the drawings, unforeseen site conditions, design changes requested by the client, rulings of building officials, or many other factors. During bidding and prior to contract award, changes are made by addenda. During construction, changes in the construction work are accomplished in one of three ways: by minor changes in the work, by construction change directive, or by formal change order.

Minor Changes in the Work

When a change does not involve a modification of the contract sum or time and is consistent with the contract documents, the interior designer may issue a written order directing the contractor to make a minor change. For example, moving a door opening over 6 in before it is framed would be a minor change. The interior designer may issue an order for such a minor change without the approval of either the owner or contractor.

Construction Change Directive

When a change needs to be made right away but the owner and contractor cannot agree on a price or time revision, the interior designer may issue a construction change directive. A *construction change directive* is a written order prepared by the interior designer directing a change in the work before the owner and contractor agree on an adjustment in contract cost, time, or both. The *construction change directive* gives the owner a way to unilaterally order changes to the contract without changing the terms of the contract. It is used in the absence of total agreement on the terms of a change order. The change in the work may involve additions, deletions, or other revisions. The construction change directive must be signed by both the interior designer and the owner but does not have to be signed by the contractor.

In addition to describing the changes required, the directive should include a proposed basis for determining the adjustment of cost or time or both. If the directive involves a cost adjustment, the interior designer's proposed basis of adjustment must be based on one of four methods: a lump sum, properly itemized; unit prices previously agreed to in the specifications; costs to be determined by mutual agreement on a fixed or percentage fee; or as provided for in a subsequent clause and summarized in the following paragraph.

Under provisions of the General Conditions of the Contract for Construction, the contractor must proceed with the work and advise the interior designer of the contractor's agreement or disagreement with the basis for cost and time adjustment. If the contractor agrees, the change is recorded as a change order. If the contractor disagrees, the interior designer determines the method and adjustment based on reasonable expenditures and savings of those performing the work. In addition to the actual cost of the work, the interior designer must include costs related to worker's benefits, equipment rental, supplies, premiums for bonds and insurance, field supervision, permit fees, and profit.

Change Orders

A *change order* is a document authorizing a variation from the original contract documents that involves a change in contract price, contract time, or both. See Fig. 23.3. Technically, it is issued by the owner because the owner has the agreement with the contractor, but it is prepared by the interior designer. It must be approved by the owner, interior designer, and contractor.

Any of the three parties may suggest a change order, but it is normally the interior designer who submits a proposal request to the contractor. This request is accompanied by supporting drawings or other documents as required to fully describe the proposed change. The contractor submits his or her quotation of price and time change. If these are acceptable to the owner, the formal change order document is prepared and signed by all three parties.

Progress Payments

During the job the contractor requests periodic payments, usually monthly, against the total contract sum. Under the General Conditions of the Contract for "Construction", the interior designer is responsible for making sure that the amounts requested are consistent with the amount of work done and the amount of materials stored.

To receive periodic payment, the contractor must submit to the interior designer a notarized application for payment at least 10 days before the date established for each payment in the owner-contractor agreement. This application should include the value of work done up until the date of the application, in addition to the value of any materials purchased and in acceptable storage but not yet incorporated into the work.

Certification of the application for payment constitutes an acknowledgment by

Figure 23.3
Change Order

Osprey Design Associates
Interior design and space planning

Date 8/16/2010

To: PQF Constructors
1534 48th Street

Name Global Transportation Hqs.

Project No. 9231

Location 427 Zeneth Ave.

Change Order No. | 1 |

You are directed to make the following changes in the Contract:

Hardware: Revisions per work authorization #1

Provide 2 ea. 3080, 4 hinge, LH, HM door frames $ 117.00
Provide 2 ea. 3070, 1-hr. hollow metal doors $ 482.92
Provide and install 1 ea. 3070 door to replace #12 $ 340.00

                        Subtotal   939.92
                        13% O & P   122.19
                        TOTAL $ 1062.11

Original contract sum $ 227,351.00
Net change by previous Change Orders $
Contract Sum prior to this Change Order $ 227,351.00
Contract Sum ☑ increased ❑ decreased by $ 1,062.11
New Contract Sum including this Change Order $ 228,413.11

Contract time ☑ increased ❑ decreased by   two (2)   days
Revised completion date: Jan. 14, 2011

Interior Designer
Name

Address

Date

Signed

Contractor
Name

Address

Date

Signed

Owner
Name

Address

Date

Signed

the interior designer that the work has progressed to the point indicated and that, to the best of the interior designer's knowledge, information, and belief, the quality of the work is according to the contract documents. Certification is not a representation that the interior designer has made exhaustive on-site inspections or that the designer has reviewed construction methods, techniques, or procedures. Further, certification is not a representation that the designer has reviewed copies of requisitions received from subcontractors and material suppliers or that the designer has determined how and for what purpose the contractor has used moneys previously paid.

If the application for payment is approved, the interior designer signs it and sends it to the owner for payment. An amount, called the *retainage*, is withheld from each application until the end of the job. This retainage, which is usually 10% of each application amount, gives the owner leverage in making sure the job is completed and can be used to provide money to satisfy any claims that may arise.

The interior designer may withhold all or a portion of the applications for payment to protect the owner if the designer cannot verify that the amount of work done or materials stored is in conformance with the application. The designer may also withhold payment for any of the following reasons.

- defective work

- third-party claims or evidence of probability of third-party claims

- failure of the contractor to make payments to subcontractors or suppliers

- reasonable evidence that the work cannot be completed for the unpaid balance of the contract sum

- damage to the owner or another contractor

- reasonable evidence that the work will not be completed on time

- persistent failure of the contractor to carry out the work in accordance with the contract documents

Installation

Installation is the final placement of furniture, fixtures, and equipment. If the project involves both construction and installation of furniture, one contractor may be responsible for both or there may be two or more contractors. In most commercial work, construction is carried out by one contractor, and the supply and installation of furniture is carried out by one or more furniture installation contractors or vendors.

In either case, the interior designer assists with the correct placement of furniture according to the contract documents and answers any questions that may arise. However, it is the owner's responsibility to provide for the following.

- adequate facilities for the delivery, unloading, staging, and storage of furniture, fixtures, and equipment

- the route to be used from the point of delivery to final placement

- that the route is free of unanticipated obstacles or other trades that might impede the installation contractor

- a firm schedule for the contractor for the use of both unloading facilities and elevators

- any costs incurred by the contractor due to the owner's failure to conform to the schedule or due to other delays caused by the owner

- security against loss or damage to the furniture and fixtures stored at the site between the dates of delivery and final acceptance by the owner

The owner is also solely responsible for inspection when the items are delivered, final inspection of the installation, and rejection of any work that is damaged or that does not conform to the contract documents. The interior designer may assist and make recommendations, but the owner has the final authority and responsibility.

When the owner inspects delivery of furniture and fixtures, it is only for identifying them and verifying quantities to provide a basis for payment to the contractor or supplier. It is not final, nor does it constitute acceptance of or taking charge or control over the furniture. If any defects are later found before final acceptance, previous acceptance may be revoked by the owner. This is an important distinction because the exchange of furniture may be governed by certain provisions of the Uniform Commercial Code or by state or provincial laws governing the sale of merchandise.

PROJECT CLOSEOUT

Project closeout is an important part of the construction administration phase. It is during this time that the building work is completed, the furniture and fixtures are finally installed, the structure is made ready for occupancy, and all remaining documentation takes place.

The contractor initiates closeout procedures by notifying the interior designer in writing and submitting a comprehensive list of items to be completed or corrected prior to final payment. The designer then makes a first inspection to determine if the work or a designated portion of it is substantially complete or if additional items need to be completed or corrected. The contractor must proceed promptly to complete or correct these items before a certificate of substantial completion can be issued.

Substantial completion is the stage when the work is sufficiently complete in accordance with the contract documents so

that the owner can occupy or utilize the work for its intended purpose. The date of substantial completion is important because it has legal implications. For example, in many states, the statute of limitations for errors possibly caused by the interior designer begins with the date of substantial completion. Warranties usually commence on the date of substantial completion.

The list of items made by the interior designer as a result of the first inspection is called the *punch list* (or *deficiency list*, in Canada). It is during this inspection that the interior designer notes anything that needs to be completed or corrected if not in accordance with the contract documents. The contractor must correct these items, after which another inspection is called for. If the final inspection shows that the work is substantially complete, the interior designer issues a certificate of substantial completion. The certificate of substantial completion may be accompanied by a list of items that still need to be completed or corrected by the contractor. The certificate also establishes the responsibilities of the owner and contractor for security, maintenance, heat, utilities, damage to the work, and insurance.

When the certificate of substantial completion is issued, final application for payment is processed and the interior designer issues a final certificate for payment. With consent of surety, the owner makes final payment, including retainage, unless some work is still incomplete or not in accordance with the requirements of the contract documents.

If the work is not substantially complete based on the interior designer's inspection, the interior designer notifies the contractor of work that must be completed before a certificate of substantial completion can be prepared. The owner may wait for the entire project to be completed or, if appropriate, may agree with the contractor to occupy or utilize only a portion of the work.

In addition to completing the work, the contractor must also submit to the owner certain other items including the following.

- all warranties, maintenance contracts, operating instructions, certificates of inspection, and bonds

- all documentation required with the application for final payment (as described previously)

- a set of record drawings if required by the Owner-Contractor Agreement

- the certificate of occupancy (CO) as issued by the building department (part of the permit process originally paid for by the contractor)

- extra stock of materials as called for in the specifications

The contractor must also complete final cleaning, instruct the owner or owner's representatives in the operation of systems and equipment, complete the keying for locks and turn keys over to the owner, and restore all items damaged by the contractor.

The interior designer's formal services may terminate when the final certificate for payment is issued, if so described in the Owner-Designer Agreement.

In addition to the administrative chores, project closeout also includes other jobs that are important for the interior designer's office and that create a good impression with the client and provide an opportunity to maintain contact with the client for future work. Some of these project closeout tasks include helping the client with problems during move-in and immediately after, making sure the client has any required operating manuals, and providing the cleaning procedures for finish materials. It is also helpful to both the client and design firm to make follow-up visits at six-month and one-year intervals to review maintenance problems, look for defects that are covered by guarantees, and see how materials and other design decision are withstanding the test of time. These services should be budgeted for in the initial agreement.

POST-OCCUPANCY EVALUATION

A post-occupancy evaluation (POE) is a review of a completed project after the client has occupied it for some time, typically from three to six months. A POE is not a standard part of the interior designer's services, and most clients are unwilling to pay extra for a formal evaluation unless the client intends to construct additional, similar facilities. In most instances, a POE is an informal review undertaken at the interior designer's own time and expense. Regardless of how it is accomplished and who pays for it, a POE provides valuable information for the interior designer.

Post-occupancy evaluations try to provide answers to some or all of the following questions.

- Does the final space layout satisfy the original program requirements?

- Is the design image consistent with the client's stated goals?

- Is adequate flexibility and expansibility provided consistent with the client's original needs?

- Are rooms and spaces of adequate size for their intended function?

- Were all adjacencies provided for?

- Are finishes holding up to normal wear and tear?

- Are any materials or finishes presenting maintenance problems?

- Are construction details adequate for their use?

- Do furniture and fixtures meet the design criteria established during programming?

- Is the furniture selected adequate for the functional requirements of the space and the type of use it receives?

- Are there any ergonomic problems with the furniture selected?

- Is the lighting adequate for the space?

- Are there any problems with the HVAC systems?

- Was adequate power and communication provided for?

- Are the acoustics adequate?

- How did the contractor, subcontractors, and other suppliers perform?

- Is the client satisfied with the project?

- Are the actual users satisfied with the performance and appearance of the finished space?

- What problems have arisen that may be covered by product or contractor warranties?

In addition to evaluating the project itself, the design firm should review how the project delivery process worked or did not work so improvements can be made for future jobs. The design office should review design processes, programming information, project management techniques, scheduling, fee allotment, specification and detailing methods, and construction documentation procedures.

SAMPLE QUESTIONS

1. The last person to see the mechanical shop drawings before they are returned to the mechanical subcontractor should be the

(A) mechanical engineer
(B) architect
(C) interior designer
(D) general contractor

2. A project is being completed subject to the standard AIA General Conditions and contract agreement. If some millwork was installed with the incorrect finish, who is responsible if no sample was submitted to the designer?

(A) millworker
(B) interior designer
(C) project manager
(D) contractor

3. During a routine site visit, the interior designer notices a lack of barricades around a floor opening while interior construction is taking place. What should the designer do?

(A) Point out the situation to the contractor and write a letter to the client stating what was observed.
(B) Tell the contractor to correct the situation.
(C) Write a letter to the contractor stating the concerns, and copy the owner on the letter.
(D) Have the contractor stop the work until the problem is corrected.

4. What is the LEAST important part of a project manager's job?

(A) planning job tasks for the project staff on a weekly basis
(B) organizing the layout of the construction drawings
(C) keeping notes on daily decisions and meetings
(D) staying current with the client's opinion of the progress of the project

5. If it appears to the interior designer that the dollar amount requested on the contractor's application for payment exceeds the work completed and material stored, the designer should

(A) certify only the amount that the designer believes represents the work completed and stored, and attach a letter explaining why the amount certified differs from the amount applied for

(B) return the application to the contractor and request that it be revised to be more in line with actual work done and materials stored

(C) reject the application and attach an explanatory letter

(D) send the application to the client for his review and opinion about what amount should be certified

6. If an interior designer did not find an error in a dimension on the shop drawings for a custom steel doorframe and the doorframe was subsequently fabricated, who is responsible for paying to have the mistake corrected?

(A) doorframe supplier

(B) wall framing subcontractor

(C) general contractor

(D) interior designer

7. In order to allow the contractor extra time to complete a project because the owner asked for minor changes, the interior designer should issue

(A) an addendum

(B) a construction change authorization

(C) a change order

(D) a minor work order

8. A contractor would be within her rights if she asked the owner to provide which of the following?

(A) extra insurance for the goods during transit from the warehouse to the site

(B) final inspection and acceptance by the owner once the furniture was off the truck

(C) extra space for storage and initial preparation of furniture delivered to the site

(D) additional workers to help with final installation

9. Which of the following is NOT a typical part of post-occupancy evaluation?

(A) review of the HVAC system

(B) interviews with representative users of the project

(C) a check on maintenance problems

(D) suggestions on how the client's next project can be improved

10. A doorway is installed by the contractor according to the drawings. After viewing the job, a building inspector tells the contractor that the door is not wide enough. Who is responsible for correcting the problem?

(A) framing subcontractor

(B) interior designer

(C) owner

(D) contractor

24

INTERIOR DESIGN BUSINESS PRACTICES

Being an interior designer involves more than just designing and preparing drawings and specifications. Business knowledge and skills are also needed. These include business management, carrying appropriate insurance, financial management, an awareness of legal issues, business development, and managing employees. This chapter discusses these topics as well as professional ethics.

BUSINESS STRUCTURES

There are several types of organizational structures that an interior designer can use to conduct business. Each has its advantages and disadvantages and may be more or less appropriate depending on the number of people in the firm, the laws of the state or states where the firm is doing business, the type of practice, the size of business, and the level of risk the owner or owners want to take.

Sole Proprietorship

The simplest business type is the *sole proprietorship*. In this structure the company is owned by an individual and operates under either the individual's name or a company name. To set up a

sole proprietorship, it is only necessary to establish a name and location for the business, open a company bank account, have stationery printed, and obtain whatever licenses are needed by the local jurisdiction. If employees are hired, other state (province) and local requirements must be met.

The advantages of this form of business include the ease of setting it up, total management control by the owner, and possible tax advantages to the owner because business expenses and losses may be deducted from the gross income of the business. The primary disadvantage is that the owner is personally liable for all debts and losses of the company. For example, if a client sues the designer, his or her personal income (and possibly co-owned property of a spouse), personal property, and other assets can be seized to pay any judgments. Another disadvantage is that it is more difficult to raise capital and establish credit as a sole proprietorship unless the owner's personal credit rating and assets are adequate. Because the business depends primarily on the work and reputation of the owner, it may be difficult to sell the business, and the company usually ceases to exist when the owner quits or dies.

Partnerships

With a *general partnership*, two or more people share in the management, profits, and risks of the business. Income from the business is taxed as ordinary income on personal tax forms. If necessary, employees can be hired as with any form of business.

Partnerships are relatively easy to form (a partnership agreement is usually advisable) and provide a business with the skills and talents of several people rather than just one, as with a sole proprietorship. In most cases, partnerships are formed because each of the partners brings to the organization a particular talent such as business development, design, or technical knowledge.

The primary disadvantage is that all the partners are responsible and liable for the actions of the others. As with a sole proprietorship, the personal assets of any of the partners are vulnerable to lawsuits and other claims. Another potential disadvantage of the partnership form is that income is taxed at individual rates. On a personal level, the partners may eventually disagree on how to run the business. If one partner wants to withdraw, the partnership is usually dissolved.

A variation of the general partnership is the *limited partnership*. This type of organization has one or more general partners and other limited partners. As with a general partnership, the general partners invest in the company, manage it, and are financially responsible. The limited partners are simply investors and receive a portion of the profits. They have no say in the management of the company and are liable only to the extent of their investment. Limited partnerships have generally

given way to the limited liability company, described in a following section.

Corporations

Another common form of business organization is the corporation. A *corporation* (sometimes called a *C corporation*) is an association of individuals, created by statutory requirements, having an existence independent from its members. The formation and conduct of corporations are governed by the laws of individual states, and formal articles of incorporation must be drawn up by an attorney and filed with the appropriate state office to legally form a corporation.

Because a corporation is a separate legal entity, it is financially and legally independent from its stockholders. As such, the stockholders are financially liable only for the amount of money invested in the corporation. If the corporation is sued, the personal assets of the stockholders are not at risk. This is the greatest advantage of the corporate form.

Another advantage is that a corporation is generally taxed at a lower rate than are individuals, which can result in considerable savings. However, a corporation is taxed at two levels: it is taxed on its profits, and shareholders are taxed on their dividends. Additionally, corporations have a continuity independent of changes in stockholders, deaths of members of its board of directors, or changes in the principals. It is also relatively easy to raise capital by selling stock in the corporation.

The primary disadvantages of a corporation are the initial set-up costs and the continuing paperwork and formal requirements necessary to maintain the business. These disadvantages, however, are usually outweighed by the reduced liability and tax benefits.

Variations on the corporate form include the subchapter S corporation and the professional corporation. *Subchapter S corporations* (also know as the *S corporation*) have certain eligibility requirements and offer all the advantages of a standard corporation, but the profits or losses are paid or deducted from the stockholders' personal income taxes in proportion to the shares of stock they hold. This can be an advantage when there are losses or when the state tax rates shift the financial benefits so that the individual is taxed rather than the corporation.

Many states allow the formation of a *professional corporation* for professionals such as interior designers, architects, lawyers, doctors, and accountants. This form of business is similar to other corporations except that liability for malpractice is generally limited to the person responsible. However, each state has its own laws regarding the burden of liability in a professional corporation.

Limited Liability Companies and Limited Liability Partnerships

A *limited liability company* (LLC) and a *limited liability partnership* (LLP) are two hybrid business organizations that combine the advantages of the corporation and the partnership. The particular requirements of LLCs and LLPs vary according to the state in which the business is established, but basically both are formed like a partnership where the investors are called members and those who manage are called managers. Unlike with partnerships, it is possible to have nonmembers as managers in an LLC or LLP. The company name must include LLC or LLP.

The main advantage of these types of organizations is that liability is limited to a member's investment; a member has no personal liability. In addition, these organizations are taxed as a partnership or corporation, at the owners' discretion, with only one level of taxation for members,

unlike a C corporation. Generally, they are easier than a corporation to set up and operate.

Joint Ventures

A *joint venture* is a temporary association of two or more persons or firms for the purpose of completing a project. This business type is typically used by interior design firms when a project is too large or complex to be completed by a single firm. It can also be used when one firm does not have the experience in a particular building type that the partnering firm has.

With joint ventures, a formal, written agreement should be developed that describes the duties and responsibilities of each firm, how profits and losses should be divided, and how the work will be done. Joint ventures are treated as partnerships and cannot be sued like a corporation can. Depending on the state (province) in which the joint venture operates, profits may be taxed as a partnership, or the individual members of the joint venture may be taxed separately.

Office Organization

In addition to the legal organization of the business, offices can be set up in various ways to complete projects. In the *departmental organization*, a project moves through the office from one department to another. There may be a marketing department, a design department, a specifications department, a contract documents department, and a construction administration department. While this type of organization is efficient and can take advantage of many types of specialists, communication between departments about any particular project can be a challenge. It also discourages or makes it impossible for anyone to gain a breadth of experience or share their knowledge in other aspects of project planning and completion.

The *studio organization* is based on various smaller groups in the business, called studios. Each studio is responsible for completing an entire project, from initial planning to production and construction administration. Members of each studio have the necessary expertise to provide all or most all of the work required on the project. Projects can be assigned to studios based on their expertise, or studios can be formed or dissolved as the need arises. For example, an office may have a studio to complete retail projects, another to do industrial work, and another to provide office planning. The advantages of the studio organization include close and immediate communication among members of the design team and the synergy that comes from sharing ideas and group problem solving. Studios also work well with a strong project management system where the project manager has daily contact with the design and production team as well as with the client. Sometimes the studio organization is combined with one or more departments that provide very specialized work, such as specification writing.

Smaller offices may work on a very informal basis in which the principal or the partners complete the client contact and design work and then hand off the production and administration to others in the office.

INSURANCE

There are many types of insurance, both required and optional, that pertain to doing business and completing an interior design project. Each of the three primary parties to a project—the designer, owner, and contractor—must have certain kinds of insurance to protect against liability, property loss, and personal loss. Because the insurance issue is so complex and the designer is not qualified to give insurance advice, it is best that the owner's insurance counselor give insurance recommendations for specific projects. The interior designer and contractor should also have their respective insurance advisers recommend needed insurance for their businesses.

Interior Designer's Insurance

Professional liability insurance protects the designer in case some action by the designer causes bodily injury or property damage. Sometimes called malpractice or errors and omissions insurance, this coverage responds to problems resulting from things such as incorrect specifications, mistakes on drawings, and incorrect installation of furniture.

General liability insurance includes a range of insurance to protect against claims of property damage, liability, and personal injury caused by the designer or employees, consultants, or other people hired by the designer. It may also include product liability insurance, which provides protection in case a product or an installation completed by the designer or a subcontractor does some injury to the client after the designer or subcontractor gives up possession of the product. Sometimes the designer will also buy insurance to cover the possibility that contractors or subcontractors do not have their own valid insurance.

Property insurance protects the designer's building and its contents against disasters such as fire, theft, and flood. Even if the designer rents space, property insurance protects the contents and any stock the designer may be holding for the client.

Personal injury protection insurance protects the interior designer against charges of slander, libel, defamation of character, misrepresentation, and other torts. A *tort* is a civil wrong (as contrasted with a criminal act) that causes injury to another person.

Automobile insurance covers liability and property damage to vehicles owned and used by the business and can include protection against claims made by employees using their own cars while on company business.

Workers' compensation insurance is mandatory in all states and protects employees in the event of injuries caused by work-related activities.

Other types of insurance that the designer may carry include health and life insurance for employees, special flood insurance, valuable papers insurance, and business life insurance.

Owner's Insurance

As stated in A275™ID, General Conditions of the Contract for Furniture, Furnishings, and Equipment, the owner is required to carry his or her own liability insurance as well as property insurance for the full insurable value of the work. This insures against physical loss or damage caused by fire, theft, vandalism, and malicious mischief. The policy must be the "all risk" type rather than the "specified peril" type. All risk insurance is broader in coverage and includes all hazards except those that are specifically excluded by the policy.

Contractor's Insurance

The General Conditions of the Contract requires that the contractor carry insurance that will protect from the following types of claims.

- claims under workers' compensation
- claims for damages because of bodily injury, occupational sickness, or death of employees
- claims for damages of bodily injury or death to people other than employees
- claims for personal injury, which include slander, libel, false arrest, and similar actions
- claims for damages other than to the work because of destruction of tangible property. This includes loss of use resulting from such damages.

- claims for damages related to use of motor vehicles

In addition, the contractor must carry insurance for any portions of the work that are stored off the job site or that are in transit to the site. Additional coverage may include "products and completed operations" insurance, which protects against claims resulting from the contractor's actions when an injury occurs after the job is complete and the contractor has left the site.

FINANCIAL MANAGEMENT

The financial management of a design firm depends on two broad categories of accounting. The first is the basic accounting that all businesses must do to keep track of money for day-to-day operations, banking, taxes, and auditing. The second is active financial management so the firm owners know the financial status of the business and can use financial reporting to help make decisions critical to the firm's survival and profit.

Financial Terminology

Financial management is a complex subject. To understand the fundamentals, there are some basic terms with which the interior designer must be familiar. These include the following.

Accounts payable: claims from the suppliers of goods or services (such as consultants) but not yet paid for

Accounts receivable: money that others owe to the business through invoices for services

Assets: any type of tangible or intangible resource that can be measured in monetary terms. Assets include current assets, fixed assets, and other assets.

Chart of accounts: a list of the various accounts a business uses to keep track of money along with corresponding account numbers used for data processing

Current assets: resources of a business that are converted into cash within one year

Direct labor: all labor of technical staff, principals, and support staff that is directly chargeable to projects

Direct personnel expense: the expense of employee salaries plus the cost of mandatory and discretionary expenses and benefits such as payroll taxes, health insurance, and the like

Discretionary distribution: voluntary distribution of profits to owners and non-owners, such as performance bonuses, profit sharing, incentive compensation, and the like. Some interior design firms view this as a necessary expense in order to be competitive in attracting qualified personnel, while other firms view it as a profit item.

Fixed assets: resources that are used by the business and that are long-term items, such as equipment and property

Gross revenue: all the revenue generated by a business for a period of time stated

Indirect labor: all labor not charged to a project or revenue-producing account, such as administration, general office time, and marketing

Liabilities: claims by people outside the business and claims by the owners of the business against the total assets of the business

Other assets: miscellaneous resources such as securities or copyrights

Overhead: expenses incurred in order to keep a business operating whether or not any revenue is being generated, such as rent, power, and telephone

Accounting Methods

There are two basic accounting methods, cash and accrual. With *cash accounting,* revenue and expenses are recognized at the actual time the business receives the cash or pays a bill. With *accrual accounting,* revenue and expenses are recognized at the time they are earned or incurred, whether or not cash changes hands. For example, if a firm sends an invoice to a client for $10,000, that money is listed as revenue even though the client has not paid the invoice.

Cash accounting is fairly simple and is often used by single-person or small firms. However, it cannot be used by a corporation or if the business maintains an inventory. The accrual method of accounting is mandatory for some types of businesses and makes it possible to get a better overall picture of the financial status of a business and produce the reports vital for active financial management.

With both types of accounting methods, revenue and expenses are grouped into individual accounts for the purposes of auditing, review, tax preparation, management, and analysis. For example, there are separate expense accounts for wages, rent, telephone, supplies, and so on. The accrual accounting method uses *double-entry bookkeeping* in which all transactions are listed chronologically in a journal. They are then posted to a ledger in which transactions are grouped into individual accounts. Although legacy terms such as "journal" and "ledger" are still used in accounting, nearly all but the smallest businesses perform accounting functions with computer programs, some of which are designed specifically for design firms.

Accounting Statements

From the basic information entered in journals and ledgers, various types of accounting reports are generated. The more common types are described here.

A *balance sheet* summarizes all assets and liabilities and shows the financial position of a business. All the assets listed must exactly equal all the liabilities listed. One important part of a balance sheet is the net worth of the business or the owner's equity. The *net worth* of a firm is the total assets less the total liabilities. *Owner's equity* is the money invested in a business by the owners or stockholders. Another way to view this, and the way it normally shows on a balance sheet, is that total assets must equal total liabilities *plus* the net worth or owner's equity.

A *profit and loss statement* (or *income statement*) lists all the income and expenses of a business for a certain period of time. The difference between all the income and all the expenses gives either the profit or the loss for that period.

A *cash flow statement* shows actual inflows and outflows of cash or cash equivalents. *Cash* is defined as money, checks, or anything else accepted by banks. *Cash equivalents* are short-term investments that can be quickly converted into cash. Cash flow statements are important reports because a business's month-to-month financial health depends on it being able to meet payroll and pay its bills.

In addition to reports that show the overall financial health of a business, the basic information obtained from journals, ledgers, and project data can be used to develop reports for individual projects in the interior design office so project managers and firm management can track the progress of each job.

Profit Planning and Financial Management

Beyond the basic bookkeeping and accounting activities a business must perform, the more important aspect of financial management is the active planning, monitoring, controlling of financial information, and acting on that information. This allows a design firm to stay in business, grow, and make a profit.

The most fundamental equation for financial planning in any profit-oriented business should be

$$profit + expenses = revenues$$

This equation is often shown in the form

$$revenue - expenses = profit$$

Even though the two equations are mathematically equal, the latter assumes that profit is whatever may be left over after expenses are subtracted from whatever revenue may be generated. The first equation assumes that the business *will* make a targeted profit and must then control expenses and generate appropriate revenue to make that happen. Controlling expenses generally means reducing overhead cost wherever possible. One of the highest percentages of overhead is for indirect labor, that is, personnel that do not directly work on projects. Increasing revenue generally means increasing the amount of work the firm does or increasing fees.

Based on information from accounting journals, time sheets, and project financial data, a variety of reports can be generated by financial management software that can help firm principals and project managers.

In addition to the basic accounting reports previously mentioned, one of the most important types of reports for interior design firms is the *project progress report*. This report is a more detailed and computer-generated version of the manually produced charts shown in Ch. 23 (Figs. 23.1 and 23.2) to monitor the progress of individual jobs. The project progress report shows the hours and labor costs for each phase of a project for the current reporting period as well as the amount to date and compares these numbers with estimated hours and dollars. Direct costs, such as for consultants, overhead allocations, and reimbursable expenses, are also shown. These reports give the project manager and firm management an accurate look at the status of a project and can be used to take corrective action as necessary.

An *office earnings report* can also be generated that summarizes each project in the office in terms of the amount of revenue it has generated, expenses, unbilled services, percent complete, and profit or loss to date. This report can help firm management find any projects that may be hurting overall profitability and need remedial action.

An *aged accounts receivable report* shows the status of all invoices for all projects, whether they have been paid, and the "age" of each invoice; that is, the amount of time that passed between invoice date and payment date. Any invoice that has not been paid for more than 60 days generally needs attention by the firm principal or whoever is responsible for getting invoices paid. For architecture and interior design businesses, the average collection period for invoices runs between 60 and 75 days.

A *time analysis report* lists each employee along with the number of hours spent on direct and indirect labor, including marketing, professional development, vacation time, sick leave, and holidays. Every office has a targeted percentage of time that technical employees should be spending on direct labor, and this report is an excellent way of monitoring such time. The most important ratio this report generates is the chargeable ratio. The *chargeable ratio* (or *utilization rate*) is the percentage of time, or dollars, spent on direct labor divided by the total time or dollars spent on direct and indirect labor in addition to vacation, holiday, and sick leave. A chargeable ratio of about 65% for the average of a design firm is generally though to be about the break-even point or the minimum that should be allowed. Of course, some employees, such as a senior designer, will have a high ratio because most of their time is spent doing

work on projects, while principals will spend more of their time on nonchargeable work like promotion, marketing, and management.

Financial Ratios

There are many other types of ratios and values that firm management, accountants, and banks use to measure the status of a business' financial health. These ratios and values can be compared with industry benchmarks and recommended values to see if corrective action needs to be taken. A few of these ratios are as follows.

Current ratio: total current assets divided by total current liabilities. This is a measure of a firm's ability to meet current obligations. The higher the ratio, the better.

Net profit before tax: the percentage of profit based on net revenue; that is, total annual revenue less consultant's fees and reimbursable expenses

Overhead rate: the ratio of total office overhead to total direct labor. When used to calculate fees, the ratio is multiplied by the estimated cost of direct labor (no fringe benefits, taxes, etc.) and the resulting product is added to the direct labor amount

Quick ratio: this is a refinement of the current ratio and includes only cash and equivalents, plus accounts receivable, divided by total current liabilities. It is a more conservative measure than the current ratio because it includes only those assets that are the most liquid.

Revenue per technical staff: the amount of net revenue produced per technical staff member, that is, those staff members most directly involved with charging direct time and producing jobs

Revenue per total staff: the amount of net revenue produced per staff member per year, including part-time people and principals

Setting Fees

One of the most important aspects of financial management and making an interior design business profitable is setting fees. Although many methods are available for charging clients, including square foot fees, percentages of project cost, or profit from the sale of furniture, the most common method is to charge an hourly rate for the people working on a project. This hourly rate is known as the *billing rate* and varies with the staff member doing the work and possibly the type of service provided. Refer to Ch. 25 for a discussion of the various methods of charging professional fees.

Billing rates are determined based on the amount of money an employee is paid (salary rate) plus the costs for the employee's fringe benefits, plus the cost of office overhead, plus an allowance for profit. A net multiplier is used to determine the billing rates. The *net multiplier* is a factor derived by dividing net revenue of the design firm (no consultants or reimbursables) by the cost of direct labor. It covers fringe benefits, indirect labor, overhead, and profit. For most design firms, this value is generally from 2.7 to 3.0. For example, for a firm using a net multiplier of 3.0, if a designer is paid $40.00 per hour, then the billing rate to the client for that employee would be $120.00 per hour.

Related to the net multiplier is a multiplier based on direct personnel expense, or DPE. With DPE, the costs of providing taxes, benefits, and the like are included with the employee's base salary. The multiplier is then calculated to account for indirect labor and profit. Because benefits are already included in the DPE, the multiplier is slightly less than the net multiplier.

Once hourly rates are established for all the employees in the firm, setting fees requires estimating the amount of time it will take to complete a project and which employees (with different billing rates) will be doing what work. Hours are then multiplied by billing rates to get the total estimated fee. In addition to the hourly fees, the person estimating the total project budget must add costs for estimated non-reimbursable direct expenses, consultants' fees (if not billed separately), and a contingency (if any).

Of course, every office has a slightly different method of determining fees, but the process described above is a common method. Many firms also develop benchmark figures so any calculation of estimated hours and fees for a new job can be compared with the fees required to complete similar projects in the past based on area, construction costs, or other measures. This comparison serves as a double check to make sure the estimated fee is sufficient to do the job.

BUSINESS ISSUES

All interior design businesses must conform to local, state, and federal laws and regulations, regardless of their size and organizational structure. Because requirements for licensing and taxation vary widely from one local and state jurisdiction to another, the following is just a short summary of some of the more common requirements. Interior designers should research the particular requirements of their local and state licensing and taxing agencies.

Business Licenses

Most local jurisdictions require all business, including professional services, to have a license. This allows the business to practice and usually serves as a basis for taxation. Most states require that interior design firms reselling goods obtain a *sales tax license*, sometimes called a *resale license* or a *transaction privilege tax license*. This type of license allows the designer to pass on the state sales tax to the client. The design business must remit the tax monthly along with standard reporting forms.

Corporations are entities formed within the state where they practice and are required to be registered with the state. Corporations have corporate identification numbers issued by a state agency, typically the secretary of state's office.

Tax Requirements

Of course, all businesses must pay tax. If a company has employees, the business must withhold taxes for each employee and forward the tax to the Internal Revenue Service (IRS). Businesses with employees must also file an IRS Form SS-4, Application for Employer Identification Number (EIN). This number is used in tax filings and other correspondence with the IRS. Businesses must also complete two additional forms. The first is Form W-4, Employee's Withholding Allowance Certificate, which indicates the number of deductions the employee is claiming. The second is Form W-2, Employer's Wage and Tax Statement, which shows all wages paid along with federal, state, and city taxes withheld and FICA taxes. FICA is the acronym for Federal Insurance Contribution Act, which is more commonly known as social security taxes. Form W-2 is sent to each employee no later than January 31 each year for the employees' use in preparing personal taxes. Most states have similar requirements for filing state income taxes.

For single proprietors and some partnerships, federal and state income tax must be filed as estimated taxes every quarter. In addition, single proprietors and some partnerships must pay self-employment tax to cover social security and Medicare taxes.

Many states also apply a use tax on goods purchased from out of state for either use by the design business or for resale. The designer must file a use tax certificate and

pay what amounts to a sales tax. Some states also charge a personal property tax on furniture and equipment that is used by the business.

An interior design business may also be subject to a variety of city taxes. These may include city income taxes, employment taxes, occupational privilege taxes, and use taxes. Property taxes are also assessed if the design business owns property.

Professional Licensing and Regulation

Many states have laws regulating the practice of interior design. Some states have *practice acts*, which require that anyone who wants to practice as an interior designer meet certain requirements and obtain a license from the state to practice. Other states have *title acts*, which regulate who may use the title of "interior designer" (or some similar title), although anyone may have a business that offers interior design services as long as they do not use the regulated title.

For the states that have practice acts and for some states that have title acts, interior designers are usually required to meet minimum educational requirements and pass the NCIDQ examination. Some states require supplemental tests in the area of codes and regulations and fire-rated construction. Some states also require license or title holders to take a certain amount of continuing education classes each year to keep their licenses or titles in force.

Human Resources

Human resource management, or personnel management as it is sometimes called, involves the entire spectrum of hiring, compensating, managing, and terminating employees along with all the legal responsibilities of having employees. Although small offices typically have fewer problems with human resources, all design firms with employees must deal with the same issues. This section highlights a few of the common components of human resource management.

Hiring

Finding employees may be done in a variety of ways. The designer can place advertisements in local newspapers and trade journals, hire an executive search firm, contact university placement offices, or post their needs on the internet. Design firms also generally receive unsolicited resumes, phone calls, and emails requesting an interview for employment. Depending on the state of the local economy, these unsolicited requests may be few or numerous. Word-of-mouth notice that a particular firm is hiring can also be an effective way to find people to interview within a local design community.

When interviewing, the interior designer must be aware of the many legal requirements for hiring employees. For example, equal employment opportunity laws make it illegal for employers to ask job candidates their age, date of birth, marital status, national origin, race, or maiden name. The Civil Rights Act of 1964, the Equal Employment Opportunity Act of 1972, and the Civil Rights Act of 1991 also make it illegal to discriminate on the basis of sex, race, color, religion, or national origin. The Americans with Disabilities Act makes it illegal to discriminate on the basis of disabilities. In most cases, these laws only apply to firms with 15 or more employees. However, to minimize potential problems, all firms should follow these hiring guidelines.

The process of considering someone for employment should include a review of their past work experience, their résumé, a portfolio review, and one or more personal interviews.

Work Organization and Job Descriptions

Every office, regardless of size, should have a defined method of completing projects and an understanding of who does what tasks and who reports to whom. For small offices this may simply be an agreed-on practice; for large offices, it is formalized into an organizational chart. In addition to an organizational structure, there should also be written job descriptions for all positions in the firm. Job descriptions list the title of each position and define the duties and responsibilities of the person holding that title. Job descriptions may also include the qualifications and experience required for the position, and how that position fits within the organizational and reporting structure of the firm.

The individual titles vary from one firm to another, but they commonly include principal, project manager, design director, designer, and assistant designer. There may also be titles like receptionist, resource coordinator, librarian, CAD operator, marketing director, and bookkeeper.

Compensation

Compensation is any kind of payment to an employee for work done. For interior design firms this includes a base salary or wage along with fringe benefits. In addition, some firms may offer bonuses based on the profitability of the firm or fixed bonuses at holidays or other times based on the employees' base salary. Fringe benefits include compensation such as paid vacations and sick leave, health insurance, educational benefits, retirement plans, dental and vision insurance, travel expenses, and life insurance. For firms that resell furniture, employees may receive a *commission*, or a percentage of the cost of the goods sold.

Evaluations

A *performance evaluation* is a formal review by an interior design firm of how each employee is working. Evaluations are normally conducted at yearly intervals for existing employees and more frequently for newly hired employees. Generally, evaluations tell each employee how they are doing and where they may need to improve. More specifically, performance evaluations serve several purposes.

- They serve as the basis for pay increases, promotions, or terminations.

- They provide a way to direct improved employee work performance.

- They help the firm understand the strengths and weaknesses of personnel and help direct hiring.

- They help protect the design firm from claims by employees.

To be useful, evaluations must be an objective process that treats all employees equally and that is based on the job description of each employee. To the extent possible, evaluations should be based on objective, measurable criteria or on goals the employer and employee jointly set. One effective way of maintaining objectivity is to have preprinted evaluation forms with some type of grading scale for the criteria used.

Termination

Termination of an employee is one of the most difficult tasks a manager or firm principal performs. Reasons for termination generally fall into one of two broad categories: Employees may be terminated because of low business volume (layoffs) or because of some non-acceptable behavior. Non-acceptable behavior may include incompetence, low productivity, chronic lateness or absences, negligence, dishonesty, sexual harassment, fraud, misappropriation of company property, insubordination, illegal activity, or noncompliance with company policies. Employees cannot be terminated for age, activities outside of work hours (except in

the case of moonlighting if it is against company policy), missing work for required military obligations or jury duty, or reporting company violations of health or safety laws.

Legal Requirements

In addition to the legal requirements for hiring previously mentioned, there are numerous other federal laws that regulate the employee-employer relationship.

The National Labor Relations Act (also called the Wagner Act) protects employees, mostly union employees, from unfair labor practices by employers.

The Equal Pay Act requires equal pay for all employees who have the same work duties, responsibilities, and experience.

The Family and Medical Leave Act requires companies with 50 or more employees to give an employee up to 12 weeks of leave for child, spousal, or parental care, without initiating retribution or jeopardizing the employee's job.

The Occupational Safety and Health Act (OSHA) requires employers to provide a safe work environment. Although primarily aimed at construction sites, factories, and industrial plants, OSHA can inspect offices and levy fines for failure to provide things such as first aid kits, posted material safety data sheets, and fire extinguishers.

In addition, for firms that do work for the federal or state government, there are other regulations with which the interior design firm must comply.

One important legal aspect of human resources is the condition under which employees are hired. In some cases, a design firm may have a formal employment contract that both the employee and employer sign. This contract spells out the employee's responsibilities, work duties, compensation, benefits, work conditions, termination procedures, and policies for working outside of the office (moonlighting), and may include a noncompete clause. A *noncompete clause*, sometimes called *restrictive covenant*, may include limits or prohibitions on such things as who the employee may work for during a specified amount of time after leaving the present employer, whether or not the employee may set up a competing business in the same geographical area, on working for the firm's clients, or passing on confidential information to others.

If an employment contract is not used, the employee works under the concept of employment at will. *Employment at will* means that there is no written contract and the employee can be terminated at any time without explanation. Likewise, the employee can quit at any time without giving a reason. However, the employee is still protected from being terminated because of age, sex, religion, or the other conditions mentioned previously.

LEGAL ISSUES

There are a multitude of legal issues with which the interior designer should be familiar. These include not only contractual issues, but also concepts on which contracts are based, liability, negligence, third-party claims, and copyright. The primary legal issues are briefly described here.

Agency

The legal concept of *agency* is that one person, the "agent," acts on behalf of another, the "principal," in dealings with another, the "third party." In interior design, the agent is the interior designer, the principal is the owner or client, and the third party is the contractor or vendor. Legally speaking, when the agent consents to act on behalf of and represent the interests of the principal, the agent is empowered to create legal relationships between the principal and third parties.

When the interior designer works with and conveys information to the contractor, the contractor may assume the interior designer has more authority than he or she has. The contractor may blame the interior designer for instructions the owner may not be aware of, and the owner may blame the interior designer for inadequately or incorrectly carrying out his or her wishes. The interior designer must be careful when conveying information about what is to be done on the owner's behalf. The standard agreement forms and general conditions of the contract attempt to minimize potential problems by clearly defining duties and responsibilities of the various parties. This is one reason, for example, why change orders must be signed by the owner as well as the interior designer.

Duties

The law attempts to define what one person "owes" another in particular relationships, including contracts. This is called *duty* and is important in the interior design and construction industry because of the multitude of formal (contractual) and informal relationships. For the interior designer, there are three ways duty is established.

The first is by the terms of a contract, whether written or oral. The standard forms of agreement by the AIA, ASID, and others attempt to outline the services and responsibilities of the interior designer as clearly as possible and state that these may not be extended without written consent of the owner.

The second way duty is established is by legislative enactment, such as building codes and interior design licensing or title laws.

The third way duty is established is by the interior designer's conduct. Courts often look to the *implied duties* based on how the parties conduct themselves in the course of performing their work. Many situations may arise that are not covered by the contracts or general conditions. In these cases the interior designer is not free to act unilaterally; he or she must consult with the client. The interior designer may be held liable for the consequences of either action or inaction.

Some examples of implied duties include the following.

- The interior designer has the duty to cooperate with the contractor or vendor. While some actions related to this duty are clearly stated in the contracts, others are not.

- The interior designer has the duty not to interfere with the contractor's or vendor's work. This includes actions that might cause delays, or additional costs, or that might cause the contractor to modify standard construction methods and procedures.

- The interior designer has the duty to inform the contractor or vendor of relevant information that may affect the job's progress, including any problems or errors observed.

- The interior designer has the duty to assist the owner in coordinating the schedules and requirements of other contractors and vendors not reporting to the general contractor.

Liability, Negligence, and Risk Management

Liability is the legal responsibility for injury or damage to another person or property. Interior designers are constantly exposed to liability for their actions or inactions or by simply being named as a responsible third party in other claims. One of the primary ways interior designers can be liable is through negligence. *Negligence* is the failure to use due care to avoid harming another person or property.

In order for an interior designer to be found negligent, three conditions must be met. First, there must be a legal duty established between the parties. Second, it must be shown that the interior designer breached that duty. Third, it must be shown that the breach of duty was the cause of the damage or injury suffered by the other party.

Because interior designers represent themselves as having special knowledge and skill, the law holds them liable for their professional actions. However, the prevailing legal concept is that the professional is not expected to be perfect. The interior designer is only expected to exercise the degree of skill, knowledge, and judgment normally possessed by other professionals in similar circumstances in similar communities. The interior designer is expected to perform to the standards of the professional community and the generally accepted knowledge, practice, and procedures of that community.

Although an interior designer cannot totally avoid liability, he or she can limit exposure to liability through good risk management, which involves the following procedures.

- Use well-written contracts and follow them thoroughly. Standard AIA or ASID documents have been written to coordinate with each other and have been based on decades of experience. If these cannot be used, the interior designer should employ an attorney to write the contract or to review a client's contract.

- Maintain an active quality control program. This should include a wide variety of elements, but the most important are establishing a well-defined program set of objectives for the project; having standard checklists of procedures; using proven construction methods, details, and specifications; maintaining communication among everyone on the design and construction team (including the client); and making sure everyone in the office who works on the project understands the contractual obligations and their responsibilities.

• Document every decision, meeting, action, and observation throughout the entire life of the project. See the section under project management in Ch. 23 for more information on documentation. Documentation is invaluable in proving the sequence of events, who made a decision, and the standards of care the interior designer took to complete the work.

• Be very careful of last-minute changes and substitutions. About half of all claims and lawsuits result from these types of actions, in cases where the interior designer did not have time to fully research and consider the modifications.

• Carry sufficient liability insurance for the types of work the office does. Refer to the discussion in this chapter on types of insurance.

• Follow the guidelines for avoiding third-party claims as discussed in the next section.

Exposure to Third-Party Claims

Through the concept of *privity*, the interior designer is theoretically protected from claims by parties with whom the designer has no direct contractual relationship. This is clearly stated in the General Conditions of the Contract for Construction, AIA A201, as well as other contracts, as an indemnification clause. *Indemnification clauses* attempt to hold harmless both the owner and interior designer for any damages, claims, or losses resulting from the performance of any work on the project, whether by the contractor or others with whom the interior designer has no contractual relationship. However, in some cases courts may not support the enforcement of this clause for a variety of reasons, one of which may be that instructions the interior designer gave or failed to give

were the primary cause of the damage or injury. In addition to making sure an indemnification clause is in the contract and general conditions, the interior designer can minimize third-party claims by following these guidelines.

• Do not include contract language that would expressly state or imply responsibility to provide management, supervision, coordination, or planning of construction, unless those services are specifically being provided by formal agreement.

• Be aware that actions taken or directions given to the contractor during construction may imply that the interior designer's responsibility extends to portions of the work beyond what the contract requires. Do not give directions concerning methods of construction.

• Point out obvious construction safety problems to the contractor. Follow up in writing to both the contractor and owner. If the problems are not corrected, suggest to the owner that the owner stop construction until the problems are corrected.

Copyright

Copyright protection for interior design work falls into two categories. The first is the traditional one and includes copyright for the drawings, specifications, and other pictorial or graphic representations of the interior designer's work. The second is for the design itself. This latter copyright protection was established under The Architectural Works Copyright Protection Act, which applies to buildings and interior designs erected after December 1, 1990. Although the law defines what an architectural work is as the design of a building, a Congressional Committee Report (Report 101-735, September 21, 1990) specifically notes that interior design is included in the definition of buildings. With the current copyright protection, the copyright holder retains rights that include the graphic representation of a building or interior as well as the overall form, arrangement, and composition of spaces and elements in the design. This means that an owner cannot make unauthorized copies of a building or interior that was designed by the architect or interior designer (copyright holder), nor can the owner make derivative works. *Derivative works* are buildings or interiors designed after the original building or interior that are either substantially similar to or modifications of the original building or interior.

Generally, the interior designer owns the copyright unless the interior designer is an employee of the owner or specifically assigns the copyright to the owner. This is something that should be clearly stated in the Owner-Designer Agreement. AIA Document B171™ ID states that the interior designer is the owner of the instruments of service and shall retain all common-law, statutory, and other reserved rights, including copyrights. In addition, the interior designer should specifically claim ownership rights of the building copyright by making such a declaration in the Owner-Designer Agreement and registering the work with the U.S. Copyright Office. Although not technically required, official registration is advisable and allows the interior designer to bring a lawsuit for infringement and collect attorneys' fees and recover statutory damages. Registration should be made within three months of "publication," which in this case means construction of the interior design project.

The interior designer can transfer the copyright to the owner, if desired, or can grant a license to reproduce the building or a derivative work one or more times.

BUSINESS DEVELOPMENT

In the competitive marketplace of professional services, it is no longer possible for an interior designer to sit in the office waiting for a phone call for a new job or for a referral from a previous client. Marketing and public relations have become integral parts of successful firms, and interior designers should be familiar with the basic techniques.

Marketing

Marketing can be defined simply as a set of activities related to facilitating an honest exchange of something one party has for something another needs. A number of marketing techniques are used by interior design firms today. Which ones should be used by any particular office depends on the type of market the office is hoping to capture, the geographical area the office markets in, the type of work the office wants to perform, and the budget and personnel available for marketing, among other factors. The following marketing techniques are some of the more common methods used.

Corporate identity: Although a corporate identity is not a specific marketing technique in itself, it is a fundamental requirement for a professional firm and something that is applicable to other marketing aspects. A corporate identity is a distinct and consistently applied graphic image that connects the graphic with the designer's firm in the minds of people who see it. It may include a specially designed logo or mark that is unique to the design firm or a unique treatment of the design firm's name. All firms should have a well-designed corporate identity program that encompasses all the graphic and promotional items produced such as letterhead, envelopes, brochures, business cards, proposals, newsletters, forms, drawing paper, and similar items. A properly designed corporate identity program can visually communicate the firm's philosophy; present a strong, visible identity to support the firm's marketing efforts; organize the firm's internal office procedures and project documentation; and give the firm a visual coherence and consistency.

Developing leads: A lead is a source of information about a potential client who may need the services of an interior designer now or in the future. A lead can also be a planned building project for which there is a need for design services. As more design firms target their marketing efforts to the types of clients they want or the kinds of projects in which they specialize, finding and developing leads is becoming increasingly important to a thriving business. For example, a design firm that specializes in law offices may develop a list of all the law firms in a given area so the marketing effort is directed only at those potential clients and not wasted on accounting firms.

Brochures: A brochure is a basic marketing tool for all design firms. It gives a brief description of the firm and its capabilities and service specialties and includes representative photographs of past projects. Brochures are produced in a wide range of sizes and styles, from simple, pocket-size folders to hardbound books. In most cases, however, a brochure should be well designed, fairly brief, and laid out to give potential clients an overall impression of the firm and its abilities. It should serve as a reminder of the firm and encourage a potential client to seek more information from the designer. Many firms now use CDs or DVDs in addition to or in place of printed brochures.

Audiovisual presentations: Audiovisual presentations are often used to present more detailed information about a firm and its work or to focus on how a designer might approach a particular client's design problem. In the past, slide shows were commonly used because they were relatively easy to assemble and could be customized for each client. Most audio-visual presentations today are placed on CDs or DVDs,

either as a stand-alone presentation or using a presentation program like Power-Point. These are fairly easy to customize for each client type and then produce and reproduce as required.

Newsletters: A newsletter is an effective way to keep a design firm's name and work in front of a large audience on a regular basis. Promotional newsletters (as opposed to the in-house type that are intended for the office staff) are well-designed pieces that are sent to past, present, and potential clients. Newsletters are a relatively inexpensive marketing tool, but to be effective they must be produced on a regular basis, which takes a commitment of time and money. Newsletters can also be produced in an electronic format and made available through a firm's website.

Websites: Most firms now have websites that provide an overview of the firm, examples of the types of projects the firm does, photographic images, and a listing of staff experience and capabilities. Websites may also contain links to other sites, basic helpful information for potential clients, a method to submit résumés, and online newsletters. For many firms, websites are replacing the traditional brochure.

Advertising: Advertising is any paid communication in some type of media, such as newspapers, magazines, or television. Although once considered professionally unethical, advertising is now being used to reach a wide market. Unlike press releases, articles, and other publicity tools, advertising has the advantage of being guaranteed to reach a given audience because firms do not have to depend on the decision of an editor to place their promotions.

Public Relations

Public relations (PR) differs from marketing in that it is not tied to a particular potential job or single potential client. Rather, it establishes and communicates the firm's presence to various groups of "publics" on many different levels. It attempts to create a positive image of the design firm on the part of some group of people. Of course, the most important audience group a designer tries to communicate with are those people who may need the designer's services or are able to recommend the firm to others.

A public relations program should be a part of any office's marketing plan. To be effective, a public relations effort must identify who the "public" is and what their needs are, because the design firm is ultimately trying to communicate the overlap of services with the interests of a particular community of people. To get the message across most effectively, all the PR efforts must communicate on the public's terms and in the language they understand best.

There are several ways to promote an interior design firm through good public relations. One of the most common is through a *press release*, a short statement concerning some newsworthy event related to the design firm that is sent to appropriate publications with the hope that the editors will use it. These may be local newspapers, trade newspapers, regional magazines, or national trade magazines.

Press releases are one of the most economical ways to publicize a design firm. Unfortunately, many releases never go to press because they are poorly written or incorrectly presented, do not conform to the requirements of the publication, or do not contain anything really newsworthy.

Another excellent form of publicity is an article about one of the design firm's projects in a magazine. It is better to be published in the magazines that potential clients receive than in a design trade magazine. (Remember, though, that it is flattering to be featured in a design trade magazine, and reprints of the article can be

sent to existing and potential clients.) For instance, a bank interior that is featured in banking magazines will be more likely to reach and impress other bankers looking for interior design services than if the interior was shown in an interior design trade journal. Technical articles written by an interior designer can also be used to promote an office name and its services.

Other methods of public relations include organizing seminars or workshops on a topic of interest to the firm's "publics," volunteering for local service groups or projects, getting involved with local politics, winning design awards, and setting up open houses for the public.

TRADE SOURCES

A *trade source* is any dealer, manufacturer, representative, subcontractor, or tradesperson who supplies goods or services to an interior designer. In some cases, a trade source (most often a subcontractor) may not work directly for or with the designer, but rather through a general contractor who is responsible for completing a project. For example, if a client has a contract directly with a general contractor to remodel a house, subcontractors such as carpenters, electricians, and plumbers will work for the general contractor and have no formal agreement with either the designer or the designer's client.

Craftworkers are people who specialize in one type of construction or accessory such as furniture, stained glass, or fiber art. Their working relationship on a project varies with the type of job and the preferred contracting methods of the designer or client. For instance, they may contract with the interior designer or work directly for the client while coordinating their efforts through the interior designer, or they may be hired by the general contractor as a subcontractor.

Refer to Ch. 16 for a discussion of the various types of trade sources related to the furniture and furnishings industry.

PROFESSIONAL ETHICS

An interior designer must conform to all the federal, state, provincial, and local laws that any other business person must follow. Beyond this, however, a professional's conduct should be guided by a general sense of what is ethically correct and incorrect. For most professions, ethics are defined by historical practice as well as by codified standards developed by a profession's trade organization.

There are several trade organizations for interior designers, including the American Society of Interior Designers (ASID) and the International Interior Design Association (IIDA). Interior designers should be familiar wth the ASID code of ethics. It establishes minimum standards of conduct for its members and sanctions for violators. Although stated differently, the IIDA code of ethics covers many of the same areas and provides for discipline of a member who is found to have violated the code. For a complete listing of these codes of ethics, visit the ASID and IIDA websites.

The ASID code of ethics is divided into five areas covering responsibility to the public, to the client, to other designers and colleagues, to the profession, and to the employer. Some of the major ethical guidelines that apply to ASID members include the following.

Responsibility to the Public

• The interior designer must at all times consider the health, safety, and welfare of the public in spaces he or she designs.

• The designer cannot seal or sign drawings or other interior design documents except where the designer or

designer's firm has prepared, supervised, or professionally reviewed the documents.

• The designer must not engage in any form of false or misleading promotion or advertising.

• The designer cannot offer or give payments or gifts to any public official with the intent of unduly influencing the official's judgment.

Responsibility to the Client

• The designer must perform services in the best interests of the client as long as those interests do not violate laws, regulations, and codes; the designer's aesthetic judgment; or the health, safety, or welfare of the occupants.

• The designer is prohibited from divulging any privileged information about the client or the client's project without the express permission of the client.

• The designer is allowed to offer services to clients for any form of legal compensation.

• The designer must fully disclose to the client all compensation the designer will receive in connection with a project and must not accept any form of compensation from a supplier of goods and services in cash or in kind.

Responsibility to Other Interior Designers and Colleagues

• The designer cannot interfere with the fulfillment of another designer's contractual arrangement with a client.

• The designer cannot initiate any discussion or activity that might cause unjust injury to another professional. However, the designer can render a second opinion to a client or may serve as an expert witness in a judicial proceeding.

• The designer can only take credit for work that has actually been created by the designer or under the designer's direction.

Responsibility to the Profession

• As a member of ASID, the designer also agrees, whenever possible and within the scope of his or her interests and abilities, to encourage and contribute to the sharing of ideas and information among designers, allied professionals, and others in the industry, and to encourage and offer support to interior design students.

• Designers should continually upgrade their professional knowledge and competency.

Responsibility to the Employer

• When leaving an employer's service, the designer cannot take drawings, data, or other material except with the permission of the employer.

• The designer cannot disclose any confidential information obtained during the course of his or her employment, without the permission of both the client and the employer.

• Employers should not unreasonably withhold from employees leaving the firm permission to take copies of materials relating to the employee's work, as long as those materials are not confidential.

In addition to the professional organization's codes of ethics, there are some standards of conduct that derive from legal or contractual relationships or that have simply developed through industry-standard practice.

One of the primary sources of ethical and business problems during design and construction is lack of communication. The designer has a duty to keep both the owner and contractor informed of problems, changes, or other information that might affect his or her work or the performance of his or her contractual obligations. In most cases, any communication should be in writing to either party and a copy should be given to the other party. This helps avoid misunderstandings and provides documentation of all actions on the job should disputes arise. Even meetings and telephone conversations should be documented with memos or notes or followed up with an email.

SAMPLE QUESTIONS

1. An interior designer could determine which clients have not paid by looking at the

(A) aged accounts receivable

(B) balance sheet

(C) cash flow statement

(D) income statement

2. If, during construction, an interior designer repeatedly tells a contractor how to install certain finishes, this could give rise to

(A) a breach of duty

(B) a claim of negligence

(C) liability exposure

(D) a third-party claim

3. The owner of a restaurant calls an interior designer and says she would like to hire the designer to complete a project because she is unhappy with the work the current architect is doing. What should be the designer's first response?

(A) Decline the offer and tell the restaurant owner the original architect must complete the project.

(B) Tell the owner that a working agreement could be discussed only if the architect were no longer working on the job.

(C) Suggest that the designer and the architect work together to complete the project to the owner's satisfaction.

(D) Tell the owner that design work could begin while waiting for a letter from the owner stating that all contractual relationships with the original architect have been severed.

4. A shipment of furniture is vandalized in a storage area at the job site. Whose insurance will cover the loss?

(A) interior designer's

(B) owner's

(C) contractor's

(D) furniture dealer's

5. Which business organization allows the most control by its founders?

(A) sole proprietorship

(B) partnership

(C) professional corporation

(D) subchapter S corporation

6. In order to reduce fees to be competitive in a local market, an interior designer should first consider reducing

(A) indirect labor costs

(B) capital expenses

(C) profit

(D) salary rates

7. What would be the most appropriate type of marketing for a design firm just beginning business?

(A) well-designed business stationery and a quarterly newsletter

(B) a direct-mail campaign to targeted client types

(C) advertising in local magazines where business is wanted

(D) a corporate identity package and a capabilities brochure

8. Which of the following is NOT generally considered a trade source?

(A) artisan

(B) general contractor

(C) manufacturer's representative

(D) furniture showroom

9. What type of insurance is LEAST necessary for a practicing interior designer?

(A) employee health

(B) worker's compensation

(C) general liability

(D) automobile

10. What type of insurance is an owner NOT required to carry?

(A) general liability

(B) worker's compensation

(C) property

(D) errors and omissions

25

OWNER-DESIGNER AGREEMENTS

For every job that an interior designer undertakes, there is some form of mutual understanding about what the designer will do and what the client will give in return for services rendered. Such understandings are formalized in a contract, whether a simple one-page letter or a formal, multipage document. This chapter describes basic contract provisions and discusses some of the standard language in the agreement forms published by professional design organizations.

BASIC ELEMENTS OF A CONTRACT

A *contract* is a bargain between two or more parties who agree to exchange something each desires to obtain. For example, the client wants an interior space designed, and the designer desires to be paid for his or her services. In a legal sense, there are two parts to this: an offer by one party and an acceptance by the other. Every contract, whether written or oral, must have both of these to be valid. If one person offers to do something and does it without acceptance by the other party and an agreement to receive something in return, a contract does not exist. There are

other elements to a valid contract, such as a fair consideration (money) to be paid, but offer and acceptance are the most fundamental elements.

A contract between an interior designer and the client can take many forms. It may be a brief letter of agreement; a document developed by the designer's or client's attorney especially for a particular project; a standardized, preprinted form developed by a professional design organization like the American Institute of Architects (AIA) or the American Society of Interior Designers (ASID); or a standardized form that the client may use on all his or her design projects.

Whatever the contract origin, it should include the following provisions.

- *Parties to the contract and date:* The full legal name of both parties must be clearly stated along with their addresses and the date of the contract. The person signing the contract must have the legal authority to do so. For residential work for a husband and wife, both should sign the contract so they are each separately responsible.

• *Scope of work and designer's responsibilities:* One of the most important parts of any agreement is the part that describes the exact amount of work the designer promises to do. This should include the actual area of the work (such as only the reception room and main conference room of an office suite) as well as a detailed description of services. The scope of work may be divided into common phases such as schematic design, design development, and construction, and each phase may be subdivided in more detail. This is useful if billing for services is being done after completion of each phase. Generally, fewer disputes will arise if services are specifically itemized.

It is also acceptable to itemize those services that will *not* be provided, such as purchasing furniture or construction observation. This technique is useful for pointing out services that are normally included in a designer's contract and that the client may expect if the services are not specifically excluded.

• *Purchasing agreements, if any:* If the interior designer will be buying furniture and fixtures and reselling them to the client, any agreement should clearly state the designer's responsibilities as well as the client's responsibilities for final payment, acceptance of the work, rejection of damaged goods, payment of delivery and installation costs, payment of deposits, and methods of purchasing furniture and equipment. Any agreement or contract should be consistent with the Uniform Commercial Code and with any specific laws of the state in which the designer is practicing. The AIA standard forms state that if the interior designer will be purchasing furniture and equipment on behalf of the owner, the duties and compensation for such additional services must be set forth in a separate document.

• *Method of payment:* Any contract should state how much the client will be charged for services and how services will be paid for. There are several ways of charging for professional services, including a fixed fee, multiple of direct personnel expense, percentage of project cost, and cost per unit area, along with several variations of these basic methods. These will be discussed in more detail in a later section. The agreement should also clearly define when payment is to be made—monthly, at the completion of each phase, or on some other schedule. It should also include payment due dates and any provision for late payments.

• *Reimbursable expenses:* Reimbursable expenses are costs that are not part of professional services but are necessary to complete the project. These include things such as travel, long-distance telephone calls, reproduction costs, and postage. On large jobs these expenses can be significant, and it is important to itemize them so the client does not think they are part of the professional fee. Fees for consultants, such as electrical and mechanical engineers, may be included here or with methods of compensation. Many designers bill their clients the cost of consultants' fees plus 10% to cover the cost of coordination and billing.

• *Extra services:* It is common for a client to request extra work from the designer once a project begins. This may include things like studying more design options, expanding the area of the job, specifying additional furniture, or requiring a longer time commitment due to delays. Many disputes can be avoided by clearly listing the types of extra services, charges for them, and how they will be billed to the client—the designer is then protected from providing extra work for free.

• *Responsibilities of the client:* Most projects require that the client perform certain actions or provide necessary information for the job to be completed. These may include things like buying and arranging for moving of client-supplied equipment, arranging for space to receive furniture delivered to the job site, or providing as-built drawings to the designer. If these responsibilities are not itemized in the General Conditions of the Contract as discussed in Ch. 22, they should be clearly stated in the contract. If timely completion of any action by the client is required to maintain the schedule, this should also be included.

• *Ownership of documents:* This provision states that the designer retains the rights of ownership to the documents and that the documents are only to be used to complete the specific project for which they were developed. The client may not reuse them to build other jobs without permission of and adequate compensation to the designer. This type of contractual provision is most often used with a copyright notice on the drawings themselves.

• *Provisions for arbitration:* Because disputes often arise, a contract should include procedures for arbitration. This is often more desirable than taking disagreements to court because it is generally faster and less costly, but both parties must agree to it in the contract.

• *Termination of the contract:* A termination clause gives both the designer and the client the right to quit the contract upon giving adequate written notice, usually at least seven days. If the contract is terminated by the client through no fault of the designer, the designer must be compensated for work performed up to the time of termination. Although a contract can be terminated without such a clause if both parties agree to it in writing, it is better to specify the conditions ahead of time.

• *Signatures:* To be legally valid, the contract need be signed only by the client, the person accepting the offer of the contract. However, it is better if both designer and client sign the agreement and date it.

In addition to these provisions, other articles may be added to cover such things as publication rights, time limits, responsibilities of third parties, and any special conditions of the project.

SCOPE OF BASIC INTERIOR DESIGN SERVICES

The amount and type of work that an interior designer does for a client vary widely and depend on the size and type of the project, what the client wants done, and which other professional consultants may be involved (such as architects, engineers, and specialized consultants). The following sections are based on the Standard Form of Agreement Between Owner and Architect for Interior Design Services, B171™ID, developed by the AIA. This agreement itemizes the most typical services that an architect or interior designer performs. Familiarity with these provisions and the particular responsibilities the designer has during each phase of a project is important for the NCIDQ exam. If the AIA documents are used, the word "architect" should be replaced by "interior designer." At the time of this writing, the American Society of Interior Designers (ASID) has a series of standard documents for residential interior design and was developing a series of documents for commercial construction. These should be reviewed when they become available.

Programming

Although many contracts do not include programming as part of basic services, the AIA Standard Form of Agreement for Interior Design Services does. During this phase, the designer consults with the owner to develop the applicable requirements of the project and studies the feasibility of meeting the requirements within the constraints of the owner's budget and the building in which the project is to be located. This information and analysis are documented in a written program. Refer to Chs. 1 and 2 for information on programming.

Schematic Design

Based on the approved written program, the designer prepares diagrams showing the general functional relationships required by the project and develops preliminary space allocation plans showing partitions, furnishings, and other pertinent planning ideas. The designer also prepares studies to establish the design concept of the project, including types and qualities of materials, finishes, and furniture. This may include color and material sample boards and preliminary selection of furniture types as appropriate. The professional also prepares a preliminary statement of probable project cost based on the design concept and current costs for projects of similar scope and quality. As with all budgets, the designer is not responsible for final project cost. Refer to Chs. 3 and 4 for information regarding schematic design.

Design Development

During the design development phase, the professional refines the approved schematic design work so that the size, scope, and character of the project are generally fixed. The drawings, color boards, samples, furniture selections, and other specifics of the job are presented to the client for approval or modification before work on the contract documents phase is commenced.

The design development documents usually include detailed plans showing partition and door locations, furniture and fixture layout, lighting design, sketches of special built-in cabinetry and furniture, and other elevation or three-dimensional drawings sufficient to describe the character of the design. In some cases, outline construction specifications may also be developed. At the end of this phase, the designer submits another statement of probable project cost for approval. This statement should reflect the changes and specific decisions made since the schematic design phase. Refer to Chs. 5, 6, 7, and 13 for additional information on design development.

Contract Documents

Based on the approved design development submissions, the designer is responsible for preparing the detailed drawings, specifications, and other documents required to have the project constructed. The contract documents may include the work for both construction and furniture purchasing, or they may be developed separately so individual contracts can be let for construction and FF&E. The AIA Standard Form states that separate documents are to be prepared. This is usually the preferred method because interior construction contracts are different from furniture and equipment contracts. The designer should advise the client of any adjustments or changes to the previous statements of probable project cost based on changes in the scope of work made during document preparation. Refer to Chs. 14, 15, and 16 for additional information on contract documents.

Bidding

The designer must assist the owner in preparing the bidding documents, necessary procurement forms, conditions of the contracts, and forms of agreement between the owner and the contractor. The designer must also assist the owner in filing documents required for various governmental approvals. Notice that the designer's responsibility is to assist the owner, and not to perform all this work alone. After the necessary documentation is prepared, the designer assists the owner in obtaining bids (or negotiated proposals, if the project is not bid) and evaluating the bids (or proposals), and he or she assists in preparing contracts for interior construction and for FF&E. The designer is responsible for providing coordination of all these activities.

Note that in Canada and elsewhere the word *tender* or *tendering* is used to refer to bidding. Refer to Ch. 21 for more information on bidding procedures.

Contract Administration and the Designer's Responsibilities

In the AIA agreement, the scope of the designer's services during the contract administration phase is extensive. Candidates should read the full text of these services in the agreement (B171™ID), but the major provisions are outlined here.

The designer is a representative of the owner and advises and consults with the owner during the contract administration phase. Instructions to the contractors are forwarded through the designer, who has the authority to act on behalf of the owner, but only to the extent provided in the contract documents.

The designer assists the owner in coordinating the schedules for delivery and installation of the various portions of the work but is not responsible for neglect or malfeasance of any of the contractors or suppliers with regard to meeting their schedules or fulfilling their contractual requirements.

To keep the owner informed and to guard against defects and deficiencies in the contractors' work, the designer must visit the project as necessary to become generally familiar with the progress and quality of the work and to determine, in general, if the work is proceeding according to the contract documents. The designer, however, is not required to make exhaustive or continual inspections.

One especially important provision is that the designer is not responsible for the means, methods, techniques, sequences, or procedures of construction. Nor is he or she responsible for fabrication, procurement, shipment, delivery, or installation of construction or furnishings. The designer is also not responsible for job site safety or for the acts or omissions of the contractors, subcontractors, or suppliers.

During the construction and installation phase, the designer determines the amounts owed to the contractors and suppliers based on observations at the project site and on evaluation of the contractors' applications for payment. On this basis, the designer issues certificates for payment, usually monthly. In most cases, a single form is used as the application and certificate for payment.

The designer is considered the interpreter of the requirements of the contract documents and is expected to be an impartial judge of performance by both the owner and the contractors. His or her decisions should be consistent with the intent of the contract documents and reasonably inferable from contract documents. The designer's decisions concerning aesthetic judgments are final if they are consistent with the intent of the contract documents.

As part of the day-to-day activities of contract administration, the designer reviews and takes appropriate action upon contractor submittals such as shop drawings and samples, prepares change orders when necessary, and may order minor changes in the work not involving an adjustment in the contract sum or an extension of the contract time. When the designer reviews shop drawings, it is only for conformance with the design concept expressed in the contract documents. The contractor is responsible for determining the accuracy and completeness of dimension, details, quantities, and other aspects of the shop drawings.

When the job is complete, the designer reviews the final state of construction and the final placement of all items and inspects for damage and function to determine if all the work has been supplied, delivered, and installed according to the contract documents.

The designer's responsibilities do not include the receipt, inspection, and acceptance on behalf of the owner of FF&E at the time of their delivery and installation. Nor is the designer authorized to stop the work, reject nonconforming work, or terminate the work on behalf of the owner. Instead, the designer can recommend to the owner that nonconforming work be rejected.

Purchase Orders

When the designer buys goods or services for the owner, either as a reseller or as an agent, a purchase order is used. This form gives the receiving party all the necessary information to supply the goods or services and authorizes the purchase of the listed items. Information given includes the buyer's name and address; the vendor's name and address; a purchase order number; the quantity, description, and price of the items; and a shipping and billing address. In addition to providing written authorization, purchase orders are used as accounting devices to track the status of ordered goods and services and to serve as a basis for billing the client.

Once purchase orders are received by the vendor, they are usually followed up with an acknowledgment from the vendor. This lets the designer know the purchase order was received and allows the order to be double-checked for accuracy. The vendor creates a bill of lading when the goods are shipped, and later the vendor provides an invoice as a bill for the supplied items. Refer to Ch. 16 for more information on the role of purchase orders in the order processing procedure.

ADDITIONAL SERVICES

The specific services that the interior designer agrees to perform are itemized in the scope of work. The most common ones are described in the previous section based on the various phases of the work.

The AIA Standard Form of Agreement lists many other services that are not commonly included in a standard contract. Including them in any type of contract helps avoid disputes because it makes clear what the client should not expect unless other arrangements are made. Additional services listed in the AIA form include

• making revisions to drawings and specifications when those revisions are inconsistent with written approvals from the client, when they are required by revisions in codes or regulations after preparation of the documents, when they are due to a change in change orders or change directive, or when they are due to proposed substitutions from contractors and vendors

• providing services to investigate existing conditions or facilities or to make measured drawings

• making surveys or detailed inventories of materials or furniture, or making valuations and detailed appraisals of existing facilities, furniture, and equipment

• providing services to verify the accuracy of information supplied by the owner

• assisting the owner in contracting for special surveys, environmental studies, and submissions required for the approvals of governmental authorities

• providing services for the design and selection of graphics and signage

• providing services in connection with the procurement of art

• subcontracting structural, mechanical, and electrical engineering consultants not mentioned in other parts of the agreement

• providing services relative to future facilities, furniture, and equipment that are not intended to be completed during the contract administration phase

• organizing and participating in selection interviews with prospective contractors if requested by the owner

• receiving, inspecting, and accepting or rejecting, on behalf of the owner, furniture, fixtures, and equipment at the time of their delivery and installation

• providing post-occupancy evaluations

• providing a set of reproducible record drawings showing significant changes to the work based on data furnished by the contractor

• providing services made necessary by the default of any contractor or supplier or the performance failure of either the owner or the contractor

• providing services in connection with a public hearing, mediation, arbitration, or legal proceeding, except where the interior designer is party thereto

OWNER'S RESPONSIBILITIES

The owner also has several responsibilities under the AIA agreement. He or she must furnish full information regarding requirements of the project, including a budget that provides for contingencies as well as for the basic cost items. The owner must furnish all legal, accounting, and insurance counseling services necessary for the project and must furnish any required laboratory tests, inspections, and reports as required by the contract documents. There must also be suitable space provided by the owner for the receipt, inspection, and storage of materials and equipment used on the job. The owner is also responsible for the removal or relocation of existing facilities, furniture, and equipment unless otherwise provided by the agreement.

The standard document also requires that the owner designate, when necessary, a representative who has the authority to act on the owner's behalf for the day-to-day decision-making required by the project. When the designer asks a question or submits documents for review, the representative must render decisions promptly to avoid delaying the job. If the designer is purchasing furniture and equipment for the project, the contract also requires that the owner maintain working funds that can be used for such purchases.

PROJECT COST

Project cost is defined as the total cost or estimated cost to the owner of all components of the project—including items designed or specified by the interior designer; labor; and materials, furniture, and equipment furnished by the owner if it was designed or selected by the designer—plus a reasonable allowance for the contractor's overhead and profit. It also includes the costs of managing or supervising construction and installation. Construction cost does not include professional fees of the designer or consultants, financing costs, or other costs that are the responsibility of the owner.

One of the most important provisions of contract language concerning project cost is that the interior designer does not warrant that bids or negotiated costs will not vary from the owner's budget or from any estimate prepared by the designer. The designer's estimated cost or statements of probable project costs represent only his or her best judgment as a design professional.

Language in the AIA agreement specifically states that no fixed limit of project cost shall be established as a condition of the agreement unless agreed to in writing by both parties. Only if the two parties thus agree to a fixed limit, and the lowest bid or negotiated price exceeds that limit, is the designer obligated to modify the drawings and specifications at no additional charge to reduce the project cost. If the lowest bid or negotiated proposal exceeds the project budget or fixed limit of project cost, the owner has four options.

1. The owner can give written approval of an increase in the budget.

2. The owner can authorize rebidding or renegotiating of the project.

3. The owner can abandon the project.

4. If there is a fixed limit of project cost, the owner can have the designer modify the drawings and specifications, without charge, to reduce the project cost.

Of course, the owner may also work with the designer to reduce the scope of the project. If this occurs and there is no contractual fixed limit of project cost, the designer must be paid for his or her extra work in modifying the plans and specifications.

PROFESSIONAL FEES

There are many ways to charge for interior design work. Broadly speaking, these fall into two categories: charges that are based only on professional services, and charges that are based on the retail method of re-selling furniture and fixtures. For interior design firms, the most common method is to charge for services only, with furniture and fixtures being purchased by the client separately or through the design firm but without the design firm having any financial interest in the transaction. This method allows the interior designer to remain more objective about what type and quality of goods are specified, because compensation is not tied to a particular manufacturer's discount or to the total cost of the installation.

The AIA Standard Form of Agreement and other professional organizations only include methods of determining fees based on professional services. Following are the five basic ways this can be done, including some variations on each method.

- *Fixed fee:* This method states a fixed sum of money that the client will pay to the interior designer for a specific set of services. The money is usually paid out monthly according to the proportion of the basic phases of services described in the previous section, although other schedules can be arranged. With a fixed fee, the designer must accurately estimate all costs and allow for a profit. The fixed fee must include the salary costs of the people doing the job, customary benefits of employees, taxes, and office overhead. Reimbursable expenses are in addition to fees for the basic services.

For a fixed fee to be profitable, the scope of services must be carefully itemized in the contract along with services that are not included. Methods and amounts of payment for additional services must be included in the contract so the client knows what to expect if extra work is requested. A fixed fee also requires the interior designer to carefully estimate the time for doing a project and to carefully monitor that time as the job progresses.

- *Hourly rate:* With an hourly rate, the client is charged for the actual amount of time that the professional spends on the project. The number of hours is multiplied by an hourly rate to arrive at the compensation charged to the client. The hourly rate must include not only the salary of the professional but also allowances for overhead and profit.

The most common form of the hourly rate is the billing rate, which is calculated with the net multiplier. As described in Ch. 24, the hourly salary of employees is multiplied by a factor to account for normal personnel expenses such as taxes, healthcare, and other required and customary benefits, as well as overhead and profit. Refer to Ch. 24 for a more detailed discussion of setting fees using this method.

The hourly method is favored by many interior designers, because for every actual hour spent on the project the designer is assured of covering expenses and making a profit. It also protects the designer when a client keeps changing his or her mind or otherwise delays the completion of the job. The designer is also compensated if unforeseen problems develop during design, construction, or installation of the project. Because some clients do not like the open-ended nature of the hourly rate system, a contract can be written for hourly rates that sets a maximum amount that the client will pay.

- *Percentage of project cost:* With this method, the professional fee is determined based on the total cost of the project. It is most appropriate for projects where the interior designer can accurately anticipate the amount of work required and has a good idea of the expected cost of the project. In many cases, this method may be ill-advised because an economical or low-cost project may require just as much or more work as an expensive project. From the client's standpoint, the designer may be encouraged to increase the cost of the project to increase the fee, or may lose incentive to reduce construction and furnishings costs.

- *Area fee:* Professional fees based on the area method are determined by multiplying the square footage of a project by some fixed rate. This method is generally used only in commercial construction and then only for project types with which the interior designer has much experience. Tenant finish planning is often priced on a square-foot basis because a designer will know what it takes to do the job and because tenants, building owners, and leasing agents do most of their negotiations on a square-foot basis.

As with a fixed fee, the scope of services with this method must be clearly defined so the designer is not forced to do more work than the fee will allow. In addition, the designer must specify how the area of the project will be calculated. For example, the area for lease spaces may be based on gross square footage, net square footage, or rentable square footage.

- *Retail method:* Using one of the variations of the retail method, the designer produces their compensation by acting as a reseller of goods: buying furniture, fixtures, and other items at a trade discount and then selling to the client at retail price. The difference in price covers the designer's cost of doing business, delivery and installation charges, overhead, and profit. This method is used by stores offering design services, but it is also used by many residential and some commercial designers. Generally, the retail method is discouraged as a method of charging for professional services.

SAMPLE QUESTIONS

1. During preparation of a construction contract, the client asks the interior designer to check with an insurance agent so the correct amounts of coverage can be included in the Supplementary General Conditions of the Contract. How should the designer respond?

(A) Suggest that his agent and the client's agent meet to make such a determination.

(B) Tell the client that insurance requirements should be placed in the General Conditions of the Contract.

(C) Call the client's insurance representative to discuss the project so the correct amounts can be determined.

(D) Remind the client that advice on insurance must come from the client.

2. Which of the following is a reimbursable expense?

(A) health insurance

(B) in-house costs for copying

(C) telephone calls made in connection with the project

(D) charges for having a model built for office design work

3. What should the interior designer do first if a client decides to make major revisions after a project has been tendered but before construction has started?

(A) Tell the contractor not to proceed until the issues have been resolved.

(B) Return any shop drawings to the contractor and tell him that revisions will be forthcoming.

(C) Advise the client that making major revisions may delay the job and increase its cost and that additional fees will be charged for design and drawing revision.

(D) Estimate the amount of time and extra fees needed to make the revisions, and suggest that the client reconsider making major changes.

4. Under the Standard Form of Agreement, what activities are included in an interior designer's services?

(A) programming, schematic design, contract administration, and post-occupancy evaluation

(B) design development, specification production, shop drawing review, and final punch list

(C) financial feasibility study, design development, working drawing production, and contract administration

(D) schematic design, assistance with bidding, contract administration, and furniture acceptance

5. If a partially completed low partition constructed according to the interior designer's drawings falls over during construction and injures a worker, who is responsible?

(A) interior designer

(B) contractor

(C) subcontractor

(D) worker

6. If the interior designer specifies file cabinets that do not fit within a space the contractor built according to the contract documents, who is responsible for paying for the correction?

(A) contractor

(B) interior designer

(C) cabinet supplier

(D) owner

7. Which type of fee is most often disadvantageous to the interior designer?

(A) hourly rate

(B) multiple of direct personnel expense

(C) fixed fee

(D) retail method

8. Which of the following is NOT an extra service?

(A) designing and detailing custom built-in furniture

(B) arranging and paying for an electrical engineering consultant

(C) designing signage for a project

(D) making a detailed survey of existing space prior to design

9. A project construction budget prepared by the interior designer should probably NOT include

(A) the contractor's profit

(B) the designer's fees and reimbursables

(C) estimates for built-in equipment

(D) fixtures to be supplied by the owner

10. What document is used to approve the release of funds for furnishing a project?

(A) application for payment

(B) certificate for payment

(C) purchase order

(D) bill of lading

26

SUSTAINABLE DESIGN

Sustainable building design (also known as "green" building) is an increasingly important part of interior design. Sustainable design includes a wide range of concerns, such as the environmental impact of an interior design project, the wise use of materials, energy conservation, use of alternative energy sources, adaptive reuse, indoor air quality, recycling, reuse, and other strategies to achieve a balance between the consumption of environmental resources and the renewal of those resources. Sustainable design considers the full life cycle of a building and the materials that comprise the building. This includes considering the impact of raw material extraction through its fabrication, installation, operation, maintenance, and disposal.

Although an architect addresses many sustainable design issues during the design of a building, there are many steps the interior designer can take to minimize the environmental impact of interior build-out.

BUILDING RATING SYSTEMS

Several organizations have emerged that provide industry-recognized ratings of the relative sustainability of a building or interior build-out. These organizations develop objective criteria that designers must follow in order to receive a particular type of rating. Although conforming to the criteria that these organizations establish is not mandatory by any building code, some governmental entities and large corporations may require their designers to follow the organizations' guidelines. The following are the major rating systems in the United States, Canada, and Britain.

Leadership in Energy and Environmental Design Certification

The Leadership in Energy and Environmental Design (LEED™) Green Building Rating System is a national, consensus-based building rating system designed to accelerate the development and implementation of green building practices. It was developed by the U.S. Green Building Council (USGBC), which is a national coalition of leaders from all aspects of the building industry working to promote buildings that are environmentally responsible and profitable and that provide healthy places to live and work. In addition to developing the rating system, the full LEED program offers training workshops, professional accreditation, resource support, and third-party certification of building performance. In order for a building to be certified, certain prerequisites must be achieved and enough points must be earned to meet or exceed the program's technical requirements. Points add up to a final score that relates to one of four possible certification levels: certified, silver, gold, and platinum. LEED is one of the primary building rating systems in the United States.

There are several rating systems for different building types. LEED for new construction was the first rating system. The LEED program now offers rating systems for commercial interiors, new construction, and existing buildings. At the time of this writing, there were also programs under development for core and shell work, homes, and neighborhood development.

Leadership in Energy and Environmental Design BC

The Canada Green Building Council (CaGBC) has adopted the United States' LEED program for use across Canada. The requirements are essentially the same except that SI units are used, reference is made to Canadian standards and regulations, protection of fish habitats is recognized, a few definitions are changed, and a few other minor modifications are made to tailor the requirements to Canada.

Building Research Establishment Environmental Assessment Method

The Building Research Establishment (BRE) is a British organization that provides research-based consultancy, testing, and certification services covering all aspects of the built environment and associated industries. The BRE Environmetal Assessment Method (BREEAM) is a method of reviewing and improving the environmental performance of buildings. There are methods to review offices, industrial buildings, retail buildings, and homes.

BREEAM evaluates the performance of buildings in the areas of management, energy use, health and well being, pollution, transportation, land use, ecology, materials, and water use. Credits are awarded in each area and are added to produce a total score. The building is then given a rating of pass, good, very good, or excellent and awarded a certificate.

The BRE also runs a certified environmental profiling system that provides a measurement of the environmental performance of building materials and products.

PRODUCT CERTIFICATION

As with entire buildings, there are organizations that certify products as being environmentally sound. The following are the most notable.

Green Seal

Green Seal is an independent, nonprofit organization that strives to achieve a more sustainable world by promoting environmentally responsible production, purchasing, and products. Among other programs, Green Seal develops environmental standards for products in specific categories and certifies products that meet these standards. The organization meets the criteria of International Standards Organization's ISO 14020 and ISO 14024 for ecolabeling. Green Seal's product evaluations are conducted using a life-cycle approach considering energy; resource use; emissions to air, water, and land; and health impacts of the product. The Green Seal is awarded to products that have less impact on the environment and also work well.

Greenguard

The Greenguard Environmental Institute is a nonprofit, industry-independent organization that oversees the Greenguard Certification Program. This program tests indoor products for emissions to ensure that they meet acceptable indoor air quality pollutant guidelines and standards. Products are tested for total volitile organic compounds (VOCs), formaldehyde, total aldehydes, respirable particles, carbon monoxide, nitrogen oxide, and carbon dioxide emissions.

If a product meets the Greenguard standard, it is added to the Greenguard Registry. Products include building materials, furnishings, furniture, cleaning and maintenance products, electronic equipment, and personal care products. Greenguard also sets allowable emission levels for their testing, using the lesser value of levels established by the Environmental Protection Agency's procurement specifications, the state of Washington's indoor air quality program, the World Health Organization, and Germany's Blue Angel Program for electronic equipment.

Scientific Certification Systems

Scientific Certification Systems (SCS) is a private organization established to advance both public and private sectors toward more environmentally sustainable policies. Under its Environmental Claims Certification program, the SCS certifies specific product attributes such as biodegradability and recycled content. It also certifies environmentally preferable products, which are products that have a reduced environmental impact when compared to similar products performing the same function. Building products that are certified include carpet, nonwoven flooring, composite panel products, adhesives and sealants, furniture, paints, and other wall coverings.

SCS also certifies well-managed forests under their Forest Certification Program, as mentioned later in this chapter under the section on wood and plastic products.

ISO 14000

The International Standards Organization (ISO) is a nongovernmental organization comprised of national standards bodies from over 120 countries. ISO 14000 is a collection of standards and guidelines that cover issues such as performance, product standards, labeling, environmental management, and life-cycle assessment as they relate to the environment. Several of the individual standards and guidelines are applicable to building products.

ISO 14020 describes a set of principles that must be followed by any practitioner of environmental labeling. ISO 14024 covers labeling programs and specifies the procedures and principles that third-party certifiers, or ecolabelers, must follow. These include requirements that an organization conduct scientific evaluations using internationally accepted methodologies, use a life-cycle approach when evaluating products, and not have any financial interest in the products it certifies. The ISO 14040 series of standards covers requirements for life-cycle assessments.

MATERIALS

The selection and use of materials in a building represents a significant part of the total sustainability of an interiors project. As with energy consumption and other sustainability issues, material selection must be made with consideration of the entire life cycle of the interior design. However, sustainability issues must be considered along with the traditional concerns of function, cost, appearance, and performance.

Life-Cycle Assessment

A *life-cycle assessment* (LCA) provides the methodology to evaluate the environmental impact of using a particular material or product in a building. (Note that this is not the same as a life-cycle cost analysis as described in Ch. 7.) There are commonly four phases to an LCA.

The first phase in the process is to determine the purpose and goals of doing the study. Limits of the study and the units for study must also be established so alternatives can be compared and the framework for data acquisition can be developed.

The second phase, inventory analysis, is often the most difficult part because it involves determining and quantifying all of the inputs and outputs of the product under study. These might include the energy required to obtain the raw materials and to process or manufacture them, the energy of transportation, the need for ancillary materials, and the pollution or waste disposal involved in the manufacturing, use, and disposal processes. The ability to recycle the material again is also considered. Some of the criteria used for evaluating building materials are given in the next section.

The impact assessment phase attempts to characterize the effects of the processes found in the inventory analysis in terms of their impacts on the environment. The analysis may include such things as resource depletion, generation of pollution, health impacts, or effects on social welfare. For example, the energy required to produce a product may necessitate the addition of electrical generating capacity, which in turn may produce both waterborne and airborne pollution.

Finally, the improvement analysis phase provides suggestions on how to reduce the environmental impact of all the raw materials, energy, and processing required for the product or construction activity.

There are four main stages of a product's life cycle. These include raw-material acquisition, manufacturing, use in the building, and disposal or reuse. The potential individual elements of each stage are as follows.

Raw-Material Acquisition

- acquisition of raw materials and energy from mining, drilling, or other activities

- processing of raw materials

- transportation of raw materials to processing points

Manufacturing

- conversion of processed raw materials into useful products

- manufacturing or fabrication of materials into the final product

- packaging of the product

- transportation of the finished product to the job site

Use and Maintenance

- installation or construction of the product into the building

- long-term use of the product throughout its life or the building's

- maintenance and repair of the product throughout its life

Disposal

- demolition of the product used in the building

- conversion of the waste into other useful products

- waste disposal of the product

- reuse or recycling of the product if not disposed of or converted

At any point in the life cycle (but most commonly during inventory analysis), consideration must be given to all the inputs and outputs of the system or product under study. These include the energy and other raw materials required to acquire, process, or use the product and emissions to the air, water, and land. A useful model for considering these factors is shown in Fig. 26.1.

Using this model is helpful in directing the required collection of data. Inputs for energy are typically given in units such as British thermal units or megajoules; inputs for raw materials are given in pounds or kilograms; and water is commonly measured in gallons or liters. Output is typically given by weight in pounds or kilograms.

Criteria for Evaluating Building Materials

Some of the criteria for evaluating how sustainable a product or construction process is include the following. Of course, not all of the criteria apply to every product.

• *Embodied energy:* The material or product should require as little energy as possible for its extraction as a raw material, initial processing, and subsequent manufacture or fabrication into a finished building product. This includes the energy required for transportation of the materials and products during their life cycle. The production of the material should also generate as little waste or pollution as possible.

• *Renewable materials:* A material is sustainable if it comes from sources that can renew themselves within a fairly short time. LEED credits are given for using rapidly renewable building materials and products for 5% of the total value of all building materials and products used in the project. These include products typically made from plants that are harvested within a cycle of 10 years or less. Products that meet this criterion include wool carpets, bamboo flooring and paneling, straw board, cotton batt insulation, linoleum flooring, poplar oriented strand board

Figure 26.1
Life-Cycle
Inventory Model

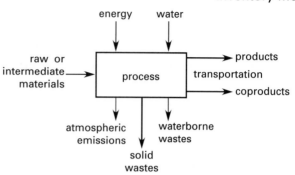

(OSB), sunflower seed board, and wheatgrass cabinetry.

• *Recycled content:* The more recycled content a material has, the less raw materials and energy are required to process the raw materials into a final product. Each of the three types of recycled content should be considered: post-consumer materials, post-industrial materials, and recovered materials. Refer to the definitions at the end of this chapter for a description of these terms.

• *Energy efficiency:* Materials, products, and assemblies should reduce the energy consumption in a building.

• *Use of local materials:* Using locally produced materials reduces transportation costs and can add to the regional character of a design. A building can receive LEED credit if 20% of its building materials and products were manufactured regionally, that is, within a radius of 500 mi (804 km). Additional credit is available if 10% or more of a buildings materials and products were extracted, harvested, or recovered, as well as manufactured, within 500 mi (804 km) of the project.

• *Durability:* Durable materials will last longer and generally require less maintenance over the life of a product or building. Even though initial costs may be higher, the life-cycle costs may be less.

- *Low volatile organic compound (VOC) content:* LEED credits are given for using low-emitting materials, including adhesives and sealants, paints and coatings, carpet systems, composite wood and laminate adhesives, and systems furniture and seating. The standards that must be met vary with the material. Refer to the LEED program for exact requirements and standards.

- *Low toxicity:* Materials should be selected that emit few or no harmful gases such as chlorofluorocarbons (CFCs), formaldehyde, and others listed on the EPA's list of hazardous substances.

- *Moisture problems:* If possible, materials should be selected that prevent or resist the growth of biological contaminants.

- *Water conservation:* Products should reduce water consumption in a building and in landscaping.

- *Maintainability:* Materials and products should be able to be cleaned and otherwise maintained with only nontoxic or low-VOC substances.

- *Potential for reuse and recycling:* Some materials and products are more readily recycled than others. Steel, for example, can usually be separated and melted down to make new steel products. On the other hand, plastics used in construction are difficult to remove and separate.

- *Reusability:* A product should be reusable after it has served its purpose in the original building. This type of product becomes a salvaged material in the life cycle of another building.

Use of Salvaged Materials

Salvaged materials should be used as much as possible. This includes items such as doors, window units, cabinetry, furnishings, and equipment. There may be extra costs involved in preparing salvaged materials for reuse, but these costs can be offset by savings on new materials and the costs associated with their production or disposal. Reusing materials, such as brick or timber from old buildings, can even add to the aesthetic appeal of a new building.

Metals

Although metals require large amounts of embodied energy for their production, they have a high potential for recycling. Steel is the most common metal used in buildings and is commonly recycled as scrap to produce more steel. Steel with a recycled content up to 30% or more is readily available. Aluminum is also widely used and is available with a recycled content of 20% or more. Copper also has great value as a recycled material, and brass, bronze, and stainless steel can also be recycled, if separated.

Problems can arise with some metals that are plated or coated with chemicals. Electroplating processes produce high levels of pollution and byproducts. Alternatives to these processes include powder coatings and plastic polymer coatings. Whatever finish is applied should be readily removable to facilitate recycling.

Wood

Lumber and wood products represent a large portion of both residential and commercial construction, from rough framing to furniture. This includes both softwoods and hardwoods from domestic and foreign sources. Deforestation and the processing and manufacture of wood products represent a large ecological problem, but interior designers can minimize the problem by applying three sustainable strategies: using reclaimed wood, specifying sustainable or alternate materials, and using certified wood products.

Reclaimed wood is basically recycled wood from old buildings or structures that has been salvaged and prepared for a new use. Preparation may include removing nails and other fasteners, drying, and cutting or planing. In addition to being ecologically sound, reclaimed wood members have a unique visual character that many interior designers and clients find desirable.

Sustainable or *alternate materials* include a wide range of products. Standard solid-wood framing products can be replaced with engineered wood products such as wood I-joists or laminated veneer lumber. Panel products that use waste material, such as particleboard and medium-density fiberboard (MDF), are good sustainable products but often require adhesives and resins that outgas formaldehyde or other pollutants. These panels are typically made from urea formaldehyde. However, formaldehyde-free MDF or low-emission panels that use phenol-formaldehyde or urethane adhesives are available. These have a formaldehyde level of 0.04 ppm (parts per million) or less, which is below the commonly accepted level of 0.05 ppm. Another alternative to urea formaldehyde is methylene-diphenyl isocyanate (MDI). This resin does not emit toxic gasses during use and requires less dryer energy and lower press temperatures than do traditional binders.

Other innovative products can be used in some instances to replace rough lumber. Straw particleboard, for example, is made from wheat straw, a waste product from farming. The straw is milled into fine particles and hot pressed together with formaldehyde-free resins. It can be used for both construction and furniture making. Other agricultural products used are rice straw and *bagasse*, the residue from the processing of sugar cane. Some products also use post-consumer recycled waste paper for making building panels. A building can receive a LEED credit for using low-emitting materials, such as wood and agrifiber products, that contain no added urea-formaldehyde resins.

For finish carpentry and architectural woodwork, many alternate products exist.

Molding can be made from MDF or molded high-density polyurethane foam. Composite wood veneers are manufactured from readily available and fast-growing trees by slicing veneers, dying them, and gluing them back into an artificial "log." The manufactured log is then sliced. By varying the dye colors and how the artificial log is cut, a wide variety of veneers is possible, from those that look like standard wood to highly figured and colored products.

Certified wood products are those that use wood obtained through sustainable forest management practices. While there are many forest certification groups in North America, the most well known is the Forest Stewardship Council (FSC). This organization is an international body that oversees the development of national and regional standards based on basic forest management principles and criteria. It accredits certifying organizations that comply with its principles. The three groups the FSC currently accredits in the United States are the SmartWood Program of the Rainforest Alliance, the Forest Conservation Program of Scientific Certification Systems (SCS), and SGS's Systems and Services Certification.

The FSC has 10 basic principles and 56 individual criteria it uses to evaluate organizations for accreditation. It has also established additional regional criteria for different parts of the United States. The 10 principles are as follows.

• Forest management practices must respect all applicable laws of the country in which they occur and must comply with FSC principles and criteria.

• Long-term tenure and use rights to the land and forests must be defined, documented, and legally established.

• The rights of indigenous peoples to own, use, and manage their land must be recognized and respected.

- Forest management practices and operations must maintain or enhance the long-term social and economic well-being of workers and local communities.

- Forest management must encourage the efficient use of the forest's products to ensure economic viability and environmental and social benefits.

- Forest management must conserve biological diversity, water resources, soils, ecosystems, and landscapes to maintain the ecological functions of the forest.

- A management plan must be written, implemented, and maintained.

- Monitoring must be conducted to assess the condition of the forest, yields, chain of custody, and management activities and their social and environmental impacts.

- Management activities in high-conservation-value forests must maintain or enhance the attributes that define such forests.

- Plantations must follow the first nine principles and the criteria that apply to plantations. Plantations should complement the management of, reduce pressures on, and promote the restoration and conservation of natural forests.

A building can receive a LEED credit if a minimum of 50% of the wood-based materials and products it uses are certified in accordance with the FSC's principles and criteria. However, even though only a very small fraction of forests comply with FSC criteria, there are many other well-managed forests in North American and elsewhere.

Plastic

Any plastics used should be identified for recycling. If possible, compostable plastics should be specified. Polyethylene terephthalate (PET) from soft-drink containers, for example, can be used to manufacture carpet with properties similar to polyesters.

Two new developments in plastic may improve the sustainability of this material type. The first is *bio-plastics*, specifically *polylactide* (PLA). This is a biodegradable plastic derived from harvested corn. It is currently used in fibers for carpet manufacture. The second is the development of *metallocene polyolefins*. This type of plastic allows polyolefins to be precisely manufactured to have specific properties. These may be used as a replacement for PVC and other plastics that are more harmful to the environment. They may be used for window frames, membrane roofing, siding, and wire sheathing.

Finishes

Interior finish materials provide a primary method of improving a building's sustainability because they are one of the main sources of potential indoor air pollution and are typically replaced several times over the life of a building. Finish types are grouped according to four categories: adhesives, flooring, wall finishes, and ceiling finishes. The following sections give some of the more traditional finish materials as well as some alternative sustainable materials that are being used more frequently for both residential and commercial construction.

Adhesives

With many types of finishes, a potential problem is due to adhesives or coatings and not the finish material itself. Most adhesives emit gases because they contain plastic resins and other materials that can outgas. There are three types of low-emission and zero-VOC adhesives that can be used for installing carpet, resilient flooring, plastic laminates, sheet metal, wood veneers, and some types of wall coverings. These adhesives include dry adhesives that contain resins stored in capsules released by pressure, water-based adhesives containing latex or polyvinyl acetate, and natural adhesives containing plant resins in a water dispersion system. A building can receive a LEED credit for using adhesives and sealants with a VOC content less than that defined in the California South Coast Air Quality Management District (SCAQMD) Rule 1168, which is among the lowest VOC content standards in the country.

Flooring

When using carpet, there are three major considerations for sustainability: raw-material use, raw-material disposal, and indoor air quality. Good raw materials include polyester and nylon-blended carpet made from recycled soft-drink containers (PET) or wool. Although wool has a higher initial cost, it is a renewable resource, wears well, and may have a lower life-cycle cost when compared to less-expensive carpet that typically needs to be replaced more frequently. In addition to carpet, carpet cushion made from recycled materials should be selected. The recycled materials used can include tire rubber and synthetic and natural fiber from textile mill waste.

Carpet disposal is a problem because of the total quantity that is placed in landfills, the fact that carpet does not decompose easily, the difficulty of separating the various components for recycling, and the costs of recycling compared with landfill disposal. Nylon 6, one type of nylon fiber, can be recycled easily. Although some manufacturers have made efforts to recycle used carpet, the amount recycled is just a fraction of the total amount of disposed carpet. Generally, carpet tiles are more sustainable than broadloom carpet. This is because only a small number need to be replaced when they are damaged or worn, the adhesives used to apply them tend to outgas less than do broadloom adhesives, and several manufactures have programs to recycle the tiles.

Carpet can affect indoor air quality because of its construction and the adhesives used in direct-glue applications. Most carpet is made by bonding the face fiber to a backing with a synthetic latex resin. The latex can be replaced with fusion bonding, in which the face fiber is heat-welded to a sponge plastic backing. Carpets made with a needlepunching process also avoid the use of latex bonding. The Carpet and Rug Institute (CRI) has a voluntary testing program under which manufacturers have their carpet tested by an independent agency for four emission types: total VOC, styrene, formaldehyde, and 4-phenylcyclohexene (4-PC). Carpet that passes the test criteria is allowed to carry the CRI IAQ carpet testing program label, or the "Green Label." The CRI also recommends that a ventilation system should be operated at maximum capacity during and for 48 to 72 hr after installation. An interior build-out can receive a LEED credit for using carpet systems that meet or exceed the requirements of the CRI IAQ carpet testing program.

Vinyl flooring provides many benefits including durability, ease of cleaning, a wide choice of patterns and colors, and relatively low cost. However, it requires highly refined petrochemicals for its manufacture and contains a large percentage of polyvinyl chloride (PVC) that can cause environmental problems during manufacture and disposal. Because of the high concentration of chloride in the tile, hazardous substances can be given off if vinyl flooring is incinerated. Some vinyl tile is manufactured from recycled PVC, and one brand is made without chloride. As with carpet, low-VOC adhesives should be specified for laying vinyl flooring.

Rubber flooring, both tile and sheet goods, made from recycled tires is also available. This flooring is durable, slip resistant, and resilient. However, because of the methods of manufacture and the binders that are used, recycled rubber flooring may give off indoor pollutants. This type of flooring should only be used where there is adequate ventilation, such as in outdoor sports areas, locker rooms, and other utility spaces.

Linoleum is available in tile or sheet form and can also be used for baseboards. Linoleum is made from natural, renewable products including linseed oil, rosin, cork powder, and pigments. It is a durable floor material and is biodegradable, waterproof, fire resistant, naturally antibacterial, and does not generate static electricity. When used with low-VOC adhesives, it emits only low levels of contaminants, less than those of vinyl flooring.

Cork flooring is made from a renewable resource, the bark of cork oak trees, which regenerate every 9 to 10 years. Cork forests are well managed and protected by the countries that have them. The only disadvantage to using cork as a natural material is that it must be imported from Mediterranean countries, increasing the transportation energy required. Although cork requires binders to hold the individual pieces together, the binders used today are phenol-formaldehyde, polyurethane, or all-natural protein products. Cork flooring using urea-formaldehyde should not be used. Cork can be finished with water-based urethanes with very low VOCs that provide durability along with water and chemical resistance. It should be installed with a water-based, low-VOC latex adhesive. Cork flooring is also an excellent absorber of sound.

Wood flooring offers many options for sustainable use. First, wood originating from well-managed forests can be selected. Both domestic and tropical hardwood is available from sustainable, FSC-accredited, certified sources. Second, veneered and laminated products using a plywood or MDF core can be used. Finally, salvaged solid-wood flooring is available. Whenever possible, prefinished flooring should be used to eliminate the need for sanding and finishing on the job site, which could create indoor air quality problems. If adhesives are required, they should be low-VOC content types. On-site finishing should only use water-dispersed urethanes. Varnishes, acid-cured varnishes, or hardening oils for on-site finishing should be avoided.

As an alternative to standard wood floors, bamboo or palm wood can be used. Bamboo is a fast-growing grass that reaches maturity in three to four years. It is almost as hard and twice as stable as red oak or maple and is sold in tongue-and-groove strips prefinished with a durable polyurethane coating. Palm wood is harvested as a byproduct of commercial coconut plantations. It is harder than maple or oak and is also sold in tongue-and-groove strips and prefinished with polyurethane.

Ceramic tile is generally considered a sustainable material in spite of the high embodied energy required to produce it and the transportation costs to get it from the factory to the job site. It uses readily available natural materials, is very durable, produces practically no harmful emissions, and requires very little maintenance. Some tile is made from post-consumer or post-industrial waste products using from 25% to 100% recycled material. Cement mortars and grouts are also environmentally friendly and produce very few emissions. Avoid epoxy-modified grout, plastic adhesives with solvents, and sealers that contain VOCs.

Wall Finishes

Gypsum wallboard is manufactured with 100% recycled content for its paper faces and with some recycled content for the core. Some manufacturers mix recycled newspaper with gypsum as the core material. In addition, about 7% of the industry's total use of gypsum is synthetic gypsum. Synthetic gypsum is chemically identical to natural, mined gypsum but is a byproduct of various manufacturing, industrial, or chemical processes. The main source of synthetic gypsum in North America is *flue-gas desulfurization*. This is the process whereby power-generating plants (and similar plants) remove polluting gases from their stacks to reduce emission of harmful materials into the atmosphere. Synthetic gypsum represents an efficient application for refuse material. By itself, gypsum wallboard does not contribute in any significant degree to indoor air pollution. However, adhesives, paints, and caulking can be pollution sources and should be specified carefully.

Disposal of gypsum wallboard is problematic because wallboard cannot be reused when taken out of an old building. Some gypsum wallboard plants are recycling old wallboard. However, the wallboard must be separated from other materials and be free of screws, nails, and lead paint. Currently, the cost of collecting and transporting the old wallboard is a disincentive for recycling. If the wallboard can be recycled, it is pulverized and can be worked into the ground as a soil additive.

Sisal wall covering is a natural material made from fibers of the henequen plant. The branches are harvested and the fiber extracted, dyed, and spun into yarn. Although fairly rough and not suitable for wet areas, sisal wall covering (and floor covering) is durable, low maintenance, and reduces sound reflection and transmission. It should be applied with a zero-VOC adhesive and detailed to allow slight expansion and contraction with the absorption and release of humidity.

Paints and other coatings should be selected and used only after careful consideration. Although federal, state, and local regulations have eliminated coatings containing dangerous components such as lead and cadmium and have limited use of the VOCs, some commercial coatings may still contain these components. Generally, paint sold now must conform to the limits of VOCs set by the Environmental Protection Agency (EPA) as required by the Clean Air Act. The limits are set in the National Volatile Organic Compound Emission Standards for Architectural Coatings, 40 CFR Part 59. Many types of coatings are listed in the standard. For example, the VOC content of flat interior paint cannot exceed 250 g/L (2.1 lbm/gal), while non-flat interior paint cannot exceed 380 g/L (3.2 lbm/gal). (Enforcement of the rule is based on SI units.) California has stricter standards, limiting paint to 100 g/L (0.84 lbm/gal) for flat paint and 150 g/L (1.3 lbm/gal) for non-flat coatings. In the future, these limits in California will be reduced even further.

A building can receive a LEED credit for using interior paints and coatings that comply with the VOC and chemical component limits of the Green Seal Standard GS-11. However, these standards are stricter for flat paint than are the EPA standards. Green Seal standards state that flat interior paint cannot exceed 50 g/L (0.42 lbm/gal).

Ceiling Finishes

Acoustical ceiling tile that uses recycled content from old tiles, newsprint, or perlite is available. Other materials, such as clay and wood fibers, may also be used. Fiberglass ceiling panels are also available with recycled content. Recycled content varies but can constitute up to 95%, depending on the manufacturer and the product type. Old tile can be repainted if the correct type of paint and procedures are used. One manufacturer offers a recycling program that allows customers to ship old tile to their plant if the manufacturers' own tile is to be used as a replacement. The cost to recycle is typically less than the cost of sending the material to a landfill. The ceiling grid itself can be recycled as scrap steel.

However, tile may shed fiber if it is damaged or as it ages. This fiber can be collected by the HVAC system if the plenum is used as a return air space. Using separate ducts for return air or cleaning the plenum regularly with a vacuum can alleviate some of the problem.

Furnishings

In addition to other sustainability issues, furnishings can be a significant source of formaldehyde in residential and commercial settings because of the particleboard, MDF, and coatings used in their construction. The following strategies can be used to improve sustainability through the selection and specification of furnishings.

- Use refurbished or previously used office furniture.

- Consider using furniture made from steel, solid wood, and glass, which are all materials that can readily be recycled.

- Specify that furnishings can be fabricated with wood certified under standards established by the Forest Stewardship Council (FSC) or with reclaimed wood.

- Require that furnishings be fabricated with formaldehyde-free MDF or strawboard.

- Use furniture with cushions, workstation panels, and fabrics made with recycled PET from soda bottles.

- Look for fabrics with biodegradable and nontoxic dyes.

- Use finish coverings for furniture made of cotton, wool, ramie, blends, or other natural materials. Use chemical-free organic cotton fabrics.

- Use low-VOC finishes.

- Use powder coatings for finishes instead of standard paint.

- Require that cushions be foamed with CO_2-injected foam or other environmentally friendly materials.

ENERGY EFFICIENCY

Although much of the energy efficiency of a building is decided by the original architecture and mechanical system design, there are many strategies that the interior designer can use to reduce energy consumption. These can be grouped into four broad categories: building commissioning, mechanical systems, electricity use, and plumbing. Refer to Ch. 18 for a review of mechanical and electrical systems and to Ch. 19 for information on lighting design.

Building Commissioning

Building commissioning is the process of inspecting, testing, starting up, and adjusting building systems and then verifying and documenting that they are operating as intended and meet the design criteria of the contract documents. Commissioning is an expansion of the traditional testing, adjusting, and balancing (TAB) that is commonly performed on mechanical systems, but with greatly broadened scope over a longer time period.

The building systems that require commissioning depend on the complexity of the building and the needs of the owner. They may include some or all of the following.

- mechanical systems, including heating and cooling equipment, air handling equipment, distribution system, pumps, sensors and controls, dampers, and cooling-tower operation

- electrical systems, including switchgear, controls, emergency generators, fire management, and safety systems

- plumbing systems, including tanks, pumps, water heaters, compressors, and fixtures

- sprinkler systems, including standpipes, alarms, hose cabinets, and controls

- fire management and life-safety systems, including alarms and detectors, air handling equipment, smoke dampers, and building communications

- vertical transportation, including elevator controls and escalators

- telecommunication and computer networks

The majority of building commissioning occurs during the design and initial occupancy of the building. During this time the architect, owner, mechanical engineer, electrical engineer, contractors, and others as required perform the main building commissioning.

For an interior design project, commissioning involves verifying and ensuring that the building elements are designed, installed, and calibrated to operate as intended for the tenant's scope of work. Following the LEED guidelines is mandatory if the project is to qualify for LEED credit. For LEED certification, a commissioning team must be used, and the team cannot include individuals directly responsible for the project design or construction management.

Mechanical Systems

There are a variety of actions the interior designer can take to reduce energy consumption with mechanical systems. These include the following.

- Design the tenant's portion of the HVAC system to conform to ASHRAE/IESNA Standard 90.1, Energy Standard for Buildings Except Low-Rise Residential Buildings, or the local energy code, whichever is more stringent. Refer to the section later in this chapter for a description of this standard. This is a mandatory requirement for LEED certification. If energy use is reduced beyond this minimum amount, a project can receive LEED credit.

- Do not use any mechanical system components for the tenant space that includes CFC-based refrigerants. This is a mandatory requirement for LEED certification.

- If possible, use displacement ventilation. Displacement ventilation is an air distribution system in which supply air originates at floor level and rises to return-air grilles in the ceiling as shown in Fig. 26.2. Because the supply air is delivered close to users, it does not have to be cooled as much, resulting in energy savings. It is also a good system for removing heat generated by ceiling-level lights and for improving indoor air quality because these systems typically use a high percentage of outdoor air. This system can also be used in conjunction with personal temperature control and flexible underfloor wiring.

Most displacement ventilation systems use an access flooring system to provide space for underfloor ducting and to allow rearrangement of air-supply outlets as the space layout changes. However, this makes displacement ventilation only appropriate for new construction, where the additional floor-to-floor height can be set to accommodate the 12 in (300) or more required for ductwork, along with coordination of stairways and elevators.

Figure 26.2
Displacement
Ventilation

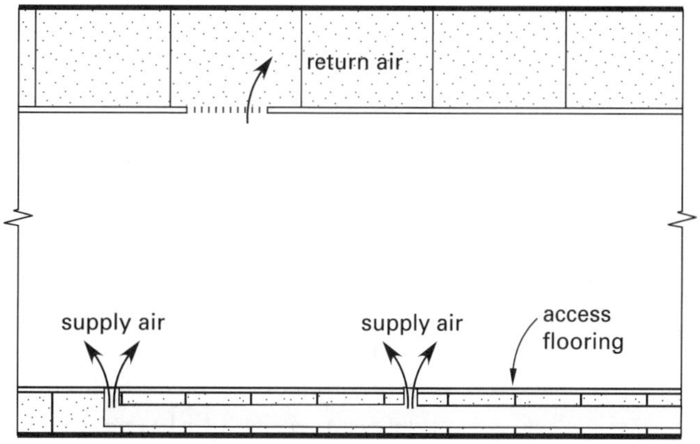

A variation of this system uses supply-air outlets located low on exterior walls, but this system only works for spaces next to the exterior wall to a depth of about 16 ft (4880).

Electricity Use

• Reduce the power required for lighting by designing task/ambient systems or by other means, such as utilizing daylighting. A project can receive LEED credit if the lighting power density is reduced a certain amount below the ASHRAE/IESNA Standard 90.1 level.

• Specify automatic occupancy lighting controls in all spaces that are not regularly occupied, such as copy rooms, storage rooms, rest rooms, and the like.

• Have the electrical engineer set up non-emergency lighting on a programmable timer that turns lighting off during non-business hours, and include a manual override capability. Of course, this requires the approval of the building owner.

• Specify daylight-responsive controls in all occupied spaces within 15 ft (4570) of windows and under skylights.

• Specify high-reflectance finishes to improve the brightness provided by daylighting.

• Specify appliances and equipment that are energy efficient. A project can receive LEED credit if minimum standards are surpassed.

• If the building owner approves, specify submetering equipment to measure and record energy uses within a tenant space. Along with this, arrange for the energy costs to be paid by the tenant but not be included in the base rent. Of course, this also requires the approval of the building owner.

Plumbing

• Specify low-flow fixtures and other strategies to reduce water consumption. A project can receive LEED credit if at least 50% of the tenant occupancy requirements include strategies for using 20% less water than the baseline amount calculated for the tenant space *after* meeting the fixture performance requirements of the Energy Policy Act of 1992. Additional credit is available if these percentages are increased.

INDOOR AIR QUALITY

Maintaining health is an important aspect of sustainable design, and one of the basic requirements of health is good indoor air quality (IAQ). In addition to simply maintaining health, the quality of indoor air affects people's sense of well-being and can affect absenteeism, productivity, creativity, and motivation. IAQ is a complex subject because there are hundreds of different contaminants, dozens of causes of poor IAQ, many possible symptoms building occupants may experience, and a wide variety of potential strategies for maintaining good IAQ. This section outlines some of the more important areas of knowledge with which examinees should be familiar. Because IAQ has become such an important topic in building design, there is no shortage of laws and standards devoted to regulating IAQ. Some of these are given at the end of this section.

Indoor Air Contaminants

Indoor air contaminants can be broadly classified into two groups: chemical contaminants and biological contaminants. Chemical contaminants include things such as volatile organic compounds, inorganic chemicals, tobacco smoke, and dozens of others, while biological contaminants include mold, pollen, bacteria, and viruses.

Volatile organic compounds (VOCs) are chemicals that contain carbon and hydrogen and that vaporize at room temperature and pressure. They are found in many indoor sources, including building materials and common household products.

Common sources of VOCs in building materials include paint, stains, adhesives, sealants, water repellents and sealers, particleboard, furniture, upholstery, and carpeting. Other sources include copy machines, cleaning agents, and pesticides.

The EPA has established regulations for VOCs in coatings. The final regulation on VOCs in architectural, industrial, and maintenance coatings was issued on September 13, 1998. This regulation listed the maximum content of VOCs in the various types of coatings. The maximum VOC levels of some common coatings were listed in the previous section. However, state laws also regulate VOCs, and each state may permit a different level. For example, the California South Coast Air Quality Management District has very strict limits on the volatile organic content of paints.

Formaldehyde is a colorless gas with a pungent odor. It is used in the preparation of the resins and adhesives most commonly found in particleboard, wall paneling, furniture, carpet adhesives, and other glues used in the construction and furnishings industry. Formaldehyde is designated as a probable human carcinogen and has irritant effects on the eyes and respiratory tract.

The maximum suggested or allowable exposure rates vary depending on the agency. ASHRAE recommends a maximum continuous indoor air concentration of 0.1 ppm. OSHA specifies concentrations not to exceed 0.75 ppm in an 8-hour time period, with a 2 ppm 15-minute short-term exposure. In order to qualify as Greenguard-certified, a product cannot emit more than 0.05 ppm.

The problems associated with formaldehyde can most easily be solved by minimizing the sources of formaldehyde within a space, using two or three coats of

sealants, or airing out the building before occupancy.

There are potentially hundreds of organic and inorganic chemicals that may be harmful to humans. The California Office of Environmental Health Hazard Assessment has a list of 76 chemicals (current at the time of this writing) that the state regulates along with the chronic inhalation reference exposure level (REL) for each, in micrograms per cubic meter ($\mu g/m^3$). These were developed as a result of California's Proposition 65, which was passed in 1986. Proposition 65 requires businesses to provide a clear and reasonable warning before knowingly and intentionally exposing anyone to a listed chemical.

The Greenguard Environmental Institute also produces a list of products, chemicals in those products, and allowable maximum emission levels. Some of the common chemicals include VOCs, formaldehyde, aldehydes, 4-phenylcyclohexene, and styrene, as well as particulates and biological contaminates. In order to be certified by Greenguard, a product must meet the Greenguard standards after being tested according to ASTM D5116 and D6670, the State of Washington's protocol for interior furnishings and construction materials, and the EPA's testing protocol for furniture.

Tobacco Smoke

Secondhand smoke, also called environmental tobacco smoke (ETS), is a mixture of the smoke given off by the burning end of a cigarette, pipe, or cigar and the smoke exhaled from the lungs of smokers. Secondhand smoke has been found to contain over 4000 substances, more than 40 of which are known to cause cancer in humans and many of which are strong irritants. The U.S. EPA and the California EPA have found that exposure to secondhand smoke causes increased risk for cancer and other serious health effects. In order to improve indoor air quality, either smoking should be banned completely from buildings and near entrances, or isolated smoking rooms should be constructed that have a separate ventilation system that vents directly to the outside.

Biological Contaminants

Potential biological contaminants in a building include the common problem of mold and mildew in addition to bacteria, viruses, mites, pollen, animal dander, dust, and insects. Even protein in urine from rats and mice is an allergen.

Molds and mildew are microscopic organisms, a type of fungi, that produce enzymes to digest organic matter. Their reproductive spores are present nearly everywhere. When exposed to these spores, a person sensitive to molds and mildew may experience eye irritation, a skin rash, a runny nose, nausea, head-aches, and similar symptoms.

Mold spores require three conditions to grow: moisture, a nutrient, and a temperature range from 40°F to 100°F (4°C to 38°C). Nutrients are simply organic materials, which can include wood, carpet, the paper coating of gypsum wallboard, paint, wallpaper, insulation, and ceiling tile, among others, that serve as a nourishing food source for organisms. Because nutrients and a suitable temperature are always present in buildings, the only ways to prevent and control mold is to prevent and control moisture in places where it should not be, or to use a material that does not provide a nutrient.

Causes of Poor Indoor Air Quality

There are four basic causes of poor IAQ. These include chemical contaminants from indoor sources, chemical contaminants from outdoor sources, biological contaminants, and poor ventilation. These factors may be present alone or

combined with one or more of the others to produce the various symptoms of poor IAQ.

One of the most common sources of poor IAQ is chemical contaminants from indoor sources. These sources include all of the contaminants previously mentioned, including VOCs, environmental tobacco smoke, respirable particles, carbon monoxide, and nitrogen dioxide. Lists of harmful chemicals can be found at the following sources.

- *Hazardous Chemicals Desk Reference*, Richard J. Lewis. New York: Van Nostrand Reinhold

- National Toxicology Program (lists chemicals known to be carcinogenic)

- International Agency for Research of Cancer (IARC) (classifies chemicals that are known to be carcinogenic)

- *Chemical Cross Index, Chemical List of Lists*, California Environmental Protection Agency (lists hazardous chemicals regulated by various state and federal agencies)

- *Chronic Reference Exposure Levels*, California Office of Environmental Health Hazard Assessment, (lists hazardous chemicals recognized by this office, with links to more information about each chemical)

- California Health and Welfare Agency, Safe Drinking Water and Toxic Enforcement Act of 1986 (Proposition 65) (lists chemicals known to cause cancer and reproductive toxicity)

- California Air Toxics, California Environmental Protection Agency, Air Resources Board (ARB)

Chemical contaminants from outdoor sources are introduced to a building when air intake vents, windows, or doors from parking garages are improperly located, allowing pollutants from the outside (carbon monoxide, for example) to be drawn into the building. Indoor pollutants from exhausts and plumbing vents can also be sucked back into the building through improperly located air intakes.

Biological contaminants such as mold, bacteria, and viruses may develop from moisture infiltration, standing water, stagnant water in mechanical equipment, and even from droppings from insects or bird that find their way into the building. Biological contaminants were discussed in the previous section.

Poor ventilation allows indoor pollutants to accumulate to unpleasant or even unhealthy levels and affects the general sense of well-being of building occupants. One of the most difficult aspects of providing proper ventilation is balancing the requirement for energy conservation. However, this problem can be solved by using heat exchangers and other mechanical engineering methods. For interior design projects, it is helpful to verify what types of mechanical equipment are installed in the building. Some of the minimum levels of ventilation are given in the following section on strategies for maintaining good IAQ.

Symptoms of Poor Indoor Air Quality

There are many symptoms of poor indoor air quality, from temporary, minor irritations to serious, life-threatening illnesses. They are generally grouped into three classifications: sick-building syndrome, building-related illnesses, and multiple chemical sensitivities. Problems with asbestos, lead, and radon are serious, long-term problems and are generally not grouped with these three classifications.

Sick-building syndrome (SBS) describes a condition in which building occupants experience a variety of health-related symptoms that cannot be directly linked to any particular cause. Generally, symptoms

disappear after the occupants leave the building. Noninclusive symptoms may include irritation of the eyes, nose, and throat; dry mucous membranes and skin; erythema (redness of the skin); mental fatigue and headache; respiratory infections and cough; hoarseness of voice and wheezing; hypersensitivity reactions; and nausea and dizziness.

Building-related illness (BRI) describes a condition in which the health-related symptom or symptoms of a building's occupants are identified and can be directly attributed to certain building contaminants. In the case of BRI, the symptoms do not immediately improve when the occupant leaves the building. Legionnaires' disease is an example of BRI.

Multiple chemical sensitivity (MCS) is a condition brought on by exposure to VOCs or other chemicals. People with MCS may develop acute, long-term sensitivity that shows symptoms each time they are exposed to the chemicals. These sensitivities can remain with some people for the rest of their lives. In many cases only a slight exposure to the chemical can be enough to produce symptoms.

Strategies for Maintaining Good Indoor Air Quality

Many of the methods for maintaining good IAQ must be implemented by the architect or mechanical engineer with the approval of the building owner. However, there are several strategies that the interior designer can implement. These can be classified into four broad categories: eliminate or reduce the sources of pollution, control the ventilation of the building, establish good maintenance procedures, and control occupant activity as it affects IAQ.

Eliminate or Reduce Sources of Pollution

• Establish the owner's criteria for IAQ early in the project. This may be part of the programming process and should include the budget available.

• Select and specify finish materials and furnishings with low emissions and VOCs. The standards listed in the next section provide guidance on choosing materials. Because it is not always possible to eliminate all sources of pollutants, set priorities by identifying materials that are the most volatile and that represent large quantities.

• Specify materials and finishes that are resistant to the growth of mold and mildew, especially in areas that may become wet or damp.

• Request emissions test data from manufacturers. This can be the material safety data sheets (MSDSs) from the manufacturer, or other data provided by the manufacturer. However, OSHA regulations require all manufacturers to develop and supply MSDSs for their products that contain chemicals.

• Prior to occupancy, the HVAC system in a new building or occupied space should be operated at full capacity for two weeks to reduce the emissions due to outgassing chemicals and moisture. If it is possible to ventilate an individual space after the completion of construction, this suggestion should be made to the client.

Control Ventilation

• During the programming phase, determine the owners' and occupants' requirements for ventilation. Also determine the energy conservation code requirements.

• Verify with the mechanical engineer or building architect that minimum outdoor air ventilation is being provided. Minimum rates are recommended by the American Society of Heating, Refrigerating, and Air-Conditioning Engineers (ASHRAE) for the specific activity of the building or individual space. These minimums, as given in ASHRAE Standard 62, range from 15 cfm/person to 60 cfm/person (8 L/s/person to 30 L/s/person). The absolute minimum now recommended is 15 cfm/person (8 L/s/person). For office spaces, 20 cfm/person (10 L/s/person) is recommended. The high range of 60 cfm/person (30 L/s/person) is used for smoking lounges.

• Provide separate rooms and ventilation for equipment that emits high concentrations of pollutants. In an office, a high-volume copier might require a separate room. Health clubs, laboratories, and kitchens are other common locations of such equipment.

• Specify independent building commissioning and testing, adjusting, and balancing (TAB) of the HVAC system.

Establish Good Maintenance Procedures

Once a building is completed it is important that it be properly maintained. Of course, the interior designer has little control over this aspect of IAQ, but through the proper selection of materials, development of maintenance manuals, and establishment of operating guidelines, the interior designer, architect, mechanical engineer, and other design professionals can provide the building owner with the basis for proper maintenance.

• Select and specify building materials and finishes that are easy to clean and maintain.

• Include in the specifications any requirements for warranties and maintenance contracts.

• Suggest that the client and building owner conduct post-occupancy evaluations at regular intervals to review procedures for maintaining good IAQ.

- Require in the specifications that the contractor assemble an operation and maintenance manual from the various suppliers of HVAC and electrical equipment. The manual should give performance criteria, operation requirements, cleaning instructions, and maintenance procedures.

- Include in the maintenance manual materials and procedures for regular cleaning of specified products, including furnishings. Cleaning products should be low-emission products recommended by the manufacturer of each product or finish.

Control Occupant Activity

As with maintenance procedures, the interior designer has little control over occupant activity once the building is completed. However, the designer can suggest to the client methods of controlling occupant activity as it affects IAQ. The interior designer can also add long-term occupancy IAQ suggestions to the operation and maintenance manual.

- Suggest a no-smoking policy for the space.

- Suggest that the building owner or manager monitor individual space use to determine if major changes to occupant load, activities, or equipment occur. The building HVAC system may need to be adjusted accordingly.

- Install sensors for carbon dioxide (CO_2), carbon monoxide (CO), VOCs, and other products, which are connected to the building management system.

INDOOR AIR QUALITY STANDARDS

The last few decades have seen the development of many laws, regulations, and standards enacted at the federal, state, and local levels that attempt to control and improve IAQ. OSHA has also proposed rules for IAQ. Some of the more important laws, standards, and regulations with which interior designers should be familiar are listed here.

For a listing of additional regulations and industry standards related to sustainablity, refer to the section later in this chapter.

- *Clean Air Act (CAA) of 1970:* This law regulates air emissions from area, stationary, and mobile sources. The law authorizes the EPA to establish the National Ambient Air Quality Standards to protect public health and the environment. It has been amended several times since 1970 to extend deadlines for compliance and add other provisions.

- *National Ambient Air Quality Standards (U.S. Environmental Protection Agency, 40 CFR 50):* This standard implements part of the Clean Air Act.

- *ASHRAE Standard 62-2001, Ventilation for Acceptable Indoor Air Quality:* This is an industry standard and, as such, compliance with it is voluntary. However, most building codes incorporate all or part of this standard by reference, thereby giving it the force of law. In addition to setting minimum outdoor air requirements for ventilation, the standard includes provisions for managing sources of contamination, controlling indoor humidity, and filtering building air, as well as requirements for HVAC system construction and startup, and operation and maintenance of systems.

- *ASHRAE Standard 62.2-2003, Ventilation and Acceptable Indoor Air Quality in Low-Rise Residential Buildings:* This is also a voluntary industry standard. The standard applies to single-family houses and multifamily buildings of three stories or less, including manufactured and modular houses. It defines the roles of and minimum requirements for mechanical and natural ventilation systems as well as the building envelope.

- *National VOC Emission Standards for Architectural Coatings (40 CFR Part 59):* This rule implements part of the Clean Air Act and sets limits on the amount of volatile organic compounds that manufacturers and importers of architectural coatings can put into their products.

• *South Coast Air Quality Management District (SCAQMD) Rule 1113, Architectural Coatings:* This rule limits the VOC content of architectural coatings used in the South Coast Air Quality Management District in California. The limits it sets are more restrictive than those of the national VOC emission standard published by the EPA. Rule 1168 limits the VOC content of adhesives and sealants.

• *California Safe Drinking Water and Toxic Enforcement Act of 1986 (Proposition 65):* This law prohibits businesses from discharging chemicals that cause cancer or reproductive harm into sources of drinking water and requires that warning be given to individuals exposed to such chemicals. The California Environmental Protection Agency's Office of Environmental Health Hazard Assessment (OEHHA) is the lead agency for the implementation of Proposition 65.

• *Greenguard Environmental Institute:* The Greenguard Environmental Institute (described earlier in this chapter) tests products following ASTM Standards D5116 and D6670, the EPA's testing protocol for furniture, and the State of Washington's protocol for interior furnishings and construction materials. Greenguard has a list of the emission levels that products must meet before they are certified by the organization.

• *Threshold Limit Values and Biological Exposure Indices, American Conference of Governmental Industrial Hygienists (ACGIH):* This document gives exposure limits for chemicals in the workplace, called threshold limit values (TLVs).

• *ASTM D5116, Standard Guide for Small-Scale Environmental Chamber Determinations of Organic Emissions from Indoor Materials/Products:* This guide describes the equipment and techniques suitable for determining organic emissions

from small samples of indoor materials. It cannot be used for testing complete assemblages or coatings. Another standard, ASTM D6803, is used for testing paint using small environmental chambers.

• *ASTM D6670, Standard Practice for Full-Scale Chamber Determination of Volatile Organic Emissions from Indoor Materials/Products:* This practice details the method to be used to determine the VOC emissions from building materials, furniture, consumer products, and equipment under environmental and product usage conditions that are typical of those found in office and residential buildings. It is referenced by other standards or laws as a standard way to determine the level of VOC emissions.

• *ASTM E1333, Standard Test Method for Determining Formaldehyde Concentrations in Air and Emission Rates from Wood Products Using a Large Chamber:* This test method measures the formaldehyde concentration in air and the emission rate from wood products in a large chamber under conditions designed to simulate product use.

HAZARDOUS MATERIAL MITIGATION

Hazardous materials are chemical or biological substances that pose a threat to the environment or to human health if released or misused. There are thousands of products and substances that can be defined as hazardous. A few of the more common ones found in buildings are described in the following sections.

In many cases, building sites or existing buildings may be contaminated with harmful chemicals, mold, mildew, and so on. These contaminants need to be identified and removed in accordance with best practices and in compliance with federal, state, or local regulations.

Asbestos

Asbestos is a naturally occurring fibrous mineral found in certain types of rock formations. After mining and processing, asbestos consists of very fine fibers. Asbestos is known to cause lung cancer, asbestosis (a scarring of the lungs), and mesothelioma (a cancer of the lining of the chest or abdominal cavity). Oral exposure may be associated with cancer of the esophagus, stomach, and intestines. In buildings, exposure generally comes from asbestos that has become friable (easily crumbled) or that has been disturbed accidentally or by construction activities. Although generally not a problem in new construction, asbestos can be found in many types of existing building materials, including pipe and blown-in insulation, asphalt flooring, vinyl sheet and tile flooring, construction mastics, ceiling tiles, textured paints, roofing shingles, cement siding, caulking, vinyl wall coverings.

Asbestos is regulated under two federal laws and one federal agency restriction: the Clean Air Act (CAA) of 1970, the Toxic Substances Control Act (TSCA) of 1976, and the U.S. Consumer Product Safety Commission (CPSC). Under authority of the TSCA, in 1989 the EPA issued a ban on asbestos. However, much of the original rule was vacated by the U.S. Fifth Circuit Court of Appeals in 1991. Products still banned include flooring felt, corrugated or specialty paper, commercial paper, and rollboard. The ban also prevents the use of asbestos in products that have not historically contained asbestos. Under authority of the CAA, the National Emission Standards for Hazardous Air Pollutants (NESHAP) rules for asbestos banned the use of sprayed-on or wet-applied asbestos-containing materials (ACM) for fireproofing and insulation. These rules took effect in 1973. NESHAP also bans the use of ACMs for decorative purposes. This took effect in 1978. The CPSC bans the use of asbestos in certain consumer products such as textured paint and wall patching compounds.

Testing for asbestos and mitigation efforts must be done by an accredited company following strict procedures. In many cases, if the asbestos has not been disturbed, it can be left in place because the EPA and NIOSH (National Institute for Occupational Safety and Health) have determined that intact and undisturbed asbestos materials do not pose a health risk. The asbestos may be encapsulated to protect it from becoming friable or from accidental damage. During building demolition or renovation, however, the EPA does require asbestos removal. This must be done by a licensed contractor certified for this type of work.

Vermiculite

Vermiculite is a hydrated laminar magnesium-aluminum-ironsilicate that resembles mica. It is separated from mineral ore that contains other materials, including the possibility of asbestos. When heated during processing, vermiculite expands into worm-like pieces. In construction, it is used for pour-in insulation, acoustic finishes, fire protection, and sound-deadening compounds. Vermiculite obtained from a mine in Montana is known to contain some amount of asbestos. The mine was closed in 1990. Vermiculite is still mined at other locations, but those have low levels of contamination. The current concern is with loose, pour-in insulation used in attics and concrete blocks.

The EPA recommends that attic insulation that may contain asbestos-contaminated vermiculite not be disturbed, and that any cracks in the ceiling be sealed. If the insulation must be removed, only a trained and certified professional contractor should perform the work.

Lead

Lead is a highly toxic metal that was once used in a variety of consumer and industrial products. Exposure to lead can cause serious health problems, especially to children, including damage to the brain and nervous system, slowed growth, behavior problems, seizures, and even death. In adults it can cause digestive and reproductive problems, nerve disorders, muscle and joint pain, and difficulties during pregnancy. Most exposure from lead comes from paint in homes built before 1978 or from soil and household dust that has picked up lead from deteriorating lead-based paint. The federal government banned lead-based paint from housing in 1978.

Federal law requires that anyone conducting lead-based paint removal be certified and that lead-based paint be removed from some types of residential occupancies and child-occupied facilities by a certified company using approved methods for removal and disposal. Removal of lead-based paint should not be done by sanding, propane torch, heat gun, or dry scraping. Sometimes, covering the wall with a new layer of gypsum wallboard or even simply repainting is an acceptable alternative. Also, lead-coated copper used in flashing, sheet metal panels, gutters, and downspouts is no longer used due to the potential for soil contamination.

Radon

Radon is a colorless, odorless, tasteless, naturally occurring radioactive gas found in soils, rock, and water throughout the world. Radon causes lung cancer, with most of the risk coming from breathing air contaminated with radon and its decay products. Most exposure occurs in places where radon accumulates, such as in homes, schools, and office buildings, so most remedial work is done in existing buildings. Testing for radon is easy and

can be done by a trained contractor or by homeowners with kits available in hardware stores or through the mail. The EPA recommends that remedial action be taken if a radon level over 4 picocuries per liter (pCi/L) is found.

Remedial work should follow the radon mitigation standards of the EPA and ASTM E2121 and can include any or a combination of the following.

• sealing cracks in floors, walls, and foundations

• venting the soil outside the foundation wall

• depressurizing the voids within a block wall foundation (block wall depressurization)

• ventilating the crawl space with a fan (crawl-space depressurization)

• using a vent pipe without a fan to draw air from under a slab to the outside (passive sub-slab depressurization)

• using a fan-powered vent to draw air from below the slab (active sub-slab depressurization)

• using a fan-powered vent to draw air from below a membrane laid on the crawl-space floor (sub-membrane depressurization)

Polychlorinated Biphenyls

Polychlorinated biphenyls (PCBs) are mixtures of synthetic organic chemicals with physical states ranging from oily liquids to waxy solids. PCBs were used in many commercial and industrial applications including building transformers, fluorescent light transformers, paints, coatings, and plastic and rubber products. PCBs are known to cause cancer and other adverse health effects afflicting the immune system, reproductive system, nervous system, and endocrine system. Because of the concerns regarding the toxicity and persistence of PCBs in the environment, their manufacture and importation were banned in 1977 under the Toxic Substances Control Act (TSCA) of 1976. There are some exceptions allowing the use of PCBs, but the TSCA strictly regulates their manufacture, processing, distribution, and disposal.

If PCBs are discovered in building components or on a site, they must be handled by a certified contractor and disposed of by incineration, dechlorination, or placement in an approved chemical waste landfill.

RECYCLING AND REUSE

Recycling and reuse of materials and products is an important part of the total life cycle of an interior space or building. As many materials as possible should be recycled into other products or previously used for their original purpose. In turn, new spaces and buildings should incorporate as many recycled and previously used materials as possible to provide a market for those products. Ideally, all materials should be durable, biodegradable, or recyclable.

Adaptive Reuse

Adaptive reuse begins with reusing as much of the existing building stock as possible instead of constructing new buildings. Buildings can be either updated to conform to their original use or adapted to a new use. Turning an old warehouse into residences is a common example of adaptive reuse. A project can receive LEED credit for maintaining at least 75% of the existing building structure and shell, excluding window assemblies and nonstructural roofing material. Additional credit is also given for using at least 50% of the non-shell areas such as walls, doors, floor coverings, and ceiling systems.

On a smaller scale, individual products can be reused in new buildings. These include building elements such as plumbing fixtures, doors, timber, and bricks. For example, heavy timber can be reused by resawing and planing. In most cases, using these old materials adds to the architectural character of the new building. A project can receive LEED credit for using salvaged, refurbished, or previously used materials, products, and furnishings for at least 5% of the total of all building materials. Additional credit is given for using 10%.

Reuse conserves natural resources, reduces the energy required to construct new buildings or products, lessens air and water pollution due to burning or dumping, and keeps materials from entering the waste stream.

Recycled Materials

Recyclability is the ability of a previously used material to be used as a resource in the manufacturer of a new product. Melting down old steel to manufacture new steel is an example of recyclability. Recycling materials is often difficult because of the problem of separating different substances so that they can be individually marketed. Most of this separating must be done by hand, and in some cases, such as with gypsum wallboard, the cost of separating all the component parts may be more than the cost of sending the material to a landfill.

Before selecting and specifying materials, the interior designer should ask product suppliers about the recycled content of their products. A project can receive LEED credit for using recycled materials if the sum of the post-consumer recycled content plus one-half of the post-industrial content constitutes at least 5% of the total value of the materials in the project. Additional credit is given for using 10%.

Recycling of consumer products can be encouraged by providing bins, recycling rooms, and other provisions as part of the building design. In some areas of the country, local codes require that a portion of trash areas be reserved for recycling bins.

Building Disposal

If old products and materials cannot be reused or recycled, they must be burned or placed in a landfill for disposal. If a material is biodegradable, it can break down quickly and return to the earth. Some materials, such as aluminum, most plastics, or steel, take a very long time to decompose naturally. A project can receive LEED credit for diverting at least 50% of construction, demolition, and land-clearing debris from landfill disposal to recycling, or by donating usable materials to charitable organizations.

Biobased products may be used to minimize disposal problems while saving depletable raw materials. *Biobased products* are made from plant or animal materials as the main ingredient. Using biobased products also helps maintain good IAC and provides a market for the rural economy. Some examples of biobased products include adhesives, composite panels, gypsum wallboard substitutes, ceiling tiles, and carpet backing. A project can receive LEED credit for using rapidly renewable building materials made from plants that are typically harvested within a cycle of 10 years or less for 5% of the total value of all building materials used.

REGULATIONS AND INDUSTRY STANDARDS RELATED TO SUSTAINABILITY

- *ASHRAE Standard 90.1, Energy Standard for Buildings Except Low-Rise Residential Buildings:* This is a voluntary industry standard that gives information on minimum energy efficiency standards; building envelope requirements; zone isolation; floor, ceiling, and roof insulation; and power allowance calculation. It is written in mandatory enforceable language suitable for code adoption.

- *ASTM E1991, Standard Guide for Environmental Life Cycle Assessment of Building Materials/Products*

- *ASTM E2114, Standard Terminology for Sustainability Relative to the Performance of Buildings*

- *ASTM E2129, Standard Practice for Data Collection for Sustainability Assessment of Building Products*

- *Green Seal, GS-11:* product standard for paints

- *Green Seal, GS-13:* product standard for windows

- *Toxic Substances Control Act (TSCA) of 1976:* This law was enacted to give the EPA the authority to track and regulate over 75,000 industrial chemicals produced or imported into the United States. It allows the EPA to ban the manufacturer and import of those chemicals that pose an unreasonable risk.

DEFINITIONS

Coproduct: a marketable by-product from a process that can include materials traditionally considered to be waste but that can be used as raw materials in a different manufacturing process

Demand control ventilation: a system designed to adjust the amount of ventilation air provided to a space, based on the extent of occupancy. The system normally uses carbon dioxide sensors but may also use occupancy sensors or air quality sensors.

Embodied energy: the total energy required to extract, produce, fabricate, and deliver a material to a job site, including the collection of raw materials, the energy used to extract and process the raw materials, transportation from the original site to the processing plant or factory, the energy required to turn the raw materials into a finished product, and the energy required to transport the material to the job site

Post-consumer: referring to a material or product that has served its intended use and has been diverted or recovered from waste destined for disposal, having completed its life as a consumer item

Post-industrial: referring to materials generated in manufacturing processes, (trimmings or scrap) that have been recovered or diverted from solid waste. Also called *Pre-consumer materials.*

Pre-consumer materials: see *Post-industrial*

Recovered materials: waste or by-products that have been recovered or diverted from solid-waste disposal. The term does not apply to materials that are generated from or reused within an original manufacturing process.

Renewable product: a product that can be grown, naturally replenished, or cleansed at a rate that exceeds human depletion of the resource

Sustainable: the condition of being able to meet the needs of the present generation without compromising the needs of future generations

SAMPLE QUESTIONS

1. Wood chips and sawdust made into panel products are examples of

(A) post-consumer materials
(B) post-industrial materials
(C) recycled products
(D) renewable products

2. Which of the following agricultural products is NOT used in the production of panel products?

(A) bagasse
(B) poplar
(C) rice straw
(D) wheat straw

3. The absolute minimum fresh air ventilation rate recommended by ASHRAE Standard 62 is

(A) 5 cfm/person (3 L/s/person)
(B) 10 cfm/person (5 L/s/person)
(C) 15 cfm/person (8 L/s/person)
(D) 20 cfm/person (10 L/s/person)

4. The building commissioning of an interior design project seeking LEED credit is the responsibility of the

(A) building architect
(B) independent commissioning team
(C) project's interior designer
(D) project's mechanical engineer

5. An interior designer is evaluating various alternatives for a particular building product as they relate to sustainability. The interior designer would most likely use

(A) an environmental impact study
(B) a life-cycle assessment
(C) an impact assessment
(D) a matrix comparison chart

6. A building can receive LEED credit if the carpet used meets the requirements of the

(A) CRI IAQ program
(B) Greenguard registry
(C) Green Seal product standards
(D) South Coast Air Quality Management District

7. Buildings constructed prior to which year are likely to contain spray-on fireproofing and insulation containing asbestos?

(A) 1968
(B) 1970
(C) 1973
(D) 1978

8. Certified contractors are required to abate all of the following hazardous materials EXCEPT

(A) asbestos

(B) lead

(C) PCBs

(D) radon

9. An interior design project that carries a gold rating has been designed and certified under which of the following systems?

(A) Greenguard

(B) Green Seal

(C) ISO 14000

(D) LEED

10. Which of the following is the LEAST effective for maximizing indoor air quality?

(A) conducting a post-occupancy evaluation

(B) developing a maintenance manual

(C) planning separate rooms for large copiers

(D) specifying materials with low VOCs

27

BUILDING CODES

Building codes are one of the main types of regulations governing the design and construction of buildings, including interior planning, construction, and finishing. The NCIDQ exam places significant emphasis on knowledge of building and barrier-free codes. It includes code questions in the multiple-choice sections and tests the candidate's ability to apply code requirements in the design practicum.

Although codes vary from one jurisdiction to another, there are basic concepts with which the candidate must be familiar. In the NCIDQ design practicum, the problem statement outlines the particular code requirements that must be incorporated into the solution. This avoids any problems with differences in code knowledge any one person may have based on the geographical area in which he or she works.

This chapter and Ch. 28 review general building code requirements. Chapter 29 summarizes the requirements for barrier-free design. Also, refer to Ch. 6 for a review of furniture and window covering flammability tests and standards.

BUILDING REGULATIONS

Building codes are only one type of regulation affecting the design and construction of buildings, along with interior construction. Additional requirements that may be applicable include legal and administrative regulations at the federal, state, and local levels. For example, a state may enforce flammability regulations for furniture, while the building code used in that state will not regulate furniture at all.

State and Federal Regulations

Most states have agencies that regulate building in some way. In addition to a state building code, state governments may enforce energy codes, environmental regulations, fabric flammability standards, and specific rules relating to state government buildings, institutions, and other facilities.

At the national level, several federal agencies may regulate a construction project, such as military construction or federal prison construction. Certain federal agencies may also regulate or issue rules covering a specific part of construction, such as the safety-glazing requirement issued by the Consumer Product Safety Commission (CPSC).

For interior designers, the most notable national federal-level law is the Americans with Disabilities Act (ADA), which regulates, among other things, the removal of barriers for the physically disabled. The ADA requirements are based on the American National Standard Institute's (ANSI) ICC/ANSI A117.1, *Accessible and Usable Buildings and Facilities.* However, additional provisions are given in the ADA regulations. Although very similar to the ICC/ANSI A117.1 standard, the ADA is not a code or standard, but a piece of civil rights legislation. However, designers must adhere to its provisions when designing the facilities covered by the law. Chapter 29 covers requirements for barrier-free design.

Local Regulations

Local codes may include amendments to the model building code in use. These amendments usually pertain to specific concerns or needs of a geographical region, or are provisions designed to alleviate local problems that are not addressed in the model codes. Local regulations may also include requirements of agencies that govern hospitals, nursing homes, restaurants, schools, and similar institutions, as well as rules of local fire departments.

Model Building Codes

Local jurisdictions (including states) may write their own building codes, but in most cases a model code is adopted into law by reference. A *model code* is one that has been written by a group comprised of experts knowledgeable in the field, without reference to any particular geographical area. Adopting a model code allows a city, county, or district to have a complete, workable building code without the difficulty and expense of writing its own. If certain provisions need to be added or changed to suit the particular requirements

of a municipality, the model code is enacted with modification. Even when a city or state writes its own code, it is usually based on a model code. Exceptions include some large cities, such as New York and Chicago, and a few states that have adopted the Life Safety Code, published by the National Fire Protection Association, or have codes of their own.

Today, the primary model code is the International Building Code (IBC) produced by the International Code Council and first published in 2000. It is a consolidation of the three model codes previously published in the United States, developed by three code-writing groups. The IBC combines provisions of all three of the previous model codes and is organized in the same format that the three code-writing groups used in the most recent editions of their codes. At the time of this writing, many jurisdictions had adopted the IBC, and others were in the process of adopting it. Some jurisdictions are still using the most recent edition of one of the three previous model codes. The intent is for the IBC to bring uniformity to code practices across the country and in other countries, and eventually to replace the other three model codes.

The three model codes previously used throughout the United States and still used by some jurisdictions are

- the Uniform Building Code (UBC)

- the BOCA National Building Code (BOCA)

- the Standard Building Code (SBC)

The primary code for Canadian provinces is the National Building Code of Canada (NBC). Other Canadian codes regulate plumbing, housing, fire safety, and other specific areas of construction.

In 2003 the three code groups merged to form the International Code Council (ICC).

The material in this chapter is based on the IBC, which will most likely become the most commonly used model code in the United States.

Adjuncts to Building Codes

In addition to a building code, there are companion codes that govern other aspects of construction. The same groups that publish the model building codes publish these. For example, the International Code Council also publishes the International Residential Code, the International Fire Code, the International Mechanical Code, the International Plumbing Code, and the International Zoning Code, among others.

The electrical code used by all jurisdictions is the National Electrical Code (NEC), published by the National Fire Protection Association (NFPA). In order to maintain greater uniformity in building regulations, the ICC does not publish an electrical code, but relies on the NEC. The ICC only publishes administrative text necessary to administer and enforce the NEC.

Model codes also make extensive use of industry standards that are developed by trade associations such as the Gypsum Association; government agencies; standards-writing organizations, such as the American Society for Testing and Materials (ASTM) and the National Fire Protection Association (NFPA); and standards-approving groups such as the American National Standards Institute (ANSI). Standards are made part of a building code by reference name and number and date of latest revision. For example, most codes adopt by reference the American National Standard ICC/ANSI A117.1-1998, *Accessible and Usable Buildings and Facilities*. This standard was developed by the International Code Council based on previous ANSI accessibility standards and is approved by ANSI.

Legal Basis of Codes

In the United States, the authority for adopting and enforcing building codes is one of the police powers given to the states by the Tenth Amendment to the United States Constitution. Each state, in turn, may retain those powers or delegate some of them to lower levels of government, such as counties or cities. Because of this division of power, the authority for adopting and enforcing building codes varies among the states.

Building codes are usually adopted and enforced by local governments, either by a municipality or, in the case of sparsely populated areas, a county or district. A few states write their own codes or adopt a model code statewide. Regulation in Canada is the responsibility of provincial and territorial governments.

Codes are enacted as laws just as any other local regulation. Before construction, a building code is enforced through the permit process, which requires that builders submit plans and specifications for checking and conduct inspections to verify that building is proceeding according to the approved plans. However, the design professional is ultimately responsible for making sure that the design meets all applicable codes and regulations.

TESTING AND MATERIAL STANDARDS

All approved materials and construction assemblies referred to in building codes are required to be manufactured according to accepted methods or tested by approved agencies according to standardized testing procedures, or both. By themselves, standards have no legal standing. Only when they are referred to in a building code and that code is adopted by a governmental jurisdiction do standards become law. There are hundreds of standardized tests and product standards for building materials and constructions. Some of the more common ones are listed in this section.

Standards-Writing Organizations

The American Society for Testing and Materials (ASTM) is one organization that publishes thousands of test procedures that prescribe, in detail, such things as how the test apparatus must be set up, how materials must be prepared for the test, the length of the test, and other requirements. If a product manufacturer has one of its materials successfully tested, it will indicate what tests the material has passed in its product literature. Standards are developed through the work of committees of experts in a particular field. Although ASTM does not actually perform tests, its procedures and standards are used by testing agencies.

The National Fire Protection Association (NFPA) is another private, voluntary organization that develops standards related to the causes and prevention of de-structive fires. NFPA publishes hundreds of codes and standards in a multivolume set that covers the entire scope of fire prevention, including sprinkler systems, fire extinguishers, hazardous materials, fire fighting, and much more.

Other standards-writing organizations are typically industry trade groups that have an interest in a particular material, product, or field of expertise. Examples of such trade groups include the American Society of Heating, Refrigerating and Air-Conditioning Engineers (ASHRAE); the Illuminating Engineering Society (IES); the Gypsum Association (GA); and the Tile Council of America (TCA). There are hundreds of these construction trade organizations.

The American National Standards Institute (ANSI) is a well-known organization in the field, but unlike the other standards groups, ANSI does not develop or write standards. Instead, it approves standards developed by other organizations and works to avoid duplications between different standards. For example, ANSI 108, *Specifications for Installation of Ceramic Tile*, was developed by the Tile Council of America and reviewed by a large committee of widely varying industry representatives. Although the ANSI approval process does not necessarily represent unanimity among committee members, it requires much more than a simple majority, and mandates that all views and objections be considered and that a concerted effort be made toward their resolution.

Testing Laboratories

When a standard describes a test procedure or requires one or more tests in its description of a material or product, a testing laboratory must perform the test. A standards-writing organization may also provide testing, but in most cases a Nationally Recognized Testing Laboratory (NRTL) must perform the test. An NRTL is an independent laboratory recognized by the Occupational Safety and Health Administration (OSHA) to test products to the specifications of applicable product safety standards.

One of the most well known testing laboratories is Underwriters Laboratories (UL). Among other activities, UL develops standards and tests products for safety. When a product successfully passes the prescribed test, it is given a UL label. There are several types of UL labels, and each means something different. When a complete and total product is successfully tested, it receives a *listed label*. This means that the product passed the safety test and is manufactured under the UL follow-up services program.

Another type of label is the *classified label.* This means that samples of the product were tested for certain types of uses only. In addition to the classified label, the product must also carry a statement specifying the conditions that were tested for. This allows field inspectors and others to determine if the product is being used correctly.

One of the most common uses of UL testing procedures is for doors and other opening protections. For example, fire doors are required to be tested in accordance with UL 10B, *Fire Tests of Door Assemblies,* and they must carry a UL label. Fire ratings for doors are discussed in Ch. 10. The results of UL tests and products that are listed are published in UL's *Building Materials Directory.*

Types of Tests and Standards

There are hundreds of types of tests and standards for building materials and assemblies that examine a wide range of properties, from fire resistance to structural integrity to durability to stain resistance. Building codes indicate what tests or standards a particular type of material must satisfy in order to be considered acceptable for a particular use. For example, gypsum wallboard must meet the standards of ASTM C1396, *Standard Specification for Gypsum Board.*

The most important types of tests for interior design components are those that rate the ability of a construction assembly to prevent the passage of fire and smoke from one space to another, and those that rate the degree of flammability of a finish material. Refer to Table 27.1 for a summary of tests for interior construction as well as furniture and finishes.

Fire Tests for Construction Assemblies

The following summaries include fire testing for building *assemblies* such as partitions, door openings, and ceiling/floor assemblies.

ASTM E119

One of the most commonly used tests for fire resistance of construction assemblies is ASTM E119, *Standard Test Methods for Fire Tests of Building Construction and Materials.* This test involves building a sample of the wall or floor/ceiling assembly in the laboratory and setting a standard fire on one side of it (actually, controlled gas burners). Monitoring devices measure temperature and other aspects of the test as it proceeds.

There are two parts to the E119 test. The first measures heat transfer through the assembly. The goal of this test is to determine the temperature at which the surface or adjacent materials on the side of the assembly not exposed to the heat source will combust. The second is the *hose stream test,* which uses a high-pressure hose stream to simulate how well the assembly stands up to an impact from falling debris and the cooling and eroding effects of water. Overall, the test evaluates an assembly's ability to prevent the passage of fire, heat, and hot gases for a given amount of time.

For construction assemblies testing according to ASTM E119, a time-based rating is given to the assembly. In general terms, this rating is the amount of time an assembly can resist a standard test fire without failing. The ratings are 1 hour, 2 hours, 3 hours, and 4 hours. Doors and other opening assemblies can also be given 20-minute, 30-minute, and 45-minute ratings.

NFPA 252

NFPA 252, *Standard Methods for Fire Tests of Door Assemblies,* evaluates the ability of a door assembly to resist the passage of flame, heat, and gases. It establishes a time-endurance rating for the door assembly, and the hose stream part of the test determines if the door will stay within its frame when subjected to a standard blast

Table 27.1

Summary of
Tests for Fire
and
Flammability of
Interior Design
Components

common name	application	test number(s)
floor finishes		
flooring radiant panel test	carpet, resilient floors, and other floor coverings in corridors	NFPA 253 (ASTM E648)
methenamine pill test	carpets and rugs	ASTM D2859
floor/ceiling construction		
wall and floor/ceiling assembly test	fire ratings of walls, structure, and floor construction assemblies	ASTM E119
wall finishes		
Steiner tunnel test	flame-spread rating of finishes	ASTM E84
room corner test	contribution of wall finish to fire growth in full-scale mockup	NFPA 265
smoke density chamber test	smoke developed from flaming and nonflaming solid materials	NFPA 258
wall construction		
wall and floor/ceiling assembly test	fire ratings of walls, structure, and floor construction assemblies	ASTM E119
ceilings		
Steiner tunnel test	flame-spread rating of finishes	ASTM E84
door/glass openings		
fire tests of door assemblies	endurance test of doors to flame and heat transfer	UL 10B
fire tests of window assemblies	endurance of glazing for 45 minutes to flame and heat transfer.	ASTM E163
furniture		
cigarette ignition resistance test of furniture components	separate fabric and fillings of upholstered furniture	NFPA 260 (CAL TB 117)
cigarette ignition resistance test of furniture composites	mockup of a seat cushion, including foam, liner, and fabric	NFPA 261 (CAL TB 116)
full seating test	actual sample of a chair tested to an open flame	NFPA 266 (CAL TB 133)
window coverings		
vertical ignition test	draperies, curtains, and other window treatment as well as banners, awnings, and fabric structures.	NFPA 701

from a fire hose after the door has been subjected to the fire-endurance part of the test. Similar tests include UL10B, UL10C, and UBC 7-2.

NFPA 257
NFPA 257, *Standard for Fire Test for Window and Glass Block Assemblies*, prescribes

specific fire and hose stream test procedures to establish a degree of fire protection, in units of time, for window openings in fire-resistive walls. It determines the degree of protection from the spread of fire, including flame, heat, and hot gasses.

Fire tests for Finish Materials

Flammability tests for finish materials determine the following.

- whether a material is flammable, and if so, if it simply burns with applied heat or if it supports combustion (adds fuel to the fire)

- the degree of flammability (how fast fire spreads across the material)

- how much smoke and toxic gas the material produces when ignited

Several tests are typically used for building and interior construction, although not all may be in any one building code. Details on these tests follow. Refer to Ch. 6 for tests related to the flammability of fabrics and furniture.

ASTM E84

ASTM E84, *Standard Test Method for Surface Burning Characteristics of Building Materials*, is one of the most common fire testing standards. It is also known as the *Steiner tunnel test* and rates the surface burning characteristics of interior finishes and other building materials by testing, in a narrow test chamber, a sample piece with a controlled flame at one end. The primary result is a material's flame-spread rating compared to glass-reinforced cement board (with a rating of 0) and red oak flooring (with an arbitrary rating of 100). ASTM E84 can also be used to generate a *smoke developed index*, which is a number representing the amount of smoke generated as a material burns in the test chamber.

With this test, materials are classified into one of three groups based on their tested flame-spread characteristics. These groups and their flame-spread indexes are given in Table 27.2.

Class A is the most fire resistant. Product literature generally indicates the flame spread of the material, either by class (letter or Roman numeral) or by numerical

class	flame-spread rating
(A) I	0–25
(B) II	26–75
(C) III	76–200

Table 27.2
Flame-Spread Ratings

value. Building codes then specify the minimum flame-spread requirements for various occupancies in specific areas of the building (see Table 27.3). These are discussed in the next section, under Finishes.

ASTM E662

ASTM E662, *Standard Test Method for Specific Optical Density of Smoke Generated by Solid Materials*, measures the amount of smoke given off by a flaming or smoldering material or finish. During this test, the material is tested when it first smolders and then when a flame source is added. A smoke density value from 0 to 800 is developed. Most codes require a smoke density of 450 or less for finish materials. This is the same test as NFPA 258.

ASTM E648

ASTM E648, *Flooring Radiant Panel Test*, tests a sample of carpet in the normal horizontal position and measures the flame spread in a corridor or exitway that is under the influence of a fully developed fire in an adjacent space. The resulting test numbers are measured in watts per square centimeter; the higher the number, the more resistant the material is to flame propagation. This is the same test as NFPA 253.

Two material classes are defined by the flooring radiant panel test: Class I and Class II. Class I materials have a critical radiant flux of not less than 0.45 W/cm^2, and Class II materials have a critical radiant flux of not less than 0.22 W/cm^2. Class I finishes are typically required in corridors and exitways of hospitals, nursing homes, and detention facilities. Class

Table 27.3

Maximum
Flame-Spread
Classes for
Occupancy
Groups

Interior Wall and Ceiling Finish Requirements
by Occupancy[k]
(IBC Table 803.5)

group	sprinklered[l]			nonsprinklered		
	vertical exits and exit passage-ways[a,b]	exit access corridors and other exitways	rooms and enclosed spaces[c]	vertical exits and exit passage-ways[a,b]	exit access corridors and other exitways	rooms and enclosed spaces[c]
A-1 & A-2	B	B	C	A	A[d]	B[e]
A-3[f], A-4, A-5	B	B	C	A	A[d]	C
B, E, M, R-1, R-4	B	C	C	A	B	C
F	C	C	C	B	C	C
H	B	B	C[g]	A	A	B
I-1	B	C	C	A	B	B
I-2	B	B	B[h,i]	A	A	B
I-3	A	A[j]	C	A	A	B
I-4	B	B	B[h,i]	A	A	B
R-2	C	C	C	B	B	C
R-3	C	C	C	C	C	C
S	C	C	C	B	B	C
U	no restrictions			no restrictions		

For SI: 1 in = 25.4 mm, 1 ft^2 = 0.0929 m^2.

a. Class C interior finish materials shall be permitted for wainscoting or paneling of not more than 1000 ft^2 of applied surface area in the grade lobby where applied directly to a noncombustible base or over furring strips applied to a noncombustible base and fireblocked as required by Sec. 803.4.1.

b. In vertical exits of buildings less than three stories in height of other than Group I-3, Class B interior finish for nonsprinklered buildings and Class C interior finish for sprinklered buildings shall be permitted.

c. Requirements for rooms and enclosed spaces shall be based upon spaces enclosed by partitions. Where a fire-resistance rating is required for structural elements, the enclosing partitions shall extend from the floor to the ceiling. Partitions that do not comply with this shall be considered enclosing spaces and the rooms or spaces on both sides shall be considered one. In determining the applicable requirements for rooms and enclosed spaces, the specific occupancy thereof shall be the governing factor regardless of the group classification of the building or structure.

d. Lobby areas in A-1, A-2 and A-3 occupancies shall not be less than Class B materials.

e. Class C interior finish materials shall be permitted in places of assembly with an occupant load of 300 persons or less.

f. For churches and places of worship, wood used for ornamental purposes, trusses, paneling, or chancel furnishing shall be permitted.

g. Class B material required where building exceeds two stories.

h. Class C interior finish materials shall be permitted in administrative spaces.

i. Class C interior finish materials shall be permitted in rooms with a capacity of four persons or less.

j. Class B materials shall be permitted as wainscoting extending not more than 48 in above the finished floor in exit access corridors.

k. Finish materials as provided for in other sections of this code.

l. Applies when the vertical exits, exit passageways, exit access corridors or exitways, or rooms and spaces are protected by a sprinkler system installed in accordance with Sec. 903.3.1.1 or Sec. 903.3.1.2.

II flooring is typically required in corridors and exitways of other occupancies, except one- and two-family dwellings. The Uniform Building Code does not establish criteria that limits the critical radiant flux of flooring material, but the IBC does for textile coverings or coverings comprised of fibers. The IBC specifically excludes traditional flooring types such as wood, vinyl, linoleum, and terrazzo. It also allows Class II materials in sprinklered buildings where Class I materials might otherwise be required.

ASTM D2859

Another test for carpet flammability is ASTM D2859, *Standard Test Method for Ignition Characteristics of Finished Textile Floor Covering Materials,* also known as the *methenamine pill test* which is required for all carpet sold and manufactured in the United States. A test sample of the carpet is placed in a draft-protected cube and held in place with a metal plate with an 8 in diameter hole. A timed methenamine pill is placed in the center and lighted. If the sample burns to within 1 in of the metal plate, it fails the test. This is also sometimes called by an older designation, DOC FF-1.

NFPA 265

The *Room Corner Test,* NFPA 265, is sometimes required in addition to or instead of an ASTM E84 rating for interior finishes. This test determines the contribution of interior wall and ceiling coverings to room fire growth. It attempts to simulate real-world conditions by testing the material in the corner of a full-sized test room. It was developed as an alternate to the E84 Steiner tunnel test. For the test, the textile wall covering is applied to three sides of an 8 ft × 12 ft × 8 ft (2.4 × 3.7 × 2.4) high room. An ignition source is placed in the room and provides a heat output of 40 kW for 5 minutes and then 150 kW for 10 minutes. Rating is based on whether (1) the flame does not spread to the ceiling during the 40 kW exposure and (2) other conditions are met during the 150 kW exposure, including no flashover and no spread of flame to the outer extremity of the 8 ft × 12 ft (2.4 × 3.7) wall. A rating is either pass or fail.

NFPA 286

NFPA 286 is the *Standard Methods of Fire Tests for Evaluating Contribution of Wall and Ceiling Interior Finish to Room Fire Growth.* This standard was developed to address concerns with interior finishes that do not remain in place during testing according to the E84 tunnel test. It evaluates materials other than textiles. It is similar to NFPA 265 in that materials are mounted on the walls or ceilings inside a room, but more of the test room wall surfaces are covered, and ceiling materials can be tested. This test evaluates the extent to which finishes contribute to fire growth in a room, assessing factors such as heat and smoke released, combustion products released, and the potential for fire spread beyond the room.

NFPA 701

NFPA 701 is the *Standard Methods of Fire Tests for Flame Propagation of Textiles and Films.* This test establishes two procedures for testing the flammability of draperies, curtains, or other window treatments. Test 1 provides a procedure for assessing the response of fabrics lighter than 21 oz/yd^2 individually and in multilayer composites used as curtains, draperies, and other window treatments. Test 2 is for fabrics weighing more than 21 oz/yd^2, such as fabric blackout linings, awnings, and similar architectural fabric structures and banners. NFPA 701 is appropriate for testing materials that are exposed to air on both sides. A sample either passes or fails the test.

FIRE-RESISTIVE STANDARDS

Building codes recognize that there is no such thing as a fireproof building; there are only degrees of fire resistance. Because of this, building codes specify requirements for two broad classifications of fire resistance as mentioned in the previous section: resistance of materials and assemblies, and surface burning characteristics of finish materials.

Construction Materials and Assemblies

In the first type of classification, the amount of fire resistance that a material or construction assembly must have is specified in terms of an hourly rating as determined by ASTM E119 for walls, ceiling/floor assemblies, columns, beam enclosures, and similar building elements. Codes also specify what time rating doors and glazing must have as determined by NFPA 252 or NFPA 257, respectively. For example, exit-access corridors are often required to have at least a 1-hour rating, and the door assemblies in such a corridor may be required to have a 20-minute rating.

Building codes typically have tables indicating what kinds of construction meet various hourly ratings. Other sources of information for acceptable construction assemblies include Underwriters Laboratories' *Building Materials Directory*, manufacturers' proprietary product literature, and other reference sources.

The assemblies that interior designers are most often concerned with include permanent partitions, doors, glazed openings, and portions of floor/ceiling constructions. Occasionally, if a project involves build-out of two or more floors, shaft enclosures, such as stairways, must also be detailed to meet the applicable fire-resistive requirements.

The fire-resistive ratings of existing building components are important in determining the construction type of the building. This topic is discussed in greater detail in the section of this chapter titled Classification Based on Construction Type.

It is important to note that many materials by themselves do not create a fire-rated barrier. It is the construction assembly of which they are a part that is fire resistant. A 1-hour-rated suspended ceiling, for example, must use rated ceiling tile, but it is the assembly of tile, the suspension system, and the structural floor above that carries the 1-hour rating. In a similar way, a 1-hour rated partition may consist of a layer of $5/8$ in (15.9 mm) Type-X gypsum board attached to both sides of a wood or metal stud according to certain conditions. A single piece of gypsum board cannot have a fire-resistance rating by itself, except under special circumstances defined by the IBC.

Types of Fire-Resistance-Rated Partitions

One of the most common types of construction assemblies the interior designer details is a partition. The new IBC makes important distinctions between various types of fire-resistance-rated walls and partitions. These include fire partitions, fire barriers, fire walls, and smoke barriers. Fire partitions are one of the most common fire-resistance-rated partitions used by interior designers.

A *fire partition* is a wall assembly with a fire-resistance rating of 1 hour, used in the following designated locations.

- walls separating dwelling units such as rooms in apartments, dormitories, and assisted living facilities

- walls separating guest rooms in Group R-1 occupancies, such as hotels, as well as R-2 and I-1 occupancies

- walls separating tenant spaces in covered mall buildings

- corridor walls

The exceptions include (1) corridor walls permitted to be nonrated and (2) dwelling and guest room separations in Type IIB, IIIB, and VB buildings equipped with automatic sprinkler systems. In these construction types, separation walls may be $^1/_2$-hour rated.

In most cases, fire partitions must provide a continuous barrier. This means that they must extend from the floor to the underside of the floor or roof slab above or to the ceiling of a fire-resistance-rated floor/ceiling or roof/ceiling assembly.

Openings in fire partitions must be a minimum of $^3/_4$-hour except for corridors, which must be protected by 20-minute fire-protection assemblies.

A *fire barrier* is a vertical or horizontal assembly that is fire-resistance rated and is designed to restrict the spread of fire, confine fire to limited areas, and/or afford safe passage for protected egress. In general terms, a fire barrier offers more protection than a fire partition. Fire barriers are used for the following purposes.

• to enclose vertical exit enclosures (stairways), exit passageways, horizontal exits, and incidental use areas

• to separate different occupancies in a mixed-occupancy situation

• to separate single occupancies into different fire areas

• to otherwise provide a fire barrier where specifically required by code provisions in the IBC as well as the other international codes

Unlike fire partitions, fire barriers must always be continuous from the floor slab to the underside of the floor or roof slab above. There are only a few exceptions. Fire barriers may also be required to have a fire-resistance rating greater than 1 hour.

A *smoke barrier* is a continuous vertical or horizontal membrane with a minimum fire-resistance rating of 1 hour, designed and constructed to restrict the movement of smoke. It is a passive form of smoke control. Openings in smoke barriers must have at least a 20-minute rating.

Finishes

In the second type of fire-resistive classification, single layers of finish material are rated according to ASTM E84 and their use is restricted to certain areas of buildings based on their rating and whether or not the building is sprinklered (see Table 27.3). The purposes of this type of regulation are to control the flame-spread rate along the surface of a material and to limit the amount of combustible material in a building.

The materials tested and rated according to surface burning characteristics include finishes such as wainscotting, paneling, heavy wall covering, or other finishes applied structurally or for decoration, acoustical correction, surface insulation, or similar purposes. In most cases, the restrictions do not apply to trim such as chair rails, baseboards, and handrails; or to doors, windows, or their frames; or to materials that are less than 1/28 in (0.9 mm) thick cemented to the surface of noncombustible walls or ceilings.

Traditionally, the E84 test was used exclusively for interior finishes, but the IBC also allows the use of finish materials other than textiles if they meet requirements set forth in the IBC when tested in accordance with NFPA 286 and when a Class A finish would otherwise be required.

The Uniform Building Code has a table similar to Table 27.3 except it uses the Roman numerals I, II, and III instead of letters and discusses the different requirements for sprinklered and unsprinklered buildings in the text rather than in the table. It still sets requirements for three areas of a building, but the most restrictive is enclosed vertical exitways; the next most restrictive includes other exitways, and the least restrictive includes rooms or areas.

If textile wall coverings are used, they must either be rated as Class A according to ASTM E84 and be protected by an automatic sprinkler system *or* they must meet the requirements of NFPA 265, which is the *Room Corner Test* described in an earlier section. In the UBC, only ASTM E84 was referenced.

The IBC now regulates the ratings of some floor coverings. These include textile coverings or coverings comprised of fibers—in other words, carpet. It specifically excludes traditional flooring types such as wood, vinyl, linoleum, and terrazzo.

The IBC requires textile or fiber floor coverings to be of one of two classes as defined by NFPA 253, the *Flooring Radiant Panel Test*. In this test the amount of radiant energy needed to sustain flame is measured and defined as the critical radiant flux. This test was described in the previous section.

Decorations and Trim

Curtains, draperies, hangings, and other decorative materials suspended from walls or ceilings in occupancies of Groups A, E, I, and R-1 and in Group R-2 dormitories must be flame resistant and pass the NFPA 701 test or must be noncombustible. In Group I-1 and I-2 occupancies, combustible decoration must be flame retardant unless quantities are so limited as to present no hazard. The amount of noncombustible decorative materials is not limited, but the amount of flame-resistant materials is limited to 10% of the aggregate area of walls and ceilings, except in Group A occupancies, where it is limited to 50% if the building is fully sprinklered.

Material used as interior trim must have a minimum Class C flame-spread index and smoke-developed index. Combustible trim (such as wood trim), excluding handrails and guardrails, cannot exceed 10% of the aggregate wall or ceiling area in which it is located.

For an explanation of the terms used in this section, refer to the definitions at the end of this chapter.

CLASSIFICATION BASED ON OCCUPANCY

Occupancy refers to the type of use assigned to a building or interior space such as an office, restaurant, private residence, or school. Buildings and spaces are grouped by occupancy classifications based on similar life safety characteristics, the presence of fire hazards, and combustible contents.

The philosophy behind occupancy classification is that some uses are more hazardous than others. For example, a building where flammable liquids are present is more dangerous than a single-family residence. Also, residents of a nursing home will have more trouble exiting than will young school children who have participated in fire drills. In order to achieve equivalent safety in building design, each occupancy group therefore varies by fire protection requirements, area and height limitations, type of construction restrictions (as described in the next section), and means of egress elements.

Occupancy Groups

Every building or portion of a building is classified according to its use and is assigned an occupancy group. This is true of the IBC as well as Canadian model codes and the three former U.S. model codes still used in some jurisdictions. The IBC classifies occupancies into 10 major groups.

A assembly

B business

E   educational
F   factory and industrial
H   hazardous
I   institutional
M   mercantile
R   residential
S   storage
U   utility

Six of these groups are further divided to distinguish subgroups that define the relative hazard of the occupancy. For example, in the assembly group, an A-1 occupancy includes assembly places, usually with fixed seats, used to view performing arts or motion pictures, while an A-2 occupancy includes places designed for food and/or drink consumption. The IBC should be consulted for a complete description of the occupancies and specific requirements for each.

Knowing the occupancy classification is important in determining other building requirements, many of which relate to the architectural design of a building, such as the maximum area, the number of floors allowed, and how the building is separated from other structures. For interior design, occupancy classification affects the following.

• calculation of occupant load

• egress design

• interior finish requirements

• use of fire partitions and fire barriers

• fire detection/suppression systems

• ventilation/sanitation requirements

• other special restrictions particular to any given classification

Mixed Occupancy and Occupancy Separation

When a building or area of a building contains two or more occupancies, it is considered to be of mixed occupancy. Mixed occupancies are common in architectural and interior design. For instance, the design of a large office space can include an office occupancy (B occupancy) adjacent to an auditorium used for training, which would be an assembly occupancy (A occupancy) if it had an occupant load over 50. Commercial interior design often involves planning a new space of one occupancy that is next to an existing space of another occupancy. Each occupancy must be separated from other occupancies with a fire barrier of the hourly rating as defined by the particular code that applies. The required hourly rating determines the specific design and detailing of the partition separating the two spaces. The IBC shows required occupancy separations with a matrix table with hourly separations ranging from 1 hour to 4 hours. When the building is equipped with an automated sprinkler system, the required hourly ratings may be reduced by 1 hour. The other model codes have similar tables.

Accessory and Incidental Use Areas

In the IBC there are two variations of the concept of mixed occupancies, each of which has its own particular requirements: accessory use areas and incidental use areas.

An *accessory use area* is a space or room that is used in conjunction with the main occupancy but does not exceed 10% of the floor area of the main occupancy. Accessory use areas do not need to be separated from the main occupancy with a fire barrier. For example, a small gift shop in a hospital would be considered an accessory use area and therefore not require the 2-hour occupancy separation normally required between an M occupancy and an I-2 occupancy. The two exceptions to this provision are Group H occupancies or incidental use areas.

An *incidental use area* is an area that is incidental to the main occupancy and has the same classification as the nearest main occupancy but, by code, must be separated from the main occupancy by a fire barrier. The incidental rooms or areas and the separations required are given in Ch. 3 of the IBC. See Table 27.4.

When the table allows a sprinkler system to substitute for a fire barrier, the incidental use area must be separated by a smoke barrier and the sprinklers only have to be in the incidental use area. Doors must be self-closing or automatic-closing.

Table 27.4
Incidental Use
Areas

Incidental Use Areas
IBC Table 302.1.1

room or area	separation*
furnace room where largest piece of equipment is over 400,000 Btu/hr input	1 hour or provide automatic fire-extinguishing system
boilers over 15 psi and 10 hp	1 hour or provide automatic fire-extinguishing system
refrigerant machinery rooms	1 hour or provide automatic fire-extinguishing system
automotive parking garage in other than Group R-3	2 hours, or 1 hour and provide automatic fire-extinguishing system
incinerator rooms	2 hours and automatic sprinkler system
paint shops, not classified as a Group H, located in occupancies Group F	2 hours, or 1 hour and provide automatic fire-extinguishing systems
laboratories and vocational shops, not classified as Group H, located in Group E and I-2 occupancies	1 hour or provide automatic fire-extinguishing system
laundry rooms over 100 ft^2	1 hour or provide automatic fire-extinguishing system
storage rooms over 100 ft^2	1 hour or provide automatic fire-extinguishing system
Group I-3 padded cells	1 hour
waste and linen collection room over 100 ft^2	1 hour or provide automatic fire-extinguishing system
stationary load-acid battery systems having a liquid capacity of more than 100 gal (380 L) used for facility standby power, emergency power, or uninterrupted power supplies	1-hour fire barriers and floor-ceiling assemblies in Group B, F, H, M, S, and U occupancies, 2-hour fire barriers and floor-ceiling assemblies in Group A, E, I, and R occupancies.

*Where an automatic fire-extinguishing system is provided, it need only be provided in the incidental use room or area.

CLASSIFICATION BASED ON CONSTRUCTION TYPE

Every building is classified into one of five major types of construction based on the fire resistance of certain building components. Under the IBC, these components include the structural frame, interior and exterior bearing walls, and floor and roof construction. The five types of construction are Types I, II, III, IV, and V. Type I buildings are the most fire resistive, while Type V are the least fire resistive. For example, the structural frame of a Type I building must have a 3-hour rating, while the frame in a Type III building must only have a 1-hour rating. Type I and II buildings are noncombustible, while Types III, IV, and V are considered combustible. In four of the types there are two subgroups designated with an A or B suffix, which indicates whether the construction is fire protected or not. In the IBC there are Types I-A, I-B, II-A, II-B, IlI-A, III-B, IV, V-A, and V-B.

The purposes of designing buildings to a certain classification are to protect the structural elements from fire and collapse and to prevent fire from spreading from one building to another. In combination with occupancy groups, building type limits the area and height of buildings. For example, a Type I building of any occupancy (except certain hazardous occupancies) can be of unlimited area and height, while a Type V building is limited to only a few thousand square feet in area and one or two stories in height, depending on its occupancy. Limiting height and area based on construction type and occupancy recognizes that it becomes more difficult to fight fires, provide time for egress, and rescue people as buildings get larger and higher. It also recognizes that the type and amount of combustibles existing due to the building's use and construction affect the building's safety.

There are several interrelated variables concerning construction type, most of which are determined by the architect during building design. For existing buildings, the construction type is already established. To determine the construction type of a project, ask the local building official, or check with the architect if the building is currently being designed or has recently been constructed.

Interior designers must know the construction type if major changes are being made. For example, if the occupancy of a building or portion of a building is being changed from a B (business) to an A (assembly) occupancy, the interior designer must know the construction type to verify that the maximum area is not exceeded. If the maximum area is being exceeded, it may be necessary to construct a firewall or add sprinklers. This is a similar situation to that described in the previous example concerning allowable area based on occupancy group. In addition, construction type can affect the required fire ratings of coverings of structural elements, floor/ceiling assemblies, and openings in rated walls. For example, during a remodeling, the required fire rating of a protected beam may be changed to accommodate new construction, and the interior designer would have to detail or specify repairs or new construction to return the assembly to its original rating.

FIRE DETECTION AND SUPPRESSION

Fire detection, alarm, and suppression systems have become important parts of a building's overall life safety and fire protection strategies. Almost all new buildings are now required to have some type of fire detection device, even if it is a single smoke detector in a residence. Other occupancies, such as high-rise buildings and hotels, must have elaborate detection and alarm systems, including communication devices on each floor to allow firefighters to talk with each other and with occupants in the event of an emergency.

The term *fire protection system* is used to describe any fire alarm or fire-extinguishing device or system that is designed and installed to detect, control, or extinguish a fire, or to alert the occupants or the fire department that a fire has occurred, or any combination of these. Most systems are designed to be automatic, which means they provide an emergency function without human intervention and are activated by the detection of one or a combination of the following.

- smoke/other products of combustion

- a rise in temperature to a predetermined level

- a rate of rise of temperature to a predetermined rate of change

For large or complex buildings, a complete fire protection system may include many elements such as smoke and heat detectors, sprinklers, alternate fire-extinguishing systems (halon, for example), portable fire extinguishers, standpipes, smoke control systems, and smoke and heat vents.

Sprinklers are the most common type of suppression system and are required in nearly all new high-rise buildings and hotels. They are also becoming commonplace in many other types of commercial buildings. One of the major changes from the UBC to the IBC was that sprinklers were either mandated in occupancies where they were not previously required, or the code gave generous tradeoffs for using sprinklers. For example, in a nonsprinklered building of A, B, E, F, M, S, or U occupancy, the corridors must have a 1-hour rating. In a sprinklered building of the same occupancy, the corridors need not be rated. The intent of the new IBC is to encourage designers, developers, and builders to install sprinkler systems, recognizing their value as a part of the entire life safety system of a building.

The design and layout of a sprinkler system are the responsibility of the mechanical engineer or fire protection contractor, but the interior designer should be aware of sprinkler system requirements, most notably the spacing of sprinkler heads and the types of heads available. Some of these requirements are given in Ch. 18.

The National Fire Protection Association has developed standards that are followed by most building departments for the design of sprinkler systems. These are NFPA13 for commercial buildings and NFPA13R for residential construction. The NFPA standards are required by reference by the model codes and the IBC.

OTHER REQUIREMENTS

In addition to the provisions mentioned in the previous sections, the IBC and the other model building codes regulate many other aspects of construction, including the use and structural design of individual materials, excavations, demolition, and elevators. In addition to the model codes, there are local, state, and federal regulations that may govern the design of a particular project. Specific requirements for means of egress and barrier-free design are discussed in Chs. 28 and 29, respectively. Other regulations with which interior designers should be familiar include the following.

Glazing

Code requirements for interior glazing focus on two basic issues: glazing use in hazardous locations, and glazing use in fire-rated assemblies such as partitions and doors.

When glass is installed in hazardous locations—that is, where it is subject to human impact—it must be safety glazing (i.e., tempered glass or laminated glass). The exact locations where safety glazing is required are discussed in Ch. 10 and shown in Fig. 10.20.

The requirements for glass used in fire-rated doors are discussed in Ch. 28.

For glass used in fire-resistance-rated partitions, the IBC differentiates between two types of glazing: fire-protection-rated glazing and fire-resistance-rated glazing.

Fire-protection-rated glazing is 1/4 in (6) thick wired glass in steel frames, or other types of glazing that meet the requirements of NFPA 257, *Standard for Fire Test for Window and Glass Block Assemblies.* Such glazing must have a 45-minute rating and is limited to 1-hour-rated fire partitions or fire barriers when the fire barrier is used to separate occupancies or to separate incidental use areas. The amount of such glazing is limited to 25% of the area of the common wall within any room using the glazing. This limitation applies to partitions separating two rooms as well as to a partition separating a room and a corridor. Individual lights of fire-protection-rated glazing cannot exceed 1296 in^2 in area (9 ft^2 (0.84 m^2)), and any one dimension cannot be more than 54 in (1372). The IBC accepts 1/4 in wired glass as meeting the requirements for a 45-minute rating without specific testing, but other glazing must meet the NFPA 257 test requirements for a 45-minute rating.

Fire-resistance-rated glazing is glass or other glazing material that has been tested as part of a fire-resistance-rated wall assembly according to ASTM E119. This glazing definition allows the use of special fire-rated glazing that can have fire-resistive ratings up to 2 hours. Refer to Ch. 10 for a discussion of these types of glazing products. This type of glazing may be used in partitions that must have a rating higher than 1 hour, although the glazing

must have the same rating as the partition in which it is used. There are no area limitations.

Guards (Guardrails)

A *guard* is a component whose function is to prevent falls from an elevated area. For example, an opening on the second floor that overlooks the first floor must be protected with a guard. In the UBC, guards were called guardrails. Guards are required along open-sided walking surfaces, mezzanines, industrial equipment platforms, stairways, ramps, and landings that are more than 30 in (762) above the floor below. There are several exceptions, including stages and raised platforms.

Guards must be a minimum of 42 in (1067) high and designed such that a sphere with a 4 in (102) diameter cannot pass through any opening up to a height of 34 in (864). Guards must be designed to resist a load of 50 lbf/ft (0.73 kN/m) applied in any direction at the top of the guard. Other design requirements and exceptions are detailed in Ch. 10 of the IBC.

Mechanical Systems

The International Mechanical Code, companion to the IBC, details the requirements for materials and design of systems for heating, ventilating, and air-conditioning systems. Most of these do not directly affect the interior designer except where mechanical elements, such as supply-air diffusers and return-air grilles, are visible in the finished space. Refer to Ch. 18 for information on coordinating with mechanical systems.

Plumbing Systems

The IBC and other model codes specify in great detail how a plumbing system must be designed. They also specify the number of sanitary fixtures required based on the type of occupancy. In most cases, satisfying the requirements is the responsibility of the mechanical engineer and architect. However, in some cases, the interior designer may be involved with remodeling toilet rooms in commercial buildings. In this case, it is helpful to know how many fixtures are required when preliminary design layouts are being developed. For example, the International Plumbing Code, which is a companion volume to the IBC, gives the minimum number of toilets, lavatories, drinking fountains, and other fixtures required in a building. For convenience, these provisions are also given in Ch. 29 of the IBC.

Electrical Systems

The IBC and the other three former model codes reference the National Electrical Code (NEC), published by the National Fire Protection Association. As with other companion codes, the NEC details the requirements for materials and design of the power supply and lighting systems of buildings. Most of these do not directly affect the interior designer except where electrical elements, such as outlets, are visible in the finished space. The NEC, for example, specifies the maximum spacing for outlets and the requirement for ground fault interrupter outlets. Refer to Ch. 18 for more information on coordinating with electrical systems.

Sound Ratings

The IBC requires that wall and floor/ceiling assemblies in residential occupancies separating dwelling units or guest rooms from each other and from public spaces be designed and constructed to provide for sound transmission control. The code specifies a minimum sound transmission class (STC) of 50 (45 if field tested) for walls. The requirement does not apply to dwelling-unit entrance doors. However, these doors must be tight-fitting to the frame and sill. The minimum impact insulation class (IIC) for floors must be 50 (45 if field tested). Construction details

that satisfy these requirements must be selected. Refer to Ch. 20 for more information on acoustics.

DEFINITIONS

The following terms are frequently used by building codes to precisely communicate meaning. Although the differences between terms are sometimes subtle, they are important. Refer to Ch. 28 for definitions related to means of egress.

Combustible: material that will ignite and burn, either as a flame or glow, and that undergoes this process in air at pressures and temperatures that might occur during a fire

Fire assembly: an assembly of a fire door, fire window, or fire damper, including all required anchorage, frames, sills, and hardware

Fire barrier: a new term in the 2000 IBC meaning a fire-resistance-rated vertical or horizontal assembly of materials designed to restrict the spread of fire in which openings are protected

Fire partition: a new term in the 2000 IBC meaning a fire-resistive component used to separate dwelling units in R-2 construction, guest rooms in R-1 construction, and tenant spaces in covered mall buildings, and also used as corridor walls. Fire partitions generally are required to have a minimum 1-hour fire-protection-rated construction except in certain circumstances. They are similar to fire barriers, but the requirements for support are not as strict.

Fire protection rating: the period of time an opening assembly, such as a door or window, can confine a fire or maintain its integrity, or both, when tested in accordance with NFPA 252, UL 10B, or UL IOC for doors, and NFPA 257 for windows. An assembly that requires a fire-protection rating must withstand fire exposure and thermal shock as would an assembly that required a fire-resistance rating, but it need not withstand heat transmission as walls, columns, and floors do.

Fire-rated: use fire-protection rating

Fire resistance: the property of a material or assembly to withstand or resist the spread of fire or give protection from it

Fire-resistance rating: the period of time a building component such as a wall, floor, roof, beam, or column can confine a fire or maintain its structural integrity, or both, when tested in accordance with ASTM E119, *Standard Test Methods for Fire Tests of Building Construction and Materials.* This is different from a fire-protection rating, which involves protected opening assemblies.

Fire-resistive construction: same as "fire resistance"

Fire retardant: should not be used as a noun. As an adjective, it should only be used as a modifier with defined compound terms such as fire-retardant-treated wood.

Flame resistance: the ability to withstand flame impingement or give protection from it. This applies to individual materials as well as combinations of components when tested in accordance to NFPA 701, *Standard Methods of Fire Tests for Flame-Resistant Textiles and Films* (see Ch. 6).

Flame retardant: should not be used as a noun. As an adjective, it should only be used as a modifier with defined compound terms such as flame-retardant treatment.

Flame spread: the propagation of flame over a surface

Flame-spread index: the numerical value assigned to a material tested in accordance with ASTM E84, *Standard Test Method for Surface Burning Characteristics of Building Materials*

Flammable: capable of burning with a flame and subject to easy ignition and rapid flaming combustion

Noncombustible: material that will not ignite and burn when subjected to a fire. The IBC and UBC classify a material as noncombustible only if it is tested in accordance with ASTM E136, *Standard Test Method for Behavior of Materials in a Vertical Tube Furnace at 750°C,* or if it has a structural base of noncombustible material with a surfacing not more than $1/8$ in (3.18) thick that has a flame-spread index no greater than 50.

Trim: includes picture molds, chair rails, baseboards, handrails, door and window frames, and similar decorative or protective materials used in fixed applications

SAMPLE QUESTIONS

1. The minimum number of toilet fixtures required for an interior design remodeling is determined by occupant load and

(A) accessibility requirements

(B) building type

(C) occupancy group

(D) square footage

2. Which test gives the most accurate evaluation of the safety of a partition system?

(A) ASTM E84, *Standard Test Method for Surface Burning Characteristics of Building Materials*

(B) Steiner tunnel test

(C) room corner test

(D) ASTM E119, *Standard Test Methods for Fire Tests of Building Construction and Materials*

3. A designer is planning a library in which tall bookshelves will be used. If the project is located in a city that has adopted the International Building Code, where would the designer look to find requirements on the minimum allowable space between the top of the shelving and the sprinkler heads in the ceiling?

(A) IBC

(B) International Mechanical Code

(C) NFPA13

(D) IPC

4. Where are flame-spread ratings in a building most restrictive?

(A) in exit enclosures

(B) on corridor floors

(C) in access ways to exits

(D) in enclosed spaces

5. Exit access corridors in nonsprinklered buildings must have a rating of

(A) 30 minutes

(B) 45 minutes

(C) 1 hour

(D) 2 hours

6. When selecting interior partition finishes to meet flame-spread standards, the most important considerations are

(A) the occupancy group, and the location in the building where the finishes will be used

(B) whether or not the building has an automatic sprinkler system, and the construction type

(C) whether or not the partition is a fire barrier, and the ratings of assemblies in the partition

(D) the hourly rating of the partition on which the finish will be installed, and the construction type

7. The majority of building codes in the United States are established by

(A) federal laws

(B) model code writing agencies

(C) state governments

(D) local governments

8. ASTM is an example of

(A) a model code group

(B) an industry standard-writing organization

(C) a testing laboratory

(D) a federal code writing agency

9. In starting a design project in a multi-use building, what information would an interior designer need to determine?

I. construction type

II. adjacent occupancies

III. sprinkler condition

IV. fire zone classification

V. accessibility requirements

(A) I, II, and III

(B) I, IV, and V

(C) II, III, and IV

(D) II, IV, and V

10. In order to specify an acceptable type of wall covering, which of the following tests should the designer require that the wall covering pass?

(A) methenamine pill test

(B) smoke density chamber test

(C) Steiner tunnel test

(D) vertical ignition test

11. In which building type are fire-resistive construction requirements likely to be LEAST restrictive?

(A) Type I

(B) Type II

(C) Type III

(D) Type IV

12. A designer selecting glass to meet the requirements for safety glazing in a hazardous location should specify

(A) tempered or laminated glass

(B) tempered or wired glass

(C) heat-strengthened glass or wired glass

(D) laminated glass or wired glass

13. Which test is most frequently used to evaluate carpet in the United States?

(A) flooring radiant panel test

(B) Steiner tunnel test

(C) methenamine pill test

(D) methods of fire tests of building construction and materials

14. If a material does not burn, it is considered to be

(A) fire retardant

(B) fire rated

(C) flame resistant

(D) noncombustible

15. In a fully sprinklered office building, how many sprinklers would be required in a room measuring 20 ft × 25 ft (6100 × 7620)?

(A) 2

(B) 3

(C) 4

(D) 6

28

EXITING

Exiting, or "means of egress" as it is called in the codes, is one of the most important requirements of any building code. Candidates must be familiar with the basic concepts and requirements of exiting and should know many of the commonly used dimensions for corridors, doors, and stairs. Because there are several model codes used throughout the United States and Canada and many jurisdictions are in the process of adopting the 2003 International Building Code (IBC), the NCIDQ exam tests knowledge of exiting concepts that are common to all codes. The current exam format puts less emphasis on detailed facts that can be easily looked up in any code and more emphasis on the important aspects of providing a safe means of egress regardless of specific dimensions.

The NCIDQ exam includes egress questions in the multiple-choice sections of the test and also requires that given code requirements be applied in the design practicum. Instead of relying on any one code, the practicum section of the exam gives the specific code requirements that must be incorporated into the design solution. To provide examples of code

concepts, this section is based primarily on the IBC. References are made to the 1997 Uniform Building Code (UBC), which some jurisdictions may still be using.

THE EGRESS SYSTEM

The UBC, IBC, and other codes define *means of egress* as a continuous and unobstructed path of vertical and horizontal egress travel from any point in a building or structure to a public way. The means of egress consists of three parts: the exit access, the exit, and the exit discharge. These must lead to a public way. A *public way* is any street, alley, or similar parcel of land essentially unobstructed from the ground to the sky that is permanently appropriated to the public for public use and has a clear width of not less than 10 ft (3048). See Fig. 28.1.

The *exit access* is that portion of the means of egress that leads to the entrance to an exit. Exit access areas may or may not be protected, depending on the specific requirements of the code based on occupancy and construction type. They may include components such as rooms,

Figure 28.1
Egress System

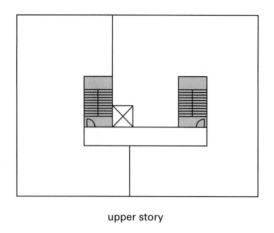

upper story

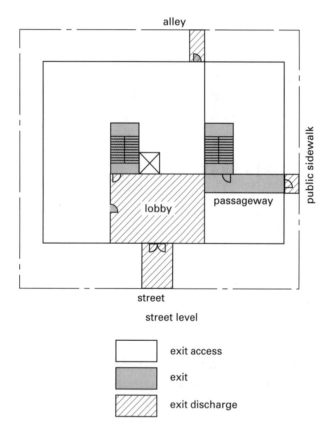

street level

exit access

exit

exit discharge

of the building where travel distance is measured and regulated (see the section on arrangement and width of exits).

The *exit* is the portion of the egress system that provides a protected path of egress between the exit access and the exit discharge. Exits are fully enclosed and protected from all other interior spaces by fire-resistance-rated construction with protected openings (doors, glass, etc.). Exits may be as simple as an exterior exit door at ground level or may include exit enclosures for stairs, exit passageways, and horizontal exits. In the 2003 IBC, exits may also include exterior exit stairways and ramps. Depending on building height, construction type, and passageway length, exits must have either a one- or two-hour rating. Travel distance is not an issue once the exit has been reached.

The *exit discharge* is the portion of the egress system between the termination of an exit and a public way. Exit discharge areas typically include portions outside the exterior walls such as exterior exit balconies, exterior exit stairways, and exit courts. Exit discharge may also include building lobbies of multistory buildings if one of the exit stairways opens onto the lobby and certain conditions are met. These conditions require that the exit door in the lobby is clearly visible, that the level of discharge is sprinklered, and that the entire area of discharge is separated from areas below by the same fire-resistance rating as for the exit enclosure that opens onto it. Note that in the 2003 IBC, exterior exit stairways and ramps are considered exits, not exit discharge areas.

OCCUPANT LOAD

The *occupant load* is the number of people that a building code assumes will occupy a given building or portion of a building. It is based on the occupancy classification as discussed in Ch. 27, including assembly, business, educational,

spaces, aisles, intervening rooms, hallways, corridors, ramps, and doorways. In concept, exit access does not provide a protected path of travel. In the 2003 IBC, even fire-rated corridors are considered exit access. The exit access is the portion and the other categories. Occupant load assumes that certain types of use will be more densely packed with people than others and that exiting provisions should respond accordingly. For example, an auditorium needs more exits to allow safe evacuation than does an office space of the same area.

The IBC requires that the occupant loads of areas without fixed seating be determined by taking the area assigned to a particular use and dividing by an occupant load factor as given in the code. In the IBC, the occupant load factor (or floor area in ft^2/occupant) is given in Table 1004.1.1. The IBC table is reproduced here as Fig. 28.2.

For areas with fixed seating, the occupant load is determined by taking the actual number of fixed seats installed and adding the occupant load of areas in which fixed seating is not installed, such as waiting spaces and wheelchair spaces. The occupant load of the open areas is calculated using the same occupant load factors as described previously. For fixed seating without dividing arms, the occupant load is based on one person for each 18 in (457) of seating length. For seating booths, the assumed unit is one person for each 24 in (610) of booth seat length.

The *occupant load factor* is the amount of floor area presumed to be occupied by one person. It is based on the generic uses of building spaces and is not the same as the occupancy groups discussed in Ch. 27. The occupant load factors, over time, have been found to consistently represent the densities found in various uses. IBC Table 1004.1.1 also shows whether the occupant load must be calculated based on net or gross area. The gross floor area includes stairs, corridors, toilet rooms, mechanical rooms, closets, and interior partition thicknesses. Net floor area includes just the space actually used. Most common uses

are included in the table, but the IBC gives the local building official the power to establish occupant load factors in cases where a use is not specifically listed.

The previous codes have tables similar to Fig. 28.2, although the exact factors may vary slightly. In previous editions of the UBC, the occupant load factor table also included a column describing the occupant load when two exits became necessary. In the IBC, this provision is now located in another part of the code and is based on occupancy as well as occupant load; it is discussed in the next section.

When an occupant load from an accessory space exits through a primary space, the egress facilities from the primary space occupant load must include their own occupant load plus the occupant load of the accessory space. This provision simply requires that the occupant loads should be cumulative as occupants exit through intervening spaces to an ultimate exit.

In determining the occupant load, all portions of the building are presumed to be occupied at the same time. However, the local building official may reduce the occupant load if the official determines that one area of a building would not normally be occupied while another area is occupied. An example of this would be the lunchroom of a factory area where the factory workers are either in the work area or the lunchroom, but not both at the same time.

If there are mixed occupancies or uses, each area is calculated with its respective occupant load factor and then all loads are added together.

Example 28.1

What is the occupant load for a restaurant dining room that is 2500 ft^2 in area?

In Fig. 28.2, dining rooms are listed under the use of "assembly areas, unconcentrated use," with an occupant load factor of 15 ft^2.

Figure 28.2
Maximum Floor
Area Allowances
per Occupant

occupancy	floor area (ft²/occupant)	occupancy	floor area (ft²/occupant)
agricultural buildings	300 gross	industrial areas	100 gross
aircraft hangars	500 gross	institutional areas	
airport terminals		inpatient treatment areas	240 gross
concourse	100 gross	outpatient areas	100 gross
waiting areas	15 gross	sleeping areas	120 gross
baggage claim	20 gross		
baggage handling	300 gross	kitchens, commercial	200 gross
assembly		libraries	
gaming floors (keno, slots, etc.)	11 gross	reading rooms	50 net
		stack areas	100 gross
assembly with fixed seats	see 1003.2.2.9	locker rooms	50 gross
assembly without fixed seats		mercantile, basement and grade floor areas	30 gross
concentrated (chair only—not fixed)	7 net	areas on other floors	60 gross
standing space	5 net	storage, stock, and shipping areas	300 gross
unconcentrated (tables and chairs)	15 net	parking garages	200 gross
bowling centers, allow 5 persons for each lane including 15 feet of runway, and for additional areas	7 net	residential	200 gross
business areas	100 gross	skating rinks, swimming pools	
		rinks and pools	50 gross
		decks	15 gross
courtrooms—other than fixed seating areas	40 net	stages and platforms	15 net
dormitories	50 gross	accessory storage areas, mechanical equipment rooms	300 gross
educational		warehouses	500 gross
classroom areas	20 net		
shops and other vocational rooms	50 net		
exercise rooms	50 gross		
H-5 fabrication and manufacturing areas	200 gross		

occupant load

$$= \frac{A}{15 \dfrac{\text{ft}^2}{\text{occupant}}} = \frac{2500 \text{ ft}^2}{15 \dfrac{\text{ft}^2}{\text{occupant}}}$$

$$= 166.67 \text{ occupants} \quad (167 \text{ occupants})$$

Example 28.2

What is the occupant load for 3700 ft² office that also has two training classrooms of 1200 ft² each?

An office ("business areas") has an occupant load factor of 100, so

office occupant load

$$= \frac{A}{100 \dfrac{\text{ft}^2}{\text{occupant}}} = \frac{3700 \text{ ft}^2}{100 \dfrac{\text{ft}^2}{\text{occupant}}}$$

$$= 37 \text{ occupants}$$

Classrooms have an occupant load factor of 20. Two classrooms of 1200 ft gives a total of 2400 ft².

classroom occupant load

$$= \frac{A}{20 \dfrac{\text{ft}^2}{\text{occupant}}} = \frac{2400 \text{ ft}^2}{20 \dfrac{\text{ft}^2}{\text{occupant}}}$$

$$= 120 \text{ occupants}$$

The total occupant load of all the spaces is therefore

total occupant load
= 37 occupants + 120 occupants
= 157 occupants

REQUIRED NUMBER OF EXITS

The number of exits or exit access doorways required from a space, a group of spaces, or an entire building is determined by several factors. The ones that may appear on the exam are the occupant load and occupancy of a space, the limitations on the common path of egress travel, and specific requirements when large occupant loads are encountered.

IBC Table 1014.1
Spaces With One Means of Egress

occupancy	maximum occupant load
A, B, E, F, M, U	50
H-1, H-2, H-3	3
H-4, H-5, I-1, I-3, I-4, R	10
S	30

2003 International Building Code.
Copyright 2003. Falls Church, Virginia:
International Code Council, Inc.
Reproduced with permission. All rights reserved.

Figure 28.3
Occupant Load Triggering Requirements for Two Exits

Every building or portion of a building must, of course, have at least one exit. When the number of occupants of a space exceeds the number given in the code, then at least two exits must be provided. The idea is to have an alternate way out of a room, group of rooms, or building if one exit is blocked. The IBC requires two exits when the occupant load of a space exceeds the numbers given in IBC Table 1014.1. This is reproduced in Fig. 28.3.

Even if the occupant load of a space or a building is less than that shown in Fig. 28.3, two exits are still required if the common path of egress travel exceeds limits given in the code. The *common path of egress travel* is that portion of an exit access that the occupants are required to traverse before two separate and distinct paths of egress travel to two exits become available. See Fig. 28.4. Even if two exits are not required based on occupant load, if the common path of travel exceeds 75 ft (32 m) for all except H-1, H-2, and H-3 occupancies, then two exits from a space are required. The distance is increased to 100 ft (30.5 m) in some occupancies if certain conditions are met. For example, in B, F, and S occupancies, if the building is fully sprinklered, the maximum length of common path of egress travel is increased to 100 ft.

Figure 28.4
Common Path of
Egress Travel

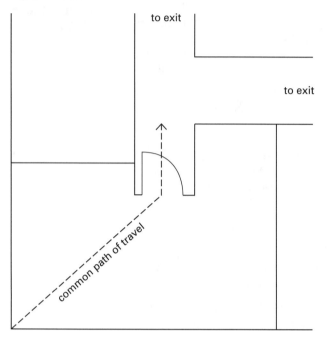

The final factor determining number of exits is a large occupant load. Three exits are required when the occupant load is between 501 and 1000, and at least four exits are required when the occupant load is greater than 1000.

In the previous UBC, only the number of occupants determined whether two exits were required. The provision of common path of egress travel was not used.

In Ex. 28.1, the restaurant dining room would require two exits because 167 persons exceeds the figure of 50 given in Fig. 28.3 (Table 1014.1 of the IBC). In Ex. 18.2, the total area of the offices and classrooms would require two exits. In addition, note that each classroom would need two exits because the occupant load for each is 60 (1200 divided by 20 ft²/occupant). This is more than the 50 occupants given in the second column of the table, which is the trigger point for requiring a minimum of two exits.

ARRANGEMENT AND WIDTH OF EXITS

Arrangement of Exits

Once the number of exits required for each room, space, or group of rooms is known, then the arrangement and width of those exits must be determined. When two exits are required, they must be placed a distance apart equal to not less than one-half the length of the maximum overall diagonal dimension of the building or area to be served, as measured in a straight line between the exits. This rule is shown diagrammatically in Fig. 28.5. The reason for this requirement is to position the exits far enough apart so that a fire or other emergency would not block both exits.

If three or more exits are required, two exits must be placed a distance apart equal to not less than one-half the length of the maximum overall diagonal dimension of the building or area to be served, measured in a straight line. Again, the additional exit or exits must be arranged a reasonable distance apart so that if one is blocked the others will be available.

In the IBC, there is a provision that reduces the minimum separation distance to one-third the maximum diagonal dimension of the room or area to be served if the building is fully sprinklered.

Maximum Travel Distance

Travel distance (or *exit access travel distance* in the IBC) is the distance that an occupant must travel from the most remote point in the occupied portions of the exit access to the entrance to the nearest exit. Once a person is safely in an exit, travel distance is not an issue. Because exit access areas are not protected, the codes limit how far someone must travel to safety. Maximum travel distances are based on the occupancy of the building and whether or not the building is sprinklered. There are special requirements in the older model codes and the IBC that decrease the allowable travel distances in some occupancies and situations such as malls, atria, and hazardous, educational, and assembly seating.

The maximum exit access travel distances are given in IBC Table 1015.1. See Fig. 28.6. The footnotes in this table refer to other sections of the code for specific occupancy requirements.

In the previous UBC, the maximum travel distances were 200 ft in an unsprinklered building and 250 ft in a sprinklered building. These distances could be increased a maximum of 100 ft when the increased travel distance was the last portion of the travel distance and was entirely within a 1-hour-rated exit corridor.

NCIDQ candidates generally do not have to worry about maximum travel distances in the design practicum section because the problems are of a much smaller scale, but knowledge of travel distance may be tested in the multiple-choice sections.

Exits Through Adjoining Rooms

Most codes allow a room to have one exit through an adjoining or intervening room if it provides a direct, obvious, and unobstructed means of travel to an exit corridor or other exit, as long as the total maximum travel distances, described in the previous section, are not exceeded. However, exiting is not permitted through kitchens, storerooms, rest rooms, closets, or spaces used for similar purposes. In the IBC, foyers, lobbies, and reception rooms constructed as required for corridors (with a 1-hour-rated wall as described in the next section) are not considered intervening rooms, so occupants can exit through these spaces.

In dwelling units there are some differences between the UBC and the new IBC. The IBC does not allow exiting from a sleeping area through other sleeping areas

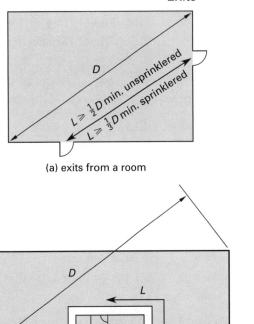

Figure 28.5
Arrangement of Exits

(a) exits from a room

$L \geq \frac{1}{2}D$ min. unsprinklered
$L \geq \frac{1}{3}D$ min. sprinklered

(b) exits from a building or group of rooms

or toilet rooms. In the design practicum, residential spaces should be planned so that toilet rooms, kitchens, and bedrooms lead to a corridor within the unit or common living area and then to a corridor or exit.

Widths of Exits

The required minimum width of an exit is determined by multiplying the occupant load by the appropriate factor given in Table 1005.1 of the IBC. The resulting number is the minimum total width in inches (or millimeters). Other codes have similar methods of calculating total exit width. In occupancies other than H-1, H-2, H-3, H-4, and I-2, in unsprinklered buildings the factor is 0.3 for stairways

Figure 28.6
Exit Access
Travel Distances

IBC Table 1015.1
Exit Access Travel Distance [1]

occupancy	without sprinkler system (ft)	with sprinkler system (ft)
A, E, F-1, I-1, M, R, S-1	200	250[2]
B	200	300[3]
F-2, S-2, U	300	400[2]
H-1	not permitted	75[3]
H-2	not permitted	100[3]
H-3	not permitted	150[3]
H-4	not permitted	175[3]
H-5	not permitted	200[3]
I-2, I-3, I-4	150	200[3]

For SI: 1 ft = 304.8 mm.

[1]See the following sections for modifications to exit access travel distance requirements:

Sec. 402:	For the distance limitation in malls.
Sec. 404:	For increased limitation through an atrium space.
Sec. 1015.2:	For increased limitation in Groups F-1 and S-1.
Sec. 1024.7:	For increased limitation in assembly seating.
Sec. 1024.7:	For increased limitation for assembly open-air seating.
Sec. 1018.2:	For buildings with one exit.
Ch. 31:	For the limitation in temporary structures.

[2]Buildings equipped throughout with an automatic sprinkler system in accordance with Sec. 903.3.1.1 or 903.3.1.2. See Sec. 903 for occupancies where sprinkler systems according to Sec. 903.3.1.2 are permitted.

[3]Buildings equipped throughout with an automatic sprinkler system in accordance with Sec. 903.3.1.1.

and 0.2 for egress components other than stairways; in sprinklered buildings, the factors are 0.2 for stairways and 0.15 for other egress components. The factors are higher for the H and I occupancies because of the increased risk these occupancies present. If a greater width is specified elsewhere in the code, the larger number must be used.

If two or more exits are required, the total width must be divided such that the loss of any one means of egress does not reduce the available capacity to less than 50% of the required capacity.

The IBC also requires that if doors are part of the required egress width, their clear width must be used, not the width of the door. For example, a 36 in (914) door actually provides about 33 in (838) of clear width when the thickness of the door in the 90° open position and the width of the stop are subtracted from the full width.

For instance, using Ex. 28.2 again and assuming the building is *not* sprinklered, the occupant load of 157 multiplied by 0.2 gives 31.4 in. A corridor serving this occupancy would have to be at least this wide. However, as described in the next section of this chapter, the minimum corridor width is 44 in (1118). For the doors, because at least two exits are required in this example, the total required exit width would be more than satisfied with two 3 ft wide (914) doors (with a clear opening width of about 33 in each) because they give a total exit width of 66 in (1676).

In most cases, for business, residential, and some educational occupancies of the square footages used on the NCIDQ exam, exit widths are usually satisfied by using the minimum 3 ft exit door width and having two exits. However, if there is an assembly occupancy (with very low occupant load factor) or a very large space, the required exit width should be verified.

For corridors, get in the habit of using at least 5 ft (1500) wide corridors for commercial occupancies. This is a good, comfortable width for functional use and allows a maximum occupancy of 300 (60 in divided by 0.2) for an unsprinklered building or a maximum occupancy of 400 (60 in divided by 0.15) for a sprinklered building. It also provides the necessary space for accessible design. If space is tight and there is not much traffic, a 4 ft wide corridor can be considered.

CORRIDORS

A *corridor* is a portion of an exit access leading to an exit. The purpose of a corridor is to provide a safe means of egress from a room or space to a building exit or to another approved exitway, such as a stairway. When two exits are required, corridors must be laid out so that it is possible to travel in two directions to an exit. If one path is blocked, then occupants always have an alternate way out. Dead-end corridors (those with only one means of exit) are generally limited to a maximum length of 20 ft (6096), but in some instances, to 50 ft (15 240). However, when completing the design practicum portion of the exam, spaces should be planned to avoid dead-end corridors altogether if possible.

The minimum width of a corridor in feet is determined (as discussed previously) by taking the occupant load the corridor serves and multiplying by 0.2, 0.15, or another factor given in the code. However, the absolute minimum width for most occupancies is 44 in (1118) if the corridor serves an occupant load of 50 or more. For occupant loads less than 50, the minimum width is 36 in (914).

Certain occupancies, most notably educational and institutional in the IBC, require wider corridors. For instance, the IBC requires that corridors in schools be 72 in (1829) when serving an occupant load of 100 or more.

For most situations in the NCIDQ exam, plan on corridors 5 ft (1500) wide, if possible, for commercial design. This dimension satisfies most exiting requirements, provides enough space for barrier-free design, and is ample space for general circulation.

The width of a corridor must be unobstructed, but handrails and fully opened doors can protrude a maximum of 7 in (178) total. Other projections such as trim may extend into the width a maximum of 4 in (102) on each side. However, horizontal projections cannot reduce the minimum clear width of accessible routes.

With a few exceptions, corridors must be built of 1-hour fire-resistive construction when serving an occupant load of 10 or more in R-1 and I occupancies and when serving an occupant load of 30 or more in other occupancies. This must include the walls and ceilings. If the ceiling of the entire story is 1-hour rated, then the rated corridor walls may terminate at the ceiling. Otherwise, the 1-hour-rated corridors must extend through the ceiling to the rated floor or roof above.

Doors placed in 1-hour corridors must have a fire rating of at least 20 minutes and include approved smoke- and draft-control seals around the door. The door must also be maintained self-closing (with a door closer) or be automatic-closing by actuation of a smoke detector. Both the door and frame must bear the label of an approved testing agency, such as Underwriters Laboratories (UL).

Glass may be used in 1-hour-rated corridor walls only if it is listed and labeled as a $^3/_4$-hour fire-protection rating and the total area does not exceed 25% of the area of the corridor wall of the room that it is separating from the corridor.

When a duct penetrates a rated corridor, it must be provided with a fire damper,

Figure 28.7
Exit Door Swing

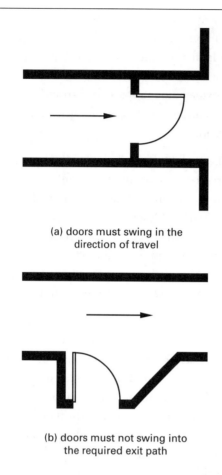

(a) doors must swing in the
direction of travel

(b) doors must not swing into
the required exit path

which is a device that automatically closes in the event of a fire.

In the IBC, the requirements for corridors have changed somewhat. First, the new definition of a corridor makes it clear that it is an *exit access* component that defines and provides a path of egress travel to an exit. A new table lists when a corridor is required to be fire-resistance rated based on occupancy, the occupant load served, and whether the building is sprinklered. All R occupancies must have a one-hour rated corridor if the occupant load is greater than 10, and all I occupancies must have one-hour corridor regardless of the occupant load. One of the most significant changes is that, in a sprinklered building of A, B, E, F, I-1, I-3, M, S, and U occupancy, corridors do not have to be fire-resistive rated.

Another change in the IBC is the requirement for dead-end corridors. The 20 ft (6096) limitation is still the basic provision, but now B and F occupancies may have 50 ft (15 240) dead-end corridors if the entire building is equipped with an automatic sprinkler system. Also, dead ends are not limited in length where the length is less than 2.5 times the least width of the dead-end corridor.

DOORS

Building code provisions apply to exit doors serving an area with an occupant load of 10 or more. Exit doors must be pivoted or side-hinged and must swing in the direction of travel when serving any hazardous area or when serving an occupant load of 50 or more. This is to avoid a door being blocked when people are trying to get out in a panic. Make sure all required exit doors swing in the correct direction, including doors to spaces with a high occupant load, stairway doors, and doors from corridors to other exitways. See Fig. 28.7. Doors also must not swing into a required travel path, such as a corridor. In many instances, doors may need to be recessed as shown in Fig. 28.7.

In the UBC, exit doors must be a minimum of 3 ft (914) wide and 6 ft 8 in (2032) high. The maximum width is 4 ft (1220). Exit doors must be operable from the inside without the use of any special knowledge or effort. Certain occupancies, such as educational and assembly, require panic hardware. This is hardware that unlatches the door when pressure is applied against it rather than requiring a turning motion as with a doorknob or lever handle. There are also requirements on the maximum force needed to unlatch the lock, set the door in motion, and swing it to a full-open position. Doors with and without closers are both covered by these types of requirements.

The IBC includes most of the same provisions as the previous model codes except that minimum width requirements have been stated differently. Now, the minimum width is required to be sufficient for the occupant load calculation, but in no case can a door provide less than 32 in (813) of clear width when the door is open at 90°. From a practical standpoint, this basically means a 36 in (914) door must be used to allow for the decrease in width due to the stop and the thickness of the door when open. There are several exceptions to this minimum width requirement.

Exit doors in fire-resistance-rated partitions are required to have a fire rating. The specific fire rating varies depending on the rating of the partition. Some of the more common ratings for interior design work are summarized in Table 28.1. Under the IBC, if a building is fully sprinklered, corridors in A, B, E, F, M, S, and U occupancies do not have to have a fire rating, so fire-protection-rated doors are not required.

In addition to having a 20-minute fire rating, doors in corridors and smoke barriers must meet the requirements for positive pressure fire testing. Positive pressure fire testing simulates actual fire conditions where there is positive pressure on the fire side of the door above a certain point on the door (called the neutral pressure level) and negative pressure below this point. Under such conditions, there is a greater tendency for smoke and gases to be forced through the crack between the door and frame. To meet the requirements of positive pressure fire testing, a door must have approved gasketing or intumescent material along its edge or frame. An intumescent material is one that swells and chars when exposed to heat to form a barrier to smoke and fire.

Exit doors must have automatic closers, and all hardware must be tested and

use of partition	rating of partition	required door assembly rating	**Table 28.1** Fire-Rated Door Classifications
corridors	1 hour or less	20 minute	
smoke barriers	1 hour	20 minute	
fire partitions	1 hour	$^3/_4$ hour	
exit passageways	1 hour	$^3/_4$ hour	
exit stairs	1 hour	1 hour	
occupancy separations	1 hour	$^3/_4$ hour	
exit stairs	2 hours	$1^1/_2$ hour	

approved for use on fire exits. When closed, they must provide a tight seal against smoke and drafts. Glass in exit doors must be wired glass, and its total area is limited depending on the door's fire rating.

In most cases, special doors such as revolving, sliding, and overhead doors are not considered required exits. Power-operated doors and revolving doors are sometimes allowed if they meet certain requirements. Revolving doors, for example, must have leaves that collapse under opposing pressure and must have a diameter of at least 6 ft 6 in (1981). There must also be at least one conforming exit door within 10 ft (3050) of the revolving door.

Refer to Ch. 10 for more details on fire door requirements.

STAIRWAYS

Stairways serving an occupant load of 50 or more must be at least 44 in (1118) wide or as wide as determined by multiplying the occupant load by 0.3 or another factor as discussed previously. Those serving an occupant load of 49 or less must not be less than 36 in (914) wide. Handrails may project into the required width $4^1/_2$ in (114) on each side. See Fig. 28.8.

The risers of the stair cannot be less than 4 in (102) or more than 7 in (178), and the tread must be no less than 11 in (279). Risers for barrier-free stairs cannot exceed

Figure 28.8
Stairway Width

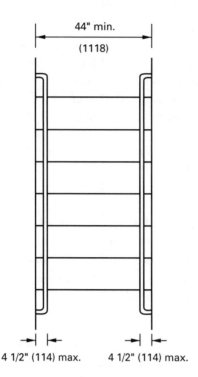

44" min.
(1118)

4 1/2" (114) max.   4 1/2" (114) max.

7 in; treads must have an acceptable nosing design as discussed in Ch. 29. For good design, determine either the required riser or tread and then use the stair formula discussed in Ch. 18 to calculate the other dimension. For residential occupancies and private stairways serving an occupant load less than 10, the maximum riser may be $7^3/4$ in (197) and the minimum tread may be 10 in (254). See Fig. 28.9.

Winding, circular, and spiral stairways may be used as exits in R-3 occupancies and in private stairways of R-1 occupancies only if they meet certain design conditions as specified in the code.

Landings must be provided at the top and bottom of every stairway. The minimum dimension in the direction of travel must not be less than the width of the stair but need not be more than 44 in (48 in in the IBC) if the stair is a straight run.

Handrails must be provided on both sides of the stair. Intermediate handrails are required so that all portions of the stairway width required for egress capacity are within 30 in (762) of a handrail. Another way of stating this is that stairways wider than 5 ft (1524) must have intermediate handrails. The IBC definition of a stair is one or more risers, so even one step now requires handrails. The exception to this applies to decks, patios, and walkways, single risers at entrance doors of R-3 occupancies, and single risers in dwelling units of Groups R-2 and R-3 occupancies.

In the previous UBC, handrails were only required on one side of the stair if the stair was less than 44 in (1118) wide or for residential use. Also, stairways needed an intermediate handrail only if they were wider than 88 in (2235).

As shown in Fig. 28.10, the top of the handrail must be between 34 in and 38 in (864 and 965) above the nosing of the treads and must extend not less than 12 in (305) beyond the top riser and not less than the depth of one tread beyond the bottom riser. The ends must be returned to the wall or floor or terminate in a newel post. The gripping portion cannot be less than $1^1/4$ in (32) or more than 2 in (51) in cross-sectional dimension. There must be a space at least $1^1/2$ in (38) wide between the wall and the handrail.

RESIDENTIAL EXITING

Exiting requirements for individual dwelling units and single-family houses are not as stringent as those for commercial occupancies. Only one exit is required from the basement or second story of a house. However, basements and bedrooms must have an escape window with a minimum openable area of 5.7 ft^2 (0.53 m^2), with the windowsill no more than 44 in (1118) above the floor. The minimum clear opening height is 24 in (610), and the minimum clear width is 20 in (508).

Unlike most commercial construction, residential exits may pass through kitchens, storerooms, and similar spaces. Because the occupant load is less than 50, corridors may be a minimum of 36 in (914) wide (but this may be too narrow for accessibility in some instances). Also, because the occupant load is less than 10, doors may swing into rooms so there is not a problem with corridors being blocked.

Houses may have dead bolts or similar secondary locking devices, provided that they are openable from the inside without a key or tool and are mounted no more than 48 in (1220) above the floor. Houses may also have doorknobs instead of lever handles because they do not have to be accessible.

DEFINITIONS

Area of refuge: an area where persons unable to use stairways can remain temporarily to await instructions or assistance during emergency evacuation

Corridor: an enclosed exit access component that defines and provides a path of egress travel to an exit. A corridor may or may not be protected depending on the particular requirements of the code.

Exit court: a court or yard (considered part of an exit discharge) that provides access to a public way for one or more required exits. In the IBC, this is now called an *egress court*.

Exit enclosure: a fully enclosed portion of an exit that is only used as a means of egress and that provides for a protected path of egress either in a vertical or horizontal direction. In most instances, however, exit enclosures mean protected stairways. Depending on construction type and building type, an exit enclosure must have either a one-hour or two-hour rating, and all

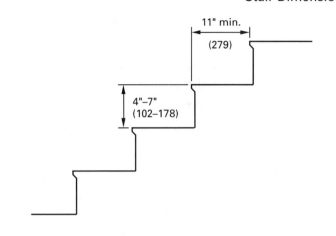

Figure 28.9
Stair Dimensions

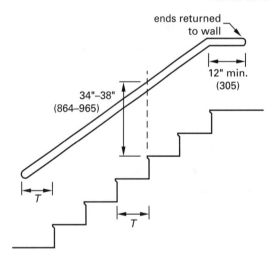

Figure 28.10
Handrail Design

openings must be protected. An exit enclosure must lead to an exit discharge or public way.

Exit passageway: a horizontal, fully enclosed portion of an exit that is only used as a means of egress. An exit passageway leads from an exit doorway to an exit discharge or public way. A common example of an exit passageway is an exit from the door at the ground level of an interior stairway that leads through the building to an outside door.

Horizontal exit: an exit through a minimum two-hour rated wall that divides a building into two or more separate exit access areas to afford safety from fire and smoke

Stair: (new to the IBC) a change in elevation, consisting of one or more risers.

Stairway: one or more flights of stairs, either exterior or interior, with the necessary landings and platforms connecting them, to form a continuous and uninterrupted passage from one level to another

Travel distance: the measurement of the distance between the most remote occupiable point of an area or room to the entrance of the nearest exit that serves it. It is part of the exit access and is measured in a straight line along the path of exit travel.

SAMPLE QUESTIONS

1. According the the IBC, dead-end corridors in unsprinklered buildings are limited to a maximum of

(A) 10 ft

(B) 20 ft

(C) 40 ft

(D) 50 ft

2. The abbreviated table shown includes requirements for occupancy loads. A restaurant on the ground floor contains 3500 ft^2 of dining area, a 1000 ft^2 kitchen, and a 1200 ft^2 bar. What is the total occupant load?

(A) 202 occupants

(B) 318 occupants

(C) 380 occupants

(D) 410 occupants

3. What is included in the rise of a stair?

(A) the vertical distance from one nosing to the next

(B) the average height of a step

(C) the distance from finish floor slab to finish floor slab

(D) the number of steps between landings

Sample Question 2 Table

use	occupant load factor (ft^2/occupant)
assembly areas, concentrated use (without fixed seats) auditoriums dance floors lodge rooms	7
assembly areas, less-concentrated use conference rooms dining rooms drinking establishments exhibit rooms lounges stages	15
hotels and apartments	200
kitchen—commercial	200
offices	100
stores, ground floor	30

4. Working under the IBC, a designer has calculated that a total exit width of 8 ft is required from a store. What combination of door widths would meet most exiting requirements?

(A) one 36 in door remotely located from a pair of 34 in doors

(B) a pair of 32 in doors remotely located from one 38 in door

(C) three 36 in doors remotely located

(D) three 34 in doors remotely located

5. In a 90,000 ft^2, single-story office building, what would be of greatest concern in space planning?

(A) dead-end corridors

(B) corridor widths

(C) horizontal exits

(D) travel distances

6. A client has requested a new entry to her consulting business, which is located in an old, unsprinklered building. The client's space must conform to current IBC requirements. Her current entrance consists of a pair of all-glass doors mounted on floor closers. The entrance opens onto a 1-hour rated building corridor. What should the designer tell her to expect regarding the new entrance?

- (A) Smoke seals will have to be located around the edges of the glass doors.
- (B) The glass doors will have to be replaced.
- (C) One of the doors will have to be removed.
- (D) The floor closers will have to be changed to hinges.

7. Which of the following is an INCORRECT statement about fire-rated door assemblies?

- (A) Either hinges or rated pivots may be used.
- (B) Under some circumstances a closer is not needed.
- (C) Labeling is required for both the door and frame.
- (D) Glass area is limited based on rating.

8. According to the UBC, the minimum width of a stair when handrails are required on either side is

- (A) 36 in
- (B) 42 in
- (C) 44 in
- (D) 60 in

9. Exits may NEVER pass through

- (A) kitchens
- (B) foyers
- (C) reception rooms
- (D) lobbies

10. The two most important factors in determining the number of exits required for a particular room or space are

- (A) occupancy and the distance from the room exit to the building exit
- (B) the exit widths and common path of egress travel

- (C) the occupant load and building size
- (D) the occupancy and the occupant load

11. The three parts of a means of egress include the

- I. public way
- II. exit
- III. exit access
- IV. exit enclosure
- V. exit discharge
- VI. corridor

- (A) I, II, and III
- (B) I, III, and VI
- (C) II, III, and V
- (D) II, IV, and V

12. Exits are always

- (A) protected by fire-rated construction
- (B) limited in length
- (C) corridors or stairways
- (D) required in buildings without sprinklers

13. Which two factors most typically determine whether a room must have at least two exits?

- (A) occupancy and travel distance
- (B) occupant load and occupancy
- (C) travel distance and occupant load
- (D) exit width factor and occupancy

14. A designer is developing a space plan for a full floor tenant in a high-rise building. What two things does the designer need to know when determining the maximum travel distance?

- (A) the construction type and height of the building
- (B) the occupancy classification and whether the design involves an exit or exit access

(C) the occupancy classification and whether the building is sprinklered

(D) the construction type and whether the building is sprinklered

15. Which of the following is an INCORRECT statement about corridors?

(A) Corridor construction must be fire-rated.

(B) Corridors are part of the exit access.

(C) Corridors must be used exclusively for egress.

(D) Corridors are included in calculating travel distance.

29

BARRIER-FREE DESIGN

Barrier-free design is an important part of the NCIDQ exam and is a topic with which all interior designers should be familiar. The exam tests knowledge of barrier-free concepts and requirements in the multiple-choice sections and the candidate's ability to apply regulations in the design practicum section. Although many model codes, state laws, and federal laws set requirements for accessibility, and there are differences between them, the overriding regulation today is the Americans with Disabilities Act (ADA). This federal law requires, among other things, that all commercial and public accommodations be accessible to people with disabilities. Al-though the ADA is not a national building code and does not depend on inspection for its enforcement, building owners must comply with the requirements or be liable for civil lawsuits. Interior designers are likewise responsible for designing interior spaces that conform to ADA requirements.

The ADA is a complex, four-title civil rights law. Title III, Public Accommodations and Commercial Facilities, is the part that most affects designers. The design requirements for construction are mainly found in the ADA Accessibility Guidelines (ADAAG), which is technically Appendix A to 28 CFR 36, the Code of Federal Regulations rule that implements Title III of the Act. When designers refer to the ADA, they are usually referring to the design criteria contained in the ADAAG.

Other local and federal laws and regulations also govern accessibility. For example, the ADA does not cover single- or multi-family housing. Multi-family housing is regulated mainly by the federal Fair Housing Act and by some state laws. In some cases, for federal buildings, the Uniform Federal Accessibility Standards govern. Although there are differences among these regulations, they all follow most of the standards set forth in ICC/ANSI A117.1-1998, Accessible and Usable Buildings and Facilities, or the older version, CABO/ANSI A117.1, American National Standard for Buildings and Facilities Providing Accessibility and Usability for Physically Handicapped People.

The differences among the standards primarily address scoping provisions and some details. *Scoping provisions* are requirements that dictate how many accessible elements must be provided. For example, scoping provisions tell the designer how many seats in a restaurant must allow for wheelchair access or how many housing units in a complex must be accessible.

The standards discussed in this chapter include the basic requirement for accessibility related to interior design as defined in the ICC/ANSI standard and the requirements that are most likely to be tested on the NCIDQ exam. Being familiar with the basic concepts and requirements of accessibility is good preparation for the exam.

ACCESSIBLE ROUTES

An *accessible route* is a continuous, unobstructed path connecting all accessible elements and spaces in a building or facility. It includes corridors, doorways, floors, ramps, elevators, lifts, and clear floor space at fixtures. The standards for accessible routes are designed primarily to accommodate a person using a wheelchair, but they should accommodate people with other disabilities.

Accessible routes and other clearances are based on some basic dimensional requirements of wheelchairs. The minimum clear width for an accessible route is 36 in (915) continuously and 32 in (815) at a passage point such as a doorway. The passage point cannot be more than 24 in (610) long. The minimum passage width for two wheelchairs is 60 in (1525). If an accessible route is less than 60 in wide, then passing spaces at least 60 in × 60 in must be provided at intervals not to exceed 200 ft (61 m). These requirements are shown in Fig. 29.1.

The minimum clear floor space required to accommodate one stationary wheelchair is 30 in × 48 in (760 × 1220). For maneuverability, a minimum 60 in (1525) diameter circle is required for a wheelchair to make a 180° turn. In place of this, a T-shaped space may be provided as shown in Fig. 29.2. When planning toilet rooms, make sure there is at least this 5 ft diameter clear space available. If turns in

Figure 29.1
Wheelchair
Clearances

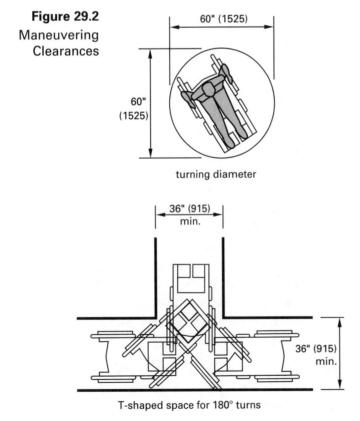

32" (815) min. door opening

36" (915) corridor

corridor and door clearances

60" (1525) min.

minimum clear width for two wheelchairs

Figure 29.2
Maneuvering
Clearances

60" (1525)

60" (1525)

turning diameter

36" (915) min.

36" (915) min.

T-shaped space for 180° turns

corridors or around obstructions must be made, the minimum dimensions are as shown in Fig. 29.3.

An accessible route may have a slope up to 1:20 (1 in of rise rise for every 20 in of distance). A slope any greater than this is classified as a ramp and must meet the requirements given later in this chapter.

DOORWAYS

A door must have a minimum clear opening width of 32 in (815) when opened at 90°. The maximum depth of a doorway 32 in wide is 24 in (610). If the area is deeper than this, then the width must be increased to 36 in (915). See Fig. 29.4.

Maneuvering clearances are required at standard swinging doors to allow easy operation of the latch and provide for a clear swing. For single doors, the clearances are shown in Fig. 29.5. The minimum space for two doors in a series is shown in Fig. 29.6. Note the 48 in (1220) space requirement. If sufficient clearance is not provided, then the doors must have power-assisted mechanisms or open automatically.

Barrier-free codes also require that door hardware meet certain specifications. Thresholds at doorways cannot exceed $1/2$ in (13) in height and must be beveled so no slope of the threshold is greater than 1:2. Operating devices must have a shape that is easy to grasp. This includes lever handles, push-type mechanisms, and U-shaped handles. Standard door knobs are not allowed. If door closers are provided, they must be adjusted to slow the closing time. The opening force required to push or pull open an interior hinged door cannot be more than 5 lbf-ft. Power-assisted doors may also be used.

PLUMBING FIXTURES AND TOILET ROOMS

ICC/ANSI A117.1-1998 governs the design of the components of toilet rooms as

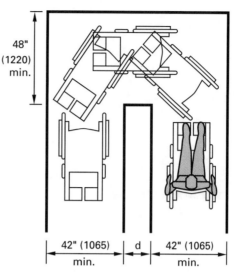

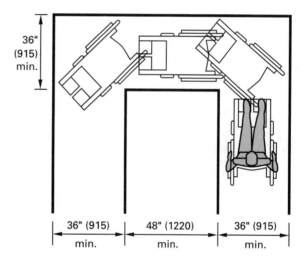

Figure 29.3
Turn in Corridors or Around Obstructions

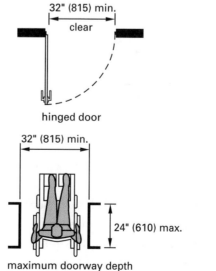

Figure 29.4
Doorway Clearances

Figure 29.5

Manuvering
Clearances
at Doors

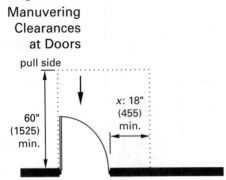

pull side

60"
(1525)
min.

x: 18"
(455)
min.

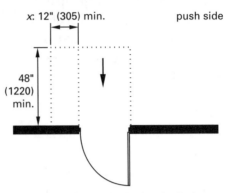

x: 12" (305) min.   push side

48"
(1220)
min.

Note: x = 12" (305) if door has both closer and latch

front approaches – swinging doors

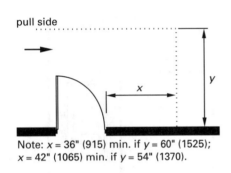

pull side

x

y

Note: x = 36" (915) min. if y = 60" (1525);
x = 42" (1065) min. if y = 54" (1370).

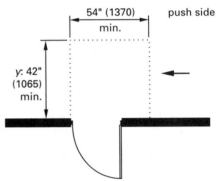

54" (1370)
min.   push side

y: 42"
(1065)
min.

Note: y = 48" (1220) min. if door has both latch and closer.

hinge side approaches – swinging doors

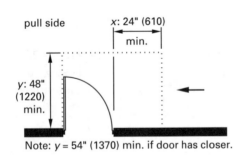

pull side   x: 24" (610)
min.

y: 48"
(1220)
min.

Note: y = 54" (1370) min. if door has closer.

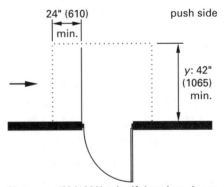

24" (610)   push side
min.

y: 42"
(1065)
min.

Note: y = 48" (1220) min. if door has closer.

latch side approaches – swinging doors

well as individual elements such as drinking fountains, bathtubs, and showers. As mentioned in the first section of this chapter, toilet rooms must have a minimum clear turning space of a 5 ft diameter circle; however, the clear floor space at fixtures and controls and at the turning space may overlap.

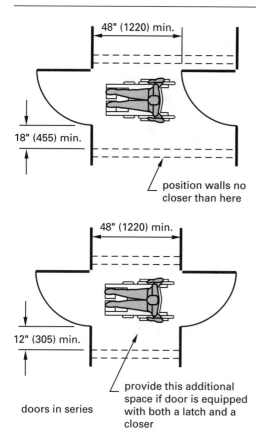

48" (1220) min.

18" (455) min.

position walls no closer than here

Figure 29.6
Double Door
Clearances

48" (1220) min.

12" (305) min.

provide this additional space if door is equipped with both a latch and a closer

doors in series

Figure 29.7
Toilet Stall
Dimensions

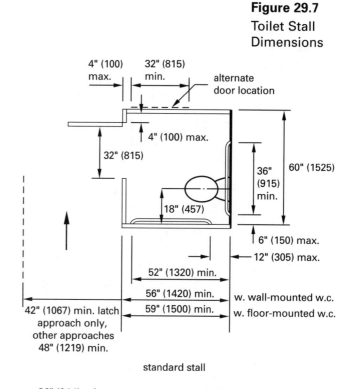

4" (100) max. 32" (815) min. alternate door location

4" (100) max.

32" (815)

36" (915) min. 60" (1525)

18" (457)

6" (150) max.
12" (305) max.

52" (1320) min.
56" (1420) min. w. wall-mounted w.c.
59" (1500) min. w. floor-mounted w.c.

42" (1067) min. latch approach only, other approaches 48" (1219) min.

standard stall

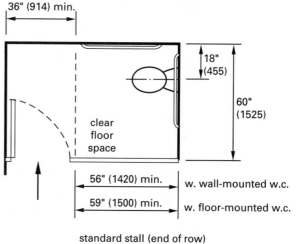

36" (914) min.

18" (455)

60" (1525)

clear floor space

56" (1420) min. w. wall-mounted w.c.
59" (1500) min. w. floor-mounted w.c.

standard stall (end of row)

Toilet Stalls

There are several acceptable layouts for toilet stalls. Minimum clearances for two standard stall layouts are shown in Fig. 29.7. Alternate layouts are also acceptable as shown in Fig. 29.8. The clearance depth in both cases varies depending on whether a wall-hung or floor-mounted water closet is used. In most cases, the door must provide a minimum clear opening of 32 in (815) and must swing out, away from the stall enclosure. Grab bars must also be provided as shown in the illustrations, mounted from 33 in to 36 in (840 to 915) above the floor.

If toilet stalls are not used, the centerline of the toilet must still be 18 in (455) from a wall with grab bars at both the back and side of the water closet. A clear space in front of and beside open water closets should be provided as shown in Fig. 29.9. Note that the dimension from the centerline of the toilet is 18 in (455) to both an

adjacent wall and the closest edge of a lavatory. This can be important to the layout of a toilet room in the design practicum section of the test.

The requirements described here are based on the ADA accessibility guidelines

Figure 29.9
Clear Floor
Space at Water
Closets

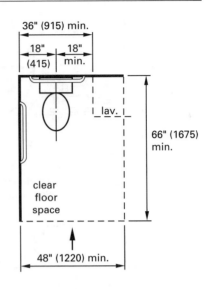

Figure 29.8
Alternate Toilet
Stall Dimensions

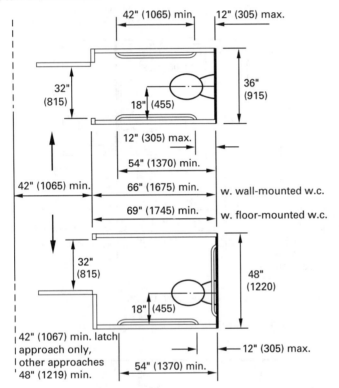

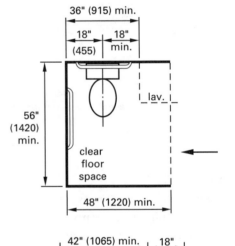

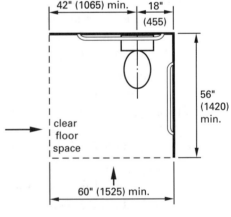

current at the time of this writing. This version of the requirements allows use of the alternate stalls shown in Fig. 29.8 for remodeling when it is technically infeasible to use a standard stall. The new regulations may eliminate the alternate stall configurations.

The following design guidelines for toilets are based on ICC/ANSI A117.1-1998, which includes a 16 in to 18 in (405 to 455) dimension range for the distance from a wall to the centerline of a toilet. The Access Board has recommended this change to allow some tolerance when installing a toilet. At the time of this writing,

their recommendation had not been formally adopted, though adoption is likely to occur. Currently, the ADA requires the 18 in (455) dimension only.

In addition, proposed regulations will not allow a lavatory or vanity to be 18 in (415) from the centerline of the toilet, as shown in Fig. 29.9; a full 60 in (1525) clear width from the adjacent wall will be required.

Urinals

Urinals must be of the stall type or wall hung with an elongated rim at a maximum height of 17 in (430) above the floor. A clear floor space of 30 in × 48 in (760 × 1220) must be provided in front of the urinal, which may adjoin or overlap an accessible route.

Lavatories

Lavatories must allow someone in a wheelchair to move under the sink and easily use the basin and water controls. The required dimensions are shown in Fig. 29.10. Notice that because of these clearances, wall-hung lavatories are the best type to use when accessibility is a concern. If pipes are exposed below the lavatory, they must be insulated or otherwise protected and there must not be any sharp or abrasive surfaces under lavatories or sinks. Faucets must be operable with one hand and cannot require tight grasping, pinching, or twisting of the wrist. Lever-operated, push-type, and automatically controlled mechanisms are acceptable.

Mirrors must be mounted with the bottom edge of the reflecting surface no higher than 40 in (1015) from the floor.

Drinking Fountains

Requirements for drinking fountains with a front approach are shown in Fig. 29.11. If a drinking fountain is freestanding or built-in without clear space below, it must have a clear floor space in front of it at least 30 in × 48 in (760 × 1220), which allows a person in a wheelchair to make a parallel approach.

Bathtubs

Bathtubs must be configured as shown in Fig. 29.12, and an in-tub seat or a seat at the head of the tub must be provided as

Figure 29.10
Clear Floor Space at Lavatories

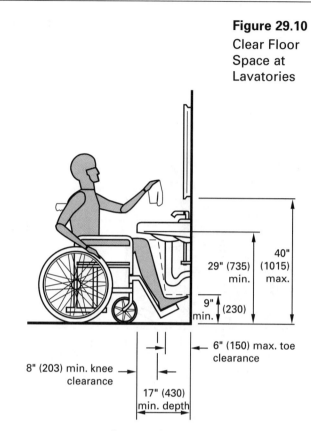

lavatory clearances

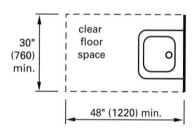

clear floor space at lavatories

shown. Grab bars must be provided as illustrated in Fig. 29.13. When there is an enclosure, it cannot obstruct the controls or the transfer from wheel-chairs onto seats or into the tub. Enclo-sure tracks cannot be mounted on the rim of the tub.

Showers

Shower stalls may be one of two basic types as shown in Fig. 29.14. When facilities with accessible sleeping rooms or suites are provided, a minimum number

Figure 29.12
Clear Floor Space at Bathtubs

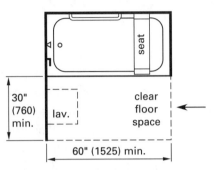

(a) with seat in tub, side approach

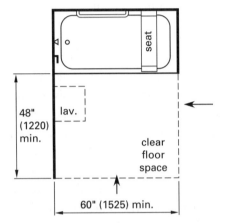

(b) with seat in tub, front approach

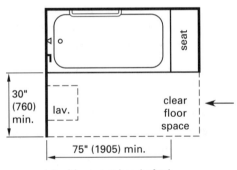

(c) with seat at head of tub

o drain
◁ shower head
⌐ shower controls

Figure 29.11
Water Fountain Access

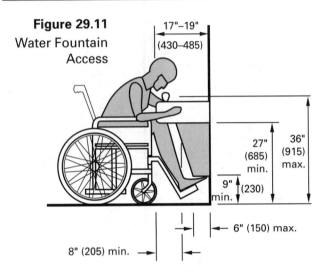

spout height and
knee clearance

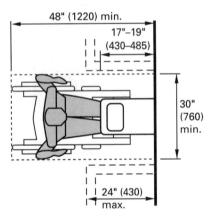

clear floor space

of rooms having roll-in showers, as specified in the ADA or the federal Fair Housing Act, is required. A seat is required in the smaller shower stall configuration, while a folding seat is required in the larger configuration if a permanent seat is not provided. Grab bars must be provided and mounted from 33 in to 36 in (840 to 915) above the floor.

FLOOR SURFACES

Floor surfaces must be stable, firm, and slip-resistant. If there is a change in level, the transition must meet the following requirements. If the change is less than $1/4$ in (6), it may be vertical and without edge treatment. If the change is between $1/4$ in and $1/2$ in (6 and 13), it must be beveled with a slope no greater than 1:2 ($1/2$ in of

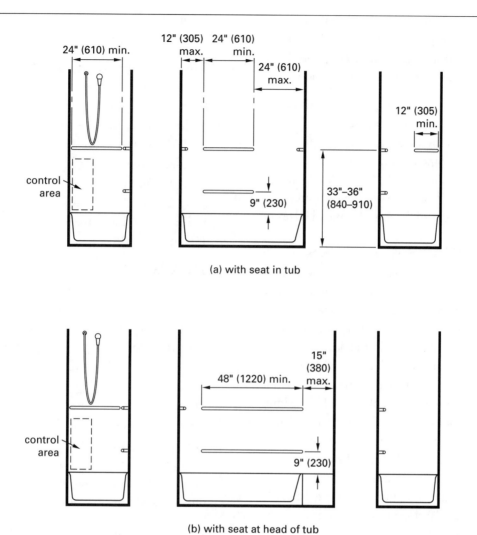

Figure 29.13
Grab Bars at
Bathtubs

(a) with seat in tub

(b) with seat at head of tub

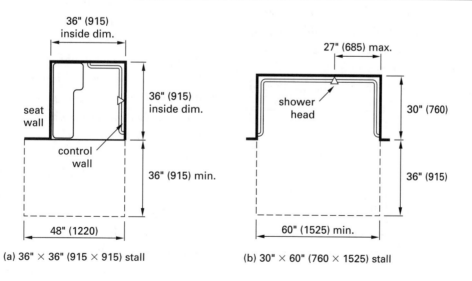

Figure 29.14
Accessible
Shower Stalls

(a) 36" × 36" (915 × 915) stall

(b) 30" × 60" (760 × 1525) stall

rise requires 1 in of length, for example). Changes greater than $^1/_2$ in (13) must be accomplished with a ramp meeting the requirements in the next section.

Carpet must have a firm cushion or backing or no cushion, as well as a level loop, textured loop, level-cut pile, or level-cut/uncut pile texture with a maximum pile height of $^1/_2$ in (13). It must be securely attached to the floor and have trim along all lengths of exposed edges.

RAMPS AND STAIRS

Ramps are required to provide a smooth transition between elevation changes, for both wheel-chair-bound persons as well as those whose mobility is otherwise restricted. In general, the least possible slope should be used, but in no case can a ramp have a slope greater than 1:12 (1 in of rise for every 12 in of run). The maximum rise for any ramp is limited to 30 in (760). Changes in elevation greater than this require a level landing before the next run of ramp is encountered. In some cases where exiting conditions prevent the 1:12 slope, a 1:10 slope is permitted if the maximum rise does not exceed 6 in (150). A 1:8 slope is permitted if the maximum rise does not exceed 3 in (75).

A ramp must have a minimum clear width of 36 in (915) and landings at least as wide as the widest ramp leading to them. Landing lengths must be a minimum of 60 in (1525). If ramps change direction at a landing, then the landing must be at least 60 in square.

Ramps with rises greater than 6 in (150) or lengths greater than 72 in (1830) must have handrails on both sides, and the top of the handrail must be from 34 in to 38 in (865 to 965) above the ramp surface. Handrails must extend at least 12 in (305) beyond the top and bottom of the ramp segment and have a diameter or width of gripping surface from $1^1/_4$ in to $1^1/_2$ in (32 to 38).

The ANSI code states that stairs that are required as a means of egress and stairs between floors not connected by an elevator must be designed according to certain standards specifying the configuration of treads, risers, nosings, and handrails. The maximum riser height is 7 in (180) and the treads must be a minimum of 11 in (280) as measured from riser to riser, as shown in Fig. 29.15. Open risers are not permitted. The undersides of the nosings must not be abrupt and must conform to one of the styles shown in Fig. 29.16.

Stairway handrails must be continuous on both sides of the stairs. The inside handrail on switchback or dogleg stairs must always be continuous as it changes direction. Other handrails must extend beyond the top and bottom riser as shown in Fig. 29.17. The top of the gripping surface must be between 34 in (865) and 38 in (965) above stair nosings. The handrail must have a diameter or width of gripping surface from $1^1/_4$ in to $1^1/_2$ in (32 to 38). There must be a clear space between the handrail and the wall of at least $1^1/_2$ in (38). When an exit stairway is part of an accessible route in an unsprinklered building (not including houses), there must be a clear width of 48 in (1220) between the handrails. The proposed regulations will allow a handrail with a circular cross-section up to 2 in (51) in diameter.

Figure 29.15
Stair Design Requirements

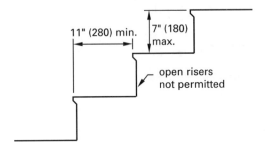

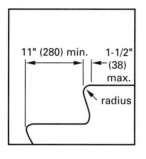

flush riser

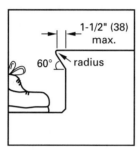

angled nosing

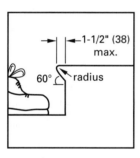

rounded nosing

Figure 29.16
Stair Nosing
Requirements

Figure 29.17
Handrail Design

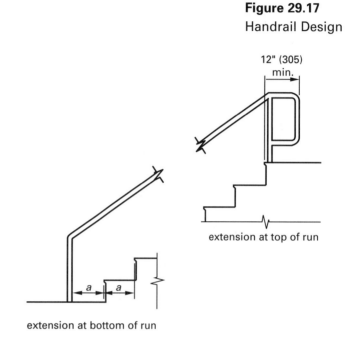

extension at top of run

extension at bottom of run

PROTRUDING OBJECTS

There are restrictions on objects and building elements that project into corridors and other walkways, because they present a hazard for visually impaired people. These restrictions are shown in Fig. 29.18 and are based on the needs of people with severe vision impairments walking with a cane. A protruding object with a lower edge less than 27 in (685) above the floor can be detected by a person using a cane, so these objects may project any amount.

Regardless of the situation, protruding objects cannot reduce the clear width required for an accessible route or maneuvering space. In addition, if the vertical

clearance of an area adjacent to an accessible route is reduced to less than 80 in (2030), a guardrail or other barrier must be provided.

DETECTABLE WARNINGS

Detectable warning surfaces are required on walking surfaces in front of stairs, in hazardous vehicular areas, and in other places where a hazard may exist without a guardrail or some other warning method. The surfaces must consist of exposed aggregate concrete, cushioned surfaces of rubber or plastic, raised strips, or grooves. Such textures must contrast with that of the surrounding surface.

At the time of this writing, the ADA's detectable warning provisions have been temporarily suspended pending further study. Local codes or other state and federal regulations should be verified to

Figure 29.18
Requirements
for Protruding
Objects

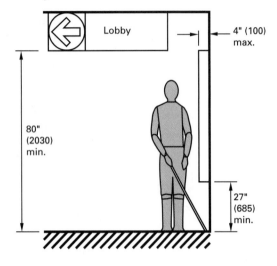

Lobby

4" (100)
max.

80"
(2030)
min.

27"
(685)
min.

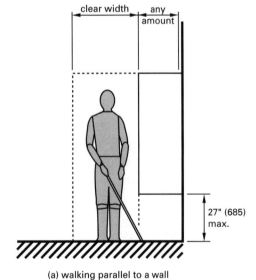

clear width | any amount

27" (685)
max.

(a) walking parallel to a wall

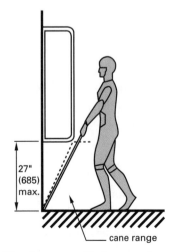

27"
(685)
max.

cane range

(b) walking perpendicular to a wall

determine what rules apply to a particular design project.

Door handles are also required to have textured surfaces if they are part of a door that leads to an area that might prove dangerous to a blind person, such as doors to loading platforms, boiler rooms, and stages.

SIGNAGE AND ALARMS

The ADA requires that certain accessible rooms and features be clearly identified with the symbol for accessibility and that identification, directional, emergency, and information signs meet certain specifications, including Braille.

Permanent rooms and spaces must be identified with signs having lettering from $5/8$ in to 2 in (16 to 51) high, raised $1/32$ in (0.8) above the surface of the sign. Lettering must be all uppercase, in sans serif or simple serif type accompanied with Grade 2 Braille. If pictograms are used, they must be at least 6 in (152) high and must be accompanied by the equivalent verbal description, placed directly below. Signs must have an eggshell matte or other nonglare finish with characters and symbols contrasting with their background. Permanent identification signs must be mounted on the wall adjacent to the latch side of the door such that a person can approach to within 3 in (75) of the signage without encountering protruding objects or standing within the door swing. Mounting height to the centerline of the sign must be 60 in (1525). When there is no wall space to the latch side of the door, including double-leaf doors, the sign must be placed on the nearest adjacent wall.

Directional and informational signs must have lettering at least 3 in (75) high (measured as a capital X) with a width-to-height ratio between 3:5 and 1:1. The stroke width-to-height ratio must be between 1:5 and 1:10. Contrast and finish requirements are the same as those for permanent room identification.

The international symbol for accessibility is required on parking spaces, passenger loading zones, accessible entrances, and toilet and bathing facilities when not all are accessible. Building directories and temporary signs do not have to comply.

Emergency warning systems that provide both a visual and audible alarm are required. Audible alarms must produce a sound that exceeds the prevailing sound level in the room or space by at least 15 dB. Visual alarms must be flashing lights that have a flashing frequency of about 1 cycle/sec.

TELEPHONES

If public telephones are provided, at least one telephone per floor must conform to the requirements as shown in Fig. 29.19 and as specified in the ADA requirements. If there are two or more banks of telephones, at least one telephone per bank must conform. When four or more public pay telephones are provided, then at least one interior public text telephone is required.

Figure 29.19
Telephone Access

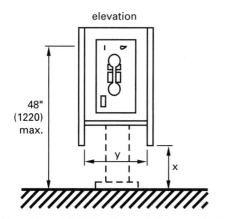

Note: if y < 30" (760), then x shall be ≥ 27" (685).

(a) front reach only

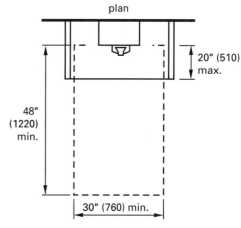

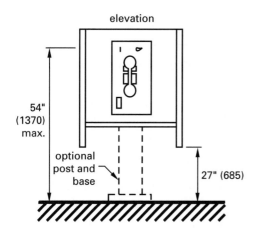

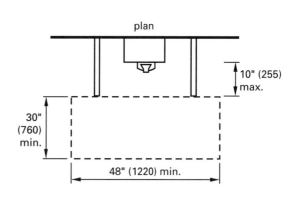

(b) side reach possible

Accessible telephones may be designed for either front or side access. The dimensions required for both of these types are shown in Fig. 29.19. In either case, a clear floor space of at least 30 in × 48 in (760 × 1220) must be provided. The telephones should have pushbutton controls and telephone directories within reach of a person in a wheelchair.

The locations of text telephones must be identified with the international TDD (text telephone) symbol, and volume-control telephones must have a sign depicting a telephone handset with radiating sound waves. In assembly areas, permanently installed assistive listening systems must display the international symbol for hearing-loss access.

ELEVATORS

The ADA prescribes many requirements for elevators. In most cases, elevators are already existing or are being designed and specified by the building architect. However, there are several regulations with which the interior designer should be familiar and that may be covered on the NCIDQ exam.

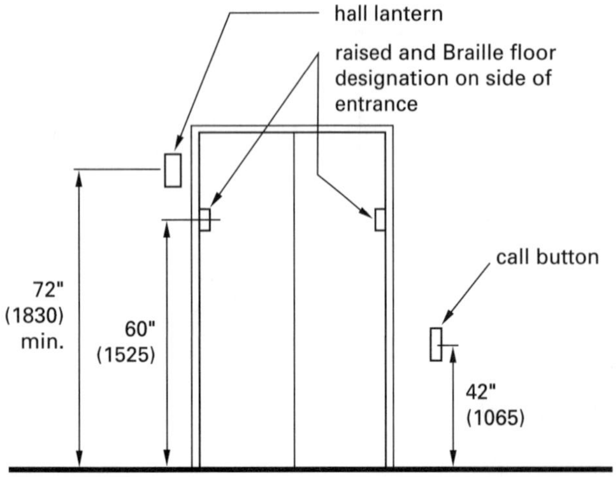

Elevator signals must be located as shown in Fig. 29.20. The call buttons, hall lantern, and floor designators must all be located within easy reach and visual access. The call button must indicate when each call is registered and answered. The hall lantern must give a visual and audible signal. For audible signals, the lantern can sound once for up and twice for down, or it may be equipped with a verbal annunciator that sounds out "up" and "down."

Inside the car, floor buttons can be no higher than 54 in (1370) above the floor for a side approach and 48 in (1220) above the floor for a front approach. Emergency controls must be grouped with the centerline of the group no higher than 35 in (890) above the floor. Refer to the ADAAG for other requirements such as the minimum size of cars, door and signal timing, and safety reopening devices. The proposed regulations will reduce the maximum side reach dimension to 48 in (1220).

SEATING

If fixed or built-in seating or tables are provided in accessible public- or common-use areas, then at least 5%, but not less than one table, of the seating areas must be accessible. This applies to facilities such as restaurants, nightclubs, churches, and similar spaces. In new construction and when possible in remodeling, the number of tables should be dispersed throughout the facility. If smoking and nonsmoking areas are provided, the required number of seating spaces must be proportioned among the smoking and nonsmoking areas. The area for this type of seating must comply with the dimensions shown in Fig. 29.21.

In places of assembly with fixed seating, the minimum number of wheelchair locations is given in a table in the ADA based on the capacity of seating in the assembly area. At least 1% (no less) of all fixed seats

Figure 29.20
Elevator Entrances

hall lantern

raised and Braille floor designation on side of entrance

call button

72" (1830) min.

60" (1525)

42" (1065)

must be aisle seats with no armrests on the aisle side, or must have removable or folding armrests on the aisle side. Signs notifying people of the availability of these seats must be posted at the ticket office. The wheelchair areas must be an integral part of the overall seating plan and must be provided so people have a choice of admission prices and lines of sight comparable to those available for members of the general public. At least one companion seat must be provided next to each wheelchair area. Wheelchair areas must adjoin an accessible route that also serves as a means of emergency egress.

When assembly areas are part of a remodeling and it is not feasible to disperse the seating areas throughout the facility, the accessible seating areas may be clustered. These clustered areas must have provisions for companion seating and must be located on an accessible route that also serves as a means of emergency egress.

Refer to the complete text of the ADA for requirements for audio-amplification systems, assisted listening devices, and signage required for assembly areas.

SAMPLE QUESTIONS

1. The minimum clear width for a door is
(A) 30 in (760)
(B) 32 in (815)
(C) 34 in (865)
(D) 36 in (915)

2. When doing design work for remodeling toilet rooms to make them accessible, the designer finds that it is impossible to provide adequate clearance on one side of a door. What is the best course of action?
(A) Propose to the client that walls be demolished and replanned to provide the necessary clearances.
(B) Apply to the building department for a variance because of the remodeling problem.

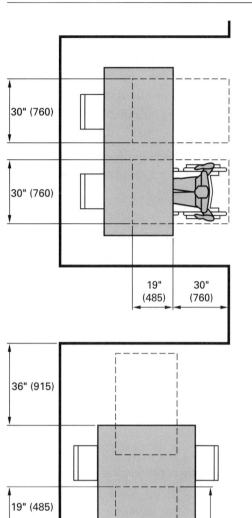

Figure 29.21
Minimum Clearances for Seating and Tables

(C) Specify a power-assisted door opener that meets accessibility standards, and incorporate this into the design.
(D) Suggest that a unisex toilet be built nearby that complies with all accessibility requirements.

3. As measured from the nosing, a handrail for barrier-free design must have a height of
(A) 28 in to 32 in (710 to 815)
(B) 30 in to 34 in (760 to 865)

(C) 32 in to 36 in (815 to 915)

(D) 34 in to 38 in (865 to 965)

4. In developing a signage system for a health care clinic, the designer decides that the room identification signs should be mounted perpendicular to the wall near the door to each room. What would be of LEAST concern in the design work?

(A) the color of the lettering and its background

(B) that the amount the Braille lettering is raised above the surface

(C) whether or not the width of the accessible route was reduced

(D) the mounting height to the center of the sign

5. Which type of sink is best for barrier-free design?

(A) vanity

(B) pedestal

(C) wall hung

(D) free standing

6. When considering the initial space planning of an accessible toilet room, which of the following design elements should be of most concern?

(A) door swing and toilet position

(B) grab bar location and approach dimension

(C) stall depth and grab bar location

(D) door swing and approach dimension

7. What are the most important design elements to incorporate into a hotel, to provide safe egress for physically disabled people?

I. visual alarms

II. audible alarms

III. flashing smoke detectors

IV. large emergency lettering

V. tactile signage

(A) I and II

(B) I and III

(C) II and IV

(D) II and V

8. An accessible route must serve

(A) all accessible spaces and parts of a building

(B) the corridors, stairs, elevators, and toilet rooms of a building

(C) entrances, parking, toilet rooms, corridors, and drinking fountains

(D) entrances, corridors, toilet rooms, and elevators except those available only for maintenance personnel

9. During space planning, the designer must locate a 36 in (915) door leading from a corridor, where limited space is available, into another room. One option is to orient the corridor either perpendicular or parallel to the wall separating the corridor from the room and to swing the door in any direction. The door will have a latch only, with no closer. In order to provide for accessibility and minimize the width of the corridor, which of the following door orientations and approach directions would best meet the criteria?

(A) front approach, door swings into room

(B) latch side approach, door swings into corridor

(C) hinge side approach, door swings into room

(D) front approach, door swings into corridor

10. In addition to meeting the requirements of the ADA, what other accessibility requirements should the interior designer be most concerned with when doing design development for a commercial project?

(A) ANSI A117.1, Accessible and Usable Buildings and Facilities

(B) scoping provisions of the local building code

(C) ADAAG

(D) the Uniform Federal Accessibility Standards

30

SAMPLE DESIGN PRACTICUM

ABOUT THE DESIGN PRACTICUM

Section III of the NCIDQ exam is the design practicum, covering schematics and design development. It is the part of the exam where candidates are required to develop a design solution and related construction document items within a sketch format.

Section III includes three user types or areas of specialization. The first two areas include residential design and office design and remain constant from one examination to the next. The third area varies and may include hospitality, retail, institutional, or healthcare. However, this does not mean that a candidate has to be an expert in one of these four building types; candidates need only be prepared for design problems related to one type or another. The main emphasis is on designing a small residential space (an apartment, for example) and a small office area.

Section III is administered in two parts: four hours for Part 1 and three hours for Part 2. Part 1 gives a program for a small multi-use facility. This means candidates will have to deal with commercial as well as residential spaces. The program requires that candidates either plan all spaces based on a minimum square footage area or develop the room or space based on a detailed list of furniture and equipment. For example, there may be a requirement to plan a functional kitchen to accommodate a particular set of appliances and linear footage of counter space without having a specific square footage area requirement.

Part 1 requires candidates to fill in an adjacency matrix, draw a floor plan with required furniture to scale (either drafted or sketched), fill in an abbreviated finish schedule, and select appropriate partition types for a few specified rooms.

Part 2 requires candidates to complete an electrical plan, a reflected ceiling plan, and an elevation and section through a small portion of the space, usually an architectural woodwork fixture. As part of the reflected ceiling plan, candidates must indicate with a brief four- or five-word description how they used ambient, task, and accent lighting in the solution.

The design practicum tests the candidate's ability to synthesize a great deal of information into a design solution floor plan and other specific kinds of drawings and diagrams. Within this overall design solution, it tests the ability to perform some basic design skills. The following list may be used to evaluate a candidate's experience and readiness to take the test. Candidates should be able to perform the following tasks if they are required on the exam. This list is not necessarily complete, but it should provide a good starting point for study. Skills necessary include the ability to

• develop an adjacency matrix from a written program

• develop a floor plan incorporating required spaces and adjacencies

• develop a functional floor plan that meets exiting and accessibility requirements

• lay out a functional kitchen based on given appliances, furnishings, and other requirements

• lay out accessible and functional toilet rooms and bathrooms based on given fixtures

• lay out public areas based on given furniture and fixture requirements

• lay out furniture in rooms of a given area in a functional manner

• make decisions on appropriate finishes for given room types

• draw all required plan elements (either sketched or hardlined), including partitions, doors, room names, furniture, and equipment, accurately and to scale on the base sheet provided

• select appropriate partition types and details for given functional requirements

• use appropriate electrical symbols for power, voice, and data, and place them on a drawing as required by a given furniture plan and equipment list

• select and apply appropriate lighting types to a ceiling layout based on program requirements, design concepts, and good lighting design principles

• use appropriate electrical symbols, including exit signs and emergency lighting, on a reflected ceiling plan

• develop switching for lighting based on functional and programmatic requirements

• develop and sketch an elevation meeting accessibility requirements, symbol orientation, and dimensional requirements

• develop and sketch a section that matches the section cut on the elevation and that uses correct materials, communicates the intent for construction, and is correctly dimensioned

THE SPACE-PLANNING PROCESS FOR THE NCIDQ EXAM

Space-planning proficiency is tested in the design practicum section of the NCIDQ exam. Although every designer has a slightly different method of space planning, each one follows an orderly process using a similar sequence of steps. Candidates with some experience with space planning may find that their particular approach will work for the NCIDQ exam. One of the most difficult challenges is completing the requirements of the problem within the allotted time. Strict time management is an absolute necessity to successfully completing the practicum. The following steps represent one possible method of completing this portion of the test.

Read Program and Sketch Constraints

The first step, of course, is to read the problem statement thoroughly. This will establish the basic rooms and areas needed as well as suggest a direction for overall design. However, for complex problems it may be helpful to translate the written word into graphic notation. One way of doing this is to lay a piece of tracing paper over the base plan and schematically mark the important requirements as given by the program. See Fig. 30.1. These may include items such as entrance points and emergency exits, special features, plumbing locations, views from windows or sources of daylight, and similar fixed constraints of the problem. A design concept may also be indicated diagrammatically. Try to complete this step in 15 minutes.

Sketch the Required Program Areas

The problem statement will give the functional spaces. For some spaces, the area in square feet (or square meters) will simply be stated. For other areas requiring a furniture layout, the detailed requirements for the furniture and accessories will be stated, and the furniture groupings will have to be arranged to satisfy the program statements. For example, the program may state that a seating group must have six chairs, two end tables, space for magazine storage, and table lamps, but these items must be located and spaced in a way that makes the arrangement work. In some cases, both the furniture required and a minimum area will be given.

However, the numbers given in the program are difficult to visualize. To give a clear, graphic image of these numbers, translate the individual programmed spaces into graphic squares or rectangles at the same scale required for the final drawings. This can be done on a separate piece of tracing paper to help the designer visualize the spaces required as space planning begins. Use a consistent dimensional increment such as 2 ft (600) for small projects or 5 ft or 10 ft (1500 or 3000) for large projects or a module suggested by the window mullions. This will save time

and help the designer to see spatial relationships between functional groupings.

For areas where furniture needs to be laid out, sketch the area to develop a block of space that can accommodate the furniture and accessories. It is easier to work with a larger block of space during initial space planning than it is to redraw all the individual items of furniture. Sketch the furniture arrangement at the same scale as the base drawing sheet so it can be traced on the final drawing. Also, calculate the square footage of the block of space so all the programmed areas can be summed to compare with the available space. Figure 30.2 shows examples of these areas and furniture sketches. Try to complete this step in 15 minutes.

It is also helpful to make graphic notes on program requirements regarding the elements that are unique to each space, such as the number of exits or the room's relationship to some existing feature in the base floor plan. If two or more spaces must be adjacent or it seems logical to keep them together, develop a block area to show them as a group. Be sure to add some circulation if required.

When finished with this step, every required space should be sketched roughly to scale on a piece of tracing paper. Remember that these diagrams are only notes to help maintain a mental image of the spaces. As work proceeds on the floor plan base sheet, remain flexible so blocks can be adjusted to fit the specific conditions of the architectural plan. Functional groupings may even need to be split with a corridor, but such divisions need not compromise the adjacency requirements implied by the large functional grouping.

Develop and Analyze Adjacencies

At this point the adjacency matrix needs to be completed. Notice that the matrix

Figure 30.1
Programming
Base Sheet

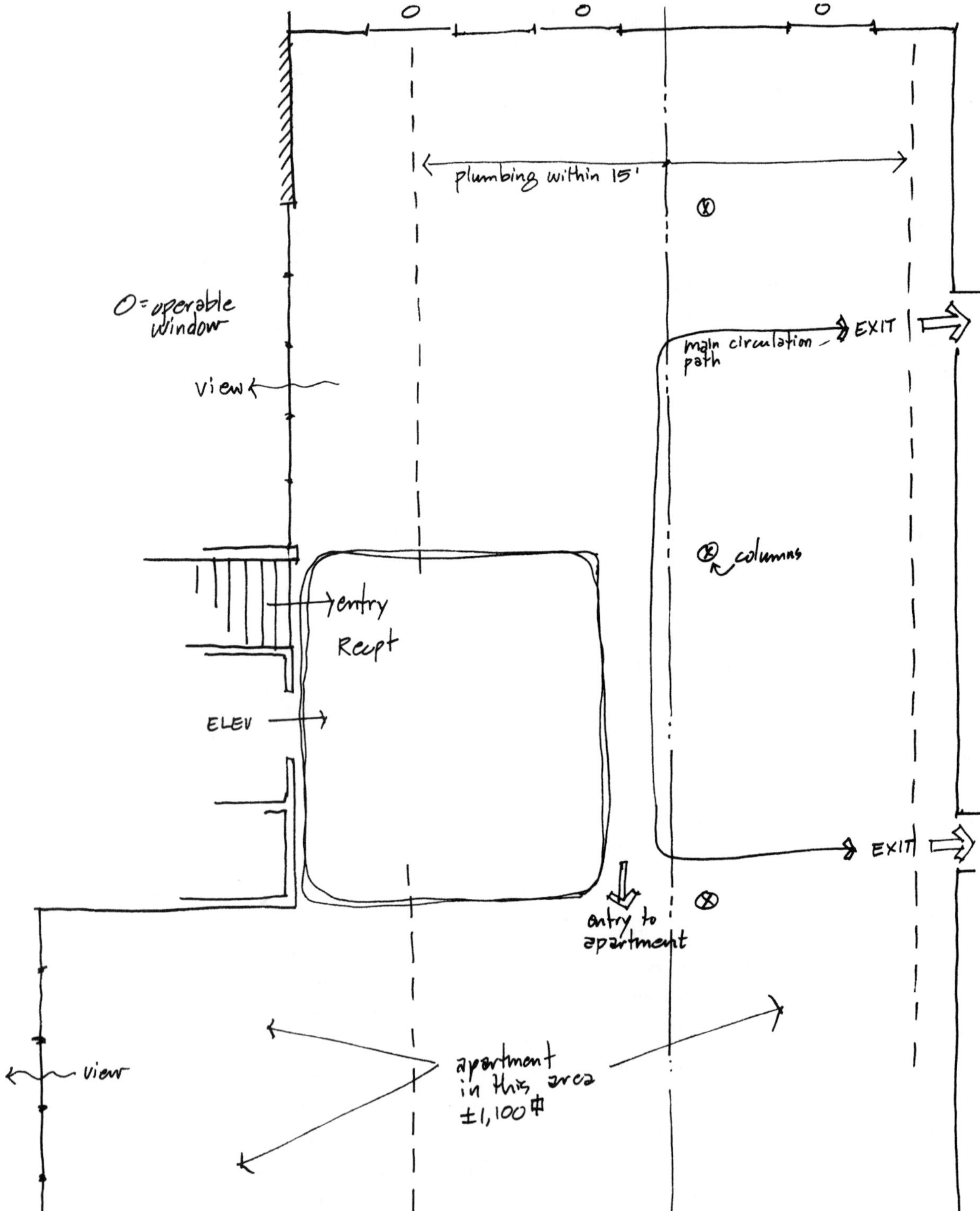

does not show all of the spaces, so the other adjacency requirements will have to be considered, whether they are specifically stated or just implied by the program. It may be easier to translate the adjacency matrix and other requirement to a simple bubble diagram. Most of the adjacencies are fairly straightforward, so this step should take no more than 10 to 15 minutes.

Locate and Understand Use of Required Exits

The number and location of exits will be shown in the base plan provided, and the problem statement will clearly specify how access to them must be provided and the minimum distance between the exits when they are connected with a corridor. In the first step, there should have been a line drawn to indicate a preliminary estimate of how the corridor would work. Take this opportunity to quickly review the program and make sure the requirements are being satisfied.

Sketch Preliminary Layouts

Before final space planning, quickly sum the areas of all the programmed spaces, multiply by 1.25 to account for circulation, and compare the total square footage with the available area. This comparison will indicate how generous the test makers have been and how carefully the space plan must be laid out. If it appears that there is more than enough space, it probably will not take as much time to plan as it would if the available space were limited.

In addition, sum the space required for just the residential part of the program. Some of the spaces will have minimum areas listed; for other spaces the minimum areas will have to be estimated. For example, an accessible residential toilet room will require from 70 ft^2 to 100 ft^2 (6.5 m^2 to 9.3 m^2) if a 5 ft 0 in (1525) diameter turning circle is required. Based on the

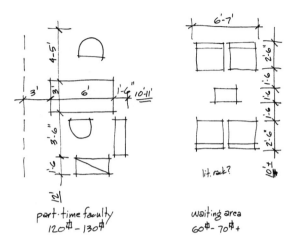

Figure 30.2
Individual Furniture Block Plans

equipment and countertop linear footage requirements, the kitchen area can be quickly estimated. Closets can be calculated by multiplying a 2 ft (600) depth by the linear footage of storage stated in the program.

Once the required usable area is established, add another 25% to account for wall thicknesses and hallways within the residential portion, to establish a total area. This approximate area can be compared with the blocks of space on the practicum's base plan. This comparison will suggest where the residential portion of the problem should be blocked out. This residential area will then have to remain as a complete unit without any exit corridors or other programmed areas impinging on it.

This space could be blocked out on the programming base sheet, developed in the first step. Compare the notation shown in Fig. 30.1 with the final solution shown in the practicum solutions in Ch. 31 (Fig. 31.2).

The individual spaces can now be laid out on the base floor plan. Use tracing paper to do this rather than the final sheet that will be turned in. The existing conditions of the architectural plan and the program requirements (that have been noted on the base sheet) will determine the locations of many of the rooms and programmed spaces. For example, rooms requiring plumbing will need to be placed close to a wet column or plumbing lines, or a window with the best view and natural light should be used for one of the major spaces rather than for a secondary space like a storage room.

As space planning begins, work from the general to the particular. That is, lay out large blocks of space in their correct relationships before starting to worry about ancillary spaces or individual furniture groupings. This way several schematic alternatives can be sketched to see which one works best for further refinement. At this time, give thought to the organizational concepts and circulation schemes discussed earlier in this chapter. If there is a direct, simple circulation path and sensible organizational scheme, the spaces allocated earlier will probably accommodate the required furniture layouts.

At this early stage, a good circulation pattern is necessary because it will help organize the other spaces, satisfy required exiting, and provide for accessibility requirements. Try to finish locating the entrances and exits, and choose a preliminary layout of blocks of space and circulation in about 30 minutes or less. This is an incredibly short time even for a problem of limited size, but it must be done quickly to leave enough time for drawing the final floor plan.

Verify Space Allocations with Problem Requirements

After selecting the one plan that seems to work, take a few minutes to check it against the following performance criteria that the graders look for.

- Does the plan include all the programmed spaces with the correct areas?

- Does the plan include the required entries and exits based on the building code requirements?

- Have the corridors been sized to meet code requirements?

- Is there adequate space in corridors and activity areas to meet barrier-free codes?

- Does the plan meet all the adjacency requirements?

- Is there an efficient, direct circulation system, both in the primary circulation system as well as any secondary circulation paths?

- Have spaces requiring plumbing been located within the specified distance to the existing wet columns or plumbing lines?

- Are the rooms functional?

Draw the Final Plan

If the preliminary layout is satisfactory, it can now be refined and drawn in it's final form on the base sheet provided. Make any necessary adjustments to the sketch plan until the questions in the previous section can be successfully answered. The drawing may either be hardlined or drawn using freehand sketching techniques. Use whichever method is easiest and fastest. Remember that no extra points are given for a perfectly drafted plan, nor are points deducted for a very sketchy plan. The important thing is to communicate the design intent and show that all the problem requirements have been met. The drawing only needs to be legible.

At this point, doors, counters, toilet fixtures, kitchen equipment, and other items as required by the program can be precisely located. Before the final door locations are drawn, make sure the required maneuvering space on both the pull and push sides of the door at the latch jamb is shown. Additional items that must be shown on the plan include the following.

• Make sure all exit doors swing in the direction of travel.

• Be sure to draw the required grab bars in the rest rooms.

• Draw the 5 ft 0 in (1525) diameter circles in hallways where the direction changes and in the rest rooms.

• Show the upper cabinets in the kitchen and other areas where they are required.

• Note the partition types around the rooms stated on the wall type details page (or elsewhere in the program, if not on the details page). Be sure to include all the walls around the specified rooms, as the details may change. Be particularly careful to use partitions with water-resistant gypsum wallboard in wet areas like bathrooms, and to use full-height, insulated walls where acoustical separation is required. Fire-rated partitions may also be required in some instances.

• Make notes as required if things are not graphically clear on the drawing. This may include items such as microwave ovens, grab bars that are difficult to see on the drawing, overhead construction (such as skylights), and dishwashers.

TIPS FOR COMPLETING THE PRACTICUM

In addition to the suggestions in the previous section, consider the following tips.

• Develop the basic circulation plan first, and keep it simple. The exits and entrances on the base plan will determine the end points of circulation. Connect these in a way that gives enough space in one area for the residential portion of the problem, with the rest for the commercial portion. The residential portion will probably need to be more or less self-contained (like an apartment), so

splitting the space with a major public corridor will make it difficult to plan.

• Imagine that the size of every door is the minimum required width plus whatever the greatest dimension is for accessible clear space. For example, if the program requires a 3 ft 0 in door with 1 ft 0 in of space on the push side and 1 ft 6 in on the pull side, make jamb marks 4 ft 6 in apart. This is a quick way of noting enough room on any preliminary sketches before laying out furniture, fixtures, or cabinetry. Planning for every corridor to be a minimum of 5 ft 0 in on center is also a good way to initially block out enough space for accessible door openings and to provide for a 5 ft 0 in turning circle at changes in corridor direction. If a door opening is at the end of a corridor and the door swings in, there must be at least 1 ft 0 in on the push side of the door.

• If the program requires a related group of furniture items in a given room, quickly sketch what seems to be the most sensible and functional grouping, and then use the overall size of the grouping for planning purposes instead of the individual pieces. This helps to lay out plans faster without coming up short on space or proportion when the time comes to draw the individual pieces of furniture. For example, a list of furniture requiring a sofa, two lounge chairs, a coffee table, two end tables, and one side table may be planned as a block of space about 9 ft wide and 11 ft long.

• Know and memorize two standard toilet room layouts: one for a public toilet with a sink and toilet, and one for a residential bathroom with a toilet, sink, and either a tub or accessible shower. Have in mind some common minimum sizes so it is possible to quickly block out rectangles of minimum sizes that will later work for laying out the individual fixtures.

The following sample design practicum is similar to what candidates can expect on the NCIDQ exam. The size of the problem is slightly smaller in square footage, to work within the confines of this book format, and the problem description and background information are formatted to fit in this book instead of the 11" × 17" drawing format of the actual exam. Also, the dimensions are in customary U.S. units; the actual exam will have both customary U.S. and SI units. Candidates may order a sample practicum problem from NCIDQ that is printed in 11" × 17" format to match the actual exam.

Remember to be prepared for any configuration of problem. Regardless of the exact nature of the practicum, it will always involve work on a combination of residential and commercial spaces, and it will test the items listed at the beginning of this chapter.

PRACTICUM PART 1

Project Description

A new company is developing a facility to provide leasable space for computer and telecommunications equipment for internet service providers. The majority of space is devoted to computer equipment and emergency backup power supplies. The front office portion of the facility includes a small office space for sales and administration of the facility.

Because of the 24-hour nature of the facility, a service technician/manager must be available at all times to respond to emergency technical problems. This technician will live in an onsite apartment on the second floor that is acoustically separated from the rest of the administration space on the floor. The apartment will consist of a living/dining room area, kitchen, bedroom, bedroom closet, and coat closet. Primary access to this apartment will be by the elevator and main stairway off the first-floor lobby. The apartment must have access to the two secondary stairways leading to the first-floor equipment area and exits.

As project designer you are required to design approximately 3000 gross square feet of mixed-use space on the second floor, to include the administration offices and the apartment. You must produce a space plan and furniture fixture along with equipment layouts for the second floor of this facility.

The administrative offices will require a small reception area in addition to the other office areas. The reception area requires lounge seating for three visitors, a custom reception desk for one receptionist, a file cabinet, and a display case for the company's product brochures. The reception area must provide direct access to the elevator and main stairway. Visitors will access the conference room by the elevator and stairway. There should also be convenient access from the reception area to the work room, conference room, and visitor's toilet. The sales office should have immediate access to the reception area as well as to the conference room. The sales office should have convenient access to the visitors' toilet. The work room must have convenient access to the conference room, the copy room, and the visitors' toilet.

The apartment must be accessible from the circulation of the general office area, but does NOT require a separate entrance. However, the apartment entrance should be reasonably remote from the reception area.

Detailed requirements for each programmed area are listed in the matrix under Project Design Requirements.

Instructions to candidates:

• Review the project description and the project code requirements.

• Review the key plan (and exterior elevation on the actual test).

• Review the detailed project design requirements.

- Complete the adjacency matrix.

- Draw the project design solution.

- Complete the material and finish schedule.

- Review the wall type details.

- Indicate the wall type details on the project design solution floor plan.

Project Code Requirements

The following code requirements apply for this practicum examination only. Do not apply requirements of other model codes or specific jurisdictional codes with which you may be familiar. Your solution will be juried for compliance only with these code requirements. Develop your design solution for the total second floor space as necessary to satisfy these code requirements. The second floor is NOT sprinklered.

a. Two means of egress are required. Egress (exit) doors must open in the direction of exit travel.

b. Egress doors must be a minimum of 35 ft 0 in apart, measured along the interior path of travel.

c. All sleeping rooms must have an operable window or an exterior means of egress.

d. The paths of exit travel leading to an exit may NOT pass through a secondary space subject to closure by doors, storage materials, or other projections.

e. The MINIMUM interior corridor width must be 44 in.

f. All paths of travel must be barrier-free and provide a 5 ft 0 in turning circle (shown as a dotted line) at changes of travel direction. Turning into a room does NOT require a 5 ft turning circle.

g. You must consider the open dimension of storage elements such as closet

doors and file drawers if you choose to locate them along the interior path of travel. This open dimension may NOT restrict the minimum required clear width of the path of travel.

h. When open in any position, doors shall NOT project more than 7 in into the building corridor.

i. All doors shall be at LEAST 3 ft 0 in wide with a 1 ft 6 in clear space at the latch edge on the pull side of the door and a 1 ft 0 in clear space at the latch edge on the push side of the door.

j. All bathrooms and toilet rooms must be accessible (barrier-free) and have a 5 ft 0 in turning circle (shown as a dotted line). A door swing may encroach upon the turning circle a MAXIMUM of 12 in.

k. Bathroom and toilet room grab bars must be indicated, where required to provide accessibility, in appropriate locations on the plan. This includes two grab bars for a bathroom and three grab bars for an accessible shower.

l. Sinks in bathrooms and toilet rooms must have clear knee access.

m. Flooring in all public rest rooms must be slip-resistant.

n. Walls in toilet rooms must be impervious to moisture.

o. All plumbing fixtures, including sinks, must be located within 15 ft 0 in of the plumbing access line. The plumbing access line is indicated on the floor plan.

p. Exit corridors must be enclosed with one-hour rated partitions.

Key Plan

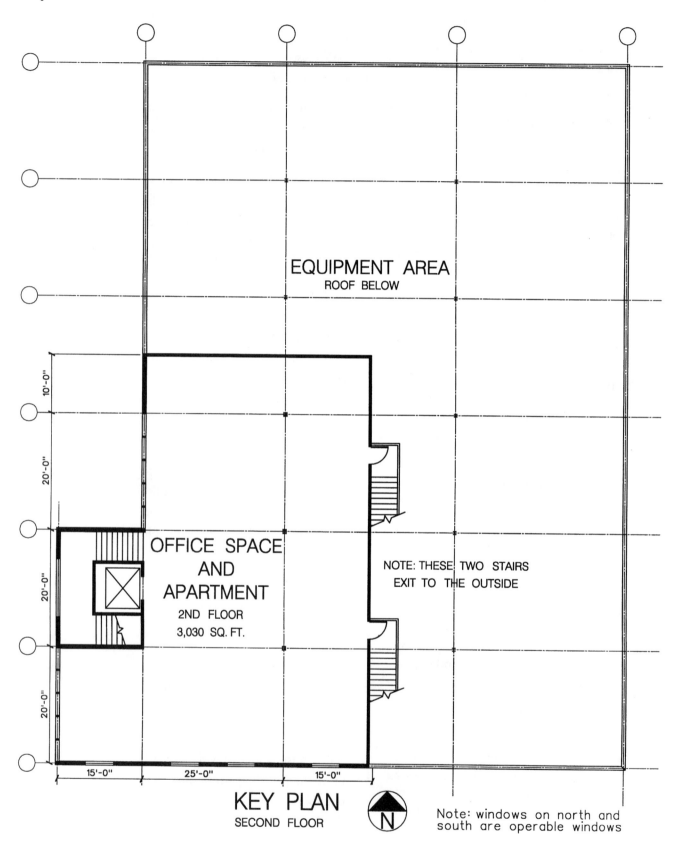

EQUIPMENT AREA
ROOF BELOW

OFFICE SPACE
AND
APARTMENT

2ND FLOOR
3,030 SQ. FT.

NOTE: THESE TWO STAIRS
EXIT TO THE OUTSIDE

10'-0"   20'-0"   20'-0"   20'-0"

15'-0"   25'-0"   15'-0"

KEY PLAN
SECOND FLOOR

N

Note: windows on north and
south are operable windows

Project Design Requirements

Instructions to candidates:

- All items listed below must be included in your design solution

- Consult the drawing instructions, found on the page prior to the project design solution sheet.

- Where items are not specifically listed below, you are NOT required to show FF&E.

room name	minimum area (ft²)	furnishings	dimensions, W × D × H (in)	notes
reception	350	three chairs	32 × 32 × 36	
		two end tables	24 × 24 × 18	
		two end lamps		
		custom built desk	30 in deep	min. 10 ft total
		one reception chair		
		one file cabinet	42 × 18 × 32	
		display cabinet	36 × 9 × 54	
sales office	200	desk	72 × 36 × 29	
		desk chair	24 × 26 × 42	
		credenza	72 × 18 × 29	
		two visitor's chairs	20 × 18 × 34	
		two lounge chairs	32 × 32 × 36	
		end table	24 × 24 × 18	
		book case	72 × 12 × 72	
conference room		table	36 × 84 × 29	
		six chairs	20 × 18 × 32	
		side table	18 × 24 × 18	
work room	175			
copy room	175			
break room		table	48 in diameter	
		four chairs	18 × 20 × 36	
		cabinets		min. 18 ft w/sink
		microwave	21 × 18 × 18	upper cabinet installation
storage	50			does not have to be in apt.
visitor's toilet		toilet, sink, grab bars		
living/dining	300			
kitchen		counter		min. 20 ft counter space
		cabinets		min. 15 ft upper cabs.
		refrigerator	36 × 30 × 75	
		sink	30 × 21 × 9	
		dishwasher	24 × 24 × 30	under counter installation
		oven with cooktop	36 × 24 × 36	
		microwave	30 × 21 × 18	over oven installation
apartment bath		toilet/sink		min. 4 ft counter
		tub/shower	60 × 36	
bedroom	225	queen size bed	60 × 80 × 26	
		two night tables	18 × 18 × 24	
		dresser	42 × 20 × 56	
		lounge chair	36 × 34 × 34	
		side table w/lamp	26 × 26 × 20	
		TV stand	20 × 32 × 30	
clothes closet				min. 10 ft of storage
coat closet				min. 3 ft of storage

Adjacency Matrix

Instructions to candidates:

- Do not mark in the shaded area.

- Using the project description, complete a correct adjacency matrix.

- Use circles as indicated for adjacencies requested.

- Not all rooms are included in the adjacency matrix.

ADJACENCY MATRIX ● direct/ primary adjacency ○ convenient/ secondary adjacency	1. reception	2. sales office	3. work room	4. conference	5. copy room	6. break room	7. visitor's toilet	8. storage	9. stairs
1. reception									
2. sales office									
3. work room									
4. conference									
5. copy room									
6. break room									
7. visitor's toilet									
8. storage									
9. stairs									

Wall Type Details

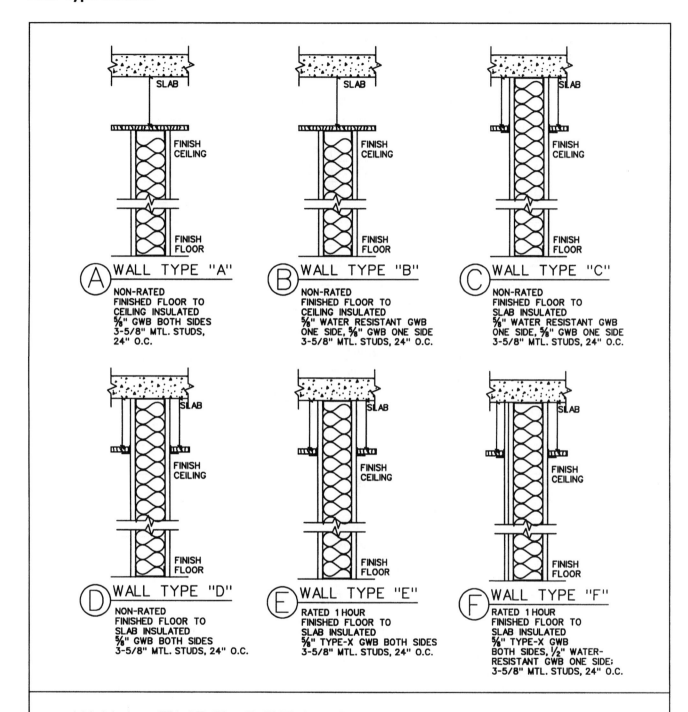

WALL TYPE "A"
NON-RATED
FINISHED FLOOR TO
CEILING INSULATED
⅝" GWB BOTH SIDES
3-5/8" MTL. STUDS,
24" O.C.

WALL TYPE "B"
NON-RATED
FINISHED FLOOR TO
CEILING INSULATED
⅝" WATER RESISTANT GWB
ONE SIDE, ⅝" GWB ONE SIDE
3-5/8" MTL. STUDS, 24" O.C.

WALL TYPE "C"
NON-RATED
FINISHED FLOOR TO
SLAB INSULATED
⅝" WATER RESISTANT GWB
ONE SIDE, ⅝" GWB ONE SIDE
3-5/8" MTL. STUDS, 24" O.C.

WALL TYPE "D"
NON-RATED
FINISHED FLOOR TO
SLAB INSULATED
⅝" GWB BOTH SIDES
3-5/8" MTL. STUDS, 24" O.C.

WALL TYPE "E"
RATED 1 HOUR
FINISHED FLOOR TO
SLAB INSULATED
⅝" TYPE-X GWB BOTH SIDES
3-5/8" MTL. STUDS, 24" O.C.

WALL TYPE "F"
RATED 1 HOUR
FINISHED FLOOR TO
SLAB INSULATED
⅝" TYPE-X GWB
BOTH SIDES, ½" WATER-
RESISTANT GWB ONE SIDE;
3-5/8" MTL. STUDS, 24" O.C.

WALL TYPE DETAILS
Instructions to candidates:
On the Project Design Solution (floor plan) indicate the
wall type for all walls in the visitor's toilet room and the bedroom.

Material and Finish Specifications

Instructions to candidates:

- Complete the material and finish schedule using the symbols given to indicate the most appropriate finish/material. Use ONLY the materials and symbols from the specifications below.

Material and Finish Specifications

symbol	flooring materials
F1	carpet, 32 oz. level loop, direct glue
F2	carpet, 50 oz. plush, installed over pad
F3	vinyl composition
F4	wood strip
F5	ceramic tile, glazed
F6	ceramic tile, slip resistant
F7	linoleum
F8	$^3/_8$ in parquet

symbol	wall materials
W1	paint, latex, eggshell
W2	paint, alkyd enamel, gloss
W3	vinyl wallcovering, Type II, Class A
W4	vinyl wallcovering, Type III, Class C
W5	wool fabric, stretched installation
W6	ceramic tile

symbol	ceiling materials
C1	acoustical tile
C2	gypsum wallboard
C3	suspended decorative wood grid
C4	linear strip metal; brass finish

Material and Finish Schedule

room	floor	walls	ceiling
reception			
visitor's toilet			
copy room			
kitchen			
bedroom			

Drawing Instructions

- Draw your solution either using a freehand sketch technique to scale or in drafted format.

- Draw and label all rooms, adhering to all adjacencies as described in the project design requirements and the adjacency matrix.

- Draw all walls, doors, door swings, and other components that are part of your design solution, adhering to all project code requirements.

- Draw all toilet room and bathroom fixtures and grab bars within the space.

- Draw and dimension the 5 ft 0 in accessible turning radius.

- Label all square footage and all lineal footage as noted in the project design requirements. Square footage and lineal footage must adhere to the project design requirements.

- Draw all furniture, fixtures, and equipment as noted on the project design requirements table.

- Label as required for clarity.

Project Design Solution

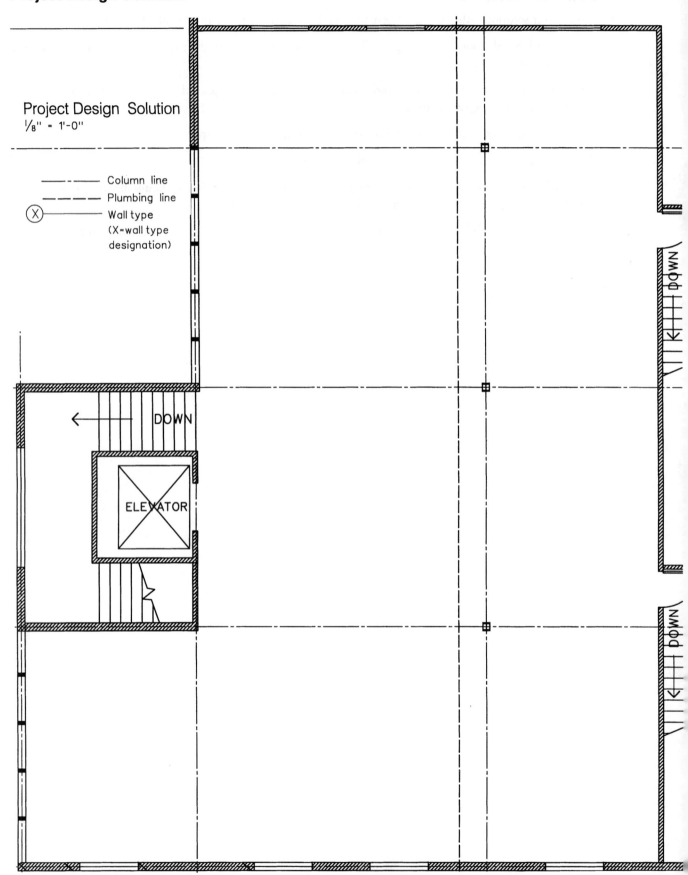

Project Design Solution
$\frac{1}{8}$" = 1'-0"

—·—·— Column line
—————— Plumbing line
(X)———— Wall type
       (X=wall type
       designation)

DOWN

DOWN

DOWN

ELEVATOR

PRACTICUM PART 2

Project Description

Due to the fast-growing nature of the facility, your client has decided to add additional reception space on the first floor to accommodate clients who need to work directly with the equipment in their leased space on the first floor. Based on the existing space plan, you also need to design an accessible reception desk, showing an elevation and section for the woodworker.

You also need to develop both a reflected ceiling plan with a lighting schedule and an electrical, voice, and date plan that will indicate the power, telephone, and data outlets for the equipment required. Power may be pulled from walls, floor, or ceiling. The floor is a concrete slab on grade.

Instructions to candidates:

- Review the project description and the floor plan.

- Review the equipment list.

- Create the electrical (power, data, and voice) plan.

- Create the elevations and section of the reception desk.

- Review the lighting required.

- Create a reflected ceiling plan.

- Complete a lighting schedule.

Base Plan

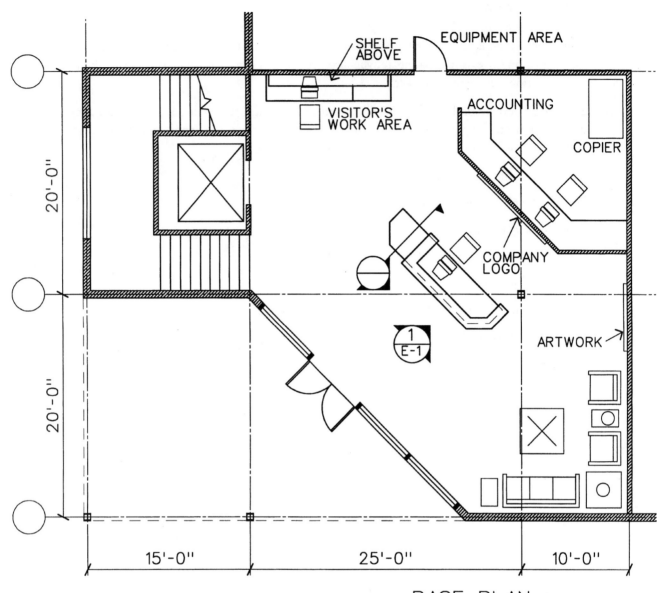

BASE PLAN
Project Design Solution
$\frac{1}{8}$" - 1'-0"

Electrical Legend and Equipment List

ELECTRICAL LEGEND

⊖ Duplex receptacle outlet

⊕ Quadruplex receptacle outlet

⊖GFI Duplex receptacle outlet with GFI

△ Special purpose receptacle outlet

◁ Telephone outlet

◀ Data outlet

◀ Data/telephone outlet

S Security card reader

C Clock hanger receptacle

⊖ Floor duplex receptacle outlet

◁ Floor telephone outlet

◀ Floor data outlet

△ Floor special purpose outlet

P Power pole

EQUIPMENT LIST

RECEPTION AREA

(1) computer with modem

(1) printer

(1) task light under reception desk counter

(1) telephone

(1) security card reader to equipment area

VISITOR'S AREA

(1) computer with modem

(1) telephone

WAITING AREA

(2) table lamps

(1) telephone

ACCOUNTING AREA

(2) computers with modems

(1) printer

(2) telephones

(2) desk lamps

(1) fax machine

(1) copier

ELECTRICAL LEGEND AND EQUIPMENT LIST

Electrical Plan

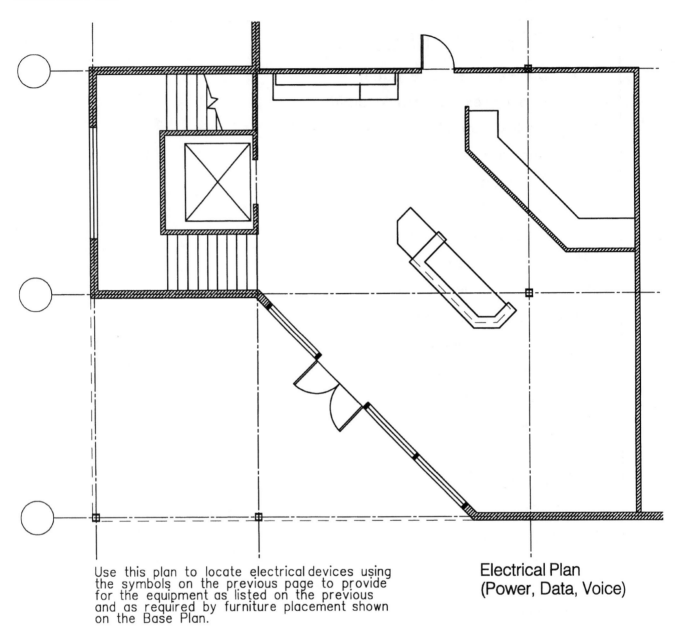

Use this plan to locate electrical devices using the symbols on the previous page to provide for the equipment as listed on the previous and as required by furniture placement shown on the Base Plan.

Electrical Plan
(Power, Data, Voice)

Elevation with Instructions

Instructions to Candidates
   Draw the elevation of the reception desk below.
   Refer to the elevation symbol on the Floor Plan.

   Indicate all dimensions.

   Label all finishes.

   The reception counter must be accessible for the disabled.

   Draw the elevation at $\frac{1}{2}$"=1'-0" scale.

ELEVATION   1-E1

Section with Instructions

Instructions to Candidates

Draw a section through the reception desk front
showing accessibility for the disabled.

Indicate the section with an appropriate symbol on the elevation.

Indicate dimensions for depth.

Indicate and label all materials and construction components
to adequately describe design intent to the woodworker.

Draw section at $\frac{1}{2}$" = 1'-0" scale.

SECTION

Reflected Ceiling Plan

The reception area requires a variety of lighting types. Provide ambient illumination with adequate light levels for reading. The reception area and desk require task lighting for the surface of the desk. The company name and logo are mounted on the wall behind the reception desk and require accent lighting. There is also a large work of art hung on the east wall that requires appropriate lighting. The accounting area requires general ambient illumination for the workers. The visitor's work area requires task illumination of the desk surface. Exit and emergency lighting must be placed in the space.

Instructions to candidates:

- Review the base plan and reflected ceiling plan.

- Complete the reflected ceiling plan and fixture schedule using the symbols on the reflected ceiling legend. Do NOT create your own symbols.

- Existing fire sprinklers and HVAC diffusers must NOT be moved.

- Place emergency and exit lighting.

- Draw a switching diagram for all light fixtures on the reflected ceiling plan.

- On the fixture schedule provided, explain how you have used ambient, task, and accent lighting in your solution.

- You do NOT have to show lighting or ceiling fixtures in the stairway.

Reflected Ceiling Legend

REFLECTED CEILING LEGEND

Lighting Symbols

Walls	Ceiling	
—○	○	Surface-mounted fixture, incandescent or compact fluorescent
	ⓡ	Recessed fixture, incandescent or compact fluorescent
—○$_{LV}$	○$_{LV}$	Surface-mounted fixture, low-voltage incandescent
	ⓡ$_{LV}$	Recessed fixture, low-voltage incandescent
	◗	Wall wash fixture, incandescent or compact fluorescent
	⊕	Pendant-mounted fixture, incandescent or compact fluorescent
	⊢○⊣	Track light fixture, incandescent or low-voltage incandescent
	▭	Surface-mounted or pendant-mounted fixture, fluorescent
	▭$_{R}$	Recessed fixture, fluorescent 2x4 or 2x2
	⌐○⌐	Under-cabinet fixture, incandescent or fluorescent
—○$_{E}$	○$_{E}$	Surface-mounted fixture on emergency power
—Ⓙ	Ⓙ	Junction box
—⊗	⊗	Exit sign
	S	Single pole switch
	S$_3$	3-way switch
	S$_4$	4-way switch
	S$_{DM}$	Dimmer switch
	S$_{LV}$	Low-voltage switch

Ceiling Symbols

⦿   Sprinkler head

⊠   HVAC ceiling diffuser

REFLECTED CEILING PLAN SYMBOLS

Reflected Ceiling Plan and Fixture Schedule

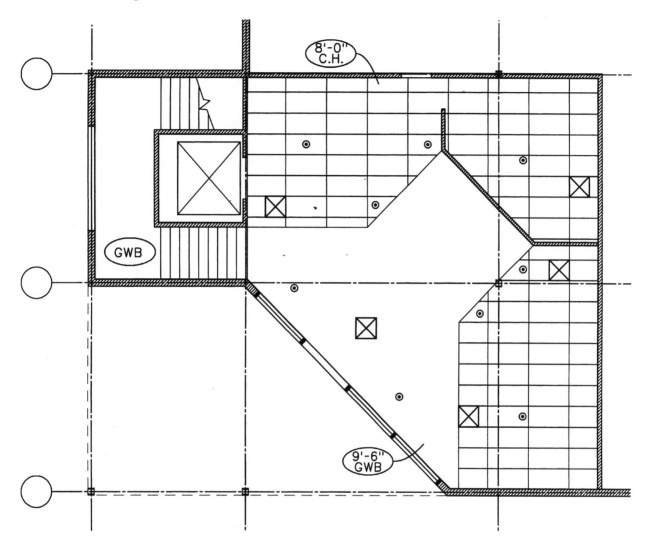

Reflected Ceiling Plan

Symbol	Concept Note (use 4-6 words to describe why the fixture was selected)

31 SOLUTIONS

1 INFORMATION GATHERING

1. *A is correct.*

All the options are important considerations for well-designed chairs, but because several people would be using the same chair for long periods of time, the chairs would have to be adjustable to accommodate variations in body size.

2. *C is correct.*

Option C is least important because glare on the screen is a function of the lighting design more than the workstation design. All the other options relate to items that could be controlled with the workstation design alone.

3. *B is correct.*

Identical furnishings organized around an imaginary (but perceived) line divide the room into two equal territories that each person could then personalize. Option A is incorrect because personal space relates to actual distance, and the question gives no information about the room's size or exactly how it is arranged.

4. *D is correct.*

Proxemics is the application of knowledge about personal space needs to actual space planning. Determining the design of seating where people will be close to each other is the most likely situation of the four options where proxemics would be used.

5. *B is correct.*

Social distance, including both the close and far phase, ranges from about 4 ft to 12 ft. Option C is incorrect because it includes only the far phase of social distance.

6. *C is correct.*

Because the question mentions an accessory and ease of use, a simple table fan would be the most logical suggestion to make. Creating air movement would increase evaporation from a person's skin, thereby cooling it.

7. *B is correct.*

Anthropometrics is primarily concerned with measuring the size of the human body and developing dimensional ranges within which certain percentages of a given population fall. Such raw data would be directly useful in comparing the height, depth, and other aspects of the benches with the percentages of children fitting those dimensions. The other options relate more to ergonomics, or the interaction of the human with the environment.

8. *A is correct.*

Options B and C directly relate to how much heat would be generated in the room and how much ventilation would be needed, both of which the mechanical engineer would have to design for. The reflected ceiling plan would tell the engineer what type of ceiling was planned and give an idea of the heat load generated by the lights. As long as the engineer knew the primary occupancy was elderly persons, the exact age is of little concern.

9. *C is correct.*

Tapestries served all four purposes listed, but the primary advantage was to decrease heat loss through radiation by covering the cold stone walls with an insulating material. This, in effect, raised the mean radiant temperature.

10. *C is correct.*

Of the four options listed, only the interior designer would have the best knowledge of the use of the conference room, which might suggest increasing the ventilation or providing extra exhaust. In the other three situations, the ventilation and exhaust requirements would be evident to the engineer and in most cases governed by the building code.

11. *C is correct.*

It is very likely that information concerning the other three questions would be available from a good, complete set of construction drawings. A field survey would be most necessary to determine what sources of noise exist and their magnitude.

12. *A is correct.*

Option B is incorrect because there are usually more design concepts than there are programmatic concepts. Option C is incorrect because a programmatic concept

is a performance requirement, not the other way around. Option D is incorrect because design concepts are based on and generated after programmatic concepts.

13. *B is correct.*

Options A, C, and D relate directly to decisions about the locations or sizes of elements in the store. If restrooms were provided at all (which they probably would be) they would be positioned away from the sales area whether or not they were available for customer use.

14. *D is correct.*

Because programming interviews consume so much time and often require two people to conduct, and because interviewees tend to talk more than is necessary, interviews are a very *inefficient*, although valuable, way to verify information.

15. *B is correct.*

Options C and D are important but would be issues considered after the overall feasibility of the project has been determined. Options A and B are very close to being the preferred response, but option A would require additional costs to the client even before the feasibility was determined. In addition, in a case like this, a client is not likely to have a good grasp of the costs required for remodeling and may not have enough of a budget to do the job as he wants to.

2 INFORMATION ANALYSIS AND PRESENTATION

1. *D is correct.*

Trade associations would be the least likely to have current information on a specific manufacturer's product. A manufacturer's website and a manufacturers' representative would have the most current information, followed by the manufacturer's catalog found in *Sweets Catalog.*

2. *D is correct.*

This is the standard BOMA (Building Owners and Managers Association) method of measuring lease space and one that is generally followed in the industry.

3. *B is correct.*

Although there are many building code requirements that the designer needs to start planning, of the options given, the number of exits and the maximum distance to exits would be critical for preliminary space layout. Option A is incorrect because neither the occupancy group nor the floor area would in themselves suggest how the space should be laid out. Option C is incorrect because glazing requirements would not be a critical element. Option D is incorrect because the details of corridor construction are not needed initially; only the corridor locations are needed.

4. *A is correct.*

In a call center, most of the work and transactions are conducted by telephone or electronically, so very few direct adjacencies are required. Even supervisors can monitor work electronically rather than being in or adjacent to other work spaces. In the other three building types, either materials or people must communicate directly so a direct, physical adjacency is necessary.

5. *B is correct.*

Regardless of how the information is collected, area is based on the actual space that a client needs to perform a function. This is the net area or the net assignable area. For example, a client would know that a 150 ft^2 office is required but would not give consideration to the corridor required to get to the space or the wall thickness needed to create the office. Based on the net area and knowledge of the project type, the programmer can estimate how much additional space is required for secondary circulation. The usable space can

then be used as a basis for calculating the rentable and, if necessary, the gross area.

6. *B is correct.*

The rentable area is calculated by multiplying the usable area by the rentable-usable ratio. The usable area includes the net assignable area plus allowance for circulation, so no increase for this is required.

$$A_{\text{rentable}} = A_{\text{usable}} \text{ (rentable-usable ratio)}$$
$$= (8000 \text{ ft}^2)(1.25)$$
$$= 10,000 \text{ ft}^2$$

7. *D is correct.*

In addition to designing the HVAC system, the mechanical engineer determines the best locations for controls such as thermostats. In cases where these locations interfere with other wall-mounted items, the interior designer can sometimes suggest minor modifications.

8. *D is correct.*

Although an executive summary is usually advisable in a formal, written programming report, it is not as necessary as the other three items, all of which are critical to define and present to the client.

9. *D is correct.*

The information listed in options A, B, and C could easily be determined by simple inspection. The adequacy of the air supply would have to be determined by a mechanical consultant, but the number of diffusers can easily be counted. Even water pressure for one additional sink could be verified by turning on a faucet. Option D relates to structural considerations and the feasibility of cutting through a loadbearing wall, which may not be obvious to an interior designer.

10. *B is correct.*

The space in a laundry workroom would be determined more by the size, number, and configuration of equipment than by the limited number of people who would operate the equipment. The other options all are highly dependent on the number of people that must be accommodated.

3 DEVELOPING AND PRESENTING DESIGN CONCEPTS

1. *A is correct.*
Environmental design research provides a scientifically studied view of how the environment affects human behavior and attitudes. Functional requirements, while usually rational, do not necessarily take into account the effects of a functional design on the users of the design. Gestalt psychology is a theory of perception rather than a study of the environment. Social influences, while an important consideration in design, are so varied that a totally rational approach to making design decisions could not be based on this factor alone.

2. *A is correct.*
Le Corbusier, Mies van der Rohe, and Walter Gropius were all part of the modern movement begun in Europe. Their designs were sparse and mechanical, with little detail. Of the designers listed, Frank Lloyd Wright's work was the most connected to human scale and nature, and used materials and detailing that most consider organic and humanistic. Although history is not specifically covered in the NCIDQ exam, there are questions that assume a knowledge of historic styles and significant names in the history of art, design, and architecture.

3. *D is correct.*
Closure is the tendency for people to view incomplete forms as complete, especially when the forms suggest a simple shape such as a circle or square. The seating arrangement shown in the diagram strongly suggests a circle.

4. *A is correct.*
For a formal, ceremonial space, the axial organization would focus attention on the altar in relationship to the nave, or seating area. Aligning the entry would also emphasize entry and procession, two elements that are important to most religions. A centralized plan could also be used, but this was not one of the options.

5. *A is correct.*
Because environmental design research typically only focuses on one variable at a time, it is often difficult to draw valid conclusions that may apply to any design situation.

6. *C is correct.*
By using the word *department*, the question implies that the company is large and will occupy a multistory building and thus will occupy multiple floors. To show overall departmental relationships (rather than individual space relationships), a stacking diagram is used. Then individual block diagrams or bubble diagrams are developed for each floor.

7. *A is correct.*
The answers given in options B and D are possible but would require that the designer make guesses and do a lot of work before the client would review the problem with the designer. Option C is risky because the adjacency that is problematic may turn out to be the most important one for the client, while the ones easily achieved may be unimportant to the client. Option A lets the client clarify the programming adjacencies and, if necessary, modify them so the designer can proceed with good information. If the client does want to see some sketches to prove that the required adjacencies cannot be made to work, these are already available from the initial work on the problem.

8. *B is correct.*

Option A is incorrect because, while the change in elevation would help define a space, the vertical perimeter of the raised platform would still need something to set the perimeter of the space. In addition, the platform and accompanying steps and ramp would not be as cost-effective as a gypsum wallboard partition. Option C is incorrect because doors provide transitions through partitions and do not define space. Option D is incorrect because transparency would minimize the space-defining element and a glazed wall would be more expensive than a simple gypsum wallboard partition.

9. *A is correct.*

The fireplace size (although important in final planning) is the most detailed aspect of the options and would probably least affect the overall design and feeling of the space.

10. *C is correct.*

In a manufacturing plant, goods travel from one station to another during the process of fabrication. A flow diagram would show both the adjacencies as well as the steps in the process of manufacturer. A bubble diagram would show the adjacencies but not necessarily the specific sequence of manufacturer. An adjacency matrix and stacking diagram would not adequately illustrate the relationships.

4 SPACE PLANNING

1. *D is correct.*

Layout D is the only one that satisfies both criteria. Layout C is also very efficient but not good for frequent visitor conferences because it would be difficult for the worker to get to his or her desk and the arrangement of the visitor chairs would make talking awkward.

2. *A is correct.*

A base plan shows the layout of the existing building and is always necessary before beginning an interior design space plan.

3. *B is correct.*

Although all the options would have some influence, the actual dimensions (which would include the existing structural columns and walls) would determine if the proposed restaurant would even fit within the space available. This would be the most important thing to determine before worrying about plumbing or reuse of millwork or lighting fixtures.

4. *D is correct.*

An atrium could be incorporated into any of the concepts listed, but it is most often used in a central scheme where most of the functions focus on the atrium and its activities.

5. *B is correct.*

A nurses' workstation requires much record keeping and temporary and long-term storage of a variety of items. Option B includes provisions for most of the elements that require a large amount of space, including patient files and movable carts. Option D is incorrect because communication equipment and electrical outlets alone do not contribute significantly to the space required for the nurse's station.

6. *A is correct.*

Because a waiting area is generally filled with strangers who prefer not to share the same sofa, a layout that provides individual seating is best, which eliminates options B and D. Option A is better than option C because it makes it easier for people to circulate to and from the chairs, and it minimizes the number of people facing each other if all chairs are occupied.

7.   *B is correct.*

This is an obvious option because the question relates to corridors, while option B is the only one that describes exiting from a room.

8.   *C is correct.*

Because a double-loaded corridor serves rooms on both sides of it in a straight line, this is the most efficient option. A radial system and grid system generally have a much higher proportion of corridor to space served than does a double-loaded system.

9.   *D is correct.*

Of the design strategies listed, the interior designer can typically only influence the surface finishes and reflectance of rooms. The other options are usually part of the building's architecture.

10.   *A is correct.*

Providing an area for the collection and storage of recyclables is a required condition before any points can be given for LEED™ credit. While the other options are desirable and each can be used to earn points, they are not required.

5   COMMUNICATION METHODS

1.   *B is correct.*

If just the top of the building is shown, it is a roof plan. If the surroundings are shown, it is a site plan.

2.   *A is correct.*

Option B refers to a plan oblique drawing. Option C refers to an orthographic drawing, while option D refers to a floor plan.

3.   *B is correct.*

Orthographic drawings assume the impossible situation that the viewer's eye is perpendicular to every point on an object at the same time, when in fact the viewer sees an object in perspective from only one point of view, even when standing directly in front of it.

4.   *D is correct.*

In a perspective drawing, SP indicates station point. Refer to Fig. 5.13.

5.   *C is correct.*

Even for laypersons, perspectives show the most realistic view of three-dimensional space on two-dimensional media.

6.   *B is correct.*

$3/32$" and $3/16$" scales should never be used because they are too close to $1/8$" and $1/4$" scales, which are used most commonly. At $3/16$", most people would assume the drawings were at $1/4$" scale, and possibly misread them.

7.   *C is correct.*

Magazines and other publications typically reduce original drawings to fit the format of the publication. Only a graphic scale would enlarge and reduce in the same proportion as the drawing.

8.   *D is correct.*

Using a perspective grid is a quick, fairly easy method for setting up an accurate perspective view. Plotting the perspective using standard methods is time consuming. A computer model could be used, but drawing the model accurately enough before a perspective view could be taken of it is equally time consuming. Creating a model would also take a significant amount of time.

9.   *B is correct.*

A full-size mockup of an actual material would be the best way to represent the material.

10.   *C is correct.*

An oblique drawing is one that has one of its planes parallel to the picture plane so an existing floor plan or elevation can be used as the starting point. The third dimension is then represented by project lines at any convenient angle. Option A is incorrect because a perspective is the most realistic view of an object. Option B is incorrect because one of the axes must be drawn at a different scale so the drawing does not look distorted. Option D is incorrect because foreshortened lines will still be distorted and foreshortened in an oblique view.

6 SELECTION OF MATERIALS, FINISHES, AND FURNISHINGS

1. *B is correct.*
Theater seating requires a fabric that is resilient, durable, and flame retardant. The only combination that meets these requirements is the wool/nylon blend.

2. *A is correct.*
A medical waiting area with high usage would benefit from a firmer cushion. Cotton batting and low-density polyurethane do not meet this requirement. Also, any material with a low ILD (indentation load deflection) implies a soft cushion.

3. *C is correct.*
Because institutional furniture takes much abuse and must last a long time, its durability is important. This suggests option C or D because quality can be considered a measure of durability. However, cost is usually an important factor in furniture selection for this type of client, so option C is the best.

4. *D is correct.*
Options B and D create the greatest hazard. However, welt cording provides the most likely condition where a cigarette could lodge and start a fire.

5. *B is correct.*
There are two ways of selecting the best option for this question. One of the most important tests for this application would

be for wearability. This includes the Wyzenbeek and Taber tests, so option A is eliminated. Because only one wearability test would probably be needed, this eliminates option C. An indentation load deflection test is for cushioning, and the question asks about the fabric only, so this eliminates option D.

Another way to view the question is to realize that wearability, flammability, and fading are three important standards for any custom-blended fabric in a public area. This leaves a choice between options A and B. Because they both include a fading test, the importance of wearability and flammability must be weighed. Any fabric can be flame-retardant treated, but only testing can determine if a custom fabric has sufficient wearability for a specific use, so option B is the better choice.

6. *A is correct.*
Of the possible choices, option A is the most correct because it implies that the amount of fuel would be reduced, regardless of the fabric material, whether or not it was fire-retardant treated, or what type of weave it had.

7. *B is correct.*
Although Class A fabric chars the least of the four classifications, it still does char but will not ignite.

8. *B is correct.*
Although chemical retardants and interliners are important considerations in upholstery flammability resistance, the combination of surface fabric and cushioning has the greatest affect.

9. *C is correct.*
Rayon is one of the least desirable fabrics in general and specifically has very poor resistance to fading from sunlight.

10. *D is correct.*

Because channeling is a method of attaching fabric to a cushion and direct attachment is the best way to avoid slippage, option D is the best choice.

11. *C is correct.*

This question refers to the Vertical Ignition Test or NFPA 701. The question may be presented as FR 701. The important thing is to recognize the 701 designation, Standard Methods of Fire Tests for Flame-Propagation of Textiles and Films, which establishes testing procedures for window treatments.

12. *B is correct.*

A fire-retardant (or flame-retardant) treated fabric may ignite, but it will not support burning. Note that the term fire retardant (or flame retardant) is used as an adjective.

13. *D is correct.*

For any environment, but especially a healthcare facility, volatile organic compound emissions should be limited, and these can be found in paint and many other materials. Option A is incorrect because if abrasion resistance were an important consideration, some material other than paint should be used. Option B is incorrect because for most areas of a hospital, chemical staining is not a problem. Option C is incorrect because paint is so thin that it is not regulated; rather, the substrate would need to be flame resistant.

14. *A is correct.*

ASTM is the American Society for Testing and Materials and is the organization that writes the majority of standards used in the United States. Although ASTM standards can be researched and purchased on the Internet, option B is too vague to be an accurate option. Option C is incorrect because the Construction Specifications Institute does not write or distribute standards. Option D is incorrect because

Sweets Catalog is a source of product data, not standards information.

15. *D is correct.*

Wool is the most fire resistant natural fiber. Cotton is the most flammable unless it is treated.

7 COORDINATION, BUDGETING, AND SCHEDULING

1. *A is correct.*

Because general contractors add their overhead and profit charges (anywhere from about 10% to 20%) to all subcontracted work, the client would be paying that much extra for the appliances without the general contractor doing much work for the extra cost. Option D is incorrect because the interior designer could get about the same discount for the client as the contractor could, without the contractor's markup.

2. *C is correct.*

The base cost of the partition is $45.00 times 350 feet or $15,750. To that you must add an additional 14%.

$$(\$15,750)(0.14) = \$2205$$
$$\$15,750 + \$2205 = \$17,955$$

For preliminary budgeting, amounts are often rounded off to the nearest ten or one hundred dollars. $17,950 is the closest to the figure so this is the correct option.

3. *C is correct.*

Because the two lowest bids are so close, it is likely that they represent a true indication of the cost for the restaurant as designed rather than an overbid. Although the client has the option of trying to get more money, it is generally the designer's responsibility to be within 10% of the expected bid. For this reason, the designer should offer to help the client redesign as necessary to reduce the cost.

4. *C is correct.*

Carpeting is a finish item (like paint or ceiling tile) that is attached to the construction and is typically part of the construction contract. Even though a sculpture is physically attached to the construction, it is commissioned directly with the artist and may be included in the FF&E budget. Vertical blinds are sometimes included in the construction contract but not as commonly as wall-to-wall carpeting is. Vending machines can also be part of a construction contract, but if there is both a construction and FF&E contract, they are usually part of FF&E. Although all four of the items mentioned may be part of either contract as the client wishes, the question asks which is *generally* not.

5. *B is correct.*

Option A is incorrect because cost books are dated by the time they are published. Option C is not the best choice because it does not account for current variations in prices or the unique nature of a particular job. Option D is a possibility, but given the choice between designers and contractors, the contractors are most likely to be the best source of data.

6. *B is correct.*

Refer to the text for a complete explanation of cost items. Option A is incorrect because it is missing professional fees. Option C is incorrect because it does not include furnishings, an obvious, major component of an interior project. Option D is incorrect because it is missing professional fees and telephone installation.

7. *D is correct.*

A quantity takeoff is the most detailed method, and therefore it is the most accurate.

8. *A is correct.*

Legal fees and specialty consulting like artwork advice are often separated from the construction and furnishing budget that the interior designer prepares. The items in the other three choices can be estimated by the interior designer (unlike legal fees) and are often placed in the designer's budget work.

9. *C is correct.*

A line item included in a budget to account for unknown conditions is called a contingency.

10. *B is correct.*

Because the furniture dealer and interior designer are the two people closest to the specification and ordering of furniture, option B is correct. Furniture manufacturers, general contractors, and clients are seldom, if ever, involved in budgeting furniture.

8 ELEMENTS OF DESIGN

1. *B is correct.*

Manipulating scale through the physical placement of walls, ceilings, and other architectural elements would be most likely to create the feeling of intimacy. The use of pattern, texture, and color, while important elements in setting a mood, can be neutralized if the physical size of the space is too great.

2. *C is correct.*

Because warm colors tend to advance and darker values tend to make objects look heavier, option C is the best choice, especially when the sofa is contrasted with a lighter background. Option B is the next most correct response, but there is no indication whether the sofa is a warm or cool hue. A warm color, as in option C, would tend to make the sofa appear heavier.

3. *D is correct.*

To accentuate the rough wall, you would want grazing light. Among the choices listed, point sources close to the wall such as recessed incandescents would do the job best. The other types of lighting would tend to flatten the surface.

4. *A is correct.*
This question obviously requires that you know what a Parsons' table looks like. It has a square or rectangular thick top with thick legs set flush with the edges of the top. Such a table is very volumetric but also has a planar quality.

5. *B is correct.*
Because highly saturated, complementary colors reinforce each other, the second combination would create the highest contrast and be the easiest to see for people of all ages. Option D would be the next closest option, but the description does not explain how the colors and white would be used. For example, a sign with yellow lettering on a white background would be very difficult to see.

6. *A is correct.*
Dark values tend to make surfaces "close in," as do heavy textures. The two in combination would lower the apparent ceiling height.

7. *C is correct.*
The Prang system (also known as the Brewster system) is simply the familiar color wheel with the primary and secondary colors organized in a circle. Option D is not correct because it states five principle hues (used in the Munsell system) rather than the three that the Prang system uses.

8. *D is correct.*
Although wallpaper can be used to show all the option choices listed, it is most commonly used for pattern because of the repetitive nature of wallpaper printing.

9. *D is correct.*
Option B and C are incorrect because they use colors that are widely separated around the color wheel. Option A is

incorrect because a monochromatic scheme uses only one hue with variations only in value and intensity.

10. *B is correct.*
As shown in Figure 8.10, as more black is added to a hue (color), the hue becomes a shade. A tone is created by adding gray.

9 PRINCIPLES OF DESIGN

1. *C is correct.*
All other things being equal, people tend to perceive the color, texture, shape, and other aspects of visual weight more than placement.

2. *B is correct.*
Option A relates more to balance and repetition. Option C describes the principle of emphasis. Option D is incorrect because harmony seeks to unify a composition rather than provide variation, even though variation is often part of a harmonious design.

3. *A is correct.*
Gradation is the gradual modification of some feature of a composition, which a series of color changes exemplifies. Option C is incorrect because repetition is the multiple use of an element.

4. *D is correct.*
By definition, bilateral symmetry is organized around only one axis so option A is incorrect. If the composition were asymmetrical the axes would probably not intersect in a common point, so option B is incorrect. Because a radial balance is a type of symmetrical balance, option C could be considered correct, but the question states that the three or more axes intersect in a common point, which makes it more likely that such a composition is radial.

5. *A is correct.*
Although all four options could emphasize the object, option A uses location, position, and lighting to focus attention on

the item. Option C is the next choice, but because the question does not specify what the item is, making an oversized model may distort its image.

6. *C is correct.*

Because the different table tops are related to each other by a common characteristic (the identical bases), this configuration best represents harmony. The symmetrical balance of the equally spaced and distributed tables represents a secondary principle that would probably not be as visible as the difference in table tops. Variety is incorrect because the table tops are closely related to the bases.

7. *A is correct.*

The golden proportion is a line divided such that the ratio of the smaller length is to the larger length as the larger length is to the whole.

8. *C is correct.*

LeCorbusier developed the Modular system.

9. *A is correct.*

Option B is incorrect because the question does not give any information about how the photographs are grouped and whether they form a regular pattern. Option C is incorrect because no single framed photograph would be different enough from the rest to create a significant contrast. Option D is incorrect because if all the frames are different, no single one dominates.

10. *D is correct.*

From the diagram there is no apparent size relationship among the different forms and no relationship to an object of known size, so options A and B are not good choices. Option C is incorrect because there is no repetition of a regular pattern even though the forms are all circles.

10 INTERIOR CONSTRUCTION

1. *A is correct.*

Option B is incorrect because a solid-core wood door in a steel frame could be used to meet the conditions. Option C is incorrect because a smoke-proof opening can be achieved with a wood door as well as with a hollow metal door. Option D is a possible choice, but minimal maintenance under heavy use does not necessarily imply a metal door.

2. *D is correct.*

A mortise lock offers a variety of locking functions and is durable enough for the heavy use of an office building. The other lock types could be used, but they are not the most appropriate.

3. *A is correct.*
Refer to Fig. 10.20.

4. *A is correct.*
Refer to Fig. 10.3.

5. *D is correct.*

Plenum access precludes the use of gypsum wallboard for the ceiling. Both integrated ceilings and linear metal strip ceilings provide for some access, but their cost in a large commercial project would not be warranted. An integrated ceiling may be a good choice, but the question does not give enough information about the parameters of the problem to make this a reasonable option.

6. *D is correct.*

Caulking or sealant seals the gap between butt glazing. A glazing bead cushions the glass against the frame. Glazing tape or putty cushions the glass against the frame. Setting blocks support the weight of the glass and separate it from the bottom frame.

7. *D is correct.*

Even in an interior environment, brass, bronze, and copper would most likely tarnish to some degree, while stainless steel would maintain its appearance.

8. *A is correct.*

In any situation that involves or might involve a structural question, an engineer or architect should be consulted.

9. *B is correct.*

The noise created by a door closer might be objectionable for the short time the door was closing, but it would have no effect on privacy once the door was closed.

10. *B is correct.*

A resilient channel allows the gypsum wallboard attached to it to "bounce" when sound strikes it and minimizes the transmission of sound through the wall.

11. *C is correct.*

A 2-hour rated stairway enclosure requires a $1^{1}/_{2}$-hour rated door.

12. *D is correct.*

Neither option B nor C is correct, because wire and float glass, which do not meet the requirements of either ANSI Z97.1 or 16 CFR Part 1201, are not considered safety glazing. Option A is also incorrect. Although there are some types of laminated ceramic glazing that meet the requirements, most are not considered safety glazing.

13. *B is correct.*

Although there are several ways to achieve a 1-hour rating, a single layer of $^{5}/_{8}$ in Type X wallboard is the easiest and least expensive. The size of the studs is not a critical variable. Two layers of $^{1}/_{2}$ in wallboard or the special $^{3}/_{4}$ in rated wallboard would work, but these are more than is required. $^{1}/_{2}$ in Type X wallboard can only achieve a 45-minute rating unless there is a veneer finish.

14. *B is correct.*

Building codes generally only require flame-spread classifications for wall finishes. Other types of woodwork such as bookshelves, cabinets, and door and window trim are not regulated.

15. *D is correct.*

Panic hardware is only required on exit doors where specifically called for by the building code, usually in occupancies such as schools and assembly areas. This may include a 1-hour rated door, but not necessarily.

11 ARCHITECTURAL WOODWORK

1. *C is correct.*

The majority of a cabinet is built with $^{3}/_{4}$ in (19) panels including the bottom, sides, and top bracing. The back is typically $^{1}/_{4}$ in (6), but this was not one of the options.

2. *A is correct.*

Flush construction is a style where the doors and drawers are installed flush with the face frame. This requires additional care in fabrication and subsequently increases the cost.

3. *C is correct.*

Composite wood veneer is an artificial product that uses readily available and fast-growing renewable trees to make veneers that are stained and reformed into an artificial log that is then sliced to produce new veneer. It is considered a sustainable or "green" product.

4. *D is correct.*

This is a drawing of a rabbet joint, which is one where a notch is cut out of the end of a piece of material. When a notch is cut somewhere between the ends of a material it is called a dado joint. Refer to Fig. 11.3 for an illustration of each joint type.

5. *B is correct.*

Although all the information listed in the options needs to be included, the most important is the clearance provided near the ceiling to allow the paneling to be installed. The installation of the panel is not really affected by the thickness of the wood cleat or the size of the base.

6. *C is correct.*

A scribe piece allows for field cutting so the edge of a cabinet or countertop can be trimmed to fit the irregularities of the wall exactly. A reveal can also be used to disguise the irregularities of the wall, but the question asks about a good fit, which implies direct contact between the cabinet and the existing construction. A reveal piece can also be a scribe piece, but the options include a scribe.

7. *B is correct.*

Refer to Fig. 11.2.

8. *B is correct.*

Of the options listed, only book matching and slip matching refer to the ways individual veneer pieces can be laid up next to each other. Of these two options, book matching is generally considered the preferred, most pleasing method. Balance matching and center matching refer to methods of applying veneers to panels.

9. *D is correct.*

Wood wall finishes of paneling or wainscoting are regulated in the same way as other wall and ceiling finishes. The minimum flame-spread rating depends on the occupancy and the location in the building.

10. *C is correct.*

Polyurethane and polyester are both very durable, synthetic finishes.

12 FINISHES

1. *A is correct.*

Type I vinyl wall covering is the lightest weight of the three types and is appropriate for residential use. There is no Type IV wall covering.

2. *C is correct.*

Both the Axminster and Wilton processes allow for complex patterns, but only the Wilton allows for varying pile heights.

3. *A is correct.*

The entry to a restaurant is a place that could be slippery due to spills or people tracking in snow, mud, or water, so a rough surface is best. A flamed-finish granite would have the roughest surface of the four options given.

4. *C is correct.*

Parquet flooring can be mastic-applied easily over most existing residential subfloors or finished floors or over a new subfloor. On a square-foot basis, the parquet would be least expensive considering both materials and installation.

5. *D is correct.*

Both nylon and polyester carpet over a cushion would be acceptable options for this application. Of the two remaining options, wool would be the least desirable because of its high cost, which could be substantial in a building with a large floor area, such as a hotel.

6. *A is correct.*

By definition, curtains are generally not intended to be opened.

7. *C is correct.*

Although the sheet material indicated in the drawing may help minimize squeaking, the fact that a wood floor is shown over a concrete floor should indicate that the material shown is a vapor barrier.

8. *A is correct.*

Because slate does not have a uniform thickness and a concrete subfloor above grade may deflect and cause cracking, the best installation is a thick-set method with a cleavage membrane. The thick-set method allows the tile setter to adjust the bed according to the exact thickness of each stone, and a cleavage membrane (with reinforcement) allows the finish floor to float above any slight deflection of the concrete floor.

9. *B is correct.*

Sheet vinyl minimizes the number of joints and is resistant to grease, oils, and water.

10. *B is correct.*

Pitch is the number of ends of surface yarn in a 27 in width. To convert this measurement to gauge (the spacing between stitches) divide 27 in into 216 stitches. This gives 8 stitches/in, or 8 surface yarns/in. The equivalent gauge is therefore $1/8$.

13 FINALIZING DESIGN DEVELOPMENT AND PRESENTATION TO THE CLIENT

1. *B is correct.*

The building owner sets standards and regulations regarding the type of building standard light fixtures, if any.

2. *D is correct.*

The tolerance of the gypsum wallboard used to build the niche would be of greatest concern because the cabinet would be built to very exact dimensions while the wallboard would be built to less exact standards. For a built-in cabinet, the fit would need to be tight and the interior designer would have to know the tolerance of wallboard construction in order to dimension the opening size and develop a method of fitting the millwork.

3. *C is correct.*

Lighting locations are shown on the interior designer's reflected ceiling plans. All of the other options listed would be on the electrical engineer's drawings or the security consultant's drawings.

4. *C is correct.*

Only broad planning issues related to barrier-free design need be made during the early design phases of programming and schematic design. While decisions about detailed items, like the locations of grab bars, can be made during the construction documents phase, it is better if accessibility research has been completed prior to beginning the construction drawings.

5. *A is correct.*

Although the correct selection of adhesive is important, the other three elements must be used correctly to prevent penetration of water to the substrates.

6. *C is correct.*

All manufacturers know the limitations of their products and should be consulted when one of their products is going to be used in a specific special situation that the interior designer knows about. Although the other sources may be consulted for additional information, only the manufacturer knows the limitations of a product.

7. *D is correct.*

Most particleboard contains formaldehyde and may contain other volatile organic compounds. The other options are incorrect because particleboard is readily available and strong enough for architectural woodwork details and other uses. Permeability, which is the ability to transfer moisture, is not a factor, because the particleboard would only be used as a substrate for other finishes.

8. *B is correct.*

A slip joint allows the floor above a partition to move without damaging the partition.

9. *C is correct.*

Ergonomic design would not be a criterion for a design of something that people did not come in direct contact with.

10. *D is correct.*

Although the cleaning agent manufacturer would possibly provide warnings about the health effects of its products, the most unbiased source is the material safety data sheet. The flooring manufacturer would only list the recommended cleaning agents and not be responsible for detailing potential hazards of the cleaning agent itself. The EPA would probably not have information about individual cleaning products; it would only have information about the base chemicals that would be a constituent part.

14 CONSTRUCTION DRAWINGS

1. *A is correct.*

The reflected ceiling plan should show slab-to-slab partitions as well as ceiling-high partitions. Although this information is usually indicated on wall-section details and sometimes on interior elevations, the reflected ceiling plan is the one place where it is all shown at once in an obvious manner.

2. *C is correct.*

Refer to Fig. 14.17.

3. *C is correct.*

The interior designer is ultimately responsible for coordinating the drawings of the various consultants.

4. *D is correct.*

An underfloor raceway system uses metal enclosures buried in the concrete floor slab. The selection would obviously involve the electrical consultant and the architect because this is part of the architectural work. The structural engineer would also be involved because the

size, spacing, and configuration of the system affects the thickness of the slab and its reinforcing.

5. *D is correct.*

Although the mechanical engineer designs and locates the ductwork along with the supply-air diffusers and return-air grilles, the portions of the mechanical system that are exposed on the ceiling, like the return-air grilles, should be shown on the interior design drawings.

6. *C is correct.*

The contractor is the person typically responsible for submitting the plans and specifications to the building department, along with the application for a permit.

7. *A is correct.*

This is a symbol for a three-way switch, which allows control from two locations. Refer to Fig. 14.19. A four-way switch allows control from three locations.

8. *C is correct.*

Because windows are part of the architectural work in a building, a window schedule would not be found on interior drawings.

9. *C is correct.*

Refer to Fig. 14.19.

10. *C is correct.*

Sometimes outlets are shown on the furniture plan and on the partition plan in small residential projects, but they would always be found on the power plan.

15 CONSTRUCTION SPECIFICATIONS

1. *A is correct.*

The first choice is the simplest and most reliable because it puts the entire burden of matching the existing finish on the contractor and painting subcontractor. They are the people most likely to have the knowledge and experience to make the match. Also, putting the notes on the drawings and specifications ensures that the general contractor would be responsible for correcting the finish if it did not match.

2. *D is correct.*

A base bid with approved equal specifically lists one product and requires that the interior designer has final approval before any other product is substituted. The other options leave the exact choice up to the contractor. Although a reference or performance specification could be written to make it very likely that the final product was acceptable, the base bid would ensure it.

3. *C is correct.*

The ceiling suspension main runners are a descriptive specification. The hangar wires are a reference standard specification. The runners are also a reference standard specification because the wording refers to the reference standards of the studs.

4. *C is correct.*

Part 3, Execution, is the portion of any standard specification section that always contains installation or application requirements.

5. *B is correct.*

The courts have held in many past cases that information in the specifications takes precedence over the other documents in the case of conflicts. This provision is often written into contracts.

6. *C is correct.*

The specifications should be outlined and begun while the drawings are being done. The specifications writer and the job captain should be in constant contact while both documents are being completed, to minimize conflicts.

7. *A is correct.*

The methods in options B and C are useful in writing concise specifications but are not as good as using industry standards, which eliminate a great deal of text. Option D is incorrect because a descriptive specification requires lengthy text to fully and accurately describe what the specifier wants.

8. *C is correct.*

Cost estimates are never placed in the project manual, because the project manual is used for bidding. Including a cost estimate would defeat the purpose of bidding.

9. *D is correct.*

A proprietary specification calls out one single item by brand name, manufacturer, and model number. With a proprietary specification, the interior designer can also require that a sample be submitted to further verify that the item meets the project needs, but this method alone is not the best way.

10. *B is correct.*

Option A is incorrect because both the interior designer and client must agree to the use of a contractor-selected product. Option C is incorrect because the alternate product must be reviewed and approved by the interior designer, not just the contractor. Option D is incorrect because the intent of the "or approved equal" language is to permit equal products, although sometimes the alternate does turn out to be better than the one specified.

16 FURNITURE AND FURNISHINGS DOCUMENTS AND PROCUREMENT

1. *C is correct.*

Consultant contract coordination should be done early in the project, prior to beginning the project or during schematic design. A code review should be performed during schematic design and design development. Shop drawing review is done during the contract administration phase.

2. *D is correct.*
A line chart lists the various products a representative handles.

3. *D is correct.*
The client must sign the sales agreement, which obligates the client to pay for the purchase of merchandise. The other documents are handled by the interior designer, dealership, or others.

4. *A is correct.*
ASTM D4157 is the Wyzenbeek abrasion resistance test and is only for fabrics, not construction of the chair itself. CAL 133 is the full seating test and is used for flammability testing. NFPA 701 is the vertical ignition test for the flammability of draperies or window treatments.

5. *B is correct.*
A drop ship order is simply a purchase order requesting that merchandise be delivered somewhere other than the address of the person or company ordering the merchandise.

6. *D is correct.*
Under Article 6 of AIA A275/ID, the owner is responsible for conducting an acceptance inspection, with the *assistance* of the architect or interior designer.

7. *C is correct.*
The furniture plan typically contains code numbers for each piece of furniture. The code number refers either to a schedule on the drawings or to the specifications where information such as manufacturer, model number, color, finish, and so on are listed.

8. *A is correct.*
A manufacturer issues an acknowledgment after receiving a purchase order.

Because the information on the purchase order is repeated, the designer can compare this with the original purchase order to make sure they match.

9. *A is correct.*
The most common method for showing clients an actual sample of furniture is to visit the nearest showroom. Because showrooms are open to the trade only, the designer must accompany the client. Option B is incorrect because the designer would probably have to accompany the client to a trade-only dealership. Option C is incorrect because a special trip would not be necessary and the manufacturer may not even have a sample of the sofa on display. Option D is incorrect because reps do not supply actual samples of large furniture items.

10. *B is correct.*
In this situation, the dealership(s) would most likely provide the ordering, delivery, and installation services, including the paperwork needed.

17 STRUCTURAL SYSTEMS

1. *B is correct.*
A flat plate concrete structure consists of just a slab of concrete and columns, making it possible to run ductwork in any direction and in any position (except for the column locations) without interference from any structure. An open-web steel joist system would be the second easiest of those listed because small ductwork can be run through the webs of the joists.

2. *D is correct.*
Live loads include the loads of people, furniture, snow, and equipment.

3. *A is correct.*
Movement joints for building expansion must be designed into the original building structure by the architect. The interior designer can design slip joints for floor

deflection, ceiling systems for seismic events, and slip joints for wind sway.

4. *A is correct.*

Option B is incorrect because an architect would have to do more than just sign the drawings; structural calculations would be necessary. Option C is incorrect because the interior designer is not qualified to determine what type of header is needed. Option D is incorrect because the opening can be made as long as it is engineered properly by a qualified professional

5. *B is correct.*

Standard residential wood house framing is 16 in (406) on center.

6. *D is correct.*

A post-tensioned concrete slab contains tendons under high tension. Normally, these tendons are located throughout the slab, which would make it very difficult, if not impossible, to drill a small hole through the structure. Concrete over steel decking has little or no reinforcement and is easy to core drill. A flat slab concrete slab has reinforcing, but that reinforcement can be located with X-raying, and cutting one reinforcing bar is not usually a problem. With a one-way pan joist system it is easy to locate the joists and drill through the thinner slab.

7. *C is correct.*

Option A is incorrect because a beam is used for structural framing and to span large openings. Option B is incorrect because a header refers to a lintel in wood frame construction. Option D is incorrect because a trimmer is a double thickness of wood framing around an opening running parallel to the direction of the joists.

8. *A is correct.*

An H-shaped symbol represents a column in plan or a beam in section.

9. *D is correct.*

Post-tensioned slabs could not be penetrated, because a stair opening would probably require cutting an area larger than the spacing of the post-tensioning cables. In addition, if one of the cables were severed, the slab could collapse. In the other types of slabs listed, the locations of reinforcing and beams could be easily determined, and those elements could be avoided or reinforced when cutting large or small openings.

10. *C is correct.*

Although all of these professionals may need to be consulted regarding book stacks, option C is the best choice. Because book stacks in libraries are very heavy, a structural engineer needs to determine if the existing floor is capable of supporting the weight. This would be the most important determining factor in early space planning and stack location. Issues of air supply, stack types, and sprinkler locations could be based on the final locations of stacks.

18 MECHANICAL AND ELECTRICAL SYSTEMS

1. *C is correct.*

A convector transfers heat from a hot water system to the air. A grille may control the distribution of air but has no provisions for controlling the volume of air. A duct simply directs the transfer of air from one point to another.

2. *A is correct.*

An all-air system can be subdivided into as many individually controlled areas as needed. Radiant panels could be used, but it would be awkward to locate them in the ceiling and the cost would be much higher than that of an all-air system.

3. *D is correct.*

Most building codes do not allow any combustible material in a return-air plenum (the space above the suspended ceiling). Electrical cable is allowed if it is enclosed in steel conduit.

4. *B is correct.*

The interior designer would not determine conduit size or put speaker locations on the power plan. This eliminates options C and D. Switch locations would be placed on the reflected ceiling plan.

5. *A is correct.*

Upright sprinklers disperse the water upward so coverage is provided above and below the suspended wood-slat ceiling.

6. *B is correct.*

The portion of stair identified is a tread. Refer to Fig. 18.6.

7. *A is correct.*

New window coverings can affect the exterior appearance of a building and the heat load, which affects the mechanical system. Also, they can put additional heat stress on the glass, causing cracking or breaking. Although light reflectance might be affected, it would be minor and probably not affect the overall light quality in the room.

8. *B is correct.*

The symbol shown indicates a suspended exit light. Refer to Fig. 18.9.

9. *C is correct.*

If space is at a premium and the floor-to-floor dimension is fixed, minimize the number of treads and the width of each one so the shortest possible total run is achieved. This can be accomplished by using an 8 in riser, which is allowed by code in this type of use. (It requires 16 risers 7 in high or 14 risers 8 in high to equal 9 ft 4 in. In turn, 16 risers require 15 treads while 14 risers require only 13 treads.) Because codes also allow a minimum 9 in tread in residential uses like this, an 8 in riser and 9 in tread is the best

combination (9 in times 13 treads requires a total run of only 9 ft 9 in).

10. *B is correct.*

Computer cable and electrical conduit are commonly placed in access floors, such as below computer rooms. Duct work is also allowed. Plumbing is not allowed because pipe breaks can cause problems.

11. *B is correct.*

In the space between a suspended ceiling and the structural floor above, fire-rated dividers are required if partitions do not extend through the plenum. Fire dampers are used in partitions and other fire-rated separations to allow fire-rated openings for duct work.

12. *A is correct.*

Card readers would be the most cost-effective solution because they could provide access control as well as notification if there was an attempt at unauthorized entry.

13. *B is correct.*

According to the UBC and other current codes, a series of two or more risers is a flight.

14. *A is correct.*
Refer to Fig. 18.9.

15. *D is correct.*

The interior designer would most likely be able to influence the design of sprinklers by coordinating with the mechanical or fire protection engineer during the construction documents phase of a project. For example, the interior designer could request that sprinklers be placed in certain positions or that additional sprinklers be installed. Compartmentation and smoke control are already designed by the architect and mechanical engineer in the original plans of the building, and there would be little the designer could do to change these elements. Fire detection is determined by the local building code and the type of building and occupancy, so little influence by the designer is possible.

16. *C is correct.*

Although all of the listed options *could* be modified to improve acoustic separation, a convector is the most troublesome and *must* be modified or it will allow sound to travel through the vents in one office, through the opening around the convector pipe, and out the vents in the adjacent office. See Fig. 18.2.

19 LIGHTING

1. *C is correct.*

Of the options given, the electrical engineer is responsible for designing the circuiting, panel box layout, and other technical aspects of a lighting layout. The interior designer may choose the types of fixtures, lamps, and light and switch locations, but a detailed drawing stamped by a licensed electrical engineer is required for submission to the building department. The one exception to this is on small projects, such as residences, where the electrical contractor can handle technical issues such as wire sizes, circuits, and the like and have the job approved and inspected by the building department. However, because the option choices included "electrical engineer," this is the better choice.

2. *D is correct.*

MR-16 lamps are the smallest of the choices given and could fit within the small area of a display case. They are also tungsten-halogen lamps, which give good color rendition and sparkle to jewelry.

3. *B is correct.*

G is the common indication for the lamp type indicated. Refer to Fig. 19.4.

4. *B is correct.*

Footlamberts describe brightness either reflected or transmitted from a source or surface, and account for the projected area (i.e., only the area that you see when looking at the source).

5. *A is correct.*

Any lights in the ceiling of a drafting room are reflected off plastic triangles, parallel bars, and similar instruments, causing veiling reflections.

6. *D is correct.*

Option A is not the best action because the illumination can easily be lowered below an acceptable level. Option B is a possibility and may ultimately be necessary, but other options should be explored first because the question asks what should be done to begin redesign. Option C is also a possibility, but the original design was developed for a reason and the first action should be to try to make that work. Option D allows everything but the lamps to be left unchanged. If this investigation did not bring the design within the budget, then the other options consistent with the design could be explored.

7. *C is correct.*

Metal-halide lamps are the best choice because they have a high efficacy (80 lm/W to 120 lm/W) and good color rendition. These two advantages would make metal-halide a better choice, even though mercury-vapor lamps have a longer life.

8. *B is correct.*

Although all the choices are possible reasons for using surface-mounted luminaires, the lighting fixtures are most often employed when space is inadequate for recessing.

9. *B is correct.*

In a fabric showroom, accurate color rendition is an important concern. Therefore options B and D are the most likely choices. Although the color temperature rating of a lamp gives a general indication of the lamp's "whiteness," the color rendering index (CRI) is a more accurate indication of how appropriate a lamp is for a specific application.

10. *A is correct.*
Any design with provided direct lighting, as in options B, C, and D might result in reflections off the screens. Because the question does not state that the video display terminals are in known locations, an ambient/task light system is best.

20 ACOUSTICS

1. *B is correct.*
Impact isolation class and sound transmission coefficient are both important ratings for evaluating transmission loss through a floor/ceiling assembly.

2. *B is correct.*
Because a change in intensity level of 3 dB is considered just perceptible, it would probably be better not to use the material, regardless of how low the added cost was. Trying to modify the material to 6 dB would also probably not be worth the trouble. If an STC rating of 6 dB or higher is needed, it would be better to look at another construction assembly instead of trying to make do with a modified material. Option D could be correct if the material was such that simply doubling it would result in a 6 dB increase rather than modifying it, but the question does not include enough information to make this determination.

3. *A is correct.*
Options B, C, and D are all important considerations in controlling both noise within a room and noise being transmitted from outside a room. A large ceiling might be useful for applying sound-absorbent material, but the size of the ceiling is already determined by the time design development begins.

4. *B is correct.*
The assembly shown would not be the best for controlling impact noise (because it is a partition) or mechanical vibration, so options A and D are incorrect. Although the partition construction shown would be good for preventing sound transmission in both directions, it would be *better* from room A to room B. This is because noise transmission between two rooms is dependent on the transmission loss of the wall, the area of the wall, and the absorption of the surfaces in the *receiving* room.

5. *C is correct.*
Refer to Table 20.2, which shows that any change above 5 dB is clearly noticeable.

6. *B is correct.*
The noise created by a door closer might be objectionable for the short time the door was closing, but it would have no affect on privacy once the door was closed.

7. *C is correct.*
For interior partitions, insulation is only good to dampen sound within the cavity of the partition.

8. *A is correct.*
Changing from wallboard to acoustic tile affects the total absorption of a room and thereby changes the reverberation time.

9. *B is correct.*
A vaulted ceiling would focus sound reflections into one concentrated area and produce annoying echoes or quiet spots in the hall.

10. *C is correct.*
Although placing absorptive materials on both sides of the wall would not hurt and would decrease the noise level in the "noisier" room, the three most important variables are the wall's transmission loss, stiffness (damping qualities), and area.

21 BIDDING AND NEGOTIATION OF CONTRACTS

1. *A is correct.*
Addenda must be sent to *all* the contractors bidding on a project.

2. *B is correct.*
The contractor should always request approval in writing so the interior designer can review the information about the tile and make a determination whether the specification was an "or equal." If the request is approved, the interior designer will issue an addendum to all contractors telling them that the new product was approved.

3. *D is correct.*
The best way to get the lowest price is to open the project for bidding, so this eliminates options B and C. Because the project is a specialized building type, it would be best to use only prequalified bidders who have had experience with data processing facilities. This leaves option D as the best choice.

4. *C is correct.*
Although most bid openings are open to anyone who wants to attend, the general contractors, owner, and interior designer are the parties commonly in attendance. On particularly large projects, the major subcontractors, such as mechanical and electrical, may also attend.

5. *C is correct.*
Of the options listed, prequalifying bidders would encourage competitive bidding while only allowing those bidders that the owner and interior designer thought were most qualified.

6. *D is correct.*
A labor and material payment bond is designed to pay subcontractors and vendors in case the general contractor defaults on his or her payments for labor and materials provided. When subcontractors or vendors are not paid for their work, they can file liens against the property. A performance bond provides money for completion of a project should the general contractor default, but it does not provide for payment of past-due bills on the original construction.

7. *B is correct.*
Because bond money is a fixed amount, the budget must be met, so this eliminates option A. Rebidding takes additional time and does not guarantee that the new bids will be any better; in fact, they may be higher because prices will probably increase in the time it takes to rebid. This eliminates option C. The designer may want to wait for direction from the city, but the project must go forward. The amounts of the bids are so close to the budget that is likely that costs could be reduced by 4% with some adjustments in the scope of the project.

8. *C is correct.*
For bidding, the procedure a contractor must follow to propose a substitution is in the instructions to bidders. After the contract is awarded, the specification requirements can be found in the General Requirements. The advertisement to bid simply states that bidding is being accepted for a particular project and gives information about how to submit a bid. There is no such document as "bidding procedures."

9. *A is correct.*
When the owner wants to make sure some amount of money is included in the bid before the exact amount of the item is known, the interior designer should use an allowance. Option B is incorrect because alternates are used to require the contractor to provide an alternate price for something that varies from the base bid. Option C is incorrect because a material bond is a

way to guarantee payment for materials by a bonding company. Option D is incorrect because a unit price is a way to obtain a price commitment from a contractor on a portion of work before the total quantity of the work is known.

10. *C is correct.*

The owner is ultimately responsible for deciding which contractor to award the contract to. The interior designer is generally involved but only assists with the process and gives advice.

22 CONSTRUCTION AND FF&E CONTRACTS

1. *B is correct.*

Although the bid form is often bound into the project manual along with the specifications, it is only a proposal and is not part of the contract documents.

2. *C is correct.*

Retainage is a percentage of each payment that is withheld by the owner and not paid until the contractor has completed the work.

3. *D is correct.*

The Uniform Commercial Code (UCC) assigns risks by allowing the factory and vendor to use "F.O.B. factory" or "F.O.B. destination" to determine at what point title is transferred and who is at risk for shipping damage.

4. *A is correct.*

Option A describes the standard procedure that is written into most general conditions, including the AIA General Conditions for the Contract for Furniture, Furnishings and Equipment. Option D is close to being correct, but the response does not specify whether or not the contractor notifies the designer in writing. In addition, although the contractor often suggests how to solve a problem, that is the designer's responsibility.

5. *C is correct.*

The General Conditions state that the interior designer may only recommend to the owner that the owner reject work.

6. *D is correct.*

As stated in the General Conditions of the Contract for Furniture, Furnishings and Equipment, the owner must provide vertical transportation necessary for the execution of the work.

7. *C is correct.*

The FF&E General Conditions state that the owner is responsible for both preliminary inspection of furniture and final acceptance.

8. *C is correct.*

The General Conditions of the Contract states that the owner has the right to perform work separate from the main construction contract.

9. *A is correct.*

The General Conditions clearly state the contractor may ask for such evidence.

10. *B is correct.*

All projects, no matter how small, should be completed under some form of written agreement, which options A, C, and D indicate.

23 PROJECT MANAGEMENT AND CONTRACT ADMINISTRATION

1. *D is correct.*

After a review by the mechanical engineer and interior designer, the shop drawings are returned to the general contractor, who reviews them again to see what comments the engineer and designer have made before returning them to the subcontractor.

2. *D is correct.*

The contractor should make sure that the necessary samples, shop drawings, and other required submittals are forwarded to the interior designer for review. Because the general contractor is responsible for coordinating the various trades and suppliers, he or she would be responsible for the mechanical shop drawings.

3. *A is correct.*

The contractor is solely responsible for job site safety, and if the interior designer told the contractor to correct an unsafe condition, the designer could be opening himself or herself to liability. The designer's duty would be to advise the owner in writing of what was observed. In addition, it would be expedient to point it out to the contractor to see why there were no barricades.

4. *B is correct.*

Although on small projects the project manager may organize drawing layout, this is usually the task of the job captain or whoever is in charge of preparing the drawings. The other three choices are more commonly activities of the project manager.

5. *A is correct.*

Option A is the most common method of processing applications for payment. The designer may certify an amount less than what is requested as long as a written explanation is attached. Applications for payment are sometimes returned to the contractor for revision, but this usually delays the normal payment schedule and keeps money from the contractor that he or she is entitled to.

6. *C is correct.*

The interior designer's review of the shop drawings is only for conformance to the general design intent of the job. The general contractor is responsible for coordinating the job, checking dimensions, and in general, building the job according to the contract documents.

7. *C is correct.*

Anything that requires a change in contract cost or time must be approved with a change order. A construction change authorization and minor work order are only for minor changes that do not require a change in contract cost or time.

8. *C is correct.*

Standard contract documents require that the owner provide adequate space for the receipt and staging of furniture, fixtures, and equipment. Option A is incorrect because the goods should already be adequately insured. Option B is incorrect because the owner inspects delivery of furniture only for the purpose of identifying and verifying quantities and checking for damage; the owner's approval does not constitute final acceptance. Option D is incorrect because the contractor should have adequately estimated the number of workers needed for installation.

9. *D is correct.*

Although the designer may use lessons learned from one job to the next, suggestions for improvement are generally not placed in a verbal or written post-occupancy evaluation.

10. *B is correct.*

The interior designer is responsible for designing the job according to governing building codes. The contractor often points out problem areas ahead of time, but he or she is under no obligation to do so.

24 INTERIOR DESIGN BUSINESS PRACTICES

1. *A is correct.*

The aged accounts receivable shows the time since each invoice was billed.

2. *D is correct.*

An interior designer is not responsible for the means and methods of construction beyond those given on the drawings and in the specifications. Advising the contractor on the exact methods of doing something may imply to the courts that the designer's responsibility extended beyond what the contract permits. This could give rise to a third-party claim.

3. *B is correct.*

Standard professional practice and ethical guidelines require that before taking on a job, an interior designer know that another design professional does not have any contractual relationships with the client.

4. *B is correct.*

According to the General Conditions of the Contract for Furniture, Furnishings and Equipment, the owner must carry property insurance to cover vandalism, loss by fire or theft, and similar causes. The contractor's insurance covers damages to the work, and the dealer's insurance does not cover furniture once it is at the site.

5. *B is correct.*

Because the question asks about founders in plural, this eliminates option A. Professional corporations and subchapter S corporations are entities in themselves and are managed by a board of directors, which may include only the founders, but overall, partnerships have the most complete, long-term control over a business founded by two or more people.

6. *A is correct.*

Indirect labor accounts for the largest percentage of overhead in a design firm. Option B is incorrect because capital expenses typically do not account for a large percentage of overhead costs and they can be deferred to a later time if necessary. Although reducing the percentage of profit is an often-used method to reduce fees, from the client's point of view profit should remain the same in order to maintain a viable business. Therefore, option C is not the best option. Option D is incorrect because salaries are already set and cutting an

employee's pay is generally not an option in a professional business.

7. *D is correct.*

A corporate identification package includes basic items such as stationery, business cards, and other items with the firm's name and address on them. A capabilities brochure is a basic tool to give to prospective clients and others, to briefly explain the firm and the type of jobs the firm does.

8. *B is correct.*

Trade sources are people who provide information and/or products to interior designers.

9. *A is correct.*

Although an interior designer may find it very difficult to find employees who would work without employer-provided health insurance, offering health insurance is not mandatory for operating a business. Workers' compensation is mandatory in all states. Even though general liability and automobile insurance may not be required by statute in every state, any business person would be foolish to be without it.

10. *D is correct.*

Errors and omissions insurance is carried by the design professional.

25 OWNER-DESIGNER AGREEMENTS

1. *D is correct.*

The Standard Form of Agreement for Interior Design Services, B171, clearly states that the client is responsible for providing all legal, accounting, and insurance counseling services necessary for the project.

2. *B is correct.*

Options B and C are the closest choices. However, only long-distance telephone calls directly related to a project are generally considered reimbursable. Models are also considered reimbursable if they are special presentation types and not just study models built for office design work.

3. *C is correct.*

This question requires knowledge of the word *tendered* as well as of the procedures for handling these types of changes. *Tender* is a term used in England and often in Canada that means the same as *to bid.* Making changes after a project has been bid can be a major problem, and the interior designer should be sure the client understands the implications of time delays and cost changes.

4. *B is correct.*

Option A is incorrect because post-occupancy evaluation is not considered a standard service. Option C is incorrect because financial feasibility studies are also not a standard service. Option D is incorrect because the owner is responsible for furniture acceptance under the Standard Form of Agreement even though the interior designer may view the furniture when it arrives and help direct the installation.

5. *B is correct.*

The contractor is responsible for all means and methods of construction and all safety concerns on the job site.

6. *B is correct.*

The interior designer is responsible for knowing the size of built-in items and for designing and detailing construction into which those items are placed.

7. *C is correct.*

A fixed fee requires that the interior designer perform the services listed in your contract for a set amount, regardless of any problems that may arise, caused by either the client or the designer.

8. *A is correct.*

The AIA/ASID standard owner-designer agreement clearly lists providing consultants, designing signage, and doing detailed surveys as extra services. Designing

and detailing custom built-in furniture is considered part of the millwork that the designer is responsible for.

9. *B is correct.*

If the budget in question is a construction budget, fees are generally not included. The other options all relate to the actual construction of the project.

10. *C is correct.*

Furnishings are bought through the purchase order process. Releasing funds for construction is done with an application and certificate for payment.

26 SUSTAINABLE DESIGN

1. *B is correct.*

Option A is incorrect because post-consumer materials are those that have served their intended use. Option C is incorrect because recycled products are finished materials or products that have been reused as they are or converted into another material. Option D is incorrect because renewable materials are those that can be grown or naturally replenished faster than humans can deplete them.

2. *B is correct.*

Bagasse (the residue from the processing of sugar cane) and rice straw are both alternative agricultural products that are made into panel products. Wheat straw is a little more common and is also used for straw particleboard.

3. *C is correct.*

Although ventilation rates vary depending on the use of the space, 15 cfm/person (8 L/s/person) is the lowest recommended by ASHRAE 62-2001.

4. *B is correct.*

In order to get LEED credit, an independent commissioning team that does not include anyone responsible for the project must be used. Even without seeking LEED credit, commissioning requires a joint effort of the mechanical engineer, the contractor, the electrical engineer, the building owner, and others.

5. *B is correct.*

A life-cycle assessment evaluates the environmental impact of using a particular material over its entire useful life, including disposal. It could be used to compare the impacts of two or more materials so the architect could select the most sustainable one.

Option A is incorrect because an EIS is used to evaluate the impact of a development on the environment. Option C is incorrect because an impact assessment is one phase of a life-cycle assessment. Option D is incorrect because there is no sustainability evaluation method by that name.

6. *A is correct.*

A building can receive a LEED credit for using a carpet system that meets or exceeds the requirements of the Carpet and Rug Institute's IAQ Carpet Testing Program. Such carpet may be on the Greenguard Registry™ or have a Green Seal label, but neither is sufficient for LEED credit. The SCAQMD sets standards for VOCs, but meeting their requirements is not sufficient for receiving LEED credit.

7. *C is correct.*

The Environmental Protection Agency (EPA) banned the spray application of asbestos-containing fireproofing and insulation materials in 1973.

8. *D is correct.*

Although it is sometimes done by a specialty contractor, radon detection and remediation can be done by anyone.

9. *D is correct.*

Options A and B are incorrect because Greenguard and Green Seal are both product rating systems. Greenguard certifies for acceptable emission levels while Green Seal certifies products that meet certain environmental standards. Option C is incorrect because ISO 14000 refers to the International Standards Organization's collection of standards and guidelines that relate to a variety of environmental standards, including labeling, life-cycle assessment, and others. ISO standards are used as a measure for performance of other organizations that certify products' other environmental claims. Only LEED certifies the entire building as it meets sustainability standards.

10. *A is correct.*

Although post-occupancy evaluations are good tools for verifying that earlier decisions regarding IAQ are being maintained, the other three options would be the best ways to establish air quality at the beginning of a project.

27 BUILDING CODES

1. *C is correct.*

The International Plumbing Code and similar model codes base toilet fixture requirements on the basic use or occupancy of the building.

2. *D is correct.*

ASTM E119 tests the entire assembly, not just the finish materials like ASTM E84 (also known as the Steiner tunnel test). The ASTM E119 test is best at evaluating any barrier, like a partition, that is intended to prevent the spread of fire.

3. *C is correct.*

The International Building Code refers to NFPA13 in detailing the requirements of sprinkler system design and installation. The other model codes refer to NFPA13 as well.

4. *A is correct.*

Refer to Table 27.3, which indicates that the most restrictive requirements for finish materials are in enclosed vertical exitway enclosures.

5. *C is correct.*

According to the IBC, exit access corridors must have a 1-hour rating.

6. *A is correct.*

As indicated in Table 27.3, building codes limit flammability of finishes based on the occupancy of the building and whether the finishes are in an exit or not. A sprinkler system may allow a reduction in one flame-spread class rating but is not the overriding variable. Flame-spread requirements are also independent of the rating of the assembly on which the finishes are placed.

7. *D is correct.*

Any rights not specifically reserved for the federal government by the United States Constitution revert to individual states. The states, in turn, can delegate control of construction to local jurisdictions. Only a few states have a state building code. In nearly all cases, the local or state code is based on the IBC or one of the model codes.

8. *B is correct.*

ASTM is the American Society for Testing and Materials and is one of the organizations that establish a wide variety of standards covering testing methods, products, definitions, and more. Although its committees develop test methods, it is not a testing laboratory.

9. *A is correct.*

This question implies that the design process cannot proceed without some basic data that the interior designer might not otherwise have about a building. The most important pieces of information are construction type, adjacent occupancies, and sprinkler condition. Construction type could affect the maximum area of the client's proposed use and how the designer would have to detail shaft walls and structural enclosures. Adjacent occupancy groups would affect what rating the designer felt would be needed between the client's space and the existing spaces.

Knowing whether or not a building was fully sprinklered would affect maximum allowable area, finishes, and other design and detailing decisions. Fire-zone classifications are generally irrelevant for interior design work. Accessibility requirements are necessary, but the requirements themselves do not relate to the building.

10. *C is correct.*

The Steiner tunnel test (ASTM E84) is used to measure the flammability of wall finishes and is the test most often required in building codes. The methenamine pill test is for carpet. The smoke density test does not measure flame spread, which is of vital importance. The vertical ignition test is for window coverings.

11. *D is correct.*

The most restrictive building type is Type I, while the least restrictive is Type V.

12. *A is correct.*

Only tempered and laminated glass are considered to be safety glazing, because they meet the requirements of 16 CFR 1201. Refer to Ch. 10 for information on glazing.

13. *C is correct.*

All carpet manufactured or sold in the United States is required to pass the pill test. The flooring radiant panel test is used for corridor flooring and types of flooring in only a few occupancies. The Steiner tunnel test can be used, but is not a realistic test on carpet because the material is tested on top of the tunnel.

14. *D is correct.*

By definition, a material that does not ignite or burn is considered noncombustible.

15. *C is correct.*

The only way to locate sprinklers such that the maximum spacing between heads is 15 ft (4570) and the maximum spacing from the walls is 7½ ft (2285) is to use four heads.

28 EXITING

1. *B is correct.*

The IBC limits dead-end corridors to 20 ft (6096) in unsprinklered buildings.

2. *B is correct.*

From the table, assembly areas including restaurants and bars have an occupant load of 15. Commercial kitchens have an occupant load of 200. Therefore,

$$\frac{3500 \text{ ft}^2}{15 \frac{\text{ft}^2}{\text{occupant}}} = 233 \text{ occupants}$$

$$\frac{1000 \text{ ft}^2}{200 \frac{\text{ft}^2}{\text{occupant}}} = 5 \text{ occupants}$$

$$\frac{1200 \text{ ft}^2}{15 \frac{\text{ft}^2}{\text{occupant}}} = 80 \text{ occupants}$$

total $\overline{318}$ occupants

3. *C is correct.*

Refer to Fig. 28.7. Option A describes a riser.

4. *C is correct.*

Options A, B, and D include doors that would provide less than a clear 32 in wide opening.

5. *D is correct.*

A 90,000 ft² building would be approximately 300 ft² or about 250 ft wide and 360 ft long. The size combined with typical rectangular planning of corridors would create very long distances to exits.

6. *B is correct.*

Smoke seals will be required, but the most important thing is that the glass doors will have to be replaced, either with solid, 20-minute rated doors or with 20-minute rated doors with glass that is also 20-minute rated. Because this will significantly change the appearance of the existing entry, it is the first thing the client should be told to expect. Either pivoted floor closers or hinges may be used as long as they are also fire-rated and the door is side-swinging.

7. *B is correct.*

Closers are always required with fire-rated door assemblies (protected openings).

8. *C is correct.*

Under the UBC, any stair 44 in or wider requires handrails on both sides.

9. *A is correct.*

Exits may never pass through kitchens.

10. *D is correct.*

The occupancy and occupant load are used to determine the number of exits. See Fig. 28.3.

11. *C is correct.*

Normally, the three parts are identified as they go from the least protected to the most protected: exit access, exit, and exit discharge.

12. *A is correct.*

Exits are not limited in length (because they are protected), can be something as simple as a door, and are usually required in buildings with sprinklers.

13. *B is correct.*

As shown in Fig. 28.3, the two most important variables are the use of the space (occupancy) and the number of people that must exit the space (occupant load). This is similar to question 10.

14. *C is correct.*

The primary consideration for travel distance is whether or not the building is sprinklered. Then the codes may decrease the distance for certain occupancies.

15. *A is correct.*

The main thing to remember is that corridors are part of the exit access. This means that they are used for calculating travel distance, but they do not necessarily have to be fire-rated (although they usually are). Also, by definition they must be used exclusively for egress.

29 BARRIER-FREE DESIGN

1. *B is correct.*

The minimum clear width for a door is 32 in (815). Refer to Fig. 29.4.

2. *C is correct.*

The solution that is least expensive and most sensitive to accessibility requirements is to provide a power-assisted door opener.

3. *D is correct.*

As measured from the nosing, a handrail for barrier-free design must be 34 in to 38 in (865 to 965) high.

4. *A is correct.*

Barrier-free design requires that objects do not protrude into the accessible path in such a way as to present a hazard. See Fig. 29.18. In addition, tactile signs must have a minimum $1/32$ in raised surface, and accessible routes must not be reduced in width.

5. *C is correct.*

All the sink installations listed as possible options can work if they meet the measurement requirements shown in Fig. 29.10, but a wall-hung lavatory gives the most open access, usually exceeding the minimum requirements.

6. *D is correct.*

The size of accessible stalls, whether standard, end, or row type, is more or less fixed. Factors that could affect the total space required would be use of an in-swing door (which adds to the area required) and whether the design uses a side or front approach (latch side takes the least room). See Fig. 29.7. Grab bar locations and the toilet position relative to the stall are fixed and would not be of initial concern.

7. *A is correct.*

Emergency warning systems must provide both visual and audible alarms.

8. *A is correct.*

An accessible route must serve all accessible spaces and parts of a building.

9. *C is correct.*

Looking at the required maneuvering clearances shown in Fig. 29.5, it is clear that the side approach with the door swinging into the room only requires a minimum of 42 in (1065) (assuming the door has no closer). This would allow the use of a 44 in (1118) minimum corridor. The front approach (door swings into room) and latch side approach (door swings into corridor) both require a minimum of 48 in (1220). The front approach (door swings into corridor) would require a 60 in (1525) corridor (a 36 in door plus 24 in of side clearance (915 plus 610)).

10. *B is correct.*

Scoping provisions tell the designer how much of something is required. Although there are scoping provisions in the ADA, local codes may be more stringent, in which case the interior designer must conform to the more restrictive requirements.

ANSI A117.1 may or may not be applicable in a given jurisdiction. If it has been adopted by the local building code, it is important to review to see if the requirements are more restrictive than those of the ADA. The latest edition of A117.1 leaves scoping up to local jurisdiction. ADAAG is the ADA Accessibility Guidelines and is part of the ADA, so this option is irrelevant. The Uniform Federal Accessibility Standards are applicable to federal buildings and projects that receive federal funding and would not be used for a commercial project.

30 SAMPLE DESIGN PRACTICUM

Part 1

This practicum requires a tightly planned solution because there is not much area to work with. An analysis of the program indicates there are few direct adjacency relationships required as shown in the completed adjacency matrix in Fig. 31.1.

Before attempting to lay out the spaces, add up the required area estimated for the residential spaces to see if there are any large blocks or logical areas in the base plan that could be used for the apartment. In this sample design practicum, minimum areas are given for the living room and bedroom. Estimate that about 100 ft^2 will be needed for an accessible bathroom and about 200 ft^2 will be needed for a kitchen to meet the counter space and equipment requirements. The closets will add about another 25 ft^2 (a 2 ft depth times a 13 ft length). This total gives about 850 ft^2. Add an allowance of 25% for circulation and wall thickness (210 ft^2), for a total of about 1062 ft^2 required for the apartment. The first structural bay at the south part of the space is 20 ft wide and 55 ft deep, for a total of approximately 1100 ft^2. This suggests that the south part should be used for the apartment.

Because the reception area must be directly adjacent to the main stairs (and elevator), the area adjacent to the elevator can be blocked out for this use. The column locations suggest one wall of a corridor, and by connecting the two back exit stairways, most of the plan becomes blocked out. Because there are no windows between the two stairways, the only logical options for spaces in this area are the copy room, break room, storage room, and visitor's toilet. One solution to this approach is shown in Fig. 31.2.

Figure 31.1 Completed Adjacency Matrix

ADJACENCY MATRIX

● direct/ primary adjacency

○ convenient/ secondary adjacency

	1. reception	2. sales office	3. work room	4. conference	5. copy room	6. break room	7. visitor's toilet	8. storage	9. stairs
1. reception									
2. sales office	●								
3. work room	○	○							
4. conference	○	●	○						
5. copy room			○						
6. break room									
7. visitor's toilet	○	○	○						
8. storage									
9. stairs	●			○					

This solution satisfies nearly all the requirements of the program. All the adjacencies are met, the spaces are labeled, and all required furniture and equipment is drawn in to the right scale. Appropriate wall types are indicated in the required areas. The only problems are that the apartment coat closet is a little short and there is not quite enough counter space for the vanity in the apartment bathroom.

The apartment could also be located in the north part of the space, but this would

Figure 31.2
Project Design
Solution

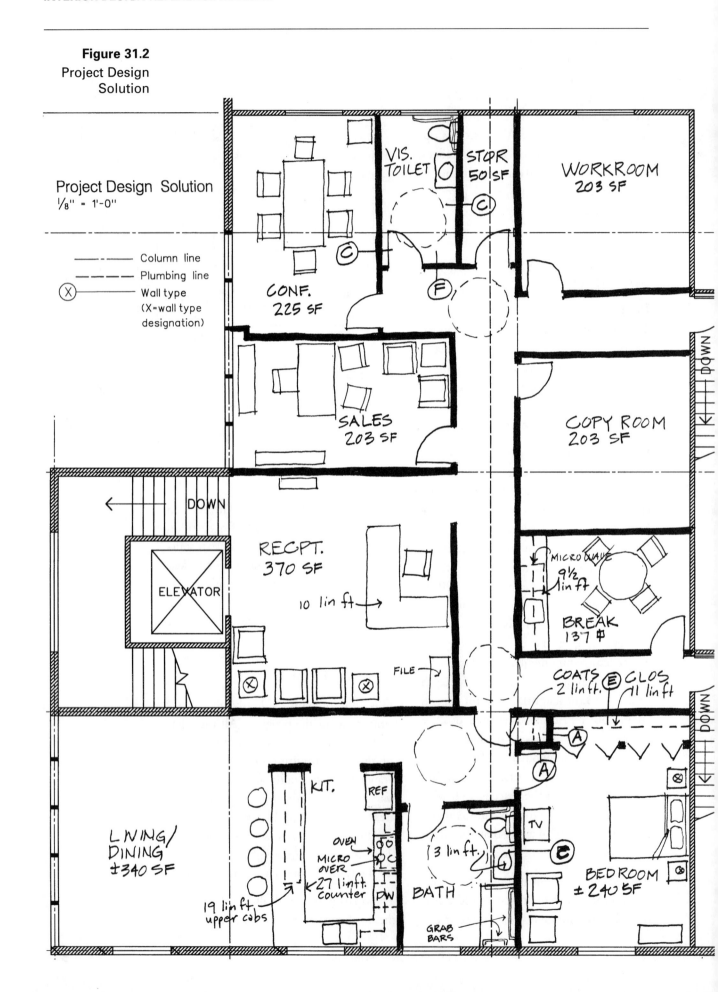

Project Design Solution
1/8" = 1'-0"

Column line
Plumbing line
Wall type
(X=wall type
designation)

VIS.
TOILET

STOR
50 SF

WORKROOM
203 SF

CONF.
225 SF

SALES
203 SF

COPY ROOM
203 SF

DOWN

RECPT.
370 SF

10 lin ft

MICROWAVE
9½ lin ft

BREAK
137 ♯

ELEVATOR

FILE

COATS
2 lin ft

CLOS
11 lin ft

DOWN

KIT.

REF

TV

LIVING/
DINING
±340 SF

OVEN

MICRO
OVER

27 lin ft
counter

19 lin ft
upper cabs

DW

BATH

3 lin ft

BEDROOM
±240 SF

GRAB
BARS

require that the apartment plan be an L-shape to fit in all the required spaces. The reception area must still be next to the stairway, and the elevator and two exits must still connect. An alternate plan using this approach is shown in Fig. 31.3.

Although this plan generally works, there are some specific problems that could cause it to fail.

• The apartment bathroom lacks enough space on the pull side of the door latch.

• No 5 ft 0 in diameter turning circle is indicated in the apartment bathroom, and there is not adequate space for such a circle.

• No grab bars are shown around the toilet in the apartment bathroom.

• Access to the bathroom shower is partially blocked by the sink.

• The apartment bedroom is undersized, and the layout as shown is crowded.

• There is insufficient space on the pull side of the bedroom door.

• There is no indication of a microwave in the break room.

• The 73 in high bookcase in the sales office is placed in front of the window, blocking the view and light.

• Although a credenza is shown in the reception area, it is not clear if this is part of the desk counter space required by the program.

• Linear footages are missing, and some square foot listings are missing.

The material and finish schedule shown in Fig. 31.4 includes finishes appropriately selected for the rooms listed.

Note that several finish selections would be appropriate for the various rooms, so there is no one correct resonse to the material and finish schedule.

Part 2

The sample solutions for Part 2 illustrate the various parts that satisfy the problem requirements. The electrical plan shown in Fig. 31.5 indicates the required power, telephone, and data outlets as well as the security card reader. It is important to indicate the heights of the outlets and other controls because many are above built-in countertops. Be sure to include quadraplex outlets or multiple duplex outlets when several electrical devices will be used.

The elevation and section shown in Fig. 31.6 and 31.7 illustrate a simple but workable design based on the reception desk shown in the base plan. In addition to showing correct woodwork construction, it is important to indicate how the item being designed and detailed is accessible for the physically disabled. Be sure to include all necessary dimensions and call out the materials.

The reflected ceiling plan shown in Fig. 31.8 indicates all lighting that may be required and includes a completed schedule briefly indicating why each fixture type was used. Exit lights are shown along with most switching. However, switching for the wallwash units is not shown.

Figure 31.3
Alternate Project
Design Soution

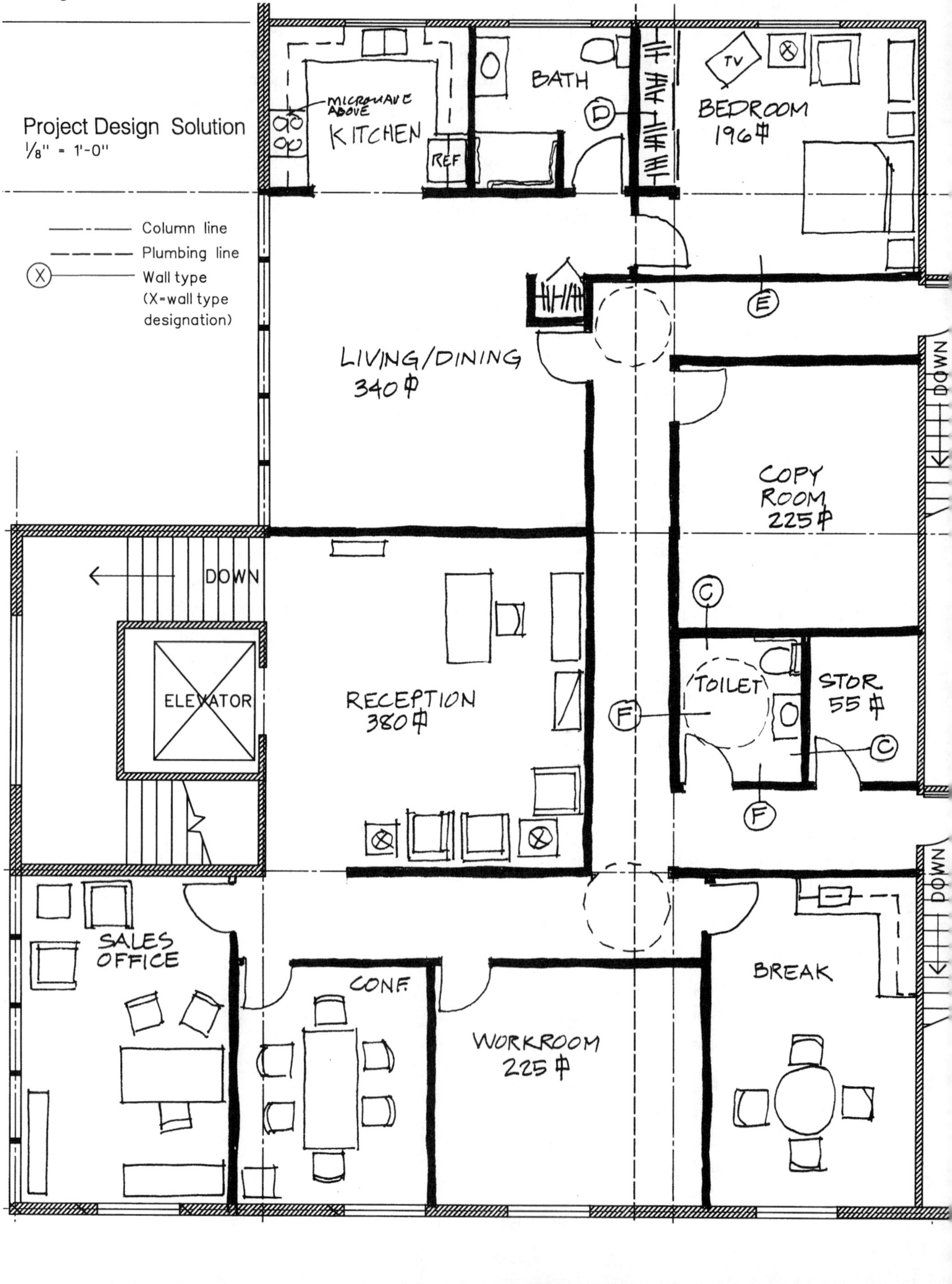

Project Design Solution
1/8" = 1'-0"

—·—·— Column line
———— Plumbing line
Ⓧ Wall type
(X=wall type designation)

KITCHEN

MICROWAVE ABOVE

REF

BATH

Ⓓ

BEDROOM 196 Φ

TV Ⓧ

Ⓔ

LIVING/DINING 340 Φ

COPY ROOM 225 Φ

DOWN

Ⓒ

DOWN

ELEVATOR

RECEPTION 380 Φ

Ⓕ

TOILET

STOR 55 Φ

Ⓒ

Ⓕ

SALES OFFICE

CONF.

WORKROOM 225 Φ

BREAK

DOWN

Material and Finish Schedule

room	floor	walls	ceiling
reception	F1	W3	C1
visitor's toilet	F6	W6	C2
copy room	F1	W1	C1
kitchen	F7	W2	C2
bedroom	F1	W1	C2

Figure 31.4
Material and
Finish Schedule

Figure 31.5
Electrical Plan

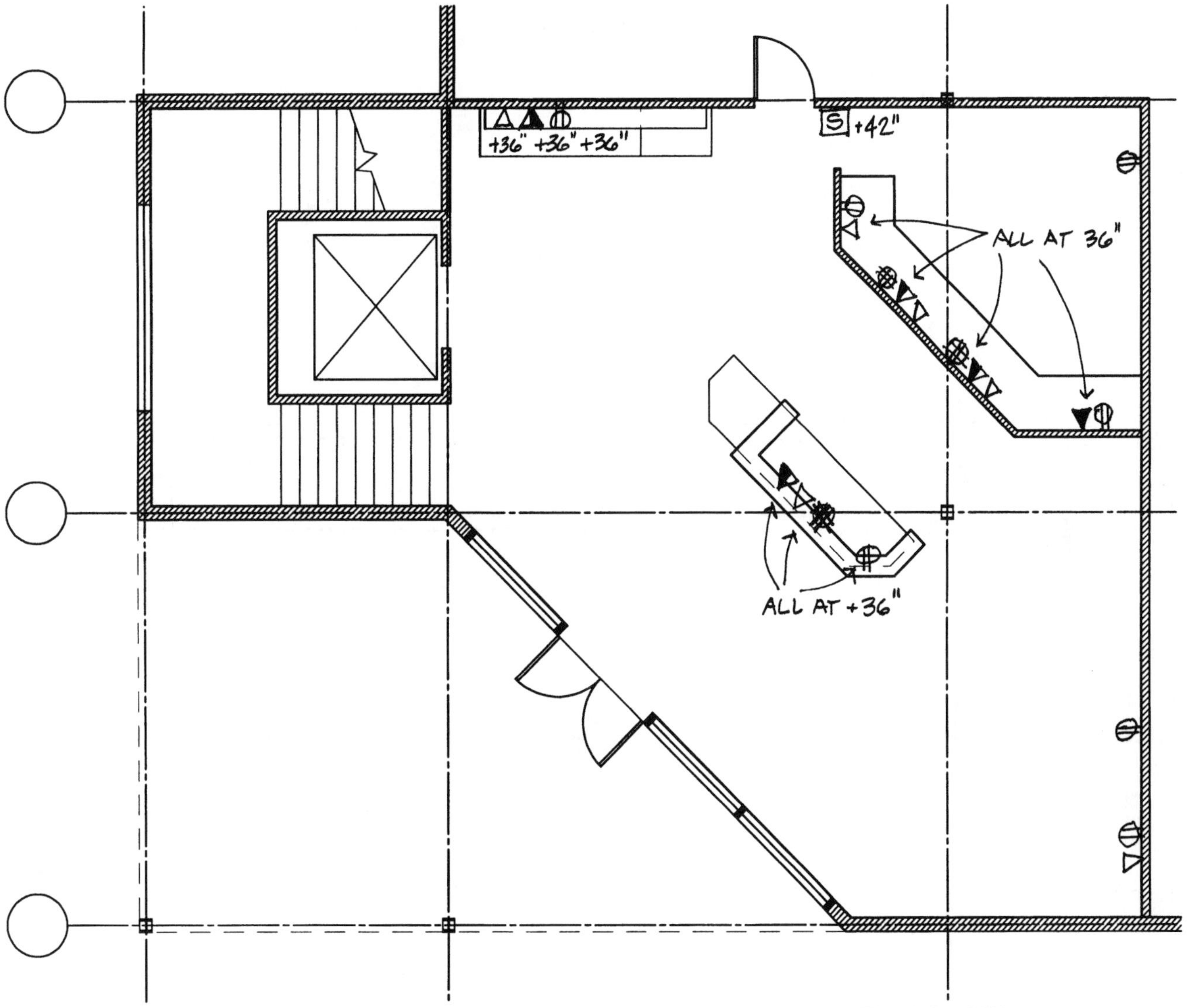

+36" +36" +36"

S +42"

ALL AT 36"

ALL AT +36"

Use this plan to locate electrical devices using the symbols on the previous page to provide for the equipment as listed on the previous and as required by furniture placement shown on the Base Plan.

Electrical Plan
(Power, Data, Voice)

Figure 31.6
Reception Desk
Elevation

Instructions to Candidates

Draw the elevation of the reception desk below.
Refer to the elevation symbol on the Floor Plan.

Indicate all dimensions.

Label all finishes.

The reception counter MUST be accessible for the disabled.

Draw the elevation at ½"=1'-0" scale.

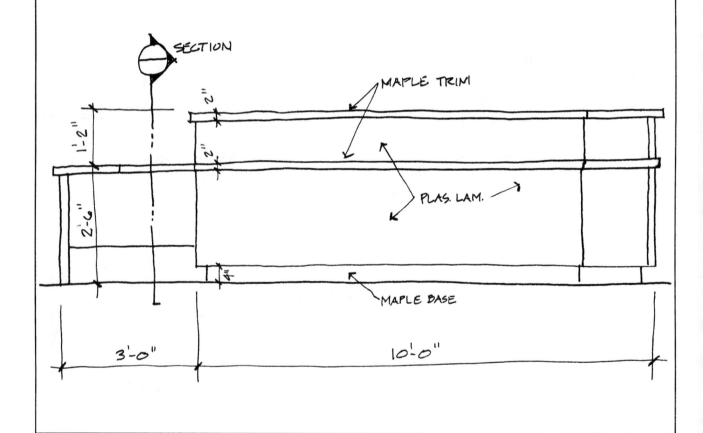

ELEVATION   1-E1

Figure 31.7
Reception Desk
Section

Instructions to Candidates

Draw a section through the reception desk front
showing accessibility for the disabled.

Indicate the section with an appropriate symbol on the elevation.

Indicate dimensions for depth.

Indicate and label all materials and construction components
to adequately describe design intent to the woodworker.

Draw section at $\frac{1}{2}$" = 1'-0" scale.

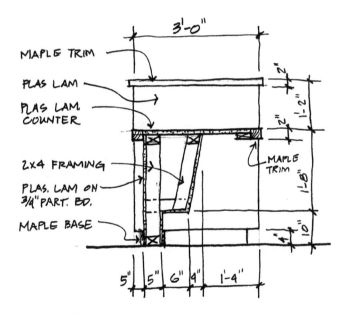

SECTION

Figure 31.8
Reflected Ceiling
Plan

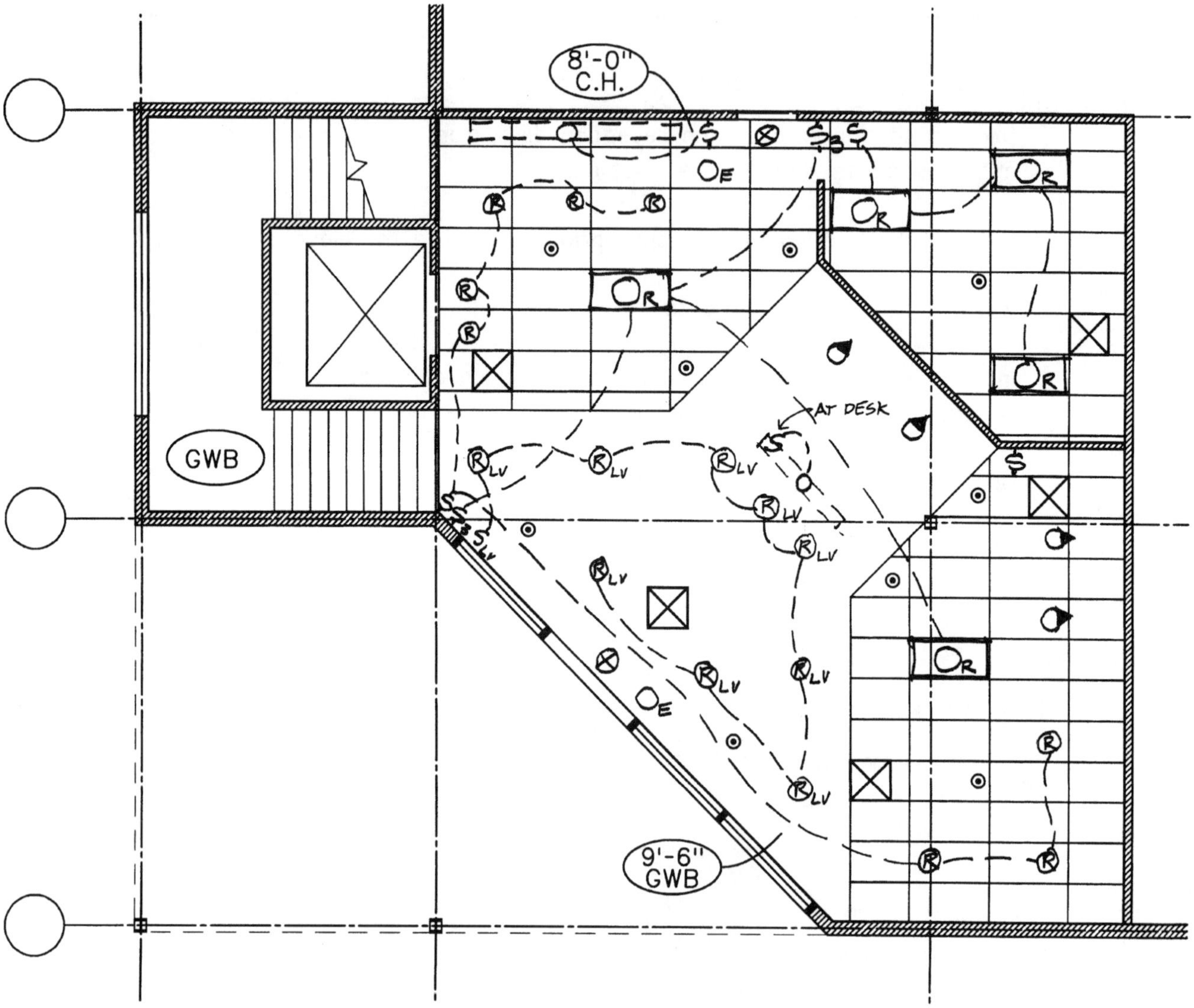

Reflected Ceiling Plan

Symbol	Concept Note (use 4-6 words to describe why the fixture was selected)
 ◗	used to highlight logo and artwork
 [-Ω-]	low-glare task lighting at work area and reception desk
Ⓡ	highlights elevator area and waiting area—low glare

RECOMMENDED READING

Ambrose, James. *Building Construction: Interior Systems.* Van Nostrand Reinhold.

Ballast, David Kent. *Interior Construction and Detailing for Designers and Architects.* Professional Publications.

Binggeli, Corky. *Building Systems for Interior Designers.* John Wiley & Sons.

Birren, Faber. *Color and Human Response.* Van Nostrand Reinhold.

Ching, Francis D. K. *Architecture: Form, Space, and Order.* John Wiley & Sons.

Ching, Francis D.K., and Corky Binggeli. *Interior Design Illustrated.* John Wiley & Sons.

Coleman, Cindy. *Interior Design Handbook of Professional Practice.* McGraw-Hill Professional Publishing.

Crawford, Tad, and Eva Doman Bruck. *Business and Legal Forms for Interior Designers.* Allworth Press.

Deasy, C. M. *Designing Places for People: A Handbook on Human Behavior for Architects, Designers, and Facility Managers.* Whitney Library of Design.

Downey, Joel, and Patricia K. Gilbert. *Successful Interior Projects Through Effective Contract Documents.* R. S. Means.

Farren, Carol E. *Planning and Managing Interior Projects.* R. S. Means.

Gordon, Gary, and James L. Nuckolls. *Interior Lighting for Designers.* John Wiley & Sons.

Hall, Edward T. *The Hidden Dimension.* Doubleday.

—. *The Silent Language.* Doubleday.

Harmon, Sharon Koomen, and Katherine E. Kennon. *The Codes Guidebook for Interiors.* John Wiley & Sons.

Henley, Pamela E. B. *Interior Design Practicum Exam Workbook.* Professional Publications.

Karlen, Mark. *Space Planning Basics.* John Wiley & Sons.

Kilmer, W. Otie and Rosemary Kilmer. *Construction Drawings and Details for Interiors: Basic Skills.* John Wiley & Sons.

Knackstedt, Mary V. *The Interior Design Business Handbook: A Complete Guide to Profitability.* John Wiley & Sons.

Mahnke, Frank H. *Color, Environment, and Human Response.* John Wiley & Sons.

McGowan, Maryrose. *Specifying Interiors: A Guide to Construction and FF&E for Commercial Interiors Projects.* John Wiley & Sons.

McGowan, Maryrose, and Kelsey Kruse, eds. *Interior Graphic Standards.* John Wiley & Sons.

Mitton, Maureen. *Interior Design Visual Presentation: A Guide to Graphics, Models, and Presentation Techniques.* John Wiley & Sons.

National Council for Interior Design Qualification. *NCIDQ Examination Study Guide.* National Council for Interior Design Qualification.

Pena, William. *Problem Seeking: An Architectural Programming Primer.* John Wiley & Sons.

Perritt, Henry H., Jr. *Americans with Disabilities Act Handbook.* John Wiley & Sons.

Piotrowski, Christine M. *Professional Practice for Interior Designers.* John Wiley & Sons.

Rengel, Roberto J. *Shaping Interior Space.* Fairchild Publications.

Reznikoff, S. C. *Interior Graphic and Design Standards.* Whitney Library of Design.

—. *Specifications for Commercial Interiors: Professional Liabilities, Regulations, and Performance Criteria.* Whitney Library of Design.

Riggs, J. Rosemary. *Materials and Components of Interior Architecture.* Prentice Hall.

Sampson, Carol A. *Estimating for Interior Designers.* Watson-Guptill.

Sommer, Robert. *Personal Space: The Behavioral Basis of Design.* Prentice Hall.

Stein, Benjamin and John S. Reynolds. *Mechanical and Electrical Equipment for Buildings.* John Wiley & Sons.

Wakita, Osamu A., and Richard M. Linde. *Professional Practice of Architectural Detailing.* John Wiley & Sons.

Yates, Marypaul. *Fabrics: A Guide for Interior Designers and Architects.* W.W. Norton & Company.

Yeager, Jan I. and Lura K. Teter-Justice. *Textiles for Residential and Commercial Interiors.* Fairchild Publications.

INDEX

PROFESSIONAL PUBLICATIONS, INC.

PROFESSIONAL PUBLICATIONS, INC.

S

S corporation, 408–409
Safe Drinking Water and Toxic Enforcement Act of 1986 (Proposition
65), 454
Safety, 397
as programmatic concept, 5
fire, of upholstery, 105–106
glazing, 172–173, 480–481
of flooring, 218
part of detailing, 231
responsibilities, 433
standard for architectural glazing materials, 16 CFR 1201, 172
Safety/health, criteria for material selection, 97–98
Salary, 417
Sales
agreement, 290
representatives, 287–288
tax license, 415
Salvaged materials, 444
Sample boards, 110
Samples, 394
Sandstone flooring, 208
Sash door, 162
SBC (see Standard Building Code)
SBS (see Sick-building syndrome)
Scale
drafting instrument, 75–77
architect's, 75–77
as design element, 131–132
criteria for fabric selection, 104
engineer's, 77
graphic communication, 75
metric, 76
of details, 251
of elevations, 249
of plans, 241
using, 77
SCAQMD (see California South Coast
Air Quality Management District)
Scarf joint, 190
Schedule
door, 253
finish, 241, 243
Scheduling, 122–125, 251, 433
Schematic design services, 431–432
Scientific Certification Systems (SCS),
441
Scope
of interior design services, 431–434
of work, 430
Scoping provisions, 503–504
Scribe piece, 191, 193
Scrubability, criteria for material selec-
tion, 96
SCS (see Scientific Certification Systems)
Seal, door, 169
Seaming, 105

Seamless flooring, 217–218
Seating, 100
arrangements, 15
barrier-free design, 516–517
dimensions, 7
Secondary circulation space, 31
Sections, 249–251 (see also Details)
drawing, 82
of specification, 270
reference mark, 259
Security, 327–331 (see also specific types)
controls, as programmatic concept, 5
criteria for material selection, 98
part of detailing, 231
Seismic
design, 300
load, 300
restraint for ceilings, 177–178, 179
Selection criteria
for fabrics, 103–105
for furniture, 101
for materials and finishes, 94–98
Self-healing quality, criteria for material
selection, 97
Semidirect lighting systems, 344
Semivitreous tile, 217
Separated flow, as programmatic concept, 5
Septum, 361
Sequence match, 194–195, 196
Sequential flow, as programmatic con-
cept, 5
Service groupings, as programmatic con-
cept, 4
Services
additional, 434–435
of interior designer, 431–435
Shape
as design element, 130–131
constancy, 46–47
Sheathing, 305, 308
Sheet
carpet, 213
size, 252–253, 254
Shop drawings, 394
Shoulder miter joint, 190
Showers, barrier-free design, 509–510,
511
Showrooms, 289
Shrinkage
criteria for material selection, 96
woodwork, 198
Sick-building syndrome (SBS), 455
Signage, barrier-free design, 514–515
Signatures on contract, 431
Silk, 102
Similarity, in Gestalt psychology, 44, 45, 46
Simultaneous contrast, 44, 135
Single tee concrete system, 297, 298
Sisal wall covering, as sustainable materi-
al, 449

Site plan, 80, 245
Site visits, 433
Size
clue, 47
constancy, 47
Skills required for design practicum, 520
Slab deflection, 301
Slate flooring, 208
Sleepers, for wood flooring, 206
Slip
joint, 301
partition, 155
matching, 194
resistance
criteria for material selection, 98
flooring, 218
Slope of drains, 322
Slot air diffuser, 315–316, 317
SmartWood Program, 445
Smoke
barrier, 174, 475, 497
control, 324
density chamber test (ASTM E662,
NFPA 258), 470, 471
detectors, 480
developed index, 471
Smoldering, 108
Snagging, 103
Social
distance, proxemics, 14
influences on design, 11-16, 48
Softwood, 188
Soil stack, 322
Soldering, 182
Sole plate, 306, 308
Sole proprietorship, 407–408
Solid
stock, 188
surfacing, 200–201
Solid-core door, 161
Sound
absorption, 358
rules of thumb, 358-359
control, 359
intensity levels, 355, 356
masking, 359
ratings, building code requirements,
482
transmission, 356
class (STC), 357, 482
ratings, 357
control, 360
qualities, 355
South Coast Air Quality Management District (SCAQMD) Rule 1113, 458
SP (see Station point)
Space allocation
for space planning, 61
for practicum, 524
Space
needs, 30–31

W

Waffle slab system, 297, 298
Wages, 417
Wagner Act, 418
Wainscot, 193
Wall finishes, 219–224
   stone, 223–224
Wallboard (*see* Gypsum wallboard)
   partitions (*see* Gypsum wallboard partitions)
Wall covering
   adhesives, 447
   fabric, 222
   vinyl, 221–222
Wall-mounted luminaire, 346
Wallpaper, 221
Walls,
   as basic design component, 54
   loadbearing, 299
Warehouse match, 194, 196
Washability, criteria for material selection, 96
Washington state indoor air quality program, 441
Waste
   stack, 322
   conservation, building materials evaluation, 444
Water supply, 320, 321
Water-dispersed urethanes, 448
Water-reducible acrylic lacquer, 200
Wearability standards for furniture, 108–110
Weaving of carpet, 214
Website, 423
Welding, 182
Welt, 105
Wertheimer, Max, 43
Wet
   columns, 323
   etching, 180
Wheelchair clearances, 504
White sound, 359
Wide-flange beam, 308
Width of exits, 493–495
Wilton carpet, 214, 215
Wind load, 300
Winding stairways, 331, 332, 498
Window
   coverings, 314
   clearance for air supply, 315
   fire test for (NFPA 701), 470, 473, 476
   screen security detector, 327
   treatment, types, 224–225
Wire glass, 170, 172
Withdrawal of bid, 371
Withholding payment, 402
Wood (*see also* Lumber)
   as sustainable material, 444
   certified products, 445

doors and frames, 161–162
flooring, 205–207
   as sustainable material, 448
framing, 304–306
grid ceiling, 177
molding, 184
paneling, 193–195
plastics, and composites, CSI division 06, 274
reclaimed, 445
stain, 200
stair construction, 332–333
structural systems, 304–306
studs, 153
sustainable, 445
Woodwork
   finishes, 198–200
   fire rating, 201–202
Wool, 102
   carpet, 214
Work
   by others, 386
   by owner, 386
   organization in design office, 417
Workers' compensation insurance, 411
Workflow, types, 35
Working
   drawings (*see* Construction drawings)
   model, 91
Workstations, 100
   design, 7, 8
   dimensions, computer, 13
World Health Organization (WHO), 441
Writing, for public relations, 424
Wyzenbeek abrasion resistance test, 108

Z

Z-clips, 195, 196
Zonal cavity method, 348

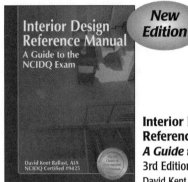
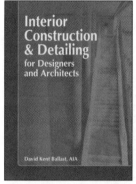
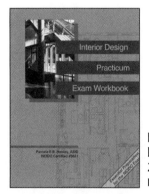